Instant Vortex Air Fryer Oven Cookbook

~1001~

Quick and Effortless Instant Vortex Air Fryer Recipes that Anyone Can Cook at Home

Emily Romero

© Copyright 2021 by Emily Romero - All rights reserved.

The content contained within this book may not be reproduced, duplicated, or transmitted without direct written permission from the author or the publisher. Under no circumstances will any blame or legal responsibility be held against the publisher, or author, for any damages, reparation, or monetary loss due to the information contained within this book. Either directly or indirectly.

Legal Notice:

This book is copyright protected. This book is only for personal use. You cannot amend, distribute, sell, use, quote, or paraphrase any part, or the content within this book, without the consent of the author or publisher.

Disclaimer Notice:

Please note the information contained within this document is for educational and entertainment purposes only. All effort has been executed to present accurate, up to date, and reliable, complete information. No warranties of any kind are declared or implied. Readers acknowledge that the author is not engaging in the rendering of legal, financial, medical, or professional advice. The content within this book has been derived from various sources. Please consult a licensed professional before attempting any techniques outlined in this book.

By reading this document, the reader agrees that under no circumstances is the author responsible for any losses, direct or indirect, which are incurred as a result of the use of the information contained within this document, including, but not limited to, errors, omissions, or inaccuracies.

TABLE OF CONTENTS

INTRODUCTION 19
BREAKFAST 21

1. Jalapeno Breakfast Muffins 22
2. Cinnamon and Cheese Pancake 22
3. Scallion Sandwich 22
4. Cinnamon Pancake 22
5. Fried Egg 22
6. Vegetable Sausage Egg Bake 22
7. Ham Egg Brunch Bake 23
8. Cheese Broccoli Bake 23
9. Cheese Ham Omelette 23
10. Sweet Potato Frittata 23
11. Squash Oat Muffins 24
12. Hashbrown Casserole 24
13. Perfect Brunch Baked Eggs 24
14. Eggs Florentine 24
15. Peanut Butter & Banana Sandwich 25
16. Spiced Apple Turnovers 25
17. Classic Corned Beef Hash and Eggs 25
18. Mini Cinnamon Sticky Rolls 25
19. Morning Mini Cheeseburger Sliders 26
20. Grilled Cheese 26
21. Buttery Chocolate Toast 26
22. Cheesy Baked-Egg Toast 26
23. Ham and Cheese Bagel Sandwiches ... 26
24. Peanut Butter and Jelly Banana Boats .. 27
25. Avocado and Spinach with Poached Eggs 27
26. Toasted Cinnamon Bananas 27
27. Tomatta Spinacha Frittata 27
28. Ultimate Breakfast Burrito 27
29. Ultimate Breakfast Sandwich 28
30. Air Fried French Toast 28
31. Wheat and Seed Bread 28
32. Crispy Ham Egg Cups 28
33. Ham and Egg Toast Cups 28
34. Air Fryer Sausage Wraps 29
35. Tasty Raspberry Scones 29
36. Air Fried Spring Rolls 29
37. Cinnamon and Honey Pancakes 29
38. Chocolate Filled Donut Holes 30
39. French Toast Sticks 30
40. Air Fryer Chicken and Waffles 30
41. Tasty Scramble Casserole 30
42. Grilled Ham and Cheese 31
43. Sausage Balls 31
44. Morning Sandwich Cheesy Stuffed 31
45. Omelette Frittata 31
46. Cheese Soufflés 31
47. Simple Egg Soufflé 32
48. Vegetable Egg Soufflé 32
49. Garlic Cheese Bread 32
50. Chili Cream Soufflé 32
51. Broccoli Stuffed Peppers 32
52. Cheese and Bacon Breakfast Bombs .. 33
53. Delicious Breakfast Soufflé 33
54. Yummy Breakfast Italian Frittata 33
55. Air-Fried English Breakfast 33
56. Sausage and Egg Breakfast Burrito 33
57. Home-Fried Potatoes 34
58. Homemade Cherry Breakfast Tarts 34
59. Sausage and Cream Cheese Biscuits . 34
60. Fried Chicken and Waffles 35
61. Cheesy Tater Tot Breakfast Bake 35
62. Savory Cheese and Bacon Muffins 35
63. Seasoned Potatoes 35

64.	Ham and Cheese Patties	36
65.	Peppers and Lettuce Salad	36
66.	Radish Hash Browns	36
67.	Artichoke Omelet	36
68.	Carrot Oatmeal	36
69.	Chicken Burrito	36
70.	Potato Frittata	37
71.	Herbed Omelet	37
72.	Cheese Toast	37
73.	Carrots and Cauliflower Mix	37
74.	Vanilla Oatmeal	37
75.	Fish Tacos Breakfast	37
76.	Tuna Sandwiches	38
77.	Tofu and Bell Peppers	38

VEGETABLE AND SIDE DISHES 39

78.	Herbed Tomatoes	40
79.	Baked Potato	40
80.	Air Fried Leeks	40
81.	Wine Glazed Mushrooms	40
82.	Veggie Stuffed Bell Peppers	40
83.	Stuffed Okra	40
84.	Fried Spicy Tofu	41
85.	Tarragon Yellow Squash	41
86.	Broccoli With Olives	41
87.	Roasted Butternut Squash With Brussels Sprouts and Sweet Potato Noodles	41
88.	Green Beans and Cherry Tomatoes	42
89.	Flatbread	42
90.	Creamy Cabbage	42
91.	Cauliflower Pizza Crust	42
92.	Olives and Artichokes	42
93.	Lemon Asparagus	42
94.	Salty Lemon Artichokes	43
95.	Pecan Brownies	43
96.	Cheesy Endives	43
97.	Cauliflower Steak	43
98.	Chard with Cheddar	43
99.	Air Fryer Crunchy Cauliflower	44
100.	Chili Squash Wedges	44
101.	Air Fryer Veg Buffalo Cauliflower	44
102.	Air Fryer Asparagus	44
103.	Almond Flour Battered and Crisped Onion Rings	44
104.	Crispy Brussels Sprouts	44
105.	Spicy Eggplant Cubes	45
106.	Supreme Air-Fried Tofu	45
107.	Zucchini Cubes	45
108.	Wrapped Asparagus	45
109.	Coconut Oil Artichokes	45
110.	Mashed Yams	46
111.	Rosemary Air Fried Potatoes	46
112.	Air Fryer Falafel Balls	46
113.	Indian Cauliflower Curry	46
114.	Carrot Fries	47
115.	Broccoli Salad Recipe	47
116.	Cajun Olives and Peppers	47
117.	Garlic-Rosemary Brussels Sprouts	47
118.	Simple Basil Potatoes	47
119.	Stuffed Mushrooms	47
120.	Green Beans with Sesame Seeds	48
121.	Black Bean and Tomato Chili	48
122.	Potatoes with Zucchinis	48
123.	Cauliflower Faux Rice	48
124.	Mediterranean Air Fried Veggies	49
125.	Easy Cinnamon Squash	49
126.	Twice-Baked Potatoes	49
127.	Golden Garlicky Potatoes	49
128.	Garlic-Roasted Red Potatoes	50
129.	Cauliflower Fried Rice	50
130.	Vegetable Medley	50

#	Recipe	Page
131.	Crispy Cheesy Asparagus	50
132.	Eggplant Parmesan	51
133.	Simple Balsamic-Glazed Carrots	51
134.	Air Fryer Vegetables	51
135.	Golden Squash Croquettes	51
136.	Quinoa Burgers	51
137.	Tofu with Broccoli	52
138.	Sweet and Spicy Parsnips	52
139.	Breaded Cheesy Broccoli Gratin	52
140.	Broccoli with Cauliflower	53
141.	Vinegar Green Beans	53
142.	Herbed Bell Peppers	53
143.	Cheesy cauliflower fritters	53
144.	Caramelized Baby Carrots	53
145.	Buttered carrot-zucchini with mayo	54
146.	Parmesan Asparagus	54
147.	Roasted vegetables salad	54
148.	Cheddar, squash and zucchini casserole	55
149.	Zucchini parmesan chips	55
150.	Jalapeño cheese balls	55
151.	Roasted Cauliflower with Nuts & Raisins	55
152.	Creamy and cheese broccoli bake	56
153.	Italian Ratatouille	56
154.	Crispy jalapeno coins	56
155.	Buffalo cauliflower	56
156.	Crisped baked cheese stuffed chile pepper	56
157.	Jicama fries	57
158.	Mushroom, Onion and Feta Frittata	57
159.	Spaghetti squash tots	57
160.	Crispy and healthy avocado fingers	57
161.	Onion rings	57
162.	Cinnamon butternut squash fries	58
163.	Cheesy Spinach	58
164.	Stuffed Bell Peppers	58
165.	Mushroom with Peas	58
166.	Buttermilk Fried Mushrooms	59
167.	Veggies Rice	59
168.	Best Ever Jalapeño Poppers	59
169.	Parmesan Breaded Zucchini Chips	60
170.	Bell PepperCorn Wrapped in Tortilla	60
171.	Baked Cheesy Eggplant with Marinara	60
172.	Spicy Sweet Potato Fries	61
173.	Creamy Spinach Quiche	61
174.	Crispy Salt and Pepper Tofu	61
175.	Brown Rice, Spinach and Tofu Frittata	61
176.	Carrots, Yellow Squash & Zucchini	62
177.	Winter Vegetarian Frittata	62
178.	Air Fried Kale Chips	62
179.	Buttered Broccoli	62
180.	Seasoned Carrots with Green Beans	63
181.	Seasoned Veggies	63
182.	Creamy Potatoes	63
183.	Sweet Potato Side Salad	63
184.	Mayo Brussels Sprouts	63
185.	Green Beans and Shallots	63
186.	Italian Mushroom Mix	64
187.	Crispy Fried Pickle Spears	64
188.	Spicy Winter Squash Bites	64
189.	Butter Squash Fritters	64
190.	Herbed Roasted Potatoes	64
191.	Indian-Style Garnet Sweet Potatoes	64
192.	Easy Frizzled Leeks	65
193.	Cremini Mushrooms in Zesty Tahini Sauce	65
194.	Pepper Jack Cauliflower Bites	65
195.	Cheesy Broccoli Croquettes	65
196.	Cauliflower Cakes Ole	65
197.	Celery and Carrot Croquettes	66
198.	Smoked Veggie Omelet	66
199.	Sweet Potato and Carrot Croquettes	66
200.	Manchego and Potato Patties	66

201. Mint-Butter Stuffed Mushrooms 66
202. Thai Green Curry Noodles 67

POULTRY 68

203. Honey Duck Breasts 69
204. Creamy Coconut Chicken 69
205. Easy Turkey Breasts With Basil 69
206. Crime Chicken 69
207. Chicken and Rice Casserole 69
208. Parmesan Chicken Meatballs 70
209. Chicken Legs With Dilled Brussels Sprouts ... 70
210. Chicken Breasts With Chimichurri 70
211. Turkey And Almonds 70
212. Teriyaki Wings 71
213. Chicken Wings With Prawn Paste 71
214. Korean Chicken Wings 71
215. Crispy Air Fryer Butter Chicken 71
216. Harissa-Rubbed Cornish Game Hens 71
217. Easy Lemon Chicken Thighs 72
218. Air Fryer Southern Fried Chicken 72
219. Air Fryer Grilled Chicken Breasts 72
220. Basil-Garlic Breaded Chicken Bake 73
221. Air Fryer Cornish Hen 73
222. Cheese and Garlic Stuffed Chicken Breasts .. 73
223. Turkey Wontons with Garlic-parmesan Sauce 73
224. Breaded Nugget In Doritos 74
225. Flavorful Chicken Drumsticks 74
226. Gluten-Free Air Fried Chicken 74
227. Barbecue with Chorizo and Chicken 74
228. Healthy Chicken Popcorn 75
229. Chicken in Beer 75
230. Herbed Turkey Breast 75
231. Marinara Sauce Cheese Chicken 75
232. Herby Chicken with Lime 75
233. Spicy Chicken Strips with Aioli Sauce 76
234. Crispy Chicken Thighs 76
235. Classic Greek Chicken 76
236. Perfect Juicy Chicken Breast 76
237. Faire-Worthy Turkey Legs 77
238. Broccoli Bacon Ranch Chicken 77
239. Jerk Chicken Legs 77
240. Western Chicken Wings 77
241. Protein Packed Baked Chicken Breasts 77
242. Flavors Balsamic Chicken 78
243. Simple and Delicious Chicken Thighs 78
244. Perfect Baked Chicken Breasts 78
245. BBQ Chicken Wings 78
246. Crunchy Munchy Chicken Tenders With Peanuts 78
247. Chinese-Style Sticky Turkey Thighs 79
248. Buffalo Chicken Tenders 79
249. Turkey Turnovers 79
250. Chicken Parm 79
251. Teriyaki Duck Legs 80
252. Almond Flour Coco-Milk Battered Chicken ... 80
253. Sweet and Sour Chicken 80
254. Zingy and Nutty Chicken Wings 80
255. Honey and Wine Chicken Breasts 81
256. Chicken Fillets, Brie and Ham 81
257. Chicken Fajitas 81
258. Thai Red Duck with Candy Onion 81
259. Buttermilk Chicken 81
260. Chicken with Avocado Mix 82
261. Chicken with Coconut and Turmeric 82
262. Crunchy Curry Chicken Strips 82
263. Easy Ritzy Chicken Nuggets 82
264. Orange Chicken Stir Fry 82
265. Chicken Curry 83
266. Pandan Chicken 83
267. Lemon Garlic Rosemary Chicken 83

268.	Paprika Chicken Legs With Brussels Sprouts	83
269.	Chicken Pie	84
270.	Easy Paprika Chicken	84
271.	Texas Thighs	84
272.	Crunchy Golden Nuggets	84
273.	Air Fried Turkey Breast	84
274.	Chicken In Bacon Wrap	85
275.	Lemon and Honey Glazed Game Hen	85
276.	Turkey And Pepper Sandwich	85
277.	Air-Fried Lemon Olive Chicken	85
278.	Chicken, Mushroom, And Pepper Kabobs	86
279.	Chicken, Potatoes & Cabbage	86
280.	Grilled Garlic Chicken	86
281.	Crisp Chicken w/ Mustard Vinaigrette	86
282.	Chicken with Oregano-Orange Chimichurri & Arugula Salad	87
283.	Stir-Fried Chicken with Water Chestnuts	87
284.	Spicy Duck Legs	87
285.	Duck Breast with Fig Sauce	87
286.	Duck Breasts with Red Wine and Orange Sauce	87
287.	Classic Air Fried Drumstick	88
288.	Duck Breasts and Raspberry Sauce	88
289.	Duck and Tea Sauce	88
290.	Lemon-Pepper Chicken Wings	88
291.	Cheesy Chicken in Leek-Tomato Sauce	89
292.	Duck and Cherries	89
293.	Oven-Fried Chicken Wings	89
294.	Beer Can Chicken	89
295.	Balsamic-Glazed Chicken Breasts	90
296.	Paprika Rotisserie-Style Chicken	90
297.	Harissa Chicken with Yogurt Sauce	90
298.	Spicy Roasted Chicken	91
299.	Spicy Rotisserie Chicken	91
300.	Cornish Hen with Montreal Chicken Seasoning	91

FISH AND SEAFOOD **92**

301.	Breaded Cod Sticks	93
302.	Grilled Sardines	93
303.	Zucchini with Tuna	93
304.	Salmon With Crisped Topped Crumbs	93
305.	Shrimp Casserole Louisiana Style	93
306.	Caramelized Salmon Fillet	94
307.	Salmon Steak Grilled with Cilantro Garlic Sauce	94
308.	Crusted Hake Fillets	94
309.	Deep Fried Prawns	94
310.	Snow Peas With Ginger Salmon Steaks	94
311.	Monkfish with Olives and Capers	95
312.	Kimchi Stuffed Squid	95
313.	Hot Smoked Trout Frittata	95
314.	Salmon with Pistachio Bark	95
315.	Baked Butter Crayfish	95
316.	Salmon Cakes	95
317.	Sautéed Trout with Almonds	96
318.	Grilled Fish with Light Mayo Sauce	96
319.	Teriyaki Glazed Halibut Steak	96
320.	Breaded Flounder	96
321.	Southern Style Catfish with Green Beans	97
322.	Air Fryer Salmon	97
323.	Beer Potato Fish	97
324.	Quick Paella	97
325.	Sesame Seeds Coated Tuna	98
326.	Tuna Veggie Stir-Fry	98
327.	Crab Legs	98
328.	Bang Bang Panko Breaded Fried Shrimp	98
329.	Crusty Pesto Salmon	99
330.	Old Bay Crab Cakes	99
331.	Scallops and Spring Veggies	99
332.	Parmesan Shrimp	99
333.	Lemon-garlic Butter Lobster	99

#	Recipe	Page
334.	Spicy Halibut	100
335.	Baked Tilapia	100
336.	Tilapia Meunière With Vegetables	100
337.	Foil Packet Salmon	100
338.	Savory Cod Fish in Soy Sauce	100
339.	Air Fryer Spicy Shrimp	101
340.	Simple Lemon Salmon	101
341.	Foil Packet Lobster Tail	101
342.	Miso White Fish Fillets	101
343.	Pecan-crusted Catfish Fillets	101
344.	Blackened Mahi Mahi	102
345.	Avocado Shrimp	102
346.	Cod Fish Nuggets	102
347.	Steamed Salmon and Sauce	102
348.	Indian Fish Fingers	102
349.	Lemony Tuna	103
350.	Grilled Soy Salmon Fillets	103
351.	Flying Fish	103
352.	Spicy Mackerel	103
353.	Salmon Noodles	103
354.	Fried Calamari	104
355.	Mustard-Crusted Fish Fillets	104
356.	Fish and Vegetable Tacos	104
357.	Lighter Fish and Chips	104
358.	Snapper with Fruit	105
359.	Thyme Scallops	105
360.	Tuna and Fruit Kebabs	105
361.	Asian Swordfish	105
362.	Tilapia & Chives Sauce	105
363.	Salmon on Bed of Fennel and Carrot	106
364.	Scallops with Green Vegetables	106
365.	Ranch Flavored Tilapia	106
366.	Butter Up Salmon	106
367.	Tasty Grilled Red Mullet	106
368.	Hearty Spiced Salmon	107
369.	Cajun Shrimp	107
370.	Air Fried Dragon Shrimp	107
371.	Garlicky-Grilled Turbot	107
372.	Crispy Paprika Fish Fillets	107
373.	Fish Tacos	108
374.	Bass Filet In Coconut Sauce	108
375.	Mahi Mahi with Herby Buttery Drizzle	108
376.	Beer Battered Cod Filet	108
377.	Fried Scallops with Saffron Cream Sauce	108
378.	Butterflied Prawns with Garlic-Sriracha	109
379.	Sweet Asian Style Salmon	109
380.	Zesty Ranch Fish Fillets	109
381.	Tempura Shrimp	109
382.	Easy Fish Sticks with Chili Ketchup Sauce	110
383.	Packet Lobster Tail	110
384.	Shrimp and Green Beans	110
385.	Crab Dip	110
386.	Sesame Shrimp	110
387.	Salmon and Cauliflower Rice	110
388.	Tuna Patties	111
389.	Garlic Tilapia	111
390.	Trout and Mint	111
391.	Salmon and Coconut Sauce	111
392.	Broiled Tilapia	111
393.	Fried French Mussels	111
394.	Salmon and Sauce	112
395.	Parmesan Cod	112
396.	Cod and Endives	112
397.	Cod and Tomatoes	112
398.	Salmon Burgers	112
399.	Bacon Wrapped Shrimp	113
400.	Crispy Coated Scallops	113
401.	Tasty Tuna Loaf	113
402.	Maryland Crab Cakes	113
403.	Mediterranean Sole	113

#	Recipe	Page
404.	Tomato Basil Scallops	114
405.	Spicy Grilled Halibut	114
406.	Tropical Shrimp Skewers	114
407.	Cheesy Fish Gratin	114
408.	Crispy Air Fried Sushi Roll	115
409.	Honey Glazed Salmon	115
410.	Parmesan Shrimp	115
411.	Bacon Wrapped Scallops	115
412.	Air Fryer Fish Tacos	115
413.	Salmon Croquettes	116
414.	Panko-Crusted Tilapia	116
415.	Friedamari	116
416.	Tuna Pie	116
417.	Louisiana Shrimp Po Boy	116
418.	Crumbled Fish	117
419.	3-Ingredient Air Fryer Catfish	117
420.	Healthy Fish and Chips	117
421.	Fish in Parchment Paper	117
422.	Buttery scallops	118
423.	Crusted scallops	118
424.	Lobster tails with white wine sauce	118
425.	Broiled lobster tails	118
426.	Paprika lobster tail	119
427.	Lobster tails with lemon butter	119
428.	Sheet pan seafood bake	119

MEAT 120

#	Recipe	Page
429.	Pork And Mixed Greens Salad	121
430.	Pork Satay	121
431.	Pork Burgers With Red Cabbage Salad	121
432.	Crispy Mustard Pork Tenderloin	121
433.	Sage 'n Thyme Rubbed Porterhouse	122
434.	Italian Beef Rolls	122
435.	Cajun Rubbed Ribeye Steaks	122
436.	Herb Crusted Lamb Chops	122
437.	Pumpkin and Pork Escallops	123
438.	Pork Taquitos	123
439.	Pork And Fruit Kebabs	123
440.	Steak And Vegetable Kebabs	123
441.	Air Fryer Baby Back Ribs	123
442.	Keto Parmesan Crusted Pork Chops	124
443.	Pork Milanese	124
444.	Crispy Fried Pork Chops the Southern Way	124
445.	Italian Sausages with Peppers and Onions	124
446.	Cilantro-Mint Pork BBQ Thai Style	125
447.	Dry Rub Baby Back Ribs	125
448.	Curry Pork Roast in Coconut Sauce	125
449.	Buckwheat with Pork Chunks	125
450.	Crispy Roast Garlic-Salt Pork	126
451.	Pulled Pork	126
452.	Light Herbed Meatballs	126
453.	Brown Rice And Beef-Stuffed Bell Peppers	126
454.	Chinese Salt and Pepper Pork Chop Stir-fry	127
455.	Garlic Putter Pork Chops	127
456.	Fried Pork with Sweet and Sour Glaze	127
457.	Oregano-Paprika on Breaded Pork	127
458.	Cajun Pork Steaks	128
459.	Cajun Bacon Pork Loin Fillet	128
460.	Country Fried Steak	128
461.	Polish Sausage with Sauerkraut	128
462.	Air Fryer Roast Beef	128
463.	Crispy Mongolian Beef	129
464.	German Sausages with Peppers and Onions	129
465.	Porchetta-Style Pork Chops	129
466.	Wonton Meatballs	129
467.	Beef Steaks with Beans	130
468.	Crispy Dumplings	130
469.	Rolled All Beef Hot Dogs	130
470.	Argentinian Style Skirt Steak	130
471.	Greek Style Lamb Chops	130

#	Recipe	Page
472.	Korean Style Meat Skewers	131
473.	Blue Cheese Stuffed Burgers	131
474.	Air Fried Strip Steak with Red Wine Sauce	131
475.	Easy Marinated Steak	131
476.	Rib Eye Steak	132
477.	Steak Bites and Mushrooms	132
478.	Korean Beef Wraps	132
479.	Hanger Steak with Red wine sauce	132
480.	Air Fried Beef Tenderloin	132
481.	Air Fried Ground Beef	133
482.	Lemon Garlic Lamb Chops	133
483.	Herb Butter Rib-eye Steak	133
484.	Classic Beef Jerky	133
485.	Pork Cutlet Rolls	133
486.	Fried Pork Scotch Egg	134
487.	Korean Barbeque Beef	134
488.	Beef Burgers	134
489.	Bacon Wrapped Filet Mignon	135
490.	Braised Pork	135
491.	Lean Beef with Green Onions	135
492.	Country Style Pork Tenderloin	135
493.	Beef Brisket Recipe from Texas	136
494.	Lamb Meatballs	136
495.	Chimichurri Skirt Steak	136
496.	Creamy Burger & Potato Bake	136
497.	Beef Brisket Recipe from Texas	136
498.	Warming Winter Beef with Celery	137
499.	Charred Onions And Steak Cube BBQ	137
500.	Beef Stroganoff	137
501.	Cheesy Ground Beef And Mac Taco Casserole	137
502.	Beefy Steak Topped with Chimichurri Sauce	137
503.	Beef Ribeye Steak	138
504.	Beef Korma	138
505.	Cumin-Paprika Rubbed Beef Brisket	138
506.	Beef & Lemon Schnitzel for One	138
507.	Crispy Beef Schnitzel	138
508.	Steak and Asparagus Bundles	139
509.	Raspberry Smoked Pork Chops	139
510.	Beef With Beans	139
511.	Swedish Meatballs	139
512.	Rice and Meatball Stuffed Bell Peppers	140
513.	Pub Style Corned Beef Egg Rolls	140
514.	Stir-Fried Steak and Cabbage	140
515.	Reuben Egg Rolls	140
516.	Air-Fried Philly Cheesesteak	141
517.	Herbed Roast Beef	141
518.	Beef Empanadas	141
519.	Beef Pot Pie	141
520.	Bolognaise Sauce	142
521.	Garlic and Rosemary Lamb Cutlets	142
522.	Garlic Sauced Lamb Chops	142
523.	Herb Encrusted Lamb Chops	142
524.	Herbed Rack of Lamb	143
525.	Lamb Roast with Root Vegetables	143
526.	Lemon and Cumin Coated Rack of Lamb	143
527.	Macadamia Rack of Lamb	144
528.	Perfect Lamb Burgers	144
529.	Simple Yet Tasty Lamb Chops	144
530.	Tandoori Lamb	144
531.	Barbecue Flavored Pork Ribs	145
532.	Rustic Pork Ribs	145
533.	Italian Parmesan Breaded Pork Chops	145
534.	Crispy Breaded Pork Chops	145
535.	Caramelized Pork Shoulder	146
536.	Roasted Pork Tenderloin	146
537.	Bacon-Wrapped Pork Tenderloin	146
538.	Dijon Garlic Pork Tenderloin	146
539.	Pork Neck with Salad	147
540.	Chinese Braised Pork Belly	147

#	Recipe	Page
541.	Air Fryer Sweet and Sour Pork	147
542.	Juicy Pork Ribs Ole	147
543.	Teriyaki Pork Rolls	148
544.	Glazed Pork Tenderloin	148
545.	Crusted Rack Of Lamb	148
546.	Greek Rotisserie Lamb Leg	148
547.	Duo Crisp Ribs	149

WRAP AND SANDWICH 150

#	Recipe	Page
548.	Cheesy Chicken Wraps	151
549.	Chicken-Lettuce Wraps	151
550.	Chicken Pita Sandwich	151
551.	Veggie Salsa Wraps	151
552.	Cheesy Shrimp Sandwich	152
553.	Smoky Chicken Sandwich	152
554.	Nugget and Veggie Taco Wraps	152
555.	Cheesy Greens Sandwich	152
556.	Cheesy Chicken Sandwich	153
557.	Thai Pork Burgers	153
558.	Easy Homemade Hamburgers	153
559.	Easy Beef Burritos	153
560.	Beef and Seeds Burgers	154
561.	Chicago-Style Beef Sandwich	154
562.	Air Fryer Veggie Quesadillas	154
563.	Crispy Cheesy Vegan Quesarito	154
564.	Mozzarella -Spinach Stuffed Burgers	155
565.	Crispy Baked Avocado Tacos	155
566.	Quick Sausage and Veggie Sandwiches	155
567.	Cheesy Beef Burrito	156
568.	Cheeseburger Egg Rolls	156
569.	Juicy Cheeseburgers	156
570.	Crunchy Chicken Egg Rolls	156
571.	Panko-Crusted Avocado and Slaw Tacos	157
572.	Golden Cabbage and Mushroom Spring Rolls	157
573.	Korean Beef and Onion Tacos	158
574.	Cabbage and Prawn Wraps	158
575.	Ricotta Spinach and Basil Pockets	158
576.	Avocado and Tomato Wraps	159
577.	Hot Bacon Sandwiches	159
578.	Chicken Sandwiches	159
579.	Easy Hot Dogs	159
580.	Turkey Burgers	159
581.	Prosciutto Sandwich	160
582.	Tasty Cheeseburgers	160
583.	Rolled Salmon Sandwich	160
584.	Chicken Capers Sandwich	160
585.	Easy Prosciutto Grilled Cheese	160
586.	Persimmon Toast with Sour Cream and Cinnamon	161
587.	Roasted Grape and Goat Cheese Crostinis	161
588.	Veggies on Toast	161
589.	Mushroom Pita Pizzas	161
590.	French Toast Sticks with Sugar and Berries	162
591.	Coconut Sandwich with Tomato and Avocado	162
592.	Avocado Taco Fry	162
593.	Breakfast Cheese Bread Cups	162
594.	Cheese and Egg Breakfast Sandwich	163
595.	Breakfast Muffins	163
596.	Tomato and Mozzarella Bruschetta	163
597.	All-in-One Toast	163
598.	Jalapeño Tacos with Guacamole	163

APPETIZER AND SNACK 164

#	Recipe	Page
599.	Air Fried Buffalo Chicken Strips	165
600.	Allspice Chicken Wings	165
601.	Friday Night Pineapple Sticky Ribs	165
602.	Egg Roll Wrapped with Cabbage and Prawns	165
603.	Sesame Garlic Chicken Wings	165
604.	Sausage and Onion Rolls	166
605.	Green Chilis Nachos	166

#	Title	Page
606.	Dehydrated Candied Bacon	166
607.	Cheesy Roasted Jalapeño Poppers	166
608.	Salty Baked Almonds	167
609.	Dehydrated Spiced Orange Slices	167
610.	Spicy and Sweet Roasted Nuts	167
611.	Steamed Pot Stickers	167
612.	Beef and Mango Skewers	167
613.	Curried Sweet Potato Fries	168
614.	Spicy Kale Chips with Yogurt Sauce	168
615.	Phyllo Artichoke Triangles	168
616.	Arancini	168
617.	Pesto Bruschetta	168
618.	Fried Tortellini with Spicy Dipping Sauce	169
619.	Shrimp Toast	169
620.	Bacon Tater Tots	169
621.	Hash Brown Bruschetta	169
622.	Mini Burgers	170
623.	Honey Roasted Carrots	170
624.	Potato Balls Stuffed with Ham and Cheese from the Air Fryer	170
625.	Garlic Mozzarella Sticks	170
626.	Sausages and Chorizos	171
627.	Air Fried French Fries	171
628.	Double-Baked Stuffed Potato	171
629.	Homemade Peanut Corn Nuts	171
630.	Walnut & Cheese Filled Mushrooms	171
631.	Cauliflower and Broccoli Dish	172
632.	Hearty Lemon Green Beans	172
633.	Stuffing hushpuppies	172
634.	Quick Zucchini Cakes	172
635.	Apple Cider Donuts	172
636.	Berry Crumble	173
637.	Butternut Squash with Thyme	173
638.	Chicken Breasts in Golden Crumb	173
639.	Yogurt Chicken Tacos	173
640.	Flawless Kale Chips	173
641.	Cheese Fish Balls	174
642.	Vermicelli Noodles and Vegetables Rolls	174
643.	Dehydrated Spiced Cauliflower	174
644.	Roasted Pumpkin Seeds	174
645.	Buttery Parmesan Broccoli Florets	174
646.	Spicy Chickpeas	175
647.	Roasted Peanuts	175
648.	Roasted Cashews	175
649.	French Fries	175
650.	Mini Popovers	176
651.	Fried Up Avocados	176
652.	Hearty Green Beans	176
653.	Parmesan Cabbage Wedges	176
654.	Extreme Zucchini Fries	176
655.	Easy Fried Tomatoes	176
656.	Caprese Stuffed Garlic Butter Portobellos	177
657.	Roasted Brussels and Pine Nuts	177
658.	Low-Calorie Beets Dish	177
659.	Grilled Avocado Caprese Crostini	177
660.	Bacon and Asparagus Spears	178
661.	Healthy Low Carb Fish Nugget	178
662.	Fried Up Pumpkin Seeds	178
663.	Decisive Tiger Shrimp Platter	178
664.	Jalapeno Poppers	178
665.	Jicama Fries	178
666.	Parmesan Potatoes	179
667.	Tasty Zucchini Fritters	179
668.	Crispy Beef Cubes	179
669.	Healthy Carrot Fries	179
670.	Easy Baked Potato Wedges	179
671.	Waffle Fry Poutine	180
672.	Spicy Almonds	180
673.	Onion Pakora	180
674.	Juicy Fish Nuggets	180

#	Item	Page
675.	Cheese Stuffed Jalapenos	181
676.	Ranch Chickpeas	181
677.	Cauliflower Hummus	181
678.	Tortilla Chips	181
679.	Apple Chips	181
680.	Herb Mushrooms	182
681.	Cinnamon Sweet Potato Bites	182
682.	Spicy Mix Nuts	182
683.	Easy Roasted Walnuts	182
684.	Rosemary Cauliflower Bites	182
685.	Sweet Potato Croquettes	182
686.	Sweet & Spicy Mixed Nuts	183
687.	Cheese Dip	183
688.	Creamy Zucchini Dip	183

DESSERT 184

#	Item	Page
689.	Lemon Mousse	185
690.	Glazed Banana	185
691.	Raspberry Danish	185
692.	Blueberry Muffins	185
693.	Cranberry Cupcakes	186
694.	Zucchini Mug Cake	186
695.	Chocolate Brownies	186
696.	Apple Crisp	187
697.	Banana and Walnut Cake	187
698.	Perfect Cinnamon Toast	187
699.	Easy Baked Chocolate Mug Cake	187
700.	Angel Food Cake	187
701.	Sweet Pear Stew	188
702.	Apple Dumplings	188
703.	Apple Pie in Air Fryer	188
704.	Air Fryer Chocolate Cake	188
705.	Banana-Choco Brownies	188
706.	Chocolate Donuts	189
707.	Easy Air Fryer Donuts	189
708.	Chocolate Soufflé for Two	189
709.	Blueberry Lemon Muffins	189
710.	Sweet Cream Cheese Wontons	189
711.	Air Fryer Cinnamon Rolls	190
712.	Raspberry Cream Rol-Ups	190
713.	Apple Hand Pies	190
714.	Chocolaty Banana Muffins	190
715.	Chocolate Rice	191
716.	Cinnamon Fried Bananas	191
717.	Awesome Chinese Doughnuts	191
718.	Crispy Bananas	191
719.	Air Fried Banana and Walnuts Muffins	191
720.	Nutty Mix	192
721.	Vanilla Spiced Soufflé	192
722.	Chocolate Cup Cakes	192
723.	Air Baked Cheesecake	192
724.	Air Roasted Nuts	193
725.	Air Fried White Corn	193
726.	Fruit Cake	193
727.	Hydrated Apples	193
728.	Nutty Slice	193
729.	Energy Brownies	194
730.	Air Fry Toaster Oven Bars	194
731.	Self-Saucing Banana Pudding	194
732.	Chocolate Lava Cake	194
733.	Banana Bread	194
734.	Choco-Peanut Mug Cake	195
735.	Raspberry-Coco Desert	195
736.	Almond Cherry Bars	195
737.	Coffee Flavored Doughnuts	195
738.	Simple Strawberry Cobbler	195
739.	Easy Pumpkin Pie	196
740.	Simple Cheesecake	196
741.	Strawberry Donuts	196
742.	Apricot Blackberry Crumble	196
743.	Ginger Cheesecake	197

#	Recipe	Page
744.	Coconut Donuts	197
745.	Blueberry Cream	197
746.	Blackberry Chia Jam	197
747.	Mixed Berries Cream	197
748.	Cinnamon-Spiced Acorn Squash	197
749.	Pear Sauce	198
750.	Brownie Muffins	198
751.	Chocolate Mug Cake	198
752.	Warm Peach Compote	198
753.	Chocolate Cake	198
754.	Chocolate Chip Air Fryer Cookies	199
755.	Doughnuts	199
756.	Cherry-Choco Bars	199
757.	Crusty Apple Hand Pies	199
758.	Pancakes Nutella-Stuffed	199
759.	Spiced Pear Sauce	200
760.	Saucy Fried Bananas	200
761.	Easy cheesecake	200
762.	Macaroons	200
763.	Orange cake	200
764.	Bread dough and amaretto	201
765.	Carrot cake	201
766.	Sweet Peach Jam	201
767.	Easy granola	201
768.	Pears and espresso cream	202
769.	Vanilla Apple Compote	202
770.	Raisins Cinnamon Peaches	202
771.	Air Fried Butter Cake	202
772.	Dried Raspberries	202
773.	Fried peaches	202
774.	Air Fryer Oreo Cookies	203
775.	Peanut Butter Cookies	203
776.	Grilled Peaches	203
777.	Honey Fruit Compote	203
778.	Lemon Pear Compote	203
779.	Simple & Delicious Spiced Apples	204
780.	Cinnamon Pear Jam	204
781.	Fried bananas with chocolate sauce	204
782.	Air Fryer S'mores	204
783.	Walnut Apple Pear Mix	204
784.	Apple Dates Mix	205
785.	Tangy Mango Slices	205
786.	Bread pudding with cranberry	205
787.	Black and white brownies	205
788.	French toast bites	205
789.	Baked apple	206
790.	Coffee and blueberry cake	206
791.	Cinnamon sugar roasted chickpeas	206
792.	Strawberry Stew	206
793.	Sweet Peach Wedges	206
794.	Coconutty lemon bars	206
795.	Simple Coffee Cake	207
796.	Lime Cheesecake	207
797.	Marvelous Lemon Biscuits	207
798.	Banana Fritters	207
799.	Tasty Banana Snack	207
800.	Strawberry Cobbler	208
801.	Super Yummy Brownies	208
802.	Air Fryer Churros with Chocolate Sauce	208

CASSEROLE, FRITTATA AND QUICHE 209

#	Recipe	Page
803.	Cheesy Chicken Divan	210
804.	Cheesy-Creamy Broccoli Casserole	210
805.	Cheesy Chorizo, Corn, and Potato Frittata	210
806.	Taco Beef and Green Chile Casserole	210
807.	Golden Asparagus Frittata	211
808.	Corn and Bell Pepper Casserole	211
809.	Creamy-Mustard Pork Gratin	211
810.	Broccoli, Carrot, and Tomato Quiche	211
811.	Herbed Cheddar Cheese Frittata	212
812.	Cauliflower, Okra, and Pepper Casserole	212

813.	Sumptuous Chicken and Vegetable Casserole	212
814.	Easy Chickpea and Spinach Casserole	213
815.	Classic Mediterranean Quiche	213
816.	Cheesy Mushrooms and Spinach Frittata	213
817.	Broccoli-Rice 'n Cheese Casserole	213
818.	Beefy 'n Cheesy Spanish Rice Casserole	214
819.	Air Fryer Beef Casserole	214
820.	Broccoli Creamy Casserole	214
821.	Chicken, Feta, and Olive Casserole	214
822.	Turkey Taco Casserole	215
823.	Italian Chicken Casserole	215

SAUCE, DIP AND DRESSING 216

824.	Spicy Buffalo Chicken Dip	217
825.	Bacon Cheeseburger Dip	217
826.	Spicy Spinach Artichoke Dip	217
827.	Peppers and Cheese Dip	217
828.	Fennel Spread	217
829.	Spinach Dip	218
830.	Spicy Sweet Potato Dip	218
831.	Smoked Salmon Dip	218
832.	Blue Cheese Dressing	218
833.	Broccoli Dip	219
834.	Crab and Artichoke Dip	219
835.	Feta Cheese Dip	219
836.	Eggplant Dip	219
837.	Naan Bread Dippers	219
838.	Cheese Artichoke Arugula Dip	220
839.	Mozzarella, Brie and Artichoke Dip	220
840.	Garlic Cheese Dip	220
841.	Cheesy Beef Dip	220
842.	Cheesy Spinach Dip	220
843.	Tomatoes Dip	221
844.	Easy Buffalo Chicken Dip	221
845.	Perfect Goat Cheese Dip	221
846.	Easy Taco Dip	221
847.	Spicy Mexican Cheese Dip	221
848.	Cheesy Crab Dip	222
849.	Perfect Crab Dip	222
850.	Yummy Chicken Dip	222
851.	Creamy Mushroom Dip	222
852.	Different Hummus	222
853.	Hot Spread	223
854.	Basil Cream Cheese Dip	223
855.	Honey Tomato Dip	223
856.	Tofu Dip	223
857.	Mango and Chili Spread	223
858.	Smoked Dip	224
859.	Meat Sauce	224
860.	Mushroom Broth	224
861.	Red Lentil Mushroom Ragu	224
862.	Fresh Tomato Marinara Sauce	225
863.	Fresh Tomato Basil Sauce	225
864.	Red Onion Marmalade	225
865.	Louisiana Crab Dip	225
866.	Three-Layer Taco Dip	226
867.	Mexican Street Corn Queso Dip	226
868.	Cheesy Bacon Dipping Sauce	226
869.	Caramel Sauce	226
870.	Alfredo Sauce	227
871.	Beef Spaghetti Sauce	227
872.	Spaghetti Sauce	227

BREAD, BAGEL AND PIZZA 228

873.	Bread Roll	229
874.	Ham Rolls	229
875.	Raspberry Roll	229
876.	Egg Rolls	229
877.	Garlic with Bacon Pizza	229
878.	Spring Roll	230
879.	Chicken Roll	230

#	Title	Page
880.	Barbeque Bacon With Chicken Pizza	230
881.	Turkey and Artichoke Pizza	230
882.	Beef Stuffed Pizza	231
883.	Vanilla and Mango Bread with Cinnamon	231
884.	Cinnamon and Vanilla Toast	231
885.	Basil Parmesan Bagel	231
886.	Buttery Orange Toasts	231
887.	Basil Prosciutto Crostini with Mozzarella	231
888.	Soda Brad	232
889.	Baguette Bread	232
890.	Yogurt Bread	232
891.	Sunflower Seed Bread	233
892.	Date Bread	233
893.	Date and Walnut Bread	233
894.	Pizza Toast	234
895.	Blueberry Overload French Toast	234
896.	Meat Lovers' Pizza	234
897.	Easy Peasy Pizza	234
898.	Mexican Pizza	235
899.	Bacon Garlic Pizza	235
900.	Tomato and Cheese Pizza	235
901.	Low-Calorie Calzones	235
902.	Baked Turnovers with Pear	235
903.	Creamy Beef Pockets	236
904.	Mini Pizza	236
905.	Artichoke with Red Pepper Pizza	236
906.	Artichoke Turkey Pizza	236
907.	Bacon Cheeseburger Pizza	236
908.	Bacon Lettuce Tomato Pizza	237
909.	Bread Pudding	237
910.	Cheesy Bread	237
911.	Peach Pie Mix	237
912.	Breakfast Pizza	237
913.	French Bread Pizza	238
914.	Quick Cheese Sticks	238
915.	Herbed Croutons with Brie Cheese	238
916.	Monkey Bread	238
917.	Southern Pimento Grilled Cheese	238
918.	Fluffy Peanut Butter Marshmallow Turnovers	239
919.	Fast and Simple Doughnuts	239
920.	Raisin and Apple Dumplings	239
921.	Homemade Donuts	239
922.	Mozzarella, Bacon and Turkey Calzone	240
923.	Nutty Bread Pudding with Honey and Raisins	240
924.	Cheesy Berry-Flavored French Toast	240
925.	Pita and Pepperoni Pizza	240
926.	Simple Cinnamon Toasts	241
927.	Sourdough Croutons	241
928.	American-Style BBQ Chicken Pizza	241
929.	Pizzas in Fryer Without Oil	241
930.	Avocado on Toast with Poached Egg	241
931.	Bread Roll and an Egg	242
932.	Cheese Ham Pluck Bread	242
933.	Green Focaccia	242
934.	Pizza Flammkuchen Style	242
935.	Beef and Onion BBQ Pizza	243
936.	Cheese Sticks	243
937.	Baltic Garlic Bread Sticks with Yogurt Dip	243
938.	Perfect Donuts	243
939.	Three-grain Bread with the Airfryer Baking Pan	244
940.	Corn Bread	244

SOUP AND STEW 245

#	Title	Page
941.	Tortilla and White Beans Soup	246
942.	Mexican Beef Soup	246
943.	Zucchini and Cauliflower Stew	246
944.	Butternut Squash and Apple Soup	246
945.	Carrot Soup with Fowl	246
946.	Lobster Bisque Soup	247

947.	Air fryer Angel Hair Soup	247
948.	Vegetable Wild Rice Soup	247
949.	English Pub Split Pea Soup	248
950.	Salmon Tortellini Soup	248
951.	Lentil Soup	248
952.	Potato Soup	248
953.	Noodle Soup with Tofu	249
954.	Tomato Soup	249
955.	Stewed Celery Stalk	249
956.	Bacon and Cauliflower Soup	249
957.	Pork Stew	250
958.	Pumpkin Tomato Soup	250
959.	Eggplant Stew	250
960.	Coconut Lime Soup	250
961.	Garlic Soup with Almonds	251
962.	Turkey And Broccoli Stew	251
963.	Leftover Stew	251
964.	Onion Soup	251
965.	Mixed Veggies Soup	252
966.	Lamb Stew	252
967.	Creamy Squash Soup	252
968.	Light Taco Soup	252
969.	Spicy Mushroom Soup	253
970.	Carrot Soup with Cardamom	253
971.	Beef Noodle Soup	253
972.	Asian Pork Soup	253
973.	Handmade Sausage Stew	254
974.	Carrot Peanut Butter Soup	254
975.	Taco Soup	254
976.	Kale Beef Soup	254
977.	Chicken Daikon Soup	255
978.	Hearty Red Wine Stew	255
979.	Butternut Cauliflower Soup	255
980.	Pho	255
981.	Beef and Guinness Stew	256
982.	Mediterranean Bamyeh Okra Tomato Stew	256
983.	Beef Barley Soup	256
984.	Potato Leek Soup	257
985.	Chicken Soup	257
986.	Corn Soup	257
987.	Golden Lentil and Spinach Soup	257
988.	Split Pea Soup	258
989.	Kale Cottage Cheese Soup	258
990.	Chicken and Wild Rice Soup	258
991.	Awesome Sea Bass Stew	258
992.	Hearty Orange Stew	259
993.	Greek Vegetable Soup	259
994.	Autumn Stew	259
995.	Awesome Rosemary Stew	259
996.	Turkey and Mushroom Stew	259
997.	Okra and Green Beans Stew	260
998.	Zucchini Stew	260
999.	Asparagus Garlic Ham Soup	260
1000.	Cabbage Soup	260
1001.	Zoodle Soup	260

CONCLUSION 261

CONVERSION CHART 262

AIR FRYER COOKING TIMES 263

INDEX 264

INTRODUCTION

Using an air fryer, the benefits are manifold. They are easy to use and clean, they do not cause odor because the air or steam they expel is infinitely less than that of conventional fryers, and of course, the lower consumption of fat and cholesterol in the food must be highlighted. In addition, food is cooked with up to 80% less oil.

The excessive consumption of fried foods has negative effects on our health. They are responsible for increased cholesterol, triglycerides, as well as body fat. In addition, it favors overweight and various cardiovascular diseases. For this reason, for some years now, hot air fryers have been an increasingly chosen alternative to oil fryers. They appeared to find a place in the kitchen for those looking for a healthier method for their daily dishes.

Instant ™ Vortex air fryer offers a healthier and more convenient alternative to prepare to fry, in addition to versatility to roast, bake and reheat. As a result, you can produce healthier versions of all your favorite fried foods. Fry juicy chicken wings, crispy fries, and fresh or frozen onion rings. Make skewers of shrimp, potato popes, and chicken nuggets. Bake broken or mini pizzas, fluffy cinnamon rolls, delicious cookies, and brownie snacks, or overflow dinner last night for lunch.

The time required to preheat this air fryer is very short. You will surely appreciate it if it happens to you like us and you are always in a hurry and have to improvise a meal at the last minute.

In addition, the capacity of this air fryer-oven is significantly higher than that of most air fryers on the market.

Thanks to the trays incorporated in the Instant Vortex Plus, you can distribute a fairly large amount of food on them in a single layer. In this way, the heat distribution will be much more uniform than in a conventional air fryer, and you will achieve much faster and more homogeneous cooking.

It is a convection oven that has been designed as a multifunction oven and is capable of performing up to 7 different functions: Broil, Air frying, Make bread, pastries, etc., Gratin, Reheat, Dehydrate, Cook with rotation.

Air frying function

Air fryers circulate hot air at high speed around food, creating a crunchy layer on the outside and cooking it on the inside.

In this way, it is possible to fry potatoes and all kinds of food using just a few drops of oil and thus to achieve frying in which the ingredients barely absorb oil. This type of frying is much less caloric than conventional frying consisting of submerging food in hot oil.

Air frying can, in many cases, reduce cooking time, which can be up to 20% less than necessary using the conventional frying method. The cooking time is also less than what you would need using a conventional convection oven.

Dehydrator function

Another very interesting function of this oven is that it allows you to dehydrate food. The dehydration technique consists of eliminating practically all of the moisture from the food.

The ideal is to carry out this operation using low temperatures. In this way, the food conserves most of its nutrients, but a much more intense and concentrated flavor is obtained by eliminating the water. Since these dry ingredients contain hardly any water, you can keep them for a long time. And you can further increase their shelf life by vacuum packaging them.

Rotary function

The Instant Vortex Plus oven includes a metal basket in which we can introduce the ingredients that we want to fry with this technique.

During frying, this basket constantly rotates, achieving uniform frying over the entire surface of the ingredients.

You can use this metal basket to fry all kinds of food: Potatoes, Sweet potato, Chicken wings, Nuggets, All kinds of vegetables, Roasting nuts, Etc.

As we have already seen, it is possible to place food in a metal basket and fry it using air and minimal oil. This metal basket rotates throughout the frying time to provide a very uniform frying and a crisp surface at all food points. This rotating metal basket can also be used when the Instant Vortex Plus functions as a convection oven.

In addition, you can remove this metal basket and replace it with a steel bar. So you can insert different foods into this bar to rotate while frying or slow cooking using the convection oven function. This allows you, for example, to grill or fry a whole chicken and get it to cook completely evenly on all sides.

An accessory is included with this Instant Vortex Plus oven that will allow you to safely remove the basket and steel bar used for cooking with the rotary cooking function without burning yourself.

Other functions of the Instant Vortex Plus multifunction oven

The functions of the Instant Vortex Plus that we have described so far are the ones that we find most interesting. However, do not forget that, in addition, this oven can also function as a conventional convection oven. So you can use this oven to roast and bake all kinds of food. When using these functions, the oven will warn you with a beep to remind you to turn the food over and thus achieve more homogeneous cooking.

You will save each time you use one of the oven functions the time and temperature settings used. These values will be the ones that the oven will use by default when you use this function.

In addition this oven includes a safety mechanism that automatically turns off if the internal temperature of 232°C is exceeded.

In this book you will find the best and healthiest recipes to use your Instant Vortex Air Fryer Oven in the most appropriate and best way possible; we have recipes of all kinds and for all tastes so that nothing is missing when you want to prepare a portion of healthy and delicious food.

Right here, I write you a multitude of recipes for the air fryer; most of them are multifunctional so that you can cook all kinds of food: chicken, potatoes, meat, vegetable, fish, pizza, etc...

BREAKFAST

1. Jalapeno Breakfast Muffins

Preparation Time: 10 minutes
Cooking Time: 15 minutes
Servings: 8

Ingredients:
- 5 eggs
- 1/3 cup coconut oil, melted
- 2 tsp baking powder
- 3 tbsp erythritol
- 3 tbsp. jalapenos, sliced
- 1/4 cup unsweetened coconut milk
- 2/3 cup coconut flour
- 3/4 tsp sea salt

Directions:
1. Preheat the air fryer to 325 F.
2. In a large bowl, mix together coconut flour, baking powder, erythritol, and sea salt.
3. Stir in eggs, jalapenos, coconut milk, and coconut oil until well combined.
4. Pour batter into the silicone muffin molds and place into the air fryer basket.
5. Cook muffins for 15 minutes
6. Serve and enjoy.

Nutrition: Calories 125 Fat 12 g Carbs 7 g Protein 3 g

2. Cinnamon and Cheese Pancake

Preparation Time: 7 minutes
Cooking Time: 20 minutes
Servings: 4

Ingredients:
- 2 eggs
- 2 cups reduced-fat cream cheese
- 1/2 tsp. cinnamon
- 1 pack Stevia

Directions:
1. Adjust the Air Fryer to 330ºF. In a blender, mix cream cheese, cinnamon, eggs, and stevia.
2. Pour a quarter of the mixture into the Air fryer basket. Cook for 2 minutes on all sides. Repeat the process with the remaining portion of the mixture. Serve.

Nutrition: Calories: 140 kcalCarbs:5.4gFat: 10.6gProtein: 22.7g

3. Scallion Sandwich

Preparation Time: 10 minutes
Cooking Time: 15 minutes
Servings: 1

Ingredients:
- 2 slices wheat bread
- 2 tsps. Low-fat butter
- 2 sliced scallions
- 1 tbsp. grated parmesan cheese
- 3/4 cup low-fat, grated cheddar cheese

Directions:
1. Adjust the Air fryer to 356ºF.
2. Apply butter to a slice of bread. Then place it inside the cooking basket with the butter side facing down.
3. Place cheese and scallions on top. Spread the rest of the butter on the other slice of bread. Then put it on top of the sandwich and sprinkle with parmesan cheese.
4. Allow to cook for 10 minutes. Serve.

Nutrition: Calories: 154 kcal Carbs: 9gFat: 2.5gProtein: 8.6g

4. Cinnamon Pancake

Preparation Time: 15 minutes
Cooking Time: 20 minutes
Servings: 4

Ingredients:
- 2 eggs
- 2 cups low-fat cream cheese
- 1/2 tsp. cinnamon
- 1 pack Stevia

Directions:
1. Adjust the temp. to 330ºF.
2. Combine cream cheese, cinnamon, eggs, and stevia in a blender.
3. Pour a quarter of the mixture in the air fryer basket.
4. Allow to cook for 2 minutes on both sides.
5. Repeat the process with the rest of the mixture. Serve.

Nutrition: Calories: 106 kcal Carbs: 10gFat: 3.2gProtein: 9g

5. Fried Egg

Preparation Time: 5 minutes
Cooking Time: 4 minutes
Servings: 1

Ingredients:
- 1 pastured egg
- 1/8 tsp. salt
- 1/8 tbsp. cracked black pepper

Directions:
1. Grease the fryer pan with olive oil then crack the egg in it.
2. Insert the fryer pan into the air fryer, close the lid. Then adjust the fryer to 370ºF.
3. After 3minutes, open the air fryer to check if the egg needs more cooking. If yes, leave it for an extra 1 minute.
4. Serve the egg. Add salt and black pepper to season it.

Nutrition: Calories: 90 kcal Carbs: 0.6 g Fat: 7 g Protein: 6.3 g

6. Vegetable Sausage Egg Bake

Preparation time: 10 minutes
Cooking time: 35 minutes
Servings: 4

Ingredients:
- 10 eggs
- 1 cup spinach, diced
- 1 cup onion, diced
- 1 cup pepper, diced
- 1 lb sausage, cut into 1/2-inch pieces
- 1 tsp garlic powder
- 1/2 cup almond milk
- Pepper
- Salt

Directions
1. Spray an 8*8-inch baking dish with cooking spray and set aside.
2. Insert wire rack in rack position 6. Select bake, set temperature 390 F, timer for 35 minutes. Press start to preheat the oven.
3. In a bowl, whisk eggs with milk and spices. Add vegetables and sausage and stir to combine.
4. Pour egg mixture into the prepared baking dish. Bake for 35 minutes.
5. Slice and serve.

Nutrition: Calories 653 Fat 50.6g Carbs 12.6g Sugar 3.3g Protein 38.3g Cholesterol 504mg

7. Ham Egg Brunch Bake

Preparation time: 10 minutes
Cooking time: 60 minutes
Servings: 6
Ingredients:
- 4 eggs
- 20 oz hash browns
- 1 onion, chopped
- 2 cups ham, chopped
- 3 cups cheddar cheese, shredded
- 1 cup sour cream
- 1 cup milk
- Pepper
- Salt

Directions
1. Spray a 9*13-inch baking dish with cooking spray and set aside.
2. Insert wire rack in rack position 6. Select bake, set temperature 375 F, timer for 35 minutes. Press start to preheat the oven.
3. In a large mixing bowl, whisk eggs with sour cream, milk, pepper, and salt. Add 2 cups cheese and stir well.
4. Cook onion and ham in a medium pan until onion is softened.
5. Add hash brown to the pan and cook for 5 minutes.
6. Add onion ham mixture into the egg mixture and mix well.
7. Pour egg mixture into the prepared baking dish. Cover dish with foil and bake for 35 minutes.
8. Remove foil and bake for 25 minutes more.
9. Slice and serve.

Nutrition: Calories 703 Fat 46.2g Carbs 41.2g Sugar 4.6g Protein 30.8g Cholesterol 214mg

8. Cheese Broccoli Bake

Preparation time: 10 minutes
Cooking time: 30 minutes
Servings: 12
Ingredients:
- 12 eggs
- 1 1/2 cup cheddar cheese, shredded
- 2 cups broccoli florets, chopped
- 1 small onion, diced
- 1 cup milk
- Pepper
- Salt

Directions
1. Spray a 9*13-inch baking dish with cooking spray and set aside.
2. Insert wire rack in rack position 6. Select bake, set temperature 390 F, timer for 30 minutes. Press start to preheat the oven.
3. In a large bowl, whisk eggs with milk, pepper, and salt. Add cheese, broccoli, and onion and stir well.
4. Pour egg mixture into the prepared baking dish and bake for 30 minutes.
5. Slice and serve.

Nutrition: Calories 138 Fat 9.5g Carbs 3.1g Sugar 1.8g Protein 10.2g Cholesterol 180mg

9. Cheese Ham Omelette

Preparation time: 10 minutes
Cooking time: 25 minutes
Servings: 6
Ingredients:
- 8 eggs
- 1 cup ham, chopped
- 1 cup cheddar cheese, shredded
- 1/3 cup milk
- Pepper
- Salt

Directions
1. Spray a 9*9-inch baking dish with cooking spray and set aside.
2. Insert wire rack in rack position 6. Select bake, set temperature 390 F, timer for 25 minutes. Press start to preheat the oven.
3. In a large bowl, whisk eggs with milk, pepper, and salt. Stir in ham and cheese.
4. Pour egg mixture into the prepared baking dish and bake for 25 minutes.
5. Slice and serve.

Nutrition: Calories 203 Fat 14.3g Carbs 2.2g Sugar 1.2g Protein 16.3g Cholesterol 252mg

10. Sweet Potato Frittata

Preparation time: 10 minutes
Cooking time: 30 minutes
Servings: 6
Ingredients:
- 10 eggs
- 1/4 cup goat cheese, crumbled
- 1 onion, diced
- 1 sweet potato, diced
- 2 cups broccoli, chopped
- 1 tbsp olive oil
- Pepper
- Salt

Directions
1. Spray a baking dish with cooking spray and set aside.
2. Insert wire rack in rack position 6. Select bake, set temperature 390 F, timer for 20 minutes. Press start to preheat the oven.
3. Heat oil in a pan over medium heat. Add sweet potato, broccoli, and onion and cook for 10-15 minutes or until sweet potato is tender.
4. In a large mixing bowl, whisk eggs with pepper and salt.
5. Transfer cooked vegetables into the baking dish. Pour egg mixture over vegetables. Sprinkle with goat cheese and bake for 15-20 minutes.
6. Slice and serve.

Nutrition: Calories 201 Fat 13g Carbs 8.4g Sugar 3.3g Protein 13.5g Cholesterol 282mg

11. Squash Oat Muffins

Preparation time: 10 minutes
Cooking time: 20 minutes
Servings: 12

Ingredients:
- 2 eggs
- 1 tbsp pumpkin pie spice
- 2 tsp baking powder
- 1 cup oats
- 1 cup all-purpose flour
- 1 tsp vanilla
- 1/3 cup olive oil
- 1/2 cup yogurt
- 1/2 cup maple syrup
- 1 cup butternut squash puree
- 1/2 tsp sea salt

Directions
1. Line 12 cups muffin pan with cupcake liners.
2. Insert wire rack in rack position 6. Select bake, set temperature 390 F, timer for 20 minutes. Press start to preheat the oven.
3. In a large bowl, whisk together eggs, vanilla, oil, yogurt, maple syrup, and squash puree.
4. In a small bowl, mix together flour, pumpkin pie spice, baking powder, oats, and salt.
5. Add flour mixture into the wet mixture and stir to combine.
6. Scoop the batter to the prepared muffin pan and bake for 20 minutes.
7. Serve and enjoy.

Nutrition: Calories 171 Fat 7.1g Carbs 23.8g Sugar 9.4g Protein 3.6g Cholesterol 28mg

12. Hashbrown Casserole

Preparation time: 10 minutes
Cooking time: 60 minutes
Servings: 10

Ingredients:
- 32 oz frozen hash browns with onions and peppers
- 2 cups cheddar cheese, shredded
- 15 eggs, lightly beaten
- 5 bacon slices, cooked and chopped
- Pepper
- Salt

Directions
1. Spray 9*13-inch casserole dish with cooking spray and set aside.
2. Insert wire rack in rack position 6. Select bake, set temperature 350 F, timer for 60 minutes. Press start to preheat the oven.
3. In a large mixing bowl, whisk eggs with pepper and salt. Add 1 cup cheese, bacon, and hash browns and mix well.
4. Pour egg mixture into the prepared casserole dish and sprinkle with remaining cheese.
5. Bake for 60 minutes or until the top is golden brown.
6. Slice and serve.

Nutrition: Calories 403 Fat 27.1g Carbs 23.6g Sugar 0.6g Protein 19g Cholesterol 280mg

13. Perfect Brunch Baked Eggs

Preparation time: 10 minutes
Cooking time: 20 minutes
Servings: 4

Ingredients:
- 4 eggs
- 1/2 cup parmesan cheese, grated
- 2 cups marinara sauce
- Pepper
- Salt

Directions
1. Spray 4 shallow baking dishes with cooking spray and set aside.
2. Insert wire rack in rack position 6. Select bake, set temperature 390 F, timer for 20 minutes. Press start to preheat the oven.
3. Divide marinara sauce into four baking dishes.
4. Break the egg into each baking dish. Sprinkle cheese, pepper, and salt on top of eggs and bake for 20 minutes.
5. Serve and enjoy.

Nutrition: Calories 208 Fat 10.1g Carbs 18g Sugar 11.4g Protein 11.4g Cholesterol 174mg

14. Eggs Florentine

Preparation time: 10 minutes
Cooking time: 12 minutes
Servings: 4

Ingredients:
- 3 cups frozen spinach, thawed and drained
- ¼ teaspoon kosher salt or ⅛ teaspoon fine salt
- 4 ounces ricotta cheese
- 2 tablespoons heavy (whipping) cream
- 2 garlic cloves, minced
- ⅛ teaspoon freshly ground white or black pepper
- 2 teaspoons unsalted butter, melted
- 3 tablespoons grated Parmesan or similar cheese
- ½ cup panko bread crumbs
- 4 large eggs

Directions
1. In a medium bowl, stir together the spinach, salt, ricotta, cream, garlic, and pepper.
2. In a small bowl, stir together the butter, cheese, and panko. Set aside.
3. Scoop the spinach mixture into four even circles on the sheet pan.
4. Select Air Roast, set temperature to 375 F, and set time to 15 minutes. Select Start/Pause to begin preheating.
5. Once the unit has preheated, slide the sheet pan into the oven.
6. After 8 minutes, press Pause and remove the pan. The spinach should be bubbling. With the back of a large spoon, make indentations in the spinach for the eggs. Crack the eggs into the indentations and sprinkle the panko mixture over the surface of the eggs.
7. Return the pan to the oven and press Start to resume cooking. After 5 minutes, check the eggs. If the eggs are done to your liking, remove the pan. If not, continue cooking.
8. When cooking is complete, remove the pan from the oven. Serve the eggs with toasted English muffins, if desired.

Nutrition: Calories 241 Fat 14g Saturated Fat 7g Cholesterol 216mg Sodium 263mg Carbs 15g Fiber 3g Protein 13g

15. Peanut Butter & Banana Sandwich

Preparation Time: 4 minutes
Cooking Time: 6 minutes
Servings: 1
Ingredients:
- 2 slices whole-wheat bread
- 1 tsp. sugar-free maple syrup
- 1 sliced banana
- 2 tbsps. Peanut butter

Directions:
1. Evenly coat each side of the sliced bread with peanut butter.
2. Add the sliced banana and drizzle with some sugar-free maple syrup.
3. Adjust the air fryer to 330°F then cook for 6 minutes. Serve warm.

Nutrition: Calories: 211 kcal Fat: 8.2g Carbs: 6.3g Protein: 11.2g

16. Spiced Apple Turnovers

Preparation time: 15 minutes
Cooking time: 20 minutes
Servings: 4
Ingredients:
- 1 cup diced apple (about 1 medium apple)
- 1 tablespoon brown sugar
- ¼ teaspoon cinnamon
- ⅛ teaspoon allspice
- 1 teaspoon freshly squeezed lemon juice
- 1 teaspoon all-purpose flour, plus more for dusting
- ½ package (1 sheet) frozen puff pastry, thawed
- 1 large egg, beaten
- 2 teaspoons granulated sugar

Directions
1. In a medium bowl, stir together the apple, brown sugar, cinnamon, allspice, lemon juice, and flour.
2. Lightly flour a cutting board. Unfold the puff pastry sheet onto the board. Using a rolling pin, gently roll the dough to smooth out the folds, seal any tears, and form it into a square. Cut the dough into four squares.
3. Scoop a quarter of the apple mixture into the center of each puff pastry square and spread it evenly in a triangle shape over half the pastry, leaving a border of about ½ inch around the edges of the pastry. Fold the pastry diagonally over the filling to form triangles. With a fork, crimp the edges to seal them. Place the turnovers on the sheet pan, spacing them evenly.
4. Cut two or three small slits in the top of each turnover. Brush with the egg. Sprinkle evenly with the granulated sugar.
5. Select Bake, set temperature to 350 F, and set time to 20 minutes. Select Start/Pause to begin preheating.
6. Once the unit has preheated, slide the sheet pan into the oven.
7. After 10 to 12 minutes, remove the pan from the oven. Check the pastries; if they are browning unevenly, rotate the pan. Return the pan to the oven and continue cooking.
8. When cooking is complete, remove the pan from the oven. The turnovers should be golden brown and the filling bubbling. Let cool for about 10 minutes before serving (the filling will be very hot).

Nutrition: Calories 399 Fat 24g Saturated Fat 6g Cholesterol 47mg Sodium 170mg Carbs 40g Fiber 2g Protein 6g

17. Classic Corned Beef Hash and Eggs

Preparation time: 10 minutes
Cooking time: 12 minutes
Servings: 4
Ingredients:
- 2 medium Yukon Gold potatoes, peeled, cut into ¼-inch cubes (about 3 cups)
- 1 medium onion, chopped (about 1 cup)
- ⅓ cup diced red bell pepper
- 3 tablespoons vegetable oil
- ½ teaspoon dried thyme
- ½ teaspoon kosher salt or ¼ teaspoon fine salt, divided
- ½ teaspoon freshly ground black pepper, divided
- ¾ pound corned beef, cut into ¼-inch pieces
- 4 large eggs

Directions
1. In a large bowl, mix the potatoes, onion, red pepper, oil, thyme, ¼ teaspoon of salt, and ¼ teaspoon of pepper. Spread the vegetables on the sheet pan in an even layer.
2. Select Air Roast, set temperature to 375 F, and set time to 25 minutes. Select Start/Pause to begin preheating.
3. Once the unit has preheated, slide the sheet pan into the oven.
4. After 15 minutes, remove the pan from the oven and add the corned beef. Stir the mixture to incorporate the corned beef. Return the pan to the oven and continue cooking for 5 minutes.
5. After 5 minutes (20 minutes total), remove the pan from the oven. Using a large spoon, create 4 circles in the hash to hold the eggs. Gently crack an egg into each circle; season eggs with remaining ¼ teaspoon of salt and ¼ teaspoon of pepper. Return the sheet pan to the oven. Continue cooking for 3 to 8 minutes, depending on how you like your eggs (3 to 4 minutes for runny yolks; 8 minutes for firm yolks).
6. When cooking is complete, remove the pan from the oven. Serve immediately.

Nutrition: Calories 397 Fat 26g Saturated Fat 7g Cholesterol 239mg Sodium 777mg Carbs 21g Fiber 3g Protein 20g

18. Mini Cinnamon Sticky Rolls

Preparation time: 10 minutes
Cooking time: 25 minutes
Servings: 18 mini rolls
Ingredients:
- 2 teaspoons cinnamon
- ⅓ cup light brown sugar
- 1 (9-by-9-inch) frozen puff pastry sheet, thawed
- All-purpose flour, for dusting
- 6 teaspoons (2 tablespoons) unsalted butter, melted, divided

Directions
1. In a small bowl, mix together the cinnamon and brown sugar.
2. Unfold the puff pastry on a lightly floured surface. Using a rolling pin, press the folds together and roll the dough out in one direction so that it measures about 9 by 11 inches. Cut it in half to form two squat rectangles of about 5½ by 9 inches.
3. Brush 2 teaspoons of butter over each pastry half, and then sprinkle with 2 generous tablespoons of the cinnamon sugar. Pat it down lightly with the palm of your hand to help it adhere to the butter.
4. Starting with the 9-inch side of one rectangle and using your hands, carefully roll the dough into a cylinder. Repeat with the other rectangle. To make slicing easier, refrigerate the rolls for 10 to 20 minutes.

5. Using a sharp knife, slice each roll into nine 1-inch pieces. Transfer the rolls to the center of the sheet pan. They should be very close to each other, but not quite touching. For neater rolls, turn the outside rolls so that the seam is to the inside. Drizzle the remaining 2 teaspoons of butter over the rolls and sprinkle with the remaining cinnamon sugar.
6. Select Bake, set temperature to 350 F, and set time to 25 minutes. Select Start/Pause to begin preheating.
7. Once the unit has preheated, slide the sheet pan into the oven.
8. When cooking is complete, remove the pan and check the rolls. They should be puffed up and golden brown. If the rolls in the center are not quite done, return the pan to the oven for another 3 to 5 minutes. If the outside rolls are dark golden brown before the inside rolls are done, you can remove those with a small spatula before returning the pan to the oven.
9. Let the rolls cool for a couple of minutes, then transfer them to a rack to cool completely.

Nutrition: Calories 149 Fat 9g Saturated Fat 5g Cholesterol 7mg Sodium 94mg Carbs 16g Fiber 1g Protein 2g

19. Morning Mini Cheeseburger Sliders

Preparation Time: 5 minutes
Cooking Time: 10 minutes
Servings: 6
Ingredients:
- 1 lb. ground beef
- 6 slices cheddar cheese
- 6 dinner rolls
- Salt and Black pepper

Directions:
1. Adjust the air fryer to 390°F.
2. Form 6 beef patties (each about 2.5 oz.) and season with salt and black pepper.
3. Add the burger patties to the cooking basket and cook them for 10 minutes.
4. Remove the burger patties from the air fryer; place the cheese on top of burgers and return to the air fryer and cook for another minute.
5. Remove and put burgers on dinner rolls and serve warm.

Nutrition: Calories: 262 kcal Fat: 9.4g Carbs: 8.2g Protein: 16.2g

20. Grilled Cheese

Preparation Time: 4 minutes
Cooking Time: 7 minutes
Servings: 2
Ingredients:
- 4 slices brown bread
- 1/2 cup shredded sharp cheddar cheese
- 1/4 cup melted butter

Directions:
1. Adjust your air fryer to 360°F.
2. In separate bowls, place cheese and butter.
3. Melt butter and brush it onto the 4 slices of bread.
4. Place cheese on 2 sides of bread slices.
5. Put sandwiches together and place them into the cooking basket.
6. Cook for 5 minutes and serve warm.

Nutrition: Calories: 214 kcal Fat: 11.2g Carbs: 9.4g Protein: 13.2g

21. Buttery Chocolate Toast

Preparation time: 5 minutes
Cooking time: 5 minutes
Servings: 1
Ingredients:
- Whole wheat bread slices
- Coconut oil
- Pure maple syrup
- Cacao powder

Directions
1. Toast the bread in air fryer oven.
2. Spread coconut oil over the toast.
3. Drizzle maple syrup in lines over the toast.
4. Sprinkle cacao powder and serve.

Nutrition: Calories 101 Sodium 133mg Dietary Fiber 2.4g Fat 3.5g Total Carbs 14.8g Protein 4.0g

22. Cheesy Baked-Egg Toast

Preparation time: 10 minutes
Cooking time: 10 minutes
Servings: 4
Ingredients:
- 4 slices wheat bread
- 4 eggs
- 1 cup shredded cheese
- 2 tablespoons softened butter

Directions
1. Start by preheating air fryer oven to 350 F.
2. Place bread on a greased baking sheet.
3. Use a teaspoon to push a square into the bread creating a little bed for the egg.
4. Sprinkle salt and pepper over the bread.
5. Break one egg into each square. Spread butter over each edge of the bread.
6. Sprinkle 1/4 cup cheese over buttered area.
7. Bake for 10 minutes or until the eggs are solid and the cheese is golden brown.

Nutrition: Calories 297 Sodium 410mg Dietary Fiber 1.9g Fat 20.4g Total Carbs 12.3g Protein 16.3g

23. Ham and Cheese Bagel Sandwiches

Preparation time: 5 minutes
Cooking time: 5 minutes
Servings: 2
Ingredients:
- 2 bagels
- 4 teaspoons honey mustard
- 4 slices cooked honey ham
- 4 slices Swiss cheese

Directions
1. Start by preheating air fryer oven to 400 F.
2. Spread honey mustard on each half of the bagel.
3. Add ham and cheese and close the bagel.
4. Bake the sandwich until the cheese is fully melted, approximately 5 minutes.

Nutrition: Calories 588 Sodium 1450mg Dietary Fiber 2.3g Fat 20.1g Total Carbs 62.9g Protein 38.4g

24. Peanut Butter and Jelly Banana Boats

Preparation time: 5 minutes
Cooking time: 15 minutes
Servings: 1
Ingredients:
- 1 banana
- 1/4 cup peanut butter
- 1/4 cup jelly
- 1 tablespoon granola

Directions
1. Start by preheating air fryer oven to 350 F.
2. Slice banana lengthwise and separate slightly.
3. Spread peanut butter and jelly in the gap.
4. Sprinkle granola over the entire banana. Bake for 15 minutes.

Nutrition: Calories 724 Sodium 327mg Fiber 9g Fat 36g Carbs 102.9g Protein 20.0g

25. Avocado and Spinach with Poached Eggs

Preparation time: 7 minutes
Cooking time: 10 minutes
Servings: 1
Ingredients:
- 2 eggs
- 1/2 avocado
- 2 slices bread
- 1 bunch spinach
- Pinch of salt
- Pinch of pepper

Directions
1. Start by preheating air fryer oven to 400 F.
2. Bring a pan of water to a rolling boil.
3. Place bread on a pan and toast it in the oven for 10 minutes.
4. Once the water is boiling, whisk it around in a circle until it creates a vortex.
5. Drop one egg in the hole and turn the heat to low, then poach for 2 minutes.
6. Repeat with the second egg.
7. Mash avocado and spread it over the toast while the eggs poach.
8. Add the eggs to the toast and top with spinach.

Nutrition: Calories 409 Sodium 553mg Dietary Fiber 14.2g Fat 29.7g Total Carbs 21.7g Protein 22.7g

26. Toasted Cinnamon Bananas

Preparation time: 10 minutes
Cooking time: 10 minutes
Servings: 1
Ingredients:
- 1 ripe banana
- Lemon juice
- 2 teaspoons honey
- Ground cinnamon

Directions
1. Start by preheating air fryer oven to 350 F.
2. Slice bananas lengthwise and place them on a greased baking sheet.
3. Brush each slice with lemon juice.
4. Drizzle honey and sprinkle cinnamon over each slice.
5. Bake for 10 minutes.

Nutrition: Calories 154 Sodium 3mg Dietary Fiber 4.2g Fat 0.5g Total Carbs 40.2g Protein 1.5g

27. Tomatta Spinacha Frittata

Preparation time: 15 minutes
Cooking time: 30 minutes
Servings: 4
Ingredients:
- 3 tablespoons olive oil
- 10 large eggs
- 2 teaspoons kosher salt
- 1/2 teaspoon black pepper
- 1 (5-ounce) bag baby spinach
- 1 pint grape tomatoes
- 4 scallions
- 8 ounces feta cheese

Directions
1. Preheat air fryer oven to 350 F.
2. Halve tomatoes and slice scallions into thin pieces.
3. Add oil to a 2-quart oven-safe pan, making sure to brush it on the sides as well as the bottom. Place the dish in toaster oven.
4. Combine the eggs, salt, and pepper in a medium mixing bowl and whisk together for a minute.
5. Add spinach, tomatoes, and scallions to the bowl and mix together until even.
6. Crumble feta cheese into the bowl and mix together gently. Remove the dish from the oven and pour in the egg mixture.
7. Put the dish back into the oven and bake for 25–30 minutes, or until the edges of the frittata are browned.

Nutrition: Calories 448 Sodium 515mg Dietary Fiber 2.3g Fat 35.4g Total Carbs 9.3g Protein 25.9g

28. Ultimate Breakfast Burrito

Preparation time: 20 minutes
Cooking time: 20 minutes
Servings: 8
Ingredients:
- 16 ounces cooked bacon ends and pieces
- 16 eggs
- 1 tablespoon butter
- 8 hash brown squares
- 8 large soft flour tortillas
- 2 diced jalapeños
- 2 cups shredded sharp cheddar

Directions
1. Place bacon on a baking sheet in air fryer oven. Bake at 450 F until it reaches desired level of crispiness and set aside.
2. Whisk together eggs in a bowl and set aside.
3. Melt butter into a sauce pan and mix in eggs until they are starting to cook but not fully hardened.
4. While eggs are cooking, microwave and cool hash brown squares.
5. Roll out tortillas and top them with hash browns, bacon, jalapeños, and cheese.
6. Wrap up the burritos and place them seam-down on a baking sheet. Bake at 375 F for 15–20 minutes.

Nutrition: Calories 698 Sodium 1821mg Dietary Fiber 3.4g Fat 43.7g Total Carbs 32.9g Protein 42.1g

29. Ultimate Breakfast Sandwich

Preparation time: 5 minutes
Cooking time: 5 minutes
Servings: 2
Ingredients:
- 2 English muffins
- 2 eggs
- 2 slices aged yellow cheddar
- 2 large spicy pork sausage patties
- Softened butter

Directions
1. Start by setting toaster oven to toast and warming up a non-stick pan.
2. Add sausages to pan and butter the insides of the muffins.
3. While the sausages cook, put the muffins in the toaster oven to toast until crispy brown, about 5–7 minutes.
4. Set the sausages aside and add eggs to the skillet.
5. Let the whites set, then carefully flip the eggs to keep the yolks intact.
6. Turn off the heat and add cheese and sausage to the top of the eggs. This will allow everything to melt together but leave the yolks with the perfect consistency.
7. Add the mixture to the muffin and enjoy the perfect breakfast.

Nutrition: Calories 332 Sodium 677mg Dietary Fiber 2.0g Fat 14.9g Total Carbs 26.1g Protein 22.7g

30. Air Fried French Toast

Preparation time: 5 minutes
Cooking time: 8 minutes
Servings: 1
Ingredients:
- 2 slices of sourdough bread
- 3 eggs
- 1 tablespoon of margarine
- 1 tsp. of liquid vanilla
- 3 tsps of honey
- 2 tablespoons of Greek yoghurt Berries

Directions
1. Preheat the air fryer to 356 F.
2. Pour the vanilla into the eggs and whisk to mix. Spread the margarine on all sides of the bread and soak in the eggs to absorb.
3. Place it in the deep fryer basket and cook for 3 minutes. Turn the bread over and cook for another 3 minutes.
4. Transfer to a place, top with yoghurt and berries with a sprinkle of honey.

Nutrition: Calories 101 Fat 3.5g Total Carbs 14.8g Protein 4.0g

31. Wheat and Seed Bread

Preparation time: 40 minutes
Cooking time: 20 minutes
Servings: 1
Ingredients:
- 3 1/2 ounces of flour
- 1 tsp. of yeast
- 1 tsp. of salt
- 3 1/2 ounces of wheat flour
- ¼ cup of pumpkin seeds

Directions
1. Mix the wheat flour, yeast, salt, seeds and the plain flour in a large bowl. Stir in ¾ cup of lukewarm water and keep stirring until dough becomes soft.
2. Knead for another 5 minutes until the dough becomes elastic and smooth.
3. Mould into a ball and cover with a plastic bag. Set aside for 30 minutes for it to rise.
4. Heat your air fryer to 392 F.
5. Transfer the dough into a small pizza pan and place in the air fryer. Bake for 18 minutes until golden. Remove the dough and then place it on a wire rack to cool.

Nutrition: Calories 154 Fat 0.5g Total Carbs 40.2g Protein 1.5g

32. Crispy Ham Egg Cups

Preparation time: 5 minutes
Cooking time: 20 minutes
Servings: 4
Ingredients:
- 4 large eggs
- 4: 1-oz. slices deli ham
- ½ cup shredded medium Cheddar cheese
- ¼ cup diced green bell pepper
- 2 tbsp. diced red bell pepper
- 2 tbsp. diced white onion
- 2 tbsp. Full-fat sour cream

Directions
1. On top of 4 baking cups, put the ham there.
2. Take a big bowl, and with sour cream, mix the eggs. With green pepper, onion and red pepper mix the ham with it.
3. Pour into a ham-lined baking cups. Top with Cheddar. Place cups into the air fryer basket. Adjust the temperature to 320 F and set the timer for 12 minutes or until the tops are browned. Serve warm.

Nutrition: Calories 203 Fat 14.3g Carbs 2.2g Sugar 1.2g Protein 16.3g Cholesterol 252mg

33. Ham and Egg Toast Cups

Preparation Time: 10 Minutes
Cooking Time: 15 Minutes
Servings: 2
Ingredients:
- 2 eggs
- 4 slices of bread
- 1 slice of ham
- Melted butter
- Salt and pepper to taste

Directions:
1. Grease the inside of the ramekin with melted butter.
2. Toast bread and flatten it with a rolling pin.
3. Press 1 piece of toast into the bottom of the ramekin to create a bread bowl.
4. Press another piece of toast onto the first one to create a double layer.
5. Cut the ham into 4 slices then line the inside of the toast cups with 2 strips of ham each.
6. Crack an egg into the middle of each cup and season with salt and pepper.
7. Cook it in the air fryer for 15 minutes at 320 degrees, if you like your eggs less runny, you may want to add a few minutes to the cook time.

Nutrition: Calories: 202 Sodium: 488 mg Dietary Fiber: 1.6 g Fat: 2.6 g Carbs: 16 g Protein: 9.2 g

BREAKFAST

34. Air Fryer Sausage Wraps

Preparation Time: 5 Minutes
Cooking Time: 3 Minutes
Servings: 2
Ingredients:
- 8 pre-cooked sausages
- 2 pieces American cheese
- 1 can of 8 count refrigerated crescent roll dough

Directions:
1. Cut each of the cheese slices into corners.
2. Unroll eat crescent roll.
3. At the wide end of the crescent roll, put down 1/4 of cheese and 1 sausage.
4. Starting at the wide end, roll the crescent up and tuck in the ends to cover the sausage and cheese.
5. Preheat the fryer to 380 degrees.
6. Put them in the basket and cook for about 3 minutes.

Nutrition: Calories: 325Sodium: 783 mg Dietary Fiber: 0.5gFat: 24.7g Carbs: 7.9 g Protein: 16.7 g

35. Tasty Raspberry Scones

Preparation time: 10 minutes
Cooking time: 15 minutes
Servings: 6
Ingredients:
1. Olive oil spray
2. 2½ tbsps. Cubed cold butter
3. 1½ tsps. baking powder
4. ¼ tsp. salt
5. 1 cup all-purpose flour
6. ½ cup milk
7. ½ cup fresh raspberries
8. 1 tbsp. granulated sugar

Directions
1. Place a parchment liner in the air fryer basket.
2. Combine the sugar, flour, baking powder, cold butter, and salt in a mixing bowl.
3. Work the ingredients together with clean hands until the mixture is crumbly.
4. Create a hole in the center of the mixture, and pour in the milk.
5. Knead the combination with your hands until it forms a thick dough.
6. Transfer to a well-floured, flat work surface.
7. Add the raspberries, and gently work them throughout the dough, taking care to not squash the berries.
8. Mold the dough into a ball and flatten out slightly, making sure to not crush the berries.
9. Cut into 6 wedges, and place on the liner in the air fryer basket.
10. Spray lightly with olive oil, and bake for 5 minutes at 400 F.
11. Reposition the scones, and bake for another 5 minutes.
12. Flip the scones over, and bake for a final 5 minutes. Serve warm.

Nutrition: Calories 152 Fat 6g Carbs 22g Protein 3g

36. Air Fried Spring Rolls

Preparation time: 20 minutes
Cooking time: 4 minutes
Servings: 4
Ingredients:
- For the filling
- 1 sliced celery stalk
- 4 oz. cooked and shredded chicken breast
- ½ cup sliced mushrooms
- 1 tsp. sugar
- ½ tsp. finely chopped ginger
- 1 tsp. chicken stock powder
- 1 sliced carrot
- For the spring roll wrappers
- 1 tsp. cornstarch
- 1 beaten egg
- 8 spring roll wrappers
- ½ tsp. vegetable oil

Directions
1. Prepare the filling. Put the meat, carrot, mushrooms, and celery in a bowl. Mix until combined. Add the chicken stock powder, sugar, and ginger. Mix well.
2. In another bowl, combine the cornstarch and egg and whisk until thick. Set aside.
3. Spoon some filling into a spring roll wrapper. Roll and seal the ends with the egg mixture. Brush the prepared spring rolls with a bit of oil. Arrange them in the cooking basket.
4. Cook for 4 minutes at 390 F.

Nutrition: Calories 257 Fat 3.5g Carbs 40.9g Protein 14.2g

37. Cinnamon and Honey Pancakes

Preparation time: 5 minutes
Cooking time: 10 minutes
Servings: 2
Ingredients:
- 2 tbsps. honey
- ½ cup coconut milk
- ¼ tsp. baking soda
- 4 tbsps. brown sugar
- 2 whisked eggs
- ¼ tsp. cinnamon powder
- Salt
- 1 cup whole wheat flour
- 1 tsp. baking powder
- ½ cup almond flour

Directions
1. In a large bowl add wheat flour, all-purpose flour, salt, baking powder, baking soda and brown sugar, mix well.
2. Now add eggs and milk whisk a little with a fork for 1-2 minutes.
3. Preheat your Air Fryer to a temperature of 400 F.
4. Grease a baking pan with some oil that can be fit into fryer basket.
5. Transfer half of the batter into pan and place into fryer basket and cook for 5 minutes.
6. Make another pancake with the same method.
7. When done transfer to serving platter and drizzle honey on top.
8. Serve with berries.

Nutrition: Calories 447 Fat 20.15g Carbs 57.93g Protein 14.92g

38. Chocolate Filled Donut Holes

Preparation Time: 10 Minutes
Cooking Time: 12 Minutes
Servings: 6

Ingredients:
- 1 (8-count) can refrigerated biscuits
- 1 bag semi-sweet chocolate chips
- 3 tablespoons melted butter
- 1/4 cup powdered sugar

Directions:
1. Cut each biscuit on into thirds.
2. Flatten each third with your hands and put a small dimple in the center with your thumb.
3. Place 2 – 3 chocolate chips inside each dimple and wrap the dough around the chocolate chips creating a ball.
4. Brush each ball with butter.
5. Cook at 320 for 10 minutes tossing at least once to ensure even baking throughout.
6. Place powdered sugar in bowl.
7. As soon as your donut holes are done put them in the powdered sugar and toss before serving.

Nutrition: Calories: 297 Sodium: 705 mg Dietary Fiber: 0.6g Fat: 15.5g Carbs: 35.4 g Protein: 4.7g.

39. French Toast Sticks

Preparation time: 5 minutes
Cooking time: 15 minutes
Servings: 12

Ingredients:
- 1 tsp. vanilla extract
- 1 tbsp. butter
- 1 tsp. ground cinnamon
- 1 egg
- 1 tsp. stevia
- ¼ cup milk
- Cooking oil
- 4 slices Texas toast

Directions
1. Divide the bread slices into 3 pieces each.
2. Place the butter in a small, microwave-safe bowl.
3. Set in the microwave for 15 seconds, or until the butter has melted.
4. Remove the bowl from the microwave. Add the egg, stevia, cinnamon, milk, and vanilla extract. Whisk until fully combined.
5. Spray the cooking basket with cooking oil.
6. Dredge each of the bread sticks in the egg mixture.
7. Place the French toast sticks in the air fryer. It is okay to stack them. Spray the French toast sticks with cooking oil. Cook for 8 minutes at 375 F.
8. Open the air fryer and flip each of the French toast sticks.
9. Allow to cook until the French toast sticks are crisp.
10. Cool before serving.

Nutrition: Calories 52 Fat 2g Carbs 7g Protein 2g

40. Air Fryer Chicken and Waffles

Preparation time: 10 minutes
Cooking time: 30 minutes
Servings: 4

Ingredients:
- 8 whole chicken wings
- 1 tsp. garlic powder
- Chicken seasoning or rub
- Pepper
- ½ cup all-purpose flour
- Cooking oil
- 8 frozen waffles
- Maple syrup

Directions
1. Rub the chicken with the chicken seasoning, garlic powder, and pepper in a sizable bowl.
2. Set the chicken in a sealable plastic bag and add the flour to coat evenly.
3. Spread the cooking basket with cooking oil.
4. Move the chicken from the bag to the air fryer with tongs.
5. Top some cooking oil on the chicken wings.
6. Allow to cook for five minutes.
7. Shake the basket.
8. Keep cooking the meat as you shake every five minutes for 20 minutes at 400 F.
9. Reserve the cooked chicken on a bowl.
10. Clean up the cooking baskets using warm water.
11. Set them back to their place.
12. Decrease the temperature of the air fryer to 370 F.
13. Set the frozen waffles in the cooker.
14. In relation to your air fryer size, you may need to cook the waffles in sets.
15. Top the waffles with cooking oil to cook for six minutes.
16. Remove the already done waffles to cook the remaining ones.
17. Enjoy the waffles with the chicken and a touch of maple syrup.

Nutrition: Calories 461 Fat 22g Carbs 45g Protein 28g

41. Tasty Scramble Casserole

Preparation time: 20 minutes
Cooking time: 10 minutes
Servings: 4

Ingredients:
- Salt
- Cooking oil
- Pepper
- ½ cup chopped green bell pepper
- 6 eggs
- ¾ cup shredded Cheddar cheese
- ½ cup chopped red bell pepper
- 6 slices bacon
- ½ cup chopped onion

Directions
1. Cook the bacon in a skillet for 5 to 7 minutes, flipping to evenly crisp over medium-high heat.
2. Drain on paper towels, crumble, and set aside.
3. In a medium bowl, whisk the eggs.
4. Add salt and pepper to taste.
5. Spray a barrel pan with cooking oil. Make sure to cover the bottom and sides of the pan.

6. Add the beaten eggs, crumbled bacon, red bell pepper, green bell pepper, and onion to the pan. Place the pan in the air fryer. Cook for 6 minutes.
7. Open the air fryer and sprinkle the cheese over the casserole. Cook for an additional 2 minutes.
8. Cool before serving.

Nutrition: Calories 348 Fat 26g Carbs 4g Protein 25g

42. Grilled Ham and Cheese

Preparation time: 5 minutes
Cooking time: 10 minutes
Servings: 2
Ingredients:
- 4 slices smoked country ham
- 4 slices bread
- 4 thick slices tomato
- 1 tsp. butter
- 4 slices Cheddar cheese

Directions
1. Spread ½ tsp. of butter onto one side of 2 slices of bread. Each sandwich will have 1 slice of bread with butter and 1 slice without.
2. Assemble each sandwich by layering 2 slices of ham, 2 slices of cheese, and 2 slices of tomato on the unbuttered pieces of bread. Top with the other bread slices, buttered side up.
3. Place the sandwiches in the air fryer buttered-side down. Cook for 4 minutes.
4. Open the air fryer. Flip the grilled cheese sandwiches. Cook for an additional 4 minutes.
5. Cool before serving.
6. Cut each sandwich in half and enjoy.

Nutrition: Calories 525 Fat 25g Carbs 34g Protein 41g

43. Sausage Balls

Preparation Time: 10 Minutes
Cooking Time: 20 Minutes
Servings: 10
Ingredients:
- 1-pound breakfast sausage
- 1 egg
- 1 cup almond meal
- 1 cup sharp cheddar cheese
- 2 teaspoons baking powder

Directions:
1. Put all of the ingredients in a bowl and mix it well. Considering the consistency of these ingredients, you may want to use and electric mixer to save your shoulders.
2. Preheat your fryer to 350 degrees.
3. Spoon out small scoops and roll them into balls and place them in your basket giving them room to breathe. This recipe makes about 30 balls, so you will probably have to do at least 2 batches.
4. Cook for 350 minutes, tossing at the 10- and 15-minute mark.

Nutrition: Calories: 262 Sodium: 533 mg Dietary Fiber: 1.2g Fat: 21.8g Carbs: 2.7g Protein: 14.2g.

44. Morning Sandwich Cheesy Stuffed

Preparation Time: 1 minute
Cooking Time: 8 minutes
Servings: 2
Ingredients:
- 1 tbsp. butter
- 4 frozen bread slices
- 2 cheddar cheese slices

Directions:
1. Evenly spread butter on each bread slice evenly.
2. Place one cheese slice between two bread slices.
3. Preheat your Air Fryer to a temperature of 360°F.
4. Transfer sandwiches into fryer basket and let them cook for 8 minutes.
5. Serve with coffee or tea, or with vegetables.

Nutrition: Calories: 272 Protein: 10.39 g Fat: 16.56 g Carbs: 20.37 g

45. Omelette Frittata

Preparation Time: 10 minutes
Cooking time: 6 minutes
Servings: 2
Ingredients:
- 3 eggs, lightly beaten
- 2 tbsp cheddar cheese, shredded
- 2 tbsp heavy cream
- 2 mushrooms, sliced
- 1/4 small onion, chopped
- 1/4 bell pepper, diced
- Pepper
- Salt

Directions
1. In a bowl, whisk eggs with cream, vegetables, pepper, and salt.
2. Preheat the air fryer to 400 F.
3. Pour egg mixture into the air fryer pan. Place pan in air fryer basket and cook for 5 minutes.
4. Add shredded cheese on top of the frittata and cook for 1 minute more.
5. Serve and enjoy.

Nutrition: Calories 160 Fat 10g Carbs 4g Sugar 2g Protein 12g Cholesterol 255mg

46. Cheese Soufflés

Preparation Time: 10 minutes
Cooking time: 6 minutes
Servings: 8
Ingredients:
- 6 large eggs, separated
- 3/4 cup heavy cream
- 1/4 tsp cayenne pepper
- 1/2 tsp xanthan gum
- 1/2 tsp pepper
- 1/4 tsp cream of tartar
- 2 tbsp chives, chopped
- 2 cups cheddar cheese, shredded
- 1 tsp salt

Directions
1. Preheat the air fryer to 325 F.
2. Spray eight ramekins with cooking spray. Set aside.
3. In a bowl, whisk together almond flour, cayenne pepper, pepper, salt, and xanthan gum.

4. Slowly add heavy cream and mix to combine.
5. Whisk in egg yolks, chives, and cheese until well combined.
6. In a large bowl, add egg whites and cream of tartar and beat until stiff peaks form.
7. Fold egg white mixture into the almond flour mixture until combined.
8. Pour mixture into the prepared ramekins. Divide ramekins in batches.
9. Place the first batch of ramekins into the air fryer basket.
10. Cook soufflé for 20 minutes.
11. Serve and enjoy.

Nutrition: Calories 210 Fat 16g Carbs 1g Sugar 0.5g Protein 12g Cholesterol 185mg

47. Simple Egg Soufflé

Preparation Time: 5 minutes
Cooking time: 8 minutes
Servings: 2
Ingredients:
- 2 eggs
- 1/4 tsp chili pepper
- 2 tbsp heavy cream
- 1/4 tsp pepper
- 1 tbsp parsley, chopped
- Salt

Directions
1. In a bowl, whisk eggs with remaining gradients.
2. Spray two ramekins with cooking spray.
3. Pour egg mixture into the prepared ramekins and place into the air fryer basket.
4. Cook soufflé at 390 F for 8 minutes.
5. Serve and enjoy.

Nutrition: Calories 116 Fat 10g Carbs 1.1g Sugar 0.4g Protein 6g Cholesterol 184mg

48. Vegetable Egg Soufflé

Preparation Time: 10 minutes
Cooking time: 20 minutes
Servings: 4
Ingredients:
- 4 large eggs
- 1 tsp onion powder
- 1 tsp garlic powder
- 1 tsp red pepper, crushed
- 1/2 cup broccoli florets, chopped
- 1/2 cup mushrooms, chopped

Directions
1. Spray four ramekins with cooking spray and set aside.
2. In a bowl, whisk eggs with onion powder, garlic powder, and red pepper.
3. Add mushrooms and broccoli and stir well.
4. Pour egg mixture into the prepared ramekins and place ramekins into the air fryer basket.
5. Cook at 350 F for 15 minutes. Make sure souffle is cooked if souffle is not cooked then cook for 5 minutes more.
6. Serve and enjoy.

Nutrition: Calories 91 Fat 5.1g Carbs 4.7g Sugar 2.6g Protein 7.4g Cholesterol 186mg

49. Garlic Cheese Bread

Preparation Time: 15 minutes
Cooking Time: 10 minutes
Servings: 4
Ingredients:
- Large egg, 1.
- Grated parmesan cheese, 1/4 cup
- Garlic powder, 1/2 tsp.
- Shredded mozzarella cheese, 1 cup

Directions:
1. Layer the air fryer basket with parchment paper.
2. Mix parmesan cheese, mozzarella cheese, garlic powder, and egg in a suitable bowl.
3. Set the mixture in a well-greased pan and place this pan in the fryer basket.
4. Return the basket to the fryer.
5. Leave them to cook for 10 minutes at 350 F on Air Fryer Mode.
6. Slice and serve warm.

Nutrition: Calories: 225 Fat: 14.3 g Carbs: 2.8 g Protein: 28.2 g

50. Chili Cream Soufflé

Preparation Time: 5 minutes
Cooking Time: 10 minutes
Servings: 4
Ingredients:
- Free-range eggs, 4.
- Large red chili pepper, 1/4 tsp.
- Chopped fresh parsley.
- Cream, 4 tbsps.
- Salt and pepper.

Directions:
1. Preheat your air fryer to 390 °F and grease some ramekin dishes.
2. Take a large bowl and add the eggs, whisking well to combine.
3. Add the cream, parsley and chili and stir well to combine.
4. Transfer the egg mixture into the ramekin dishes up to about halfway.
5. Pop into the air fryer and cook for 10 minutes until perfect.
6. Serve and enjoy.

Nutrition: Calories: 127 Carbs: 3g Protein: 10g Fat: 7g

51. Broccoli Stuffed Peppers

Preparation Time: 10 minutes
Cooking time: 40 minutes
Servings: 2
Ingredients:
- 4 eggs
- 1/2 cup cheddar cheese, grated
- 2 bell peppers, cut in half and remove seeds
- 1/2 tsp garlic powder
- 1 tsp dried thyme
- 1/4 cup feta cheese, crumbled
- 1/2 cup broccoli, cooked
- 1/4 tsp pepper
- 1/2 tsp salt

Directions
1. Preheat the air fryer to 325 F.
2. Stuff feta and broccoli into the bell peppers halved.

3. Beat egg in a bowl with seasoning and pour egg mixture into the pepper halved over feta and broccoli.
4. Place bell pepper halved into the air fryer basket and cook for 35-40 minutes.
5. Top with grated cheddar cheese and cook until cheese melted.
6. Serve and enjoy.

Nutrition: Calories 340 Fat 22g Carbs 12g Sugar 8.2g Protein 22g Cholesterol 374mg

52. Cheese and Bacon Breakfast Bombs

Preparation Time: 10 minutes
Cooking Time: 5 minutes
Servings: 2
Ingredients:
- Large eggs, 3.
- Centre-cut bacon slices, 3.
- Low carb pizza dough, 4 oz.
- Chopped fresh chives, 1 tbsp.
- Softened cream cheese, 1 oz.

Directions:
1. Pop a pan over medium heat and cook the bacon for ten minutes until crisp.
2. Remove from the heat and crumble, then pop to one side.
3. Stir the eggs to the pan and cook until set. Remove from the heat.
4. Place the eggs into a bowl with the cream cheese, chives and bacon.
5. Preheat your air fryer to 350°F.
6. Next take the pizza dough and carefully cut it into four pieces.
7. Roll each piece into a circle.
8. Place ¼ of the egg mixture into the middle and fold over the sides of the dough to meet in the middle.
9. Pop into the air fryer and cook for 5 minutes until perfectly cooked.

Nutrition: Calories: 305 Carbs: 23g Protein: 19g Fat: 15g

53. Delicious Breakfast Soufflé

Preparation Time: 5 minutes
Cooking Time: 15 minutes
Servings: 4
Ingredients:
- 6 eggs
- 1/3 of cup of milk
- ½ cup of shredded mozzarella cheese
- 1 tablespoon of freshly chopped parsley
- ½ cup of chopped ham
- 1 teaspoon of salt
- 1 teaspoon of black pepper
- ½ teaspoon of garlic powder

Directions:
1. Grease 4 ramekins with a nonstick cooking spray. Preheat your air fryer to 350 F.
2. Using a large bowl, add and stir all the ingredients until it mixes properly.
3. Pour the egg mixture into the greased ramekins and place it inside your air fryer.
4. Cook it inside your air fryer for 8 minutes. Then carefully remove the soufflé from your air fryer and allow it to cool off.
5. Serv and enjoy!

Nutrition: Calories 195 Fat 15g Carbs 6g Protein 9g

54. Yummy Breakfast Italian Frittata

Preparation Time: 5 minutes
Cooking Time: 10 minutes
Servings: 6
Ingredients:
- 6 eggs
- 1/3 cup of milk
- 4-ounces of chopped Italian sausage
- 3 cups of stemmed and roughly chopped kale
- 1 red deseeded and chopped bell pepper
- ½ cup of a grated feta cheese
- 1 chopped zucchini
- 1 tablespoon of freshly chopped basil
- 1 teaspoon of garlic powder
- 1 teaspoon of onion powder
- 1 teaspoon of salt
- 1 teaspoon of black pepper

Directions:
1. Turn on your air fryer to 360 F.
2. Grease the air fryer pan with a nonstick cooking spray.
3. Add the Italian sausage to the pan and cook it inside your air fryer for 5 minutes.
4. While doing that, add and stir in the remaining ingredients until it mixes properly.
5. Add the egg mixture to the pan and allow it to cook inside your air fryer for 5 minutes
6. Thereafter carefully remove the pan and allow it to cool off until it gets chill enough to serve.
7. Serve and enjoy!

Nutrition: Calories 225 Fat 14g Carbs 4.5g Protein 20g

55. Air-Fried English Breakfast

Preparation Time: 5 minutes
Cooking time: 20 minutes
Servings: 4
Ingredients:
- 8 sausages
- 8 bacon slices
- 4 eggs
- 1 (16-ounce) can of baked beans
- 8 slices of toast

Directions:
1. Add the sausages and bacon slices to your air fryer and cook them for 10 minutes at a 320 F.
2. Using a ramekin or heat-safe bowl, add the baked beans, then place another ramekin and add the eggs and whisk.
3. Change the temperature to 290 F.
4. Place it inside your air fryer and cook it for an additional 10 minutes or until everything is done.
5. Serve and enjoy!

Nutrition: Calories 850 Fat 40g Carbs 20g Protein 48g

56. Sausage and Egg Breakfast Burrito

Preparation Time: 5 minutes
Cooking time: 30 minutes
Servings: 6
Ingredients:
- 6 eggs
- Salt
- Pepper
- Cooking oil

- ½ cup chopped red bell pepper
- ½ cup chopped green bell pepper
- 8 ounces ground chicken sausage
- ½ cup salsa
- 6 medium (8-inch) flour tortillas
- ½ cup shredded Cheddar cheese

Directions:
1. In a medium bowl, whisk the eggs. Add salt and pepper to taste.
2. Place a skillet on medium-high heat. Spray with cooking oil. Add the eggs. Scramble for 2 to 3 minutes, until the eggs are fluffy. Remove the eggs from the skillet and set aside.
3. If needed, spray the skillet with more oil. Add the chopped red and green bell peppers. Cook for 2 to 3 minutes, once the peppers are soft.
4. Add the ground sausage to the skillet. Break the sausage into smaller pieces using a spatula or spoon. Cook for 3 to 4 minutes, until the sausage is brown.
5. Add the salsa and scrambled eggs. Stir to combine. Remove the skillet from heat.
6. Spoon the mixture evenly onto the tortillas.
7. To form the burritos, fold the sides of each tortilla in toward the middle and then roll up from the bottom. You can secure each burrito with a toothpick. Or you can moisten the outside edge of the tortilla with a small amount of water. I prefer to use a cooking brush, but you can also dab with your fingers.
8. Spray the burritos with cooking oil and place them in the air fryer. Do not stack. Cook the burritos in batches if they do not all fit in the basket. Cook for 8 minutes
9. Open the air fryer and flip the burritos. Heat it for an additional 2 minutes or until crisp.
10. If necessary, repeat steps 8 and 9 for the remaining burritos.
11. Sprinkle the Cheddar cheese over the burritos. Cool before serving.

Nutrition: Calories 236 Fat 13g Carbs 16g Protein 15g

57. Home-Fried Potatoes

Preparation Time: 5 minutes
Cooking time: 25 minutes
Servings: 4

Ingredients:
- 3 large russet potatoes
- 1 tablespoon canola oil
- 1 tablespoon extra-virgin olive oil
- 1 teaspoon paprika
- Salt
- Pepper
- 1 cup chopped onion
- 1 cup chopped red bell pepper
- 1 cup chopped green bell pepper

Directions:
1. Cut the potatoes into ½-inch cubes. Place the potatoes in a large bowl of cold water and allow them to soak for at least 30 minutes, preferably an hour.
2. Dry out the potatoes and wipe thoroughly with paper towels. Return them to the empty bowl.
3. Add the canola and olive oils, paprika, and salt and pepper to flavor. Toss to fully coat the potatoes.
4. Transfer the potatoes to the air fryer. Cook for 20 minutes, shaking the air fryer basket every 5 minutes (a total of 4 times).
5. Put the onion and red and green bell peppers to the air fryer basket. Fry for an additional 3 to 4 minutes, or until the potatoes are cooked through and the peppers are soft.
6. Cool before serving.

Nutrition: Calories 279 Fat 8g Carbs 50g Protein 6g

58. Homemade Cherry Breakfast Tarts

Preparation Time: 15 minutes
Cooking time: 20 minutes
Servings: 6

Ingredients:
- For the tarts:
- 2 refrigerated piecrusts
- ⅓ Cup cherry preserves
- 1 teaspoon cornstarch
- Cooking oil
- For the frosting:
- ½ cup vanilla yogurt
- 1-ounce cream cheese
- 1 teaspoon stevia
- Rainbow sprinkles

Directions:
1. To make the tarts:
2. Place the piecrusts on a flat surface. Make use of a knife or pizza cutter, cut each piecrust into 3 rectangles, for 6 in total. (I discard the unused dough left from slicing the edges.)
3. In a small bowl, combine the preserves and cornstarch. Mix well.
4. Scoop 1 tablespoon of the preserve mixture onto the top half of each piece of piecrust.
5. Fold the bottom of each piece up to close the tart. Press along the edges of each tart to seal using the back of a fork.
6. Sprinkle the breakfast tarts with cooking oil and place them in the air fryer. Cook for 10 minutes
7. Allow the breakfast tarts to cool fully before removing from the air fryer.
8. If needed, repeat steps 5 and 6 for the remaining breakfast tarts.
9. To make the frosting:
10. In a small bowl, mix the yogurt, cream cheese, and stevia. Mix well.
11. Spread the breakfast tarts with frosting and top with sprinkles, and serve.

Nutrition: Calories 119 Fat 4g Carbs 19g Protein 2g

59. Sausage and Cream Cheese Biscuits

Preparation Time: 5 minutes
Cooking Time: 15 minutes
Servings: 5

Ingredients:
- 12 ounces chicken breakfast sausage
- 1 (6-ounce) can biscuits
- ⅛ cup cream cheese

Direction:
1. Form the sausage into 5 small patties.
2. Place the sausage patties in the air fryer. Cook for 5 minutes.
3. Open the air fryer. Flip the patties. Cook for an additional 5 minutes
4. Remove the cooked sausages from the air fryer.
5. Separate the biscuit dough into 5 biscuits.
6. Place the biscuits in the air fryer. Cook for 3 minutes
7. Open the air fryer. Flip the biscuits. Cook for an additional 2 minutes

8. Remove the cooked biscuits from the air fryer.
9. Split each biscuit in half. Spread 1 teaspoon of cream cheese onto the bottom of each biscuit. Top with a sausage patty and the other half of the biscuit, and serve.

Nutrition: Calories 24g Fat 13g Carbs 20g Protein 9g

60. Fried Chicken and Waffles

Preparation Time: 10 minutes
Cooking Time: 30 minutes
Servings: 4

Ingredients:
- 8 whole chicken wings
- 1 teaspoon garlic powder
- Chicken seasoning or rub
- Pepper
- ½ cup all-purpose flour
- Cooking oil
- 8 frozen waffles
- Maple syrup (optional)

Directions:
1. In a medium bowl, spice the chicken with the garlic powder and chicken seasoning and pepper to flavor.
2. Put the chicken to a sealable plastic bag and add the flour. Shake to thoroughly coat the chicken.
3. Sprinkle the air fryer basket with cooking oil.
4. With the use of tongs, put the chicken from the bag to the air fryer. It is okay to pile the chicken wings on top of each other. Sprinkle them with cooking oil. Heat for five minutes
5. Unlock the air fryer and shake the basket. Presume to cook the chicken. Keep shaking every 5 minutes until 20 minutes has passed and the chicken is completely cooked.
6. Take out the cooked chicken from the air fryer and set aside.
7. Wash the basket and base out with warm water. Put them back to the air fryer.
8. Ease the temperature of the air fryer to 370°F.
9. Put the frozen waffles in the air fryer. Do not pile. Depends on how big your air fryer is, you may need to cook the waffles in batches. Sprinkle the waffles with cooking oil. Cook for 6 minutes
10. If necessary, take out the cooked waffles from the air fryer, then repeat step 9 for the leftover waffles.
11. Serve the waffles with the chicken and a bit of maple syrup if desired.

Nutrition: Calories 461 Fat 22g Carbs 45g Protein 28g

61. Cheesy Tater Tot Breakfast Bake

Preparation Time: 5 minutes
Cooking Time: 20 minutes
Servings: 4

Ingredients:
- 4 eggs
- 1 cup milk
- 1 teaspoon onion powder
- Salt
- Pepper
- Cooking oil
- 12 ounces ground chicken sausage
- 1-pound frozen tater tots
- ¾ cup shredded Cheddar cheese

Directions:
1. In a medium bowl, whisk the eggs. Add the milk, onion powder, and salt and pepper to taste. Stir to combine.
2. Spray a skillet with cooking oil and set over medium-high heat. Add the ground sausage. Using a spatula or spoon, break the sausage into smaller pieces. Cook for 3 to 4 minutes, until the sausage is brown. Remove from heat and set aside.
3. Spray a barrel pan with cooking oil. Make sure to cover the bottom and sides of the pan.
4. Place the tater tots in the barrel pan. Cook for 6 minutes
5. Open the air fryer and shake the pan, then add the egg mixture and cooked sausage. Cook for an additional 6 minutes. Open the air fryer and sprinkle the cheese over the tater tot bake. Cook for an additional 2 to 3 minutes
6. Cool before serving.

Nutrition: Calories 518 Fat 30g Carbs 31g Protein 30g

62. Savory Cheese and Bacon Muffins

Preparation Time: 5 minutes
Cooking time: 17 minutes
Servings: 4

Ingredients:
- 1 ½ cup of all-purpose flour
- 2 teaspoons of baking powder
- ½ cup of milk
- 2 eggs
- 1 tablespoon of freshly chopped parsley
- 4 cooked and chopped bacon slices
- 1 thinly chopped onion
- ½ cup of shredded cheddar cheese
- ½ teaspoon of onion powder
- 1 teaspoon of salt
- 1 teaspoon of black pepper

Directions:
1. Turn on your air fryer to 360 F.
2. Using a large bowl, add and stir all the ingredients until it mixes properly.
3. Then grease the muffin cups with a nonstick cooking spray or line it with a parchment paper. Pour the batter proportionally into each muffin cup.
4. Place it inside your air fryer and bake it for 15 minutes
5. Thereafter, carefully remove it from your air fryer and allow it to chill. Serve and enjoy!

Nutrition: Calories 180 Fat 18g Carbs 16g Protein 15g

63. Seasoned Potatoes

Preparation Time: 5 minutes
Cooking time: 40 minutes
Servings: 2

Ingredients:
- 2 Russet potatoes, scrubbed
- ½ tbsp. Butter, melted
- ½ tsp. Garlic and herb blend seasoning
- ½ tsp. Garlic powder
- Salt, as required

Directions:
1. In a bowl, mix all of the spices and salt.
2. With a fork, prick the potatoes. Coat the potatoes with butter and sprinkle with spice mixture.
3. Preheat the air fryer to 400 F.
4. Arrange the potatoes onto the cooking rack, insert the cooking rack in the center position and cook for 40 minutes. Serve hot.

Nutrition: Calories 176 Carbs 34.2g Fat 2.1g Protein 3.8g

64. Ham and Cheese Patties

Preparation Time: 20 minutes
Servings: 4
Ingredients:
- 8 ham slices; chopped.
- 4 handfuls mozzarella cheese; grated
- 1 puff pastry sheet
- 4 tsp. mustard

Directions:
1. Roll out puff pastry on a working surface and cut it in 12 squares. Divide cheese, ham and mustard on half of them, top with the other halves and seal the edges
2. Place all the patties in your air fryer's basket and cook at 370°F for 10 minutes. Divide the patties between plates and serve

Nutrition: Calories: 214 Carbs: 2g Fat: 16g Protein: 18g

65. Peppers and Lettuce Salad

Preparation Time: 15 minutes
Servings: 4
Ingredients:
- 2 oz. rocket leaves
- 4 red bell peppers
- 1 lettuce head; torn
- 2 tbsp. olive oil
- 1 tbsp. lime juice
- 3 tbsp. heavy cream
- Salt and black pepper to taste

Directions:
1. Place the bell peppers in your air fryer's basket and cook at 400°F for 10 minutes
2. Remove the peppers, peel, cut them into strips and put them in a bowl. Add all remaining ingredients, toss and serve

Nutrition: Calories: 255 Carbs: 1g Fat: 20g Protein: 4.

66. Radish Hash Browns

Preparation Time: 10 minutes
Cooking Time: 13 minutes
Servings: 4
Ingredients:
- 1 lb. radishes, washed and cut off roots
- 1 tbsp. olive oil
- 1/2 tsp paprika
- 1/2 tsp onion powder
- 1/2 tsp garlic powder
- 1 medium onion
- 1/4 tsp pepper
- 3/4 tsp sea salt

Directions:
1. Slice onion and radishes using a mandolin slicer.
2. Add sliced onion and radishes in a large mixing bowl and toss with olive oil.
3. Transfer onion and radish slices in air fryer basket and cook at 360 F for 8 minutes Shake basket twice.
4. Return onion and radish slices in a mixing bowl and toss with seasonings.
5. Again, cook onion and radish slices in air fryer basket for 5 minutes at 400 F. Shake the basket halfway through.
6. Serve and enjoy.

Nutrition: Calories 62 Fat 3.7 g Carbs 7.1 g Protein 1.2 g Sugar 3.5

67. Artichoke Omelet

Preparation Time: 20 minutes
Servings:
Ingredients:
- 3 artichoke hearts; canned, drained and chopped.
- 6 eggs; whisked
- 2 tbsp. avocado oil
- 1/2 tsp. oregano; dried
- Salt and black pepper to taste

Directions:
1. In a bowl, mix all ingredients except the oil; stir well. Add the oil to your air fryer's pan and heat it up at 320°F.
2. Add the egg mixture, cook for 15 minutes, divide between plates and serve

Nutrition: Calories: 250 Carbs: 11g Fat: 21g Protein: 14g

68. Carrot Oatmeal

Preparation Time: 20 minutes
Servings: 4
Ingredients:
- 1/2 cup steel cut oats
- 2 cups almond milk
- 1 cup carrots; shredded
- 2 tsp. sugar
- 1 tsp. cardamom; ground
- Cooking spray

Directions:
1. Spray your air fryer with cooking spray, add all ingredients, toss and cover. Cook at 365°F for 15 minutes. Divide into bowls and serve

Nutrition: Calories: 161 Carbs: 25g Fat: 2g Protein: 6g

69. Chicken Burrito

Preparation Time: 15 minutes
Servings: 2
Ingredients:
- 4 chicken breast slices; cooked and shredded
- 2 tortillas
- 1 avocado; peeled, pitted and sliced
- 1 green bell pepper; sliced
- 2 eggs; whisked
- 2 tbsp. mild salsa
- 2 tbsp. cheddar cheese; grated
- Salt and black pepper to taste

Directions:
1. In a bowl, whisk the eggs with the salt and pepper and pour them into a pan that fits your air fryer. Put the pan in the air fryer's basket, cook for 5 minutes at 400°F and transfer the mix to a plate
2. Place the tortillas on a working surface and between them divide the eggs, chicken, bell peppers, avocado and the cheese; roll the burritos
3. Line your air fryer with tin foil, add the burritos and cook them at 300°F for 3-4 minutes. Serve for breakfast-or lunch, or dinner!

Nutrition: Calories: 324 Carbs: 21g Fat: 16g Protein: 22g

BREAKFAST

70. Potato Frittata

Preparation Time: 25 minutes
Servings: 6
Ingredients:
- 1 lb. small potatoes; chopped.
- 1 oz. parmesan cheese; grated
- 1/2 cup heavy cream
- 2 red onions; chopped.
- 8 eggs; whisked
- 1 tbsp. olive oil
- Salt and black pepper to taste

Directions:
1. In a bowl, mix all ingredients except the potatoes and oil; stir well.
2. Heat up your air fryer's pan with the oil at 320°F. Add the potatoes, stir and cook for 5 minutes
3. Add the egg mixture, spread and cook for 15 minutes more. Divide the frittata between plates and serve

Nutrition: Calories: 775 Carbs: 56g Fat: 75g Protein: 31g

71. Herbed Omelet

Preparation Time: 20 minutes
Servings: 4
Ingredients:
- 6 eggs; whisked
- 2 tbsp. parmesan cheese; grated
- 4 tbsp. heavy cream
- 1 tbsp. parsley; chopped.
- 1 tbsp. tarragon; chopped.
- 2 tbsp. chives; chopped.
- Salt and black pepper to taste

Directions:
1. In a bowl, mix all ingredients except for the parmesan and whisk well. Pour this into a pan that fits your air fryer, place it in preheated fryer and cook at 350°F for 15 minutes
2. Divide the omelet between plates and serve with the parmesan sprinkled on top

Nutrition: Calories: 220 Carbs: 3.6g Fat: 13g Protein: 19g

72. Cheese Toast

Preparation Time: 13 minutes
Servings: 2
Ingredients:
- 4 bread slices
- 4 cheddar cheese slices
- 4 tsp. butter; softened

Directions:
1. Spread the butter on each slice of bread. Place 2 cheese slices each on 2 bread slices, then top with the other 2 bread slices; cut each in half
2. Arrange the sandwiches in your air fryer's basket and cook at 370°F for 8 minutes. Serve hot and enjoy!

Nutrition: Calories: 380 Carbs: 50g Fat: 15g Protein: 16g

73. Carrots and Cauliflower Mix

Preparation Time: 30 minutes
Servings: 4
Ingredients:
- 1 cauliflower head; stems removed, florets separated and steamed
- 2 oz. milk
- 2 oz. cheddar cheese; grated
- 3 carrots; chopped and steamed
- 3 eggs
- 2 tsp. cilantro; chopped.
- Salt and black pepper to taste

Directions:
1. In a bowl, mix the eggs with the milk, parsley, salt and pepper; whisk. Put the cauliflower and the carrots in your air fryer, add the egg mixture and spread. Then sprinkle the cheese on top
2. Cook at 350°F for 20 minutes, divide between plates and serve

Nutrition: Calories: 507 Carbs: 1g Fat: 32g Protein: 11g

74. Vanilla Oatmeal

Preparation Time: 22 minutes
Servings: 4
Ingredients:
- 1 cup steel cut oats
- 1 cup milk
- 2½ cups water
- 2 tsp. vanilla extract
- 2 tbsp. brown sugar

Directions:
1. In a pan that fits your air fryer, mix all ingredients and stir well. Place the pan in your air fryer and cook at 360°F for 17 minutes. Divide into bowls and serve

Nutrition: Calories: 291 Carbs: 41g Fat: 3.7g Protein: 12g

75. Fish Tacos Breakfast

Preparation Time: 23 Minutes
Servings: 4
Ingredients:
- 4 big tortillas
- 1 yellow onion; chopped
- 1 cup corn
- 1 red bell pepper; chopped
- 1/2 cup salsa
- 4 white fish fillets; skinless and boneless
- A handful mixed romaine lettuce; spinach and radicchio
- 4 tbsp. parmesan; grated

Directions:
1. Put fish fillets in your air fryer and cook at 350°F, for 6 minutes
2. Meanwhile; heat up a pan over medium high heat, add bell pepper, onion and corn; stir and cook for 1 - 2 minutes
3. Arrange tortillas on a working surface, divide fish fillets, spread salsa over them; divide mixed veggies and mixed greens and spread parmesan on each at the end.
4. Roll your tacos; place them in preheated air fryer and cook at 350°F, for 6 minutes more. Divide fish tacos on plates and serve for breakfast

Nutrition: Calories: 232 Carbs: 17g Fat: 3.5g Protein: 27g

76. Tuna Sandwiches

Preparation Time: 14 minutes
Servings: 4
Ingredients:
- 16 oz. canned tuna; drained
- 6 bread slices
- 6 provolone cheese slices
- 2 spring onions; chopped.
- 1/4 cup mayonnaise
- 2 tbsp. mustard
- 1 tbsp. lime juice
- 3 tbsp. butter; melted

Directions:
1. In a bowl, mix the tuna, mayo, lime juice, mustard and spring onions; stir until combined.
2. Spread the bread slices with the butter, place them in preheated air fryer and bake them at 350°F for 5 minutes
3. Spread tuna mix on half of the bread slices and top with the cheese and the other bread slices
4. Place the sandwiches in your air fryer's basket and cook for 4 minutes more. Divide between plates and serve.

Nutrition: Calories: 581 Carbs: 35g Fat: 37g Protein: 41g

77. Tofu and Bell Peppers

Preparation Time: 15 minutes
Servings: 8
Ingredients:
- 3 oz. firm tofu; crumbled
- 1 green onion; chopped.
- 1 yellow bell pepper; cut into strips
- 1 orange bell pepper; cut into strips
- 1 green bell pepper; cut into strips
- 2 tbsp. parsley; chopped.
- Salt and black pepper to taste

Directions:
1. In a pan that fits your air fryer, place the bell pepper strips and mix
2. Then add all remaining ingredients, toss and place the pan in the air fryer. Cook at 400°F for 10 minutes. Divide between plates and serve

Nutrition: Calories: 20 Carbs: 4g Fat: 2g Protein: 1g

VEGETABLE AND SIDE DISHES

78. Herbed Tomatoes

Preparation Time: 10 minutes
Cooking Time: 15 minutes
Servings: 2
Ingredients:
- 2 big tomatoes, halved and insides scooped out
- Salt and black pepper, to taste
- ½ tablespoon olive oil
- 1 clove garlic, minced
- ¼ teaspoon thyme, chopped

Directions:
1. In the air fryer, mix tomatoes with thyme, garlic, oil, salt, and pepper.
2. Mix and cook at 390F for 15 minutes.
3. Serve.

Nutrition: Calories: 112 Fat: 1g Carb: 4g Protein: 4g

79. Baked Potato

Preparation time: 5 minutes
Cooking time: 45 minutes
Servings: 3
Ingredients:
- 3 Idaho or Russet Baking Potatoes
- 1 to 2 tablespoons olive oil
- 1 teaspoon parsley
- 1 tablespoon garlic
- 1 tablespoon salt

Directions
1. Wash the potatoes very well.
2. Poke several holes in the potatoes with a fork.
3. Sprinkle the potatoes with olive oil. Evenly rub the potatoes with parsley, garlic, and salt.
4. Arrange the potatoes in the air fryer basket and cook for 35 to 40 minutes at 392 F until fork tender.
5. Serve with your favorite dipping, sour cream or fresh parsley.
6. Enjoy!

Nutrition: Calories 213 Fat 4g Carbs 39 Sodium 2336mg Dietary Fiber 2g Total Sugars 1g Protein 4g

80. Air Fried Leeks

Preparation Time: 10 minutes
Cooking Time: 7 minutes
Servings: 2
Ingredients:
- 2 leeks, washed, ends cut, and halved
- Salt and black pepper, to taste
- ½ tablespoon butter, melted
- ½ tablespoon lemon juice

Directions:
1. Rub leeks with melted butter and season with salt and pepper.
2. Lay it inside the air fryer and cook at 350F for 7 minutes.
3. Arrange on a platter. Drizzle with lemon juice and serve.

Nutrition: Calories: 100 Fat: 4g Carb: 6g Protein: 2g

81. Wine Glazed Mushrooms

Preparation Time: 10 minutes
Cooking Time: 32 minutes
Servings: 4
Ingredients:
- 1 tablespoon butter
- 2 teaspoons Herbs de Provence
- ½ teaspoon garlic powder
- 2 lbs. fresh mushrooms, quartered
- 2 tablespoons white wine

Directions:
1. In a frying pan, mix together the butter, herbs de Provence, wine, and garlic powder over medium-low heat and stir fry for about 2 minutes.
2. Add in the mushrooms and remove from the heat.
3. Transfer the mushroom mixture into the Air fryer. Put on the Air Fryer and cook on Bake mode for 30 minutes at 320 degrees F. Serve.

Nutrition: Calories: 218 Protein: 5.4g Carbs: 31.3g Fat: 3.8g

82. Veggie Stuffed Bell Peppers

Preparation time: 5 minutes
Cooking time: 25 minutes
Servings: 6
Ingredients:
- 6 large bell peppers, tops and seeds removed
- 1 carrot, peeled and finely chopped
- 1 potato, peeled and finely chopped
- ½ cup fresh peas, shelled
- 1/3 cup cheddar cheese, grated
- 2 garlic cloves, minced
- Salt and black pepper, to taste

Directions
1. Preheat the Air fryer to 350 F and grease an Air fryer basket.
2. Mix vegetables, garlic, salt and black pepper in a bowl.
3. Stuff the vegetable mixture in each bell pepper and arrange in the Air fryer pan.
4. Cook for about 20 minutes and top with cheddar cheese.
5. Cook for about 5 more minutes and dish out to serve warm.

Nutrition: Calories 101 Fat 2.5g Carbs 17.1g Sugar 7.4g Protein 4.1g Sodium 51mg

83. Stuffed Okra

Preparation time: 5 minutes
Cooking time: 12 minutes
Servings: 2
Ingredients:
- 8 ounces large okra
- ¼ cup chickpea flour
- ¼ of onion, chopped
- 2 tablespoons coconut, grated freshly
- 1 teaspoon garam masala powder
- ½ teaspoon ground turmeric
- ½ teaspoon red chili powder
- ½ teaspoon ground cumin
- Salt, to taste

Directions
1. Preheat the Air fryer to 390 F and grease an Air fryer basket.
2. Mix the flour, onion, grated coconut, and spices in a bowl and toss to coat well.

3. Stuff the flour mixture into okra and arrange into the Air fryer basket.
4. Cook for about 12 minutes and dish out in a serving plate.

Nutrition: Calories 166 Fat 3.7g Carbs 26.6g Sugar 5.3g Protein 7.6g Sodium 103mg

84. Fried Spicy Tofu

Preparation time: 5 minutes
Cooking time: 20 minutes
Servings: 4
Ingredients:
- 16 ounces firm tofu, pressed and cubed
- 1 tablespoon vegan oyster sauce
- 1 tablespoon tamari sauce
- 1 teaspoon cider vinegar
- 1 teaspoon pure maple syrup
- 1 teaspoon sriracha
- 1/2 teaspoon shallot powder
- 1/2 teaspoon porcini powder
- 1 teaspoon garlic powder
- 1 tablespoon sesame oil
- 2 tablespoons golden flaxseed meal

Directions
1. Toss the tofu with the oyster sauce, tamari sauce, vinegar, maple syrup, sriracha, shallot powder, porcini powder, garlic powder, and sesame oil. Let it marinate for 30 minutes.
2. Toss the marinated tofu with the flaxseed meal.
3. Cook at 360 F for 10 minutes; turn them over and cook for 12 minutes more.

Nutrition: Calories 173 Fat 13g Carbs 5g Protein 8g Fiber 1g

85. Tarragon Yellow Squash

Preparation Time: 10 minutes
Cooking Time: 15 minutes
Servings: 4
Ingredients:
- 4 teaspoons olive oil
- 2 lbs. yellow squash, sliced
- 1 teaspoon salt
- ½ teaspoon ground white pepper
- 1 tablespoon tarragon leaves, chopped

Directions:
1. In a large-sized bowl, mix together the oil, yellow squash, salt, and white pepper. Spread the squash in the Air fryer. Put on the Air Fryer and cook on Roast mode for 15 minutes at 390 degrees F. Serve.
2. Transfer the yellow squash into a bowl with tarragon leaves and mix until well. Serve warm.

Nutrition: Calories: 288 Protein: 24g Carbs: 41g Fat: 3g

86. Broccoli With Olives

Preparation time: 5 minutes
Cooking time: 19 minutes
Servings: 4
Ingredients:
- 2 pounds broccoli, stemmed and cut into 1-inch florets
- 1/3 cup Kalamata olives, halved and pitted
- ¼ cup Parmesan cheese, grated
- 2 tablespoons olive oil
- Salt and ground black pepper, as required
- 2 teaspoons fresh lemon zest, grated

Directions
1. Preheat the Air fryer to 400 F and grease an Air fryer basket.
2. Boil the broccoli for about 4 minutes and drain well.
3. Mix broccoli, oil, salt, and black pepper in a bowl and toss to coat well.
4. Arrange broccoli into the Air fryer basket and cook for about 15 minutes.
5. Stir in the olives, lemon zest and cheese and dish out to serve.

Nutrition: Calories 169 Fat 10.2g Carbs 16g Sugar 3.9g Protein 8.5g Sodium 254mg

87. Roasted Butternut Squash With Brussels Sprouts and Sweet Potato Noodles

Preparation time: 5 minutes
Cooking time: 15 minutes
Servings: 2
Ingredients:
- Squash:
- 3 cups chopped butternut squash
- 2 teaspoons extra light olive oil
- 1/8 teaspoon sea salt
- Veggies:
- 5-6 Brussels sprouts
- 5 fresh shiitake mushrooms
- 2 cloves garlic
- 1/2 teaspoon black sesame seeds
- 1/2 teaspoon white sesame seeds
- A few sprinkles ground pepper
- A small pinch red pepper flakes
- 1 tablespoon extra light olive oil
- 1 teaspoon sesame oil
- 1 teaspoon onion powder
- 1 teaspoon garlic powder
- 1/4 teaspoon sea salt
- Noodles:
- 1 bundle sweet potato vermicelli
- 2-3 teaspoons low-sodium soy sauce

Directions
1. Start by soaking potato vermicelli in water for at least 2 hours.
2. Preheat toaster oven to 375 F.
3. Place squash on a baking sheet with edges, then drizzle with olive oil and sprinkle with salt and pepper. Mix together well on pan.
4. Bake the squash for 30 minutes, mixing and flipping half way through.
5. Remove the stems from the mushrooms and chop the Brussels sprouts.
6. Chop garlic and mix the veggies.
7. Drizzle sesame and olive oil over the mixture, then add garlic powder, onion powder, sesame seeds, red pepper flakes, salt, and pepper.
8. Bake veggie mix for 15 minutes.
9. While the veggies bake, put noodles in a small sauce pan and add just enough water to cover.

10. Bring water to a rolling boil and boil noodles for about 8 minutes.
11. Drain noodles and combine with squash and veggies in a large bowl.
12. Drizzle with soy sauce, sprinkle with sesame seeds, and serve.

Nutrition: Calories 409 Sodium 1124mg Dietary Fiber 12.2g Fat 15.6g Total Carbs 69.3g Protein 8.8g

88. Green Beans and Cherry Tomatoes

Preparation Time: 10 minutes
Cooking Time: 15 minutes
Servings: 2
Ingredients:
- 8 ounces cherry tomatoes
- 8 ounces green beans
- 1 tablespoon olive oil
- Salt and black pepper, to taste

Directions:
1. In a bowl, mix cherry tomatoes with green beans, olive oil, salt, and pepper. Mix.
2. Cook in the air fryer at 400 degrees F for 15 minutes. Shake once.
3. Serve.

Nutrition: Calories: 162 Fat: 6g Carb: 8g Protein: 9g

89. Flatbread

Preparation Time: 5 minutes
Cooking Time: 7 minutes
Servings: 2
Ingredients:
- 1 cup shredded mozzarella cheese
- ¼ cup almond flour
- 1-ounce full-fat cream cheese softened

Directions:
1. Melt mozzarella in the microwave for 30 seconds. Stir in almond flour until smooth.
2. Add cream cheese. Continue mixing until dough forms. Knead with wet hands if necessary.
3. Divide the dough into two pieces and roll out to ¼-inch thickness between two pieces of parchment.
4. Cover the air fryer basket with parchment and place the flatbreads into the air fryer basket. Work in batches if necessary.
5. Cook at 320F for 7 minutes. Flip once at the halfway mark.
6. Serve.

Nutrition: Calories: 296 Fat: 22.6g Carb: 3.3g Protein: 16.3g

90. Creamy Cabbage

Preparation Time: 10 minutes
Cooking Time: 20 minutes
Servings: 2
Ingredients:
- ½ green cabbage head, chopped
- ½ yellow onion, chopped
- Salt and black pepper, to taste
- ½ cup whipped cream
- 1 tablespoon cornstarch

Directions:
1. Put cabbage and onion in the air fryer.
2. In a bowl, mix cornstarch with cream, salt, and pepper. Stir and pour over cabbage.
3. Toss and cook at 400F for 20 minutes.
4. Serve.

Nutrition: Calories: 208 Fat: 10g Carb: 16g Protein: 5g

91. Cauliflower Pizza Crust

Preparation Time: 26 minutes
Cooking time: 20 minutes
Servings: 2
Ingredients:
- 1 (12-oz.) Steamer bag cauliflower
- 1 large egg.
- ½ cup shredded sharp cheddar cheese.
- 2 tbsp. Blanched finely ground almond flour
- 1 tsp. Italian blend seasoning

Directions
1. Cook cauliflower according to package Preparation. Remove from bag and place into cheesecloth or paper towel to remove excess water. Place cauliflower into a large bowl.
2. Cut a piece of parchment to fit your air fryer basket. Press cauliflower into 6-inch round circle. Place into the air fryer basket. Adjust the temperature to 360 F and set the timer for 11 minutes. After 7 minutes, flip the pizza crust
3. Add preferred toppings to pizza. Place back into air fryer basket and cook for an additional 4 minutes or until fully cooked and golden. Serve right away.

Nutrition: Calories 230 Protein 14.9g Fiber 4.7g Fat 14.2g Carbs 10.0g

92. Olives and Artichokes

Preparation Time: 20 minutes
Cooking time: 15 minutes
Servings: 4
Ingredients:
- 14 oz. canned artichoke hearts, drained
- ½ cup tomato sauce
- 2 cups black olives, pitted
- 3 garlic cloves; minced
- 1 tbsp. Olive oil
- 1 tsp. Garlic powder

Directions
1. In a pan that fits your air fryer, mix the olives with the artichokes and the other ingredients, toss, put the pan in the fryer and cook at 350 F for 15 minutes
2. Divide the mix between plates and serve.

Nutrition: Calories 180 Fat 4g Fiber 3g Carbs 5g Protein 6g

93. Lemon Asparagus

Preparation Time: 17 minutes
Cooking time: 12 minutes
Servings: 4
Ingredients:
- 1 lb. Asparagus, trimmed
- 3 garlic cloves; minced
- 3 tbsp. Parmesan, grated
- 2 tbsp. Olive oil
- Juice of 1 lemon
- A pinch of salt and black pepper

Directions
1. Take a bowl and mix the asparagus with the rest of the ingredients and toss.
2. Put the asparagus in your air fryer's basket and cook at 390 F for 12 minutes. Divide between plates and serve!

VEGETABLE AND SIDE DISHES

Nutrition: Calories 175 Fat 5g Fiber 2g Carbs 4g | Protein 8g

94. Salty Lemon Artichokes

Preparation Time: 15 minutes
Cooking Time: 45 minutes
Servings: 2
Ingredients:
- 1 lemon
- 2 artichokes
- 1 teaspoon kosher salt
- 1 garlic head
- 2 teaspoon olive oil

Directions:
1. Cut off the edges of the artichokes.
2. Cut the lemon into the halves.
3. Peel the garlic head and chop the garlic cloves roughly.
4. Then place the chopped garlic in the artichokes.
5. Sprinkle the artichokes with the olive oil and kosher salt.
6. Then squeeze the lemon juice into the artichokes.
7. Wrap the artichokes in the foil.
8. Preheat the air fryer to 330 F.
9. Place the wrapped artichokes in the air fryer and cook for 45 minutes.
10. When the artichokes are cooked – discard the foil and serve.
11. Enjoy!

Nutrition: Calories 133 Fat 5 Fiber 9.7 Carbs 21.7 Protein 6

95. Pecan Brownies

Preparation Time: 30 minutes
Cooking time: 20 minutes
Servings: 6
Ingredients:
- ¼ cup chopped pecans
- ¼ cup low carb
- Sugar: -free chocolate chips.
- ¼ cup unsalted butter; softened.
- 1 large egg.
- ½ cup blanched finely ground almond flour.
- ½ cup powdered erythritol
- 2 tbsp. Unsweetened cocoa powder
- ½ tsp. Baking powder.

Directions
1. Take a large bowl, mix almond flour, erythritol, cocoa powder and baking powder. Stir in butter and egg.
2. Adjust the temperature to 300 F and set the timer for 20 minutes. When fully cooked a toothpick inserted in center will come out clean. Allow 20 minutes to fully cool and firm up.

Nutrition: Calories 215 Protein 4.2g Fiber 2.8g Fat 18.9g Carbs 21.8g

96. Cheesy Endives

Preparation Time: 20 minutes
Cooking time: 15 minutes
Servings: 4
Ingredients:
- 4 endives, trimmed
- ¼ cup goat cheese, crumbled
- 1 tbsp. Lemon juice
- 2 tbsp. Chives; chopped.
- 2 tbsp. Olive oil
- 1 tsp. Lemon zest, grated
- A pinch of salt and black pepper

Directions
1. Take a bowl and mix the endives with the other ingredients except the cheese and chives and toss well.
2. Put the endives in your air fryer's basket and cook at 380 F for 15 minutes.
3. Divide the corn between plates.
4. Serve with cheese and chives sprinkled on top.

Nutrition: Calories 140 Fat 4g Fiber 3g Carbs 5g Protein 7g

97. Cauliflower Steak

Preparation Time: 12 minutes
Cooking time: 7 minutes
Servings: 4
Ingredients:
- 1 medium head cauliflower
- ¼ cup blue cheese crumbles
- ¼ cup hot sauce
- ¼ cup full-fat ranch dressing
- 2 tbsp. Salted butter; melted.

Directions
1. Remove cauliflower leaves. Slice the head in ½-inch-thick slices.
2. In a small bowl, mix hot sauce and butter. Brush the mixture over the cauliflower.
3. Place each cauliflower steak into the air fryer, working in batches if necessary. Adjust the temperature to 400 F and set the timer for 7 minutes
4. When cooked, edges will begin turning dark and caramelized. To serve, sprinkle steaks with crumbled blue cheese. Drizzle with ranch dressing.

Nutrition: Calories 122 Protein 4.9g Fiber 3.0g Fat 8.4g Carbs 7.7g

98. Chard with Cheddar

Preparation Time: 10 minutes
Cooking Time: 11 minutes
Servings: 2
Ingredients:
- 3 oz Cheddar cheese, grated
- 10 oz Swiss chard
- 3 tablespoon cream
- 1 tablespoon sesame oil
- salt and pepper to taste

Directions:
1. Wash Swiss chard carefully and chop it roughly.
2. After this, sprinkle chopped Swiss chard with the salt and ground white pepper.
3. Stir it carefully.
4. Sprinkle Swiss chard with the sesame oil and stir it carefully with the help of 2 spatulas.
5. Preheat the air fryer to 260 F.
6. Put chopped Swiss chard in the air fryer basket and cook for 6 minutes.
7. Shake it after 3 minutes of cooking.
8. Then pour the cream into the air fryer basket and mix it up.
9. Cook the meal for 3 minutes more.
10. Then increase the temperature to 400 F.
11. Sprinkle the meal with the grated cheese and cook for 2 minutes more.
12. After this, transfer the meal in the serving plates. Enjoy!

Nutrition: Calories 272 Fat 22.3 Fiber 2.5 Carbs 6.7 Protein 13.3

99. Air Fryer Crunchy Cauliflower

Preparation Time: 20 minutes
Cooking time: 15 minutes
Servings: 5
Ingredients:
- 16 oz. cauliflower
- 1 tbsp. potato starch
- 1 tsp. olive oil
- Salt and pepper to taste

Directions
1. Set the air fryer toaster oven to 400 F and preheat it for 3 minutes. Slice cauliflower into equal pieces and if you are using potato starch then toss with the florets into bowl. Add some olive oil and mix to coat. Use olive oil cooking spray for spraying the inside of air fryer toaster oven basket then add cauliflower. Cook for eight minutes then shake the basket and cook for another 5 minutes depending on your desired level of crisp. Sprinkle roasted cauliflower with fresh parsley, kosher salt, and your seasonings or sauce of your choice.

Nutrition: Calories: 36 Fat 1g Protein 1g Carbs 5g Fiber 2g

100. Chili Squash Wedges

Preparation Time: 10 minutes
Cooking Time: 18 minutes
Servings: 2
Ingredients:
- 11 oz Acorn squash
- ½ teaspoon salt
- tablespoon olive oil
- ½ teaspoon chili pepper
- ½ teaspoon paprika

Directions:
- Cut Acorn squash into the serving wedges.
- Sprinkle the wedges with the salt, olive oil, chili pepper, and paprika.
- Massage the wedges gently.
- Preheat the air fryer to 400 F.
- Put Acorn squash wedges in the air fryer basket and cook for 18 minutes.
- Flip the wedges into another side after 9 minutes of cooking.
- Serve the cooked meal hot. Enjoy!

Nutrition: Calories 125 Fat 7.2 Fiber 2.6 Carbs 16.7 Protein 1.4

101. Air Fryer Veg Buffalo Cauliflower

Preparation Time: 20 minutes
Cooking time: 15 minutes
Servings: 3
Ingredients:
- 1 medium head cauliflower
- 2 tsp. avocado oil
- 3 tbsp. red hot sauce
- 2 tbsp. nutritional yeast
- 1 1/2 tsp. maple syrup
- 1/4 tsp. sea salt
- 1 tbsp. cornstarch or arrowroot starch

Directions
1. Set your air fryer toaster oven to 360 F. Place all the ingredients to bowl except cauliflower. Mix them to combine. Put the cauliflower and mix to coat equally. Put half of your cauliflower to air fryer and cook for 15 minutes but keep shaking them until your get desired consistency. Do the same for the cauliflower which is left except lower Cooking Time to 10 minutes. Keep the cauliflower tightly sealed in refrigerator for 3-4 days. For heating again add back to air fryer for 1-2 minutes until crispness.

Nutrition: Calories 248 Fat 20g Protein 4g Carbs 13g Fiber 2g

102. Air Fryer Asparagus

Preparation Time: 5 minutes
Cooking time: 13 minutes
Servings: 2
Ingredients:
- Nutritional yeast
- Olive oil nonstick spray
- One bunch of asparagus

Directions
1. Wash asparagus and then trim off thick, woody ends.
2. Spray asparagus with olive oil spray and sprinkle with yeast.
3. Add the asparagus to air fryer rack/basket in a singular layer. Set temperature to 360 F and set time to 8 minutes. Select Start/Stop to begin.

Nutrition: Calories 17 Fat 8g Total Carbs 2g Protein 9g

103. Almond Flour Battered and Crisped Onion Rings

Preparation Time: 5 minutes
Cooking time: 20 minutes
Servings: 3
Ingredients:
- ½ cup almond flour
- ¾ cup coconut milk
- 1 big white onion, sliced into rings
- 1 egg, beaten
- 1 tablespoon baking powder
- 1 tablespoon smoked paprika
- Salt and pepper to taste

Directions
1. Preheat the air fryer Oven for 5 minutes.
2. In a mixing bowl, mix the almond flour, baking powder, smoked paprika, salt and pepper.
3. In another bowl, combine the eggs and coconut milk.
4. Soak the onion slices into the egg mixture.
5. Dredge the onion slices in the almond flour mixture.
6. Pour into the Oven rack/basket. Set temperature to 325 F and set time to 15 minutes. Select Start/Stop to begin. Shake the fryer basket for even cooking.

Nutrition: Calories 217 Fat 17g Total Carbs 2g Fiber 6g Protein 5g

104. Crispy Brussels Sprouts

Preparation Time: 5 minutes
Cooking time: 16 minutes
Servings: 2
Ingredients:
- 2 tbsps. Parmesan, freshly grated
- ½ lb. Brussels sprouts, thinly sliced
- 1 tsp. garlic powder
- 1 tbsp. extra-virgin olive oil
- Caesar dressing for dipping
- Freshly ground black pepper to taste

- Kosher salt to taste

Directions
1. Add oil, Brussels sprouts, garlic powder and Parmesan in a large mixing bowl. Toss to combine thoroughly. Season with salt and pepper.
2. Put the coated sprouts in the air fryer basket.
3. Insert trivet into your air fryer oven and lay the air fryer basket on top. Attach the air fryer lid and cook at 350 F for 8 minutes. Toss and cook for another 8 minutes until sprouts are crisp and golden brown.
4. Garnish with Parmesan. You can serve with Caesar salad for a dip.

Nutrition: Calories 202 Carbs 15.9g Fat 12.32g Protein 6.89g Sugar 4.18g Sodium 330mg

105. Spicy Eggplant Cubes

Preparation Time: 10 minutes
Cooking Time: 20 minutes
Servings: 2

Ingredients:
- 12 ounces eggplants
- ½ teaspoon cayenne pepper
- ½ teaspoon ground black pepper
- ½ teaspoon cilantro
- ½ teaspoon ground paprika

Directions:
1. Rinse the eggplants and slice them into cubes.
2. Sprinkle the eggplant cubes with the cayenne pepper and ground black pepper.
3. Add the cilantro and ground paprika.
4. Stir the mixture well and let it rest for 10 minutes.
5. After this, sprinkle the eggplants with olive oil and place in the air fryer basket.
6. Cook the eggplants for 20 minutes at 380° F, stirring halfway through.
7. When the eggplant cubes are done, serve them right away!

Nutrition: Calories 67 Fat 2.8 Fiber 6.5 Carbs 10.9 Protein 1.9

106. Supreme Air-Fried Tofu

Preparation Time: 5 minutes
Cooking Time: 50 minutes
Servings: 4

Ingredients:
- 1 block of pressed and sliced into 1-inch cubes of extra-firm tofu
- 2 tablespoons of soy sauce
- 1 teaspoon of seasoned rice vinegar
- 2 teaspoons of toasted sesame oil
- 1 tablespoon of cornstarch

Directions:
1. Using a bowl, add and toss the tofu, soy sauce, seasoned rice vinegar, sesame oil until it is properly covered.
2. Place it inside your refrigerator and allow to marinate for 30 minutes.
3. Preheat your air fryer to 370 F.
4. Add the cornstarch to the tofu mixture and toss it until it is properly covered.
5. Grease your air fryer basket with a nonstick cooking spray and add the tofu inside your basket.
6. Cook it for 20 minutes at a 370 F, and shake it after 10 minutes.
7. Serve and enjoy!

Nutrition: Calories: 80 Fat: 5.8g Protein: 5g Carbs: 3g Dietary Fiber: 1.2g

107. Zucchini Cubes

Preparation Time: 7 minutes
Cooking Time: 8 minutes
Servings: 2

Ingredients:
- 1 zucchini
- ½ teaspoon ground black pepper
- 1 teaspoon oregano
- 2 tablespoons chicken stock
- ½ teaspoon coconut oil

Directions:
1. Chop the zucchini into cubes.
2. Combine the ground black pepper, and oregano; stir the mixture.
3. Sprinkle the zucchini cubes with the spice mixture and stir well.
4. After this, sprinkle the vegetables with the chicken stock.
5. Place the coconut oil in the air fryer basket and preheat it to 360° F for 20 seconds.
6. Then add the zucchini cubes and cook the vegetables for 8 minutes at 390° F, stirring halfway through.
7. Transfer to serving plates and enjoy!

Nutrition: Calories 30 Fat 1.5 Fiber 1.6 Carbs 4.3 Protein 1.4

108. Wrapped Asparagus

Preparation Time: 10 minutes
Cooking Time: 5 minutes
Servings: 4

Ingredients:
- 12 ounces asparagus
- ½ teaspoon ground black pepper
- 3-ounce turkey fillet, sliced
- ¼ teaspoon chili flakes

Directions:
1. Sprinkle the asparagus with the ground black pepper and chili flakes. Stir carefully.
2. Wrap the asparagus in the sliced turkey fillet and place in the air fryer basket.
3. Cook the asparagus at 400° F for 5 minutes, turning halfway through cooking.
4. Let the wrapped asparagus cool for 2 minutes before serving.

Nutrition: Calories 133 Fat 9 Fiber 1.9 Carbs 3.8 Protein 9.8

109. Coconut Oil Artichokes

Preparation Time: 10 minutes
Cooking Time: 13 minutes
Servings: 4

Ingredients:
- 1-pound artichokes
- 1 tablespoon coconut oil
- 1 tablespoon water
- ½ teaspoon minced garlic
- ¼ teaspoon cayenne pepper

Directions:
1. Trim the ends of the artichokes, sprinkle them with the water, and rub them with the minced garlic.
2. Sprinkle with the cayenne pepper and the coconut oil.
3. After this, wrap the artichokes in foil and place in the air fryer basket.
4. Cook for 10 minutes at 370° F.
5. Then remove the artichokes from the foil and cook them for 3 minutes more at 400° F.

6. Transfer the cooked artichokes to serving plates and allow to cool a little.
7. Serve!

Nutrition: Calories 83 Fat 3.6 Fiber 6.2 Carbs 12.1 Protein 3.7

110. Mashed Yams

Preparation Time: 10 minutes
Cooking Time: 10 minutes
Servings: 5
Ingredients:
- 1 pound yams
- 1 teaspoon olive oil
- 1 tablespoon almond milk
- ¾ teaspoon salt
- 1 teaspoon dried parsley

Directions:
1. Peel the yams and chop.
2. Place the chopped yams in the air fryer basket and sprinkle with the salt and dried parsley.
3. Add the olive oil and stir the mixture.
4. Cook the yams at 400° F for 10 minutes, stirring twice during cooking.
5. When the yams are done, blend them well with a hand blender until smooth.
6. Add the almond milk and stir carefully.
7. Serve, and enjoy!

Nutrition: Calories 120 Fat 1.8 Fiber 3.6 Carbs 25.1 Protein 1.4

111. Rosemary Air Fried Potatoes

Preparation Time: 10 minutes
Cooking time: 15 minutes
Servings: 4
Ingredients:
- 3 tbsps. vegetable oil
- 4 yellow baby potatoes, quartered
- 2 tsps. dried rosemary, minced
- 1 tbsp. minced garlic
- 1 tsp. ground black pepper
- ¼ cup chopped parsley
- 1 tbsp. fresh lime or lemon juice
- 1 tsp. salt

Directions
1. Add potatoes, garlic, rosemary, oil, pepper, and salt in a large bowl. Mix thoroughly.
2. Arrange seasoned potatoes in the air fryer basket and place inside the Air fryer oven. Cover with the air fryer lid and air-fry at 400 F for about 15 minutes.
3. Check to see if potatoes are cooked through.
4. Once cooked, take it out of the air fryer and place in a platter.
5. Sprinkle with lemon juice and parsley.
6. Serve warm.

Nutrition: Calories 201 Carbs 22.71g Fat 10.71g Protein 3.34g Sugar 1.32g Fiber 3.5g Sodium 592.97mg

112. Air Fryer Falafel Balls

Preparation Time: 30 minutes
Cooking time: 12 minutes
Servings: 3
Ingredients:
- ½ cup sweet onion, diced
- 2 tbsps. olive oil
- ½ tsp. turmeric
- ½ cup carrots, minced
- 1 cup rolled oats
- ½ cup roasted and salted cashews
- 2 cups canned chickpeas, drained and rinsed
- Juice of 1 fresh lemon
- 2 tbsps. soy sauce
- 1 tbsp. flax meal
- ½ tsp. garlic powder
- ½ tsp. ground cumin

Directions
1. Put a little olive oil and sauté onions and carrots in the Air Fryer. Cook for about 7 minutes and transfer onions and carrots to a large bowl. Use the pressure cooker lid and do not forget to detach it after using.
2. Place cashews and oats in a food processor and process until you achieve a coarse meal consistency. Add the mixture to the bowl with the vegetables.
3. Next, place chickpeas with the lemon juice and soy sauce into the food processor, puree until semi-smooth in consistency.
4. Transfer to the bowl and add in the flax meal and spices. Stir to blend. Make sure that everything is well mixed.
5. Using your hands, form falafel balls from the dough and arrange them into single layer in the air fryer basket lined with parchment paper. You may use two-layered air fryer to accommodate all in a single batch. Place the air fryer basket into the Air Fryer Oven and attach the air fryer lid to cover. Secure lock and air fry at 370 F for 12 minutes. Shake the basket after 8 minutes for even cooking,
6. Serve dish on top of salad greens with Magical Tahini Dressing.

Nutrition: Calories 735 Carbs 74.07g Fat 38.91g Protein 22.02g Sugar 15.71g Sodium 316mg

113. Indian Cauliflower Curry

Preparation Time: 5 minutes
Cooking Time: 15 minutes
Servings: 4
Ingredients:
- 240ml of vegetable stock
- 180ml of light coconut milk
- 1 ½ teaspoon of garam masala
- 1 teaspoon of mild curry powder
- 1 teaspoon of garlic puree
- 1/3 teaspoon of turmeric
- ¼ teaspoon of salt
- 350g of cauliflower florets
- 200g of sweet corn kernels
- 3 scallions

Directions:
1. Preheat your Air Fryer to 375 F.
2. Mix the vegetable stock, light coconut milk, garam masala, mild curry powder, garlic puree, turmeric and salt in a large bowl.
3. Add in the cauliflower, sweet corn and the scallions. Mix them in until coated.
4. Place in a dish and put inside the Air Fryer, cook at 375 F for 12 to 15 minutes

Nutrition: Calories 166 Fat 4g Carbs 29g Protein 4g

VEGETABLE AND SIDE DISHES

114. Carrot Fries

Preparation Time: 5 minutes
Cooking time: 13 minutes
Servings: 1

Ingredients:
- 3 carrots
- 2 tablespoon olive oil
- ¼ cup mayonnaise
- 2 tablespoon honey
- 1 teaspoon sriracha, more if desired
- 1 teaspoon black pepper and salt

Directions
1. Set the air fryer to 400 F/204 degrees Celsius.
2. Slice the carrots into stick fries and arrange them in one layer on a rack. (you can do two racks at a time.)
3. Air fry them for four minutes and move the fries around. Switch the racks (if you have two) for even cooking.
4. Check every four minutes until they are golden brown. Serve as a snack or side dish anytime.

Nutrition: Calories 831 Carbs 53g Fat 70g Protein 2g

115. Broccoli Salad Recipe

Preparation Time: 5 minutes
Cooking Time: 20 minutes
Servings: 4

Ingredients:
- 1 broccoli head; florets separated
- 1 tbsp. Chinese rice wine vinegar
- 1 tbsp. peanut oil
- 6 garlic cloves; minced
- Salt and black pepper to the taste

Directions:
1. In a bowl; mix broccoli with salt, pepper and half of the oil, toss, transfer to your air fryer and cook at 350 °F, for 8 minutes; shaking the fryer halfway
2. Transfer broccoli to a salad bowl, add the rest of the peanut oil, garlic and rice vinegar, toss really well and serve.

Nutrition: Calories: 12 Fat: 3 Fiber: 4 Carbs: 4 Protein: 4

116. Cajun Olives and Peppers

Preparation Time: 4 minutes
Cooking Time: 12 minutes
Servings: 4

Ingredients:
- 1 tablespoon olive oil
- ½ pound mixed bell peppers, sliced
- 1 cup black olives, pitted and halved
- ½ tablespoon Cajun seasoning

Directions:
1. In a pan that fits the air fryer, combine all the ingredients.
2. Put the pan it in your air fryer and cook at 390 degrees F for 12 minutes.
3. Divide the mix between plates and serve.

Nutrition: Calories 151 Fat 3 Fiber 2 Carbs 4 Protein 5

117. Garlic-Rosemary Brussels Sprouts

Preparation Time: 5 minutes
Cooking time: 30 minutes
Servings: 4

Ingredients:
- 3 tablespoons olive oil
- 2 garlic cloves, minced
- ½ teaspoon salt
- ¼ teaspoon pepper
- 1 lb. brussels sprouts
- ½ cup panko breadcrumbs
- 1 ½ teaspoon rosemary, freshly minced

Directions
1. Trim and slice the sprouts into halves.
2. Set the temperature of the air fryer at 350 F/177 degrees Celsius.
3. Measure and add in the first four ingredients (cloves, oil, salt, and pepper) in a small microwave-safe bowl. Set the timer on high for ½ minute.
4. Toss the sprouts with two tablespoons of the oil mixture.
5. Arrange the sprouts on the tray in the fryer basket. Fry for 4-5 minutes.
6. Stir the sprouts and continue to fry until they are lightly browned and near the desired tenderness (8 more min.), stirring halfway through the cooking cycle.
7. Toss the breadcrumbs with rosemary and the rest of the oil mixture. Drizzle it over the sprouts.
8. Continue cooking until the crumbs are browned and sprouts are tender (3-5 min.). Serve immediately.

Nutrition: Calories 164 Carbs 15g Fat 11g Protein 5g

118. Simple Basil Potatoes

Preparation Time: 15 Minutes
Cooking Time: 40 Minutes
Servings: 4

Ingredients:
- 18 Medium Potatoes
- 5 Tablespoons Olive Oil
- 4 Teaspoons Basil, Dried
- 1 ½ Teaspoons Garlic Powder
- Salt & Pepper to Taste
- Ounces Butter

Directions:
1. Turn on your air fryer to 390.
2. Cut your potatoes lengthwise, and make sure to cut them thin.
3. Lightly coat your potatoes with both your butter and oil.
4. Add in salt and pepper, and then cook for 40 minutes.

Nutrition: Calories: 140 Fat: 5 Carbs: 8 Protein: 9

119. Stuffed Mushrooms

Preparation Time: 5 minutes
Cooking time: 15 minutes
Servings: 3

Ingredients:
- 3 portobello mushrooms
- 1 teaspoon garlic
- 1 medium onion
- 3 tablespoons grated mozzarella cheese
- 2 slices chopped ham
- 1 tomato

- Green pepper
- ½ teaspoon sea salt
- ¼ teaspoon pepper
- 1 tablespoon olive oil

Directions
1. Heat the air fryer to reach 320 F /160 degrees Celsius.
2. Dice/chop the tomato, pepper, onion, garlic, and ham.
3. Wash, dry, and remove the stems from the mushrooms. Drizzle with oil and set aside for now.
4. Combine the pepper, salt, cheese, tomato, onion, garlic, bell peppers, and ham. Stuff the mixture into the mushroom caps.
5. Add the mushrooms to the fryer for eight minutes.
6. Serve with your favorite entrée.

Nutrition: Calories 271 Carbs 8g Fat 18.3g Protein 19g

120. Green Beans with Sesame Seeds

Preparation Time: 5 minutes
Cooking Time: 8 minutes
Servings: 4
Ingredients:
- 1 tablespoon reduced-sodium soy sauce or tamari
- 1/2 tablespoon Sriracha sauce
- 4 teaspoons toasted sesame oil, divided
- 12 ounces (340 g) trimmed green beans
- 1/2 tablespoon toasted sesame seeds

Directions:
1. Whisk together the Sriracha sauce, soy sauce, and 1 teaspoon of sesame oil in a small bowl until smooth. Set aside.
2. Toss the green beans with the remaining sesame oil in a large bowl until evenly coated.
3. Place the green beans in the air fry basket in a single layer.
4. Place the basket on the air fry position.
5. Select Air Fry, set temperature to 375°F (190°C), and set time to 8 minutes. Stir the green beans halfway through the cooking time.
6. When cooking is complete, the green beans should be lightly charred and tender. Remove from the air fryer grill to a platter. Pour the prepared sauce over the top of green beans and toss well. Serve sprinkled with the toasted sesame seeds.

Nutrition: Calories 214 Carbs 0.1g Fat 2.8g Protein 9.8g

121. Black Bean and Tomato Chili

Preparation Time: 15 minutes
Cooking time: 23 minutes
Servings: 6
Ingredients:
- 1 tablespoon olive oil
- 1 medium onion, diced
- 3 garlic cloves, minced
- 1 cup vegetable broth
- 3 cans black beans, drained and rinsed
- 2 cans diced tomatoes
- 2 chipotle peppers, chopped
- 2 teaspoons cumin
- 2 teaspoons chili powder
- 1 teaspoon dried oregano
- ½ teaspoon salt

Directions
1. Over a medium heat, fry the garlic and onions in the olive oil for 3 minutes.
2. Add the remaining ingredients, stirring constantly and scraping the bottom to prevent sticking.
3. Take a dish and place the mixture inside. Put a sheet of aluminum foil on top.
4. Press "Power Button" turn the dial to select "bake".
5. Push "Temp" to set the temperature at 400 F.
6. Press "Timer" to set the cooking time to 20 minutes.
7. When ready, plate up and serve immediately.

Nutrition: Calories 82 Carbs 6.3g Fat 5.66g Protein 1.5g Fiber 2.4g Sodium 46mg

122. Potatoes with Zucchinis

Preparation Time: 10 minutes
Cooking time: 45 minutes
Servings: 4
Ingredients:
- 2 potatoes, peeled and cubed
- 4 carrots, cut into chunks
- 1 head broccoli, cut into florets
- 4 zucchinis, sliced thickly
- Salt and ground black pepper, to taste
- ¼ cup olive oil
- 1 tablespoon dry onion powder

Directions
1. In a baking dish, add all the ingredients and combine well.
2. Press "Power Button" turn the dial to select "bake".
3. Push "Temp" to set the temperature at 400 F.
4. Press "Timer" to set the cooking time to 45 minutes. Cook ensuring the vegetables are soft and the sides have browned before serving.

Nutrition: Calories 201 Carbs 22.71g Fat 10.71g Protein 3.34g Fiber 3.5g Sodium 592.97mg

123. Cauliflower Faux Rice

Preparation Time: 15 minutes
Cooking time: 40 minutes
Servings: 8
Ingredients:
- 1 large head cauliflower, rinsed and drained, cut into florets
- ½ lemon, juiced
- 2 garlic cloves, minced
- 2 (8-ounce / 227-g) cans mushrooms
- 1 (8-ounce / 227-g) can water chestnuts
- ¾ cup peas
- 1 egg, beaten
- 4 tablespoons soy sauce
- 1 tablespoon peanut oil
- 1 tablespoon sesame oil
- 1 tablespoon minced fresh ginger
- Cooking spray

Directions
1. Mix the peanut oil, soy sauce, sesame oil, minced ginger, lemon juice, and minced garlic to combine well.
2. In a food processor, pulse the florets in small batches to break them down to resemble rice grains. Drain the chestnuts and roughly chop them. Pour into the basket.
3. Press "Power Button" turn the dial to select "air fry".
4. Push "Temp" to set the temperature at 350 F.

5. Press "Timer" to set the cooking time to 20 minutes. Add the mushrooms and the peas to the air fryer oven and continue to air fry for another 15 minutes.
6. Lightly spritz a frying pan with cooking spray. Prepare an omelet with the beaten egg, ensuring it is firm. Lay on a cutting board and slice it up. When the cauliflower is ready, throw in the omelet and select Bake, and cook for an additional 5 minutes. Serve hot.

Nutrition: Calories 261 Carbs 9g Fat 21g Protein 11g

124. Mediterranean Air Fried Veggies

Preparation Time: 10 minutes
Cooking time: 6 minutes
Servings: 4
Ingredients:
- 1 large zucchini, sliced
- 1 cup cherry tomatoes, halved
- 1 parsnip, sliced
- 1 green pepper, sliced
- 1 carrot, sliced
- 1 teaspoon mixed herbs
- 1 teaspoon mustard
- 1 teaspoon garlic purée
- 6 tablespoons olive oil
- Salt and ground black pepper, to taste

Directions
1. Preheat the air fryer oven to 400 F (204 degrees Celsius).
2. Combine all the ingredients in a bowl, making sure to coat the vegetables well.
3. Press "Power Button" turn the dial to select "air fry".
4. Push "Temp" to set the temperature at 400 F.
5. Press "Timer" to set the cooking time to 6 minutes and air fry, ensuring the vegetables are tender and browned.
6. Serve immediately.

Nutrition: Calories 229 Fat 1.6g Carbs 45.5g Sodium 189mg Dietary Fiber 5.6g Sugars 3.5g Protein 7.8g

125. Easy Cinnamon Squash

Preparation Time: 5 minutes
Cooking Time: 15 minutes
Servings: 4
Ingredients:
- 1 medium acorn squash, halved crosswise and deseeded
- 1 teaspoon coconut oil
- 1 teaspoon light brown sugar
- Few dashes of ground cinnamon
- Few dashes of ground nutmeg

Directions:
1. On a clean work surface, rub the cut sides of the acorn squash with coconut oil. Scatter with the cinnamon, nutmeg, and brown sugar.
2. Put the squash halves in the air fry basket, cut-side up.
3. Place the basket on the air fry position.
4. Select Air Fry, set temperature to 325°F (163°C), and set time to 15 minutes.
5. When cooking is complete, the squash halves should be just tender when pierced in the center with a paring knife. Remove the basket from the air fryer grill. Rest for 5 to 10 minutes and serve warm.

Nutrition: Calories 290 Carbs 0.1g Fat 1.8g Protein 10.8g

VEGETABLE AND SIDE DISHES

126. Twice-Baked Potatoes

Preparation Time: 15 minutes
Cooking time: 50 minutes
Servings: 8
Ingredients:
- 4 large russet potatoes
- 4 slices bacon
- 2 tablespoons butter
- ½ cup milk
- 1 teaspoon garlic powder
- Salt
- Pepper
- 2 scallions, green parts (white parts optional), chopped
- 2 tablespoons sour cream
- 1¼ cups shredded Cheddar cheese, divided

Directions
1. Using a fork, poke three holes into the top of each potato.
2. Place the potatoes in the air fryer. Cook for 40 minutes.
3. Meanwhile, in a skillet over medium-high heat, cook the bacon for about 5 to 7 minutes, flipping to evenly crisp. Drain on paper towels, crumble, and set aside.
4. Remove the cooked potatoes from the air fryer and allow them to cool for 10 minutes.
5. While the potatoes cool, heat a saucepan over medium-high heat. Add the butter and milk. Stir. Allow the mixture to cook for 2 to 3 minutes, until the butter has melted.
6. Halve each of the potatoes lengthwise. Scoop half of the flesh out of the middle of each potato half, leaving the flesh on the surrounding edges. This will hold the potato together when you stuff it.
7. Place the potato flesh in a large bowl and mash with a potato masher. Add the warm butter and milk mixture and stir to combine. Season with the garlic powder and salt and pepper to taste.
8. Add the cooked bacon, scallions, sour cream, and 1 cup of Cheddar cheese. Stir to combine.
9. Stuff each potato half with 1 to 2 tablespoons of the mashed potato mixture. Sprinkle the remaining ¼ cup of Cheddar cheese on top of the potato halves.
10. Place 4 potato halves in the air fryer. Do not stack. Cook for 2 to 3 minutes at 400 F, or until the cheese has melted.
11. Remove the cooked potatoes from the air fryer, then repeat step 10 for the remaining 4 potato halves.
12. Cool before serving.

Nutrition: Calories 292 Fat 14g Saturated Fat 8g Cholesterol 39mg Sodium 389mg Carbs 31g Fiber 5g Protein 12g

127. Golden Garlicky Potatoes

Preparation Time: 5 minutes
Cooking Time: 18 minutes
Servings: 4
Ingredients:
- 2 cup sliced frozen potatoes, thawed
- 3 cloves garlic, minced
- Pinch salt
- Freshly ground black pepper, to taste
- ¾ cup heavy cream

Directions:
1. Toss the potatoes with the salt, garlic, and black pepper in a baking pan until evenly coated. Pour the heavy cream over the top.
2. Place the pan on the bake position.

3. Select Bake, set temperature to 380°F (193°C), and set time to 15 minutes.
4. When cooking is complete, the potatoes should be tender and the top golden brown. Check for doneness and bake for another 5 minutes if needed. Remove from the air fryer grill and serve hot.

Nutrition: Calories 236 Carbs 0.1g Fat 2.8g Protein 10.8g

128. Garlic-Roasted Red Potatoes

Preparation Time: 5 minutes
Cooking time: 20 minutes
Servings: 4

Ingredients:
- 6 red potatoes, cut into 1-inch cubes
- 3 garlic cloves, minced
- Salt
- Pepper
- 1 teaspoon chopped chives
- 1 tablespoon extra-virgin olive oil

Directions
1. In a sealable plastic bag, combine the potatoes, garlic, salt and pepper to taste, chives, and olive oil. Seal the bag and shake to coat the potatoes.
2. Transfer the potatoes to the air fryer. Cook for 10 minutes at 370 F.
3. Open the air fryer and shake the basket. Cook for an additional 10 minutes.
4. Cool before serving.

Nutrition: Calories 257 Fat 4g Saturated Fat 1g Sodium 58mg Carbs 52g Fiber 6g Protein 6g

129. Cauliflower Fried Rice

Preparation Time: 25 minutes
Cooking time: 20 minutes
Servings: 5

Ingredients:
- 2½ cups riced cauliflower (1 head cauliflower if making your own)
- 2 teaspoons sesame oil, divided
- 1 medium green bell pepper, chopped
- 1 cup peas
- 1 cup diced carrots
- ½ cup chopped onion
- Salt
- Pepper
- 1 tablespoon soy sauce
- 2 medium eggs, scrambled

Directions
1. 1.If you choose to make your own riced cauliflower, grate the head of cauliflower using the medium-size holes of a cheese grater. Or you can cut the head of cauliflower into florets and pulse in a food processor until it has the appearance of rice.
2. 2.Coat the bottom of a barrel pan with 1 teaspoon of sesame oil.
3. 3.In a large bowl, combine the riced cauliflower, green bell pepper, peas, carrots, and onion. Drizzle the remaining 1 teaspoon of sesame oil over the vegetables and stir. Add salt and pepper to taste.
4. 4.Transfer the mixture to the barrel pan. Cook for 10 minutes at 375 F.
5. 5.Remove the barrel pan. Drizzle the soy sauce all over and add the scrambled eggs. Stir to combine.
6. 6.Serve warm.

Nutrition: Calories 81 Fat 4g Saturated Fat 1g Cholesterol 65mg Sodium 280mg Carbs 9g Fiber 4g Protein 5g

130. Vegetable Medley

Preparation Time: 5 minutes
Cooking time: 15 minutes
Servings: 4

Ingredients:
- 1 head broccoli, chopped (about 2 cups)
- 2 medium carrots, cut into 1-inch pieces
- Salt
- Pepper
- Cooking oil
- 1 zucchini, cut into 1-inch chunks
- 1 medium red bell pepper, seeded and thinly sliced

Directions
1. 1.In a large bowl, combine the broccoli and carrots. Season with salt and pepper to taste. Spray with cooking oil.
2. 2.Transfer the broccoli and carrots to the air fryer basket. Cook for 6 minutes at 390 F.
3. 3.Place the zucchini and red pepper in the bowl. Season with salt and pepper to taste. Spray with cooking oil.
4. 4.Add the zucchini and red pepper to the broccoli and carrots in the air fryer basket. Cook for 6 minutes.
5. 5.Cool before serving.

Nutrition: Calories 47 Fat 1g Sodium 80mg Carbs 10g Fiber 3g Protein 2g

131. Crispy Cheesy Asparagus

Preparation Time: 15 minutes
Cooking Time: 6 minutes
Servings: 4

Ingredients:
- 2 egg whites
- ¼ cup water
- ¼ cup plus 2 tablespoons grated Parmesan cheese, divided
- ¾ cup panko bread crumbs
- ¼ teaspoon salt
- 12 ounces (340 g) fresh asparagus spears, woody ends trimmed
- Cooking spray

Directions:
1. In a shallow dish, whisk together the egg whites and water until slightly foamy. In a separate shallow dish, thoroughly combine ¼ cup of Parmesan cheese, bread crumbs, and salt.
2. Dip the asparagus in the egg white, then roll in the cheese mixture to coat well.
3. Place the asparagus in the air fry basket in a single layer, leaving space between each spear. Spritz the asparagus with cooking spray.
4. Place the basket on the air fry position.
5. Select Air Fry, set temperature to 390°F (199°C), and set time to 6 minutes.
6. When cooking is complete, the asparagus should be golden brown and crisp. Remove the basket from the air fryer grill. Sprinkle with the remaining 2 tablespoons of cheese and serve hot.

Nutrition: Calories 246 Carbs 0.1g Fat 2.8g Protein 10.8g

132. Eggplant Parmesan

Preparation Time: 15 minutes
Cooking time: 20 minutes
Servings: 4

Ingredients:
- 1 medium eggplant, peeled
- 2 eggs
- ½ cup all-purpose flour
- ¾ cup Italian bread crumbs
- 2 tablespoons grated Parmesan cheese
- Salt
- Pepper
- ¾ cup marinara sauce
- ½ cup shredded Parmesan cheese
- ½ cup shredded mozzarella cheese

Directions
1. 1.Cut the eggplant into ½-inch-thick rounds. Blot the eggplant with paper towels to dry completely. You can also sprinkle with a teaspoon of salt to sweat out the moisture.
2. 2.In a small bowl, beat the eggs. Place the flour in another small bowl. In a third small bowl, combine the bread crumbs, grated Parmesan cheese, and salt and pepper to taste, and mix well.
3. 3.Spray the air fryer basket with cooking oil.
4. 4.Dip each eggplant round in the flour, then the eggs, and then the bread crumb mixture.
5. 5.Place the eggplant rounds in the air fryer basket. Do not stack. Cook in batches. Spray the eggplant with cooking oil. Cook for 7 minutes at 400 F.
6. 6.Open the air fryer. Top each of the rounds with 1 teaspoon of marinara sauce and ½ tablespoon each of shredded Parmesan and mozzarella cheese. Cook for an additional 2 to 3 minutes, until the cheese has melted.
7. 7.Remove the cooked eggplant from the air fryer, then repeat steps 5 and 6 for the remaining eggplant.
8. ·8.Cool before serving.

Nutrition: Calories 310 Fat 9g Saturated Fat 4g Cholesterol 97mg Sodium 844mg Carbs 42g Fiber 7g Protein 16g

133. Simple Balsamic-Glazed Carrots

Preparation Time: 5 minutes
Cooking Time: 18 minutes
Servings: 4

Ingredients:
- 3 medium-size carrots, cut into 2-inch × 1/2-inch sticks
- 1 tablespoon orange juice
- 2 teaspoons balsamic vinegar
- 1 teaspoon maple syrup
- 1 teaspoon avocado oil
- 1/2 teaspoon dried rosemary
- ¼ teaspoon sea salt
- ¼ teaspoon lemon zest

Directions:
1. Put the carrots in a baking pan and sprinkle with the balsamic vinegar, orange juice, maple syrup, and avocado oil, and sea salt, rosemary, finished by the lemon zest. Toss well.
2. Place the pan on the toast position.
3. Select Toast, set temperature to 390ºF (200ºC), and set time to 18 minutes. Stir the carrots several times during the cooking process.
4. When cooking is complete, the carrots should be nicely glazed and tender. Remove from the air fryer grill and serve hot.

Nutrition: Calories 209 Carbs 0.1g Fat 2.8g Protein 11.8g

134. Air Fryer Vegetables

Preparation Time: 5 minutes
Cooking Time: 10 minutes
Servings: 4

Ingredients:
- 1/2 lb. broccoli fresh
- 1/2 lb. cauliflower fresh
- 1 tbsp. olive oil
- 1/4 tsp. seasoning
- 1/3 c water

Directions:
1. Mix vegetables, olive oil and seasonings in a medium bowl.
2. Pour 1/3 c. water in the Air Fryer base to prevent from smoking.
3. Place vegetables in the air fryer basket.
4. Cook at 400 degrees for 7-10 minutes
5. Shake vegetables half way through the 7-10 minutes

Nutrition: Calories 65kcal Carbs 7g Protein 3g Fat 4g

135. Golden Squash Croquettes

Preparation Time: 5 minutes
Cooking Time: 17 minutes
Servings: 4

Ingredients:
- 1/3 butternut squash, peeled and grated
- 1/3 cup all-purpose flour
- 2 eggs, whisked
- 4 cloves garlic, minced
- 1 1/2 tablespoons olive oil
- 1 teaspoon fine sea salt
- 1/3 teaspoon freshly ground black pepper, or more to taste
- 1/3 teaspoon dried sage
- A pinch of ground allspice

Directions:
1. Line the air fry basket with parchment paper. Set aside.
2. In a mixing bowl, stir together all the ingredients until well combined.
3. Make the squash croquettes: Use a small cookie scoop to drop tablespoonfuls of the squash mixture onto a lightly floured surface and shape into balls with your hands. Transfer them to the air fry basket.
4. Place the basket on the air fry position.
5. Select Air Fry, set temperature to 345ºF (174ºC), and set time to 17 minutes.
6. When cooking is complete, the squash croquettes should be golden brown. Remove from the air fryer grill to a plate and serve warm.

Nutrition: Calories 216 Carbs 0.1g Fat 3.8g Protein 10.8g

136. Quinoa Burgers

Preparation Time: 10 minutes
Cooking time: 10 minutes
Servings: 4

Ingredients:
- ½ cup cooked and cooled quinoa
- 1 cup rolled oats
- 2 eggs, lightly beaten
- ¼ cup white onion, minced
- ¼ cup feta cheese, crumbled

- Salt and ground black pepper, as required
- Olive oil cooking spray

Directions
1. In a large bowl, add all ingredients and mix until well combined.
2. Make 4 equal-sized patties from the mixture.
3. Lightly spray the patties with cooking spray.
4. Press "Power Button" of Air fryer oven and turn the dial to select "Air Fry" mode.
5. Press "Time Button" and again turn the dial to set the cooking time to 10 minutes.
6. Now push "Temp Button" and rotate the dial to set the temperature at 400 F.
7. Press "Start/Pause" button to start.
8. When the unit beeps to show that it is preheated, open the lid.
9. Arrange the patties into the greased air fry basket and insert in the oven.
10. Flip the patties once halfway through.
11. When cooking time is completed, open the lid and transfer the patties onto a platter.
12. Serve warm.

Nutrition: Calories 215 Fat 6.6g Carbs 28.7g Fiber 3.7g Sugar 1.1g Protein 9.9g

137. Tofu with Broccoli

Preparation Time: 15 minutes
Cooking time: 15 minutes
Servings: 2

Ingredients:
- 8 ounces block firm tofu, pressed and cubed
- 1 small head broccoli, cut into florets
- 1 tablespoon canola oil
- 1 tablespoon nutritional yeast
- ¼ teaspoon dried parsley
- Salt and ground black pepper, as required

Directions
1. In a bowl, mix together the tofu, broccoli and the remaining ingredients.
2. Press "Power Button" of Air fryer oven and turn the dial to select "Air Fry" mode.
3. Press "Time Button" and again turn the dial to set the cooking time to 15 minutes.
4. Now push "Temp Button" and rotate the dial to set the temperature at 390 F.
5. Press "Start/Pause" button to start.
6. When the unit beeps to show that it is preheated, open the lid.
7. Arrange the tofu mixture into the greased air fry basket and insert in the oven.
8. Flip the tofu mixture once halfway through.
9. When cooking time is completed, open the lid and serve hot.

Nutrition: Calories 206 Fat 13.1g Carbs 12.7g Fiber 5.4g Sugar 2.6g Protein 15g

138. Sweet and Spicy Parsnips

Preparation Time: 15 minutes
Cooking time: 44 minutes
Servings: 5

Ingredients:
- 1½ pound parsnip, peeled and cut into 1-inch chunks
- 1 tablespoon butter, melted
- 2 tablespoons honey
- 1 tablespoon dried parsley flakes, crushed
- ¼ teaspoon red pepper flakes, crushed
- Salt and ground black pepper, as required

Directions
1. In a large bowl, mix together the parsnips and butter.
2. Press "Power Button" of Air fryer oven and turn the dial to select "Air Fry" mode.
3. Press "Time Button" and again turn the dial to set the cooking time to 44 minutes.
4. Now push "Temp Button" and rotate the dial to set the temperature at 355 F.
5. Press "Start/Pause" button to start.
6. When the unit beeps to show that it is preheated, open the lid.
7. Arrange the squash chunks into the greased air fry basket and insert in the oven.
8. Meanwhile, in another large bowl, mix together the remaining ingredients.
9. After 40 minutes of cooking, press "Start/Pause" button to pause the unit.
10. Transfer the parsnips chunks into the bowl of honey mixture and toss to coat well.
11. Again, arrange the parsnip chunks into the air fry basket and insert in the oven.
12. When cooking time is completed, open the lid and serve hot.

Nutrition: Calories 149 Fat 2.7g Carbs 31.5g Fiber 6.7g Sugar 13.5g Protein 1.7g

139. Breaded Cheesy Broccoli Gratin

Preparation Time: 5 minutes
Cooking Time: 14 minutes
Servings: 2

Ingredients
- 1/3 cup fat-free milk
- 1 tablespoon all-purpose or gluten-free flour
- 1/2 tablespoon olive oil
- 1/2 teaspoon ground sage
- ¼ teaspoon kosher salt
- 1/8 teaspoon freshly ground black pepper
- 2 cups roughly chopped broccoli florets
- 6 tablespoons shredded Cheddar cheese
- 2 tablespoons panko bread crumbs
- 1 tablespoon grated Parmesan cheese
- Olive oil spray

Directions:
1. Spritz a baking dish with olive oil spray.
2. Mix the milk, olive oil, flour, salt, sage, and pepper in a medium bowl and whisk to combine. Stir in the broccoli florets, bread crumbs, Parmesan cheese, and Cheddar cheese and toss to coat.
3. Pour the broccoli mixture into the prepared baking dish.
4. Place the baking dish on the bake position.
5. Select Bake, set temperature to 330°F (166°C), and set time to 14 minutes.
6. When cooking is complete, the top should be golden brown and the broccoli should be tender. Remove from the air fryer grill and serve immediately.

Nutrition: Calories 246 Carbs 0.1g Fat 2.8g Protein 10.8g

140. Broccoli with Cauliflower

Preparation Time: 15 minutes
Cooking time: 20 minutes
Servings: 4
Ingredients:
- 1½ cups broccoli, cut into 1-inch pieces
- 1½ cups cauliflower, cut into 1-inch pieces
- 1 tablespoon olive oil
- Salt, as required

Directions:
1. In a bowl, add the vegetables, oil, and salt and toss to coat well.
2. Press "Power Button" of Air fryer oven and turn the dial to select "Air Fry" mode.
3. Press "Time Button" and again turn the dial to set the cooking time to 20 minutes.
4. Now push "Temp Button" and rotate the dial to set the temperature at 375 F.
5. Press "Start/Pause" button to start.
6. When the unit beeps to show that it is preheated, open the lid.
7. Arrange the veggie mixture into the greased air fry basket and insert in the oven.
8. When cooking time is completed, open the lid and serve hot.

Nutrition: Calories 51 Fat 3.7g Carbs 4.3g Fiber 1.8g Sugar 1.5g Protein 1.7g

141. Vinegar Green Beans

Preparation Time: 10 minutes
Cooking time: 20 minutes
Servings: 2
Ingredients:
- 1 (10-ounce) bag frozen cut green beans
- ¼ cup nutritional yeast
- 3 tablespoons balsamic vinegar
- Salt and ground black pepper, as required

Directions:
7. In a bowl, add the green beans, nutritional yeast, vinegar, salt, and black pepper and toss to coat well.
8. Press "Power Button" of Air fryer oven and turn the dial to select "Air Fry" mode.
9. Press "Time Button" and again turn the dial to set the cooking time to 20 minutes.
10. Now push "Temp Button" and rotate the dial to set the temperature at 400 F.
11. Press "Start/Pause" button to start.
12. When the unit beeps to show that it is preheated, open the lid.
13. Arrange the green beans into the greased air fry basket and insert in the oven.
14. When cooking time is completed, open the lid and serve hot.

Nutrition: Calories 115 Fat 1.3g Carbs 18.5g Fiber 9.3g Sugar 1.8g Protein 11.3g

142. Herbed Bell Peppers

Preparation Time: 10 minutes
Cooking time: 8 minutes
Servings: 4
Ingredients:
- 1½ pounds mixed bell peppers, seeded and sliced
- 1 small onion, sliced
- ½ teaspoon dried thyme, crushed
- ½ teaspoon dried savory, crushed
- Salt and ground black pepper, as required
- 2 tablespoon butter, melted

Directions:
1. In a bowl, add the bell peppers, onion, herbs, salt and black pepper and toss to coat well.
2. Press "Power Button" of Air fryer oven and turn the dial to select "Air Fry" mode.
3. Press "Time Button" and again turn the dial to set the cooking time to 8 minutes.
4. Now push "Temp Button" and rotate the dial to set the temperature at 360 F.
5. Press "Start/Pause" button to start.
6. When the unit beeps to show that it is preheated, open the lid.
7. Arrange the bell peppers into the air fry basket and insert in the oven.
8. When cooking time is completed, open the lid and transfer the bell peppers into a bowl.
9. Drizzle with butter and serve immediately.

Nutrition: Calories 73 Fat 5.9g Carbs 5.2g Fiber 1.1g Sugar 3g Protein 0.7g

143. Cheesy cauliflower fritters

Preparation time: 10 minutes
cooking time: 7 minutes
Servings: 8
Ingredients
- ½ c. Chopped parsley
- 1 c. Italian breadcrumbs
- 1/3 c. Shredded mozzarella cheese
- 1/3 c. Shredded sharp cheddar cheese
- 1 egg
- 2 minced garlic cloves
- 3 chopped scallions
- 1 head of cauliflower

Directions:
1. Cut cauliflower up into florets. Wash well and pat dry. Place into a food processor and pulse 20-30 seconds till it looks like rice.
2. Place cauliflower rice in a bowl and mix with pepper, salt, egg
3. cheeses, breadcrumbs, garlic, and scallions.
4. With hands, form 15 patties of the mixture. Add more breadcrumbs if needed.
5. With olive oil, spritz patties, and place into your air fryer oven basket in a single layer. Set temperature to 390°f, and set time to 7 minutes, flipping after 7 minutes.

Nutrition: calories: 209 fat: 17g protein: 6g sugar: 0.5

144. Caramelized Baby Carrots

Preparation Time: 10 minutes
Cooking Time: 15 minutes
Servings: 4
Ingredients:
- 1/2 cup butter, melted
- 1/2 cup brown sugar
- 1 lb. bag baby carrots

Directions:
1. In a bowl, mix together the butter, brown sugar and carrots. Press Power Button of Air Fry Oven and turn the dial to select the Air Fry mode.

2. Press the Time button and again turn the dial to set the cooking time to 15 minutes.
3. Now push the Temp button and rotate the dial to set the temperature at 400 degrees F. Press Start/Pause button to start.
4. When the unit beeps to show that it is preheated, open the lid.
5. Arrange the carrots in greased Air Fry Basket and insert in the oven.
6. Serve warm.

Nutrition: Calories 312, Fat 23.2 g, Carbs 27.1 g Protein 1 g

145. Buttered carrot-zucchini with mayo

Preparation time: 10 minutes
cooking time: 25 minutes
Servings: 4

Ingredients
- 1 tablespoon grated onion
- 2 tablespoons butter, melted
- 1/2-pound carrots, sliced
- 1-1/2 zucchinis, sliced
- 1/4 cup water
- 1/4 cup mayonnaise
- 1/4 teaspoon prepared horseradish
- 1/4 teaspoon salt
- 1/4 teaspoon ground black pepper
- 1/4 cup italian bread crumbs

Directions:
1. Lightly grease baking pan of air fryer with cooking spray. Add carrots. For 8 minutes, cook on 360°f. Add zucchini and continue cooking for another 5 minutes.
2. Meanwhile, in a bowl whisk well pepper, salt, horseradish, onion, mayonnaise, and water. Pour into pan of veggies. Toss well to coat.
3. In a small bowl mix melted butter and bread crumbs. Sprinkle over veggies.
4. Pour into the oven rack/basket. Place the rack on the middle-shelf of the air fryer oven. Set temperature to 490°f, and set time to 10 minutes until tops are lightly browned.
5. Serve and enjoy.

Nutrition: calories: 223 fat: 17g protein: 2.7g sugar: 0.5

146. Parmesan Asparagus

Preparation Time: 10 minutes
Cooking Time: 10 minutes
Servings: 3

Ingredients:
- 1 lb. fresh asparagus, trimmed
- 1 tablespoon Parmesan cheese, grated
- 1 tablespoon butter, melted
- 1 teaspoon garlic powder
- Salt and ground black pepper

Directions:
1. In a bowl, mix together the asparagus, cheese, butter, garlic powder, salt, and black pepper.
2. Press Power Button of Air Fry Oven and turn the dial to select the Air Fry mode.
3. Press the Time button and again turn the dial to set the cooking time to 10 minutes
4. Now push the Temp button and rotate the dial to set the temperature at 400 degrees F.
5. Press Start/Pause button to start. When the unit beeps to show that it is preheated, open the lid.
6. Arrange the veggie mixture in greased Air Fry Basket and insert in the oven.
7. Serve hot.

Nutrition: Calories 73 Fat 4.4 g Carbs 6.6 g Protein 4.2 g

147. Roasted vegetables salad

Preparation time: 5 minutes
cooking time: 85 minutes
Servings: 5

Ingredients
- 3 eggplants
- 1 tbsp of olive oil
- 3 medium zucchini
- 1 tbsp of olive oil
- 4 large tomatoes, cut them in eighths
- 4 cups of one shaped pasta
- 2 peppers of any color
- 1 cup of sliced tomatoes cut into small cubes
- 2 teaspoon of salt substitute
- 8 tbsp of grated parmesan cheese
- ½ cup of italian dressing
- Leaves of fresh basil

Directions:
1. Wash your eggplant and slice it off then discard the green end. Make sure not to peel.
2. Slice your eggplant into 1/2 inch of thick rounds. 1/2 inch)
3. Pour 1tbsp of olive oil on the eggplant round.
4. Put the eggplants in the basket of the air fryer and then toss it in the air fryer oven. Cook the eggplants for 40 minutes. Set the heat to 360 ° f
5. Meanwhile, wash your zucchini and slice it then discard the green end. But do not peel it.
6. Slice the zucchini into thick rounds of ½ inch each.
7. In the basket of the air fryer, toss your ingredients
8. Add 1 tbsp of olive oil.
9. Cook the zucchini for 25 minutes on a heat of 360° f and when the time is off set it aside.
10. Wash and cut the tomatoes.
11. Arrange your tomatoes in the basket of the air fryer. Set the timer to 30 minutes. Set the heat to 350° f
12. When the time is off, cook your pasta according to the pasta guiding directions, empty it into a colander. Run the cold water on it and wash it and drain the pasta and put it aside.
13. Meanwhile, wash and chop your peppers and place it in a bow
14. Wash and thinly slice your cherry tomatoes and add it to the bowl. Add your roasted veggies.
15. Add the pasta, a pinch of salt, the topping dressing
16. add the basil and the parm and toss everything together. Set the ingredients together in the refrigerator, and let it chill
17. Serve your salad and enjoy it.

Nutrition: calories: 223 fat: 17g protein: 2.7g sugar: 0.5

148. Cheddar, squash and zucchini casserole

Preparation time: 5 minutes
cooking time: 30 minutes
Servings: 4

Ingredients
- 1 egg
- 5 saltine crackers, or as needed, crushed
- 2 tablespoons bread crumbs
- 1/2-pound yellow squash, sliced
- 1/2-pound zucchini, sliced
- 1/2 cup shredded cheddar cheese
- 1-1/2 teaspoons white sugar
- 1/2 teaspoon salt
- 1/4 onion, diced
- 1/4 cup biscuit baking mix
- 1/4 cup butter

Directions:
1. Lightly grease baking pan of air fryer with cooking spray. Add onion, zucchini, and yellow squash. Cover pan with foil and for 15 minutes, cook on 360° f or until tender.
2. Stir in salt, sugar, egg
3. butter, baking mix, and cheddar cheese. Mix well. Fold in crushed crackers. Top with bread crumbs.
4. Cook for 15 minutes at 390° f until tops are lightly browned.
5. Serve and enjoy.

Nutrition: calories: 285 fat: 20.5g protein: 8.6g

149. Zucchini parmesan chips

Preparation time: 10 minutes
cooking time: 8 minutes
Servings: 10

Ingredients
- ½ tsp. Paprika
- ½ c. Grated parmesan cheese
- ½ c. Italian breadcrumbs
- 1 lightly beaten egg
- 2 thinly sliced zucchinis

Directions:
1. Use a very sharp knife or mandolin slicer to slice zucchini as thinly as you can. Pat off extra moisture.
2. Beat egg with a pinch of pepper and salt and a bit of water.
3. Combine paprika, cheese, and breadcrumbs in a bowl.
4. Dip slices of zucchini into the egg mixture and then into breadcrumb mixture. Press gently to coat.
5. With olive oil cooking spray, mist coated zucchini slices. Place into your air fryer oven basket in a single layer. Set temperature to 350°f, and set time to 8 minutes.
6. Sprinkle with salt and serve with salsa.

Nutrition: calories: 211fat: 16g protein: 8g sugar: 0g

150. Jalapeño cheese balls

Preparation time: 10 minutes
cooking time: 8 minutes
Servings: 12

Ingredients
- 4 ounces cream cheese
- ⅓ cup shredded mozzarella cheese
- ⅓ cup shredded cheddar cheese
- 2 jalapeños, finely chopped
- ½ cup bread crumbs
- 2 eggs
- ½ cup all-purpose flour
- Salt
- Pepper
- Cooking oil

Directions:
1. In a medium bowl, combine the cream cheese, mozzarella, cheddar, and jalapeños. Mix well.
2. Form the cheese mixture into balls about an inch thick. Using a small ice cream scoop works well.
3. Arrange the cheese balls on a sheet pan and place in the freezer for 15 minutes. This will help the cheese balls maintain their shape while frying.
4. Spray the air fryer oven basket with cooking oil. Place the bread crumbs in a small bowl. In another small bowl, beat the eggs. In a third small bowl, combine the flour with salt and pepper to taste, and mix well. Remove the cheese balls from the freezer. Dip the cheese balls in the flour, then the eggs, and then the bread crumbs.
5. Place the cheese balls in the air fryer. Spray with cooking oil. Cook for 8 minutes.
6. Open the air fryer oven and flip the cheese balls. I recommend flipping them instead of shaking so the balls maintain their form. Cook an additional 4 minutes. Cool before serving.

Nutrition: calories: 96 fat: 6g protein: 4g sugar: 0g

151. Roasted Cauliflower with Nuts & Raisins

Preparation Time: 5 minutes
Cooking Time: 20 minutes
Servings: 4

Ingredients:
- 1 small cauliflower head, cut into florets
- 2 tablespoons pine nuts, toasted
- 2 tablespoons raisins soak in boiling water and dried
- 1 teaspoon curry powder
- ½ teaspoon sea salt
- 3 tablespoons olive oil

Directions:
1. Preheat your air fryer to 320°Fahrenheit for 2-minutes Add ingredients into a bowl and toss to combine.
2. Add the cauliflower mixture to air fryer basket and cook for 15-minutes

Nutrition: Calories 264 Fat 26g Carbs 8g Protein 2g

152. Creamy and cheese broccoli bake

Preparation time: 5 minutes
cooking time: 30 minutes
Servings: 2

Ingredients
- 1-pound fresh broccoli, coarsely chopped
- 2 tablespoons all-purpose flour
- Salt to taste
- 1 tablespoon dry bread crumbs, or to taste
- 1/2 large onion, coarsely chopped
- 1/2 (14 ounce) can evaporated milk, divided
- 1/2 cup cubed sharp cheddar cheese
- 1-1/2 teaspoons butter, or to taste
- 1/4 cup water

Directions:
1. Lightly grease baking pan of air fryer with cooking spray. Mix in half of the milk and flour in pan and for 5 minutes, cook on 360°f. Halfway through cooking time, mix well. Add broccoli and remaining milk. Mix well and cook for another 5 minutes.
2. Stir in cheese and mix well until melted.
3. In a small bowl mix well, butter and bread crumbs. Sprinkle on top of broccoli.
4. Place the baking pan in the air fryer oven. Cook for 20 minutes at 360°f until tops are lightly browned.
5. Serve and enjoy.

Nutrition: calories: 444 fat: 22.3g protein: 23g

153. Italian Ratatouille

Preparation Time: 25 minutes
Cooking Time: 25 minutes
Servings: 4

Ingredients:
- ½ Small eggplants
- 1 zucchini
- 1 medium tomato
- ½ large yellow bell pepper
- ½ large red bell peppers
- ½ onions
- 1 cayenne pepper
- 5 basil sprigs
- 2 oregano sprigs
- 1 garlic clove
- ½ teaspoon of salt
- ½ teaspoon of pepper
- 1 tablespoon of olive oil
- 1 tablespoon of white wine
- 1 teaspoon of vinegar

Directions:
1. Preheat your Air Fryer to 400 F.
2. Next, cut the zucchini, tomato, both bell peppers, onion, cayenne pepper into cubes. Then steam and chop the basil and oregano leaves.
3. Mix the eggplant, zucchini, tomato, bell peppers, onions, cayenne pepper, basil, oregano, garlic, salt and pepper in a bowl. Drizzle with the mixture in oil, wine and vinegar.
4. Find a baking dish that fits inside of your Air Fryer and pour the vegetable mixture into the bowl.
5. Put the baking dish into the Air Fryer and cook for 8 minutes Once the 8 minutes are up, stir and then cook for a further 8 minutes Stir again and keep cooking until the vegetables become tender, make sure to stir every 5 minutes for another 10 minutes

Nutrition: Calories 79 Calories Fat 3.8g Carbs 10.2g Protein 2.1g

154. Crispy jalapeno coins

Preparation time: 10 minutes
cooking time: 5 minutes
Servings: 2

Ingredients
- 1 egg
- 2-3 tbsp. Coconut flour
- 1 sliced and seeded jalapeno
- Pinch of garlic powder
- Pinch of onion powder
- Pinch of cajun seasoning (optional)
- Pinch of pepper and salt

Directions:
1. Ensure your air fryer oven is preheated to 400 degrees.
2. Mix together all dry ingredients.
3. Pat jalapeno slices dry. Dip coins into egg wash and then into dry mixture. Toss to thoroughly coat.
4. Add coated jalapeno slices to air fryer basket in a singular layer. Spray with olive oil.
5. Set temperature to 350°f, and set time to 5 minutes. Cook just till crispy.

Nutrition: calories: 128 fat: 8g protein: 7g sugar:0g

155. Buffalo cauliflower

Preparation time: 5 minutes
cooking time: 15 minutes
Servings: 2

Ingredients
- Cauliflower:
- 1 c. Panko breadcrumbs
- 1 tsp. Salt
- 4 c. Cauliflower florets
- Buffalo coating:
- ¼ c. Vegan buffalo sauce
- ¼ c. Melted vegan butter

Directions:
1. Melt butter in microwave and whisk in buffalo sauce.
2. Dip each cauliflower floret into buffalo mixture, ensuring it gets coated well. Hold over a bowl till floret is done dripping.
3. Mix breadcrumbs with salt.
4. Dredge dipped florets into breadcrumbs and place into air fryer basket. Set temperature to 350°f, and set time to 15 minutes. When slightly browned, they are ready to eat!
5. Serve with your favorite keto dipping sauce.

Nutrition: calories: 194 fat: 17g protein: 10g sugar: 3

156. Crisped baked cheese stuffed chile pepper

Preparation time: 10 minutes
cooking time: 30 minutes
Servings: 3

Ingredients
- 1 (7 ounce) can whole green chile peppers, drained
- 1 egg
- beaten

- 1 tablespoon all-purpose flour
- 1/2 (5 ounce) can evaporated milk
- 1/2 (8 ounce) can tomato sauce
- 1/4-pound monterey jack cheese, shredded
- 1/4-pound longhorn or cheddar cheese, shredded
- 1/4 cup milk

Directions:
1. Lightly grease baking pan of air fryer with cooking spray. Evenly spread chilies and sprinkle cheddar and jack cheese on top.
2. In a bowl whisk well flour, milk, and eggs. Pour over chilies.
3. For 20 minutes, cook on 360°f
4. Add tomato sauce on top.
5. Cook for 10 minutes at 390°f until tops are lightly browned.
6. Serve and enjoy.

Nutrition: calories: 392 fat: 27.6g protein: 23.9g

157. Jicama fries

Preparation time: 10 minutes
cooking time: 5 minutes
Servings: 8

Ingredients
- 1 tbsp. Dried thyme
- ¾ c. Arrowroot flour
- ½ large jicama
- Eggs

Directions:
1. Sliced jicama into fries.
2. Whisk eggs together and pour over fries. Toss to coat.
3. Mix a pinch of salt, thyme, and arrowroot flour together. Toss egg-coated jicama into dry mixture, tossing to coat well.
4. Spray the air fryer oven basket with olive oil and add fries. Set temperature to 350°f, and set time to 5 minutes. Toss halfway into the cooking process.

Nutrition: calories: 211 fat: 19g protein: 9g sugar:1

158. Mushroom, Onion and Feta Frittata

Preparation Time: 15 minutes
Cooking Time: 10 minutes
Servings: 4

Ingredients:
- 3 whole eggs
- 2 cup sliced button mushrooms
- ½ red onions
- 1 tbsp. Olive oil
- 3 tbsp crumbled feta
- 1 pinch salt

Directions:
1. Peel and slice half a red onion into ¼ inch thin slices.
2. Wash button mushrooms; then slice into ¼ inch thin slices.
3. Place a pan under a medium flame, add olive oil sweat onions and mushrooms and sauté until tender. Take onions and mushrooms off the heat and place on kitchen towel to cool.
4. Preheat Air fryer to 320°F.
5. In a mixing bowl crack 3 eggs and whisk thoroughly and vigorously.
6. Coat the outside and bottom of a 6-ounce ramekin lightly with pan spray.
7. Pour eggs into the ramekin, add ¼ cup onion and mushrooms mixture, and then add cheese.
8. Place in Air fryer and cook for 10 to 12 minutes

Nutrition: Calories 90 Fat 4.5g Carbs 8g Protein 13g

159. Spaghetti squash tots

Preparation time: 10 minutes
cooking time: 15 minutes
Servings: 8

Ingredients
- ¼ tsp. Pepper
- ½ tsp. Salt
- 1 thinly sliced scallion
- 1 spaghetti squash

Directions:
1. Wash and cut the squash in half lengthwise. Scrape out the seeds.
2. With a fork, remove spaghetti meat by strands and throw out skins.
3. In a clean towel, toss in squash and wring out as much moisture as possible. Place in a bowl and with a knife slice through meat a few times to cut up smaller.
4. Add pepper, salt, and scallions to squash and mix well.
5. Create "tot" shapes with your hands and place in the air fryer oven basket. Spray with olive oil. Set temperature to 350°f, and set time to 15 minutes. Cook until golden and crispy.

Nutrition: calories: 231 fat: 18g protein: 5g sugar: 0g

160. Crispy and healthy avocado fingers

Preparation time: 10 minutes
cooking time: 10 minutes
Servings: 4

Ingredients
- ½ cup panko breadcrumbs
- ½ teaspoon salt
- 1 pitted haas avocado, peeled and sliced
- Liquid from 1 can white beans or aquafaba

Directions:
1. Preheat the air fryer oven at 350°f.
2. In a shallow bowl, toss the breadcrumbs and salt until well combined.
3. Dredge the avocado slices first with the aquafaba then in the breadcrumb mixture.
4. Place the avocado slices in a single layer inside the air fryer basket.
5. Cook for 10 minutes and shake halfway through the cooking time.

Nutrition: calories: 51 fat: 7.5g protein:1.39g

161. Onion rings

Preparation time: 10 minutes
cooking time: 10 minutes
Servings: 4

Ingredients
- 1 large spanish onion
- 1/2 cup buttermilk
- 2 eggs, lightly beaten
- 3/4 cups unbleached all-purpose flour
- 3/4 cups panko bread crumbs
- 1/2 teaspoon baking powder
- 1/2 teaspoon cayenne pepper, to taste
- Salt

Directions:
1. Start by cutting your onion into 1/2 thick rings and separate. Smaller pieces can be discarded or saved for other recipes.
2. Beat the eggs in a large bowl and mix in the buttermilk, then set it aside.
3. In another bowl combine flour, pepper, bread crumbs, and baking powder.
4. Use a large spoon to dip a whole ring in the buttermilk, then pull it through the flour mix on both sides to completely coat the ring.
5. Pour into the oven rack/basket. Place the rack on the middle-shelf of the air fryer oven. Set temperature to 360°f, and set time to 8 minutes. Cook about 8 rings for 8-10 minutes at shaking half way through.

Nutrition: calories: 225 fat: 3.8g protein:19g fiber:2.4g

162. Cinnamon butternut squash fries

Preparation time: 5 minutes
cooking time: 10 minutes
Servings: 8
Ingredients
- 1 pinch of salt
- 1 tbsp. Powdered unprocessed sugar
- ½ tsp. Nutmeg
- 2 tsp. Cinnamon
- 1 tbsp. Coconut oil
- 10 ounces pre-cut butternut squash fries

Directions:
1. In a plastic bag
2. pour in all ingredients. Coat fries with other components till coated and sugar is dissolved.
3. Spread coated fries into a single layer in the air fryer basket. Set temperature to 390°f, and set time to 10 minutes. Cook until crispy.

Nutrition: calories: 175 fat: 8g protein:1g sugar

163. Cheesy Spinach

Preparation Time: 15 minutes
Cooking time: 15 minutes
Servings: 3
Ingredients:
- 1 (10-ounce) package frozen spinach, thawed
- ½ cup onion, chopped
- 2 teaspoons garlic, minced
- 4 ounces cream cheese, chopped
- ½ teaspoon ground nutmeg
- Salt and ground black pepper, as required
- ¼ cup Parmesan cheese, shredded

Directions:
1. In a bowl, mix well spinach, onion, garlic, cream cheese, nutmeg, salt, and black pepper.
2. Place spinach mixture into a baking pan.
3. Arrange the "Inner Basket" in Air Fryer Toaster Oven and press "Preheat".
4. Select "Start/Cancel" to begin preheating.
5. When the unit beeps to show that it is preheated, arrange the baking pan in "Inner Basket".
6. Insert the "Inner Basket" and select "Air Fry".
7. Set the temperature to 350 degrees F for 10 minutes.
8. Select "Start/Cancel" to begin cooking.
9. Now, set the temperature to 400 degrees F for 5 minutes.
10. Select "Start/Cancel" to stop cooking.
11. Serve hot.

Nutrition: Calories: 194 Cal Fat: 15.5 g Cholesterol: 46 mg Sodium: 351 mg Carbs: 7.3 g Fiber: 2.6 g Sugar: 1.4 g Protein: 8.4 g

164. Stuffed Bell Peppers

Preparation Time: 20 minutes
Cooking time: 25 minutes
Servings: 6
Ingredients:
- 6 large bell peppers
- 1 bread roll, finely chopped
- 1 carrot, peeled and finely chopped
- 1 onion, finely chopped
- 1 potato, peeled and finely chopped
- ½ cup fresh peas, shelled
- 2 garlic cloves, minced
- 2 teaspoons fresh parsley, chopped
- Salt and ground black pepper, as required
- 1/3 cup cheddar cheese, grated

Directions:
1. Remove the tops of each bell pepper and discard the seeds.
2. Finely chop the bell pepper tops.
3. In a bowl, place bell pepper tops, bread loaf, vegetables, garlic, parsley, salt and black pepper and mix well.
4. Stuff each bell pepper with the vegetable mixture.
5. Arrange the greased "Inner Basket" in Air Fryer Toaster Oven and press "Preheat".
6. Select "Start/Cancel" to begin preheating.
7. When the unit beeps to show that it is preheated, arrange the bell peppers in "Inner Basket".
8. Insert the "Inner Basket" and select "Air Fry".
9. Set the temperature to 350 degrees F for 25 minutes.
10. Select "Start/Cancel" to begin cooking.
11. After 20 minutes, sprinkle each bell pepper with cheddar cheese.
12. Select "Start/Cancel" to stop cooking.
13. Serve hot.

Nutrition: Calories: 123 Cal Fat: 2.7 g Cholesterol: 7 mg Sodium: 105 mg Carbs: 21.7 g Fiber: 3.7 g Sugar: 8.7 g Protein: 4.8 g

165. Mushroom with Peas

Preparation Time: 15 minutes
Cooking time: 15 minutes
Servings: 4
Ingredients:
- ½ cup soy sauce
- 4 tablespoons maple syrup
- 4 tablespoons rice vinegar
- 4 garlic cloves, finely chopped
- 2 teaspoons Chinese five spice powder
- ½ teaspoon ground ginger
- 16 ounces cremini mushrooms, halved
- ½ cup frozen peas

Directions:
1. In a bowl, mix well soy sauce, maple syrup, vinegar, garlic, five spice powder, and ground ginger. Set aside.
2. Place the mushroom into a greased baking pan in a single layer.
3. Arrange the "Wire Rack" in Air Fryer Toaster Oven and press "Preheat".
4. Select "Start/Cancel" to begin preheating.

VEGETABLE AND SIDE DISHES

5. When the unit beeps to show that it is preheated, arrange the baking pan on top of "Wire Rack".
6. Insert the "Wire Rack" and select "Air Fry".
7. Set the temperature to 350 degrees F for 15 minutes.
8. Select "Start/Cancel" to begin cooking.
9. After 10 minutes of cooking, in the pan, add the peas and vinegar mixture and stir to combine.
10. Select "Start/Cancel" to stop cooking.
11. Serve hot.

Nutrition: Calories: 132 Cal Fat: 0.3 g Sodium: 1100 mg Carbs: 25 g Fiber: 2.4 g Sugar: 15.4 g Protein: 6.1 g Potassium: 428 mg

166. Buttermilk Fried Mushrooms

Preparation Time: 30 minutes
Cooking Time: 15 minutes
Servings: 2
Ingredients:
- 1 ½ c. all-purpose flour
- 2 heaping cups oyster mushrooms
- 1 Tbsp oil
- 1 tsp each salt, pepper, garlic powder, onion powder, smoked paprika, cumin
- 1 c. buttermilk

Directions:
1. Preheat the air fryer to 190 ° C. Clean the mushrooms and place in a large bowl with buttermilk. Let marinate for 15 minutes.
2. Mix the flour and spices in a large bowl. Put the mushrooms out of the buttermilk (keep the buttermilk). Dip each mushroom in the flour mixture, shake off excess flour, dip again in the buttermilk and then again in the flour (short: wet> dry> wet> dry).
3. Grease the bottom of your air pan well and place the mushrooms in a layer, leaving space between the mushrooms. Let it cook for 5 minutes, then roughly coat all sides with a little oil to promote browning. Cook for another 5 to 10 minutes until golden brown and crispy.

Nutrition: Calories: 345 kcal Protein: 13 g Fat: 10 g Carbs: 57 g

167. Veggies Rice

Preparation Time: 20 minutes
Cooking time: 18 minutes
Servings: 4
Ingredients:
- 2 cups cooked white rice
- 1 tablespoon vegetable oil
- 2 teaspoons sesame oil, toasted and divided
- 1 tablespoon water
- Salt and ground white pepper, as required
- 1 large egg, lightly beaten
- ½ cup frozen peas, thawed
- ½ cup frozen carrots, thawed
- 1 teaspoon soy sauce
- 1 teaspoon Sriracha sauce
- ½ teaspoon sesame seeds, toasted

Directions:
1. In a large bowl, add the rice, vegetable oil, one teaspoon of sesame oil, water, salt, and white pepper and mix well.
2. Place the rice mixture into the prepared pan.
3. Arrange the "Wire Rack" in Air Fryer Toaster Oven and press "Preheat".
4. Select "Start/Cancel" to begin preheating.
5. When the unit beeps to show that it is preheated, arrange the baking pan on top of "Wire Rack".
6. Insert the "Wire Rack" and select "Air Fry".
7. Set the temperature to 380 degrees F for 12 minutes.
8. Select "Start/Cancel" to begin cooking.
9. Stir the rice mixture once halfway through.
10. Select "Start/Cancel" to stop cooking.
11. Remove the baking pan from oven and place the beaten egg over rice.
12. Insert the "Wire Rack" and select "Air Fry".
13. Set the temperature to 380 degrees F for 6 minutes.
14. Select "Start/Cancel" to begin cooking.
15. After 4 minutes, stir in the peas and carrots.
16. Meanwhile, in a bowl, mix together soy sauce, Sriracha sauce, sesame seeds and the remaining sesame oil.
17. Select "Start/Cancel" to stop cooking.
18. Transfer the rice mixture into a serving bowl.
19. Drizzle with the sauce and serve.

Nutrition: Calories: 438 Cal Fat: 8.6 g Cholesterol: 47 mg Carbs: 78 g Fiber: 2.7 g Sugar: 1.9 g Protein: 9.5 g Potassium: 194 mg

168. Best Ever Jalapeño Poppers

Preparation Time: 10 minutes
Cooking time: 10 minutes
Servings: 4
Ingredients:
- 12-18 whole fresh jalapeño
- 1 cup nonfat refried beans
- 1 cup shredded Monterey Jack or extra-sharp cheddar cheese
- 1 scallion, sliced
- 1 teaspoon salt, divided
- 1/4 cup all-purpose flour
- 2 large eggs
- 1/2 cup fine cornmeal
- Olive oil or canola oil cooking spray

Directions:
1. Start by slicing each jalapeño lengthwise on one side. Place the jalapeños side by side in a microwave safe bowl and microwave them until they are slightly soft; usually around 5 minutes.
2. While your jalapeños cook; mix refried beans, scallions, 1/2 teaspoon salt, and cheese in a bowl.
3. Once your jalapeños are softened you can scoop out the seeds and add one tablespoon of your refried bean mixture (It can be a little less if the pepper is smaller.) Press the jalapeño closed around the filling.
4. Beat your eggs in a small bowl and place your flour in a separate bowl. In a third bowl mix your cornmeal and the remaining salt in a third bowl.
5. Roll each pepper in the flour, then dip it in the egg, and finally roll it in the cornmeal making sure to coat the entire pepper.
6. Place the peppers on a flat surface and coat them with a cooking spray; olive oil cooking spray is suggested.
7. Pour into the Oven rack/basket. Place the Rack on the middle-shelf of the Chef man Air Fryer Oven. Set temperature to 400°F, and set time to 5 minutes. Select START/STOP to begin. Turn each pepper and then cook for another 5 minutes; serve hot.

Nutrition: Calories: 244 Cal Fat: 12 g Fiber: 2.4 g Protein: 12 g

169. Parmesan Breaded Zucchini Chips

Preparation Time: 15 minutes
Cooking time: 20 minutes
Servings: 5
Ingredients:
- For the zucchini chips:
- 2 medium zucchini
- 2 eggs
- ⅓ Cup bread crumbs
- ⅓ Cup grated Parmesan cheese
- Salt
- Pepper
- Cooking oil
- For the lemon aioli:
- ½ cup mayonnaise
- ½ tablespoon olive oil
- Juice of ½ lemons
- 1 teaspoon minced garlic
- Salt
- Pepper

Directions:
1. To make the zucchini chips:
2. Slice the zucchini into thin chips (about ⅛ inch thick) using a knife or mandolin.
3. In a small bowl, beat the eggs. In another small bowl, combine the bread crumbs, Parmesan cheese, and salt and pepper to taste.
4. Spray the air fryer basket with cooking oil.
5. Dip the zucchini slices one at a time in the eggs and then the bread crumb mixture. You can also sprinkle the bread crumbs onto the zucchini slices with a spoon.
6. Place the zucchini chips in the air fryer basket, but do not stack.
7. Pour into the Oven rack/basket Place the Rack on the middle-shelf of the Chef man Air Fryer Oven. Cook in batches. Spray the chips with cooking oil from a distance (otherwise, the breading may fly off). Cook for 10 minutes.
8. Remove the cooked zucchini chips from the Chef man Air Fryer Oven, and then repeat with the remaining zucchini.
9. To make the lemon aioli:
10. While the zucchini is cooking, combine the mayonnaise, olive oil, lemon juice, and garlic in a small bowl, adding salt and pepper to taste. Mix well until fully combined.
11. Cool the zucchini and serve alongside the aioli.

Nutrition: Calories: 192 Cal Fat: 13 g Fiber: 4 g Protein: 6 g

170. Bell PepperCorn Wrapped in Tortilla

Preparation Time: 5 minutes
Cooking time: 15 minutes
Servings: 4
Ingredients:
- 1 small red bell pepper, chopped
- 1 small yellow onion, diced
- 1 tablespoon water
- 2 cobs grilled corn kernels
- 4 large tortillas
- 4 pieces commercial vegan nuggets, chopped
- Mixed greens for garnish

Directions:
1. Preheat the Chef man Air Fryer Oven to 400°F.
2. In a skillet heated over medium heat, water sauté the vegan nuggets together with the onions, bell peppers, and corn kernels. Set aside.
3. Place filling inside the corn tortillas.
4. Pour the tortillas into the Oven rack/basket. Place the Rack on the middle-shelf of the Chef man Air Fryer Oven. Set temperature to 400°F, and set time to 15 minutes until the tortilla wraps are crispy.
5. Serve with mix greens on top.

Nutrition: Calories: 548 Cal Fat: 20.7 g Carbs: 0 g Protein: 46 g

171. Baked Cheesy Eggplant with Marinara

Preparation Time: 5 minutes
Cooking time: 45 minutes
Servings: 3
Ingredients:
- 1 clove garlic, sliced
- 1 large eggplant
- 1 tablespoon olive oil
- 1 tablespoon olive oil
- 1/2 pinch salt, or as needed
- 1/4 cup and 2 tablespoons dry bread crumbs
- 1/4 cup and 2 tablespoons ricotta cheese
- 1/4 cup grated Parmesan cheese
- 1/4 cup grated Parmesan cheese
- 1/4 cup water, plus more as needed
- 1/4 teaspoon red pepper flakes
- 1-1/2 cups prepared marinara sauce
- 1-1/2 teaspoons olive oil
- 2 tablespoons shredded pepper jack cheese
- Salt and freshly ground black pepper to taste

Directions:
1. Cut eggplant crosswise in 5 pieces. Peel and chop two pieces into ½-inch cubes.
2. Lightly grease baking pan of air fryer with 1 tbsp. olive oil for 5 minutes, heat oil at 390°F. Add half eggplant strips and cook for 2 minutes per side. Transfer to a plate.
3. Add 1 ½ tsp olive oil and add garlic. Cook for a minute. Add chopped eggplants.
4. Season with pepper flakes and salt
5. Cook for 4 minutes Lower heat to 330°F and continue cooking eggplants until soft, around 8 minutes more.
6. Stir in water and marinara sauce. Cook for 7 minutes until heated through
7. Stirring every now and then
8. Transfer to a bowl.
9. In a bowl, whisk well pepper, salt, pepper jack cheese, Parmesan cheese, and ricotta. Evenly spread cheeses over eggplant strips and then fold in half.
10. Lay folded eggplant in baking pan. Pour marinara sauce on top.
11. In a small bowl whisk well olive oil, and bread crumbs
12. Sprinkle all over sauce.
13. Place the baking dish in the Chef Man Air Fryer Oven cooking basket. Cook for 15 minutes at 390°F until tops are lightly browned.
14. Serve and enjoy.

Nutrition: Calories: 405 Cal Fat: 21.4 g Carbs: 0 g Protein: 12.7 g

172. Spicy Sweet Potato Fries

Preparation Time: 5 minutes
Cooking time: 37 minutes
Servings: 4
Ingredients:
- 2 tbsp. sweet potato fry seasoning mix
- 2 tbsp. olive oil
- 2 sweet potatoes
- Seasoning Mix:
- 2 tbsp. salt
- 1 tbsp. cayenne pepper
- 1 tbsp. dried oregano
- 1 tbsp. fennel
- 2 tbsp. coriander

Directions:
1. Slice both ends off sweet potatoes and peel. Slice lengthwise in half and again crosswise to make four pieces from each potato.
2. Slice each potato piece into 2-3 slices, and then slice into fries.
3. Grind together all of seasoning mix ingredients and mix in the salt.
4. Ensure the Air Fryer Oven is preheated to 350 degrees.
5. Toss potato pieces in olive oil, sprinkling with seasoning mix and tossing well to coat thoroughly.
6. Add fries to air fryer basket. Set temperature to 350°F, and set time to 27 minutes. Select START/STOP to begin.
7. Take out the basket and turn fries. Turn off air fryer and let cook 10-12 minutes till fries are golden.

Nutrition: Calories: 89 Cal Fat: 14 g Sugar: 3 g Protein: 8 g

173. Creamy Spinach Quiche

Preparation Time: 10 minutes
Cooking time: 20 minutes
Servings: 4
Ingredients:
- Premade quiche crust, chilled and rolled flat to a 7-inch round
- Eggs
- ¼ cup of milk
- Pinch of salt and pepper
- 1 clove of garlic, peeled and finely minced
- ½ cup of cooked spinach, drained and coarsely chopped
- ¼ cup of shredded mozzarella cheese
- ¼ cup of shredded cheddar cheese

Directions:
1. Preheat the Air Fryer Oven to 360 degrees.
2. Press the premade crust into a 7-inch pie tin, or any appropriately sized glass or ceramic heat-safe dish. Press and trim at the edges if necessary. With a fork, pierce several holes in the dough to allow air circulation and prevent cracking of the crust while cooking.
3. In a mixing bowl, beat the eggs until fluffy and until the yolks and white are evenly combined.
4. Add milk, garlic, spinach, salt and pepper, and half the cheddar and mozzarella cheese to the eggs. Set the rest of the cheese aside for now, and stir the mixture until completely blended. Make sure the spinach is not clumped together, but rather spread among the other ingredients.
5. Pour the mixture into the pie crust, slowly and carefully to avoid splashing. The mixture should almost fill the crust, but not completely – leaving a ¼ inch of crust at the edges.
6. Place the baking dish in the Air Fryer Oven cooking basket. Set the Air Fryer Oven timer for 15 minutes. After 15 minutes, the air fryer will shut off, and the quiche will already be firm and the crust beginning to brown. Sprinkle the rest of the cheddar and mozzarella cheese on top of the quiche filling. Reset the Air Fryer Oven at 360 degrees for 5 minutes. After 5 minutes, when the air fryer shuts off, the cheese will have formed an exquisite crust on top and the quiche will be golden brown and perfect. Remove from the air fryer using oven mitts or tongs, and set on a heat-safe surface to cool for a few minutes before cutting.

Nutrition: Calories: 371 Cal Fat: 33 g Cholesterol: 231 mg Sodium: 407 mg Carbs: 6 g Fiber: 1 g Sugar: 3 g Protein: 14 g

174. Crispy Salt and Pepper Tofu

Preparation Time: 5 minutes
Cooking Time: 15 minutes
Servings: 4
Ingredients:
- ¼ cup chickpea flour
- ¼ cup arrowroot (or cornstarch)
- 1 teaspoon sea salt
- 1 teaspoon granulated garlic
- ½ teaspoon freshly grated black pepper
- 1 (15-ounce) package tofu, firm or extra-firm
- Cooking oil spray (sunflower, safflower, or refined coconut)
- Asian Spicy Sweet Sauce, optional

Directions:
1. In a medium bowl, combine the flour, arrowroot, salt, garlic, and pepper. Stir well to combine.
2. Cut the tofu into cubes (no need to press—if it's a bit watery, that's fine!). Place the cubes into the flour mixture. Toss well to coat. Spray the tofu with oil and toss again. (The spray will help the coating better stick to the tofu.)
3. Spray the air fryer basket with the oil. Place the tofu in a single layer in the air fryer basket (you may have to do this in 2 batches, depending on the size of your appliance) and spray the tops with oil. Fry for 8 minutes. Remove the air fryer basket and spray again with oil. Toss gently or turn the pieces over. Spray with oil again and fry for another 7 minutes, or until golden-browned and very crisp.
4. Serve immediately, either plain or with the Asian Spicy Sweet Sauce.

Nutrition: Calories: 148 Fat: 5g Saturated fat: 0g Cholesterol: 0mg Sodium: 473mg Carbs: 14g Fiber: 1g Protein: 11g

175. Brown Rice, Spinach and Tofu Frittata

Preparation Time: 5 minutes
Cooking time: 55 minutes
Servings: 4
Ingredients:
- ½ cup baby spinach, chopped
- ½ cup kale, chopped
- ½ onion, chopped
- ½ teaspoon turmeric
- 1 ¾ cups brown rice, cooked
- 1 flax egg (1 tablespoon flaxseed meal + 3 tablespoon cold water)
- 1 package firm tofu
- 1 tablespoon olive oil
- 1 yellow pepper, chopped

- 2 tablespoons soy sauce
- 2 teaspoons arrowroot powder
- 2 teaspoons Dijon mustard
- 2/3 cup almond milk
- 3 big mushrooms, chopped
- 3 tablespoons nutritional yeast
- 4 cloves garlic, crushed
- 4 spring onions, chopped
- A handful of basil leaves, chopped

Directions:
1. Preheat the Air Fryer Oven to 375°F. Grease a pan that will fit inside the Air Fryer Oven.
2. Prepare the frittata crust by mixing the brown rice and flax egg. Press the rice onto the baking dish until you form a crust. Brush with a little oil and cook for 10 minutes.
3. Meanwhile, heat olive oil in a skillet over medium flame and sauté the garlic and onions for 2 minutes.
4. Add the pepper and mushroom and continue stirring for 3 minutes.
5. Stir in the kale, spinach, spring onions, and basil. Remove from the pan and set aside.
6. In a food processor, pulse together the tofu, mustard, turmeric, soy sauce, nutritional yeast, vegan milk and arrowroot powder. Pour in a mixing bowl and stir in the sautéed vegetables.
7. Pour the vegan frittata mixture over the rice crust and cook in the Air Fryer Oven for 40 minutes.

Nutrition: Calories: 226 Cal Fat: 8.05 g Carbs: 0 g Protein: 10.6 g

176. Carrots, Yellow Squash & Zucchini

Preparation Time: 5 minutes
Cooking time: 35 minutes
Servings: 4

Ingredients:
- 1 tbsp. chopped tarragon leaves
- ½ tsp. white pepper
- 1 tsp. salt
- 1 pound yellow squash
- 1 pound zucchini
- 6 tsp. olive oil
- ½ pound carrots

Directions:
1. Stem and root the end of squash and zucchini and cut in ¾-inch half-moons. Peel and cut carrots into 1-inch cubes Combine carrot cubes with 2 teaspoons of olive oil, tossing to combine.
2. Pour into the Air Fryer Oven basket, set temperature to 400°F, and set time to 5 minutes.
3. As carrots cook, drizzle remaining olive oil over squash and zucchini pieces, then season with pepper and salt. Toss well to coat.
4. Add squash and zucchini when the timer for carrots goes off. Cook 30 minutes, making sure to toss 2-3 times during the cooking process.
5. Once done, take out veggies and toss with tarragon. Serve up warm.

Nutrition: Calories: 122 Cal Fat: 9 g Carbs: 0 g Protein: 6 g

177. Winter Vegetarian Frittata

Preparation Time: 5 minutes
Cooking time: 30 minutes
Servings: 4

Ingredients:
- 1 leek, peeled and thinly sliced into rings
- 2 cloves garlic, finely minced
- 3 medium-sized carrots, finely chopped
- 2 tablespoons olive oil
- 6 large-sized eggs
- Sea salt and ground black pepper, to taste
- 1/2 teaspoon dried marjoram, finely minced
- 1/2 cup yellow cheese of choice

Directions:
1. Sauté the leek, garlic, and carrot in hot olive oil until they are tender and fragrant; reserve
2. In the meantime, preheat your Air Fryer Oven to 330 degrees F.
3. In a bowl, whisk the eggs along with the salt, ground black pepper, and marjoram.
4. Then, grease the inside of your baking dish with a nonstick cooking spray. Pour the whisked eggs into the baking dish. Stir in the sautéed carrot mixture. Top with the cheese shreds.
5. Place the baking dish in the Air Fryer Oven cooking basket. Cook about 30 minutes and serve warm.

Nutrition: Calories: 153 Cal Fat: 10.9 g Cholesterol: 178.6 mg Sodium: 316 mg Carbs: 3.7 g Fiber: 1 g Sugar: 1.1 g Protein: 6.7 g

178. Air Fried Kale Chips

Preparation Time: 5 minutes
Cooking time: 10 minutes
Servings: 6

Ingredients:
- ¼ tsp. Himalayan salt
- 3 tbsp. yeast
- Avocado oil
- 1 bunch of kale

Directions:
1. Rinse kale and with paper towels, dry well.
2. Tear kale leaves into large pieces. Remember they will shrink as they cook so good sized pieces are necessary.
3. Place kale pieces in a bowl and spritz with avocado oil till shiny. Sprinkle with salt and yeast.
4. With your hands, toss kale leaves well to combine.
5. Pour half of the kale mixture into the Air Fryer Oven basket, set temperature to 350°F, and set time to 5 minutes. Remove and repeat with another half of kale.

Nutrition: Calories: 55 Cal Fat: 10 g Carbs: 0 g Protein: 1 g

179. Buttered Broccoli

Preparation Time: 5 minutes
Cooking time: 15 minutes
Servings: 4

Ingredients:
- 1 lb Broccoli florets – 1 lb.
- 1 tbsp. Butter, melted
- ½ tsp. Red pepper flakes, crushed
- Salt and ground black pepper, as required

Directions
1. Gather all of the ingredients in a bowl and toss to coat well.

2. Place the broccoli florets in the rotisserie basket and attach the lid.
3. Arrange the drip pan in the bottom of the Air Fryer Oven cooking chamber.
4. Take to the preheated air fryer at 400 F for 15 minutes.
5. Serve immediately.

Nutrition: Calories 55 Carbs 6.1g Fat 3g Protein 2.3g

180. Seasoned Carrots with Green Beans

Preparation Time: 5 minutes
Cooking time: 10 minutes
Servings: 4

Ingredients:
- ½ lb. Green beans, trimmed
- ½ lb. Carrots, peeled and cut into sticks
- 1 tbsp. Olive oil
- Salt and ground black pepper, as required

Directions
1. Gather all the ingredients into a bowl and toss to coat well.
2. Place the vegetables in the rotisserie basket and attach the lid.
3. Arrange the drip pan in the bottom of the Air Fryer Oven cooking chamber. Take to the preheated air fryer at 400 F for 10 minutes.
4. Serve hot.

Nutrition: Calories 94 Carbs 12.7g Fat 4.8g Protein 2g

181. Seasoned Veggies

Preparation Time: 5 minutes
Cooking time: 12 minutes
Servings: 4

Ingredients:
- 1 cup Baby carrots
- 1 cup Broccoli florets
- 1 cup Cauliflower florets
- 1 tbsp. Olive oil
- 1 tbsp. Italian seasoning
- Salt and ground black pepper, as required

Directions
1. Gather all of the ingredients into a bowl and toss to coat well.
2. Place the vegetables in the rotisserie basket and attach the lid.
3. Arrange the drip pan in the bottom of the Air Fryer Oven cooking chamber.
4. Take to the preheated air fryer at 380 F for 18 minutes.
5. Serve

Nutrition: Calories 66 Carbs 5.7g Fat 4.7g Protein 1.4g

182. Creamy Potatoes

Preparation time: 5 minutes
Cooking time: 20 minutes
Servings: 4

Ingredients:
- `2 gold potatoes, cut into medium pieces
- `1 tablespoon olive oil
- `Salt and black pepper to taste
- `3 tablespoons sour cream

Directions:
1. In a baking dish that fits your air fryer, mix all the ingredients and toss.
2. Place the dish in the air fryer and cook at 370 degrees F for 20 minutes.
3. Divide between plates and serve as a side dish.

Nutrition: Calories: 201 Fat: 8 Fiber: 9 Carbs: 18 Protein: 5

183. Sweet Potato Side Salad

Preparation time: 5 minutes
Cooking time: 20 minutes
Servings: 2

Ingredients:
- `2 sweet potatoes, peeled and cut into wedges
- `Salt and black pepper to taste
- `2 tablespoons avocado oil
- `½ teaspoon curry powder
- `¼ teaspoon coriander, ground
- `4 tablespoons mayonnaise
- `½ teaspoon cumin, ground
- `A pinch of ginger powder
- `A pinch of cinnamon powder

Directions:
1. In your air fryer's basket, mix the sweet potato wedges with salt, pepper, coriander, curry powder, and the oil; toss well.
2. Cook at 370 degrees F for 20 minutes, flipping them once.
3. Transfer the potatoes to a bowl, then add the mayonnaise, cumin, ginger and the cinnamon.
4. Toss and serve as a side salad.

Nutrition: Calories: 190 Fat: 5 Fiber: 8 Carbs: 14 Protein: 5

184. Mayo Brussels Sprouts

Preparation time: 5 minutes
Cooking time: 15 minutes
Servings: 4

Ingredients:
- `1 pound Brussels sprouts, trimmed and halved
- `Salt and black pepper to taste
- `6 teaspoons olive oil
- `½ cup mayonnaise
- `2 tablespoons garlic, minced

Directions:
1. In your air fryer, mix the sprouts, salt, pepper, and oil; toss well.
2. Cook the sprouts at 390 degrees F for 15 minutes.
3. Transfer them to a bowl; then add the mayo and the garlic and toss.
4. Divide between plates and serve as a side dish.

Nutrition: Calories: 202 Fat: 6 Fiber: 8 Carbs: 12 Protein: 8

185. Green Beans and Shallots

Preparation time: 5 minutes
Cooking time: 25 minutes
Servings: 4

Ingredients:
- `1½ pounds green beans, trimmed
- `Salt and black pepper to taste
- `½ pound shallots, chopped
- `¼ cup walnuts, chopped
- `2 tablespoons olive oil

Directions:
1. In your air fryer, mix all ingredients and toss.
2. Cook at 350 degrees F for 25 minutes.
3. Divide between plates and serve as a side dish.

Nutrition: Calories: 182 Fat: 3 Fiber: 6 Carbs: 11 Protein: 5

186. Italian Mushroom Mix

Preparation time: 5 minutes
Cooking time: 15 minutes
Servings: 4
Ingredients:
- `1 pound button mushrooms, halved
- `2 tablespoons parmesan cheese, grated
- `1 teaspoon Italian seasoning
- `A pinch of salt and black pepper
- `3 tablespoons butter, melted

Directions:
1. In a pan that fits your air fryer, mix all the ingredients and toss.
2. Place the pan in the air fryer and cook at 360 degrees F for 15 minutes.
3. Divide the mix between plates and serve.

Nutrition: Calories: 194 Fat: 4 Fiber: 4 Carbs: 14 Protein: 7

187. Crispy Fried Pickle Spears

Preparation Time: 15 minutes
Servings 6
Ingredients
- `1/3 cup milk
- `1 teaspoon garlic powder
- `2 medium-sized eggs
- `1 teaspoon fine sea salt
- `1/3 teaspoon chili powder
- `1/3 cup all-purpose flour
- `1/2 teaspoon shallot powder
- `2 jars sweet and sour pickle spears

Directions
1. Pat the pickle spears dry with a kitchen towel. Then, take two mixing bowls.
2. Whisk the egg and milk in a bowl. In another bowl, combine all dry ingredients.
3. Firstly, dip the pickle spears into the dry mix; then coat each pickle with the egg/milk mixture; dredge them in the flour mixture again for additional coating.
4. Air fry battered pickles for 15 minutes at 385 degrees. Enjoy!

Nutrition: 58 Calories; 2g Fat; 6.8g Carbs; 3.2g Protein; 0.9g Sugars

188. Spicy Winter Squash Bites

Preparation Time: 23 minutes
Servings 8
Ingredients
- `2 teaspoons fresh mint leaves, chopped
- `1/3 cup brown sugar
- `1 ½ teaspoons red pepper chili flakes
- `2 tablespoons melted butter
- `3 pounds winter squash, peeled, seeded, and cubed

Directions
1. Toss all of the above ingredients in a large-sized mixing dish.
2. Roast the squash bites for 30 minutes at 325 degrees F in your Air Fryer, turning once or twice. Serve with a homemade dipping sauce.

Nutrition: 113 Calories; 3g Fat; 22.6g Carbs; 1.6g Protein; 4.3g Sugars

189. Butter Squash Fritters

Preparation Time: 22 minutes
Servings 4
Ingredients
- `1/3 cup all-purpose flour
- `1/3 teaspoon freshly ground black pepper, or more to taste
- `1/3 teaspoon dried sage
- `4 cloves garlic, minced
- `1 ½ tablespoons olive oil
- `1/3 butternut squash, peeled and grated
- `2 eggs, well whisked
- `1 teaspoon fine sea salt
- `A pinch of ground allspice

Directions
1. Thoroughly combine all ingredients in a mixing bowl.
2. Preheat your air fryer to 345 degrees and set the timer for 17 minutes; cook until your fritters are browned; serve right away.

Nutrition: 152 Calories; 10g Fat; 9.4g Carbs; 5.8g Protein; 0.3g Sugars

190. Herbed Roasted Potatoes

Preparation Time: 24 minutes
Servings 4
Ingredients
- `1 teaspoon crushed dried thyme
- `1 teaspoon ground black pepper
- `2 tablespoons olive oil
- `1/2 tablespoon crushed dried rosemary
- `3 potatoes, peeled, washed and cut into wedges
- `1/2 teaspoon seasoned salt

Directions
1. Lay the potatoes in the air fryer cooking basket; drizzle olive oil over your potatoes.
2. Then, cook for 17 minutes at 353 degrees F.
3. Toss with the seasonings and serve warm with your favorite salad on the side.

Nutrition: 208 Calories; 7g Fat; 33.8g Carbs; 3.6g Protein; 2.5g Sugars

191. Indian-Style Garnet Sweet Potatoes

Preparation Time: 24 minutes
Servings 4
Ingredients
- `1/3 teaspoon white pepper
- `1 tablespoon butter, melted
- `1/2 teaspoon turmeric powder
- `5 garnet sweet potatoes, peeled and diced
- `1 ½ tablespoons maple syrup
- `2 teaspoons tamarind paste
- `1 1/2 tablespoons fresh lime juice
- `1 1/2 teaspoon ground allspice

Directions
1. In a mixing bowl, toss all ingredients until sweet potatoes are well coated.
2. Air-fry them at 335 degrees F for 12 minutes.
3. Pause the air fryer and toss again. Increase the temperature to 390 degrees F and cook for an additional 10 minutes. Eat warm.

Nutrition: 103 Calories; 9g Fat; 4.9g Carbs; 1.9g Protein; 1.2g Sugars

192. Easy Frizzled Leeks

Preparation Time: 52 minutes
Servings 6
Ingredients
- `1/2 teaspoon porcini powder
- `1 1/2 cup rice flour
- `1 tablespoon vegetable oil
- `3 medium-sized leeks, slice into julienne strips
- `2 large-sized dishes with ice water
- `2 teaspoons onion powder
- `Fine sea salt and cayenne pepper, to taste

Directions
1. Allow the leeks to soak in ice water for about 25 minutes; drain well.
2. Place the rice flour, salt, cayenne pepper, onions powder, and porcini powder into a resealable bag. Add the celery and shake to coat well.
3. Drizzle vegetable oil over the seasoned leeks. Air fry at 390 degrees F for about 18 minutes; turn them halfway through the cooking time. Serve with homemade mayonnaise or any other sauce for dipping. Enjoy!

Nutrition: 291 Calories; 6g Fat; 53.3g Carbs; 5.7g Protein; 4.3g Sugars

193. Cremini Mushrooms in Zesty Tahini Sauce

Preparation Time: 22 minutes
Servings 5
Ingredients
- `1/2 tablespoon tahini
- `1/2 teaspoon turmeric powder
- `1/3 teaspoon cayenne pepper
- `2 tablespoons lemon juice, freshly squeezed
- `1 teaspoon kosher salt
- `1/3 teaspoon freshly cracked black pepper
- `1 1/2 tablespoons vermouth
- `1 ½ tablespoons olive oil
- `1 ½ pound Cremini mushrooms

Directions
1. Grab a mixing dish and toss the mushrooms with the olive oil, turmeric powder, salt, black pepper, and cayenne pepper.
2. Cook them in your air fryer for 9 minutes at 355 degrees F.
3. Pause your air fryer, give it a good stir and cook for 10 minutes longer.
4. Meanwhile, thoroughly combine lemon juice, vermouth, and tahini. Serve warm mushrooms with tahini sauce.

Nutrition: 372 Calories; 4g Fat; 80g Carbs; 11.2g Protein; 2.6g Sugars

194. Pepper Jack Cauliflower Bites

Preparation Time: 24 minutes
Servings 2
Ingredients
- 1/3 teaspoon shallot powder
- 1 teaspoon ground black pepper
- 1 ½ large-sized heads of cauliflower, broken into florets
- 1/4 teaspoon cumin powder
- ½ teaspoon garlic salt
- 1/4 cup Pepper Jack cheese, grated
- 1 ½ tablespoons vegetable oil
- 1/3 teaspoon paprika

Directions
1. Boil cauliflower in a large pan of salted water approximately 5 minutes. After that, drain the cauliflower florets; now, transfer them to a baking dish.
2. Toss the cauliflower florets with the rest of the above ingredients.
3. Roast at 395 degrees F for 16 minutes, turn them halfway through the process. Enjoy!

Nutrition: 271 Calories; 23g Fat; 8.9g Carbs; 9.8g Protein; 2.8g Sugars

195. Cheesy Broccoli Croquettes

Preparation Time: 50 minutes
Servings 6
Ingredients
- 1 1/2 cups Monterey Jack cheese
- 1 teaspoon dried dill weed
- 1/3 teaspoon ground black pepper
- 3 eggs, whisked
- 1 teaspoon cayenne pepper
- 1/2 teaspoon kosher salt
- 1 cup Panko crumbs
- ½ cups broccoli florets
- 1/3 cup Parmesan cheese

Directions
1. Blitz the broccoli florets in a food processor until finely crumbed. Then, combine the broccoli with the rest of the above ingredients.
2. Roll the mixture into small balls; place the balls in the fridge for approximately half an hour.
3. Preheat your air fryer to 335 degrees F and set the timer to 14 minutes; cook until broccoli croquettes are browned and serve warm.

Nutrition: 246 Calories; 14g Fat; 15g Carbs; 14.5g Protein; 1.6g Sugars

196. Cauliflower Cakes Ole

Preparation Time: 48 minutes
Servings 6
Ingredients
- 2 teaspoons chili powder
- 1 1/2 teaspoon kosher salt
- 1 teaspoon dried marjoram, crushed
- 1/2 cups cauliflower, broken into florets
- 1 1/3 cups tortilla chip crumbs
- 1/2 teaspoon crushed red pepper flakes
- 3 eggs, whisked
- 1 ½ cups Queso cotija cheese, crumbled

Directions
1. Blitz the cauliflower florets in your food processor until they're crumbled -it is the size of rice. Then, combine the cauliflower "rice" with the other items.
2. Now, roll the cauliflower mixture into small balls; refrigerate for 30 minutes.
3. Preheat your air fryer to 345 degrees and set the timer for 14 minutes; cook until the balls are browned and serve right away.

Nutrition: 190 Calories; 14g Fat; 4.7g Carbs; 11.5g Protein; 1.3g Sugars

197. Celery and Carrot Croquettes

Preparation Time: 25 minutes
Servings 4
Ingredients
- 2 small eggs, lightly beaten
- 1/3 teaspoon freshly cracked black pepper
- 1/3 cup Colby cheese, grated
- 1/2 tablespoon fresh dill, finely chopped
- 1/2 tablespoon garlic paste
- 1/3 cup onion, finely chopped
- 1/3 cup all-purpose flour
- 3 medium-sized carrots, trimmed and grated
- 2 teaspoons fine sea salt
- 3 medium-sized celery stalks, trimmed and grated
- 1/3 teaspoon baking powder

Directions
1. Place the carrots and celery on a paper towel and squeeze them to remove the excess liquid.
2. Combine the vegetables with the other ingredients in the order listed above. Shape the balls using 1 tablespoon of the vegetable mixture.
3. Then, gently flatten each ball with your palm or a wide spatula. Spritz the croquettes with a nonstick cooking oil.
4. Bake the vegetable cakes in a single layer for 17 minutes at 318 degrees F. Serve warm with sour cream.

Nutrition: 142 Calories; 6g Fat; 15.8g Carbs; 7.2g Protein; 3g Sugars

198. Smoked Veggie Omelet

Preparation Time: 14 minutes
Servings 2
Ingredients
- 1/3 cup cherry tomatoes, chopped
- 1 bell pepper, seeded and chopped
- 1/3 teaspoon freshly ground black pepper
- 1/2 purple onion, peeled and sliced
- 1 teaspoon smoked cayenne pepper
- 5 medium-sized eggs, well-beaten
- 1/3 cup smoked tofu, crumbled
- 1 teaspoon seasoned salt
- 1 1/2 tablespoons fresh chives, chopped

Directions
1. Brush a baking dish with a spray coating.
2. Throw all ingredients, minus fresh chives, into the baking dish; give it a good stir.
3. Cook about 15 minutes at 325 degrees F. Garnish with fresh chopped chives. Bon appétit!

Nutrition: 226 Calories; 11.5g Fat; 14.2g Carbs; 16.3g Protein; 5.2g Sugars

199. Sweet Potato and Carrot Croquettes

Preparation Time: 22 minutes
Servings 4
Ingredients
- 1/3 cup Swiss cheese, grated
- 1/3 teaspoon fine sea salt
- 1/3 teaspoon baking powder
- 1/3 cup scallions, finely chopped
- 1/2 tablespoon fresh basil, finely chopped
- 3 carrots, trimmed and grated
- 1/2 teaspoon freshly cracked black pepper
- 3 sweet potatoes, grated
- 1/3 cup all-purpose flour
- 2 small eggs, lightly beaten

Directions
1. Place grated sweet potatoes and carrots on a paper towel and pat them dry.
2. Combine the potatoes and carrots with the other ingredients in the order listed above. Then, create the balls using 1½ tablespoons of the vegetable mixture.
3. Then, gently flatten each ball. Spritz the croquettes with a nonstick cooking oil.
4. Bake your croquettes for 13 minutes at 305 degrees F; work with batches. Serve warm with tomato ketchup and mayonnaise.

Nutrition: 206 Calories; 5g Fat; 32g Carbs; 8.3g Protein; 5.7g Sugars

200. Manchego and Potato Patties

Preparation Time: 15 minutes
Servings 8
Ingredients
- 1 cup Manchego cheese, shredded
- 1 teaspoon paprika
- 1 teaspoon freshly ground black pepper
- 1/2 tablespoon fine sea salt
- 2 cups scallions, finely chopped
- 2 pounds Russet potatoes, peeled and grated
- 2 tablespoons canola oil
- 2 teaspoons dried basil

Directions
1. Thoroughly combine all of the above ingredients. Then, shape the balls using your hands. Now, flatten the balls to make the patties.
2. Next, cook your patties at 360 degrees F approximately 10 minutes. Bon appétit!

Nutrition: 191 Calories; 8.7g Fat; 22g Carbs; 7g Protein; 1.4g Sugars

201. Mint-Butter Stuffed Mushrooms

Preparation Time: 19 minutes
Servings 3
Ingredients
- 3 garlic cloves, minced
- 1 teaspoon ground black pepper, or more to taste
- 1/3 cup seasoned breadcrumbs
- 1½ tablespoons fresh mint, chopped
- 1 teaspoon salt, or more to taste
- 1½ tablespoons melted butter
- 3 medium-sized mushrooms, cleaned, stalks removed

Directions
1. Mix all of the above ingredients, minus the mushrooms, in a mixing bowl to prepare the filling.
2. Then, stuff the mushrooms with the prepared filling.
3. Air-fry stuffed mushrooms at 375 degrees F for about 12 minutes. Taste for doneness and serve at room temperature as a vegetarian appetizer.

Nutrition: 290 Calories; 14.7g Fat; 13.4g Carbs; 28g Protein; 3.3g Sugars

202. Thai Green Curry Noodles

Preparation Time: 1 hour and 15 minutes
Cooking Time: 20 minutes
Servings: 6
Ingredients:
- 1kg of shirataki noodles
- 6 tablespoons of soy sauce
- 1 ½ tablespoon of fish sauce
- 1 teaspoon of sesame oil
- ½ teaspoon garlic powder
- 350g of tofu
- 150g of snow peas
- 1 red pepper
- 1 green pepper
- 100g of mushrooms
- 150g of water chestnuts
- 1 teaspoon of coriander paste
- 3 tablespoons of lime juice
- 2 teaspoons of lemongrass paste
- 4 tablespoons of rice wine vinegar
- 350g of napa cabbage
- 2 medium carrots
- 4 green onions
- 6 tablespoons of thai green curry paste

Directions
1. Firstly, to prepare the vegetables make sure both peppers, mushrooms water chestnuts are sliced thinly. The carrots and cabbage need to be shredded and lastly, the green onions chopped finely. Set aside for later.
2. Place the noodles in a large bowl with 500 ml of boiling water, stirring in 1 tablespoon of the soy sauce. Set aside.
3. Mix 3 tablespoons of the soy sauce, fish sauce, sesame oil and garlic powder together to make a marinade.
4. Cut the tofu into bite-size cubes and put into the marinade, making sure to mix together. Set aside.
5. In a bowl to make the stir-fry veg, mix the snow peas, peppers, mushrooms and water chestnuts. Set aside.
6. To make the dressing, mix the coriander paste, lime juice, lemongrass paste and 4 tablespoons of the Thai green curry paste and 2 tablespoons of the rice vinegar. Set aside.
7. To make the veg base, mix the shredded cabbage, shredded carrots and the chopped green onion. Set aside.
8. Set the Air Fryer temperature to 360 F and spray the basket with cooking oil.
9. Remove the tofu from the marinade and place into the Air Fryer basket, cook for 12 to 13 minutes Make sure to turn halfway through the cooking process. Once done, set aside with a plate on top to keep them warm.
10. Mix the leftover marinade, 2 tablespoons of rice vinegar, 2 tablespoons of soy sauce, 2 tablespoons of the Thai green curry paste, place into a bowl suitable for the Air Fryer, mix in the stir-fry veg and spray with the cooking oil. Cook for 5 minutes
11. Dry out the noodles.
12. In a large bowl, put in: the noodles, the dressing, the tofu cubes, the stir-fry veg and the veg base. Toss with tongs to mix everything together.

Nutrition: Calories 183 Fat 6.1g Carbs 22.7g Protein 9.9g

EMILY ROMERO

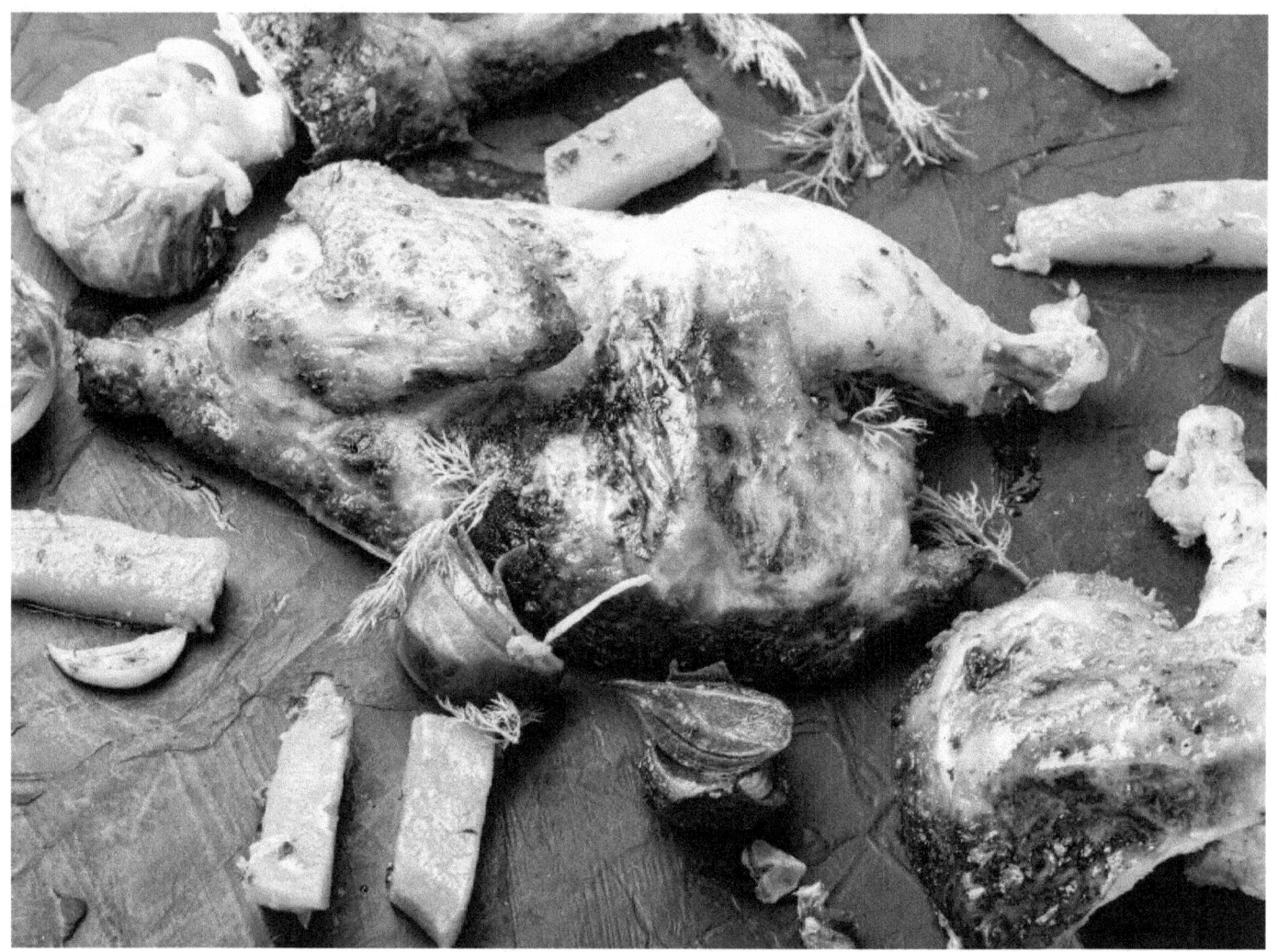

POULTRY

203. Honey Duck Breasts

Preparation Time: 5 minutes
Cooking Time: 25 minutes
Servings: 2
Ingredients:
- Smoked duck breast – 1, halved
- Honey – 1 tsp.
- Tomato paste – 1 tsp.
- Mustard – 1 tbsp.
- Apple vinegar – ½ tsp.

Directions:
1. Mix tomato paste, honey, mustard, and vinegar in a bowl. Whisk well. Add duck breast pieces and coat well. Cook in the air fryer at 370F for 15 minutes.
2. Remove the duck breast from the air fryer and add to the honey mixture. Coat again. Cook again at 370F for 6 minutes. Serve.

Nutrition: Calories 274 Carbs 22g Fat 11g Protein 13g

204. Creamy Coconut Chicken

Preparation Time: 5 minutes
Cooking Time: 20 minutes
Servings: 4
Ingredients:
- Big chicken legs 4
- Turmeric powder 5 tsps.
- Ginger 2 tbsps. grated
- Salt and black pepper to taste
- Coconut cream 4 tbsps.

Directions:
1. In a bowl, mix salt, pepper, ginger, turmeric, and cream. Whisk. Add chicken pieces, coat and marinate for 2 hours.
2. Transfer chicken to the preheated air fryer and cook at 370F for 25 minutes. Serve.

Nutrition: Calories 300 Carbs 22g Fat 4g Protein 20g

205. Easy Turkey Breasts With Basil

Preparation time: 5 minutes
Cooking time: 10 minutes
Servings: 4
Ingredients:
- 2 tablespoons olive oil
- 2 pounds turkey breasts, bone-in skin-on
- Coarse sea salt and ground black pepper, to taste
- 1 teaspoon fresh basil leaves, chopped
- 2 tablespoons lemon zest, grated

Directions
1. Rub olive oil on all sides of the turkey breasts; sprinkle with salt, pepper, basil, and lemon zest.
2. Place the turkey breasts skin side up on a parchment-lined cooking basket.
3. Cook in the preheated Air Fryer at 330 F for 30 minutes. Now, turn them over and cook an additional 28 minutes.
4. Serve with lemon wedges, if desired.

Nutrition: Calories 416 Fat 26g Protein 49g Sugars 0g Fiber 2g

206. Crime Chicken

Preparation Time: 5 minutes
Cooking Time: 25 minutes
Servings: 4
Ingredients:
- 2 tbsp. minced garlic
- 1 ½ lbs. boneless skinless chicken thighs
- Pepper and salt as desired
- 1-2 jars of artichokes hearts (10 oz. jars)
- 2 tbsp. oregano

Directions:
1. In a large bowl, mix chicken thighs and artichokes hearts (including liquid) and let it marinate for about 20-30 minutes.
2. After chicken marinates, strain the liquid and toss in remaining spices and garlic. Combine all ingredients.
3. Set broiler on the oven to high and put marinated chicken in for about 18 -25 minutes, so chicken thoroughly cooks.
4. Broil on the second rack for about 18-20 minutes, then broil on the first rack for the last 5 minutes to make chicken a little crispy.

Nutrition: Calories: 261 Protein: 33g Net Carbs: 5g Fat 10

207. Chicken and Rice Casserole

Preparation time: 5 minutes
Cooking time: 40 minutes
Servings: 6
Ingredients:
- 2 lbs. bone-in chicken thighs
- Salt and black pepper
- 1 teaspoon olive oil
- 5 cloves garlic, chopped
- 2 large onions, chopped
- 2 large red bell peppers, chopped
- 1 tablespoon sweet Hungarian paprika
- 1 teaspoon hot Hungarian paprika
- 2 tablespoons tomato paste
- 2 cups chicken broth
- 3 cups brown rice, thawed
- 2 tablespoons parsley, chopped
- 6 tablespoons sour cream

Directions
1. Mix broth, tomato paste, and all the spices in a bowl.
2. Add chicken and mix well to coat.
3. Spread the rice in a casserole dish and add chicken along with its marinade.
4. Top the casserole with the rest of the Ingredients:.
5. Press "Power Button" of Air Fry Oven and turn the dial to select the "Bake" mode.
6. Press the Time button and again turn the dial to set the cooking time to 40 minutes.
7. Now push the Temp button and rotate the dial to set the temperature at 350 F.
8. Once preheated, place the baking pan inside and close its lid.
9. Serve warm.

Nutrition: Calories 440 Fat 7.9g Cholesterol 5mg Sodium 581mg Total Carbs 21.8g Fiber 2.6g Sugar 7.1g Protein 37.2g

208. Parmesan Chicken Meatballs

Preparation time: 5 minutes
Cooking time: 12 minutes
Servings: 4

Ingredients:
- 1-lb. ground chicken
- 1 large egg, beaten
- ½ cup Parmesan cheese, grated
- ½ cup pork rinds, ground
- 1 teaspoon garlic powder
- 1 teaspoon paprika
- 1 teaspoon kosher salt
- ½ teaspoon pepper
- Crust:
- ½ cup pork rinds, ground

Directions
1. Toss all the meatball Ingredients: in a bowl and mix well.
2. Make small meatballs out this mixture and roll them in the pork rinds.
3. Place the coated meatballs in the air fryer basket.
4. Press "Power Button" of Air Fry Oven and turn the dial to select the "Bake" mode.
5. Press the Time button and again turn the dial to set the cooking time to 12 minutes.
6. Now push the Temp button and rotate the dial to set the temperature at 400 F.
7. Once preheated, place the air fryer basket inside and close its lid.
8. Serve warm.

Nutrition: Calories 529 Fat 17g Saturated Fat 3g Cholesterol 65mg Sodium 391mg Total Carbs 55g Fiber 6g Sugar 8g Protein 41g

209. Chicken Legs With Dilled Brussels Sprouts

Preparation time: 5 minutes
Cooking time: 10 minutes
Servings: 2

Ingredients:
- 2 chicken legs
- 1/2 teaspoon paprika
- 1/2 teaspoon kosher salt
- 1/2 teaspoon black pepper
- 1/2 pound Brussels sprouts
- 1 teaspoon dill, fresh or dried

Directions
1. Start by preheating your Air Fryer to 370 F.
2. Now, season your chicken with paprika, salt, and pepper. Transfer the chicken legs to the cooking basket. Cook for 10 minutes.
3. Flip the chicken legs and cook an additional 10 minutes. Reserve.
4. Add the Brussels sprouts to the cooking basket; sprinkle with dill. Cook at 380 F for 15 minutes, shaking the basket halfway through.
5. Serve with the reserved chicken legs.

Nutrition: Calories 365 Fat 21g Protein 36g Sugars 2g Fiber 3g Carbs 3g

210. Chicken Breasts With Chimichurri

Preparation time: 5 minutes
Cooking time: 35 minutes
Servings: 1

Ingredients:
- 1 chicken breast, bone-in, skin-on
- Chimichurri
- ½ bunch fresh cilantro
- 1/4 bunch fresh parsley
- ½ shallot, peeled, cut in quarters
- ½ tablespoon paprika ground
- ½ tablespoon chili powder
- ½ tablespoon fennel ground
- ½ teaspoon black pepper, ground
- ½ teaspoon onion powder
- 1 teaspoon salt
- ½ teaspoon garlic powder
- ½ teaspoon cumin ground
- ½ tablespoon canola oil
- 2 tablespoons olive oil
- 4 garlic cloves, peeled
- Zest and juice of 1 lemon
- 1 teaspoon kosher salt

Directions
1. Preheat the Air fryer to 300 degree Fahrenheit and grease an Air fryer basket.
2. Combine all the spices in a suitable bowl and season the chicken with it.
3. Sprinkle with canola oil and arrange the chicken in the Air fryer basket.
4. Cook for about 35 minutes and dish out in a platter.
5. Put all the ingredients in the blender and blend until smooth.
6. Serve the chicken with chimichurri sauce.

Nutrition: Calories 140 Fat 7.9g Protein 7.2g Sugars 7.1g Sodium 581mg Carbs 1.8g

211. Turkey And Almonds

Preparation time: 5 minutes
Cooking time: 10 minutes
Servings: 2

Ingredients:
- 1 big turkey breast, skinless; boneless and halved
- 2 shallots; chopped
- 1/3 cup almonds; chopped
- 1 tbsp. sweet paprika
- 2 tbsp. olive oil
- Salt and black pepper to taste.

Directions
1. In a pan that fits the air fryer, combine the turkey with all the other ingredients, toss.
2. Put the pan in the machine and cook at 370 F for 25 minutes
3. Divide everything between plates and serve.

Nutrition: Calories 274 Fat 12g Fiber 3g Protein 14g Carbs 5g

212. Teriyaki Wings

Preparation Time: 5 minutes
Cooking Time: 20 minutes
Servings: 4
Ingredients:
- Chicken wings – 2 pounds
- Teriyaki sauce – ½ cup
- Minced garlic – 2 tsp.
- Ground ginger - ¼ tsp.
- Baking powder – 2 tsp.

Directions:
1. Except for the baking powder, place all ingredients in a bowl and marinate for 1 hour in the refrigerator. Place wings into the air fryer basket and sprinkle with baking powder.
2. Gently rub into wings. Cook at 400F for 25 minutes. Shake the basket two- or three-times during cooking. Serve.

Nutrition: Calories 446 Carbs 3.1g Fat 29.8g Protein 41.8g

213. Chicken Wings With Prawn Paste

Preparation time: 5 minutes
Cooking time: 8 minutes
Servings: 6
Ingredients:
- Corn flour, as required
- 2 pounds mid-joint chicken wings
- 2 tablespoons prawn paste
- 4 tablespoons olive oil
- 1½ teaspoons sugar
- 2 teaspoons sesame oil
- 1 teaspoon Shaoxing wine
- 2 teaspoons fresh ginger juice

Directions
1. Preheat the Air fryer to 360 degree Fahrenheit and grease an Air fryer basket.
2. Mix all the ingredients in a bowl except wings and corn flour.
3. Rub the chicken wings generously with marinade and refrigerate overnight.
4. Coat the chicken wings evenly with corn flour and keep aside.
5. Set the Air fryer to 390 degree Fahrenheit and arrange the chicken wings in the Air fryer basket.
6. Cook for about 8 minutes and dish out to serve hot.

Nutrition: Calories 416 Fat 31.5g Sugar 1.6g Protein 24.4g Carbs 11.2g Sodium 661mg

214. Korean Chicken Wings

Preparation time: 5 minutes
Cooking time: 10 minutes
Servings: 8
Ingredients:
- Wings:
- 1 tsp. pepper
- 1 tsp. salt
- 2 pounds chicken wings
- Sauce:
- 2 packets Splenda
- 1 tbsp. minced garlic
- 1 tbsp. minced ginger
- 1 tbsp. sesame oil
- 1 tsp. agave nectar
- 1 tbsp. mayo
- 2 tbsp. gochujang
- Finishing:
- ¼ cup chopped green onions
- 2 tsp. sesame seeds

Directions
1. Preparing the ingredients.
2. Ensure air fryer is preheated to 400 F.
3. Line a small pan with foil and place a rack onto the pan, then place into air fryer.
4. Season wings with pepper and salt and place onto the rack.
5. Air Frying.
6. Set temperature to 160 F, and set time to 20 minutes and air fry 20 minutes, turning at 10 minutes. As chicken air fries, mix together all the sauce Ingredients.
7. Once a thermometer says that the chicken has reached 160 F, take out wings and place into a bowl. Pour half of the sauce mixture over wings, tossing well to coat. Put coated wings back into air fryer for 5 minutes or till they reach 165 F. Remove and sprinkle with green onions and sesame seeds. Dip into extra sauce.

Nutrition: Calories 356 Fat 26g Protein 23g Sugar 2g

215. Crispy Air Fryer Butter Chicken

Preparation Time: 5 minutes
Cooking Time: 15 minutes
Servings: 4
Ingredients:
- 2 (8-ounce) boneless, skinless chicken breasts
- 1 sleeve Ritz crackers
- 4 tablespoons (½ stick) cold unsalted butter, cut into 1-tablespoon slices

Directions:
1. Preparing the Ingredients. Spray the air fryer basket with olive oil, or spray an air fryer–size baking sheet with olive oil or cooking spray.
2. Dip the chicken breasts in water. Put the crackers in a resealable plastic bag. Using a mallet or your hands, crush the crackers. Place the chicken breasts inside the bag one at a time and coat them with the cracker crumbs.
3. Place the chicken in the greased air fryer basket, or on the greased baking sheet set into the air fryer basket. Put 1 to 2 dabs of butter onto each piece of chicken.
4. Air Frying. Set the temperature of your AF to 370°F. Set the timer and bake for 7 minutes.
5. Using tongs, flip the chicken. Spray the chicken generously with olive oil to avoid uncooked breading. Reset the timer and bake for 7 minutes more.
6. Check that the chicken has reached an internal temperature of 165°F. Add Cooking Time if needed. Using tongs, remove the chicken from the air fryer and serve.

Nutrition: Calories: 750 Fat: 40g Carbs: 38g Protein: 57g

216. Harissa-Rubbed Cornish Game Hens

Preparation time: 10 minutes plus 30 minutes to marinate
Cooking time: 20 minutes
Servings: 4
Ingredients:
- For the Harissa
- ½ cup olive oil
- 6 cloves garlic, minced
- 2 tablespoons smoked paprika

- 1 tablespoon ground coriander
- 1 tablespoon ground cumin
- 1 teaspoon ground caraway
- 1 teaspoon kosher salt
- ½ to 1 teaspoon cayenne pepper
- For the Hens
- ½ cup yogurt
- Cornish game hens, any giblets removed, split in half lengthwise

Directions
1. Preparing the Ingredients
2. For the harissa: In a medium microwave-safe bowl, combine the oil, garlic, paprika, coriander, cumin, caraway, salt, and cayenne. Microwave on high for 1 minute, stirring halfway through the cooking time. (You can also heat this on the stovetop until the oil is hot and bubbling. Or, if you must use your air fryer for everything, cook it in the air fryer at 350 F for 5 to 6 minutes, or until the paste is heated through.)
3. For the hens: In a small bowl, combine 1 to 2 tablespoons harissa and the yogurt. Whisk until well combined. Place the hen halves in a resealable plastic bag and pour the marinade over. Seal the bag and massage until all of the pieces are thoroughly coated. Marinate at room temperature for 30 minutes or in the refrigerator for up to 24 hours.
4. Air Frying
5. Arrange the hen halves in a single layer in the air fryer basket. (If you have a smaller air fryer, you may have to cook this in two batches.) Set the Air fryer to 400 F for 20 minutes. Use a meat thermometer to ensure the game hens have reached an internal temperature.

Nutrition: Calories 590 Fat 38g Carbs 3.2g Protein 32.5g

217. Easy Lemon Chicken Thighs

Preparation time: 5 minutes
Cooking time: 10 minutes
Servings: 4

Ingredients:
- 1 teaspoon salt
- 1 teaspoon freshly ground black pepper
- 2 tablespoons olive oil
- 2 tablespoons Italian seasoning
- 2 tablespoons freshly squeezed lemon juice
- 1 lemon, sliced

Directions
1. Preparing the Ingredients.
2. Place the chicken thighs in a medium mixing bowl and season them with the salt and pepper. Add the olive oil, Italian seasoning, and lemon juice and toss until the chicken thighs are thoroughly coated with oil. Add the sliced lemons. Place the chicken thighs into the Air fryer basket in a single layer.
3. Air Frying.
4. Set the temperature of your Air fryer to 350 F. Set the timer and cook for 10 minutes. Using tongs, flip the chicken. Reset the timer and cook for 10 minutes more. Check that the chicken has reached an internal temperature of 165 F. Add cooking time if needed. Once the chicken is fully cooked, plate, serve, and enjoy.

Nutrition: Calories 325 Fat 26g Saturated Fat 6g Carbs 1g Protein 20g Sugar 1g Iron 1mg Sodium 670mg

218. Air Fryer Southern Fried Chicken

Preparation time: 15 minutes plus 1 hour to marinate
Cooking time: 26 minutes
Servings: 4

Ingredients:
- ½ cup buttermilk
- 2 teaspoons salt, plus 1 tablespoon
- 1 teaspoon freshly ground black pepper
- 1 pound chicken thighs and drumsticks
- 1 cup all-purpose flour
- 2 teaspoons onion powder
- 2 teaspoons garlic powder
- ½ teaspoon sweet paprika

Directions
1. Preparing the Ingredients
2. In a large mixing bowl, whisk together the buttermilk, 2 teaspoons of salt, and pepper. Add the chicken pieces to the bowl, and let the chicken marinate for at least an hour, covered, in the refrigerator. About 5 minutes before the chicken is done marinating, prepare the dredging mixture. In a large mixing bowl, combine the flour, 1 tablespoon of salt, onion powder, garlic powder, and paprika. Spray the Air fryer basket with olive oil. Remove the chicken from the buttermilk mixture and dredge it in the flour mixture. Shake off any excess flour. Place the chicken pieces into the greased Air fryer basket in a single layer, leaving space between each piece. Spray the chicken generously with olive oil.
3. Air Frying
4. Set the temperature of your Air fryer to 390 F. Set the timer and cook for 13 minutes. Using tongs, flip the chicken. Spray generously with olive oil. Reset the timer and fry for 13 minutes more. Check that the chicken has reached an internal temperature of 165 F. Add cooking time if needed. Once the chicken is fully cooked, plate, serve, and enjoy!

Nutrition: Calories 377 Fat 18g Saturated Fat 5g Carbs 28g Fiber 1g Protein 25g Sugar 2g Iron 3mg Sodium 1182mg

219. Air Fryer Grilled Chicken Breasts

Preparation time: 5 minutes
Cooking time: 14 minutes
Servings: 4

Ingredients:
- ½ teaspoon garlic powder
- 1 teaspoon salt
- ½ teaspoon freshly ground black pepper
- 1 teaspoon dried parsley
- 2 tablespoons olive oil, divided
- 3 boneless, skinless chicken breasts

Directions
1. Preparing the Ingredients.
2. In a small mixing bowl, mix together the garlic powder, salt, pepper, and parsley. Using 1 tablespoon of olive oil and half of the seasoning mix, rub each chicken breast with oil and seasonings. Place the chicken breast in the air fryer basket.
3. Air Frying.
4. Set the temperature of your Air fryer to 370 F. Set the timer and grill for 7 minutes.
5. Using tongs, flip the chicken and brush the remaining olive oil and spices onto the chicken. Reset the timer and grill for 7 minutes more. Check that the chicken has reached an internal temperature of 165 F. Add cooking time if needed.
6. Once the chicken is fully cooked, transfer it to a platter and serve.

Nutrition: Calories 182 Fat 9g Saturated Fat 1g Protein 26g Iron 1mg Sodium 657mg

220. Basil-Garlic Breaded Chicken Bake

Preparation time: 5 minutes
Cooking time: 25 minutes
Servings: 2
Ingredients:
- 2 boneless skinless chicken breast halves
- 1 tablespoon butter, melted
- 1 large tomato, seeded and chopped
- 2 garlic cloves, minced
- 1 1/2 tablespoons minced fresh basil
- 1/2 tablespoon olive oil
- 1/2 teaspoon salt
- 1/4 cup all-purpose flour
- 1/4 cup egg substitute
- 1/4 cup grated Parmesan cheese
- 1/4 cup dry bread crumbs
- 1/4 teaspoon pepper

Directions
1. Preparing the Ingredients.
2. In shallow bowl, whisk well egg substitute and place flour in a separate bowl. Dip chicken in flour, then egg, and then flour. In small bowl whisk well butter, bread crumbs and cheese. Sprinkle over chicken. Lightly grease baking pan of air fryer with cooking spray. Place breaded chicken on bottom of pan. Cover with foil.
3. Air Frying.
4. For 20 minutes, cook on 390 F.
5. Meanwhile, in a bowl whisk well remaining ingredient. Remove foil from pan and then pour over chicken the remaining Ingredients. Cook for 8 minutes. Serve and enjoy.

Nutrition: Calories 311 Fat 11g Carbs 22g Protein 31g

221. Air Fryer Cornish Hen

Preparation time: 5 minutes
Cooking time: 30 minutes
Servings: 2
Ingredients:
- 2 tablespoons Montreal chicken seasoning
- 1 (1½ to 2 pounds) Cornish hen

Directions
1. Preparing the Ingredients.
2. Preheat the Air fryer to 390 F. Rub the seasoning over the chicken, coating it thoroughly.
3. Air Frying.
4. Place the chicken in the air fryer basket. Set the timer and roast for 15 minutes.
5. Flip the chicken and cook for another 15 minutes. Check that the chicken has reached an internal temperature of 165 F. Add cooking time if needed.

Nutrition: Calories 520 Fat 36g Saturated Fat 10g Protein 45g Iron 2mg Sodium 758mg

222. Cheese and Garlic Stuffed Chicken Breasts

Preparation time: 5 minutes
Cooking time: 30 minutes
Servings: 2
Ingredients:
- 1/2 cup Cottage cheese 2 eggs, beaten
- 2 medium-sized chicken breasts, halved
- 2 tablespoons fresh coriander, chopped 1tsp. fine sea salt
- Seasoned breadcrumbs
- 1/3 tsp. freshly ground black pepper, to savor 3 cloves garlic, finely minced

Directions
1. Firstly, flatten out the chicken breast using a meat tenderizer.
2. In a medium-sized mixing dish, combine the Cottage cheese with the garlic, coriander, salt, and black pepper.
3. Spread 1/3 of the mixture over the first chicken breast. Repeat with the remaining ingredients. Roll the chicken around the filling; make sure to secure with toothpicks.
4. Now, whisk the egg in a shallow bowl. In another shallow bowl, combine the salt, ground black pepper, and seasoned breadcrumbs.
5. Coat the chicken breasts with the whisked egg; now, roll them in the breadcrumbs.
6. Cook in the air fryer cooking basket at 365 F for 22 minutes. Serve immediately.

Nutrition: Calories 424 Fat 24.5g Carbs 7.5g Protein 43.4g Sugar 5.3g

223. Turkey Wontons with Garlic-parmesan Sauce

Preparation time: 5 minutes
Cooking time: 15 minutes
Servings: 8
Ingredients:
- 8 ounces cooked turkey breasts, shredded 16 wonton wrappers
- 1½ tablespoons margarine, melted
- 1/3 cup cream cheese, room temperature 8 ounces Asiago cheese, shredded
- 3 tablespoons Parmesan cheese, grated
- 1 tsp. garlic powder
- Fine sea salt and freshly ground black pepper, to taste

Directions
1. In a small-sized bowl, mix the margarine, Parmesan, garlic powder, salt, and black pepper; give it a good stir.
2. Lightly grease a mini muffin pan; lay 1 wonton wrapper in each mini muffin cup. Fill each cup with the cream cheese and turkey mixture.
3. Air fry for 8 minutes at 335 F. Immediately top with Asiago cheese and serve warm.

Nutrition: Calories 362 Fat 13.5g Carbs 40.4g Protein 18.5g Sugar 1.2g

224. Breaded Nugget In Doritos

Preparation Time: 10 minutes
Cooking Time: 15 minutes
Servings: 4
Ingredients:
- ½ lb. boneless, skinless chicken breast
- ¼ lb. Doritos snack
- 1 cup of wheat flour
- 1 egg
- Salt, garlic and black pepper to taste.

Directions:
1. Cut the chicken breast in the width direction, 1 to 1.5 cm thick, so that it is already shaped like pips.
2. Season with salt, garlic, black pepper to taste and some other seasonings if desired.
3. You can also season with those seasonings or powdered onion soup.
4. Put the Doritos snack in a food processor or blender and beat until everything is crumbled, but don't beat too much, you don't want flour.
5. Now bread, passing the pieces of chicken breast first in the wheat flour, then in the beaten eggs and finally in the Doritos, without leaving the excess flour, eggs or Doritos.
6. Place the seeds in the Air Fryer basket and program for 15 minutes at 400°F, and half the time they brown evenly.

Nutrition: Calories: 42 Carbs: 1.65g Fat: 1.44g Protein: 5.29g Sugar: 0.1g Cholesterol: 20mg

225. Flavorful Chicken Drumsticks

Preparation Time: 10 minutes
Cooking time: 30 minutes
Servings: 4
Ingredients:
- 8 chicken drumsticks
- ¼ tsp cayenne pepper
- 1 tbsp onion powder
- 1 tbsp garlic powder
- 1 ½ tbsp honey
- 1 ½ tbsp fresh lemon juice
- 1 tbsp Worcestershire sauce
- ¼ cup soy sauce, low-sodium
- 1 tbsp sesame oil
- 2 tbsp olive oil
- ½ tsp kosher salt

Directions
1. Add all ingredients except chicken in a large mixing bowl and mix well.
2. Add chicken drumsticks to the bowl and mix until well coated.
3. Place chicken drumsticks on the Kalorix Maxx air fryer rack air fry at 400 F for 15 minutes.
4. Turn chicken drumsticks to another side and cook for 15 minutes more.
5. Serve and enjoy.

Nutrition: Calories 296 Fat 15.8g Carbs 11.6g Sugar 8.7g Protein 26.9g Cholesterol 81mg

226. Gluten-Free Air Fried Chicken

Preparation Time: 10 minutes
Cooking time: 25 minutes
Servings: 6
Ingredients:
- 6 chicken drumsticks, rinse and pat dry with a paper towel
- 1 tsp ginger
- 1 tsp onion powder
- 1 tsp garlic powder
- 1 tsp paprika
- 1 cup buttermilk
- ¼ cup brown sugar
- ½ cup breadcrumbs
- 1 cup all-purpose flour
- ½ tsp pepper
- 1 tsp salt

Directions
1. Preheat the air fryer using bake mode at 390 F.
2. Add breadcrumbs, spices, and flour into the zip-lock bag and mix well.
3. In a bowl, mix together chicken and buttermilk and let sit for 2 minutes.
4. Now put a single piece of chicken into the zip-lock bag and shake it until chicken is evenly coated with breadcrumb mixture. Do this same with remaining chicken pieces.
5. Spray coated chicken with cooking spray.
6. Place chicken into the bottom tray of air fryer and bake for 25 minutes.
7. Serve and enjoy.

Nutrition: Calories 234 Fat 3.8g Carbs 31.5g Sugar 8.7g Protein 17.6g Cholesterol 42mg

227. Barbecue with Chorizo and Chicken

Preparation Time: 5 minutes
Cooking Time: 35 minutes
Servings: 4
Ingredients:
- 4 chicken thighs
- 2 Tuscan sausages
- 4 small onions

Directions:
1. Preheat the fryer to 400°F for 5 minutes. Season the meat the same way you would if you were going to use the barbecue.
2. Put in the fryer, lower the temperature to 160°C and set for 30 minutes.
3. After 20 minutes, check if any of the meat has reached the point of your preference. If so, take whichever is ready and return to the fryer with the others for another 10 minutes, now at 400°F. If not, return them to Air Fryer for the last 10 minutes at 400°F.

Nutrition: Calories: 135 Fat: 5g Protein: 6g Cholesterol: 300mg

228. Healthy Chicken Popcorn

Preparation Time: 10 minutes
Cooking time: 10 minutes
Servings: 4
Ingredients:
- 1 lb chicken breast, skinless, boneless, and cut into 1-inch pieces
- 1 egg, lightly beaten
- ½ tbsp Tabasco sauce
- 1 cup buttermilk
- 1 tsp baking powder
- 1 cup all-purpose flour
- ½ tsp pepper
- 1 tsp salt

Directions
1. Season chicken pieces with pepper and salt.
2. In a medium bowl, mix together all-purpose flour and baking powder.
3. In another mixing bowl, mix together egg, buttermilk, and Tabasco sauce.
4. Coat chicken with flour mixture then dip chicken into the egg mixture then again coat with flour mixture.
5. Place coated chicken pieces on air fryer tray. Spray coated chicken pieces with cooking spray.
6. Air fry chicken popcorn at 400 F for minutes. Turn chicken popcorn to another side and air fry for 5 minutes more.
7. Serve and enjoy.

Nutrition: Calories 285 Fat 4.8g Carbs 27.6g Sugar 3.1g Protein 30.7g Cholesterol 116mg

229. Chicken in Beer

Preparation Time: 5 minutes
Cooking Time: 10 minutes
Servings: 4
Ingredients:
- 2 ¼ lbs chicken thigh and thigh
- ½ can of beer
- 4 cloves of garlic
- 1 large onion
- Pepper and salt to taste

Directions:
1. Wash the chicken pieces and, if desired, remove the skin to be healthier.
2. Place on an ovenproof plate.
3. In the blender, beat the other ingredients: beer, onion, garlic, and add salt and pepper, all together.
4. Cover the chicken with this mixture; it has to stay like swimming in the beer.
5. Take to the preheated air fryer at 390F for 45 minutes.
6. It will roast when it has a brown cone on top and the beer has dried a bit.

Nutrition: Calories: 674 Carbs: 5.47g Fat: 41.94g Protein: 61.94g Sugar: 1.62g Cholesterol: 206mg

230. Herbed Turkey Breast

Preparation Time: 10 minutes
Cooking time: 50 minutes
Servings: 6
Ingredients:
- 3 lbs turkey breast
- 3 garlic cloves, minced
- 1 tbsp fresh sage leaves, chopped
- 1 tbsp rosemary leaves, chopped
- 1 tbsp fresh thyme
- 3 tbsp butter
- 1 tsp lemon zest, grated
- ½ tsp pepper
- 1 tsp kosher salt

Directions
1. In a bowl, mix together butter, garlic, sage, rosemary, thyme, lemon zest, pepper, and salt.
2. Rub the butter mixture all over the turkey breast.
3. Place turkey breast into the bottom rack of air fryer and cook at 350 F for 20 minutes.
4. Turn turkey breast to the other side and cook for 30 minutes more or until the internal temperature of turkey breast reaches 160 F.
5. Slice and serve.

Nutrition: Calories 294 Fat 9.7g Carbs 11.1g Sugar 8g Protein 39g Cholesterol 113mg

231. Marinara Sauce Cheese Chicken

Preparation Time: 10 minutes
Cooking time: 15 minutes
Servings: 2
Ingredients:
- 2 chicken breasts, sliced
- 1 egg, beaten
- ½ cup breadcrumbs
- A pinch of salt and black pepper
- 2 tbsp tomato sauce
- 2 tbsp Romano cheese, grated
- 2 slices mozzarella cheese

Directions
1. Dip the breasts into the egg, then into the crumbs, and arrange in the basket. Fit in the baking tray and cook for 5 minutes at 400 F on Air Fry function. Turn and top with tomato sauce, Romano and mozzarella cheeses. Cook for 5 more minutes until the cheese is melted. Serve.

Nutrition: Calories 529 Fat 17g Saturated Fat 3g Cholesterol 65mg Sodium 391mg Total Carbs 55g Fiber 6g Sugar 8g Protein 41g

232. Herby Chicken with Lime

Preparation Time: 25 minutes
Cooking time: 40 minutes
Servings: 4
Ingredients:
- 1 (2 ½ lb) whole chicken
- Salt and black pepper to taste
- 1 tbsp chili powder
- 1 tbsp garlic powder
- 4 tbsp oregano
- 2 tbsp cilantro powder
- 2 tbsp cumin powder
- 2 tbsp olive oil
- 4 tbsp paprika
- 1 lime, juiced

Directions
1. In a bowl, pour oregano, garlic powder, chili powder, ground cilantro, paprika, cumin, pepper, salt, and olive oil. Mix well

and rub the mixture onto the chicken. Refrigerate for 20 minutes.
2. Preheat Air Fryer Oven on Air Fry function to 350 F. Remove the chicken from the refrigerator; place in the greased basket and fit in the baking tray; cook for 20 minutes. Use a skewer to poke the chicken to ensure that it is clear of juices. If not, cook further for 5 to 10 minutes; let it rest for 10 minutes. Drizzle lime juice all over and serve with green salad.

Nutrition: Calories 311 Fat 11g Carbs 22g Protein 31g

233. Spicy Chicken Strips with Aioli Sauce

Preparation Time: 5 minutes
Cooking time: 15 minutes
Servings: 4
Ingredients:
- 3 chicken breasts, cut into strips
- 2 tbsp olive oil
- 1 cup breadcrumbs
- Salt and black pepper to taste
- ½ tbsp garlic powder
- ½ cup mayonnaise
- 1 tbsp lemon juice
- ½ tbsp ground chili

Directions
1. Mix breadcrumbs, salt, pepper, and garlic and spread onto a plate. Brush the chicken with olive oil then roll up in the breadcrumb mixture. Arrange on the oiled Air Fryer basket and fit in the baking tray; cook for 10-12 minutes at 360 F on Air Fry function, turning once halfway through.
2. To prepare the aioli: mix well mayonnaise with lemon juice and ground chili. Serve the chicken with hot aioli.

Nutrition: Calories 311 Fat 11g Carbs 22g Protein 31g

234. Crispy Chicken Thighs

Preparation Time: 10 minutes
Cooking time: 35 minutes
Servings: 6
Ingredients:
- 6 chicken thighs
- 1 tbsp olive oil
- For rub:
- 1/2 tsp basil
- 1/2 tsp oregano
- 1/2 tsp pepper
- 1 tsp garlic powder
- 1 tsp onion powder
- 1/2 tsp salt

Directions
1. Insert wire rack in rack position 6. Select bake, set temperature 390 F, timer for 35 minutes. Press start to preheat the oven.
2. Brush chicken thighs with olive oil. In a small bowl, mix together rub ingredients and rub all over the chicken.
3. Arrange chicken on roasting pan and bake for 30-35 minutes.
4. Serve and enjoy.

Nutrition: Calories 49 Fat 3.4g Carbs 0.9g Protein 4.1g Cholesterol 12mg

235. Classic Greek Chicken

Preparation Time: 10 minutes
Cooking time: 30 minutes
Servings: 4
Ingredients:
- 1 lb chicken breasts, skinless and boneless
- For marinade:
- 1/2 tsp dill
- 1 tsp onion powder
- 1/4 tsp basil
- 1/4 tsp oregano
- 3 garlic cloves, minced
- 1 tbsp lemon juice
- 3 tbsp olive oil
- 1/4 tsp pepper
- 1/2 tsp salt

Directions
1. Add all marinade ingredients into the mixing bowl and mix well.
2. Add chicken into the marinade and coat well. Cover bowl and place in the refrigerator overnight.
3. Insert wire rack in rack position 6. Select bake, set temperature 390 F, timer for 30 minutes. Press start to preheat the oven.
4. Arrange marinated chicken on roasting pan and bake for 25-30 minutes.
5. Serve and enjoy.

Nutrition: Calories 313 Fat 19g Sugar 0.3g Protein 33.1g Cholesterol 101mg

236. Perfect Juicy Chicken Breast

Preparation Time: 10 minutes
Cooking time: 15 minutes
Servings: 8
Ingredients:
- 4 chicken breasts, skinless and boneless
- 1 tbsp olive oil
- For rub:
- 1 tsp garlic powder
- 1 tsp onion powder
- 4 tsp brown sugar
- 4 tsp paprika
- 1 tsp black pepper
- 1 tsp salt

Directions
1. Insert wire rack in rack position 6. Select bake, set temperature 390 F, timer for 30 minutes. Press start to preheat the oven.
2. Brush chicken breasts with olive oil. In a small bowl, mix together rub ingredients and rub all over chicken breasts.
3. Arrange chicken breasts on roasting pan and bake for 12-15 minutes or until internal temperature reaches 165 F.
4. Serve and enjoy.

Nutrition: Calories 165 Fat 7.3g Carbs 2.7g Sugar 1.8g Protein 21.4g Cholesterol 65mg

237. Faire-Worthy Turkey Legs

Preparation Time: 5 minutes
Cooking Time: 10 minutes
Servings: 4
Ingredients:
- 1 turkey leg
- 1 teaspoon olive oil
- 1 teaspoon poultry seasoning
- 1 teaspoon garlic powder
- salt and black pepper to taste

Directions:
1. Warm up the air fryer to 350°F for about 4 minutes.
2. Coat the leg with the olive oil. Just use your hands and rub it in.
3. In a small bowl, mix the poultry seasoning, garlic powder, salt and pepper. Rub it on the turkey leg.
4. Coat the inside of the air fryer basket with nonstick spray and place the turkey leg in.
5. Cook for 27 minutes, turning at 14 minutes. Be sure the leg is done by inserting a meat thermometer in the fleshy part of the leg and it should read 165 degrees F.

Nutrition: Calories: 325 Carbs: 8.3g Fat: 10g Protein: 18g

238. Broccoli Bacon Ranch Chicken

Preparation Time: 10 minutes
Cooking time: 30 minutes
Servings: 4
Ingredients:
- 4 chicken breasts, skinless and boneless
- 1/3 cup mozzarella cheese, shredded
- 1 cup cheddar cheese, shredded
- 1/2 cup ranch dressing
- 5 bacon slices, cooked and chopped
- 2 cups broccoli florets, blanched and chopped

Directions
1. Insert wire rack in rack position 6. Select bake, set temperature 375 F, timer for 30 minutes. Press start to preheat the oven.
2. Add chicken into the 13*9-inch casserole dish. Top with bacon and broccoli.
3. Pour ranch dressing over chicken and top with shredded mozzarella cheese and cheddar cheese.
4. Bake chicken for 30 minutes.
5. Serve and enjoy.

Nutrition: Calories 551 Fat 30.8g Carbs 5.4g Sugar 1.7g Protein 60.4g Cholesterol 187mg

239. Jerk Chicken Legs

Preparation Time: 10 minutes
Cooking time: 50 minutes
Servings: 10
Ingredients:
- 10 chicken legs
- 1/2 tsp ground nutmeg
- 1/2 tsp ground cinnamon
- 1 tsp ground allspice
- 1 tsp black pepper
- 1 tbsp fresh thyme
- 1 1/2 tbsp brown sugar
- 1/4 cup soy sauce
- 1/3 cup fresh lime juice
- 1 tbsp ginger, sliced
- 2 habanera peppers, remove the stem
- 4 garlic cloves, peeled and smashed
- 6 green onions, chopped

Directions
1. Add chicken into the large zip-lock bag.
2. Add remaining ingredients into the food processor and process until coarse.
3. Pour mixture over chicken. Seal bag and shake well to coat the chicken and place it in the refrigerator overnight.
4. Insert wire rack in rack position 6. Select bake, set temperature 375 F, timer for 50 minutes. Press start to preheat the oven.
5. Line baking sheet with foil. Arrange marinated chicken legs on a baking sheet and bake for 45-50 minutes.
6. Serve and enjoy.

Nutrition: Calories 232 Fat 14.2g Carbs 4.8g Sugar 2.2g Protein 21.9g Cholesterol 95mg

240. Western Chicken Wings

Preparation Time: 10 minutes
Cooking Time: 15 minutes
Servings: 4
Ingredients:
- 2 lbs. chicken wings
- 1 tsp Herb de Provence
- 1 tsp paprika
- 1/2 cup parmesan cheese, grated
- Salt and Pepper

Directions:
1. Add cheese, paprika, herb de Provence, pepper, and salt into the large mixing bowl. Place the chicken wings into the bowl and toss well to coat.
2. Preheat the air fryer to 350 F.
3. Place the chicken wings into the air fryer basket. Spray top of chicken wings with cooking spray.
4. Cook chicken wings for 15 minutes. Turn chicken wings halfway through.
5. Serve and enjoy.

Nutrition: Calories 473 Fat 19.6 g Carbs 0.8 g Sugar 0.1 g Protein 69.7 g Cholesterol 211 mg

241. Protein Packed Baked Chicken Breasts

Preparation Time: 10 minutes
Cooking time: 25 minutes
Servings: 6
Ingredients:
- 6 chicken breasts, skinless and boneless
- 1/4 tsp paprika
- 1/2 tsp garlic salt
- 1 tsp Italian seasoning
- 2 tbsp olive oil
- 1/4 tsp pepper

Directions
1. Insert wire rack in rack position 6. Select bake, set temperature 390 F, timer for 25 minutes. Press start to preheat the oven.
2. Brush chicken with oil. Mix together Italian seasoning, garlic salt, paprika, and pepper and rub all over the chicken.
3. Arrange chicken breasts on roasting pan and bake for 25 minutes or until internal temperature reaches 165 F.

4. Slice and serve.

Nutrition: Calories 321 Fat 15.7g Carbs 0.4g Sugar 0.1g Protein 42.3g Cholesterol 130mg

242. Flavors Balsamic Chicken

Preparation Time: 10 minutes
Cooking time: 25 minutes
Servings: 4
Ingredients:
- 4 chicken breasts, skinless and boneless
- 2 tsp dried oregano
- 2 garlic cloves, minced
- 1/2 cup balsamic vinegar
- 2 tbsp soy sauce
- 1/4 cup olive oil
- Pepper
- Salt

Directions
1. Insert wire rack in rack position 6. Select bake, set temperature 390 F, timer for 25 minutes. Press start to preheat the oven.
2. In a bowl, mix together soy sauce, oil, black pepper, oregano, garlic, and vinegar.
3. Place chicken in a baking dish and pour soy sauce mixture over chicken. Let it sit for 10 minutes.
4. Bake chicken for 25 minutes.
5. Serve and enjoy.

Nutrition: Calories 401 Fat 23.5g Carbs 1.9g Sugar 0.3g Protein 42.9g Cholesterol 130mg

243. Simple and Delicious Chicken Thighs

Preparation Time: 10 minutes
Cooking time: 35 minutes
Servings: 6
Ingredients:
- 6 chicken thighs
- 2 tsp poultry seasoning
- 2 tbsp olive oil
- Pepper
- Salt

Directions
1. Insert wire rack in rack position 6. Select bake, set temperature 390 F, timer for 40 minutes. Press start to preheat the oven.
2. Brush chicken with oil and rub with poultry seasoning, pepper, and salt.
3. Arrange chicken on roasting pan and bake for 35-40 minutes or until internal temperature reaches 165 F.
4. Serve and enjoy.

Nutrition: Calories 319 Fat 15.5g Carbs 0.3g Protein 42.3g Cholesterol 130mg

244. Perfect Baked Chicken Breasts

Preparation Time: 10 minutes
Cooking time: 30 minutes
Servings: 4
Ingredients:
- 4 chicken breasts, bone-in and skin-on
- 1 tsp olive oil
- 1/4 tsp black pepper
- 1/2 tsp kosher salt

Directions
1. Insert wire rack in rack position 6. Select bake, set temperature 375 F, timer for 30 minutes. Press start to preheat the oven.
2. Brush chicken with olive oil and season with pepper and salt.
3. Place chicken on roasting pan and bake for 30 minutes.
4. Serve and enjoy.

Nutrition: Calories 288 Fat 12g Carbs 0.1g Protein 42.3g Cholesterol 130mg

245. BBQ Chicken Wings

Preparation Time: 10 minutes
Cooking time: 55 minutes
Servings: 8
Ingredients:
- 32 chicken wings
- 1 1/2 cups BBQ sauce
- 1/4 cup olive oil
- Pepper
- Salt

Directions
1. Line baking sheet with parchment paper and set aside.
2. Insert wire rack in rack position 6. Select bake, set temperature 375 F, timer for 55 minutes. Press start to preheat the oven.
3. In a mixing bowl, toss chicken wings with olive oil, pepper, and salt.
4. Arrange chicken wings on a baking sheet and bake for 50 minutes.
5. Toss chicken wings with BBQ sauce and bake for 5 minutes more.
6. Serve and enjoy.

Nutrition: Calories 173 Fat 8.3g Carbs 17g Sugar 12.2g Protein 7.4g Cholesterol 23mg

246. Crunchy Munchy Chicken Tenders With Peanuts

Preparation Time: 25 minutes
Cooking Time: 20 minutes
Servings: 4
Ingredients:
- 1 ½ pounds chicken tenderloins
- 2 tablespoons peanut oil
- 1/2 cup tortilla chips, crushed
- Sea salt and ground black pepper, to taste
- 1/2 teaspoon garlic powder
- 1 teaspoon red pepper flakes
- 2 tablespoons peanuts, roasted and roughly chopped

Directions:
1. Start by preheating your Air Fryer to 360 degrees F.
2. Brush the chicken tenderloins with peanut oil on all sides.

POULTRY

3. In a mixing bowl, thoroughly combine the crushed chips, salt, black pepper, garlic powder, and red pepper flakes. Dredge the chicken in the breading, shaking off any residual coating.
4. Lay the chicken tenderloins into the cooking basket. Cook for 12 to 13 minutes or until it is no longer pink in the center. Work in batches; an instant-read thermometer should read at least 165 degrees F.
5. Serve garnished with roasted peanuts. Bon appétit!

Nutrition: 343 Calories 16.4g Fat 10.6g Carbs 36.8g Protein 1g Sugar

247. Chinese-Style Sticky Turkey Thighs

Preparation Time: 20 minutes
Cooking Time: 35 minutes
Servings: 6

Ingredients:
- 1 tablespoon sesame oil
- 2 pounds turkey thighs
- 1 teaspoon Chinese Five-spice powder
- 1 teaspoon pink Himalayan salt
- 1/4 teaspoon Sichuan pepper
- 6 tablespoons honey
- 1 tablespoon Chinese rice vinegar
- 2 tablespoons soy sauce
- 1 tablespoon sweet chili sauce
- 1 tablespoon mustard

Directions:
1. Preheat your Air Fryer to 360 degrees F.
2. Brush the sesame oil all over the turkey thighs. Season them with spices.
3. Cook for 23 minutes, turning over once or twice. Make sure to work in batches to ensure even cooking
4. In the meantime, combine the remaining ingredients in a wok (or similar type pan) that is preheated over medium-high heat. Cook and stir until the sauce reduces by about a third.
5. Add the fried turkey thighs to the wok; gently stir to coat with the sauce.
6. Let the turkey rest for 10 minutes before slicing and serving. Enjoy!

Nutrition: 279 Calories 10.1g Fat 19g Carbs 27.7g Protein 17.9g Sugars

248. Buffalo Chicken Tenders

Preparation Time: 60 minutes
Cooking time: 25 minutes
Servings: 5

Ingredients:
- Nonstick cooking spray
- 2/3 cup panko bread crumbs
- ½ tsp cayenne pepper
- ½ tsp paprika
- ½ tsp garlic powder
- ½ tsp salt
- 3 chicken breasts, boneless, skinless and cut in 10 strips
- ½ cup butter, melted
- ½ cup hot sauce

Directions
1. Line a baking sheet with foil and spray with cooking spray.
2. In a shallow dish combine, bread crumbs and seasonings.
3. Dip chicken in crumb mixture to coat all sides. Lay on prepared pan and refrigerate 1 hour.
4. In a small bowl, whisk together butter and hot sauce.
5. Place baking pan in position 2 of the oven. Lightly spray the fryer basket with cooking spray.
6. Dip each piece of chicken in the butter mixture and place in basket. Place the basket on the baking pan.
7. Set oven to air fry on 400 F for 25 minutes. Cook until outside is crispy and golden brown and chicken is no longer pink. Turn chicken over halfway through cooking time. Serve immediately.

Nutrition: Calories 371 Fat 23g Saturated Fat 12g Carbs 10g Fiber 1g Sugar 1g Protein 31g

249. Turkey Turnovers

Preparation Time: 10 minutes
Cooking time: 10 minutes
Servings: 8

Ingredients:
- 2 cups turkey, cooked and chopped
- 1 cup cheddar cheese, grated
- 1 cup broccoli, cooked and chopped
- ½ cup mayonnaise
- ½ tsp salt
- ¼ tsp pepper
- 2 cans refrigerated crescent rolls

Directions
1. Place the baking pan in position 1 of the oven.
2. In a large bowl, combine all ingredients, except rolls, mix well.
3. Separate each can of rolls into 4 squares, press perforations to seal.
4. Spoon turkey mixture on center of each square Fold over diagonally and seal the edges.
5. Set oven to bake on 375 F for 15 minutes.
6. Brush tops of turnovers lightly with additional mayonnaise. After oven has preheated 5 minutes, place turnovers on baking pan and cook 10-12 minutes or until golden brown
7. Serve warm.

Nutrition: Calories 309 Fat 21g Saturated Fat 6g Carbs 15g Fiber 2g Sugar 1g Protein 15g

250. Chicken Parm

Preparation Time: 10 minutes
Cooking time: 35 minutes
Servings: 4

Ingredients:
- Nonstick cooking spray
- ½ cup flour
- 2 eggs
- 2/3 cup panko bread crumbs
- 2/3 cup Italian seasoned bread crumbs
- 1/3 + ¼ cup parmesan cheese, divided
- 2 tbsp. fresh parsley, chopped
- ½ tsp salt
- ¼ tsp pepper
- 4 chicken breast halves, skinless and boneless
- 24 oz. marinara sauce
- 1 cup mozzarella cheese, grated

Directions
1. Place the baking pan in position 2 of the oven. Lightly spray the fryer basket with cooking spray.
2. Place flour in a shallow dish.
3. In a separate shallow dish, beat the eggs.

4. In a third shallow dish, combine both bread crumbs, 1/3 cup parmesan cheese, 2 tablespoons parsley, salt, and pepper.
5. Place chicken between two sheets of plastic wrap and pound to ½-inch thick.
6. Dip chicken first in flour, then eggs, and bread crumb mixture to coat. Place in basket and place the basket on the baking pan.
7. Set oven to air fry on 375 F for 10 minutes. Turn chicken over halfway through cooking time.
8. Remove chicken and baking pan from the oven. Place the rack in position 1. Set oven to bake on 425 F for 30 minutes.
9. Pour 1 ½ cups marinara in the bottom of 8x11-inch baking dish. Place chicken over sauce and add another 2 tablespoons marinara to tops of chicken. Top chicken with mozzarella and parmesan cheese
10. Once oven preheats for 5 minutes, place the dish in the oven and bake 20-25 minutes until bubbly and cheese is golden brown. Serve.

Nutrition: Calories 529 Fat 13g Saturated Fat 5g Sodium 1437mg Carbs 52g Fiber 5g Sugar 9g Protein 51g

251. Teriyaki Duck Legs

Preparation Time: 15 minutes
Cooking time: 2 hours
Servings: 6
Ingredients:
- 3 lbs. duck legs
- ½ cup teriyaki sauce
- 2 tbsp. soy sauce
- 2 tbsp. malt vinegar

Directions
1. Place the rack in position 1 of the oven.
2. Place the duck legs, skin side up, in an 8x11-inch baking dish.
3. In a small bowl, whisk together remaining ingredients and pour around duck legs. Liquid needs to reach the skin level of duck, if not add water until it does.
4. Set the oven to convection bake on 300 F for 60 minutes. After 5 minutes, place the ducks in the oven and cook 90 minutes, or until tender.
5. Remove duck from the oven. Pour off cooking liquid into a small saucepan. Skim off fat and reserve. Bring sauce to a boil and cook until it reduces down, about 10 minutes, stirring occasionally.
6. Place the baking pan in position 2 of the oven. Place the duck legs in the fryer basket and brush with reserved fat and sauce. Place the basket in the oven and set to broil on 400 F for 10 minutes. Turn duck over halfway through and brush with fat and sauce again. Serve.

Nutrition: Calories 608 Fat 20g Saturated Fat 5g Sodium 1063mg Carbs 6g Sugar 5g Protein 101g

252. Almond Flour Coco-Milk Battered Chicken

Preparation Time: 5 minutes
Cooking time: 30 minutes
Servings: 4
Ingredients:
- ¼ cup coconut milk
- ½ cup almond flour
- 1 ½ tablespoons old bay Cajun seasoning
- 1 egg, beaten
- 4 small chicken thighs
- Salt and pepper to taste

Directions
1. Preheat the air fryer oven for 5 minutes.
2. Mix the egg and coconut milk in a bowl.
3. Soak the chicken thighs in the beaten egg mixture.
4. In a mixing bowl, combine the almond flour, Cajun seasoning, salt and pepper.
5. Dredge the chicken thighs in the almond flour mixture.
6. Place in the air fryer basket.
7. Cook for 30 minutes at 350 F.

Nutrition: Calories 590 Fat 38g Carbs 3.2g Protein 32.5g

253. Sweet and Sour Chicken

Preparation Time: 5 minutes
Cooking time: 20 minutes
Servings: 6
Ingredients:
- 3 Chicken Breasts, cubed
- 1/2 Cup Flour
- 1/2 Cup Cornstarch
- 2 Red Peppers, sliced
- 1 Onion, chopped
- 2 Carrots, julienned
- 3/4 Cup Sugar
- 2 Tbsps Cornstarch
- 1/3 Cup Vinegar
- 2/3 Cup Water
- 1/4 cup Soy sauce
- 1 Tbsp Ketchup

Directions
1. Preheat the air fryer oven to 375 F.
2. Combine the flour, cornstarch and chicken in an air tight container and shake to combine
3. Remove chicken from the container and shake off any excess flour.
4. Add chicken to the Air Fryer tray and cook for 20 minutes.
5. In a saucepan, whisk together sugar, water, vinegar, soy sauce and ketchup. Bring to a boil over medium heat, reduce the heat then simmer for 2 minutes
6. After cooking the chicken for 20 minutes, add the vegetables and sauce mixture to the air fryer oven and cook for another 5 minutes
7. Serve over hot rice

Nutrition: Calories 300 Sodium 260mg Carbs 40g Fiber 1g Sugar 24g

254. Zingy and Nutty Chicken Wings

Preparation Time: 5 minutes
Cooking time: 18 minutes
Servings: 4
Ingredients:
- 1 tablespoon fish sauce
- 1 tablespoon fresh lemon juice
- 1 teaspoon sugar
- 12 chicken middle wings cut into half
- 2 fresh lemongrass stalks, chopped finely
- ¼ cup unsalted cashews, crushed

Directions
1. In a bowl, mix together fish sauce, lime juice and sugar.
2. Add wings ad coat with mixture generously. Refrigerate to marinate for about 1-2 hours.
3. Preheat the air fryer oven to 355 F.

4. In the air fryer oven pan, place lemongrass stalks. Cook for about 2-3 minutes. Remove the cashew mixture from Air fryer and transfer into a bowl. Now, set the air fryer oven to 390 F.
5. Place the chicken wings in Air fryer pan. Cook for about 13-15 minutes further.
6. Transfer the wings into serving plates. Sprinkle with cashew mixture and serve.

Nutrition: Calories 233 Fat 20g Saturated Fat 9g Sodium 26mg Carbs 15g Fiber 2g Sugar 11g Protein 2g

255. Honey and Wine Chicken Breasts

Preparation Time: 5 minutes
Cooking time: 15 minutes
Servings: 4
Ingredients:
- 2 chicken breasts, rinsed and halved
- 1 tablespoon melted butter
- 1/2 teaspoon freshly ground pepper, or to taste
- 3/4 teaspoon sea salt, or to taste
- 1 teaspoon paprika
- 1 teaspoon dried rosemary
- 2 tablespoons dry white wine
- 1 tablespoon honey

Directions
1. Firstly, pat the chicken breasts dry. Lightly coat them with the melted butter.
2. Then, add the remaining ingredients.
3. Transfer them to the air fryer basket; bake about 15 minutes at 330 F.
4. Serve warm and enjoy!

Nutrition: Calories 189 Fat 14g Sugar 1g Protein 11g

256. Chicken Fillets, Brie and Ham

Preparation Time: 5 minutes
Cooking time: 15 minutes
Servings: 4
Ingredients:
- 2 Large Chicken Fillets
- Freshly Ground Black Pepper
- 4 Small Slices of Brie (Or your cheese of choice)
- 1 Tbsp. Freshly Chopped Chives
- 4 Slices Cured Ham

Directions
1. Slice the fillets into four and make incisions as you would for a hamburger bun. Leave a little "hinge" uncut at the back. Season the inside and pop some brie and chives in there. Close them, and wrap them each in a slice of ham. Brush with oil and pop them into the basket.
2. Heat your fryer to 350 F. Pour into the Oven rack/basket. Place the Rack on the middle-shelf of the Air fryer oven. Set temperature to 400 F, and set time to 15 minutes. Roast the little parcels until they look tasty (15 minutes)

Nutrition: Calories 375 Fat 18.3g Cholesterol 142mg Sodium 553mg Carbs 0.8g Protein 49.2g

257. Chicken Fajitas

Preparation Time: 10 minutes
Cooking time: 10 minutes
Servings: 4
Ingredients:
- 4 boneless, skinless chicken breasts, sliced
- 1 small red onion, sliced
- 2 red bell peppers, sliced
- ½ cup spicy ranch salad dressing, divided
- ½ teaspoon dried oregano
- 8 corn tortillas
- 2 cups torn butter lettuce
- 2 avocados, peeled and chopped

Directions
1. Place the chicken, onion, and pepper in the air fryer basket. Drizzle with 1 tablespoon of the salad dressing and add the oregano. Toss to combine.
2. Place the Rack on the middle-shelf of the Air fryer oven. Set temperature to 165 F, and set time to 14 minutes. Grill for 10 to 14 minutes or until the chicken is 165 F on a food thermometer. Transfer the chicken and vegetables to a bowl and toss with the remaining salad dressing. Serve the chicken mixture with the tortillas, lettuce, and avocados and let everyone make their own creations.

Nutrition: Calories 783 Fat 38g

258. Thai Red Duck with Candy Onion

Preparation Time: 25 minutes
Cooking Time: 25 minutes
Servings: 4
Ingredients:
- 1 ½ pounds duck breasts, skin removed
- 1 teaspoon kosher salt
- 1/2 teaspoon cayenne pepper
- 1/3 teaspoon black pepper
- 1/2 teaspoon smoked paprika
- 1 tablespoon Thai red curry paste
- 1 cup candy onions, halved
- 1/4 small pack coriander, chopped

Directions:
1. Place the duck breasts between 2 sheets of foil; then, use a rolling pin to bash the duck until they are 1-inch thick.
2. Preheat your Air Fryer to 395 degrees F.
3. Rub the duck breasts with salt, cayenne pepper, black pepper, paprika, and red curry paste. Place the duck breast in the cooking basket.
4. Cook for 11 to 12 minutes. Top with candy onions and cook for another 10 to 11 minutes.
5. Serve garnished with coriander and enjoy!

Nutrition: 362 Calories 18.7g Fat 4g Carbs 42.3g Protein 1.3g Sugars

259. Buttermilk Chicken

Preparation Time: 5 minutes
Cooking time: 55 minutes
Servings: 2
Ingredients:
- ½ teaspoon cayenne pepper
- 200 ml buttermilk
- 1 teaspoon garlic, minced
- 2 pieces of chicken breast fillet
- 4 tablespoons flour

- Salt and pepper to taste
- 1 egg, beaten
- 8 ounces panko breadcrumbs
- 2 sweet potatoes, sliced into chips
- 1 tablespoon sweet smoked paprika
- 1 tablespoon olive oil

Directions:
1. In a bowl, combine cayenne pepper, buttermilk and garlic.
2. Marinate chicken breasts in this mixture for 2 hours or overnight.
3. Preheat your air fryer for 3 minutes.
4. Season flour with salt and pepper.
5. Dredge chicken with seasoned flour.
6. Dip in the beaten egg and coat with breadcrumbs.
7. Cook the chicken in the air fryer at 350 F for 20 minutes.
8. Coat the sweet potato chips with paprika and oil.
9. Cook in the air fryer at 380 F for 20 minutes.
10. Shake to cook evenly.
11. Serve the chicken with the sweet potatoes.

Nutrition: Calories 934 Fat 16.1g Net Carbs 79.5g Protein 58.4g

260. Chicken with Avocado Mix

Preparation Time: 5 minutes
Cooking time: 20 minutes
Servings: 2
Ingredients:
- 2 cups Chicken
- ½ Avocado (sliced)
- Salt and pepper to taste
- 2 Radish (sliced)
- Parsley (chopped) for dressing

Directions:
1. Cut the chicken into slices and add it to the bowl.
2. Slice the radish and cut the avocado by placing it on top of the chicken.
3. When done, dress it with parsley and mix.
4. Add it to the round baking tray and place it in the air fryer.
5. Let it cook for 14 minutes at 300 F.
6. When ready, add salt and pepper at the end to enjoy the salad.

Nutrition: Calories 90 Fat 16g Net Carbs 45g Protein 110g

261. Chicken with Coconut and Turmeric

Preparation Time: 5 minutes
Cooking time: 27 minutes
Servings: 3
Ingredients:
- 1 ½ OZ. coconut milk
- 3 teaspoons ginger, grated
- 4 teaspoons ground turmeric
- ½ teaspoon of sea salt
- 3 chicken legs (skin removed)

Directions:
1. Combine the coconut milk, ginger, turmeric, and salt.
2. Make a few slits on the chicken meat.
3. Marinate the chicken in the mixture for 4 hours.
4. Keep inside the refrigerator.
5. Preheat air fryer at 375 F.
6. Cook for 10 minutes.
7. Flip and cook for another 10 to 12 minutes.

Nutrition: Calories 112 Fat 6.5g Carbs 4g Protein 9.6g

262. Crunchy Curry Chicken Strips

Preparation Time: 5 minutes
Cooking time: 25 minutes
Servings: 4
Ingredients:
- 12 OZ. chicken breast, cut into strips
- Salt and pepper to taste
- 1 egg, beaten
- ¼ cup whole wheat flour
- ½ cup panko breadcrumbs
- ¼ cup curry powder

Directions:
1. Season the chicken strips with the salt and pepper.
2. Dip each of the chicken strips into the flour, then into the egg.
3. In a bowl, mix the curry powder and breadcrumbs.
4. Coat each of the chicken strips with the curry powder mixture.
5. Cook in the air fryer at 350 F for 10 minutes.
6. Flip and cook for another 5 minutes.

Nutrition: Calories 170 Fat 4.1g Carbs 11.4g Protein 21.2g

263. Easy Ritzy Chicken Nuggets

Preparation Time: 20 minutes
Cooking Time: 8 minutes
Servings: 4
Ingredients:
- 1 ½ pounds chicken tenderloins, cut into small pieces
- 1/2 teaspoon garlic salt
- 1/2 teaspoon cayenne pepper
- 1/4 teaspoon black pepper, freshly cracked
- 4 tablespoons olive oil
- 1/3 cup saltines (e.g. Ritz crackers), crushed
- 4 tablespoons Parmesan cheese, freshly grated

Directions:
1. Start by preheating your Air Fryer to 390 degrees F.
2. Season each piece of the chicken with garlic salt, cayenne pepper, and black pepper.
3. In a mixing bowl, thoroughly combine the olive oil with crushed saltines. Dip each piece of chicken in the cracker mixture.
4. Finally, roll the chicken pieces over the Parmesan cheese. Cook for 8 minutes, working in batches.
5. Later, if you want to warm the chicken nuggets, add them to the basket and cook for 1 minute more. Serve with French fries, if desired.

Nutrition: 355 Calories 20.1g Fat 5.3g Carbs 36.6g Protein 0.2g Sugars

264. Orange Chicken Stir Fry

Preparation Time: 5 minutes
Cooking time: 30 minutes
Servings: 4
Ingredients:
- Olive oil to mist
- 1 sliced red onion
- 1 bell pepper, yellow
- 3/4 lbs. chicken thighs
- 3 teaspoons curry powder
- 1 tablespoon cornstarch
- ¼ cup of orange juice
- 2 tablespoons honey

- ¼ cup chicken stock

Directions:
1. Add the red onion, pepper, and chicken thighs into the air fryer basket and missed all of it with some olive oil.
2. Cook these together for about 12 minutes so that the chicken can be cooked through.
3. Make sure to shake the basket around a bit halfway through the cooking time.
4. Take the vegetables and chicken out of the basket and set to the side.
5. Bring out a metal bowl and combine the curry powder, cornstarch, orange juice, honey, and stock and mix well.
6. Add in the vegetables and chicken to this and add them to the basket.
7. Cook for a few minutes until the sauce is thick and bubbly and then serve.

Nutrition: Calories 230 Fat 7g Carbs 16g Protein 26g

265. Chicken Curry

Preparation Time: 5 minutes
Cooking time: 25 minutes
Servings: 4

Ingredients:
- 1 teaspoon olive oil
- 1-pound chicken breast; skinless, boneless
- 1/2 cup chicken stock
- 2 tablespoons curry paste
- 1 onion diced
- 2 tablespoons minced garlic
- 1 tablespoon apple cider vinegar
- 1 tablespoon lemongrass
- 1/2 cup coconut milk

Directions:
1. Cut the chicken breast into the cubes.
2. Peel the onion and dice it.
3. Then combine the chicken cubes and diced onion together in the air fryer basket tray.
4. Preheat the air fryer to 365 F.
5. Put chicken mixture in the air fryer and cook it for 5 minutes.
6. Now; add minced garlic, apple cider vinegar, lemongrass, coconut milk, chicken stock; and curry paste.
7. Mix the mixture up with the help of a wooden spatula.
8. Cook the chicken curry for 10 minutes more at the same temperature.
9. When the time is over and the chicken curry is cooked; remove it from the air fryer and stir on more time.
10. Now transfer the dish to the serving plates.

Nutrition: Calories 275 Fat 15.7g Carbs 7.2g Protein 25.6g

266. Pandan Chicken

Preparation Time: 5 minutes
Cooking time: 30 minutes
Servings: 4

Ingredients:
- 15-ounce chicken
- 1 Pandan leaf
- 1/2 onion; diced
- 1 teaspoon turmeric
- 1 tablespoon butter
- 1/4 cup coconut milk
- 1 tablespoon chives
- 1 teaspoon minced garlic
- 1 teaspoon chili flakes
- 1 teaspoon Stevie
- 1 teaspoon ground black pepper

Directions:
1. Cut the chicken into 4 big cubes.
2. Put chicken cubes in the big bowl.
3. Sprinkle the chicken with the minced garlic, diced onion, chili flakes, Stevie, ground black pepper, chives, and turmeric.
4. Mix the meat up with the help of hands.
5. Then cut the Pandan leaf into 4 parts. Wrap the chicken cubs into Pandan leaf.
6. Pour the coconut milk into the bowl with the wrapped chicken and leave it for 10 minutes.
7. The preheat the air fryer to 380 F.
8. Put Pandan chicken in the air fryer basket and cook the dish for 10 minutes.
9. When the chicken is cooked; transfer it to the serving plates and let it chill for at least 2-3 minutes.

Nutrition: Calories 250 Fat 12.6g Carbs 3.1g Protein 29.9g

267. Lemon Garlic Rosemary Chicken

Preparation Time: 5 minutes
Cooking time: 27 minutes
Servings: 2

Ingredients:
- 2 chicken thighs (skin removed)
- Sea salt and pepper to taste
- 1 tablespoon lemon juice
- 3 teaspoon dried rosemary
- 3 cloves garlic, crushed and minced
- 1 teaspoon olive oil

Directions:
1. Season the chicken thighs with the sea salt, pepper, lemon juice, and dried rosemary.
2. Marinate for 1 hour.
3. Meanwhile, sauté the crushed garlic in the olive oil.
4. Cook the chicken thighs in the air fryer at 400 F for 6 minutes.
5. Flip the chicken and cook for another 6 minutes.
6. Pour the garlic oil on top of the chicken before serving.

Nutrition: Calories 188 Fat 12.3g Carbs 3.2g Protein 16g

268. Paprika Chicken Legs With Brussels Sprouts

Preparation Time: 30 minutes
Cooking Time: 20 minutes
Servings: 2

Ingredients:
- 2 chicken legs
- 1/2 teaspoon paprika
- 1/2 teaspoon kosher salt
- 1/2 teaspoon black pepper
- 1-pound Brussels sprouts
- 1 teaspoon dill, fresh or dried

Directions:
1. Start by preheating your Air Fryer to 370 degrees F.
2. Now, season your chicken with paprika, salt, and pepper. Transfer the chicken legs to the cooking basket. Cook for 10 minutes.
3. Flip the chicken legs and cook an additional 10 minutes. Reserve.

4. Add the Brussels sprouts to the cooking basket; sprinkle with dill. Cook at 380 degrees F for 15 minutes, shaking the basket halfway through.
5. Serve with the reserved chicken legs. Bon appétit!

Nutrition: 355 Calories 20.1g Fat 5.3g Carbs 36.6g Protein 0.2g Sugars

269. Chicken Pie

Preparation Time: 5 minutes
Cooking time: 31 minutes
Servings: 8 to 10

Ingredients:
- 2 chicken thighs (boneless, sliced into cubes)
- 1 teaspoon reduced-sodium soy sauce
- 1 onion, diced
- 1 carrot, diced
- 2 potatoes, diced
- 1 cup mushrooms
- 1 teaspoon garlic powder
- 1 teaspoon flour
- ½ cup milk
- 2 hard-boiled eggs, sliced in half
- 2 sheets puff pastry

Directions:
1. Season the chicken cubes with the low sodium soy sauce.
2. In a pan over low heat, sauté the onions, carrots, and potatoes,
3. Add the chicken cubes and mushrooms.
4. Season with the garlic powder,
5. Add the flour and milk. Mix well.
6. Lay the pastry sheet on the tray of the air fryer.
7. Poke it with holes using a fork.
8. Arrange the eggs on top of the pastry sheet.
9. Pour in the chicken mixture on top of the eggs.
10. Top with the second pastry sheet. Press a little.
11. Air fryer at 300 F for 6 minutes.
12. Slice into several portions and serve.

Nutrition: Calories 114 Fat 3.4g Carbs 9.7g Protein 11.2g

270. Easy Paprika Chicken

Preparation Time: 7 minutes
Cooking Time: 18 minutes
Servings: 4

Ingredients:
- 4 chicken breasts
- 1 tablespoon paprika
- ¼ teaspoon garlic powder
- 2 tablespoons fresh thyme, chopped
- From the cupboard:
- Salt and ground black pepper, to taste
- 2 tablespoons butter, melted

Directions:
1. Preheat the air fryer to 360°F (182°C). Spritz the air fryer basket with cooking spray.
2. On a clean work surface, rub the chicken breasts with paprika, garlic powder, salt, and black pepper, then brush with butter.
3. Cook the chicken in the preheated air fryer for 18 minutes or until the internal temperature reaches at least 165°F (74°C). Flip the chicken with tongs halfway through the cooking time.
4. Serve the cooked chicken on a plate immediately with thyme on top.

Nutrition: Calories: 368 Fat: 14.1g Carbs: 2.3g Protein: 57.9g

271. Texas Thighs

Preparation Time: 10 minutes
Cooking Time: 20 minutes
Servings: 8

Ingredients:
- 8 chicken thighs
- 2 teaspoons Texas BBQ Jerky seasoning
- 2 tablespoons cilantro, chopped
- From the Cupboard:
- 1 tablespoon olive oil
- Salt and ground black pepper, to taste

Directions:
1. Preheat air fryer to 380°F (193°C). Spritz the air fryer basket with cooking spray.
2. Arrange the chicken thighs in the air fryer basket, then brush with olive oil on all sides. Sprinkle with BBQ seasoning, salt, and black pepper.
3. Cook for 20 minutes or until the internal temperature of the thighs reaches at least 165°F (74°C). Flip the thighs three times during the cooking time.
4. Remove the chicken thighs from the air fryer basket and serve with cilantro on top.

Nutrition: Calories: 444 Fat: 33.8g Carbs: 1.0g Protein: 31.9g

272. Crunchy Golden Nuggets

Preparation Time: 5 minutes
Cooking Time: 10 minutes
Servings: 4

Ingredients:
- 2 chicken breasts, cut into nuggets
- 4 tablespoons sour cream
- ½ cup bread crumbs
- ½ tablespoon garlic powder
- From the Cupboard:
- ½ teaspoon cayenne pepper
- Salt and ground black pepper, to taste

Directions:
1. Preheat the air fryer to 360°F (182°C). Spritz the air fryer basket with cooking spray.
2. Put the sour cream in a large bowl. Combine the bread crumbs, cayenne pepper, garlic powder, salt, and black pepper on a large plate.
3. Dredge the chicken nuggets in the bowl of sour cream, shake the excess off, then roll the nuggets through the bread crumbs mixture to coat well.
4. Place the nuggets in the air fryer basket and cook for 10 minutes or until the chicken nuggets are golden brown and crispy. Flip the nuggets halfway through the cooking time.
5. Remove the nuggets from the basket and serve warm.

Nutrition: Calories: 324 Fat: 15.5g Carbs: 11.7g Protein: 32.7g

273. Air Fried Turkey Breast

Preparation Time: 10 minutes
Cooking Time: 40 minutes
Servings: 6

Ingredients
- 2 3/4 pounds turkey breast
- 2 tablespoons unsalted butter
- 1 tablespoon chopped fresh rosemary
- 1 teaspoon chopped fresh chives
- 1 teaspoon minced fresh garlic
- 1/4 teaspoon black pepper

- 1/2 teaspoon salt

Directions
1. Preheat your air fryer toast oven to 350° F.
2. In a bowl, mix chives, rosemary, garlic, salt, and pepper until well combined. Cut in butter and mash until well blended.
3. Rub the turkey breast with the herbed butter and then add to the air fryer toast oven basket; fry for 20 minutes. turn the turkey breast and cook for another 20 minutes.
4. Transfer the cooked turkey onto an aluminum foil and wrap; let rest for at least 10 minutes and then slice it up. Serve warm.

Nutrition: Calories: 263 kcal Carbs: 0.3 g Fat: 10.1 g Protein: 40.2 g

274. Chicken In Bacon Wrap

Preparation Time: 5 minutes
Cooking Time: 15 minutes
Servings: 4
Ingredients:
- 2 chicken breasts
- 8 ounces (227 g) onion and chive cream cheese
- 6 slices turkey bacon
- 1 tablespoon fresh parsley, chopped
- Juice from ½ lemon
- From the Cupboard:
- 1 tablespoon butter
- Salt, to taste
- Special Equipment:
- 2 or 4 toothpicks, soaked for at least 30 minutes

Directions:
1. Preheat the air fryer to 390°F (199°C). Spritz the air fryer basket with cooking spray.
2. On a clean work surface, brush the chicken breasts with cream cheese and butter on both sides. Sprinkle with salt.
3. Wrap each chicken breast with 3 slices of bacon and secure with 1 or 2 toothpicks.
4. Arrange the bacon-wrapped chicken in the preheated air fryer and cook for 14 minutes or until the bacon is well browned and a meat thermometer inserted in the chicken reads at least 165°F (74°C). Flip them halfway through the cooking time.
5. Remove them from the air fryer basket and serve with parsley and lemon juice on top.

Nutrition: Calories: 437 Fat: 28.6g Carbs: 5.2g Protein: 39.8g

275. Lemon and Honey Glazed Game Hen

Preparation Time: 10 minutes
Cooking Time: 20 minutes
Servings: 2
Ingredients:
- 1 (2-pound / 907-g) Cornish game hen, split in half
- ¼ teaspoon dried thyme
- Juice and zest of 1 lemon
- ¼ cup honey
- 1½ teaspoons chopped fresh thyme leaves
- From the Cupboard:
- 1 tablespoon olive oil
- Salt and ground black pepper, to taste
- ½ teaspoon soy sauce

Directions:
1. Preheat the air fryer to 390°F (199°C). Spritz the air fryer basket with cooking spray.
2. On a clean work surface, brush the game hen halves with olive oil, then sprinkle with dried thyme, salt, and black pepper to season.
3. Cook the hen in the preheated air fryer for 15 minutes or until the hen is lightly browned. Flip the hen halfway through.
4. Meanwhile, mix the lemon juice and zest, honey, thyme leaves, soy sauce, and black pepper in a bowl.
5. Baste the game hen with the honey glaze, then cook for an additional 4 minutes or until the hen is well glazed and a meat thermometer inserted in the hen reads at least 165°F (74°C).
6. Remove the game hen from the air fryer basket. Allow to cool for a few minutes and slice to serve.

Nutrition: Calories: 724 Fat: 22.0g Carbs: 37.5g Protein: 91.3g

276. Turkey And Pepper Sandwich

Preparation Time: 5 minutes
Cooking Time: 5 minutes
Servings: 1
Ingredients:
- 2 slices whole grain bread
- 2 teaspoons Dijon mustard
- 2 ounces (57 g) cooked turkey breast, thinly sliced
- 2 slices low-fat Swiss cheese
- 3 strips roasted red bell pepper
- From the Cupboard:
- Salt and ground black pepper, to taste

Directions:
1. Preheat the air fryer to 330°F (166°C). Spritz the air fryer basket with cooking spray.
2. Assemble the sandwich: On a dish, place a slice of bread, then top the bread with 1 teaspoon of Dijon mustard, use a knife to smear the mustard evenly.
3. Layer the turkey slices, Swiss cheese slices, and red pepper strips on the bread according to your favorite order. Top them with remaining teaspoon of Dijon mustard and remaining bread slice.
4. Place the sandwich in the preheated air fryer and spritz with cooking spray. Sprinkle with salt and black pepper.
5. Cook for 5 minutes until the cheese melts and the bread is lightly browned. Flip the sandwich halfway through the cooking time.
6. Serve the sandwich immediately.

Nutrition: Calories: 328 Fat: 5.0g Carbs: 38.0g Protein: 29.0g

277. Air-Fried Lemon Olive Chicken

Preparation Time: 10 minutes
Cooking Time: 15 minutes
Servings: 4
Ingredients
- 4 Boneless Skinless Chicken Breasts
- 1/2 teaspoon organic cumin
- 1 teaspoon sea salt (real salt)
- 1/4 teaspoon black pepper
- 1/2 cup butter, melted
- 1 lemons 1/2 juiced, 1/2 thinly sliced
- 1 cup chicken bone-broth
- 1 can pitted green olives
- 1/2 cup red onions, sliced

Directions
1. Liberally season the chicken breasts with sea salt, cumin, and black pepper

2. Preheat your air fryer toast oven to 370 degrees and brush the chicken breasts with the melted butter.
3. Cook in the pan of your air fryer toast oven for about 5 minutes until evenly browned.
4. Add all remaining ingredients and cook at 320 degrees for 10 minutes.
5. Serve hot!

Nutrition: Calories: 310 kcal Carbs: 10.2 g Fat: 9.4 g Protein: 21.8 g.

278. Chicken, Mushroom, And Pepper Kabobs

Preparation Time: 1 hour 5 minutes
Cooking Time: 15-20 minutes
Servings: 4
Ingredients:
- ⅓ cup raw honey
- 2 tablespoons sesame seeds
- 2 boneless chicken breasts, cut into cubes
- 6 white mushrooms, cut in halves
- 3 green or red bell peppers, diced

From the Cupboard:
- ⅓ cup soy sauce
- Salt and ground black pepper, to taste
- Special Equipment:
- 4 wooden skewers, soaked for at least 30 minutes

Directions:
1. Combine the honey, soy sauce, sesame seeds, salt, and black pepper in a large bowl. Stir to mix well.
2. Dunk the chicken cubes in this bowl, then wrap the bowl in plastic and refrigerate to marinate for at least an hour.
3. Preheat the air fryer to 390°F (199°C). Spritz the air fryer basket with cooking spray.
4. Remove the chicken cubes from the marinade, then run the skewers through the chicken cubes, mushrooms, and bell peppers alternatively.
5. Baste the chicken, mushrooms, and bell peppers with the marinade, then arrange them in the preheated air fryer.
6. Spritz them with cooking spray and cook for 15 to 20 minutes or until the mushrooms and bell peppers are tender and the chicken cubes are well browned. Flip them halfway through the cooking time.
7. Transfer the skewers to a large plate and serve hot.

Nutrition: Calories: 380 Fat: 16.0g Carbs: 26.1g Protein: 34.0g

279. Chicken, Potatoes & Cabbage

Preparation Time: 30 minutes
Cooking Time: 40 minutes
Servings: 8
Ingredients:
- 1 cup apple cider vinegar
- 2 lb. chicken thigh fillets
- 6 oz. barbecue sauce
- 2 lb. cabbage, sliced into wedges and steamed
- 1 lb. potatoes, roasted
- Salt and pepper to taste

Directions:
1. Pour apple cider vinegar to the inner pot.
2. Add grill grate to the Air Fryer Oven.
3. Place the chicken on top of the grill.
4. Sprinkle both sides with salt and pepper.
5. Grill the chicken for 15 to 20 minutes per side at 350 degrees F.
6. Baste the chicken with the barbecue sauce.
7. Serve chicken with potatoes and cabbage.

Nutrition: Calories:385 kcal Protein: 22.59 g Fat: 20 g Carbs: 28.03 g

280. Grilled Garlic Chicken

Preparation Time: 10 minutes
Cooking Time: 20 minutes
Servings: 8
Ingredients:
- 3 lb. chicken thigh fillets
- Garlic salt to taste

Directions:
1. Add grill plate to the Air Fryer Oven.
2. Preheat to medium heat.
3. Sprinkle chicken with garlic salt on both sides.
4. Cook for 8 to 10 minutes.
5. Flip and cook for another 7 minutes.

Nutrition: Calories: 386 kcal Protein: 28.9 g Fat: 29.01 g Carbs: 0.43 g

281. Crisp Chicken w/ Mustard Vinaigrette

Preparation Time: 15 minutes
Cooking Time: 10 minutes
Servings: 1
Ingredients
- Salad:
- 250g chicken breast
- 1 cup shaved Brussels sprouts
- 2 cups baby spinach
- 2 cups mixed greens
- 1/2 avocado sliced
- Segments of one orange
- 1 teaspoon raw pumpkin seeds
- 1 teaspoon toasted almonds
- 1 teaspoon hemp seeds

Dressing:
- 1/2 shallot, chopped
- 1 garlic clove, chopped
- 2 teaspoons balsamic vinegar
- 1 teaspoon extra virgin olive oil
- ½ cup fresh orange juice
- 1 teaspoon Dijon mustard
- 1 teaspoon raw honey
- Fresh ground pepper

Directions
1. In a blender, blend all dressing ingredients until very smooth; set aside.
2. Set your air fryer toast oven to 350 degrees and brush the basket of the air fryer toast oven with oil.
3. Place the chicken breast on the basket and cook for10 minutes, 5 minutes per side.
4. Take out of the air fryer toast oven and transfer to a plate. Let sit for 5 minutes then cut into bite-sized chunks.
5. Combine all salad ingredients in a large bowl; drizzle with dressing and toss to coat well before serving.

Nutrition: Calories: 457 kcal, Carbs: 13.6 g Fat: 37 g Protein: 31.8 g.

282. Chicken with Oregano-Orange Chimichurri & Arugula Salad

Preparation Time: 5 minutes
Cooking Time: 12 minutes
Servings: 4

Ingredients
- 1 teaspoon finely grated orange zest
- 1 teaspoon dried oregano
- 1 small garlic clove, grated
- 2 teaspoon vinegar (red wine, cider, or white wine)
- 1 tablespoon fresh orange juice
- 1/2 cup chopped fresh flat-leaf parsley leaves
- 700g chicken breast, cut into 4 pieces
- Sea salt and pepper
- 1/4 cup and 2 teaspoons extra virgin olive oil
- 4 cups arugula
- 2 bulbs fennel, shaved
- 2 tablespoons whole-grain mustard

Directions
1. Make chimichurri: In a medium bowl, combine orange zest, oregano, and garlic. Mix in vinegar, orange juice, and parsley and then slowly whisk in ¼ cup of olive oil until emulsified. Season with sea salt and pepper.
2. Sprinkle the chicken with salt and pepper and set your air fryer toast oven to 350 degrees F.
3. Brush the chicken steaks with the remaining olive oil and cook for about 6 minutes per side or until evenly browned. Take out from the fryer and let rest for at least 10 minutes.
4. Toss the cooked chicken, greens, and fennel with mustard in a medium bowl; season with salt and pepper.
5. Serve steak with chimichurri and salad. Enjoy!

Nutrition: Calories: 312 kcal Carbs: 12.8 g Fat: 33.6 g Protein: 29 g

283. Stir-Fried Chicken with Water Chestnuts

Preparation Time: 10 minutes
Cooking Time: 15 minutes
Servings: 4

Ingredients
- 2 tablespoons sesame oil
- ¼ cup wheat-free tamari
- 4 small chicken breasts, sliced
- 1 small cabbage, chopped
- 3 garlic cloves, chopped
- 1 teaspoon Chinese five-spice powder
- 1 cup dried plums
- 1 cup water chestnuts
- Toasted sesame seeds

Directions
1. Start by preheating your air fryer toast oven at 370 degrees F.
2. Heat sesame oil in your air fryer toast oven's pan set over medium heat; stir in all the ingredients, except sesame seeds, and transfer to the air fryer toast oven.
3. Cook until cabbage and chicken are tender for 15-20 minutes.
4. Serve warm sprinkled with toasted sesame seeds.
5. Enjoy!

Nutrition: Calories: 404 kcal, Carbs: 11.3 g Fat: 29 g Protein: 22 g.

284. Spicy Duck Legs

Preparation Time: 5 minutes
Cooking Time: 30 minutes
Servings: 2

Ingredients:
- 2 duck legs, bone-in, and skin on
- Salt and pepper to taste
- 1 teaspoon five spice powder
- 1 tablespoon herbs that you like such as thyme, parsley, etc., chopped

Directions:
1. Rub the spices over duck legs.
2. Place duck legs in the air fryer and cook for 25-minutes at 325°Fahrenheit.
3. Then air fries them at 400°Fahrenheit for 5-minutes

Nutrition: Calories 207 Fat 10.6g Carbs 1.9g Protein 25g

285. Duck Breast with Fig Sauce

Preparation Time: 10 minutes
Cooking Time: 20 minutes
Servings: 4

Ingredients:
- 2 duck breasts, skin on, halved
- 1 tablespoon olive oil
- ½ teaspoon thyme, chopped
- ½ teaspoon garlic powder
- ¼ teaspoon sweet paprika
- Salt and black pepper to the taste
- 1 cup beef stock
- 3 tablespoons butter, melted
- 1 shallot, chopped
- ½ cup port wine
- 4 tablespoons fig preserves
- 1 tablespoon white flour

Directions:
1. Season duck breasts with salt and pepper, Drizzle with half of the melted butter, rub well, put in your air fryer's basket and cook at 350 degrees F for 5 minutes on each side.
2. Meanwhile, heat up a pan with the olive oil and the rest of the butter over medium high heat, add shallot, stir and cook for 2 minutes
3. Add thyme, garlic powder, paprika, stock, salt, pepper, wine and figs, stir and cook for 7-8 minutes
4. Add flour, stir well, cook until sauce thickens a bit and take off heat.
5. Divide duck breasts on plates, Drizzle with figs sauce all over and serve. Enjoy!

Nutrition: Calories 246 Fat 12 Carbs 22 Protein 3

286. Duck Breasts with Red Wine and Orange Sauce

Preparation Time: 10 minutes
Cooking Time: 35 minutes
Servings: 4

Ingredients:
- ½ cup honey
- 2 cups orange juice
- 4 cups red wine
- 2 tablespoons sherry vinegar
- 2 cups chicken stock
- 2 teaspoons pumpkin pie spice

- 2 tablespoons butter
- 2 duck breasts, skin on and halved
- 2 tablespoons olive oil
- salt and black pepper to the taste

Directions:
1. Heat up a pan with the orange juice over medium heat, add honey, stir well and cook for 10 minutes Add wine, vinegar, stock, pie spice and butter, stir well, cook for 10 minutes more and take off heat.
2. Season duck breasts with salt and pepper, rub with olive oil, place in preheated air fryer at 370 degrees F and cook for 7 minutes on each side.
3. Divide duck breasts on plates, Drizzle with wine and orange juice all over and serve right away. Enjoy!

Nutrition: Calories 300 Fat 8 Carbs 24 Protein 11

287. Classic Air Fried Drumstick

Preparation Time: 5-10 min.
Cooking Time: 20 Minutes
Servings: 4-6
Ingredients:
- 8 chicken drumsticks
- 1 teaspoon black pepper
- 1 teaspoon garlic powder
- 2 tablespoon olive oil
- 1 teaspoon salt
- 1 teaspoon paprika
- 1/2 teaspoon cumin

Directions:
1. In a mixing bowl, add olive oil with salt, black pepper, garlic powder, paprika, and cumin. Combine the ingredients to mix well with each other.
2. Rub drumsticks with the spice mix.
3. Place The air fryer over the kitchen platform. Arrange to drip pan in the lower position. Press "Air Fry," set the timer to 20 minutes, and set the temperature to 375°F. The air fryer will start pre-heating.
4. When The air fryer is pre-heated, it will display "Add Food" on its screen. Open the door and take out the middle roasting tray.
5. Place drumsticks over the tray and push it back; close door and cooking will start. Midway, it will display "Turn Food" on its screen, flip drumsticks, and close door.
6. Open the door after the cooking cycle is over; serve warm.

Nutrition: Calories: 239 Fat: 12g Saturated Fat: 1.5g Trans Fat: 0g Carbs: 16g Fiber: 4.5g Sodium: 387mg Protein: 16g

288. Duck Breasts and Raspberry Sauce

Preparation Time: 10 minutes
Cooking Time: 15 minutes
Servings: 4
Ingredients:
- 2 duck breasts, skin on and scored
- Salt and black pepper to the taste
- Cooking spray
- ½ teaspoon cinnamon powder
- ½ cup raspberries
- 1 tablespoon of sugar
- 1 teaspoon red wine vinegar
- ½ cup water

Directions:
1. Season duck breasts with salt and pepper, spray them with cooking spray, put in preheated air fryer skin side down and cook at 350 degrees F for 10 minutes Heat up a pan with the water over medium heat, add raspberries, cinnamon, sugar and wine, stir, bring to a simmer, transfer to your blender, puree and return to pan.
2. Add air fryer duck breasts to pan as well, toss to coat, divide among plates and serve right away. Enjoy!

Nutrition: Calories 456 Fat 22 Carbs 14 Protein 45

289. Duck and Tea Sauce

Preparation Time: 10 minutes
Cooking Time: 20 minutes
Servings: 4
Ingredients:
- 2 duck breast halves, boneless
- 2 and ¼ cup chicken stock
- ¾ cup shallot, chopped
- 1 and ½ cup orange juice
- Salt and black pepper to the taste
- 3 teaspoons earl gray tea leaves
- 3 tablespoons butter, melted
- 1 tablespoon honey

Directions:
1. Season duck breast halves with salt and pepper, put in preheated air fryer and cook at 360 degrees F for 10 minutes Meanwhile, heat up a pan with the butter over medium heat, add shallot, stir and cook for 2-3 minutes Add stock, stir and cook for another minute.
2. Add orange juice, tea leaves and honey, stir, cook for 2-3 minutes more and strain into a bowl. Divide duck on plates, Drizzle with tea sauce all over and serve. Enjoy!

Nutrition: Calories 228 Fat 11 Carbs 20 Protein 12

290. Lemon-Pepper Chicken Wings

Preparation Time: 10 minutes
Cooking Time: 20 minutes
Servings: 4
Ingredients
- 8 whole chicken wings
- Juice of ½ lemon
- ½ teaspoon garlic powder
- 1 teaspoon onion powder
- Salt
- Pepper
- ¼ cup low-fat buttermilk
- ½ cup all-purpose flour
- Cooking oil

Directions:
1. Place the wings in a sealable plastic bag. Drizzle the wings with the lemon juice. Season the wings with the garlic powder, onion powder, and salt and pepper to taste.
2. Seal the bag. Shake thoroughly to combine the seasonings and coat the wings.
3. Pour the buttermilk and the flour into separate bowls large enough to dip the wings.
4. Spray the air fryer oven basket with cooking oil.
5. One at a time, dip the wings in the buttermilk and then the flour.
6. Place the wings in the air fryer oven basket. It is okay to stack them on top of each other. Spray the wings with cooking oil, being sure to spray the bottom layer. Cook for 5 minutes.

7. Remove the basket and shake it to ensure all of the pieces will cook fully.
8. Return the basket to the air fryer oven and continue to cook the chicken. Repeat shaking every 5 minutes until a total of 20 minutes has passed.
9. Cool before serving.

Nutrition: Calories: 347; Fat: 12G Protein: 46G Fiber: 1g

291. Cheesy Chicken in Leek-Tomato Sauce

Preparation Time: 10 minutes
Cooking Time: 20 minutes
Servings: 4

Ingredients
- 2 large-sized chicken breasts, cut in half lengthwise
- Salt and ground black pepper, to taste
- 4 ounces Cheddar cheese, cut into sticks
- 1 tablespoon sesame oil
- 1 cup leeks, chopped
- 2 cloves garlic, minced
- 2/3 cup roasted vegetable stock
- 2/3 cup tomato puree
- 1 teaspoon dried rosemary
- 1 teaspoon dried thyme

Directions:
1. Firstly, season chicken breasts with the salt and black pepper; place a piece of Cheddar cheese in the middle. Then, tie it using a kitchen strinG
2. drizzle with sesame oil and reserve.
3. Add the leeks and garlic to the oven-safe bowl.
4. Cook in the air fryer oven at 390 degrees F for 5 minutes or until tender.
5. Add the reserved chicken. Throw in the other ingredients and cook for 12 to 13 minutes more or until the chicken is done. Enjoy.

Nutrition: Calories 257.7 Fat 1.5g Carbs 40.8g Fiber 6.2g Protein 22.1g Sugar 7.5g Sodium 69.9mg

292. Duck and Cherries

Preparation Time: 10 minutes
Cooking Time: 20 minutes
Servings: 4

Ingredients:
- ½ cup sugar
- ¼ cup honey
- 1/3 cup balsamic vinegar
- 1 teaspoon garlic, minced
- 1 tablespoon ginger, grated
- 1 teaspoon cumin, ground
- ½ teaspoon clove, ground
- ½ teaspoon cinnamon powder
- 4 sage leaves, chopped
- 1 jalapeno, chopped
- 2 cups rhubarb, sliced
- ½ cup yellow onion, chopped
- 2 cups cherries, pitted
- 4 duck breasts, boneless, skin on and scored
- Salt and black pepper to the taste

Directions:
1. Season duck breast with salt and pepper, put in your air fryer and cook at 350 degrees F for 5 minutes on each side.
2. Meanwhile, heat up a pan over medium heat, add sugar, honey, vinegar, garlic, ginger, cumin, clove, cinnamon, sage, jalapeno, rhubarb, onion and cherries, stir, bring to a simmer and cook for 10 minutes
3. Add duck breasts, toss well, divide everything on plates and serve. Enjoy!

Nutrition: Calories 456 Fat 13 Carbs 64 Protein 31

293. Oven-Fried Chicken Wings

Preparation Time: 10 minutes
Cooking Time: 25 minutes
Servings: 3

Ingredients
- 1 ½ lb. chicken wings
- 1/3 c. grated Parmesan cheese
- 1/3 c. breadcrumbs
- 1/8 tsp. garlic powder
- 1/8 tsp. onion powder
- ¼ c. melted butter
- Salt and black pepper to taste
- Cooking spray

Directions
1. In a baking sheet, spray with cooking spray.
2. In a large bowl mix Parmesan cheese, garlic powder, onion powder, black pepper, breadcrumbs, and salt. Stir to combine well.
3. Dip chicken wings one at a time into melted butter and then into bread mixture until thoroughly covered. Arrange wings in a single layer on the baking sheet.
4. Place on 1-inch rack and cook on High power (350 degrees F) for 10 minutes. Flip wings over and cook for another 10-12 minutes until no longer pink in center and juices run clear. Remove promptly from NuWave Oven and serve.

Nutrition: Calories: 371 Fat: 22.6g Carbs: 11.8g Protein: 27.8g

294. Beer Can Chicken

Preparation Time: 10 minutes
Cooking time: 40 minutes
Servings: 4

Ingredients:
- `Brine
- `2 cups water
- `2 cans beer
- `¼ cup kosher salt
- `½ cup brown sugar
- `8 thyme sprigs
- `3-lb whole chicken, cleaned
- `Rub
- `2 tsp. paprika
- `1 tbsp. thyme, dried
- `½ tsp. salt
- `¼ tsp. onion powder
- `¼ tsp. garlic powder
- `¼ tsp. freshly ground black pepper
- `2 tbsp. extra virgin olive oil

Directions
1. Bring 1 cup water to a simmer in a pot.
2. Dissolve the kosher salt, sugar, and thyme in the simmering water. Add 1 cup water and the beer to the brine.
3. Marinate the chicken in the brine overnight.
4. Combine the rub ingredients in a bowl.

5. Remove the chicken from the brine and pat the chicken dry.
6. Brush the chicken with the olive oil and apply the rub to the chicken.
7. Assemble the Adjustable Skewer Racks with the Rotisserie Shaft and secure the Shaft with the Rotisserie Forks and Set Screws.
8. Set the Shaft through the chicken and tie butcher's twine around
9. the chicken's legs, center, and wings.
10. Set the Shaft into the Air fryer oven's Rotisserie Shaft sockets.
11. Press the Power Button and then the Rotisserie Button (400 F for 30 minutes).
12. Carefully remove the chicken using the Fetch Tool.

Nutrition: Calories 311 Fat 11g Carbs 22g Protein 31g

295. Balsamic-Glazed Chicken Breasts

Preparation Time: 10 minutes
Cooking time: 19 minutes
Servings: 6
Ingredients:
- Balsamic Glaze
- 2/3 cup balsamic vinegar
- cloves garlic, grated
- ¼ cup Dijon mustard
- ¼ cup honey
- 1 tsp. salt
- ½ tsp. freshly ground black pepper
- 1 cup extra virgin olive oil
- small boneless and skinless chicken breasts

Directions
1. Whisk the balsamic vinegar, garlic, Dijon mustard, honey, salt, and pepper together in a bowl. Drizzle the olive oil into the glaze while whisking to emulsify the glaze.
2. Marinate the chicken breasts in the marinade for 45 minutes in the refrigerator. Toss the chicken breasts halfway through the cooking time (22 ½ minutes).
3. Fold the chicken in half on the Rotisserie Shaft and secure the Shaft with the Rotisserie Forks and Set Screws. Set the Shaft into the Power AirFryer Oven's Rotisserie Shaft sockets.
4. Press the Power Button and then the Rotisserie Button (400 F for 30 minutes). Brush the chicken with the glaze every 10 minutes while the chicken is cooking.
5. Carefully remove the chicken using the Fetch Tool.

Nutrition: Calories 127 Fat 0.5g Protein 26g

296. Paprika Rotisserie-Style Chicken

Preparation Time: 5 minutes
Cooking time: 80 minutes + marinating time
Servings: 4
Ingredients:
- `1 (3 ½- 4 lb) whole chicken
- `2 tbsp salt
- `2 cups buttermilk
- `1 tsp lime juice
- `3 tbsp butter, melted
- `1 tbsp paprika
- `Black pepper and sea salt to taste

Directions
1. Mix the salt, lemon juice, and buttermilk and mix until the salt is dissolved in a large bowl. Submerge the chicken. Cover the bowl and place it in your refrigerator for 2 hours or overnight.
2. Remove the chicken from the fridge, discard the marinade, and pat it dry with kitchen towels. Tie the legs with a butcher's twine and brush with butter. Rub the top and sides of the chicken with paprika, sea salt, and black pepper.
3. Insert the rotisserie rod through the chicken and attach the forks to secure the rod. Select Roast function on your Air fryer oven and adjust the temperature to 380 F and the time to 50 minutes. Slide the chicken into the oven. Press Start/Pause. Make sure the chicken rotates as it cooks.
4. Approximately 10-15 minutes before the end of the suggested cooking time, start checking for doneness using a meat thermometer. Chicken should have an internal temperature of 165 F. When the chicken is cooked through, remove from the air fryer oven with the removal tool.
5. Put the chicken on a cutting board, and using gloves, carefully remove the chicken from the rod. Cover with foil and leave to rest 10-15 minutes before carving. Serve warm.

Nutrition: Calories 127 Fat 0.5g Protein 26g

297. Harissa Chicken with Yogurt Sauce

Preparation Time: 5 minutes
Cooking time: 80 minutes + marinating time
Servings: 4
Ingredients:
- `2 cups sour cream
- `Salt and black pepper to taste
- `3 tbsp olive oil
- `3 cloves garlic, minced
- `2 tsp harissa seasoning
- `1 tsp dried dill
- `1 tsp dried tarragon
- `1 (4-lb) whole chicken
- `Yogurt Sauce:
- `2 tbsp olive oil
- `Salt to taste
- `¼ tsp red pepper flakes, crushed
- `1 cup full-fat yogurt
- `1 tsp dried dill weed

Directions
1. Mix all the sauce ingredients and place in the refrigerator until ready to use.
2. Put the chicken in a large bowl and pour the sour cream over. Cover with a lid and place in the fridge for 2-3 hours. Pull the chicken from the refrigerator and let it sit for 30 minutes at room temperature.
3. Remove the chicken from the marinade. Tie the legs with a butcher's twine.
4. In a small bowl, whisk the olive oil, garlic, paprika, sage, thyme, tarragon, salt, and pepper to taste. Rub the top and sides of the chicken with the mixture.
5. Insert the rotisserie rod through the chicken and attach the forks to secure the rod.
6. Select Roast function on your Air fryer oven and adjust the temperature to 380 F and the cooking time to 60 minutes.
7. Place the chicken in the air fryer oven. Press Start/Pause to begin cooking.
8. When cooking is complete, remove the pan from the oven. Cover with foil and leave to rest 10-15 minutes before carving. Serve the chicken with chilled yogurt sauce.

Nutrition: Calories 274 Fat 12g Fiber 3g Protein 14g Carbs 5g

POULTRY

298. Spicy Roasted Chicken

Preparation Time: 5 minutes
Cooking time: 75 minutes + marinating time
Servings: 4

Ingredients:
- `1 (4 lb) whole chicken
- `4 tbsp olive oil
- `1 tbsp ground coriander
- `2 tsp garlic powder
- `1 tsp onion powder
- `1 tsp chili pepper
- `1 tbsp allspice

Directions
1. Mix the olive oil, coriander, garlic powder, onion powder, chili pepper, and allspice in a large ziplock bag; shake to combine well.
2. Place the chicken in the bag and massage to coat. Transfer to the refrigerator and allow marinating for 30 minutes.
3. Select Air Fry function on Air fryer oven and adjust the temperature to 380 F. Press Start/Pause to begin cooking.
4. Remove the chicken from the bag, place it on the rotisserie rod, and insert it in the air fryer oven. Roast for 40-50 minutes or until the chicken skin is golden and charred, making sure the chicken rotates as it cooks. Check for doneness with a meat thermometer.
5. Remove and let the chicken sit for 10 minutes before serving.

Nutrition: Calories 127 Fat 0.5g Protein 26g

299. Spicy Rotisserie Chicken

Preparation Time: 10 minutes
Cooking time: 45 minutes
Servings: 4

Ingredients:
- `3 pounds (1.4 kg) tied whole chicken
- `3 cloves garlic, halved
- `1 whole lemon, quartered
- `2 sprigs fresh rosemary whole
- `2 tablespoons olive oil
- `Chicken Rub:
- `½ teaspoon fresh ground pepper
- `½ teaspoon salt
- `1 teaspoon garlic powder
- `1 teaspoon dried oregano
- `1 teaspoon paprika
- `1 sprig rosemary (leaves only)

Directions
1. Mix together the rub ingredients in a small bowl. Set aside.
2. Place the chicken on a clean cutting board. Ensure the cavity of the chicken is clean. Stuff the chicken cavity with the garlic, lemon, and rosemary.
3. Tie your chicken with twine if needed. Pat the chicken dry.
4. Drizzle the olive oil all over and coat the entire chicken with a brush.
5. Shake the rub on the chicken and rub in until the chicken is covered.
6. Using the rotisserie shaft, push through the chicken and attach the rotisserie forks.
7. If desired, place aluminum foil onto the drip pan. (It makes for easier clean-up!)
8. Select Air Fry, Super Convection of the oven, set the temperature to 375 F (190 degrees Celsius). Set the time to 40 minutes. Check the temp in 5 minute increments after the 40 minutes. Select Start to begin preheating.
9. Once the unit has preheated, place the prepared chicken with the rotisserie shaft into the oven.
10. At 40 minutes, check the temperature every 5 minutes until the chicken reaches 165 F (74 degrees Celsius) in the breast, or 165 F (85 degrees Celsius) in the thigh.
11. Once cooking is complete, remove the chicken using the rotisserie handle and, using hot pads or gloves, carefully remove the chicken from the shaft.
12. Let the chicken sit, covered, for 5 to 10 minutes.
13. Slice and serve.

Nutrition: Calories 127 Fat 0.5g Protein 26g

300. Cornish Hen with Montreal Chicken Seasoning

Preparation Time: 5 minutes
Cooking time: 30 minutes
Servings: 2

Ingredients:
- `2 tablespoons Montreal chicken seasoning
- `1 (1½- to 2-pound / 680- to 907-g) Cornish hen

Directions
1. Preheat the air fryer to 390 F (199 degrees Celsius).
2. Rub the seasoning over the chicken, coating it thoroughly.
3. Place the chicken in the Rotisserie Spit. Set the timer and Roast for 15 minutes.
4. Flip the chicken and roast for another 15 minutes.
5. Check that the chicken has reached an internal temperature of 165 F (74 degrees Celsius). Add cooking time if needed.

Nutrition: Calories 127 Fat 0.5g Protein 26g

FISH AND SEAFOOD

FISH AND SEAFOOD

301. Breaded Cod Sticks

Preparation Time: 5 minutes
Cooking Time: 20 minutes
Servings: 4

Ingredients:
- Large eggs (2)
- Milk (3 tbsp.)
- Breadcrumbs (2 cups)
- Almond flour (1 cup)
- Cod (1 lb.)

Directions:
1. Heat the Air Fryer at 350° Fahrenheit.
2. Prepare three bowls; one with the milk and eggs, one with the breadcrumbs (salt and pepper if desired), and another with almond flour.
3. Dip the sticks in the flour, egg mixture, and breadcrumbs.
4. Place in the basket and set the timer for 12 minutes. Toss the basket halfway through the cooking process. Serve with your favorite sauce.

Nutrition: Calories 254 Fat 14.2 g Carbs 5.7 g Protein 39.1 g;

302. Grilled Sardines

Preparation Time: 5 minutes
Cooking Time: 20 minutes
Servings: 4

Ingredients:
- 5 sardines
- Herbs of Provence

Direction:
1. Preheat the air fryer to 160C. Spray the basket and place your sardines in the basket of your fryer.
2. Set the timer for 14 minutes. After 7 minutes, remember to turn the sardines so that they are roasted on both sides.

Nutrition: Calories 189g Fat 10g Protein 22g Cholesterol 128mg

303. Zucchini with Tuna

Preparation Time: 10 minutes
Cooking Time: 30 minutes
Servings: 4

Ingredients:
- 4 medium zucchinis
- 120g of tuna in oil (canned) drained
- 30g grated cheese
- 1 tsp pine nuts
- Salt, pepper to taste

Direction:
1. Cut the zucchini in half laterally and empty it with a small spoon (set aside the pulp that will be used for filling); place them in the basket.
2. In a food processor, put the zucchini pulp, drained tuna, pine nuts and grated cheese. Mix everything until you get a homogeneous and dense mixture.
3. Fill the zucchini. Set the air fryer to 180C.
4. Simmer for 20 min. depending on the size of the zucchini. Let cool before serving

Nutrition: Calories 389 Carbs 10g Fat 29g Sugars 5g Protein 23g Cholesterol 40mg

304. Salmon With Crisped Topped Crumbs

Preparation Time: 10 minutes
Cooking time: 15 minutes
Servings: 2

Ingredients:
- 1-1/2 cups soft bread crumbs
- 2 tbsp. minced fresh parsley
- 1 tbsp. Minced fresh thyme or 1 tsp. dried thyme
- Two garlic cloves, minced
- 1 tsp. grated lemon zest
- 1/2 tsp. salt
- 1/4 tsp. lemon-pepper seasoning
- 1/4 tsp. paprika
- 1 tbsp. butter, melted
- Two salmon fillets (6 ounces each)

Directions
1. In a medium bowl, mix well bread crumbs, fresh parsley thyme, garlic, lemon zest, salt, lemon-pepper seasoning, and paprika.
2. Place the air fryer lid on; lightly grease the baking pan with cooking spray. Add salmon fillet with skin side down. Evenly sprinkle crumbs on the tops of salmon and place the baking pan in the oven.
3. Close the air fryer lid and cook at 390 F for 10 minutes.
4. Let it rest for 5 minutes.
5. Serve and enjoy.

Nutrition: Calories 331 Carbs 9.0g Protein 31.0g Fat 19.0g

305. Shrimp Casserole Louisiana Style

Preparation Time: 10 minutes
Cooking time: 35 minutes
Servings: 2

Ingredients:
- 3/4 cup uncooked instant rice
- 3/4 cup water
- 1/2-pound small shrimp, peeled and deveined
- 1 tbsp. butter
- 1/2 (4 ounces) can sliced mushrooms, drained
- 1/2 (8 ounces) container sour cream
- 1/3 cup shredded Cheddar cheese

Directions
1. Place the air fryer lid on, lightly grease the baking pan with cooking spray. Add rice, water, mushrooms, and butter. Cover with foil and place the baking pan in the oven.
2. Close the air fryer lid and cook at 360 F for 20 minutes.
3. Open foil cover, stir in shrimps, return foil and let it rest for 5 minutes.
4. Eradicate foil and stir in sour cream. Mix well and evenly spread rice. Top with cheese.
5. Cook for 7 minutes at 390 F until tops are lightly browned.
6. Serve and enjoy.

Nutrition: Calories 569 Carbs 38.5g Protein 31.8g Fat 31.9g

306. Caramelized Salmon Fillet

Preparation Time: 5 minutes
Cooking Time: 25 minutes
Servings: 4
Ingredients:
- 2 salmon fillets
- 60g cane sugar
- 4 tbsp. soy sauce
- 50g sesame seeds
- Unlimited Ginger

Direction:
1. Preheat the air fryer at 180C for 5 minutes.
2. Put the sugar and soy sauce in the basket.
3. Cook everything for 5 minutes.
4. In the meantime, wash the fish well, pass it through sesame to cover it completely and place it inside the tank and add the fresh ginger.
5. Cook for 12 minutes.
6. Turn the fish over and finish cooking for another 8 minutes.

Nutrition: Calories 569 Fat 14.9 g Carbs 40 g Sugars 27.6 g Protein 66.9 g Cholesterol 165.3 mg

307. Salmon Steak Grilled with Cilantro Garlic Sauce

Preparation Time: 10 minutes
Cooking time: 15 minutes
Servings: 2
Ingredients:
- Two salmon steaks
- Salt and pepper to taste
- 2 tbsp. vegetable oil
- Two cloves of garlic, minced
- 1 cup cilantro leaves
- ½ cup Greek yogurt
- 1 tsp. honey

Directions
1. Place the air fryer lid on and preheat the oven at 390 F.
2. Place the grill pan accessory in the grill.
3. Put seasoning to the salmon steaks with salt and pepper. Brush with oil.
4. Place on the grill pan, close the air fryer lid and grill for 15 minutes and make sure to flip halfway through the cooking time.
5. In a food processor, mix the garlic, cilantro leaves, yogurt, and honey—season with salt and pepper to taste. Pulse until smooth.
6. Serve the salmon steaks with the cilantro sauce.

Nutrition: Calories 485 Carbs 6.3g Protein 47.6g Fat 29.9g

308. Crusted Hake Fillets

Preparation Time: 10 minutes
Cooking Time: 12 minutes
Servings: 4
Ingredients:
- 1 egg
- 4 oz. breadcrumbs
- 2 tablespoons vegetable oil
- 4 (6-oz.) hake fillets
- 1 lemon, cut into wedges

Directions:
1. In a shallow bowl, whisk the egg. In another bowl, add the breadcrumbs and oil and mix until a crumbly mixture form. Dip fish fillets into the egg and then coat with the breadcrumb's mixture. Arrange the hake fillets in greased Air Fryer basket inside the Air fryer.
2. Put on the Air Fryer and cook on Air Fry mode for 12 minutes at 350 degrees F. Serve.

Nutrition: Calories: 244 Protein: 32g Carbs: 41g Fat: 4g

309. Deep Fried Prawns

Preparation Time: 15 minutes
Cooking Time: 20 minutes
Servings: 6
Ingredients:
- 12 prawns
- 2 eggs
- Flour to taste
- Breadcrumbs
- 1 tsp oil

Direction:
1. Remove the head of the prawns and shell carefully.
2. Pass the prawns first in the flour, then in the beaten egg and then in the breadcrumbs.
3. Preheat the air fryer for 1 minute at 150C.
4. Add the prawns and cook for 4 minutes. If the prawns are large, it will be necessary to cook 6 at a time.
5. Turn the prawns and cook for another 4 minutes.
6. They should be served with a yogurt or mayonnaise sauce.

Nutrition: Calories 2385.1 Fat 23 Carbs 52.3g Sugar 0.1g Protein 21.4g

310. Snow Peas With Ginger Salmon Steaks

Preparation time: 10 minutes
Cooking time: 8 minutes
Servings: 1
Ingredients:
- 1 tbsp. ginger, minced
- One salmon steak
- Salt and pepper, to taste
- 1 tsp. olive oil
- 1 tbsp. lemon juice
- ½ cup snow peas
- ½ small red bell pepper
- 1 tbsp. fresh cilantro, chopped

Directions
1. Preheat the air fryer up to 350 F /180 degrees Celsius.
2. Rub the ginger into the salmon steak and season with salt and pepper on both sides.
3. Drizzle over with the olive oil and lemon juice.
4. Place the fish in the air fryer baking pan with the snow peas, bell peppers, and fresh cilantro.
5. Season again with pepper.
6. Place the air fryer baking pan in the air fryer basket and set the timer for 8 minutes or until the salmon is has cooked.
7. Serve and enjoy!

Nutrition: Calories 340 Fat 20g Carbs 9g Protein 30g

311. Monkfish with Olives and Capers

Preparation Time: 25 minutes
Cooking Time: 40 minutes
Servings: 4
Ingredients:
- 1 monkfish
- 10 cherry tomatoes
- 50 g cailletier olives
- 5 capers

Direction:
1. Spread aluminum foil inside the air fryer basket and place the monkfish clean and skinless.
2. Add chopped tomatoes, olives, capers, oil, and salt.
3. Set the temperature to 160C.
4. Cook the monkfish for about 40 minutes.

Nutrition: Calories 404 Fat 29g Carbs 36g Sugars 7g Protein 24g Cholesterol 36mg

312. Kimchi Stuffed Squid

Preparation time: 5 minutes
Cooking time: 12 minutes
Servings: 2
Ingredients:
- 1 large squid, cleaned
- 1 cup kimchi

Directions
1. Preheat the air fryer up to 350 F /180 degrees Celsius.
2. Stuff the squid with the kimchi and secure it with a toothpick.
3. Place the squid in the air fryer basket and spray it with some cooking spray.
4. Turn the timer for 12 minutes or until the squid is cooked. Halfway through the cooking time, use kitchen tongs to rearrange the squid to be cooked evenly.
5. Serve and enjoy!

Nutrition: Calories 175 Fat 2g Carbs 30g Protein 9g

313. Hot Smoked Trout Frittata

Preparation time: 5 minutes
Cooking time: 25 minutes
Servings: 2
Ingredients:
- 1 onion, sliced
- 1 tablespoon olive oil
- 3 eggs
- 1 teaspoon horseradish sauce
- 1 tablespoon crème fraiche
- 1 hot smoked trout fillet
- Salt to taste
- Pepper to taste
- 2 tablespoons chopped fresh dill

Directions
1. Place a skillet over medium heat. Add oil and heat. Add onions and sauté until translucent. Transfer into the baking accessory or a small baking dish that can fit well into the air fryer.
2. Place the trout over the onion.
3. Whisk the eggs in a bowl. Add crème fraiche and horseradish and whisk well. Pour over the trout and onions. Sprinkle salt and pepper over it.
4. Air fry in a preheated air fryer at 320 F for 20 minutes or until set.
5. Sprinkle dill on top. Cut into wedges and serve.

Nutrition: Calories 485 Carbs 6.3g Protein 47.6g Fat 29.9g

314. Salmon with Pistachio Bark

Preparation Time: 10 minutes
Cooking Time: 30 minutes
Servings: 4
Ingredients:
- 600 g salmon fillet
- 50g pistachios
- Salt to taste

Direction:
1. Put the parchment paper on the bottom of the air fryer basket and place the salmon fillet in it (it can be cooked whole or already divided into four portions).
2. Cut the pistachios in thick pieces; grease the top of the fish, salt (little because the pistachios are already salted) and cover everything with the pistachios.
3. Set the air fryer to 180C and simmer for 25 minutes.

Nutrition: Calories 371.7 Fat 21.8 g Carbs 9.4 g Sugars 2.2g Protein 34.7 g Cholesterol 80.5 mg

315. Baked Butter Crayfish

Preparation time: 5 minutes
Cooking time: 25 minutes
Servings: 6
Ingredients:
- 6 crayfish, rinsed, scrubbed
- 6 small cubes butter
- 6 small cream cubes
- 2 teaspoons garlic powder
- ¼ teaspoon salt or to taste
- ¼ teaspoon pepper powder
- Cooked spaghetti with sauce of your choice, to serve (optional)

Directions
1. Place a sheet of aluminum foil on your countertop. Place the crayfish with its bottom side up.
2. Place butter and cream cubes all over the crayfish.
3. Season with salt, pepper and garlic powder.
4. Wrap the crayfish with sides of the foil. It should be well sealed.
5. Place the sealed crayfish packet in the air fryer basket.
6. Air fry in a preheated air fryer at 375 F for 18 to 20 minutes.
7. Serve with spaghetti and a spaghetti sauce of your choice if desired.

Nutrition: Calories 602 Fat 23.9g Carbs 46.5g Sugar 2.9g Protein 11.3g Sodium 886mg

316. Salmon Cakes

Preparation time: 5 minutes
Cooking time: 15 minutes
Servings: 4
Ingredients:
- 4 cans (7.5 ounces each) unsalted pink salmon with skin and bones, drained
- ¼ cup chopped, fresh dill
- 4 teaspoons Dijon mustard
- 2 large eggs
- 1 cup whole wheat panko breadcrumbs
- 4 tablespoons mayonnaise

- Pepper to taste
- Lemon wedges to serve

Directions
1. Remove any large bones and skin from the salmon and add into a bowl. Add rest of the ingredients and mix until well incorporated.
2. Divide the mixture into 4 equal portions and shape into patties.
3. Spray the cakes on both the sides with cooking spray and place in the air fryer basket.
4. Grill in a preheated air fryer at 350 F for about 7-12, depending on the desired doneness.
5. Flip sides half way through grilling.
6. Serve with a dip of your choice.

Nutrition: Cal 532 Fat 32g Carbs 3g Protein 28g Sugars 3g Fiber 6g

317. Sautéed Trout with Almonds

Preparation Time: 35 minutes
Cooking Time: 20 minutes
Servings: 4
Ingredients:
- 700 g salmon trout
- 15 black peppercorns
- Dill leaves to taste
- 30g almonds
- Salt to taste

Direction:
1. Cut the trout into cubes and marinate it for half an hour with the rest of the ingredients (except salt).
2. Cook in air fryer for 17 minutes at 160C. Pour a drizzle of oil and serve.

Nutrition: Calories 238 Fat 20g Carbs 11.5g Sugars 1g Protein4g Cholesterol 46mg

318. Grilled Fish with Light Mayo Sauce

Preparation time: 5 minutes
Cooking time: 35 minutes
Servings: 2
Ingredients:
- 2 fish fillets
- ½ teaspoon smoked paprika
- ½ teaspoon ground coriander
- 1 tablespoon vegetable oil
- ½ red bell pepper, deseeded
- Lemon juice to taste
- 2 tablespoon light mayonnaise
- ½ tablespoon olive oil
- Salt to taste
- Pepper to taste
- ½ teaspoon ground cumin
- ¼ teaspoon ground ginger
- 2 tablespoons chopped fresh cilantro

Directions
1. Brush bell pepper with oil and place in the air fryer basket.
2. Grill in a preheated air fryer at 350 F for about 12-15 minutes, until slightly charred.
3. Remove the pepper from the air fryer and place in a bowl. Cover the bowl with plastic wrap and let it rest for 10-12 minutes. Remove the pepper and peel off the skin. Place on your cutting board and chop into fine pieces.
4. Transfer into a bowl. Also add olive oil, mayonnaise, salt, pepper, cilantro and a little lemon juice into a bowl. Mix well. Cover and set aside for a while for the flavors to set in.
5. Add vegetable oil, coriander, cumin, lemon juice, pepper, paprika and salt into a bowl and stir well. Rub this mixture onto the fish fillets and place in the air fryer.
6. Grill in a preheated air fryer at 350 F for about 12-15 minutes, depending on the desired doneness.
7. Flip sides half way through grilling.
8. Serve with chilled mayonnaise sauce mixture.

Nutrition: Calories 485 Carbs 6.3g Protein 47.6g Fat 29.9g

319. Teriyaki Glazed Halibut Steak

Preparation time: 5 minutes
Cooking time: 35 minutes
Servings: 1-2
Ingredients:
- ½ pound halibut steak
- For the marinade:
- 1/3 cup low sodium soy sauce
- 2 tablespoons sugar
- 2 tablespoons orange juice
- 4 tablespoons mirin, (Japanese cooking wine)
- 1 tablespoon lime juice
- 1/8 teaspoon ground ginger
- 1/8 teaspoon chili flakes, crushed
- 1 garlic clove, smashed

Directions
1. Place a saucepan over medium heat. Add all the ingredients of the marinade into the saucepan and bring to a boil.
2. Boil until the marinade is reduced to half its original quantity. Turn off the heat and set aside to cool.
3. Place the halibut in a Ziploc bag.
4. Slowly pour marinade over the halibut. Seal the bag and shake to coat well.
5. Chill for about 30-40 minutes.
6. Place the halibut in the air fryer basket.
7. Air fry in a preheated air fryer at 390 F for 10- 12 minutes.
8. Place steak over rice.
9. Pour the remaining glaze over the halibut and serve hot with basil or mint chutney if desired.

Nutrition: Calories 485 Carbs 6.3g Protein 47.6g Fat 29.9g

320. Breaded Flounder

Preparation Time: 15 minutes
Cooking Time: 12 minutes
Servings: 3
Ingredients:
- 1 egg
- 1 cup dry breadcrumbs
- ¼ cup vegetable oil
- 3 (6-oz.) flounder fillets
- 1 lemon, sliced

Directions
1. In a shallow bowl, beat the egg
2. In another bowl, add the breadcrumbs and oil and mix until crumbly mixture is formed.
3. Dip flounder fillets into the beaten egg and then, coat with the breadcrumb mixture.
4. Press "Power Button" of Air Fry Oven and turn the dial to select the "Air Fry" mode.
5. Press the Time button and again turn the dial to set the Cooking Time to 12 minutes.

FISH AND SEAFOOD

6. Now push the Temp button and rotate the dial to set the temperature at 350 degrees F.
7. Press "Start/Pause" button to start.
8. When the unit beeps to show that it is preheated, open the lid.
9. Arrange the flounder fillets in greased "Air Fry Basket" and insert in the oven.
10. Plate with lemon slices and serve hot.

Nutrition: Calories 524 Total Fat 24.2 g Cholesterol 170 mg Sodium 463 mg Total Carbs 26.5 g Fiber 1.5 g Sugar 2.5 g Protein 47.8g

321. Southern Style Catfish with Green Beans

Preparation time: 5 minutes
Cooking time: 25 minutes
Servings: 1

Ingredients:
- 6 ounces fresh green beans, trimmed
- ½ teaspoon light brown sugar
- Salt to taste
- 2 tablespoons all-purpose flour
- 3 tablespoons panko bread crumbs
- 1 tablespoon mayonnaise
- ½ teaspoon dill pickle relish
- A pinch granulated sugar
- ¼ teaspoon crushed red pepper (optional)
- 1 catfish fillet
- 1 small egg, lightly beaten
- Pepper to taste
- 1 teaspoon minced fresh dill
- ¼ teaspoon apple cider vinegar
- Lemon wedges to serve

Directions
1. Add green beans, brown sugar, salt and crushed red pepper into a bowl. Toss well.
2. Spray some cooking spray generously over the beans and toss well.
3. Transfer into the air fryer basket.
4. Roast in a preheated air fryer at 400 F for 12 minutes or until brown and tender as well.
5. Remove from the air fryer and place in a bowl. Cover the bowl with foil and set aside.
6. Dredge catfish in flour. Shake to drop off excess flour. Next dip in egg. Shake to drop off excess egg. Finally dredge in panko breadcrumbs and place in the air fryer basket.
7. Spray the fillet with some cooking spray.
8. Roast in a preheated air fryer at 400 F for 8 minutes or until cooked through inside and crisp outside.
9. Remove from the air fryer and season with salt.
10. Meanwhile, add mayonnaise, vinegar, sugar, dill and dill pickle relish in a bowl and whisk until sugar dissolves completely.
11. Serve roasted catfish fillet with roasted green beans, lemon wedges and sauce.

Nutrition: Calories 331 Carbs 9.0g Protein 31.0g Fat 19.0g

322. Air Fryer Salmon

Preparation time: 5 minutes
Cooking time: 10 minutes
Servings: 2

Ingredients:
- ½ tsp. salt
- ½ tsp. garlic powder
- ½ tsp. smoked paprika
- Salmon

Directions
1. Preparing the Ingredients. Mix spices together and sprinkle onto salmon.
2. Place seasoned salmon into the Air fryer oven.
3. Air Frying. Close air fryer lid. Set temperature to 400 F, and set time to 10 minutes.

Nutrition: Calories 185 Fat 11g Protein 21g

323. Beer Potato Fish

Preparation time: 15 minutes
Cooking time: 45 minutes
Servings: 6

Ingredients:
- 1 pound fish fillet
- 4 medium size potatoes, peeled and diced
- 1 cup beer
- 1 red pepper sliced
- 1 tablespoon oil
- 1 tablespoon oyster flavored sauce
- 1 tablespoon rock candy
- 1 teaspoon salt

Directions
1. Preparing the Ingredients. Put all ingredients into your Air Fryer.
2. High pressure for 40 minutes. Lock the pressure cooking lid on the Air Fryer and then cook for 40 minutes. To get 40-minutes cook time, press "Pressure" button and use the Time Adjustment button to adjust the cook time to 40 minutes.
3. Pressure Release. Release the pressure using natural release method.
4. Finish the dish. Close the air fryer lid. Select Broil, and set the time to 5 minutes. Select Start to begin. Cook until top is browned. Then that is it! Simple, fast, delicious, retaining flavour and nutrition, consistent results all the time. Serve and Enjoy!

Nutrition: Calories 250.3 Fat 4.8g Sodium 1146.8mg Fiber 2.5g Protein 25.6g

324. Quick Paella

Preparation time: 7 minutes
Cooking time: 15 minutes
Servings: 4

Ingredients:
- 1 (10-ounce) package frozen cooked rice, thawed
- 1 (6-ounce) jar artichoke hearts, drained and chopped
- ¼ cup vegetable broth
- ½ teaspoon turmeric
- ½ teaspoon dried thyme
- 1 cup frozen cooked small shrimp
- ½ cup frozen baby peas
- 1 tomato, diced

Directions
1. Preparing the Ingredients. In a 6-by-6-by-2-inch pan, combine the rice, artichoke hearts, vegetable broth, turmeric, and thyme, and stir gently.
2. Air Frying. Place in the Air Fryer, close air fryer lid and bake for 8 to 9 minutes or until the rice is hot. Remove from the Air Fryer and gently stir in the shrimp, peas, and tomato. Cook for 5 to 8 minutes or until the shrimp and peas are hot and the paella is bubbling.

Nutrition: Calories 345 Fat 1g Fiber 4g Protein 18g

325. Sesame Seeds Coated Tuna

Preparation Time: 15 minutes
Cooking Time: 6 minutes
Servings: 2
Ingredients:
- 1 egg white
- ¼ cup white sesame seeds
- 1 tablespoon black sesame seeds
- Salt and ground black pepper, as required
- 2 (6-oz.) tuna steaks

Directions
1. In a bowl, beat the egg white.
2. In another bowl, mix together the sesame seeds, salt, and black pepper.
3. Dip the tuna steaks into egg white and then, coat with the sesame seeds mixture.
4. Press "Power Button" of Air Fry Oven and turn the dial to select the "Air Fry" mode.
5. Press the Time button and again turn the dial to set the Cooking Time to 6 minutes.
6. Now push the Temp button and rotate the dial to set the temperature at 400 degrees F.
7. Press "Start/Pause" button to start.
8. When the unit beeps to show that it is preheated, open the lid.
9. Arrange the tuna steaks in greased "Air Fry Basket" and insert in the oven.
10. Flip the tuna steaks once halfway through.
11. Serve hot.

Nutrition: Calories 450 Total Fat 21.9 g Cholesterol 83 mg Sodium 182 mg Total Carbs 5.4 g Fiber 2.7 g Sugar 0.2 g Protein 56.7 g

326. Tuna Veggie Stir-Fry

Preparation time: 5 minutes
Cooking time: 12 minutes
Servings: 4
Ingredients:
- 1 tablespoon olive oil
- 1 red bell pepper, chopped
- 1 cup green beans, cut into 2-inch pieces
- 1 onion, sliced
- 2 cloves garlic, sliced
- 2 tablespoons low-sodium soy sauce
- 1 tablespoon honey
- ½ pound fresh tuna, cubed

Directions
1. Preparing the Ingredients. In a 6-inch metal bowl, combine the olive oil, pepper, green beans, onion, and garlic.
2. Air Frying. Close air fryer lid. Cook in the Air Fryer for 4 to 6 minutes, stirring once, until crisp and tender. Add soy sauce, honey, and tuna, and stir. Cook for another 3 to 6 minutes, stirring once, until the tuna is cooked as desired. Tuna can be served rare or medium-rare, or you can cook it until well done.

Nutrition: Calories 187 Fat 8g Fiber 2g Protein 17g

327. Crab Legs

Preparation Time: 10 minutes
Cooking Time: 10 minutes
Servings: 4
Ingredients:
- 3 lb. crab legs
- ¼ cup salted butter, melted and divided
- ½ lemon, juiced
- ¼ tsp. garlic powder

Directions:
1. In a bowl, toss the crab legs and two tablespoons of the melted butter together. Place the crab legs in the basket of the fryer.
2. Cook at 400°F for fifteen minutes, giving the basket a good shake halfway through.
3. Combine the remaining butter with the lemon juice and garlic powder.
4. Crack open the cooked crab legs and remove the meat. Serve with the butter dip on the side, and enjoy!

Nutrition: Calories 27 Fat 19 Fiber 9 Carbs 18 Protein 12

328. Bang Bang Panko Breaded Fried Shrimp

Preparation time: 5 minutes
Cooking time: 8 minutes
Servings: 4
Ingredients:
- 1 tsp. paprika
- Montreal chicken seasoning
- ¾ cup panko bread crumbs
- ½ cup almond flour
- 1 egg white
- 1 pound raw shrimp (peeled and deveined)
- Bang Bang Sauce:
- ¼ cup sweet chili sauce
- tbsp. sriracha sauce
- 1/3 cup plain Greek yogurt

Directions
1. Preparing the Ingredients. Ensure your Air Fryer is preheated to 400 F.
2. Season all shrimp with seasonings.
3. Add flour to one bowl, egg white in another, and breadcrumbs to a third.
4. Dip seasoned shrimp in flour, then egg whites, and then breadcrumbs.
5. Spray coated shrimp with olive oil and add to Air Fryer basket.
6. Air Frying. Close air fryer lid. Set temperature to 400 F, and set time to 4 minutes. Cook 4 minutes, flip, and cook an additional 4 minutes.
7. To make the sauce, mix together all sauce ingredients until smooth.

Nutrition: Calories 212 Carbs 12g Fat 1g Sugar 0.5g Protein 37g

329. Crusty Pesto Salmon

Preparation Time: 5 minutes
Cooking Time: 12 minutes
Servings: 2

Ingredients:
- ¼ cup almonds, roughly chopped
- ¼ cup pesto
- 2 x 4-oz. salmon fillets
- 2 tbsp. unsalted butter, melted

Directions:
1. Mix the almonds and pesto together.
2. Place the salmon fillets in a round baking dish, roughly six inches in diameter.
3. Brush the fillets with butter, followed by the pesto mixture, ensuring to coat both the top and bottom. Put the baking dish inside the fryer.
4. Cook for twelve minutes at 390°F.
5. The salmon is ready when it flakes easily when prodded with a fork. Serve warm.

Nutrition: Calories 354 Fat 21 Carbs 23 Protein 19

330. Old Bay Crab Cakes

Preparation time: 10 minutes
Cooking time: 20 minutes
Servings: 4

Ingredients:
- slices dried bread, crusts removed
- Small amount of milk
- 1 tablespoon mayonnaise
- 1 tablespoon Worcestershire sauce
- 1 tablespoon baking powder
- 1 tablespoon parsley flakes
- 1 teaspoon Old Bay® Seasoning
- 1/4 teaspoon salt
- 1 egg
- 1 pound lump crabmeat

Directions
1. Preparing the Ingredients. Crush your bread over a large bowl until it is broken down into small pieces. Add milk and stir until bread crumbs are moistened. Mix in mayo and Worcestershire sauce. Add remaining ingredients and mix well. Shape into 4 patties.
2. Air Frying. Close air fryer lid. Cook at 360 F for 20 minutes, flip half way through.

Nutrition: Calories 165 Carbs 5.8g Fat 4.5g Protein 24g

331. Scallops and Spring Veggies

Preparation time: 10 minutes
Cooking time: 8 minutes
Servings: 4

Ingredients:
- ½ pound asparagus, ends trimmed, cut into 2-inch pieces
- 1 cup sugar snap peas
- 1 pound sea scallops
- 1 tablespoon lemon juice
- teaspoons olive oil
- ½ teaspoon dried thyme
- Pinch salt
- Freshly ground black pepper

Directions
1. Preparing the Ingredients. Place the asparagus and sugar snap peas in the Air Fryer basket.
2. Air Frying. Close air fryer lid. Cook for 2 to 3 minutes or until the vegetables are just starting to get tender.
3. Meanwhile, check the scallops for a small muscle attached to the side, and pull it off and discard.
4. In a medium bowl, toss the scallops with the lemon juice, olive oil, thyme, salt, and pepper. Place into the Air Fryer basket on top of the vegetables.
5. Air Frying. Close air fryer lid. Steam for 5 to 7 minutes, tossing the basket once during cooking time, until the scallops are just firm when tested with your finger and are opaque in the center, and the vegetables are tender. Serve immediately.

Nutrition: Calories 162 Carbs 10g Fat 4g Fiber 3g Protein 22g

332. Parmesan Shrimp

Preparation time: 5 minutes
Cooking time: 10 minutes
Servings: 4

Ingredients:
- tbsp. olive oil
- 1 tsp. onion powder
- 1 tsp. basil
- ½ tsp. oregano
- 1 tsp. pepper
- 2/3 cup grated parmesan cheese
- minced garlic cloves
- pounds of jumbo cooked shrimp (peeled/deveined)

Directions
1. Preparing the Ingredients. Mix all seasonings together and gently toss shrimp with mixture.
2. Air Frying. Spray olive oil into the Air Fryer basket and add seasoned shrimp. Close air fryer lid and cook 8-10 minutes at 350 F.
3. Squeeze lemon juice over shrimp right before devouring!

Nutrition: Calories 351 Carbs 11g Sugar 1g Protein 19g

333. Lemon-garlic Butter Lobster

Preparation time: 5 minutes
Cooking time: 10 minutes
Servings: 2

Ingredients:
- oz lobster tails
- 1 tsp garlic, minced
- 1 tbsp butter
- Salt and black pepper to taste
- ½ tbsp lemon Juice

Directions
1. Add all the ingredients to a food processor except for lobster and blend well. Wash lobster and halve using a meat knife; clean the skin of the lobster and cover with the marinade.
2. Preheat your Air Fryer Oven to 380 F on Air Fry function. Place the lobster in the cooking basket and fit in the baking tray; cook for 10 minutes. Serve with fresh herbs.

Nutrition: Calories 602 Fat 23.9g Carbs 46.5g Sugar 2.9g Protein 11.3g Sodium 886mg

334. Spicy Halibut

Preparation time: 5 minutes
Cooking time: 12 minutes
Servings: 4
Ingredients:
- 1 lb halibut fillets
- 1/2 tsp chili powder
- 1/2 tsp smoked paprika
- 1/4 cup olive oil
- 1/4 tsp garlic powder
- Pepper
- Salt

Directions
1. Fit the Air fryer oven with the rack in position
2. Place halibut fillets in a baking dish.
3. In a small bowl, mix oil, garlic powder, paprika, pepper, chili powder, and salt.
4. Brush fish fillets with oil mixture.
5. Set to bake at 425 F for 17 minutes. After 5 minutes place the baking dish in the preheated oven.
6. Serve and enjoy.

Nutrition: Calories 236 Fat 15.3g Carbs 0.5g Sugar 0.1g Protein 24g Cholesterol 36mg

335. Baked Tilapia

Preparation time: 5 minutes
Cooking time: 12 minutes
Servings: 4
Ingredients:
- 1 1/4 lbs tilapia fillets
- tsp onion powder
- tbsp olive oil
- 1/2 tsp garlic powder
- 1/2 tsp dried thyme
- 1/2 tsp oregano
- 1/2 tsp chili powder
- tbsp sweet paprika
- 1 tsp pepper
- 1/2 tsp salt

Directions
1. Fit the Air fryer oven with the rack in position
2. Brush fish fillets with oil and place in baking dish.
3. Mix together spices and sprinkle over the fish fillets.
4. Set to bake at 425 F for 15 minutes. After 5 minutes place the baking dish in the preheated oven.
5. Serve and enjoy.

Nutrition: Calories 195 Fat 8.9g Carbs 3.9g Sugar 0.9g Protein 27.2g Cholesterol 96mg

336. Tilapia Meunière With Vegetables

Preparation time: 10 minutes
Cooking time: 20 minutes
Servings: 4
Ingredients:
- 10 ounces (283g) Yukon Gold potatoes, sliced ¼-inch thick
- tablespoons unsalted butter, melted, divided
- 1 teaspoon kosher salt, divided
- (8-ounce / 227g) tilapia fillets
- ½ pound (227g) green beans, trimmed
- Juice of 1 lemon
- tablespoons chopped fresh parsley, for garnish

Directions
1. In a large bowl, drizzle the potatoes with 2 tablespoons of melted butter and ¼ teaspoon of kosher salt. Transfer the potatoes to the baking pan.
2. Slide the baking pan into Rack Position 2, select Roast, set temperature to 375 F (190ºC), and set time to 20 minutes.
3. Meanwhile, season both sides of the fillets with ½ teaspoon of kosher salt. Put the green beans in the medium bowl and sprinkle with the remaining ¼ teaspoon of kosher salt and 1 tablespoon of butter, tossing to coat.
4. After 10 minutes, remove from the oven and push the potatoes to one side. Put the fillets in the middle of the pan and add the green beans on the other side. Drizzle the remaining 2 tablespoons of butter over the fillets. Return the pan to the oven and continue cooking, or until the fish flakes easily with a fork and the green beans are crisp-tender.
5. When cooked, remove from the oven. Drizzle the lemon juice over the fillets and sprinkle the parsley on top for garnish. Serve hot.

Nutrition: Calories 195 Fat 8.9g Carbs 3.9g Sugar 0.9g Protein 27.2g Cholesterol 96mg

337. Foil Packet Salmon

Preparation Time: 5 minutes
Cooking Time: 10 minutes
Servings: 4
Ingredients:
- 2 x 4-oz. skinless salmon fillets
- 2 tbsp. unsalted butter, melted
- ½ tsp. garlic powder
- 1 medium lemon
- ½ tsp. dried dill

Directions:
1. Take a sheet of foil and cut into two squares measuring roughly 5" x 5". Lay each of the salmon fillets at the center of each piece. Brush both fillets with a tablespoon of bullet and season with a quarter-teaspoon of garlic powder.
2. Halve the lemon and grate the skin of one half over the fish. Cut four half-slices of lemon, using two to top each fillet. Season each fillet with a quarter-teaspoon of dill.
3. Fold the tops and sides of the aluminum foil over the fish to create a kind of packet. Place each one in the fryer.
4. Cook for twelve minutes at 400°F.
5. The salmon is ready when it flakes easily. Serve hot.

Nutrition: Calories 365 Fat 16 Carbs 18 Protein 23

338. Savory Cod Fish in Soy Sauce

Preparation time: 5 minutes
Cooking time: 20 minutes
Servings: 4
Ingredients:
- cod fish fillets
- tbsp chopped cilantro
- Salt to taste
- green onions, chopped
- 1 cup water
- slices of ginger
- tbsp light soy sauce
- tbsp oil
- 1 tsp dark soy sauce
- cubes rock sugar

Directions
1. Sprinkle the cod with salt and cilantro and drizzle with olive oil. Place in the cooking basket and fit in the baking tray; cook for 15 minutes at 360 F on Air Fry function.
2. Place the remaining ingredients in a frying pan over medium heat and cook for 5 minutes until sauce reaches desired consistency. Pour the sauce over the fish and serve.

Nutrition: Calories 190 Fat 1g Carbs 5g Protein 9g

339. Air Fryer Spicy Shrimp

Preparation time: 5 minutes
Cooking time: 6 minutes
Servings: 4

Ingredients:
- 1 lb shrimp, peeled and deveined
- 1/4 tsp chili powder
- 1 tsp dried oregano
- 1 tsp garlic powder
- 1 tsp onion powder
- tsp paprika
- 1/4 tsp cayenne
- tbsp olive oil
- Pepper
- Salt

Directions
1. Fit the Air fryer oven with the rack in position 2.
2. In a bowl, toss shrimp with remaining ingredients.
3. Add shrimp to the air fryer basket then place an air fryer basket in the baking pan.
4. Place a baking pan on the oven rack. Set to air fry at 400 F for 6 minutes.
5. Serve and enjoy.

Nutrition: Calories 204 Fat 9.2g Carbs 3.7g Sugar 0.5g Protein 26.2g Cholesterol 239mg

340. Simple Lemon Salmon

Preparation time: 5 minutes
Cooking time: 15 minutes
Servings: 2

Ingredients:
- salmon fillets
- Salt to taste
- Zest of a lemon

Directions
1. Spray the fillets with olive oil and rub them with salt and lemon zest. Line baking paper in a baking dish. Cook the fillets in your Air fryer oven for 10 minutes at 360 F on Air Fry, turning once.

Nutrition: Calories 185 Fat 11g Protein 21g

341. Foil Packet Lobster Tail

Preparation Time: 5 minutes
Cooking Time: 10 minutes
Servings: 4

Ingredients:
- 2 x 6-oz. lobster tail halves
- 2 tbsp. salted butter, melted
- ½ medium lemon, juiced
- ½ tsp. Old Bay seasoning
- 1 tsp. dried parsley

Directions:
1. Lay each lobster on a sheet of aluminum foil. Pour a light drizzle of melted butter and lemon juice over each one, and season with Old Bay.
2. Fold down the sides and ends of the foil to seal the lobster. Place each one in the fryer.
3. Cook at 375°F for twelve minutes.
4. Just before serving, top the lobster with dried parsley.

Nutrition: Calories 369 Fat 19 Carbs 25 Protein 28

342. Miso White Fish Fillets

Preparation time: 5 minutes
Cooking time: 10 minutes
Servings: 2

Ingredients:
- cod fish fillets
- tbsp brown sugar
- tbsp miso
- 1 tbsp garlic, chopped

Directions
1. Fit the Air fryer oven with the rack in position 2.
2. Add all ingredients to the zip-lock bag and marinate fish in the refrigerator overnight.
3. Place marinated fish fillets in the air fryer basket then place an air fryer basket in the baking pan.
4. Place a baking pan on the oven rack. Set to air fry at 350 F for 10 minutes.
5. Serve and enjoy.

Nutrition: Calories 9 Fat 0.1g Carbs 0.5g Protein 1.5g Sugars 0.3g Cholesterol 3mg

343. Pecan-crusted Catfish Fillets

Preparation time: 5 minutes
Cooking time: 12 minutes
Servings: 4

Ingredients:
- ½ cup pecan meal
- 1 teaspoon fine sea salt
- ¼ teaspoon ground black pepper
- (4-ounce / 113g) catfish fillets
- Avocado oil spray
- For Garnish (Optional):
- Fresh oregano
- Pecan halves

Directions
1. Spray the air fryer basket with avocado oil spray.
2. Combine the pecan meal, sea salt, and black pepper in a large bowl. Dredge each catfish fillet in the meal mixture, turning until well coated. Spritz the fillets with avocado oil spray, then transfer to the basket.
3. Put the air fryer basket on the baking pan and slide into Rack Position 2, select Air Fry, set temperature to 375 F (190 degrees Celsius), and set time to 12 minutes.
4. Flip the fillets halfway through the cooking time.
5. When cooking is complete, the fish should be cooked through and no longer translucent. Remove from the oven and sprinkle the oregano sprigs and pecan halves on top for garnish, if desired. Serve immediately.

Nutrition: Calories 331 Carbs 9.0g Protein 31.0g Fat 19.0g

344. Blackened Mahi Mahi

Preparation time: 5 minutes
Cooking time: 12 minutes
Servings: 4
Ingredients:
- mahi-mahi fillets
- 1 tsp cumin
- 1 tsp paprika
- 1/2 tsp cayenne pepper
- 1 tsp oregano
- 1 tsp garlic powder
- 1 tsp onion powder
- 1/2 tsp pepper
- tbsp olive oil
- 1/2 tsp salt

Directions
1. Fit the Air fryer oven with the rack in position
2. Brush fish fillets with oil and place them into the baking dish.
3. Mix together the remaining ingredients and sprinkle over fish fillets.
4. Set to bake at 450 F for 17 minutes. After 5 minutes place the baking dish in the preheated oven.
5. Serve and enjoy.

Nutrition: Calories 189 Carbs 2.1g Sugar 0.5g Protein 19.4g Fat 11.7g Cholesterol 86mg

345. Avocado Shrimp

Preparation Time: 5 minutes
Cooking Time: 10 minutes
Servings: 4
Ingredients:
- ½ cup onion, chopped
- 2 lb. shrimp
- 1 tbsp. seasoned salt
- 1 avocado
- ½ cup pecans, chopped

Directions:
1. Pre-heat the fryer at 400°F.
2. Put the chopped onion in the basket of the fryer and spritz with some cooking spray. Leave to cook for five minutes.
3. Add the shrimp and set the timer for a further five minutes. Sprinkle with some seasoned salt, then allow to cook for an additional five minutes.
4. During these last five minutes, halve your avocado and remove the pit. Cube each half, then scoop out the flesh.
5. Take care when removing the shrimp from the fryer. Place it on a dish and top with the avocado and the chopped pecans.

Nutrition: Calories 384 Fat 24 Carbs 13 Protein 39

346. Cod Fish Nuggets

Preparation Time: 5 minutes
Cooking Time: 20 minutes
Servings: 4
Ingredients:
1. Cod fillet (1 lb.)
2. Eggs (3)
3. Olive oil (4 tbsp.)
4. Almond flour (1 cup)
5. Gluten-free breadcrumbs (1 cup)

Directions:
- Warm the Air Fryer at 390° Fahrenheit.
- Slice the cod into nuggets.
- Prepare three bowls. Whisk the eggs in one. Combine the salt, oil, and breadcrumbs in another. Sift the almond flour into the third one.
- Cover each of the nuggets with the flour, dip in the eggs, and the breadcrumbs.
- Arrange the nuggets in the basket and set the timer for 20 minutes.
- Serve the fish with your favorite dips or sides.

Nutrition: Calories 334 Fat 10g Carbs 8 g Protein 32g;

347. Steamed Salmon and Sauce

Preparation time: 5 minutes
Cooking time: 10 minutes
Servings: 2
Ingredients:
- 1 cup Water
- x 6 oz Fresh Salmon
- Tsp Vegetable Oil
- A Pinch of Salt for Each Fish
- ½ cup Plain Greek Yogurt
- ½ cup Sour Cream
- Tbsp Finely Chopped Dill (Keep a bit for garnishing)
- A Pinch of Salt to Taste

Directions
1. Pour the water into the tray of the air fryer oven and start heating to 285 F.
2. Drizzle oil over the fish and spread it. Salt the fish to taste.
3. Now pop it into the air fryer oven for 10 min.
4. In the meantime, mix the yogurt, cream, dill and a bit of salt to make the sauce. When the fish is done, serve with the sauce and garnish with sprigs of dill..

Nutrition: Calories 185 Fat 11g Protein 21g

348. Indian Fish Fingers

Preparation time: 35 minutes
Cooking time: 15 minutes
Servings: 4
Ingredients:
- 1/2 pound fish fillet
- 1 tablespoon finely chopped fresh mint leaves or any fresh herbs
- 1/3 cup bread crumbs
- 1 teaspoon ginger garlic paste or ginger and garlic powders
- 1 hot green chili finely chopped
- 1/2 teaspoon paprika
- Generous pinch of black pepper
- Salt to taste
- 3/4 tablespoons lemon juice
- 3/4 teaspoons garam masala powder
- 1/3 teaspoon rosemary
- 1 egg

Directions
1. Start by removing any skin on the fish, washing, and patting dry. Cut the fish into fingers.
2. In a medium bowl mix together all ingredients except for fish, mint, and bread crumbs. Bury the fingers in the mixture and refrigerate for 30 minutes.
3. Remove from the bowl from the fridge and mix in mint leaves.

4. In a separate bowl beat the egg, pour bread crumbs into a third bowl. Dip the fingers in the egg bowl then toss them in the bread crumbs bowl.
5. Pour into the Oven rack/basket. Place the Rack on the middle-shelf of the Air fryer oven. Set temperature to 360 F, and set time to 15 minutes, toss the fingers halfway through.

Nutrition: Calories 187 Fat 7g Protein 11g Fiber 1g

349. Lemony Tuna

Preparation time: 10 minutes
Cooking time: 10 minutes
Servings: 4
Ingredients:
- (6-ounce) cans water packed plain tuna
- teaspoons Dijon mustard
- ½ cup breadcrumbs
- 1 tablespoon fresh lime juice
- tablespoons fresh parsley, chopped
- 1 egg
- air fryer of hot sauce
- tablespoons canola oil
- Salt and freshly ground black pepper, to taste

Directions
1. Drain most of the liquid from the canned tuna.
2. In a bowl, add the fish, mustard, crumbs, citrus juice, parsley and hot sauce and mix till well combined. Add a little canola oil if it seems too dry. Add egg, salt and stir to combine. Make the patties from tuna mixture. Refrigerate the tuna patties for about 2 hours.
3. Pour into the Oven rack/basket. Place the Rack on the middle-shelf of the Air fryer oven. Set temperature to 355 F, and set time to 12 minutes.

Nutrition: Calories 480 Fat 37g Carbs 9g Protein 49g

350. Grilled Soy Salmon Fillets

Preparation time: 5 minutes
Cooking time: 8 minutes
Servings: 4
Ingredients:
- salmon fillets
- 1/4 teaspoon ground black pepper
- 1/2 teaspoon cayenne pepper
- 1/2 teaspoon salt
- 1 teaspoon onion powder
- 1 tablespoon fresh lemon juice
- 1/2 cup soy sauce
- 1/2 cup water
- 1 tablespoon honey
- tablespoons extra-virgin olive oil

Directions
1. Firstly, pat the salmon fillets dry using kitchen towels. Season the salmon with black pepper, cayenne pepper, salt, and onion powder.
2. To make the marinade, combine together the lemon juice, soy sauce, water, honey, and olive oil. Marinate the salmon for at least 2 hours in your refrigerator.
3. Arrange the fish fillets on a grill basket in your air fryer oven.
4. Bake at 330 F for 8 to 9 minutes, or until salmon fillets are easily flaked with a fork.
5. Work with batches and serve warm.

Nutrition: Calories 185 Fat 11g Protein 21g

351. Flying Fish

Preparation time: 5 minutes
Cooking time: 12 minutes
Servings: 6
Ingredients:
- Tbsp Oil
- 3–4 oz Breadcrumbs
- 1 Whisked Whole Egg in a Saucer/Soup Plate
- Fresh Fish Fillets
- Fresh Lemon (For serving)

Directions
1. Preheat the air fryer to 350 F. Mix the crumbs and oil until it looks nice and loose.
2. Dip the fish in the egg and coat lightly, then move on to the crumbs. Make sure the fillet is covered evenly.
3. Cook in the air fryer oven basket for roughly 12 minutes – depending on the size of the fillets you are using.
4. Serve with fresh lemon and chips to complete the duo.

Nutrition: Calories 480 Fat 37g Carbs 9g Protein 49g

352. Spicy Mackerel

Preparation Time: 5 minutes
Cooking Time: 10 minutes
Servings: 4
Ingredients:
- 2 mackerel fillets
- 2 tbsp. red chili flakes
- 2 tsp. garlic, minced
- 1 tsp. lemon juice

Directions:
1. Season the mackerel fillets with the red pepper flakes, minced garlic, and a drizzle of lemon juice. Allow to sit for five minutes.
2. Preheat your fryer at 350°F.
3. Cook the mackerel for five minutes, before opening the drawer, flipping the fillets, and allowing to cook on the other side for another five minutes.
4. Plate the fillets, making sure to spoon any remaining juice over them before serving.

Nutrition: Calories 393 Fat 12 Carbs 13 Protein 35

353. Salmon Noodles

Preparation time: 5 minutes
Cooking time: 16 minutes
Servings: 4
Ingredients:
- 1 Salmon Fillet
- 1 Tbsp Teriyaki Marinade
- ½ Ozs Soba Noodles, cooked and drained
- Ozs Firm Tofu
- Ozs Mixed Salad
- 1 Cup Broccoli
- Olive Oil
- Salt and Pepper to taste

Directions
1. Season the salmon with salt and pepper to taste, then coat with the teriyaki marinate. Set aside for 15 minutes
2. Preheat the air fryer oven at 350 F, then cook the salmon for 8 minutes.
3. Whilst the air fryer is cooking the salmon, start slicing the tofu into small cubes.

4. Next, slice the broccoli into smaller chunks. Drizzle with olive oil.
5. Once the salmon is cooked, put the broccoli and tofu into the air fryer oven tray for 8 minutes.
6. Plate the salmon and broccoli tofu mixture over the soba noodles. Add the mixed salad to the side and serve.

Nutrition: Calories 185 Fat 11g Protein 21g

354. Fried Calamari

Preparation time: 8 minutes
Cooking time: 7 minutes
Servings: 6-8

Ingredients:
- ½ tsp. salt
- ½ tsp. Old Bay seasoning
- 1/3 cup plain cornmeal
- ½ cup semolina flour
- ½ cup almond flour
- 5-6 cup olive oil
- 1 ½ pounds baby squid

Directions
1. Rinse squid in cold water and slice tentacles, keeping just ¼-inch of the hood in one piece.
2. Combine 1-2 pinches of pepper, salt, Old Bay seasoning, cornmeal, and both flours together. Dredge squid pieces into flour mixture and place into the air fryer basket.
3. Spray liberally with olive oil. Cook 15 minutes at 345 F till coating turns a golden brown.

Nutrition: Calories 211 Carbs 55g Fat 6g Protein 21g

355. Mustard-Crusted Fish Fillets

Preparation time: 5 minutes
Cooking time: 8 to 11 minutes
Servings: 4

Ingredients:
- teaspoons low-sodium yellow mustard
- 1 tablespoon freshly squeezed lemon juice
- (3.5-ounce) sole fillets
- ½ teaspoon dried thyme
- ½ teaspoon dried marjoram
- ⅛ teaspoon freshly ground black pepper
- 1 slice low-sodium whole-wheat bread, crumbled
- teaspoons olive oil

Directions:
1. 1 In a small bowl, mix the mustard and lemon juice. Spread this evenly over the fillets. Place them in the air fryer basket.
2. In another small bowl, mix the thyme, marjoram, pepper, bread crumbs, and olive oil. Mix until combined.
3. Gently but firmly press the spice mixture onto the top of each fish fillet.
4. Bake for 8 to 11 minutes at 320 F, or until the fish reaches an internal temperature of at least 145 degrees Fahrenheit on a meat thermometer and the topping is browned and crisp. Serve immediately.

Nutrition: Calories 142 Fat 4g Saturated Fat 1g Protein 20g Carbs 5g Sodium 140g Fiber 1g Sugar 1g

356. Fish and Vegetable Tacos

Preparation time: 15 minutes
Cooking time: 9 to 12 minutes
Servings: 4

Ingredients:
- 1 pound white fish fillets, such as sole or co
- teaspoons olive oil
- tablespoons freshly squeezed lemon juice, divided
- 1½ cups chopped red cabbage
- 1 large carrot, grated
- ½ cup low-sodium salsa
- ⅓ cup low-fat Greek yogurt
- soft low-sodium whole-wheat tortillas

Directions:
1. 1 Brush the fish with the olive oil and sprinkle with 1 -tablespoon of lemon juice. Air-fry in the air fryer basket for 9 to 12 minutes at 390 F, or until the fish just flakes when tested with a fork.
2. Meanwhile, in a medium bowl, stir together the remaining 2 tablespoons of lemon juice, the red cabbage, carrot, salsa, and yogurt.
3. When the fish is cooked, remove it from the air fryer basket and break it up into large pieces.
4. Offer the fish, tortillas, and the cabbage mixture, and let each person assemble a taco.

Nutrition: Calories 209 Fat 3g Protein 18g Carbs 30g Sodium 116g Fiber 1g Sugar 4g

357. Lighter Fish and Chips

Preparation time: 10 minutes
Cooking time: 11 to 15 minutes (chips); 10 to 14 minutes (cod fillets)
Servings: 4

Ingredients:
- russet potatoes, peeled, thinly sliced, rinsed, and patted dry
- 1 egg white
- 1 tablespoon freshly squeezed lemon juice
- ⅓ cup ground almonds
- slices low-sodium whole-wheat bread, finely crumbled
- ½ teaspoon dried basil
- (4-ounce) cod fillets

Directions:
1. 1 Preheat the oven to warm.
2. Put the potato slices in the air fryer basket and air-fry for 11 to 15 minutes at 390 F, or until crisp and brown. With tongs, turn the fries twice during cooking.
3. Meanwhile, in a shallow bowl, beat the egg white and lemon juice until frothy.
4. On a plate, mix the almonds, bread crumbs, and basil.
5. One at a time, dip the fillets into the egg white mixture and then into the almond–bread crumb mixture to coat. Place the coated fillets on a wire rack to dry while the fries cook.
6. When the potatoes are done, transfer them to a baking sheet and keep warm in the oven on low heat.
7. Air-fry the fish in the air fryer basket for 10 to 14 minutes, or until the fish reaches an internal temperature of at least 140 F on a meat thermometer and the coating is browned and crisp. Serve immediately with the potatoes.

Nutrition: Calories 247 Fat 5g Protein 27g Carbs 25g Sodium 131g Fiber 3g Sugar 3g

358. Snapper with Fruit

Preparation time: 15 minutes
Cooking time: 9 to 13 minutes
Servings: 4

Ingredients:
- (4-ounce) red snapper fillets
- teaspoons olive oil
- nectarines, halved and pitted
- plums, halved and pitted
- 1 cup red grapes
- 1 tablespoon freshly squeezed lemon juice
- 1 tablespoon honey
- ½ teaspoon dried thyme

Directions:
1. Put the red snapper in the air fryer basket and drizzle with the olive oil. Air-fry for 4 minutes at 390 F.
2. Remove the basket and add the nectarines and plums. Scatter the grapes over all.
3. Drizzle with the lemon juice and honey and sprinkle with the thyme.
4. Return the basket to the air fryer and air-fry for 5 to 9 minutes more, or until the fish flakes when tested with a fork and the fruit is tender. Serve immediately.

Nutrition: Calories 245 Fat 4g Saturated Fat 1g Protein 25g Carbs 28g Sodium 73g Fiber 3g Sugar 24g

359. Thyme Scallops

Preparation Time: 5 minutes
Cooking Time: 10 minutes
Servings: 4

Ingredients:
- 1 lb. scallops
- Salt and pepper
- ½ tbsp. butter
- ½ cup thyme, chopped

Directions:
1. Wash the scallops and dry them completely. Season with pepper and salt, then set aside while you prepare the pan.
2. Grease a foil pan in several spots with the butter and cover the bottom with the thyme. Place the scallops on top.
3. Pre-heat the fryer at 400°F and set the rack inside.
4. Place the foil pan on the rack and allow to cook for seven minutes.
5. Take care when removing the pan from the fryer and transfer the scallops to a serving dish. Spoon any remaining butter in the pan over the fish and enjoy.

Nutrition: Calories 454 Fat 18 Carbs 27 Protein 34

360. Tuna and Fruit Kebabs

Preparation time: 15 minutes
Cooking time: 8 to 12 minutes
Servings: 4

Ingredients:
- 1 pound tuna steaks, cut into 1-inch cubes
- ½ cup canned pineapple chunks, drained, juice reserved
- ½ cup large red grapes
- 1 tablespoon honey
- teaspoons grated fresh ginger
- 1 teaspoon olive oil
- Pinch cayenne pepper

Directions:
1. Thread the tuna, pineapple, and grapes on 8 bamboo or 4 metal skewers that fit in the air fryer.
2. In a small bowl, whisk the honey, 1 tablespoon of reserved pineapple juice, the ginger, olive oil, and cayenne. Brush this mixture over the kebabs. Let them stand for 10 minutes.
3. Grill the kebabs for 8 to 12 minutes at 370 F, or until the tuna reaches an internal temperature of at least 145 F on a meat thermometer, and the fruit is tender and glazed, brushing once with the remaining sauce. Discard any remaining marinade. Serve immediately.

Nutrition: Calories 181 Fat 2g Protein 18g Carbs 13g Sodium 43g Fiber 1g Sugar 12g

361. Asian Swordfish

Preparation time: 10 minutes
Cooking time: 6 to 11 minutes
Servings: 4

Ingredients:
- (4-ounce) swordfish steaks
- ½ teaspoon toasted sesame oil
- 1 jalapeño pepper, finely minced
- garlic cloves, grated
- 1 tablespoon grated fresh ginger
- ½ teaspoon Chinese five-spice powder
- ⅛ teaspoon freshly ground black pepper
- tablespoons freshly squeezed lemon juice

Directions:
1. Place the swordfish steaks on a work surface and drizzle with the sesame oil.
2. In a small bowl, mix the jalapeño, garlic, ginger, five-spice powder, pepper, and lemon juice. Rub this mixture into the fish and let it stand for 10 minutes.
3. Roast the swordfish in the air fryer for 6 to 11 minutes at 380 F, or until the swordfish reaches an internal temperature of at least 140 F on a meat thermometer. Serve immediately.

Nutrition: Calories 187 Fat 6g Saturated Fat 1g Protein 29g Carbs 2g Sodium 132g Sugar 1g

362. Tilapia & Chives Sauce

Preparation Time: 5 minutes
Cooking Time: 10 minutes
Servings: 4

Ingredients:
- 4 medium tilapia fillets
- 2 tsp. honey
- Juice from 1 lemon
- 2 tbsp. chives; chopped
- Salt and black pepper to the taste

Directions:
1. Flavor fish with salt and pepper, spray with cooking spray, place in preheated air fryer 350 °F and cook for 8 minutes; flipping halfway.
2. Meanwhile; in a bowl, mix honey, salt, pepper, chives and lemon juice and whisk really well. Divide air fryer fish on plates, drizzle yogurt sauce all over and serve right away.

Nutrition: Calories: 261 Fat: 8 Fiber: 18 Carbs: 24 Protein: 21

363. Salmon on Bed of Fennel and Carrot

Preparation time: 15 minutes
Cooking time: 13 to 14 minutes
Servings: 4

Ingredients:
- 1 fennel bulb, thinly sliced
- 1 large carrot, peeled and sliced
- 1 small onion, thinly sliced
- ¼ cup low-fat sour cream
- ¼ teaspoon coarsely ground pepper
- (5 ounce) salmon fillets

Directions:
1. 1 Combine the fennel, carrot, and onion in a bowl and toss.
2. Put the vegetable mixture into a 6-inch metal pan. Roast in the air fryer for 4 minutes at 400 F or until the vegetables are crisp tender.
3. Remove the pan from the air fryer. Stir in the sour cream and sprinkle the vegetables with the pepper.
4. Top with the salmon fillets.
5. Return the pan to the air fryer. Roast for another 9 to 10 minutes or until the salmon just barely flakes when tested with a fork.

Nutrition: Calories 253 Fat 9g Saturated Fat 1g Protein 31g Carbs 12g Sodium 115g Fiber 3g Sugar 5g

364. Scallops with Green Vegetables

Preparation time: 15 minutes
Cooking time: 8 to 11 minutes
Servings: 4

Ingredients:
- 1 cup green beans
- 1 cup frozen peas
- 1 cup frozen chopped broccoli
- teaspoons olive oil
- ½ teaspoon dried basil
- ½ teaspoon dried oregano
- ounces sea scallops

Directions:
1. 1 In a large bowl, toss the green beans, peas, and broccoli with the olive oil. Place in the air fryer basket. Air-fry for 4 to 6 minutes, or until the vegetables are crisp-tender.
2. Remove the vegetables from the air fryer basket and sprinkle with the herbs. Set aside.
3. In the air fryer basket, put the scallops and air-fry for 4 to 5 minutes at 400 F, or until the scallops are firm and reach an internal temperature of just 145 F on a meat thermometer.
4. Toss scallops with the vegetables and serve immediately.

Nutrition: Calories 124 Fat 3g Protein 14g Carbs 11g Sodium 56g Fiber 3g Sugar 5g

365. Ranch Flavored Tilapia

Preparation Time: 15 minutes
Cooking Time: 13 minutes
Servings: 4

Ingredients:
- ¾ cup cornflakes, crushed
- 1-ounce dry ranch mix
- and ½ tablespoons vegetable oil
- whole eggs
- pieces 6 ounces each tilapia fillets

Directions:
1. Take a shallow bowl, crack in eggs and beat them well
2. Take another bowl and add cornflakes, ranch dressing
3. oil and mix well until you have a crumbly ix
4. Dip fish fillets into the egg
5. coat well with bread crumbs mixture
6. Press "Power Button" on your Air Fryer and select "Air Fry" mode
7. Press the Time Button and set time to 13 minutes
8. Push Temp Button and set temp to 356 degrees F
9. Press the "Start/Pause" button and start the device
10. Once the appliance beeps to indicated that it is pre-heated, arrange prepared tilapia into Air Fryer basket, insert into oven
11. Let it cook until done, serve, and enjoy!

Nutrition: Calories: 267 Fat: 12 g Saturated Fat: 3 g Carbs: 5 g Fiber: 0.2 g Sodium: 168 mg Protein: 34 g

366. Butter Up Salmon

Preparation Time: 10 minutes
Cooking Time: 10 minutes
Servings: 2

Ingredients:
- pieces 6 ounces salmon fillets
- Salt and pepper to taste
- tablespoon butter, melted

Directions:
1. Season salmon fillet well with salt and pepper, coat them with butter
2. Press "Power Button" on your Air Fryer and select "Air Fry" mode
3. Press the Time Button and set time to 20 minutes
4. Push Temp Button and set temp to 320 degrees F
5. Press the "Start/Pause" button and start the device
6. Once the appliance beeps to indicated that it is pre-heated, transfer fillets to a greased Air Fryer basket and push into oven
7. Serve and enjoy!

Nutrition: Calories: 270 Fat: 16 g Saturated Fat: 5.2 g Carbs: 0 g Sodium: 193 mg Protein: 33 g

367. Tasty Grilled Red Mullet

Preparation Time: 5 minutes
Cooking Time: 10 minutes
Servings: 8

Ingredients:
- 8 whole red mullets, gutted and scales removed
- Salt and pepper to taste
- Juice from 1 lemon
- 1 tablespoon olive oil

Directions:
1. Preheat the air fryer at 390F.
2. Place the grill pan attachment in the air fryer.
3. Season the red mullet with salt, pepper, and lemon juice.
4. Brush with olive oil.
5. Grill for 15 minutes.

Nutrition: Calories: 152 Carbs: 0.9g Protein: 23.1g Fat: 6.2g

368. Hearty Spiced Salmon

Preparation Time: 10 minutes
Cooking Time: 11 minutes
Servings: 2
Ingredients:
- teaspoon smoked paprika
- 1 teaspoon cayenne pepper
- 1 teaspoon onion powder
- 1 teaspoon garlic powder
- Salt and pepper to taste
- pieces 6 ounces salmon fillets
- teaspoons olive oil

Directions:
1. Take a small bowl and add spices, mix them well
2. Drizzle salmon fillets with oil, rub the fillets with spice mixture
3. Press "Power Button" on your Air Fryer and select "Air Fry" mode
4. Press the Time Button and set time to 11 minutes
5. Push Temp Button and set temp to 390 degrees F
6. Press the "Start/Pause" button and start the device
7. Once the appliance beeps to indicated that it is pre-heated, arrange salmon fillets in the Air Fryer cooking basket
8. Push into Air Fryer Oven and cook until the timer runs out
9. Serve and enjoy!

Nutrition: Calories: 280 Fat: 15 g Saturated Fat: 2 g Carbs: 3 g Fiber: 1 g Sodium: 0.8 mg Protein: 33 g

369. Cajun Shrimp

Preparation Time: 10 minutes
Cooking Time: 7 minutes
Servings: 4
Ingredients:
- and ¼ pound tiger shrimp, about 16-20 pieces
- ¼ teaspoon cayenne pepper
- ½ teaspoon old bay seasoning
- ¼ teaspoon smoked paprika
- 1 pinch of salt
- 1 tablespoon olive oil

Directions:
1. Preheat your Air Fryer to 390 degrees F in "AIR FRY" mode
2. Take a mixing bowl and add ingredients (except shrimp), mix well
3. Dip the shrimp into spice mixture and oil
4. Transfer the prepared shrimp to your cooking basket and cook for 5 minutes
5. Serve and enjoy!

Nutrition: Calories: 180 Fat: 2 g Saturated Fat: 1 g Carbs: 5 g Sodium: 970 mg Protein: 23 g

370. Air Fried Dragon Shrimp

Preparation Time: 10 minutes
Cooking Time: 10 minutes
Servings: 4
Ingredients:
- 1-pound raw shrimp, peeled and deveined
- A ½ cup of soy sauce
- eggs
- tablespoons olive oil
- cup yellow onion, diced
- ¼ cup flour
- ½ teaspoon red pepper, ground
- ½ teaspoon ginger, grounded

Directions:
1. Preheat your air fryer to 350 degrees F in "AIR FRY" mode
2. Add all the ingredients except for the shrimp to make the batter
3. Set it aside for 10 minutes
4. Dip each shrimp into the batter to coat all sides
5. Place them on the air fryer basket
6. Cook for 10 minutes
7. Serve and enjoy!

Nutrition: Calories: 600 Fat: 6 g Saturated Fat: 2 g Carbs: 59 g Fiber: 8 g Sodium: 690 mg Protein: 31 g

371. Garlicky-Grilled Turbot

Preparation Time: 5 minutes
Cooking Time: 20 minutes
Servings: 2
Ingredients:
- 2 whole turbot, scaled and head removed
- Salt and pepper to taste
- 1 clove of garlic, minced
- ½ cup chopped celery leaves
- 2 tablespoons olive oil

Directions:
1. Preheat the air fryer at 390F.
2. Place the grill pan attachment in the air fryer.
3. Flavor the turbot with salt, pepper, garlic, and celery leaves.
4. Brush with oil.
5. Cook in the grill pan for 20 minutes until the fish becomes flaky.

Nutrition: Calories: 269 Carbs: 3.3g Protein: 66.2g Fat: 25.6g

372. Crispy Paprika Fish Fillets

Preparation time: 5 minutes
Cooking time: 15 minutes
Servings: 4
Ingredients
- 1/2 cup seasoned breadcrumbs
- tablespoon balsamic vinegar
- 1/2 teaspoon seasoned salt
- 1 teaspoon paprika
- 1/2 teaspoon ground black pepper
- 1 teaspoon celery seed
- fish fillets halved
- 1 egg
- beaten

Directions:
1. Preparing the Ingredients. Add the breadcrumbs, vinegar, salt, paprika, ground black pepper, and celery seeds to your food processor. Process for about 30 seconds.
2. Coat the fish fillets with the beaten egG
3. then, coat them with the breadcrumbs mixture.
4. Air Frying. Cook at 350 degrees F for about 15 minutes.

Nutrition: Calories 210 Fat 10g Carbs 21g Protein 9g

373. Fish Tacos

Preparation Time: 10 Minutes
Cooking Time: 9 Minutes
Servings: 4
Ingredients:
- cod fillets, cut into 1-inch cubes
- Salt and black pepper to taste
- ½ lime, juiced
- ½ cup all-purpose flour
- large egg
- lightly beaten
- 1 cup panko breadcrumbs
- Olive oil for brushing
- medium corn tortillas
- ½ cup shredded red cabbage
- 1 medium avocado, pitted, peeled, and chopped
- tbsp chopped fresh cilantro
- 1 cup sour cream
- Lime wedges for serving

Directions:
1. Insert the dripping pan in the bottom part of the air fryer and preheat the oven at Air Fry mode at 400 F for 2 to 3 minutes. Lightly brush the rotisserie basket with some olive oil and set aside.
2. Season the fish with salt, black pepper, and lime juice.
3. Pour the flour onto a plate and the breadcrumbs onto another. Dredge the fish pieces lightly on the flour, then in the eggs, and the breadcrumbs. Put the coated fish in the rotisserie basket and fit into the oven using the rotisserie lift.
4. Set the timer for 9 minutes or until the fish pieces are golden brown.
5. To serve, lay the tortillas individually on a clean, flat surface and add the fish pieces. Top with the cabbage, avocado, cilantro, sour cream, and lime wedges.
6. Serve immediately.

Nutrition: Calories 275 Fat 11.34g Carbs 19.39g Fiber 25g Protein 23.37g Sugar 1.5g Sodium 422mg

374. Bass Filet In Coconut Sauce

Preparation Time: 20 minutes
Cooking Time: 15 minutes
Servings: 4
Ingredients:
- ¼ cup coconut milk
- ½ pound bass fillet
- 1 tablespoon olive oil
- 2 tablespoons jalapeno, chopped
- 2 tablespoons lime juice, freshly squeezed
- 3 tablespoons parsley, chopped
- Salt and pepper to taste

Directions:
1. Preheat the air fryer for 5 minutes.
2. Season the bass with salt and pepper to taste.
3. Brush the surface with olive oil.
4. Place in the air fryer and cook for 15 minutes at 350F.
5. Meanwhile, place in a saucepan, the coconut milk, lime juice, jalapeno and parsley.
6. Heat over medium flame.
7. Serve the fish with the coconut sauce.

Nutrition: Calories: 139 Carbs: 2.7g Protein: 8.7g Fat: 10.3

375. Mahi Mahi with Herby Buttery Drizzle

Preparation Time: 10 minutes
Cooking Time: 12 minutes
Servings: 4
Ingredients:
- (6 oz) Mahi Mahi fillets
- Salt and black pepper to taste
- Olive oil for spraying
- 2/3 cup butter, melted
- tbsp chopped fresh parsley
- ½ tbsp chopped fresh dill

Directions:
1. Insert the dripping pan in the bottom part of the air fryer and preheat the oven at Bake mode at 400 F for 2 to 3 minutes.
2. Season the Mahi Mahi fillets with salt, black pepper, and grease lightly with some olive oil. Lay the fish on the cooking tray and fit onto the middle rack of the oven.
3. Close the lid and set the timer for 12 minutes.
4. Once the fish cooks, transfer to a serving platter. Whisk the butter with the parsley and dill, and drizzle the mixture on the fish before serving.
5. Enjoy immediately.

Nutrition: Calories 529 Fat 46.54g Carbs 9.25g Fiber 5.6g Protein 20.26g Sugar 1.28g Sodium 422mg

376. Beer Battered Cod Filet

Preparation Time: 10 minutes
Cooking Time: 15 minutes
Servings: 2
Ingredients:
- ½ cup all-purpose flour
- ¾ teaspoon baking powder
- 1 ¼ cup lager beer
- 2 cod fillets
- 2 eggs, beaten
- Salt and pepper to taste

Directions:
1. Preheat the air fryer to 390F.
2. Pat the fish fillets dry then set aside.
3. In a bowl, combine the rest of the ingredients to create a batter.
4. Dip the fillets on the batter and place on the double layer rack.
5. Cook for 15 minutes.

Nutrition: Calories: 229 Carbs: 33.2g Protein: 31.1g Fat: 10.2g

377. Fried Scallops with Saffron Cream Sauce

Preparation Time: 5 Minutes
Cooking Time: 2 minutes
Servings: 4
Ingredients:
- Olive oil for greasing
- 24 scallops, cleaned
- 2/3 cup heavy cream
- tbsp freshly squeezed lemon juice
- ¼ tsp dried crushed saffron threads

Directions:
1. Insert the dripping pan in the bottom part of the air fryer and preheat the oven at Air Fry mode 400 F for 2 to 3 minutes.
2. Lightly brush the rotisserie basket with some olive oil and fill with the scallops.
3. Close and fit the basket in the oven using the rotisserie lift and set the timer for 2 minutes or until the scallops are golden brown on the outside.
4. Meanwhile, in a medium bowl, quickly whisk the heavy cream lemon juice and saffron threads.
5. When the scallops are ready, transfer to a serving plate and drizzle the sauce on top.
6. Enjoy immediately.

Nutrition: Calories 77 Fat 7.73g Carbs 1.05g Protein 1.15g Sugar 0.66g Sodium 31mg

378. Butterflied Prawns with Garlic-Sriracha

Preparation Time: 10 minutes
Cooking Time: 15 minutes
Servings: 2

Ingredients:
- 1 tablespoon lime juice
- 1 tablespoon sriracha
- 1-pound large prawns, shells removed and cut lengthwise or butterflied
- 1 teaspoon fish sauce
- 2 tablespoons melted butter
- 2 tablespoons minced garlic
- Salt and pepper to taste

Directions:
1. Preheat the air fryer to 390F.
2. Place the grill pan accessory in the air fryer.
3. Season the prawns with the rest of the ingredients.
4. Place on the grill pan and cook for 15 minutes. Make sure to flip the prawns halfway through the cooking time.

Nutrition: Calories: 443 Carbs:9.7 g Protein: 62.8g Fat: 16.9g

379. Sweet Asian Style Salmon

Preparation Time: 10 Minutes
Cooking Time: 12 minutes
Servings: 4

Ingredients:
- garlic cloves, minced
- tbsp fresh ginger paste
- tsp fresh orange zest
- ½ cup fresh orange juice
- ¼ cup of soy sauce
- tbsp plain vinegar
- 1 tbsp olive oil
- Salt to taste
- (5 oz) salmon fillets

Directions:
1. In a large bowl, mix all the ingredients except for the fish and place the fish in the sauce. Spoon the sauce well on top and cover the bowl with a plastic wrap. Allow marinating at room temperature for 30 minutes.
2. After 30 minutes, insert the dripping pan in the bottom part of the air fryer and preheat the oven at Bake mode at 400 F for 2 to 3 minutes.
3. Using tongs, remove the fish from the sauce, making sure to shake off some marinade of the fish and place the cooking tray. You can work in two batches.
4. Slide the tray onto the top rack of the oven, close the oven, and set the timer for 12 minutes, flipping the fish after 6 minutes.
5. Once ready, transfer the fish to serving plates and serve warm with steamed greens.

Nutrition: Calories 132, Fat 7.39g Carbs 8.72g Fiber 0.5g Protein 7.2g Sugar 5.96g Sodium 257mg

380. Zesty Ranch Fish Fillets

Preparation Time: 10 Minutes
Cooking Time: 13 minutes
Servings: 4

Ingredients:
- ¾ cup finely crushed cornflakes or panko breadcrumbs
- tbsp dry ranch-style dressing mix
- tsp fresh lemon zest
- ½ tbsp olive oil
- eggs, beaten
- white fish fillets
- Lemon wedges to garnish

Directions:
1. Insert the dripping pan in the bottom part of the air fryer and preheat the oven at Air Fry mode at 400 F for 2 to 3 minutes.
2. Mix the cornflakes, dressing mix, lemon zest, and oil on a shallow plate and then pour the eggs on another.
3. Working in two batches, dip the fish into the egg
4. drip off excess egg
5. and coat well in the cornflakes mixture on both sides.
6. Place the fish on the cooking tray and fix the tray on the middle rack of the oven. Close the oven and set the timer for 13 minutes, and cook until the fish is golden brown and the fish flaky within.
7. Transfer to a serving plate and serve with the lemon wedges.

Nutrition: Calories 409 Fat 23.84g Carbs 3.79g Fiber 0.5g Protein 42.55g Sugar 1.41g Sodium 322mg

381. Tempura Shrimp

Preparation Time: 15 minutes
Cooking Time: 10 minutes
Servings: 4

Ingredients:
- 1 package frozen shrimp tempura

Directions:
1. Spread shrimp tempura on the air fryer basket or tray; don't let them overlap to allow even cooking
2. Put them in air fryer and air fry at 380f for 10 minutes, check and flip halfway through cooking
3. Serve and enjoy

Nutrition: Calories: 21 kcal Protein: 1.6 g Fat: 1.52 g

382. Easy Fish Sticks with Chili Ketchup Sauce

Preparation Time: 10 Minutes
Cooking Time: 12 Minutes
Servings: 4
Ingredients:
- fish sticks, store-bought
- ½ cup tomato ketchup
- tbsp Sriracha sauce
- 1 tbsp chopped fresh parsley to garnish
- Sliced pickles for serving

Directions:
1. Insert the dripping pan in the bottom part of the air fryer and preheat the oven at Air Fry mode at 390 F for 2 to 3 minutes.
2. Arrange the fish sticks on the cooking tray and fit onto the middle rack of the oven. Close and set the timer for 12 minutes and cook until the fish sticks are golden brown and crispy.
3. Meanwhile, in a small bowl, mix the tomato ketchup, Sriracha sauce, and parsley until well combined and set aside for serving.
4. When the fish is ready, transfer onto serving plates and serve warm with the sauce and pickles.

Nutrition: Calories 341 Fat 2.53g Carbs 1.13g Fiber 0.4g Protein 73.57g Sugar 0.69g Sodium 568m

383. Packet Lobster Tail

Preparation Time: 10 minutes
Cooking time: 27 minutes
Servings: 2
Ingredients:
- (6-oz. lobster tails, halved
- tbsp. salted butter; melted.
- 1 tsp. dried parsley.
- ½ tsp. Old Bay seasoning
- Juice of ½ medium lemons

Directions:
1. Place the two halved tails on a sheet of aluminum foil. Drizzle with butter, Old Bay seasoning and lemon juice.
2. Seal the foil packets, completely covering tails. Place into the air fryer basket
3. Adjust the temperature to 375 Degrees F and set the timer for 12 minutes. Once done, sprinkle with dried parsley and serve immediately.

Nutrition: Calories: 234 Fat: 19 g Carbs: 7 g Fiber: 1 g Protein: 23 g

384. Shrimp and Green Beans

Preparation Time: 10 minutes
Cooking time: 20 minutes
Servings: 4
Ingredients:
- ½ lb. green beans; trimmed and halved
- 1 lb. shrimp; peeled and deveined
- ¼ cup ghee; melted
- tbsp. cilantro; chopped.
- Juice of 1 lime
- A pinch of salt and black pepper

Directions:
1. In a pan that fits your air fryer, mix all the Ingredients:, toss, Introduce in the fryer and cook at 360°F for 15 minutes shaking the fryer halfway. Divide into bowls and serve

Nutrition: Calories: 222 Fat: 8 g Carbs: 5 g Fiber: 3 g Protein: 10 g

385. Crab Dip

Preparation Time: 8 minutes
Cooking time: 18 minutes
Servings: 4
Ingredients:
- oz. full-fat cream cheese; softened.
- (6-oz. cans lump crabmeat
- ¼ cup chopped pickled jalapeños.
- ¼ cup full-fat sour cream.
- ¼ cup sliced green onion
- ½ cup shredded Cheddar cheese
- ¼ cup full-fat mayonnaise
- 1 tbsp. lemon juice
- ½ tsp. hot sauce

Directions:
1. Place all Ingredients: into a 4-cup round baking dish and stir until fully combined. Place dish into the air fryer basket Adjust the temperature to 400 Degrees F and set the timer for 8 minutes. Dip will be bubbling and hot when done. Serve warm.

Nutrition: Calories: 441 Fat: 38 g Carbs: 2 g Fiber: 6 g Protein: 18 g

386. Sesame Shrimp

Preparation Time: 8 minutes
Cooking time: 15 minutes
Servings: 4
Ingredients:
- 1 lb. shrimp; peeled and deveined
- 1 tbsp. olive oil
- 1 tbsp. sesame seeds, toasted
- ½ tsp. Italian seasoning
- A pinch of salt and black pepper

Directions:
1. Take a bowl and mix the shrimp with the rest of the Ingredients: and toss well Put the shrimp in the air fryer's basket, cook at 370°F for 12 minutes, and divide into bowls and serve,

Nutrition: Calories: 199 Fat: 11 g Carbs: 4 g Fiber: 2 g Protein: 11 g

387. Salmon and Cauliflower Rice

Preparation Time: 10 minutes
Cooking time: 30 minutes
Servings: 4
Ingredients:
- salmon fillets; boneless
- ½ cup chicken stock
- 1 cup cauliflower, riced
- 1 tbsp. butter; melted
- 1 tsp. turmeric powder
- Salt and black pepper to taste

Directions:
1. In a pan that fits your air fryer, mix the cauliflower rice with the other Ingredients: except the salmon and toss Arrange the salmon fillets over the cauliflower rice, put the pan in the

fryer and cook at 360°F for 25 minutes, flipping the fish after 15 minutes Divide everything between plates and serve

Nutrition: Calories: 241 Fat: 12 g Carbs: 6 g Fiber: 2 g Protein: 12 g

388. Tuna Patties

Preparation Time: 15 minutes
Cooking Time: 10 minutes
Servings: 4
Ingredients:
- 1 egg
- 5–6 ounces of tuna
- 1 tsp. lemon zest
- 1 tbsp. Italian seasoning
- 1/2 cup bread crumbs
- 1 tsp. Dijon mustard
- 1 tbsp. of lemon juice

Directions:
1. Combine together egg, Dijon mustard, lemon zest, tuna, lemon juice, Italian seasoning and bread crumbs in a bowl
2. Spray olive oil in the air fryer basket
3. Form patties with about 1/4 cup of tuna mixture
4. Then place them in the air fryer basket and softly spray with olive oil to make the tuna patties crispy
5. Place the basket in the air fryer and set to 360 F for 5 minutes
6. Flip tuna patties and air fry for more 5 minutes
7. Serve and enjoy

Nutrition: Calories: 104 kcal Protein: 11.28 g Fat: 4.47 g Carbs: 4.09 g

389. Garlic Tilapia

Preparation Time: 10 minutes
Cooking time: 25 minutes
Servings: 4
Ingredients:
- tilapia fillets; boneless
- 1 bunch kale; chopped.
- garlic cloves; minced
- tbsp. olive oil
- 1 tsp. fennel seeds
- ½ tsp. red pepper flakes, crushed
- Salt and black pepper to taste

Directions:
1. In a pan that fits the fryer, combine all the Ingredients:, put the pan in the fryer and cook at 360°F for 20 minutes Divide everything between plates and serve.

Nutrition: Calories: 240 Fat: 12 g Carbs: 4 g Fiber: 2 g Protein: 12 g

390. Trout and Mint

Preparation Time: 10 minutes
Cooking time: 21 minutes
Servings: 4
Ingredients:
- 1 avocado, peeled, pitted and roughly chopped.
- rainbow trout
- 1/3 pine nuts
- 1 cup olive oil + 3 tbsp.
- 1 cup parsley; chopped.
- garlic cloves; minced
- ½ cup mint; chopped.
- Zest of 1 lemon
- Juice of 1 lemon
- A pinch of salt and black pepper

Directions:
1. Pat dries the trout, season with salt and pepper and rub with 3 tbsp. oil
2. Put the fish in your air fryer's basket and cook for 8 minutes on each side. Divide the fish between plates and drizzle half of the lemon juice all over In a blender, combine the rest of the oil with the remaining lemon juice, parsley, garlic, mint, lemon zest, pine nuts and the avocado and pulse well. Spread this over the trout and serve.

Nutrition: Calories: 240 Fat: 12 g Carbs: 6 g Fiber: 4 g Protein: 9 g

391. Salmon and Coconut Sauce

Preparation Time: 25 minutes
Cooking time: 10 minutes
Servings: 4
Ingredients:
- salmon fillets; boneless
- 1/3 cup heavy cream
- ¼ cup lime juice
- ½ cup coconut; shredded
- ¼ cup coconut cream
- 1 tsp. lime zest; grated
- A pinch of salt and black pepper

Directions:
1. Take a bowl and mix all the Ingredients: except the salmon and whisk.
2. Arrange the fish in a pan that fits your air fryer, drizzle the coconut sauce all over, put the pan in the machine and cook at 360°F for 20 minutes Divide between plates and serve

Nutrition: Calories: 227 Fat: 12 g Carbs: 4 g Fiber: 2 g Protein: 9 g

392. Broiled Tilapia

Preparation Time: 15 minutes
Cooking Time: 7 minutes
Servings: 2
Ingredients:
- Tilapia fillets
- Light spritz of canola oil from an oil spritz
- Old bay seasoning
- Lemon pepper
- Salt
- Molly Mcbutter or butter buds

Directions:
1. Defrost fillets, if frozen then Spray air fryer basket with cooking spray.
2. Place fillets in the basket and season to taste with the spices. Spray little oil.
3. Set air fryer to 400f for 7 minutes. Check for doneness after the timer goes off, Fish should flake easily with a fork.
4. Serve and enjoy with your favorite veggies.

Nutrition: Calories: 106 kcal Protein: 15.3 g Fat: 4.06 g Carbs: 2.13 g

393. Fried French Mussels

Preparation Time: 20 minutes
Cooking Time: 15 minutes
Servings: 4
Ingredients:
- 1-pound mussels
- 2 tbsp. minced garlic
- 4tbsps. melted butter

- 2 tbsp. dry white wine
- 2 tbsp. heavy cream

Directions:
1. Put in a bowl the mussels, garlic, butter, white wine, and heavy cream and mix together
2. Pour the mussels mixture into the air fryer basket
3. Set the air fryer to 400f for 5 minutes, shake after 5 minutes and set for more 5 minutes
4. Serve and enjoy

Nutrition: Calories: 172 Protein: 15.95 g Fat: 6.91 g Carbs: 10.47 g

394. Salmon and Sauce

Preparation Time: 10 minutes
Cooking time: 25 minutes
Servings: 4

Ingredients:
- salmon fillets; boneless
- garlic cloves; minced
- ¼ cup ghee; melted
- ½ cup heavy cream
- 1 tbsp. chives; chopped.
- 1 tsp. lemon juice
- 1 tsp. dill; chopped.
- A pinch of salt and black pepper

Directions:
1. Take a bowl and mix all the Ingredients: except the salmon and whisk well.
2. Arrange the salmon in a pan that fits the air fryer, drizzle the sauce all over, introduce the pan in the machine and cook at 360°F for 20 minutes. Divide everything between plates and serve

Nutrition: Calories: 220 Fat: 14 g Carbs: 5 g Fiber: 2 g Protein: 12 g

395. Parmesan Cod

Preparation Time: 10 minutes
Cooking time: 20 minutes
Servings: 4

Ingredients:
- cod fillets; boneless
- A drizzle of olive oil
- spring onions; chopped.
- 1 cup parmesan
- tbsp. balsamic vinegar
- Salt and black pepper to taste

Directions:
1. Season fish with salt, pepper, grease with the oil and coat it in parmesan.
2. Put the fillets in your air fryer's basket and cook at 370°F for 14 minutes. Meanwhile, in a bowl, mix the spring onions with salt, pepper and the vinegar and whisk Divide the cod between plates, drizzle the spring onions mix all over and serve with a side salad

Nutrition: Calories: 220 Fat: 12 g Carbs: 5 g Fiber: 2 g Protein: 13 g

396. Cod and Endives

Preparation Time: 10 minutes
Cooking time: 25 minutes
Servings: 4

Ingredients:
- salmon fillets; boneless
- endives; shredded
- tbsp. olive oil
- ½ tsp. sweet paprika
- Salt and black pepper to the taste

Directions:
1. In a pan that fits the air fryer, combine the fish with the rest of the Ingredients:, toss, introduce in the fryer and cook at 350°F for 20 minutes, flipping the fish halfway Divide between plates and serve right away

Nutrition: Calories: 243 Fat: 13 g Carbs: 6 g Fiber: 3 g Protein: 14 g

397. Cod and Tomatoes

Preparation Time: 10 minutes
Cooking time: 20 minutes
Servings: 4

Ingredients:
- 1 cup cherry tomatoes; halved
- cod fillets, skinless and boneless
- tbsp. olive oil
- tbsp. cilantro; chopped.
- Salt and black pepper to taste

Directions:
1. In a baking dish that fits your air fryer, mix all the Ingredients:, toss gently.
2. Introduce in your air fryer and cook at 370°F for 15 minutes
3. Divide everything between plates and serve right away.

Nutrition: Calories: 248 Fat: 11 g Carbs: 5 g Fiber: 2 g Protein: 11 g

398. Salmon Burgers

Preparation Time: 10 minutes
Cooking time: 10 minutes
Servings: 4

Ingredients:
- 14.75 oz. can salmon, drain & flake
- ¼ cup onion, chopped fine
- 1 egg
- ¼ cup multi-grain crackers, crushed
- tsp fresh dill, chopped
- ¼ tsp pepper
- Nonstick cooking spray

Directions:
1. In a medium bowl, combine all ingredients until combined. Form into 4 patties.
2. Lightly spray fryer basket with cooking spray. Place the baking pan in position 2 of the oven.
3. Set oven to air fryer on 350°F.
4. Place the patties in the basket and set on baking pan. Set timer for 8 minutes. Cook until burgers are golden brown, turning over halfway through cooking time. Serve on toasted buns with choice of toppings.

Nutrition: Calories: 330 Fat: 10 g Saturated Fat: 2 g Sodium: 643 mg Carbs: 11 g Protein: 24 g

FISH AND SEAFOOD

399. Bacon Wrapped Shrimp

Preparation Time: 5 minutes
Cooking Time: 5 minutes
Servings: 4
Ingredients:
- 1¼ pound tiger shrimp, peeled and deveined
- 1-pound bacon

Directions:
1. Wrap each shrimp with a slice of bacon.
2. Refrigerate for about 20 minutes. Preheat the air fryer to 390 degrees F.
3. Arrange the shrimp in the Air fryer basket. Cook for about 5-7 minutes.

Nutrition: Calories: 514 Protein: 42.66 g Fat: 36.92 g Carbs: 7.17 g

400. Crispy Coated Scallops

Preparation Time: 10 minutes
Cooking time: 10 minutes
Servings: 4
Ingredients:
- Nonstick cooking spray
- 1 lb. sea scallops, patted dry
- 1 teaspoon onion powder
- ½ tsp pepper
- 1 egg
- 1 tbsp. water
- ¼ cup Italian breadcrumbs
- Paprika
- 1 tbsp. fresh lemon juice

Directions:
1. Lightly spray fryer basket with cooking spray. Place baking pan in position 2 of the oven.
2. Sprinkle scallops with onion powder and pepper.
3. In a shallow dish, whisk together egg and water.
4. Place bread crumbs in a separate shallow dish.
5. Dip scallops in egg then bread crumbs coating them lightly. Place in fryer basket and lightly spray with cooking spray. Sprinkle with paprika.
6. Place the basket on the baking pan and set oven to air fryer on 400°F. Bake 10-12 minutes until scallops are firm on the inside and golden brown on the outside. Drizzle with lemon juice and serve.

Nutrition: Calories: 122 Fat: 2 g Saturated Fat: 1 g Sodium: 563 mg Carbs: 10 g Fiber: 1 g Sugar: 1 g

401. Tasty Tuna Loaf

Preparation Time: 10 minutes
Cooking time: 40 minutes
Servings: 6
Ingredients:
- Nonstick cooking spray
- oz. can chunk white tuna in water, drain & flake
- ¾ cup bread crumbs
- 1 onion, chopped fine
- eggs, beaten
- ¼ cup milk
- ½ tsp fresh lemon juice
- ½ tsp dill
- 1 tbsp. fresh parsley, chopped
- ½ tsp salt
- ½ tsp pepper

Directions:
1. Place rack in position 1 of the oven. Spray a 9-inch loaf pan with cooking spray.
2. In a large bowl, combine all ingredients until thoroughly mixed. Spread evenly in prepared pan.
3. Set oven to bake on 350°F for 45 minutes. After 5 minutes, place the pan in the oven and cook 40 minutes, or until top is golden brown. Slice and serve.

Nutrition: Calories: 169 Fat: 5 g Saturated Fat: 1 g Sodium: 540 mg Carbs: 13 g Fiber: 1 g Sugar: 3 g Protein: 18 g

402. Maryland Crab Cakes

Preparation Time: 10 minutes
Cooking time: 10 minutes
Servings: 6
Ingredients:
- Nonstick cooking spray
- eggs
- 1 cup Panko breadcrumbs
- 1 stalk celery, chopped
- tbsp. mayonnaise
- 1 tsp Worcestershire sauce
- ¼ cup mozzarella cheese, grated
- 1 tsp Italian seasoning
- 1 tbsp. fresh parsley, chopped
- 1 tsp pepper
- ¾ lb. Lump crabmeat, drained

Directions:
1. Place baking pan in position 2 of the oven. Lightly spray the fryer basket with cooking spray.
2. In a large bowl, combine all ingredients except crab meat, mix well.
3. Fold in crab carefully so it retains some chunks. Form mixture into 12 patties.
4. Place patties in a single layer in the fryer basket. Place the basket on the baking pan.
5. Set oven to air fryer on 350°F for 10 minutes. Cook until golden brown, turning over halfway through cooking time. Serve immediately.

Nutrition: Calories: 172 Fat: 8 g Saturated Fat: 2 g Sodium: 527 mg Carbs: 14 g Fiber: 1 g Sugar: 1 g Protein: 16 g

403. Mediterranean Sole

Preparation Time: 15 minutes
Cooking time: 20 minutes
Servings: 6
Ingredients:
- Nonstick cooking spray
- tbsp. olive oil
- scallions, sliced thin
- cloves garlic, diced fine
- tomatoes, chopped
- ½ cup dry white wine
- tbsp. fresh parsley, chopped fine
- 1 tsp oregano
- 1 tsp pepper
- lbs. sole, cut in 6 pieces
- oz. feta cheese, crumbled

Directions:
1. Place the rack in position 1 of the oven. Spray an 8x11-inch baking dish with cooking spray.

2. Heat the oil in a medium skillet over medium heat. Add scallions and garlic and cook until tender, stirring frequently.
3. Add the tomatoes, wine, parsley, oregano, and pepper. Stir to mix. Simmer for 5 minutes, or until sauce thickens. Remove from heat.
4. Pour half the sauce on the bottom of the prepared dish. Lay fish on top then pour remaining sauce over the top. Sprinkle with feta.
5. Set the oven to bake on 400°F for 25 minutes. After 5 minutes, place the baking dish on the rack and cook 15-18 minutes or until fish flakes easily with a fork. Serve immediately.

Nutrition: Calories: 220 Fat: 12 g Saturated Fat: 4 g Sodium: 631 mg Carbs: 6 g Fiber: 2 g Sugar: 4 g Protein: 22 g

404. Tomato Basil Scallops

Preparation Time: 5 minutes
Cooking Time: 15 minutes
Servings: 2
Ingredients:
- 8 jumbo sea scallops, wild-caught
- 1 tablespoon tomato paste
- 12 ounces frozen spinach, thawed and dry outed
- 1 tablespoon chopped fresh basil
- 1 teaspoon ground black pepper
- 1 teaspoon minced garlic
- 1 teaspoon salt
- 3/4 cup heavy whipping cream, reduced Fat

Directions:
1. Switch on the air fryer, insert fryer basket, grease it with olive oil, then shut with its lid, set the fryer at 350 degrees F and preheat for 5 minutes
2. Meanwhile, take a 7 inches baking pan, grease it with oil and place spinach in it in an even layer.
3. Spray the scallops with oil, sprinkle with ½ teaspoon each of salt and black pepper and then place scallops over the spinach.
4. Place tomato paste in a bowl, whisk in cream, basil, garlic, and remaining salt and black pepper until smooth, and then pour over the scallops.
5. Open the fryer, place the pan in it, close with its lid and cook for 10 minutes until thoroughly cooked and sauce is hot.
6. Serve straight away.

Nutrition: Calories 359 Cal Carbs 6g Fat 33g Protein 9g

405. Spicy Grilled Halibut

Preparation Time: 30 minutes
Cooking time: 10 minutes
Servings: 4
Ingredients:
- ½ cup fresh lemon juice
- jalapeno peppers, seeded & chopped fine
- 6 oz. halibut fillets
- Nonstick cooking spray
- ¼ cup cilantro, chopped

Directions:
1. In a small bowl, combine lemon juice and chilies, mix well.
2. Place fish in a large Ziploc bag and add marinade. Toss to coat. Refrigerate 30 minutes.
3. Lightly spray the baking pan with cooking spray. Set oven to broil on 400°F for 15 minutes.
4. After 5 minutes, lay fish on the pan and place in position 2 of the oven. Cook 10 minutes, or until fish flakes easily with a fork. Turn fish over and brush with marinade halfway through cooking time.
5. Sprinkle with cilantro before serving.

Nutrition: Calories: 328 Fat: 24 g Saturated Fat: 4 g Sodium: 137 mg Carbs: 3 g Sugar: 1 g Protein: 25 g

406. Tropical Shrimp Skewers

Preparation Time: 15 minutes
Cooking time: 5 minutes
Servings: 4
Ingredients:
- 1 tbsp. lime juice
- 1 tbsp. honey
- ¼ tsp red pepper flakes
- ¼ tsp pepper
- ¼ tsp ginger
- Nonstick cooking spray
- 1 lb. medium shrimp, peel, devein & leave tails on
- cups peaches drain & chop
- ½ green bell pepper, chopped fine
- ¼ cup scallions, chopped

Directions:
1. Soak 8 small wooden skewers in water for 15 minutes.
2. In a small bowl, whisk together lime juice, honey and spices Transfer 2 tablespoons of the mixture to a medium bowl.
3. Place the baking pan in position 2 of the oven. Lightly spray fryer basket with cooking spray. Set oven to broil on 400°F for 10 minutes.
4. Thread 5 shrimp on each skewer and brush both sides with marinade. Place in basket and after 5 minutes, place on the baking pan. Cook 4-5 minutes or until shrimp turn pink.
5. Add peaches, bell pepper, and scallions to reserved honey mixture, mix well. Divide salsa evenly between serving plates and top with 2 skewers each. Serve immediately.

Nutrition: Calories: 181 Fat: 1 g Sodium: 650 mg Carbs: 27 g Fiber: 2 g Sugar: 21 g Protein: 16 g

407. Cheesy Fish Gratin

Preparation Time: 30 minutes
Cooking Time: 20 minutes
Servings: 4
Ingredients:
- tablespoon avocado oil
- 1-pound hake fillets
- 1 teaspoon garlic powder
- Sea salt and ground white pepper, to taste
- tablespoons shallots, chopped
- 1 bell pepper, seeded and chopped
- 1/2 cup cottage cheese
- 1/2 cup sour cream
- 1 egg, well whisked
- 1 teaspoon yellow mustard
- 1 tablespoon lime juice
- 1/2 cup swiss cheese, shredded

Directions:
1. Brush the bottom and sides of a casserole dish with avocado oil. Add the hake fillets to the casserole dish and sprinkle with garlic powder, salt, and pepper.
2. Add the chopped shallots and bell peppers.
3. In a mixing bowl, thoroughly combine the cottage cheese, sour cream, egg, mustard, and lime juice. Pour the mixture over fish and spread evenly.

FISH AND SEAFOOD

4. Cook in the preheated air fryer at 370 degrees f for 10 minutes.
5. Top with the Swiss cheese and cook an additional 7 minutes. Let it rest for 10 minutes before slicing and serving.

Nutrition: 335 calories 18.1g fats 7.8g carbs 33.7g protein 2.6g sugars

408. Crispy Air Fried Sushi Roll

Preparation Time: 5 minutes
Cooking time: 15 minutes
Servings: 12

Ingredients:
- Kale Salad:
- 1 tbsp. sesame seeds
- ¾ tsp. soy sauce
- ¼ tsp. ginger
- 1/8 tsp. garlic powder
- ¾ tsp. toasted sesame oil
- ½ tsp. rice vinegar
- 1 ½ C. chopped kale
- Sushi Rolls:
- ½ of a sliced avocado
- sheets of sushi nori
- 1 batch cauliflower rice
- Sriracha Mayo:
- Sriracha sauce
- ¼ C. vegan mayo
- Coating:
- ½ C. panko breadcrumbs

Directions:
1. Combine all of kale salad ingredients together, tossing well. Set to the side.
2. Lay out a sheet of nori and spread a handful of rice on. Then place 2-3 tbsp. of kale salad over rice, followed by avocado. Roll up sushi.
3. To make mayo, whisk mayo ingredients together until smooth.
4. Add breadcrumbs to a bowl. Coat sushi rolls in crumbs till coated and add to air fryer.
5. Cook rolls 10 minutes at 390 degrees, shaking gently at 5 minutes.
6. Slice each roll into 6-8 pieces and enjoy!

Nutrition: Calories: 267 Fat: 13 g Carbs: 0 g Sugar: 3 g Protein: 6 g

409. Honey Glazed Salmon

Preparation Time: 5 minutes
Cooking time: 5 minutes
Servings: 2

Ingredients:
- 1 tsp. water
- tsp. rice wine vinegar
- tbsp. low-sodium soy sauce
- tbsp. raw honey
- salmon fillets

Directions:
1. Combine water, vinegar, honey, and soy sauce together. Pour half of this mixture into a bowl.
2. Place salmon in one bowl of marinade and let chill 2 hours.
3. Ensure your air fryer is preheated to 356 degrees and add salmon.
4. Cook 8 minutes, flipping halfway through. Baste salmon with some of the remaining marinade mixture and cook another 5 minutes.
5. To make a sauce to serve salmon with, pour remaining marinade mixture into a saucepan, heating till simmering. Let simmer 2 minutes. Serve drizzled over salmon!

Nutrition: Calories: 390 Fat: 8 g Carbs: 0 g Sugar: 5 g Protein: 16 g

410. Parmesan Shrimp

Preparation Time: 5 minutes
Cooking time: 10 minutes
Servings: 4 - 6

Ingredients:
- tbsp. olive oil
- 1 tsp. onion powder
- 1 tsp. basil
- ½ tsp. oregano
- 1 tsp. pepper
- 2/3 C. grated parmesan cheese
- minced garlic cloves
- pounds of jumbo cooked shrimp (peeled/deveined)

Directions:
1. Mix all seasonings together and gently toss shrimp with mixture.
2. Spray olive oil into air fryer basket and add seasoned shrimp.
3. Cook 8-10 minutes at 350 degrees.
4. Squeeze lemon juice over shrimp right before devouring!

Nutrition: Calories: 351 Fat: 11 g Carbs: 0 g Sugar: 1 g Protein: 19 g

411. Bacon Wrapped Scallops

Preparation Time: 5 minutes
Cooking time: 10 minutes
Servings: 4

Ingredients:
- 1 tsp. paprika
- 1 tsp. lemon pepper
- slices of center-cut bacon
- 20 raw sea scallops

Directions:
1. Rinse and drain scallops, placing on paper towels to soak up excess moisture.
2. Cut slices of bacon into 4 pieces.
3. Wrap each scallop with a piece of bacon, using toothpicks to secure. Sprinkle wrapped scallops with paprika and lemon pepper.
4. Spray air fryer basket with olive oil and add scallops.
5. Cook 5-6 minutes at 400 degrees, making sure to flip halfway through.

Nutrition: Calories: 389 Fat: 17 g Carbs: 0 g Sugar: 1 g Protein: 210 g

412. Air Fryer Fish Tacos

Preparation Time: 5 minutes
Cooking time: 5 minutes
Servings: 4

Ingredients:
- 1 pound cod
- 1 tbsp. cumin
- ½ tbsp. chili powder
- 1 ½ C. almond flour
- 1 ½ C. coconut flour

- ounces Mexican beer
- eggs

Directions:
1. Whisk beer and eggs together.
2. Whisk flours, pepper, salt, cumin, and chili powder together.
3. Slice cod into large pieces and coat in egg mixture then flour mixture.
4. Spray bottom of your air fryer basket with olive oil and add coated codpieces.
5. Cook 15 minutes at 375 degrees.
6. Serve on lettuce leaves topped with homemade salsa!

Nutrition: Calories: 178 Fat: 10 g Carbs: 0 g Sugar: 1 g Protein: 19 g

413. Salmon Croquettes

Preparation Time: 5 minutes
Cooking time: 15 minutes
Servings: 6 - 8
Ingredients:
- Panko breadcrumbs
- Almond flour
- egg whites
- tbsp. chopped chives
- tbsp. minced garlic cloves
- ½ C. chopped onion
- 2/3 C. grated carrots
- 1 pound chopped salmon fillet

Directions:
1. Mix together all ingredients minus breadcrumbs, flour, and egg whites.
2. Shape mixture into balls. Then coat them in flour, then egg
3. and then breadcrumbs. Drizzle with olive oil.
4. Add coated salmon balls to air fryer and cook 6 minutes at 350 degrees. Shake and cook an additional 4 minutes until golden in color.

Nutrition: Calories: 503 Fat: 9 g Carbs: 61 g Sugar: 4 g Protein: 5 g

414. Panko-Crusted Tilapia

Preparation Time: 5 minutes
Cooking time: 5 minutes
Servings: 3
Ingredients:
- tsp. Italian seasoning
- tsp. lemon pepper
- 1/3 C. panko breadcrumbs
- 1/3 C. egg whites
- 1/3 C. almond flour
- tilapia fillets
- Olive oil

Directions:
1. Place panko, egg whites, and flour into separate bowls. Mix lemon pepper and Italian seasoning in with breadcrumbs.
2. Pat tilapia fillets dry. Dredge in flour, then egg
3. then breadcrumb mixture. Add to air fryer basket and spray lightly with olive oil.
4. Cook 10-11 minutes at 400 degrees, making sure to flip halfway through cooking.

Nutrition: Calories: 256 Fat: 9 g Carbs: 0 g Sugar: 5 g Protein: 39 g

415. Friedamari

Preparation Time: 5 minutes
Cooking time: 15 minutes
Servings: 6 - 8
Ingredients:
- ½ tsp. salt
- ½ tsp. Old Bay seasoning
- 1/3 C. plain cornmeal
- ½ C. semolina flour
- ½ C. almond flour
- 5-6 C. olive oil
- 1 ½ pounds baby squid

Directions:
1. Rinse squid in cold water and slice tentacles, keeping just ¼-inch of the hood in one piece.
2. Combine 1-2 pinches of pepper, salt, Old Bay seasoning
3. cornmeal, and both flours together. Dredge squid pieces into flour mixture and place into air fryer. Spray liberally with olive oil.
4. Cook 15 minutes at 345 degrees till coating turns a golden brown.

Nutrition: Calories: 211 Fat: 6 g Carbs: 0 g Sugar: 1 g Protein: 21 g

416. Tuna Pie

Preparation Time: 10 minutes
Cooking Time: 30 minutes
Servings: 4
Ingredients:
- 2 hard-boiled eggs
- 2 tuna cans
- 200 ml fried tomato
- 1 sheet of broken dough

Directions:
1. Cut the eggs into small pieces and mix with the tuna and tomato.
2. Spread the sheet of broken dough and cut into two equal squares.
3. Put the mixture of tuna, eggs, and tomato on one of the squares.
4. Cover with the other, join at the ends and decorate with leftover little pieces.
5. Preheat the air fryer a few minutes at 180C.
6. Enter in the air fryer basket and set the timer for 15 minutes at 180C

Nutrition: Calories 244 Fat 13.67g Carbs 21.06g Protein 8.72g

417. Louisiana Shrimp Po Boy

Preparation Time: 10 minutes
Cooking time: 15 minutes
Servings: 4
Ingredients:
- 1 tsp. creole seasoning
- slices of tomato
- Lettuce leaves
- ¼ C. buttermilk
- ½ C. Louisiana Fish Fry
- 1 pound deveined shrimp
- Remoulade sauce:
- 1 chopped green onion
- 1 tsp. hot sauce
- 1 tsp. Dijon mustard

FISH AND SEAFOOD

- ½ tsp. creole seasoning
- 1 tsp. Worcestershire sauce
- Juice of ½ a lemon
- ½ C. vegan mayo

Directions:
1. To make the sauce, combine all sauce ingredients until well incorporated. Chill while you cook shrimp.
2. Mix seasonings together and liberally season shrimp.
3. Add buttermilk to a bowl. Dip each shrimp into milk and place in a Ziploc bag. Chill half an hour to marinate.
4. Add fish fry to a bowl. Take shrimp from marinating bag and dip into fish fry, then add to air fryer.
5. Ensure your air fryer is preheated to 400 degrees.
6. Spray shrimp with olive oil. Cook 5 minutes, flip and then cook another 5 minutes.
7. Assemble "Keto" Po Boy by adding sauce to lettuce leaves, along with shrimp and tomato.

Nutrition: Calories: 337 Fat: 12 g Carbs: 55 g Sugar: 2 g Protein: 24 g

418. Crumbled Fish

Preparation Time: 5 minutes
Cooking Time: 15 minutes
Servings: 4

Ingredients:
1. Breadcrumbs (.5 cup)
2. Vegetable oil (4 tbsp.)
3. Egg (1)
4. Fish fillets (4)
5. Lemon (1)

Directions:
- Heat the Air Fryer to reach 356° Fahrenheit.
- Whisk the oil and breadcrumbs until crumbly.
- Dip the fish into the egg, then the crumb mixture.
- Arrange the fish in the cooker and air-fry for 12 minutes.
- Garnish using the lemon.

Nutrition: Calories: 320 Carbs: 8 g Fat: 10 g Protein: 28 g

419. 3-Ingredient Air Fryer Catfish

Preparation Time: 5 minutes
Cooking time: 15 minutes
Servings: 4

Ingredients:
- 1 tbsp. chopped parsley
- 1 tbsp. olive oil
- ¼ C. seasoned fish fry
- catfish fillets

Directions:
1. Ensure your air fryer is preheated to 400 degrees.
2. Rinse off catfish fillets and pat dry.
3. Add fish fry seasoning to Ziploc baggie, then catfish. Shake bag and ensure fish gets well coated.
4. Spray each fillet with olive oil.
5. Add fillets to air fryer basket. Cook 10 minutes. Then flip and cook another 2-3 minutes.

Nutrition: Calories: 208 Fat: 5 g Carbs: 8 g Sugar: 0.5 g Protein: 17 g

420. Healthy Fish and Chips

Preparation Time: 5 minutes
Cooking time: 15 minutes
Servings: 3

Ingredients:
- Old Bay seasoning
- ½ C. panko breadcrumbs
- 1 egg
- tbsp. almond flour
- 4-6 ounce tilapia fillets
- Frozen crinkle cut fries

Directions:
1. Add almond flour to one bowl, beat egg in another bowl, and add panko breadcrumbs to the third bowl, mixed with Old Bay seasoning.
2. Dredge tilapia in flour, then egg
3. and then breadcrumbs.
4. Place coated fish in air fryer along with fries.
5. Cook 15 minutes at 390 degrees.

Nutrition: Calories: 219 Fat: 5 g Carbs: 18 g Sugar: 1 g Protein: 25 g

421. Fish in Parchment Paper

Preparation Time: 10 minutes
Cooking time: 25 minutes
Servings: 2

Ingredients:
- oz. cod fillets thawed
- 1 tbsp. Oil
- 1/2 cup julienned carrots
- sprigs tarragon
- 1/2 cup red peppers
- 1/2 tsp. Black Pepper
- pats melted butter
- 1 tbsp. lemon juice
- 1 tbsp. Salt divided
- 1/2 cup julienned fennel bulbs

Directions:
1. Take a bowl and add melted butter, tarragon, 1/2 tsp. salt, and lemon juice. Combine well until unless you get a creamy sauce. Put the julienned vegetable and stir well. Set it aside.
2. Slice two squares of parchment big enough to hold the fish and vegetables. Spray the fish fillets with cooking oil spray and apply salt & pepper to all sides of the fillets. Lay down one filet down on each parchment square.
3. Top each fillet with half of the vegetables. Pour any leftover sauce over the vegetables. Fold over the parchment paper and crimp the sides to hold fish, veggies and sauce carefully inside the packet.
4. Place the packets inside the air fryer toaster oven basket. Set your air fryer toaster oven to 350F for 15 minutes.
5. Put each packet to a plate and open just before serving.

Nutrition: Calories: 251 Fat: 12 g Carbs: 8 g Fiber: 2 g Protein: 26 g

422. Buttery scallops

Preparation Time: 10 minutes
Cooking Time: 25 minutes
Serving: 8

Ingredients
- `2 lb. Scallops
- `6 tablespoons butter, melted
- `2 tablespoons dry white wine
- `1 tablespoon lemon juice
- `1/2 cup parmesan cheese, grated
- `1 teaspoon salt
- `1/2 teaspoon black pepper
- `1 teaspoon garlic powder
- `1 teaspoon dried parsley
- `1/8 teaspoon cayenne pepper
- `1/4 teaspoon sweet paprika
- `2 tablespoons parsley chopped

Directions:
1. Mix everything in a bowl except scallops.
2. Toss in scallops and mix well to coat them.
3. Spread the scallops with the sauce in a baking tray.
4. Press "power button" of air fry oven and turn the dial to select the "bake" mode.
5. Press the time button and again turn the dial to set the cooking time to 25 minutes.
6. Now push the temp button and rotate the dial to set the temperature at 350 degrees f.
7. Once preheated, place the scallop's baking tray in the oven and close its lid.
8. Serve warm.

Nutrition: Calories 227 Fat: 10.1g Carbs 5.6g protein 27.8g

423. Crusted scallops

Preparation Time: 10 minutes
Cooking Time: 20 minutes
Serving: 4

Ingredients
- `1-1/2 lbs. Bay scallops, rinsed
- `3 garlic cloves, minced
- `1/2 cup panko crumbs
- `1 teaspoon onion powder
- `4 tablespoons butter, melted
- `1/2 teaspoon cayenne pepper
- `1 teaspoon garlic powder
- `1/4 cup parmesan cheese, shredded

Directions:
1. Mix everything in a bowl except scallops.
2. Toss in scallops and mix well to coat them.
3. Spread the scallops with the sauce in a baking tray.
4. Press "power button" of air fry oven and turn the dial to select the "bake" mode.
5. Press the time button and again turn the dial to set the cooking time to 20 minutes.
6. Now push the temp button and rotate the dial to set the temperature at 400 degrees f.
7. Once preheated, place the scallop's baking tray in the oven and close its lid.

Nutrition: Calories 242 Fat: 11.1g Carbs 11.1g protein 23.8g

424. Lobster tails with white wine sauce

Preparation Time: 10 minutes
Cooking Time: 14 minutes
Serving: 4

Ingredients
- `4 lobster tails, shell cut from the top
- `1/2 onion, quartered
- `1/2 cup butter
- `1/3 cup wine
- `1/4 cup honey
- `6 garlic cloves crushed
- `1 tablespoon lemon juice
- `1 teaspoon salt or to taste
- `Cracked pepper to taste
- `Lemon slices to serve
- `2 tablespoons fresh chopped parsley

Directions:
1. Place the lobster tails in the oven's baking tray.
2. Whisk rest of the ingredients in a bowl and pour over the lobster tails.
3. Press "power button" of air fry oven and turn the dial to select the "broil" mode.
4. Press the time button and again turn the dial to set the cooking time to 14 minutes.
5. Now push the temp button and rotate the dial to set the temperature at 350 degrees f.
6. Once preheated, place the lobster's baking tray in the oven and close its lid.
7. Serve warm.

Nutrition: Calories 340 Fat: 23.1g Carbs 20.4g protein 0.7g

425. Broiled lobster tails

Preparation Time: 10 minutes
Cooking Time: 6 minutes
Serving: 4

Ingredients
- `2 lobster tails, shell cut from the top
- `1/2 cup butter, melted
- `1/2 teaspoon ground paprika
- `Salt to taste
- `White pepper, to taste
- `1 lemon, juiced

Directions:
1. Place the lobster tails in the oven's baking tray.
2. Whisk rest of the ingredients in a bowl and pour over the lobster tails.
3. Press "power button" of air fry oven and turn the dial to select the "broil" mode.
4. Press the time button and again turn the dial to set the cooking time to 6 minutes.
5. Now push the temp button and rotate the dial to set the temperature at 350 degrees f.
6. Once preheated, place the lobster's baking tray in the oven and close its lid.
7. Serve warm.

Nutrition: Calories 227 Fat: 23.1g Carbs 0.2g protein 20.3g

426. Paprika lobster tail

Preparation Time: 10 minutes
Cooking Time: 10 minutes
Serving: 4
Ingredients
- `2 (4 to 6 oz) lobster tails, shell cut from the top
- `1/8 teaspoon salt
- `1/8 teaspoon black pepper
- `1/8 teaspoon paprika
- `2 tablespoon butter
- `1/2 lemon, cut into wedges
- `Chopped parsley for garnish

Directions:
1. Place the lobster tails in the oven's baking tray.
2. Whisk rest of the ingredients in a bowl and pour over the lobster tails.
3. Press "power button" of air fry oven and turn the dial to select the "broil" mode.
4. Press the time button and again turn the dial to set the cooking time to 10 minutes.
5. Now push the temp button and rotate the dial to set the temperature at 350 degrees f.
6. Once preheated, place the lobster's baking tray in the oven and close its lid.
7. Serve warm.

Nutrition: Calories 204 Fat: 12.5g Carbs 0.2g protein 21.7g

427. Lobster tails with lemon butter

Preparation Time: 10 minutes
Cooking Time: 8 minutes
Serving: 4
Ingredients
- `4 lobster tails, shell cut from the top
- `1 tablespoon fresh parsley, chopped
- `2 garlic cloves, pressed
- `1 teaspoon dijon mustard
- `1/4 teaspoon salt
- `1/8 teaspoon black pepper
- `1-1/2 tablespoon olive oil
- `1-1/2 tablespoon fresh lemon juice
- `4 tablespoon butter, divided

Directions:
1. Place the lobster tails in the oven's baking tray.
2. Whisk rest of the ingredients in a bowl and pour over the lobster tails.
3. Press "power button" of air fry oven and turn the dial to select the "broil" mode.
4. Press the time button and again turn the dial to set the cooking time to 8 minutes.
5. Now push the temp button and rotate the dial to set the temperature at 350 degrees f.
6. Once preheated, place the lobster's baking tray in the oven and close its lid.
7. Serve warm.

Nutrition: Calories 281/ fat 18.1g/Carbs 0.8g/ protein 27.9g

428. Sheet pan seafood bake

Preparation Time: 10 minutes
Cooking Time: 14 minutes
Serving: 4
Ingredients
- `2 corn ears, husked and diced
- `1 lb. Red potatoes, boiled, diced
- `2 lbs. Clams, scrubbed
- `1 lb. Shrimp, peeled and de-veined
- `12 oz. Sausage, sliced
- `1/2 red onion, sliced
- `4 lobster tails, peeled
- `Black pepper to taste
- `1 lemon, cut into wedges
- `1 cup butter
- `3 teaspoons minced garlic
- `1 tablespoon old bay seasoning
- `Fresh parsley for garnish

Directions:
1. Toss all the veggies, corn, seafood, oil, and seasoning in a baking tray.
2. Press "power button" of air fry oven and turn the dial to select the "broil" mode.
3. Press the time button and again turn the dial to set the cooking time to 14 minutes.
4. Now push the temp button and rotate the dial to set the temperature at 425 degrees f.
5. Once preheated, place the seafood's baking tray in the oven and close its lid.
6. Serve warm.

Nutrition: `Calories 532 Fat: 35.6g Carbs 26.3g protein 28.7g

MEAT

429. Pork And Mixed Greens Salad

Preparation Time: 10 minutes
Cooking Time: 15 minutes
Servings: 4
Ingredients:
- 2 pounds pork tenderloin, cut into 1-inch slices
- 1 teaspoon olive oil
- 1 teaspoon dried marjoram
- ⅛ teaspoon freshly ground black pepper
- 6 cups mixed salad greens
- 1 red bell pepper, sliced
- 1 (8-ounce) package button mushrooms, sliced
- ⅓ cup low-sodium low-fat vinaigrette dressing

Directions:
1. In a medium bowl, mix the pork slices and olive oil. Toss to coat.
2. Sprinkle with the marjoram and pepper and rub these into the pork.
3. Grill the pork in the air fryer, in batches, for about 4 to 6 minutes, or until the pork reaches at least 145°F on a meat thermometer.
4. Meanwhile, in a serving bowl, mix the salad greens, red bell pepper, and mushrooms. Toss gently.
5. When the pork is cooked, add the slices to the salad. -Drizzle with the vinaigrette and toss gently. Serve immediately.

Nutrition: Calories: 172 Fat: 5 g Saturated Fat: 1g Protein: 27g Carbs: 28g Sodium: 124mg Fiber: 2g Sugar: 3g

430. Pork Satay

Preparation Time: 15 minutes
Cooking Time: 9-14 minutes
Servings: 4
Ingredients:
- 1 (1-pound) pork tenderloin, cut into 1½-inch cubes
- ¼ cup minced onion
- 2 garlic cloves, minced
- 1 jalapeño pepper, minced
- 2 tablespoons freshly squeezed lime juice
- 2 tablespoons coconut milk
- 2 tablespoons unsalted peanut butter
- 2 teaspoons curry powder

Directions:
1. In a medium bowl, mix the pork, onion, garlic, jalapeño, lime juice, coconut milk, peanut butter, and curry powder until well combined. Let stand for 10 minutes at room temperature.
2. With a slotted spoon, remove the pork from the marinade. Reserve the marinade.
3. Thread the pork onto about 8 bamboo or metal skewers. Grill for 9 to 14 minutes, brushing once with the reserved marinade, until the pork reaches at least 145°F on a meat thermometer. Discard any remaining marinade. Serve immediately.

Nutrition: Calories: 194 Fat: 7g Saturated Fat: 3g Protein: 25g Carbs: 7g Sodium: 65mg Fiber: 1g Sugar: 3g

431. Pork Burgers With Red Cabbage Salad

Preparation Time: 20 minutes
Cooking Time: 7-9 minutes
Servings: 4
Ingredients:
- ½ cup Greek yogurt
- 2 tablespoons low-sodium mustard, divided
- 1 tablespoon lemon juice
- ¼ cup sliced red cabbage
- ¼ cup grated carrots
- 1-pound lean ground pork
- ½ teaspoon paprika
- 1 cup mixed baby lettuce greens
- 2 small tomatoes, sliced
- 8 small low-sodium whole-wheat sandwich buns, cut in half

Directions:
1. In a small bowl, combine the yogurt, 1 tablespoon mustard, lemon juice, cabbage, and carrots; mix and refrigerate.
2. In a medium bowl, combine the pork, remaining 1 tablespoon mustard, and paprika. Form into 8 small patties.
3. Put the sliders into the air fryer basket. Grill for 7 to 9 minutes, or until the sliders register 165°F as tested with a meat thermometer.
4. Assemble the burgers by placing some of the lettuce greens on a bun bottom. Top with a tomato slice, the -burgers, and the cabbage mixture. Add the bun top and serve immediately.

Nutrition: Calories: 472 Fat 15g Saturated Fat: 0g Protein: 35g Carbs: 51g Sodium 138mg Sugar 8g Fiber 8g

432. Crispy Mustard Pork Tenderloin

Preparation Time: 10 minutes | Cooking Time: 12-16 minutes
Servings: 4
Ingredients:
- 3 tablespoons low-sodium grainy mustard
- 2 teaspoons olive oil
- ¼ teaspoon dry mustard powder
- 1 (1-pound) pork tenderloin, silverskin and excess fat trimmed and discarded (see Tip, here)
- 2 slices low-sodium whole-wheat bread, crumbled
- ¼ cup ground walnuts (see Tip)
- 2 tablespoons cornstarch

Directions:
1. In a small bowl, stir together the mustard, olive oil, and mustard powder. Spread this mixture over the pork.
2. On a plate, mix the bread crumbs, walnuts, and cornstarch. Dip the mustard-coated pork into the crumb mixture to coat.
3. Air-fry the pork for 12 to 16 minutes, or until it registers at least 145°F on a meat thermometer. Slice to serve.

Nutrition: Calories: 239 Fat: 9g Saturated Fat: 2g Protein: 26g Carbs: 15g Sodium: 118m Fiber: 2g Sugar: 3g

433. Sage 'n Thyme Rubbed Porterhouse

Preparation Time: 2 hours
Cooking Time: 20 minutes
Servings: 4
Ingredients:
- ¼ cup fish sauce
- 2 porterhouse steaks
- 2 tablespoons sage
- 2 tablespoons thyme
- Salt and pepper to taste

Directions:
1. Place all of the ingredients in a resealable bag and allow to marinate in the fridge for at least 2 hours.
2. Preheat the air fryer to 400F.
3. Cook one side for 10 minutes, flip and cook the other side for another 10 minutes. Cook in batches.

Nutrition: Calories Nutrition: 1178; Carbs: 6.3g; Protein: 112.5g; Fat: 75.5g; Sugar: 2.6g; Sodium: 3086mg; Fiber: 2.2g

434. Italian Beef Rolls

Preparation time: 5 minutes
Cooking time: 15 minutes
Servings: 6
Ingredients:
- `1 cup fresh basil
- `1 cup fresh parsley
- `¼ cup pine nuts
- `2 cloves garlic
- `1 teaspoon lemon zest
- `½ teaspoon salt
- `½ teaspoon black pepper
- `¼ cup Parmesan cheese, freshly grated
- `3 tablespoons olive oil
- `1 ½ pounds flank steak, butterfly cut
- `1 cup fresh mozzarella cheese, sliced
- `1 cup fresh spinach, torn
- `1 cup roasted red peppers, sliced

Directions
1. In a blender or food processor combine the basil, parsley, pine nuts, garlic, lemon zest, salt, black pepper, Parmesan, and olive oil. Pulse until well blended.
2. Lay the steak out on the counter and open up the butterfly cut.
3. Spread the herb sauce over the steak.
4. Next, layer on the mozzarella cheese, spinach, and roasted red bell peppers.
5. Roll the steak up and secure it with cooking twine or toothpicks throughout.
6. Set the air fryer to 400 F.
7. Place the steak roll in the air fryer and cook for 15 minutes, or until the desired doneness is reached.
8. Remove the steak roll from the air fryer and let it rest for 10 minutes before removing the twine or toothpicks and slicing.

Nutrition: Calories 277.7 Fat 15.9g Saturated Fat 6.2g Carbs 3.1g Dietary Fiber 0.7g Sugars 1.2 g Protein 29.5g

435. Cajun Rubbed Ribeye Steaks

Preparation time: 5 minutes
Cooking time: 15 minutes
Servings: 4
Ingredients:
- 1 tablespoon Cajun seasoning
- 1 teaspoon black pepper, coarsely ground
- 1 teaspoon garlic powder
- 1 teaspoon powdered ground coffee
- 1 tablespoon olive oil
- 1 ½ pounds ribeye steaks

Directions
1. Set the air fryer to 400 F.
2. Combine the Cajun seasoning, black pepper, garlic powder, and powdered ground coffee.
3. Add the olive oil to the spice mixture and combine until a paste forms.
4. Rub both sides of each steak with the Cajun spice paste.
5. Place the steaks in the basket of the air fryer and cook for 15 minutes, adjusting for desired doneness. Turn once halfway through cooking.
6. Remove the steaks from the air fryer and let them rest for 10 minutes before serving.

Nutrition: Calories 358.0 Fat 15.5g Saturated Fat 4.5g Protein 50.0g

436. Herb Crusted Lamb Chops

Preparation time: 5 minutes
Cooking time: 15 minutes
Servings: 4
Ingredients:
- 1 ½ pounds lamb chops
- ½ teaspoon salt
- ½ teaspoon black pepper
- 1 tablespoon fresh tarragon, chopped
- 1 tablespoon fresh mint, chopped
- 1 tablespoon fresh parsley, chopped
- 1 tablespoon shallots, finely diced
- 1 teaspoon lemon zest, freshly grated
- ¼ cup Parmesan cheese, freshly grated
- ½ cup panko bread crumbs
- 1 tablespoon Dijon mustard
- 1 tablespoon olive oil

Directions
1. Set the air fryer to 390 F.
2. Season the lamb chops with salt and black pepper.
3. In a blender or food processor, combine the tarragon, mint, parsley, shallots, lemon zest, Parmesan cheese, and panko bread crumbs. Pulse until well blended.
4. Add the Dijon mustard and olive oil and mix well.
5. Spread the herb mixture on both sides of each of the lamb chops.
6. Place the lamb chops in the basket of the air fryer.
7. Cook for 10-12 minutes, or until the desired doneness is reached.
8. Remove the chops to a platter, and let them rest for at least 5 minutes before serving.

Nutrition: Calories 306.6 Fat 13.5g Saturated Fat 4.8g Carbs 6.6g Dietary Fiber 0.3g Sugars 0.5g Protein 37.6g

437. Pumpkin and Pork Escallops

Preparation Time: 10 minutes
Cooking Time: 40 minutes
Servings: 4
Ingredients:
- 40 oz pork, ground
- 1 medium-sized pumpkin, cut into eighths
- 4 tbsp. dried sage
- 2 tbsp. clarified and unsalted butter
- 2 teaspoons dried thyme
- 2 teaspoons ground cinnamon
- 1 cup of fish broth
- 1 teaspoon of salt
- 1 teaspoon pepper

Directions:
1. Fix your Air fryer to sauté mode and melt the unsalted butter or use the skillet to melt the butter and then pour in your Air fryer.
2. Put all the spices in a bowl. Flavor the pork with the spices mix. Form the pork escallops. Add them into the Air fryer.
3. Then, add in the pumpkin and pour in the fish broth.
4. Make sure to lock the lid and set on a HIGH pressure for 40 minutes.
5. Quick-release the pressure and transfer the pork escallops to a plate.
6. Combine the pumpkin with the pork escallops and ladle up the sauce (if any) all over the meat.

Nutrition: Calories – 254 Protein 57 g. Fat 63 g. Carbs 199 g.

438. Pork Taquitos

Preparation time: 10 minutes
Cooking time: 16 minutes
Servings: 8
Ingredients:
- 1 juiced lime
- whole wheat tortillas
- ½ cup shredded mozzarella cheese
- 30 ounces of cooked and shredded pork tenderloin

Directions
1. Preparing the Ingredients.
2. Ensure your air fryer is preheated to 380 F.
3. Drizzle pork with lime juice and gently mix.
4. Heat up tortillas in the microwave with a dampened paper towel to soften.
5. Add about 3 ounces of pork and ¼ cup of shredded cheese to each tortilla. Tightly roll them up.
6. Spray the Air fryer basket with a bit of olive oil.
7. Air Frying.
8. Set temperature to 380 F, and set time to 10 minutes. Air fry taquitos 7-10 minutes till tortillas turn a slight golden color, making sure to flip halfway through cooking process.

Nutrition: Calories 309 Fat 11g Protein 21g Sugar 2g

439. Pork And Fruit Kebabs

Preparation Time: 15 minutes
Cooking Time: 9-12 minutes
Servings: 4
Ingredients:
- ⅓ cup apricot jam
- 2 tablespoons freshly squeezed lemon juice
- 2 teaspoons olive oil
- ½ teaspoon dried tarragon
- 1 (1-pound) pork tenderloin, cut into 1-inch cubes
- 4 plums, pitted and quartered (see Tip)
- 4 small apricots, pitted and halved (see Tip)

Directions:
1. In a large bowl, mix the jam, lemon juice, olive oil, and tarragon.
2. Add the pork and stir to coat. Let stand for 10 minutes at room temperature.
3. Alternating the items, thread the pork, plums, and -apricots onto 4 metal skewers that fit into the air fryer. Brush with any remaining jam mixture. Discard any remaining marinade.
4. Grill the kebabs in the air fryer for 9 to 12 minutes, or until the pork reaches 145°F on a meat thermometer and the fruit is tender. Serve immediately.

Nutrition: Calories: 256 Fat; 5g Saturated Fat; 1g Protein: 24g Carbs: 30g Sodium: 60mg Fiber: 2g Sugar: 22g

440. Steak And Vegetable Kebabs

Preparation Time: 15 minutes
Cooking Time: 5 to 7 minutes
Servings: 4
Ingredients:
- 2 tablespoons balsamic vinegar
- 2 teaspoons olive oil
- ½ teaspoon dried marjoram
- ⅛ teaspoon freshly ground black pepper
- ¾ pound round steak, cut into 1-inch pieces
- 1 red bell pepper, sliced
- 16 button mushrooms
- 1 cup cherry tomatoes (

Directions:
1. In a medium bowl, stir together the balsamic vinegar, olive oil, marjoram, and black pepper.
2. Add the steak and stir to coat. Let stand for 10 minutes at room temperature.
3. Alternating items, thread the beef, red bell pepper, mushrooms, and tomatoes onto 8 bamboo (see Tip, here) or metal skewers that fit in the air fryer.
4. Grill in the air fryer for 5 to 7 minutes, or until the beef is browned and reaches at least 145°F on a meat thermo-meter. Serve immediately.

Nutrition: Calories: 194 Fat: 6g Saturated Fat: 2g Protein: 31g Carbs: 7g Sodium: 53mg Fiber: 2g Sugar: 2g

441. Air Fryer Baby Back Ribs

Preparation time: 5 minutes
Cooking time: 25 minutes
Servings: 4
Ingredients:
- `1 rack baby back ribs
- `1 tablespoon garlic powder
- `1 teaspoon freshly ground black pepper
- `2 tablespoons salt
- `1 cup barbecue sauce (any type)

Directions
1. Preparing the Ingredients
2. Dry the ribs with a paper towel.
3. Season the ribs with the garlic powder, pepper, and salt.
4. Place the seasoned ribs into the air fryer.
5. Air Frying.
6. Set the temperature of your Air fryer to 400 F. Set the timer and grill for 10 minutes.
7. Using tongs, flip the ribs.

8. Reset the timer and grill for another 10 minutes.
9. Once the ribs are cooked, use a pastry brush to brush on the barbecue sauce, then set the timer and grill for a final 3 to 5 minutes.

Nutrition: Calories 422 Fat 27g Saturated Fat 10g Carbs 25g Fiber 1g Sugar 17g Protein 18g Iron 1mg Sodium 4273mg

442. Keto Parmesan Crusted Pork Chops

Preparation time: 10 minutes
Cooking time: 15 minutes
Servings: 8
Ingredients:
- `3 tbsp. grated parmesan cheese
- `1 cup pork rind crumbs
- `2 beaten eggs
- `¼ tsp. chili powder
- `½ tsp. onion powder
- `1 tsp. smoked paprika
- `¼ tsp. pepper
- `½ tsp. salt
- `4-6 thick boneless pork chops

Directions
1. Preparing the Ingredients.
2. Ensure your air fryer is preheated to 400 F.
3. With pepper and salt, season both sides of pork chops.
4. In a food processor, pulse pork rinds into crumbs. Mix crumbs with other seasonings.
5. Beat eggs and add to another bowl.
6. Dip pork chops into eggs then into pork rind crumb mixture.
7. Air Frying.
8. Spray down air fryer with olive oil and add pork chops to the basket. Set temperature to 400 degree Fahrenheit, and set time to 15 minutes.

Nutrition: Calories 422 Fat 19g Sugar 2g Protein 38g

443. Pork Milanese

Preparation time: 10 minutes
Cooking time: 12 minutes
Servings: 4
Ingredients:
- (1-inch) boneless pork chops
- Fine sea salt and ground black pepper
- large eggs
- ¾ cup powdered Parmesan cheese about 2¼ ounces
- Chopped fresh parsley, for garnish
- Lemon slices, for serving

Directions
1. Preparing the Ingredients.
2. Spray the Air fryer basket with avocado oil. Preheat the Air fryer to 400 F. Place the pork chops between 2 sheets of plastic wrap and pound them with the flat side of a meat tenderizer until they're ¼ inch thick. Lightly season both sides of the chops with salt and pepper. Lightly beat the eggs in a shallow bowl. Divide the Parmesan cheese evenly between 2 bowls and set the bowls in this order: Parmesan, eggs, Parmesan. Dredge a chop in the first bowl of Parmesan, then dip it in the eggs, and then dredge it again in the second bowl of Parmesan, making sure both sides and all edges are well coated. Repeat with the remaining chops.
3. Air Frying.

4. Place the chops in the Air fryer basket and cook for 12 minutes, or until the internal temperature reaches 145 F, flipping halfway through.
5. Garnish with fresh parsley and serve immediately with lemon slices. Store leftovers in an airtight container in the refrigerator for up to 3 days. Reheat in a preheated 390 F air fryer for 5 minutes, or until warmed through.

Nutrition: Calories 351 Fat 18g Total Carbs 3g Fiber 1g Protein 42g

444. Crispy Fried Pork Chops the Southern Way

Preparation time: 10 minutes
Cooking time: 25 minutes
Servings: 4
Ingredients:
- ½ cup all-purpose flour
- ½ cup low fat buttermilk
- ½ teaspoon black pepper
- ½ teaspoon Tabasco sauce
- ½ teaspoon paprika
- bone-in pork chops

Directions
1. Preparing the Ingredients.
2. Place the buttermilk and hot sauce in a Ziploc bag and add the pork chops. Allow to marinate for at least an hour in the fridge.
3. In a bowl, combine the flour, paprika, and black pepper.
4. Remove pork from the Ziploc bag and dredge in the flour mixture.
5. Preheat the Air fryer to 390 F.
6. Spray the pork chops with cooking oil.
7. Air Frying.
8. Place in the Air fryer basket and cook for 25 minutes.

Nutrition: Calories 427 Fat 21.2g Sugar 2g Protein 46.4g

445. Italian Sausages with Peppers and Onions

Preparation time: 5 minutes
Cooking time: 28 minutes
Servings: 3
Ingredients:
- 1 medium onion, thinly sliced
- 1 yellow or orange bell pepper, thinly sliced
- 1 red bell pepper, thinly sliced
- ¼ cup avocado oil or melted coconut oil
- 1 teaspoon fine sea salt
- Italian sausages
- Dijon mustard, for serving (optional)

Directions
1. Preparing the Ingredients.
2. Preheat the Air fryer to 400 F. Place the onion and peppers in a large bowl. Drizzle with the oil and toss well to coat the veggies. Season with the salt.
3. Place the onion and peppers in a 6-inch pie pan and cook in the air fryer for 8 minutes, stirring halfway through. Remove from the air fryer and set aside.
4. Air Frying.
5. Spray the Air fryer basket with avocado oil. Place the sausages in the Air fryer basket and cook for 20 minutes, or until crispy and golden brown. During the last minute or two

of cooking, add the onion and peppers to the basket with the sausages to warm them through.
6. Place the onion and peppers on a serving platter and arrange the sausages on top. Serve Dijon mustard on the side, if desired.
7. Store leftovers in an airtight container in the fridge for up to 7 days or in the freezer for up to a month. Reheat in a preheated 390 F air fryer for 3 minutes, or until heated through.

Nutrition: Calories 576 Fat 49g Total Carbs 8g Fiber 2g Protein 25g

446. Cilantro-Mint Pork BBQ Thai Style

Preparation time: 5 minutes
Cooking time: 15 minutes
Servings: 3
Ingredients:
- 1 minced hot chile
- 1 minced shallot
- 1-pound ground pork
- tablespoons fish sauce
- tablespoons lime juice
- tablespoons basil
- tablespoons chopped mint
- tablespoons cilantro

Directions
1. Preparing the Ingredients.
2. In a shallow dish, mix well all Ingredients with hands. Form into 1-inch ovals. Thread ovals in skewers. Place on skewer rack in air fryer.
3. Air Frying.
4. For 15 minutes, cook on 360 F. Halfway through cooking time, turnover skewers. If needed, cook in batches. Serve and enjoy.

Nutrition: Calories 455 Fat 31.5g Protein 40.4g

447. Dry Rub Baby Back Ribs

Preparation time: 5 minutes
Cooking time: 35 minutes
Servings: 2
Ingredients:
- `2 teaspoons fine sea salt
- `1 teaspoon ground black pepper
- `2 teaspoons smoked paprika
- `1 teaspoon garlic powder
- `1 teaspoon onion powder
- `½ teaspoon chili powder (optional)
- `1 rack baby back ribs, cut in half crosswise

Directions
1. Preparing the Ingredients.
2. Spray the Air fryer basket with avocado oil. Preheat the Air fryer to 350 F. In a small bowl, combine the salt, pepper, and seasonings. Season the ribs on all sides with the seasoning mixture.
3. Air Frying.
4. Place the ribs in the Air fryer basket and cook for 15 minutes, then flip the ribs over and cook for another 15 to 20 minutes, until the ribs are cooked through and the internal temperature reaches 145 F.

Nutrition: Calories 515 Fat 40g Protein 37g Carbs 3g Fiber 1g

448. Curry Pork Roast in Coconut Sauce

Preparation time: 10 minutes
Cooking time: 60 minutes
Servings: 6
Ingredients:
- ½ teaspoon curry powder
- ½ teaspoon ground turmeric powder
- 1 can unsweetened coconut milk
- 1 tablespoons sugar
- tablespoons fish sauce
- tablespoons soy sauce
- pounds pork shoulder
- Salt and pepper to taste

Directions
1. Preparing the Ingredients.
2. Place all ingredients in bowl and allow the meat to marinate in the fridge for at least 2 hours.
3. Preheat the Air fryer to 390 F.
4. Place the grill pan accessory in the air fryer.
5. Air Frying.
6. Grill the meat for 20 minutes making sure to flip the pork every 10 minutes for even grilling and cook in batches.
7. Meanwhile, pour the marinade in a saucepan and allow to simmer for 10 minutes until the sauce thickens.
8. Baste the pork with the sauce before serving.

Nutrition: Calories 688 Fat 52g Protein 17g

449. Buckwheat with Pork Chunks

Preparation Time: 10 minutes
Cooking Time: 30 minutes
Servings: 4
Ingredients:
- 28 oz (1 can) pork chunks with broth, canned
- 1 cup of buckwheat, rinsed
- 4 medium onions, peeled and sliced
- 3 cups of water
- ½ teaspoon salt and pepper

Directions:
1. Immerse the buckwheat in the warm water for around 10 minutes. Then add in the buckwheat to your pot.
2. In a skillet or wok, fry the onions for 10 minutes until clear and caramelized. In a bowl, mash the pork using a fork.
3. Combine the buckwheat, pork chunks and caramelized onions and add to your Air fryer.
4. Make sure to lock the lid and cook on a HIGH pressure for 20 minutes.
5. Naturally release the pressure over 10 minutes.
6. Portion the buckwheat and pork chunks into four deep containers and dollop each bowl with the salt and pepper. Serve the buckwheat porridge and pork chunks with the coffee.

Nutrition: Calories 285 Protein 52 g .Fat 79g.Carbs 237 g

450. Crispy Roast Garlic-Salt Pork

Preparation time: 5 minutes
Cooking time: 45 minutes
Servings: 4
Ingredients:
- 1 teaspoon Chinese five spice powder
- 1 teaspoon white pepper
- pounds pork belly
- teaspoons garlic salt

Directions
1. Preheat the Air fryer oven to 390 F.
2. Mix all the spices in a bowl to create the dry rub.
3. Score the skin of the pork belly with a knife and season the entire pork with the spice rub.
4. Place in the air fryer basket and cook for 40 to 45 minutes until the skin is crispy.
5. Chop before serving.

Nutrition: Calories 785 Fat 80.7g Protein 14.2g

451. Pulled Pork

Preparation Time: 5 minutes
Cooking Time: 45 minutes
Servings: 6-8
Ingredients:
- 1 (4-pound) boneless pork roast, trimmed of excess fat
- 3 packed tablespoons brown sugar
- 2 tablespoons chili powder
- 2 tablespoons smoked paprika
- 1 teaspoon ground cumin
- 1 teaspoon kosher salt
- ½ teaspoon freshly ground white pepper
- ¾ cup apple cider or water
- ½ cup apple cider vinegar
- ½ cup ketchup
- 6 to 8 soft hamburger buns

Directions:
1. Cut the pork roast against the grain into 4 equal pieces.
2. In a small bowl, combine the brown sugar, chili powder, paprika, cumin, salt, and pepper. Rub the pork roast until covered with the spice mixture.
3. Add the apple cider or water, vinegar, and ketchup to the Air fryer and stir. Add the spice-rubbed pork and secure the lid.
4. Select Manual or Pressure Cook and cook at high pressure for 45 minutes.
5. Once done cooking, select Cancel and use a natural release. This will take about 15 minutes.
6. Move the pork to a plate and let it cool slightly. Shred with a fork, trimming off and discarding any extra fat.
7. Skim excess fat from the cooking liquid. Choose Sauté and simmer the sauce for about 20 minutes, or until it measures at the 2-cup line. Season with salt and pepper if needed.
8. Put half of the sauce to the pork and stir to combine. Serve on soft hamburger buns with more sauce.

Nutrition: Calories 624 Protein 84 g. Fat 4 g. Carbs 37 g.

452. Light Herbed Meatballs

Preparation Time: 10 minutes
Cooking Time: 12 to 17 minutes
Servings: 24
Ingredients:
- 1 medium onion, minced
- 2 garlic cloves, minced
- 1 teaspoon olive oil
- 1 slice low-sodium whole-wheat bread, crumbled
- 3 tablespoons 1 percent milk
- 1 teaspoon dried marjoram
- 1 teaspoon dried basil
- 1-pound 96 percent lean ground beef

Directions:
1. In a 6-by-2-inch pan, combine the onion, garlic, and olive oil. Air-fry for 2 to 4 minutes, or until the vegetables are crisp-tender.
2. Transfer the vegetables to a medium bowl, and add the bread crumbs, milk, marjoram, and basil. Mix well.
3. Add the ground beef. With your hands, work the mixture gently but thoroughly until combined. Form the meat mixture into about 24 (1-inch) meatballs.
4. Bake the meatballs, in batches, in the air fryer basket for 12 to 17 minutes, or until they reach 160°F on a meat thermometer. Serve immediately.

Nutrition: Calories: 190 Fat: 6g Saturated Fat: 2g Protein: 25g Carbs: 8g Sodium: 120mg Fiber: 1g; Sugar: 2g

453. Brown Rice And Beef-Stuffed Bell Peppers

Preparation Time: 10 minutes
Cooking Time: 11 to 16 minutes
Servings: 4
Ingredients:
- 4 medium bell peppers, any colors, rinsed, tops removed
- 1 medium onion, chopped
- ½ cup grated carrot
- 2 teaspoons olive oil
- 2 medium beefsteak tomatoes, chopped
- 1 cup cooked brown rice
- 1 cup chopped cooked low-sodium roast beef (see Tip)
- 1 teaspoon dried marjoram

Directions:
1. Remove the stems from the bell pepper tops and chop the tops.
2. In a 6-by-2-inch pan, combine the chopped bell pepper tops, onion, carrot, and olive oil. Cook for 2 to 4 minutes, or until the vegetables are crisp-tender.
3. Transfer the vegetables to a medium bowl. Add the tomatoes, brown rice, roast beef, and marjoram. Stir to mix.
4. Stuff the vegetable mixture into the bell peppers. Place the bell peppers in the air fryer basket. Bake for 11 to 16 minutes, or until the peppers are tender and the filling is hot. Serve immediately.

Nutrition: Calories: 206 Fat: 6g Saturated Fat: 1g Protein: 18g Carbs: 20g Sodium: 105mg Fiber: 3g Sugar: 5g

454. Chinese Salt and Pepper Pork Chop Stir-fry

Preparation time: 10 minutes
Cooking time: 15 minutes
Servings: 4
Ingredients:
- Pork Chops:
- Olive oil
- ¾ cup almond flour
- ¼ tsp. pepper
- ½ tsp. salt
- 1 egg white
- Pork Chops
- Stir-fry:
- ¼ tsp. pepper
- 1 tsp. sea salt
- tbsp. olive oil
- sliced scallions
- sliced jalapeno peppers

Directions
1. Coat the Air fryer oven basket with olive oil.
2. Whisk pepper, salt, and egg white together till foamy.
3. Cut pork chops into pieces, leaving just a bit on bones. Pat dry.
4. Add pieces of pork to egg white mixture, coating well. Let sit for marinade 20 minutes.
5. Put marinated chops into a large bowl and add almond flour. Dredge and shake off excess and place into air fryer.
6. Set temperature to 360 F, and set time to 12 minutes. Cook 12 minutes at 360 degrees.
7. Turn up the heat to 400 F and cook another 6 minutes till pork chops are nice and crisp.
8. To make stir-fry, remove jalapeno seeds and chop up. Chop scallions and mix with jalapeno pieces.
9. Heat a skillet with olive oil. Stir-fry pepper, salt, scallions, and jalapenos 60 seconds. Then add fried pork pieces to skills and toss with scallion mixture. Stir-fry 1-2 minutes till well coated and hot.

Nutrition: Calories 294 Fat 17g Protein 36g Sugar 4g

455. Garlic Putter Pork Chops

Preparation time: 10 minutes
Cooking time: 7 minutes
Servings: 4
Ingredients:
- `2 tsp. parsley
- `2 tsp. grated garlic cloves
- `1 tbsp. coconut oil
- `1 tbsp. coconut butter
- `4 pork chops

Directions
1. Ensure your Air fryer oven is preheated to 350 F.
2. Mix butter, coconut oil, and all seasoning together. Then rub seasoning mixture over all sides of pork chops. Place in foil, seal, and chill for 1 hour.
3. Remove pork chops from foil and place into air fryer.
4. Pour into the Oven rack/basket. Place the Rack on the middle-shelf of the Air fryer oven. Set temperature to 350 F, and set time to 7 minutes. Cook 7 minutes on one side and 8 minutes on the other.
5. Drizzle with olive oil and serve alongside a green salad.

Nutrition: Calories 526 Fat 23g Protein 41g Sugar 4g

456. Fried Pork with Sweet and Sour Glaze

Preparation time: 5 minutes
Cooking time: 30 minutes
Servings: 4
Ingredients:
- ¼ cup rice wine vinegar
- ¼ teaspoon Chinese five spice powder
- 1 cup potato starch
- 1 green onion, chopped
- large eggs, beaten
- pounds pork chops cut into chunks
- tablespoons cornstarch + 3 tablespoons water
- tablespoons brown sugar
- Salt and pepper to taste

Directions
1. Preheat the Air fryer oven to 390 F.
2. Season pork chops with salt and pepper to taste.
3. Dip the pork chops in egg. Set aside.
4. In a bowl, combine the potato starch and Chinese five spice powder.
5. Dredge the pork chops in the flour mixture.
6. Place in the double layer rack and cook for 30 minutes.
7. Meanwhile, place the vinegar and brown sugar in a saucepan. Season with salt and pepper to taste. Stir in the cornstarch slurry and allow to simmer until thick.
8. Serve the pork chops with the sauce and garnish with green onions.

Nutrition: Calories 420 Fat 11.8g Protein 69.2g

457. Oregano-Paprika on Breaded Pork

Preparation time: 10 minutes
Cooking time: 30 minutes
Servings: 4
Ingredients:
- ¼ cup water
- ¼ teaspoon dry mustard
- ½ teaspoon black pepper
- ½ teaspoon cayenne pepper
- ½ teaspoon garlic powder
- ½ teaspoon salt
- 1 cup panko breadcrumbs
- 1 egg, beaten
- teaspoons oregano
- lean pork chops
- teaspoons paprika

Directions
1. Preheat the Air fryer oven to 390 F.
2. Pat dry the pork chops.
3. In a mixing bowl, combine the egg and water. Then set aside.
4. In another bowl, combine the rest of the Ingredients.
5. Dip the pork chops in the egg mixture and dredge in the flour mixture.
6. Place in the air fryer basket and cook for 25 to 30 minutes until golden.

Nutrition: Calories 364 Fat 20.2g Protein 42.9g

458. Cajun Pork Steaks

Preparation time: 5 minutes
Cooking time: 20 minutes
Servings: 6
Ingredients:
- 4-6 pork steaks
- BBQ sauce:
- Cajun seasoning
- 1 tbsp. vinegar
- 1 tsp. low-sodium soy sauce
- ½ cup brown sugar
- ½ cup vegan ketchup

Directions
1. Ensure your Air fryer oven is preheated to 290 F.
2. Sprinkle pork steaks with Cajun seasoning.
3. Combine remaining ingredients and brush onto steaks. Add coated steaks to air fryer.
4. Pour into the Oven rack/basket. Place the Rack on the middle-shelf of the Air fryer oven. Set temperature to 290 F, and set time to 20 minutes. Cook 15-20 minutes till just browned.

Nutrition: Calories 209 Fat 11g Protein 28g Sugar 2g

459. Cajun Bacon Pork Loin Fillet

Preparation Time: 10 minutes
Cooking Time: 20 minutes
Servings: 6
Ingredients:
- 1½ pounds pork loin fillet or pork tenderloin
- 3 tablespoons olive oil
- 2 tablespoons Cajun Spice Mix
- Salt
- 6 slices bacon
- Olive oil spray

Directions:
1. Preparing the Ingredients. Cut the pork in half so that it will fit in the air fryer basket.
2. Place both pieces of meat in a resealable plastic bag. Add the oil, Cajun seasoning, and salt to taste, if using. Seal the bag and massage to coat all of the meat with the oil and seasonings. Marinate in the refrigerator for at least 1 hour or up to 24 hours.
3. Air Frying. Remove the pork from the bag and wrap 3 bacon slices around each piece. Spray the air fryer basket with olive oil spray. Place the meat in the air fryer. Set the air fryer to 350°F for 15 minutes. Increase the temperature to 400°F for 5 minutes. Use a meat thermometer to ensure the meat has reached an internal temperature of 145°F.
4. Let the meat rest for 10 minutes. Slice into 6 medallions and serve.

Nutrition: Calories: 355 kcal Protein: 34.83 g Fat: 22.88 g Carbs: 0.6 g

460. Country Fried Steak

Preparation time: 5 minutes
Cooking time: 12 minutes
Servings: 2
Ingredients
- `1 tsp. pepper
- `2 cup almond milk
- `2 tbsp. almond flour
- `6 ounces ground sausage meat
- `1 tsp. pepper
- `1 tsp. salt
- `1 tsp. garlic powder
- `1 tsp. onion powder
- `1 cup panko breadcrumbs
- `1 cup almond flour
- `3 beaten eggs
- `6 ounces sirloin steak, pounded till thin

Directions
1. Preparing the Ingredients. Season panko breadcrumbs with spices.
2. Dredge steak in flour, then egg, and then seasoned panko mixture.
3. Place into air fryer rack/basket.
4. Air Frying. Set temperature to 370 F, and set time to 12 minutes.
5. To make sausage gravy, cook sausage and drain off fat, but reserve 2 tablespoons.
6. Add flour to sausage and mix until incorporated. Gradually mix in milk over medium to high heat till it becomes thick.
7. Season mixture with pepper and cook 3 minutes longer.
8. Serve steak topped with gravy and enjoy!

Nutrition: Calories 395 Fat 11g Protein 39g Sugar 5g

461. Polish Sausage with Sauerkraut

Preparation Time: 10 minutes
Cooking Time: 15 minutes
Servings: 6
Ingredients:
- 1 tablespoon extra-virgin olive oil
- 1 medium yellow onion, chopped
- 2 garlic cloves, minced
- 2 cups low-sodium chicken broth
- 1 (12-ounce) package fully cooked Polish sausage, cut into 1-inch-thick slices
- 1 (32-ounce) jar sauerkraut
- 1 apple, chopped
- 3 medium red potatoes, chopped into bite-size pieces

Directions:
1. Choose Sauté and add the olive oil to the inner pot. Once the oil is warm enough, add the onion and garlic and sauté for 3 minutes, stirring occasionally.
2. Press Cancel and pour in the broth. Using a wooden spoon, remove any browned bits stuck to the bottom of the pot. Add the sausage slices, sauerkraut, apple, and potatoes; stir to combine.
3. Secure the lid into place. Choose Pressure Cook or Manual; fix the pressure to High and the time to 10 minutes. Ensure the steam release knob is in the sealed position. Once done cooking, naturally release the pressure for 10 minutes, then quick release any remaining pressure.
4. Unlock and remove the lid. Serve immediately, or place the sausages and veggies in an airtight container and refrigerate for up to 4 days.

Nutrition: Calories 341 Protein 12 g. Fat 19 g. Carbs 32 g.

462. Air Fryer Roast Beef

Preparation time: 5 minutes
Cooking time: 45 minutes
Servings: 6
Ingredients:
- Roast beef
- 1 tbsp. olive oil

MEAT

- Seasonings of choice

Directions
1. Preparing the Ingredients. Ensure your air fryer oven is preheated to 160 F.
2. Place roast in bowl and toss with olive oil and desired seasonings.
3. Put seasoned roast into the Air fryer oven.
4. Air Frying. Set temperature to 160 F, and set time to 30 minutes and cook 30 minutes.
5. Turn roast when the timer sounds and cook another 15 minutes.

Nutrition: Calories 267 Fat 8g Protein 2g

463. Crispy Mongolian Beef

Preparation time: 5 minutes
Cooking time: 10 minutes
Servings: 6
Ingredients:
- `Olive oil
- `½ cup almond flour
- `2 pounds beef tenderloin or beef chuck, sliced into strips
- `Sauce:
- `½ cup chopped green onion
- `1 tsp. red chili flakes
- `1 tsp. almond flour
- `½ cup brown sugar
- `1 tsp. hoisin sauce
- `½ cup water
- `½ cup rice vinegar
- `½ cup low-sodium soy sauce
- `1 tbsp. chopped garlic
- `1 tbsp. finely chopped ginger
- `2 tbsp. olive oil

Directions
1. Preparing the Ingredients. Toss strips of beef in almond flour, ensuring they are coated well. Add to the Air fryer oven.
2. Air Frying. Set temperature to 300 F, and set time to 10 minutes, and cook 10 minutes at 300 F.
3. Meanwhile, add all sauce ingredients to the pan and bring to a boil. Mix well.
4. Add beef strips to the sauce and cook 2 minutes.
5. Serve over cauliflower rice!

Nutrition: Calories 290 Fat 14g Protein 22g Sugar 1g

464. German Sausages with Peppers and Onions

Preparation Time: 12 minutes
Cooking Time: 10 minutes
Servings: 4
Ingredients:
- 2 tablespoons butter or canola oil
- 4 large German sausages, such as bratwurst
- 1 large onion, halved and cut into ¼-inch slices
- 1 green bell pepper, cut into ¼-inch rings
- 1 red bell pepper, cut into ¼-inch rings
- 1 (12-ounce) bottle German-style lager
- Kosher salt
- Freshly ground black pepper
- 4 hoagie rolls
- Good-quality mustard, for serving

Directions:
1. To preheat the Air fryer, select Sauté. Add the butter or oil.
2. Once hot, add the sausages. Brown them on both sides. This will take 5 to 10 minutes.
3. Remove the sausages and turn the heat to high. Add the onion and stir. Cook for 4 to 5 minutes until the onion starts to brown.
4. Add the peppers and lager and stir. Cook for 1 minute. Season with salt and pepper. Add the sausages and secure the lid.
5. Select Manual or Pressure Cook and cook at high pressure for 10 minutes
6. Once done cooking, use a natural release. Serve the sausages on hoagie rolls topped with the peppers and onions and mustard.

Nutrition: Calories 624 Protein 23 g. Fat 13 g. Carbs 57 g.

465. Porchetta-Style Pork Chops

Preparation Time: 10 minutes
Cooking Time: 15 minutes
Servings: 2
Ingredients:
- 1 tablespoon extra-virgin olive oil
- Grated zest of 1 lemon
- 2 cloves garlic, minced
- 2 teaspoons chopped fresh rosemary
- 1 teaspoon finely chopped fresh sage
- 1 teaspoon fennel seeds, lightly crushed
- ¼ to ½ teaspoon red pepper flakes
- 1 teaspoon kosher salt
- 1 teaspoon black pepper
- (8-ounce) center-cut bone-in pork chops, about 1 inch thick

Directions:
1. Preparing the Ingredients. In a small bowl, combine the olive oil, zest, garlic, rosemary, sage, fennel seeds, red pepper, salt, and black pepper. Stir, crushing the herbs with the back of a spoon, until a paste forms. Spread the seasoning mix on both sides of the pork chops.
2. Air Frying. Place the chops in the air fryer basket. Set the air fryer to 375°F for 15 minutes. Use a meat thermometer to ensure the chops have reached an internal temperature of 145°F.

Nutrition: Calories: 200 kcal Protein: 23.45 g Fat: 9.69 g Carbs: 4.46 g

466. Wonton Meatballs

Preparation Time: 15 minutes
Cooking Time: 10 minutes
Servings: 4
Ingredients:
- 1-pound ground pork
- 2 large eggs
- ¼ cup chopped green onions (white and green parts)
- ¼ cup chopped fresh cilantro or parsley
- 1 tablespoon minced fresh ginger
- 3 cloves garlic, minced
- 2 teaspoons soy sauce
- 1 teaspoon oyster sauce
- ½ teaspoon kosher salt
- 1 teaspoon black pepper

Directions:
1. Preparing the Ingredients. In the bowl of a stand mixer fitted with the paddle attachment, combine the pork, eggs, green

onions, cilantro, ginger, garlic, soy sauce, oyster sauce, salt, and pepper. Mix on low speed until all of the ingredients are incorporated, 2 to 3 minutes.
2. Form the mixture into 12 meatballs and arrange in a single layer in the air fryer basket.
3. Air Frying. Set the air fryer to 350°F for 10 minutes. Use a meat thermometer to ensure the meatballs have reached an internal temperature of 145°F.
4. Transfer the meatballs to a bowl and serve.

Nutrition: Calories: 402 kcal Protein: 32.69 g Fat: 27.91 g Carbs: 3.1 g

467. Beef Steaks with Beans

Preparation time: 5 minutes
Cooking time: 10 minutes
Servings: 4

Ingredients:
- `4 beef steaks, trim the fat and cut into strips
- `1 cup green onions, chopped
- `2 cloves garlic, minced
- `1 red bell pepper, seeded and thinly sliced
- `1 can tomatoes, crushed
- `1 can cannellini beans
- `3/4 cup beef broth
- `1/4 teaspoon dried basil
- `1/2 teaspoon cayenne pepper
- `1/2 teaspoon sea salt
- `1/4 teaspoon ground black pepper, or to taste

Directions
1. Preparing the Ingredients. Add the steaks, green onions and garlic to the Oven rack/basket. Place the Rack on the middle-shelf of the Air fryer oven.
2. Air Frying. Cook at 390 F for 10 minutes, working in batches.
3. Stir in the remaining ingredients and cook for an additional 5 minutes.

Nutrition: Calories 148 Fat 5g Sugars 1g Protein 24g

468. Crispy Dumplings

Preparation Time: 10 minutes
Cooking Time: 10 minutes
Servings: 8

Ingredients:
- .5 lb. Ground pork
- 1 tbsp. Olive oil
- .5 tsp each Black pepper and salt
- Half of 1 pkg. Dumpling wrappers

Directions:
1. Set the Air Fryer temperature setting at 390° Fahrenheit.
2. Mix the fixings together.
3. Prepare each dumpling using two teaspoons of the pork mixture.
4. Seal the edges with a portion of water to make the triangle form.
5. Lightly spritz the Air Fryer basket using a cooking oil spray as needed. Add the dumplings to air-fry for eight minutes.
6. Serve when they're ready.

Nutrition: Calories:110 kcal Protein: 8.14 g Fat: 8.34 g Carbs: 0.27 g

469. Rolled All Beef Hot Dogs

Preparation time: 5 minutes
Cooking time: 10 minutes
Servings: 4

Ingredients:
- Package of 8 All Beef Hot Dog Wieners
- Package of 8 Pop Open Crescent Rolls

Directions
1. Set the oven temperature at 375 F.
2. Start with separating the crescent rolls into 8 triangles.
3. Roll each triangle around each individual hot dog and drop them into the Air Fryer Oven Basket leaving space between each one.
4. Bake for 10 minutes, serve with dipping sauce and enjoy.

Nutrition: Calories 576 Fat 49g Total Carbs 8g Fiber 2g Protein 25g

470. Argentinian Style Skirt Steak

Preparation time: 5 minutes + marinate time
Cooking time: 10 minutes
Servings: 4

Ingredients:
- `16 oz. skirt steak
- `1 cup parsley, washed and finely chopped
- `¼ cup mint, washed and finely chopped
- `2 tbsp. oregano, washed and finely chopped
- `3 cloves garlic, finely chopped
- `1 tsp. crushed red pepper
- `1 tbsp. ground cumin
- `1 tsp. cayenne pepper
- `2 tsp. smoked paprika
- `1 tsp. salt
- `¼ tsp. black pepper
- `3 tbsp. Red wine vinegar

Directions
1. Set the oven temperature at 350 F.
2. Start with mixing all of the ingredients together.
3. Cut the steak in portions.
4. Place the steak and ¼ of the sauce in a re-sealable bag.
5. Marinate in the fridge for 2 hours.
6. Remove the steak and let rest for 30 minutes.
7. Place the chicken in the Air Fryer Oven Basket and cook for 8 minutes.
8. Garnish with the sauce, serve and enjoy.

Nutrition: Calories 515 Fat 40g Protein 37g Carbs 3g Fiber 1g

471. Greek Style Lamb Chops

Preparation time: 10 minutes
Cooking time: 20 minutes
Servings: 8

Ingredients:
- `Olive oil, 1/4 cup
- `Lemon juice, 1/4 cup
- `2 dried oregano teaspoons
- `2 teaspoons of garlic minced
- `1 salt teaspoon
- `One-half teaspoon of black pepper
- `Lamb chops, 2 pounds

Directions
1. Combine the olive oil, lemon juice, dried oregano, minced garlic, salt and pepper with your lamb chops in a large mixing bowl.
2. In the air fryer basket, or on your air fryer tray, put the lamb chops.
3. Place them in the furnace

4. Set the timer at 400 degrees F for 5 minutes, flip the lamb chops after 5 minutes and cook for a further 5 minutes.
5. Plate, serve and enjoy yourself!

Nutrition: Calories 306.6 Fat 13.5g Carbs 6.6g Protein 37.6g

472. Korean Style Meat Skewers

Preparation time: 1 hour 5 minutes
Cooking time: 6 minutes
Servings: 2-4

Ingredients:
- g ssamjang
- 20g gochujang
- ml of soy sauce
- ml of sesame oil
- ml of honey
- ml of rice wine vinegar
- 454 g of veal cut into 38 mm pieces
- wooden skewers, cut in half

Directions
1. Combine the ssamjang, gochujang, soy sauce, sesame oil, honey, and vinegar in a bowl.
2. Mix the cut meat in the marinade and marinate for an hour.
3. Select Preheat on the Air Fryer and press Start / Pause.
4. Thread the pieces of meat onto the skewers and place the skewers in the preheated air fryer.
5. Select Steak and press Start / Pause.

Nutrition: Calories 422 Fat 27g Sugar 17g Protein 18g

473. Blue Cheese Stuffed Burgers

Preparation time: 5 minutes
Cooking time: 22 minutes
Servings: 6

Ingredients:
- `2 lb. beef, ground
- `2 tbsp. Worcestershire sauce
- `1 tbsp. salt
- `1/2 tbsp. ground black pepper
- `4 slices of bacon, cooked and chopped
- `8 tbsp. crumbled blue cheese
- `1/4 cup butter
- `4 brioche buns
- `8 slices tomato
- `4 Bibb lettuce leaves
- `4 slices red onion

Directions:
1. In a mixing bowl, mix beef, sauce, salt, and pepper until well mixed. Make 4 balls from the mixture then divide each ball into a half.
2. Press the ball on a flat surface. Stuff half of it with bacon and 2 tbsp. cheese. Top with the unstuffed meat and seal the edges.
3. Place the burgers on the air fryer rack.
4. Select the air fry setting of your Air fryer oven and set the temperature at 400 F for 18 minutes. Press start.
5. Remove the burgers from the rack and set aside to cool. Transfer the rack to position 1 and butter the buns. Place the buns on the rack, butter side up.
6. Select the broil setting. Set temperature at 400 F for 10 minutes. Broil the buns until golden brown.
7. Assemble the buns and burgers with tomatoes, lettuce leaves, and onions.
8. Serve and enjoy.

Nutrition: Calories 590 Carbs 33g Fat 35g Protein 34g

474. Air Fried Strip Steak with Red Wine Sauce

Preparation time: 5 minutes
Cooking time: 20 minutes
Servings: 4

Ingredients:
- 1 lb. strip steak, 1 inch thick
- `Salt and pepper
- `1 tbsp. butter, unsalted
- `1/4 cup shallots, chopped
- `1 tbsp. garlic, minced
- `1/2 cup dry red wine
- `2 tbsp. beef bouillon base
- `3 tbsp. heavy cream

Directions:
1. Season the steak with salt and pepper and transfer it into the air fryer tray.
2. Select the air fry setting. Set the temperature at 400 F for 10 minutes. When the steak is halfway cooked, turn it so that it can be evenly cooked. Let the steak rest for 10 minutes.
3. Meanwhile, prepare the steak. Melt butter in a saucepan over medium heat. Add shallots, garlic, salt, and pepper. Sauté for 1 minute.
4. Add red wine and bring the mixture to boil. Stir with bouillon base until well mixed. Add heavy cream and cook for 1 more minute.
5. Remove the sauce from heat but keep warm.
6. Slice the steak and serve with the sauce.

Nutrition: Calories 649 Carbs 7.5g Fat 34g Protein 69g

475. Easy Marinated Steak

Preparation time: 5 minutes
Cooking time: 15 minutes
Servings: 2

Ingredients:
- `2 8oz Butcher Box New York strip steaks
- `1 tbsp. soy sauce, low sodium
- `1 tbsp. liquid smoke
- `1 tbsp. McCormick's steak seasoning
- `1/2 tbsp. cocoa powder, unsweetened
- `Salt and pepper to taste
- ` Melted butter

Directions:
1. Season the steak with soy sauce and liquid smoke until the steak is well seasoned. Refrigerate for a few hours.
2. Place the steak in the air fryer tray.
3. Select the air fry setting and set the temperature at 370 F for 5 minutes.
4. When the steak is well-cooked, with an internal temperature 160 F, remove from heat and serve it with melted butter. Enjoy.

Nutrition: Calories 476 Carbs 1g Fat 28g Protein 49g

476. Rib Eye Steak

Preparation time: 5 minutes
Cooking time: 22 minutes
Servings: 1
Ingredients:
- oz. Rib eye steak
- 1 tbsp. salt
- 3/4 tbsp. pepper
- 1/2 tbsp. garlic powder
- 3/4 steak seasoning

Directions:
1. Season the steak with the spices and set aside.
2. Place the steak in the air fryer tray.
3. Select the air fry setting. Set the temperature at 390 F for 12 minutes. Press start.
4. When the steak is halfway cooked, flip it.
5. Transfer the steak to a plate and cover it with a paper foil. Let it rest for 8 minutes before serving it.

Nutrition: Calories 651 Carbs 7.5g Fat 49g Protein 44g

477. Steak Bites and Mushrooms

Preparation time: 5 minutes
Cooking time: 20 minutes
Servings: 3
Ingredients:
- `1 lb. steaks
- `8 oz. mushrooms
- `2 tbsp. butter
- `1 tbsp. Worcestershire sauce
- `1/2 tbsp. garlic powder
- `Salt to taste
- ` Black pepper to taste
- `Minced parsley
- `Melted butter
- `Chili flakes

Directions:
1. Pat dry the steak and mushrooms then coat them with butter. Season with Worcestershire sauce, garlic, salt, and pepper.
2. Spread the steak and mushrooms in the air fryer tray.
3. Select the air fry setting of your Air fryer oven then set the temperature at 400 F for 18 minutes.
4. Ensure you shake and flip the steak and mushrooms at least 2 times through the cooking process.
5. Garnish with parsley, butter, and chili flakes.
6. Serve when warm.

Nutrition: Calories 300 Carbs 2g Fat 21g Protein 24g

478. Korean Beef Wraps

Preparation time: 5 minutes
Cooking time: 20 minutes
Servings: 4
Ingredients:
- ` 1/4 cup soy sauce, low sodium
- `2 tbsp. orange juice, fresh
- `1 tbsp. dark brown sugar
- `1 tbsp. red pepper flakes
- `1 tbsp. garlic, minced
- `1 bunch scallions, white part
- `2 tbsp. sesame oil
- `1 lb. sirloin steak
- `2 tbsp. sesame seeds, toasted
- `Steamed white rice
- `Kimchi
- `Romaine Lettuce hearts

Directions:
1. In a mixing bowl, mix the first 7 ingredients until well combined. Add the steak and toss to coat well.
2. Let the steak stand for at least 4 hours to marinate.
3. Transfer the steak to the air fryer tray.
4. Select the air fry setting of your Air fryer oven and set the temperature at 400 F for 10 minutes. Press the start button.
5. When the steak with rice, kimchi wrapped in a lettuce leaf. Enjoy.

Nutrition: Calories 298 Carbs 11g Fat 12g Protein 35g

479. Hanger Steak with Red wine sauce

Preparation time: 5 minutes
Cooking time: 25 minutes
Servings: 2
Ingredients:
- 7oz hanger steaks
- Salt and pepper
- Oil

For the Sauce
- `1 shallot, thinly sliced
- `2 tbsp. butter
- `1 bottle red wine
- `1 cup bee stock
- `1 tbsp. wholegrain mustard

Directions:
1. Season the hanger steak with salt and pepper and transfer it into the air fryer tray.
2. Select the air fry setting on your Air fryer oven then set the temperature at 400 F and timer for 10 minutes. When the steak is halfway cooked, turn it so that it can be evenly cooked. Let the steak rest for 10 minutes.
3. Meanwhile, heat a saucepan over medium heat. Cook shallots with butter until translucent. Add wine and cook until almost all the wine has evaporated.
4. Add beef stock and cook until it is reduced by a half.
5. Add mustard and swirl until well combined. Season with salt and pepper to taste.
6. Add a tablespoon of cold butter and swirl the saucepan until it melts. Serve immediately with the hanger steak.

Nutrition: Calories 619 Carbs 6.5g Fat 32g Protein 63g

480. Air Fried Beef Tenderloin

Preparation time: 5 minutes
Cooking time: 47 minutes
Servings: 8
Ingredients:
- `2 lb. beef tenderloin
- `1 tbsp. vegetable oil
- `1 tbsp. dried oregano
- `1 tbsp. salt
- `1/2 tbsp. black pepper, cracked

Directions:
1. Pat dry the tenderloin with a paper towel and place it on a platter.
2. Drizzle vegetable oil and sprinkle oregano, salt, and pepper. Rub the spices on the meat until well coated.
3. Place the roast on the air fryer tray.

4. Select the air fry setting. Set temperature at 390 F for 22 minutes. Reduce the temperature to 360 F and cook for 10 minutes.
5. Transfer the meat to a plate and allow to rest while tented with paper foil for 10 minutes before serving.

Nutrition: Calories 235 Carbs 0.2g Fat 10.6g Protein 32.4g

481. Air Fried Ground Beef

Preparation time: 5 minutes
Cooking time: 12 minutes
Servings: 6
Ingredients:
- 1-1/2 lb. ground beef
- 1 tbsp. salt
- 1/2 tbsp. pepper
- 1/2 tbsp. garlic powder

Directions:
1. Put the beef in a baking tray then season well with salt, pepper, and garlic powder.
2. Stir well using a wooden spoon.
3. Select the air fry setting on the Air fryer oven.
4. Set the temperature at 400 F for 5 minutes.
5. Stir well when halfway cooked and continue cooking for the remaining minutes.
6. Crumble the meat well and leave the broth. Use the beef in your favorite recipe.

Nutrition: Calories 134 Carbs 0.3g Fat 7.5g Protein 15.1g

482. Lemon Garlic Lamb Chops

Preparation Time: 10 minutes
Cooking Time: 6 minutes
Servings: 6
Ingredients:
- 6 lamb loin chops
- 2 tbsp. fresh lemon juice
- 1 ½ tbsp. lemon zest
- 1 tbsp. dried rosemary
- 1 tbsp. olive oil
- 1 tbsp. garlic, minced
- Pepper
- Salt

Directions:
1. Add lamb chops in a mixing bowl. Add remaining ingredients on top of lamb chops and coat well.
2. Arrange lamb chops on air fryer oven tray and air fry at 400 F for 3 minutes. Turn lamb chops to another side and air fry for 3 minutes more. Serve and enjoy.

Nutrition: Calories 69 Fat 6 g Carbs 1.2 g Protein 3 g

483. Herb Butter Rib-eye Steak

Preparation Time: 10 minutes
Cooking Time: 14 minutes
Servings: 4
Ingredients:
- 2 lbs. rib eye steak, bone-in
- 1 tsp fresh rosemary, chopped
- 1 tsp fresh thyme, chopped
- 1 tsp fresh chives, chopped
- 2 tsp fresh parsley, chopped
- 1 tsp garlic, minced
- ¼ cup butter softened
- Pepper
- Salt

Directions:
1. In a small bowl, combine together butter and herbs.
2. Rub herb butter on rib-eye steak and place it in the refrigerator for 30 minutes.
3. Place marinated steak on air fryer oven pan and cook at 400 F for 12-14 minutes. Serve and enjoy.

Nutrition: Calories 416 Fat 36.7 g Carbs 0.7 g Protein 20.3 g

484. Classic Beef Jerky

Preparation Time: 10 minutes
Cooking Time: 4 hours
Servings: 4
Ingredients:
- 2 lbs. London broil, sliced thinly
- 1 tsp onion powder
- 3 tbsp. brown sugar
- 3 tbsp. soy sauce
- 1 tsp olive oil
- 3/4 tsp garlic powder

Directions:
2. Add all ingredients except meat in the large zip-lock bag.
3. Mix until well combined. Add meat in the bag.
4. Seal bag and massage gently to cover the meat with marinade.
5. Let marinate the meat for 1 hour.
6. Arrange marinated meat slices on air fryer tray and dehydrate at 160 F for 4 hours.

Nutrition: Calories 133 Fat 4.7 g Carbs 9.4 g Protein 13.4 g

485. Pork Cutlet Rolls

Preparation time: 10 minutes
Cooking time: 15 minutes
Servings: 4
Ingredients:
- `4 Pork Cutlets
- `4 Sundried Tomatoes in oil
- `2 Tbsps Parsley, finely chopped
- `1 Green Onion, finely chopped
- `Black Pepper to taste
- `2 Tsps Paprika
- `1/2 Tbsp Olive Oil
- ` String for Rolled Meat

Directions:
1. Preparing the Ingredients. Preheat the Air fryer oven to 390 F.
2. Finely chop the tomatoes and mix with the parsley and green onion. Add salt and pepper to taste
3. Spread out the cutlets and coat them with the tomato mixture. Roll up the cutlets and secure intact with the string
4. Rub the rolls with salt, pepper, and paprika powder and thinly coat them with olive oil
5. Air Frying. Put the cutlet rolls in the Air fryer oven tray and cook for 15 minutes. Roast until nicely brown and done.
6. Serve with tomato sauce.

Nutrition: Calories 422 Fat 27g Protein 18g

486. Fried Pork Scotch Egg

Preparation time: 10 minutes
Cooking time: 25 minutes
Servings: 2
Ingredients:
- `3 soft-boiled eggs, peeled
- `8 ounces of raw minced pork, or sausage outside the casings
- `2 teaspoons of ground rosemary
- `2 teaspoons of garlic powder
- `Pinch of salt and pepper
- `2 raw eggs
- `1 cup of breadcrumbs (Panko, but other brands are fine, or home-made bread crumbs work too)

Directions:
1. Preparing the Ingredients. Cover the basket of the Air fryer oven with a lining of tin foil, leaving the edges uncovered to allow air to circulate through the basket. Preheat the air fryer oven to 350 F.
2. In a mixing bowl, combine the raw pork with the rosemary, garlic powder, salt, and pepper. This will probably be easiest to do with your masher or bare hands (though make sure to wash thoroughly after handling raw meat!); combine until all the spices are evenly spread throughout the meat.
3. Divide the meat mixture into three equal portions in the mixing bowl, and form each into balls with your hands.
4. Lay a large sheet of plastic wrap on the countertop, and flatten one of the balls of meat on top of it, to form a wide, flat meat-circle.
5. Place one of the peeled soft-boiled eggs in the center of the meat-circle and then, using the ends of the plastic wrap, pull the meat-circle so that it is fully covering and surrounding the soft-boiled egg.
6. Tighten and shape the plastic wrap covering the meat so that if forms a ball, and make sure not to squeeze too hard lest you squish the soft-boiled egg at the center of the ball! Set aside.
7. Repeat steps 5-7 with the other two soft-boiled eggs and portions of meat-mixture.
8. In a separate mixing bowl, beat the two raw eggs until fluffy and until the yolks and whites are fully combined.
9. One by one, remove the plastic wrap and dunk the pork-covered balls into the raw egg, and then roll them in the bread crumbs, covering fully and generously.
10. Place each of the bread-crumb covered meat-wrapped balls onto the foil-lined surface of the air fryer oven. Three of them should fit nicely, without touching.
11. Air Frying. Set the air fryer oven timer to 25 minutes.
12. About halfway through the cooking time, shake the handle of the air-fryer vigorously, so that the scotch eggs inside roll around and ensure full coverage.
13. After 25 minutes, the air fryer oven will shut off, and the scotch eggs should be perfect – the meat fully cooked, the egg-yolks still runny on the inside, and the outsides crispy and golden-brown. Using tongs, place them on serving plates, slice in half, and enjoy.

Nutrition: Calories 785 Fat 80.7g Protein 14.2g

487. Korean Barbeque Beef

Preparation Time: 15 minutes
Cooking time: 30 minutes
Servings: 4
Ingredients:
- `1 Lb. flank steak
- `1/4 Cup corn starch
- `1 Tablespoon Pompeian oil
- `1/2 Cup soy sauce
- `1/2 Cup brown sugar
- `2 Tablespoons Pompeian while vinegar
- `1 Tablespoon garlic (crushed)
- `½ Tablespoon sesame seeds
- `1 Tablespoon corn starch
- `1 Tablespoon water

Direction
1. The steak should be sliced into thin pieces and rubbed with corn starch and oil. The air fryer oven should be preheated at 390 F for 5 minutes. The basket should be covered by aluminum foil. The steaks are placed in the basket and heated for 20 minutes with intermittent flipping. In the meantime, all other ingredients are heated in a pan except water and cornstarch in medium heat to form the sauce. The sauce should be heated until reduced to half. The sauce should be poured over the steak and served with green beans and cooked rice.

Nutrition: Calories 487 Fat 10g Carbs 32g Protein 39g

488. Beef Burgers

Preparation Time: 15 minutes
Cooking Time: 18 minutes
Servings: 4
Ingredients:
For Burgers:
- 1-pound ground beef
- ½ cup panko breadcrumbs
- ¼ cup onion, chopped finely
- 3 tablespoons Dijon mustard
- 3 teaspoons low-sodium soy sauce
- 2 teaspoons fresh rosemary, chopped finely
- Salt, to taste

For Topping:
- 2 tablespoons Dijon mustard
- 1 tablespoon brown sugar
- 1 teaspoon soy sauce
- 4 Gruyere cheese slices

Directions:
1. In a large bowl, add all the ingredients and mix until well combined.
2. Make 4 equal-sized patties from the mixture.
3. Arrange the patties onto a cooking tray.
4. Arrange the drip pan in the bottom of Air Fryer Oven cooking chamber.
5. Select "Air Fry" and then adjust the temperature to 370 degrees F.
6. Set the timer for 15 minutes and press the "Start".
7. When the display shows "Add Food" insert the cooking rack in the center position.
8. When the display shows "Turn Food" turn the burgers.
9. Meanwhile, for sauce: in a small bowl, add the mustard, brown sugar and soy sauce and mix well.
10. When cooking time is complete, remove the tray and coat the burgers with the sauce.
11. Top each burger with 1 cheese slice.
12. Return the tray to the cooking chamber and select "Broil".
13. Set the timer for 3 minutes and press the "Start".
14. When cooking time is complete, remove the tray and serve hot.

Nutrition: Calories 402 Fat 18 g Carbs 6.3 g Protein 44.4 g

MEAT

489. Bacon Wrapped Filet Mignon

Preparation Time: 10 minutes
Cooking Time: 15 minutes
Servings: 2
Ingredients:
- 2 bacon slices
- 2 (4-ounce) filet mignon
- Salt and ground black pepper, as required
- Olive oil cooking spray

Directions:
6. Wrap 1 bacon slice around each filet mignon and secure with toothpicks.
7. Season the filets with the salt and black pepper lightly.
8. Arrange the filet mignon onto a coking rack and spray with cooking spray.
9. Arrange the drip pan in the bottom of Air Fryer Oven cooking chamber.
10. Select "Air Fry" and then adjust the temperature to 375 degrees F.
11. Set the timer for 15 minutes and press the "Start".
12. When the display shows "Add Food" insert the cooking rack in the center position.
13. When the display shows "Turn Food" turn the filets.
14. When cooking time is complete, remove the rack and serve hot.

Nutrition: Calories 360 Fat 19.6 g Carbs 0.4 g Protein 42.6 g

490. Braised Pork

Preparation Time: 40 minutes
Cooking time: 40 minutes
Servings: 2
Ingredients
- 1-pound pork loin roast, boneless and cubed
- tablespoons butter, melted and divided
- Salt and black pepper, to taste
- 1 cup chicken stock
- ¼ cup dry white wine
- 1 clove garlic, minced
- ½ teaspoon thyme, chopped
- ½ thyme sprig
- 1 bay leaf
- ¼ yellow onion, chopped
- 1 tablespoon white flour
- ¼ pound red grapes

Directions
1. Season pork cubes with salt and pepper. Rub with half the melted butter and put in the air fryer. Cook at 370 F for 8 minutes.
2. Meanwhile, heat a pan on the stove with 2 tablespoons of butter over medium heat. Add onion and garlic, and stir-fry for 2 minutes.
3. Add bay leaf, flour, thyme, salt, pepper, stock, and wine. Mix well. Bring to a simmer and take off the heat.
4. Add grapes and pork cubes. Cook in the air fryer at 360 F for 30 minutes.
5. Serve.

Nutrition: Calories 320 Fat 4g Carbs 29g Protein 38g

491. Lean Beef with Green Onions

Preparation Time: 10 minutes
Cooking time: 20 minutes
Servings: 2
Ingredients
- ½ cup green onion, chopped
- ½ cup soy sauce
- ¼ cup water
- tablespoons brown sugar
- tablespoons sesame seeds
- cloves garlic, minced
- ½ teaspoon black pepper
- ½ pound lean beef

Directions
1. In a bowl, mix the onion with water, soy sauce, garlic, sugar, sesame seeds, and pepper. Whisk and add meat. Marinate for 10 minutes.
2. Drain beef. Preheat the air fryer to 390 F, then cook beef for 20 minutes.
3. Serve.

Nutrition: Calories 329 Fat 8g Carbs 26g Protein 22g

492. Country Style Pork Tenderloin

Preparation Time: 15 minutes
Cooking Time: 25 minutes
Servings: 3
Ingredients:
- 1-pound pork tenderloin
- 1 tablespoon garlic, minced
- 2 tablespoons soy sauce
- 2 tablespoons honey
- 1 tablespoon Dijon mustard
- 1 tablespoon grain mustard
- 1 teaspoon Sriracha sauce

Directions:
1. In a large bowl, add all the ingredients except pork and mix well.
2. Add the pork tenderloin and coat with the mixture generously.
3. Refrigerate to marinate for 2-3 hours.
4. Remove the pork tenderloin from bowl, reserving the marinade.
5. Place the pork tenderloin onto the lightly greased cooking tray.
6. Arrange the drip pan in the bottom of Air Fryer Oven cooking chamber.
7. Select "Air Fry" and then adjust the temperature to 380 degrees F.
8. Set the timer for 25 minutes and press the "Start".
9. When the display shows "Add Food" insert the cooking tray in the center position.
10. When the display shows "Turn Food" turn the pork and oat with the reserved marinade.
11. When cooking time is complete, remove the tray and place the pork tenderloin onto a platter for about 10 minutes before slicing.
12. With a sharp knife, cut the pork tenderloin into desired sized slices and serve.

Nutrition: Calories 277 Fat 5.7 g Carbs 14.2 g Protein 40.7 g

493. Beef Brisket Recipe from Texas

Preparation time: 15 minutes
Cooking time: 1hour and 30 minutes
Servings: 8
Ingredients
- ½ cup beef stock
- 1 bay leaf
- 1 tablespoon garlic powder
- 1 tablespoon onion powder
- 1pounds beef brisket, trimmed
- 1tablespoons chili powder
- 1teaspoons dry mustard
- 1tablespoons olive oil
- Salt and pepper to taste

Directions:
1. Preheat the Air Fryer Oven for 5 minutes. Place all ingredients in a deep baking dish that will fit in the air fryer.
2. Bake for 1 hour and 30 minutes at 400°F.
3. Stir the beef every after 30 minutes to soak in the sauce.

Nutrition: Calories: 306; Fat: 24.1G Protein:18.3g

494. Lamb Meatballs

Preparation Time: 5 minutes
Cooking Time: 15 minutes
Servings: 4
Ingredients:
- 1 lb. ground lamb
- 1 egg white
- ½ teaspoon sea salt
- 2 tablespoons parsley, fresh, chopped
- 1 tablespoon coriander, chopped
- 2 garlic cloves, minced
- 1 tablespoon olive oil
- 1 tablespoon mint, chopped

Directions:
1. Preheat your air fryer to 320°Fahrenheit.
2. Add all the ingredients in a mixing bowl and combine well.
3. Shape small meatballs from the mixture and place them in air fryer basket and cook for 15-minutes serve hot!

Nutrition: Calories 312 Fat 9.8g Carbs 12.3g Protein 23g

495. Chimichurri Skirt Steak

Preparation time: 10 minutes
Cooking time: 8 minutes
Servings: 2
Ingredients
- x 8 oz Skirt Steak
- cup Finely Chopped Parsley
- ¼ cup Finely Chopped Mint
- Tbsp Fresh Oregano (Washed & finely chopped)
- Finely Chopped Cloves of Garlic
- 1 Tsp Red Pepper Flakes (Crushed)
- 1 Tbsp Ground Cumin
- 1 Tsp Cayenne Pepper
- Tsp Smoked Paprika
- 1 Tsp Salt
- ¼ Tsp Pepper
- ¾ cup Oil
- Tbsp Red Wine Vinegar

Directions:
1. Throw all the ingredients in a bowl (besides the steak) and mix well.
2. Put ¼ cup of the mixture in a plastic baggie with the steak and leave in the fridge overnight (2–24hrs).
3. Leave the bag out at room temperature for at least 30 min before popping into the air fryer. Preheat for a minute or two to 390° F before cooking until med–rare (8–10 min). Pour into the Oven rack/basket. Place the Rack on the middle-shelf of the Air Fryer Oven. Set temperature to 390°F, and set time to 10 minutes.
4. Put 2 Tbsp of the chimichurri mix on top of each steak before serving.

Nutrition: Calories 308.6 Fat 22.6g Carbs 3.0g Fiber 1.0g Protein 23.7g Sugar 0.1g Sodium 233.3mg

496. Creamy Burger & Potato Bake

Preparation time: 5 minutes
Cooking time: 55 minutes
Servings: 3
Ingredients
- salt to taste
- freshly ground pepper, to taste
- 1/2 (10.75 ounces) can condense cream of mushroom soup
- 1/2-pound lean ground beef
- 1-1/2 cups peeled and thinly sliced potatoes
- 1/2 cup shredded Cheddar cheese
- 1/4 cup chopped onion
- 1/4 cup and 2 tablespoons milk

Directions:
1. Lightly grease baking pan of the air fryer with cooking spray. Add ground beef. For 10 minutes, cook on 360°F. Stir and crumble halfway through cooking time.
2. Meanwhile, in a bowl, whisk well pepper, salt, milk, onion, and mushroom soup. Mix well.
3. Drain fat off ground beef and transfer beef to a plate.
4. In the same air fryer baking pan, layer ½ of potatoes on the bottom, then ½ of soup mixture, and then ½ of beef. Repeat process.
5. Cover pan with foil.
6. Cook for 30 minutes. Remove foil and cook for another 15 minutes or until potatoes are tender.
7. Serve and enjoy.

Nutrition: Calories: 399; Fat: 26.9G Protein: 22.1g

497. Beef Brisket Recipe from Texas

Preparation Time: 15 minutes
Cooking Time: 1 hour and 30 minutes
Servings: 8
Ingredients:
- 1 ½ cup beef stock
- 1 bay leaf
- 1 tablespoon garlic powder
- 1 tablespoon onion powder
- 2 pounds beef brisket, trimmed
- 2 tablespoons chili powder
- 2 teaspoons dry mustard
- 4 tablespoons olive oil
- Salt and pepper to taste

Directions:
1. Preheat the Air Fryer Oven for 5 minutes Place all ingredients in a deep baking dish that will fit in the air fryer.

2. Bake it for 1 hour and 30 minutes at 400°F.
3. Stir the beef every after 30 minutes to soak in the sauce.

Nutrition: Calories 306 Cal Fat 24.1 g Carbs 0 g Protein 18.3 g

498. Warming Winter Beef with Celery

Preparation time: 5 minutes
Cooking time: 12 minutes
Servings: 4

Ingredients
- 9ounces tender beef, chopped
- 1/2 cup leeks, chopped
- 1/2 cup celery stalks, chopped
- 2cloves garlic, smashed
- 2tablespoons red cooking wine
- 3/4 cup cream of celery soup
- sprigs rosemary, chopped
- 1/4 teaspoon smoked paprika
- 3/4 teaspoons salt
- 1/4 teaspoon black pepper, or to taste

Directions:
1. Add the beef, leeks, celery, and garlic to the baking dish; cook for about 5 minutes at 390 degrees F.
2. Once the meat is starting to tender, pour in the wine and soup. Season with rosemary, smoked paprika, salt, and black pepper. Now, cook an additional 7 minutes.

Nutrition: Calories 555 Fat 21g Carbs 79g Protein 27g

499. Charred Onions And Steak Cube BBQ

Preparation time: 5 minutes
Cooking time: 40 minutes
Servings: 3

Ingredients
- 1cup red onions, cut into wedges
- 1 tablespoon dry mustard
- 1 tablespoon olive oil
- 1-pound boneless beef sirloin, cut into cubes
- Salt and pepper to taste

Directions:
1. Preheat the air fryer to 390°F.
2. Place the grill pan accessory in the air fryer.
3. Toss all ingredients in a bowl and mix until everything is coated with the seasonings.
4. Place on the grill pan and cook for 40 minutes.
5. Halfway through the cooking time, give a stir to cook evenly.

Nutrition: Calories: 260; Fat: 10.7G Protein:35.5g

500. Beef Stroganoff

Preparation time: 10 minutes
Cooking time: 14 minutes
Servings: 4

Ingredients
- 9Ozs Tender Beef
- 1Onion, chopped
- 1 Tbsp Paprika
- 3/4 Cup Sour Cream
- Salt and Pepper to taste
- Baking Dish

Directions:
1. Preheat the Air Fryer Oven to 390 degrees.
2. Chop the beef and marinate it using paprika.
3. Add the chopped onions into the baking dish and heat for about 2 minutes in the Air Fryer Oven.
4. Add the beef into the dish when the onions are transparent, and cook for 5 minutes.
5. Once the beef is starting to tender, pour in the sour cream and cook for another 7 minutes.
6. At this point, the liquid should have reduced. Season with salt and pepper and serve.

Nutrition: Calories 391 Fat 23g Carbs 21g Fiber 1.3g Protein 25g Sugar 3.2g Sodium 300mg

501. Cheesy Ground Beef And Mac Taco Casserole

Preparation time: 10 minutes
Cooking time: 25 minutes
Servings: 5

Ingredients
- 1-ounce shredded Cheddar cheese
- 1-ounce shredded Monterey Jack cheese
- 1tablespoons chopped green onions
- 1/2 (10.75 ounces) can condensed tomato soup
- 1/2-pound lean ground beef
- 1/2 cup crushed tortilla chips
- 1/4-pound macaroni, cooked according to manufacturer's Instructions
- 1/4 cup chopped onion
- 1/4 cup sour cream (optional)
- 1/2 (1.25 ounce) package taco seasoning mix
- 1/2 (14.5 ounces) can diced tomatoes

Directions:
1. Lightly grease baking pan of the air fryer with cooking spray. Add onion and ground beef. For 10 minutes, cook on 360°F. Halfway through cooking time, stir and crumble ground beef.
2. Add taco seasoning
3. diced tomatoes, and tomato soup. Mix well. Mix in pasta.
4. Sprinkle crushed tortilla chips. Sprinkle cheese.
5. Cook for 15 minutes at 390°F until tops are lightly browned and cheese is melted.
6. Serve and enjoy.

Nutrition: Calories: 329; Fat: 17G Protein:15.6g

502. Beefy Steak Topped with Chimichurri Sauce

Preparation time: 5 minutes
Cooking time: 60 minutes
Servings: 6

Ingredients
- 1cup commercial chimichurri
- 1pounds steak
- 1Salt and pepper to taste

Directions:
1. Place all ingredients in a Ziploc bag and marinate in the fridge for 2 hours.
2. Preheat the air fryer to 390°F.
3. Place the grill pan accessory in the air fryer.
4. Grill the skirt steak for 20 minutes per batch.
5. Flip the steak every 10 minutes for even grilling.

Nutrition: Calories: 507; Fat: 27G Protein:63 g

503. Beef Ribeye Steak

Preparation time: 5 minutes
Cooking time: 20 minutes
Servings: 4
Ingredients
- (8-ounce) ribeye steaks
- 1tablespoon McCormick Grill Mates Montreal Steak Seasoning
- Salt
- Pepper

Directions:
1. Season the steaks with the steak seasoning and salt and pepper to taste. Place 2 steaks in the Air Fryer Oven. You can use an accessory grill pan, a layer rack, or the air fryer basket.
2. Cook for 4 minutes. Open the air fryer and flip the steaks.
3. Cook for an additional 4 to 5 minutes. Check for doneness to determine how much additional Cooking Time: is a need. Remove the cooked steaks from the Air Fryer Oven, then repeat for the remaining 2 steaks. Cool before serving.

Nutrition: Calories: 293; Fat: 22G Protein:23G Fiber:0g

504. Beef Korma

Preparation time: 10 minutes
Cooking time: 20 minutes
Servings: 6
Ingredients
- ½ cup yogurt
- 1tablespoon curry powder
- 1 tablespoon olive oil
- 1 onion, chopped
- cloves garlic, minced
- 1 tomato, diced
- ½ cup frozen baby peas, thawed

Directions:
1. In a medium bowl, combine the steak, yogurt, and curry powder. Stir and set aside.
2. In a 6-inch metal bowl, combine the olive oil, onion, and garlic.
3. Cook for 3 to 4 minutes or until crisp and tender.
4. Add the steak along with the yogurt and the diced tomato. Cook for 12 to 13 minutes or until steak is almost tender.
5. Stir in the peas and cook for 2 to 3 minutes or until hot.

Nutrition: Calories: 289; Fat: 11G Protein: 38G Fiber:2g

505. Cumin-Paprika Rubbed Beef Brisket

Preparation time: 5 minutes
Cooking time: 2 hours   Servings: 12
Ingredients
- ¼ teaspoon cayenne pepper
- ½ tablespoons paprika
- 1 teaspoon garlic powder
- 1 teaspoon ground cumin
- 1 teaspoon onion powder
- 1easpoons dry mustard
- 1teaspoons ground black pepper
- 1teaspoons salt
- 1pounds brisket roast
- 1tablespoons olive oil

Directions:
1. Place all ingredients in a Ziploc bag and allow to marinate in the fridge for at least 2 hours.
2. Preheat the Air Fryer Oven for 5 minutes.
3. Place the meat in a baking dish that will fit in the air fryer.
4. Place in the air fryer and cook for 2 hours at 350°F.

Nutrition: Calories: 269; Fat: 12.8G Protein:35.6G Fiber:2g

506. Beef & Lemon Schnitzel for One

Preparation time: 5 minutes
Cooking time: 12 minutes
Servings: 1
Ingredients
- 2 Tbsp Oil
- 2–3 oz Breadcrumbs
- Whisked Egg in a Saucer/Soup Plate
- 1 Beef Schnitzel
- 1 Freshly Picked Lemon

Directions:
1. Mix the oil and breadcrumbs until loose and crumbly. Dip the meat into the egg
2. then into the crumbs. Make sure that it is evenly covered.
3. Gently place in the air fryer basket, and cook at 350° F (preheat if needed) until done. The timing will depend on the thickness of the schnitzel, but for a relatively thin one, it should take roughly 12 min. Serve with a lemon half and a garden salad.

Nutrition: Calories 234.8 Fat 15.7g Carbs 4.4g Fiber 0.2g Protein 18.8g Sugar 0.2g Sodium 88.7mg

507. Crispy Beef Schnitzel

Preparation time: 5 minutes
Cooking time: 12 minutes
Servings: 1
Ingredients
- beef schnitzel
- Salt and ground black pepper, to taste
- 1tablespoons olive oil
- 1/3 cup breadcrumbs
- 1 egg
- whisked

Directions:
1. Season the schnitzel with salt and black pepper.
2. In a mixing bowl, combine the oil and breadcrumbs. In another shallow bowl, beat the egg until frothy.
3. Dip the schnitzel in the egG
4. then, dip it in the oil mixture.
5. Pour into the Oven rack/basket. Place the Rack on the middle-shelf of the Air Fryer Oven. Set temperature to 350°F, and set time to 12 minutes.
6. Enjoy!

Nutrition: Calories 274 Fat 11g Carbs 11.8g Fiber 0.4g Protein 32.8g Sugar 0.7g Sodium 545mg

508. Steak and Asparagus Bundles

Preparation Time: 15 minutes
Cooking Time: 15 minutes
Servings: 4
Ingredients:
- 2 - 2 1/2 pounds Flank steak - cut into 6 pieces
- Kosher salt/black pepper
- 2 cloves Garlic - crushed
- 1-pound Asparagus - trimmed
- 3 Bell peppers - seeded and sliced thinly
- 1/3 cup Beef broth
- 2 tablespoons unsalted butter
- Olive oil spray

Directions:
1. Season the fillets with salt and pepper and place in a large zippered bag.
2. Add garlic. Close the bag and massage the fillets so that they are completely covered.
3. Put in the fridge and marinate at least 1 hour overnight. When you're done, remove the marinade fillets and place them on a chopping board or sheet.
4. Throw away the marinade. Spread the mass evenly and place the asparagus and peppers in the middle of each steak.
5. Roll the steak around the vegetables and secure them.
6. Preheat the fryer. Depending on the size of your air fryer, the packages are stacked in the frying basket.
7. Spray the vegetables with olive oil. Cook for 5 minutes at 400 degrees.
8. Remove the meat packaging and let it rest for 5 minutes before serving / cutting. At rest in a small to medium hot pan: balsamic vinegar, broth and butter over medium heat.
9. Mix and continue cooking until the sauce thicken and halves. Season it with salt and pepper and pour the sauce over the meat packets before serving.

Nutrition: Calories 220 Fat 10g Carbs 3.8g Protein 27.6g

509. Raspberry Smoked Pork Chops

Preparation Time: 15 minutes
Cooking Time: 15 minutes
Servings: 4
Ingredients:
- Cooking spray
- 2 Large eggs
- 1/4 cup Coconut milk
- 1 cup Panko bread crumbs
- 1 cup finely chopped walnuts
- 4 Smoked bone-in pork chops (7-1/2 ounces each)
- 1/4 cup Coconut flour
- 2 tablespoons Stevia
- 2 tablespoons Raspberry
- 1 tablespoon Fresh orange juice

Directions:
1. Preheat the fryer to 400°. Spray some oil in the frying basket.
2. Mix the eggs and coconut milk in a flat bowl. Mix the panko breadcrumbs with walnuts in another flat bowl and cover the pork chops with the flour. Shake off excess.
3. Dip into the egg mixture and then into the crumb mixture and tap on it to help it stick. If necessary,
4. Work in batches and place the chops in a single layer in the basket of the air fryer oven. Spray with oil, cook for 12 to 15 minutes until golden brown, turn after half the cooking time and sprinkle with additional cooking spray.
5. Remove and keep warm.
6. Repeat with the remaining chops. In the meantime, put the remaining ingredients in a small saucepan. Bring to a boil. Boil and stir until it gets a little thick, 6-8 minutes. Serve with chops.

Nutrition: Calories 542 Fat 31.8g Carbs 24.9g Protein 41.3g

510. Beef With Beans

Preparation time: 10 minutes
Cooking time: 13 minutes
Servings: 8
Ingredients
- 12Ozs Lean Steak
- Onion, sliced
- 1 Can Chopped Tomatoes
- 3/4 Cup Beef Stock
- 1Tsp Fresh Thyme, chopped
- 1 Can Red Kidney Beans
- Salt and Pepper to taste
- Oven Safe Bowl

Directions:
1. Preheat the Air Fryer Oven to 390 degrees.
2. Trim the fat from the meat and cut into thin 1cm strips
3. Add onion slices to the oven-safe bowl and place it in the air fryer.
4. Pour into the Oven rack/basket. Place the Rack on the middle-shelf of the Air Fryer Oven. Set temperature to 390°F, and set time to 13 minutes, Cook for 3 minutes. Add the meat and continue cooking for 5 minutes.
5. Add the tomatoes and their juice, beef stock, thyme, and the beans and cook for an additional 5 minutes
6. Season with black pepper to taste.

Nutrition: Calories 264 Fat 9.6g Carbs 34g Fiber 8.4g Protein 16g Sugar 4.2g Sodium 1083mg

511. Swedish Meatballs

Preparation time: 10 minutes
Cooking time: 14 minutes
Servings: 4
Ingredients
- For the meatballs
- 1pound 93% lean ground beef
- 1 (1-ounce) packet Lipton Onion Recipe Soup & Dip Mix
- ⅓ cup bread crumbs
- 1 egg beaten
- Salt
- Pepper
- For the gravy
- 1 cup beef broth
- ⅓ cup heavy cream
- 1tablespoons all-purpose flour

Directions:
1. In a large bowl, combine the ground beef, onion soup mix, bread crumbs, egg
2. and salt and pepper to taste. Mix thoroughly.
3. Using 2 tablespoons of the meat mixture, create each meatball by rolling the beef mixture around in your hands. This should yield about 10 meatballs.
4. Place the meatballs in the air fryer basket. It is okay to stack them. Cook for 14 minutes.
5. While the meatballs cook, prepare the gravy. Heat a saucepan over medium-high heat.
6. Add the beef broth and heavy cream. Stir for 1 to 2 minutes.

7. Add the flour and stir. Cover and allow the sauce to simmer for 3 to 4 minutes, or until thick.
8. Drizzle the gravy over the meatballs and serve.

Nutrition: Calories: 178; Fat: 14G Protein:9G Fiber:0g

512. Rice and Meatball Stuffed Bell Peppers

Preparation time: 13 minutes
Cooking time: 15 minutes
Servings: 4

Ingredients
- 4 bell peppers
- tablespoon olive oil
- 1 small onion, chopped
- cloves garlic, minced
- 1 cup of frozen cooked rice, thawed
- 1 to 20 small frozen precooked meatballs, thawed
- ½ cup tomato sauce
- 1 tablespoons Dijon mustard

Directions:
1. To prepare the peppers, cut off about ½ inch of the tops. Carefully remove the membranes and seeds from inside the peppers. Set aside.
2. In a 6-by-6-by-2-inch pan, combine the olive oil, onion, and garlic.
3. Bake in the Air Fryer Oven for 2 to 4 minutes or until crisp and tender. Remove the vegetable mixture from the pan and set aside in a medium bowl.
4. Add the rice, meatballs, tomato sauce, and mustard to the vegetable mixture and stir to combine. Stuff the peppers with the meat-vegetable mixture.
5. Place the peppers in the air fryer basket and bake for 9 to 13 minutes or until the filling is hot and the peppers are tender.

Nutrition: Calories: 487; Fat: 21G Protein:26G Fiber:6g

513. Pub Style Corned Beef Egg Rolls

Preparation time: 15 minutes
Cooking time: 10 minutes
Servings: 10

Ingredients
- Olive oil
- ½ C. orange marmalade
- 1 slices of Swiss cheese
- egg
- egg roll wrappers
- Brandy Mustard Sauce:
- 1/16th tsp. pepper
- 1 tbsp. whole grain mustard
- 1 tsp. dry mustard powder
- 1 C. heavy cream
- ½ C. chicken stock
- ¼ C. brandy
- ¾ C. dry white wine
- ¼ tsp. curry powder
- ½ tbsp. cilantro
- 1 minced shallot
- 1 tbsp. ghee

Directions:
1. To make mustard sauce, add shallots and ghee to skillet, cooking until softened. Then add brandy and wine, heating to a low boil. Cook 5 minutes for liquids to reduce. Add stock and seasonings. Simmer 5 minutes.
2. Turn down the heat and add heavy cream. Cook on low till sauce reduces and it covers the back of a spoon.
3. Place sauce in the fridge to chill.
4. Crack the egg in a bowl and set to the side.
5. Layout an egg wrapper with the corner towards you. Brush the edges with egg wash.
6. Place 1/3 cup of corned beef mixture into the center along with 2 tablespoons of marmalade and ½ a slice of Swiss cheese.
7. Fold the bottom corner overfilling. As you are folding the sides, make sure they are stick well to the first flap you made.
8. Place filled rolls into prepared air fryer basket. Spritz rolls with olive oil.
9. Set temperature to 390°F, and set time to 10 minutes. Cook 10 minutes at 390 degrees, shaking halfway through cooking.
10. Serve rolls with Brandy Mustard sauce.

Nutrition: Calories: 415; Fat: 13G Protein:38G Sugar:4g

514. Stir-Fried Steak and Cabbage

Preparation time: 15 minutes
Cooking time: 10 minutes
Servings: 4

Ingredients
- ½ pound sirloin steak, cut into strips
- 1 teaspoons cornstarch
- tablespoon peanut oil
- 1 cups chopped red or green cabbage
- 1 yellow bell pepper, chopped
- 1 green onions, chopped
- cloves garlic, sliced
- ½ cup commercial stir-fry sauce

Directions:
1. Toss the steak with the cornstarch and set aside.
2. In a 6-inch metal bowl, combine the peanut oil with the cabbage.
3. Place in the basket and cook for 3 to 4 minutes.
4. Remove the bowl from the basket and add the steak, pepper, onions, and garlic. Return to the Air Fryer Oven and cook for 3 to 5 minutes or until the steak is cooked to desired doneness and vegetables are crisp and tender.
5. Add the stir-fry sauce and cook for 2 to 4 minutes or until hot. Serve over rice.

Nutrition: Calories: 180; Fat: 7G Protein:20G Fiber:2g

515. Reuben Egg Rolls

Preparation time: 5 minutes
Cooking time: 20 minutes
Servings: 6

Ingredients
- Swiss cheese
- Can of sauerkraut
- Sliced deli corned beef
- Egg roll wrappers

Directions:
1. Cut corned beef and Swiss cheese into thin slices.
2. Drain sauerkraut and dry well.
3. Take egg roll wrapper and moisten edges with water.
4. Stack the center with corned beef and cheese till you reach the desired thickness. Top off with sauerkraut.
5. Fold the corner closest to you over the edge of filling. Bring up sides and glue with water.

MEAT

6. Add to the Air Fryer Oven basket and spritz with olive oil.
7. Set temperature to 400°F, and set time to 4 minutes. Cook 4 minutes at 400 degrees, then flip and cook another 4 minutes.

Nutrition: Calories: 251; Fat: 12G Protein:31G Sugar:4g

516. Air-Fried Philly Cheesesteak

Preparation time: 5 minutes
Cooking time: 16 minutes
Servings: 6

Ingredients
- Large hoagie bun, sliced in half
- 6ounces of sirloin or flank steak, sliced into bite-sized pieces
- ½ white onion, rinsed and sliced
- ½ red pepper, rinsed and sliced
- 1slices of American cheese

Directions:
1. Set the Air Fryer Oven to 320 degrees for 10 minutes.
2. Arrange the steak pieces, onions, and peppers on a piece of tin foil, flat and not overlapping
3. and set the tin foil on one side of the air-fryer basket. The foil should not take up more than half of the surface; the juices from the steak and the moisture from the vegetables will mingle while cooking.
4. Lay the hoagie-bun halves, crusty-side up and soft-side down, on the other half of the air fryer.
5. After 10 minutes, the air fryer will shut off; the hoagie buns should be starting to crisp and the steak and vegetables will have begun to cook.
6. Carefully, flip the hoagie buns so they are now crusty-side down and soft-side up; cover both sides with one slice each of American cheese.
7. With a long spoon, gently stir the steak, onions, and peppers in the foil to ensure even coverage.
8. Set the air fryer to 360 degrees for 6 minutes.
9. After 6 minutes, when the fryer shuts off, the cheese will be perfectly melted over the toasted bread, and the steak will be juicy on the inside and crispy on the outside.
10. Remove the cheesy hoagie halves first, using tongs, and set on a serving plate; then cover one side with the steak, and top with the onions and peppers. Close with the other cheesy hoagie-half, slice into two pieces, and enjoy.

Nutrition: Calories 540 Carbs 50g Fiber 8.4g Protein 32g Sugar 4g Sodium720 mg

517. Herbed Roast Beef

Preparation time: 5 minutes
Cooking time: 20 minutes
Servings: 6

Ingredients
- ½ tsp. fresh rosemary
- 1tsp. dried thyme
- ¼ tsp. pepper
- 1 tsp. salt
- 4-pound top round roast beef
- 1tsp. olive oil

Directions:
1. Ensure your Air Fryer Oven is preheated to 360 degrees.
2. Rub olive oil all over beef.
3. Mix rosemary, thyme, pepper, and salt and proceed to rub all sides of beef with spice mixture.
4. Pour into the Oven rack/basket. Place the Rack on the middle-shelf of the Air Fryer Oven. Set temperature to 360°F, and set time to 20 minutes.
5. Allow roast to rest 10 minutes before slicing to serve.

Nutrition: Calories: 502; Fat: 18G Protein:48G Sugar:2g

518. Beef Empanadas

Preparation time: 5 minutes
Cooking time: 20 minutes
Servings: 6

Ingredients
- 1tsp. water
- 1 egg white
- 1 C. picadillo
- Goya empanada discs (thawed)

Directions:
1. Ensure your Air Fryer Oven is preheated to 325. Spray basket with olive oil.
2. Place 2 tablespoons of picadillo into the center of each disc. Fold the disc in half and use a fork to seal edges. Repeat with all ingredients.
3. Whisk egg white with water and brush tops of empanadas with egg wash.
4. Add 2-3 empanadas to the air fryer.
5. Set temperature to 325°F, and set time to 8 minutes, cook until golden. Repeat till you cook all filled empanadas.

Nutrition: Calories: 183; Fat: 5G Protein:11G Sugar:2g

519. Beef Pot Pie

Preparation time: 5 minutes
Cooking time: 90 minutes
Servings: 2

Ingredients
- 1tablespoon olive oil
- 1 pound beef stewing steak, cubed
- 1 large onion, chopped
- 1 tablespoon tomato puree
- 1 canale
- Warm water, as required
- 1beef bouillon cubes
- Salt and freshly ground black pepper, to taste
- 1 tablespoon plain flour plus more for dusting
- 1 prepared shortcrust pastry

Directions:
1. In a pan, heat oil on medium heat. Add steak and cook for about 4-5 minutes. Add onion and cook for about 4-5 minutes.
2. Add tomato puree and cook for about 2-3 minutes.
3. In a jug
4. add the ale and enough water to double the mixture.
5. Add the ale mixture, cubes, salt, and black pepper in the pan with beef and bring to a boil on high heat. Reduce the heat to low and simmer for about 1 hour.
6. In a bowl, mix flour and 3 tablespoons of warm water.
7. Slowly, add the flour mixture in beef mixture, stirring continuously.
8. Remove from heat and keep aside. Roll out the shortcrust pastry.
9. Line 2 ramekins with pastry and dust with flour.
10. Divide the beef mixture in the ramekins evenly.
11. Place extra pastry on top.
12. Preheat the Air Fryer Oven to 390 degrees F, and Cook for about 10 minutes.
13. Now, set the Air Fryer Oven to 335 degrees F, and Cook for about 6 minutes more.

Nutrition: Calories 390 Fat 22g Carbs 36g Fiber 3g Protein 12g Sugar 5g Sodium 1010mg

520. Bolognaise Sauce

Preparation time: 5 minutes
Cooking time: 30 minutes
Servings: 2

Ingredients
- 13Ozs Ground Beef
- 1Carrot
- 1 Stalk of Celery
- 1Ozs Diced Tomatoes
- 1/2 Onion
- Salt and Pepper to taste
- Oven-safe bowl

Directions:
1. Preheat the Air Fryer Oven to 390 degrees.
2. Finely dice the carrot, celery, and onions. Place into the oven-safe bowl along with the ground beef and combine well
3. Place the bowl into the Air Fryer Oven tray and cook for 12 minutes until browned.
4. Pour the diced tomatoes into the bowl and replace it in the air fryer.
5. Season with salt and pepper, then cook for another 18 minutes
6. Serve over cooked pasta or freeze for later use.

Nutrition: Calories 151 Fat 11.3g Carbs 3.1g Fiber 0.6g Protein 10.6g Sugar 2.5g Sodium 588mg

521. Garlic and Rosemary Lamb Cutlets

Preparation Time: 30 Minutes
Cooking Time: 25 Minutes
Servings: 2

Ingredients
- 2lamb racks (with 3 cutlets per rack)
- 2cloves garlic, peeled and thinly sliced into slivers
- 2long sprigs of fresh rosemary, leaves removed
- 2tablespoons wholegrain mustard
- 1 tablespoon honey
- 2tablespoons mint sauce (I use mint jelly)

Directions
1. Trim fat from racks and cut slits with a sharp knife in the top of the lamb. Insert slices of the garlic and rosemary leaves in the slits and set the lamb aside.
2. Make the marinade by whisking the mustard, honey, and mint sauce together and brush over the lamb racks. Let the marinade in a cool area for 20 minutes.
3. Preheat the air fryer to 360 degrees for about 5 minutes.
4. Spray the basket using cooking spray and place the lamb rack or racks into the basket, propping them up however you can get them in to fit.
5. Cook 10 minutes, open and turn the racks and cook 10 more minutes.
6. Place on a platter and cover with foil to let sit 10 minutes before slicing and serving.

Nutrition Calories 309 Fat 2 g Protein 33 g Fiber 16 g

522. Garlic Sauced Lamb Chops

Preparation Time: 15 Minutes
Cooking Time: 25 Minutes
Servings: 4

Ingredients
- 1 garlic bulb
- 1 teaspoon + 3 tablespoons olive oil
- 1 tablespoon fresh oregano, chopped fine
- ¼ teaspoon ground pepper
- ½ teaspoon sea salt
- 8lamb chops

Directions
1. Preheat the air fryer to 400 degrees F 5 minutes and while it is preheating take the excess paper from the garlic bulb.
2. Coat the garlic bulb with the 1 teaspoon of olive oil and drop it in the basket that has been treated with cooking spray. Roast for 12 minutes.
3. Combine the 3 tablespoons of olive oil, oregano, salt, and pepper and lightly coat the lamb chops on both with the resulting oil. Let them sit at room temperature for 5 minutes.
4. Remove the garlic bulb from the basket and if it is cool, preheat again to 400 degrees for 3 minutes.
5. Spray the air fryer basket with cooking oil and place 4 chops in cooking at 400 degrees F for 5 minutes. Place them on a platter and cover to keep them warm while you do the other chops.
6. Squeeze each garlic clove between the thumb and index finger into a small bowl.
7. Taste and add salt and pepper and mix. Serve along with the chops like serving ketchup.

Nutrition Calories 194 Fat 11 g Protein 29 g Fiber 13 g

523. Herb Encrusted Lamb Chops

Preparation Time: 5 Minutes
Cooking Time: 15 Minutes
Servings: 2

Ingredients
- 1 teaspoon oregano
- 1 teaspoon coriander
- 1 teaspoon thyme
- 1 teaspoon rosemary
- ½ teaspoon salt
- ¼ teaspoon pepper
- 2tablespoons lemon juice
- 1tablespoons olive oil
- 1 pound lamb chops

Directions
1. In a closeable bag
2. combine the oregano, coriander, thyme, rosemary, salt, pepper, lemon juice, and olive oil and shake well so it mixes.
3. Place the chops in the bag and squish around so the mixture is on them. Refrigerate 1 hour.
4. Preheat the air fryer to 390 degrees F for 5 minutes.
5. Place the chops in the basket that has been sprayed with cooking spray.
6. Cook for 3 minutes and pause. Flip the chops to the other side and cook for another 4 minutes for medium rare. If you want them more well done, cook 4 minutes, pause, turn and cook 5 more minutes.

Nutrition Calories 321 Fat 34g Protein 18 g Fiber 15 g

524. Herbed Rack of Lamb

Preparation Time: 15 Minutes
Cooking Time: 35 Minutes
Servings: 2

Ingredients
- 1 tablespoon olive oil
- 1 clove garlic, peeled and minced
- 1 ½ teaspoons fresh ground pepper
- 1 tablespoon fresh rosemary, chopped
- 1 tablespoon fresh thyme, chopped
- ¾ cup breadcrumbs
- 1 egg
- 1 to 2 pounds rack of lamb

Directions
1. Place the olive oil in a small dish and add the garlic. Mix well.
2. Brush the garlic on the rack of lamb and season with pepper.
3. In one bowl combine the rosemary, thyme, and breadcrumbs and break the egg and whisk in another bowl.
4. Preheat air fryer 350 degrees F for 5 minutes. Spray with cooking spray.
5. Dip the rack in the egg and then place in the breadcrumb mixture and coat the rack.
6. Place rack in the air fryer basket and cook 20 minutes.
7. Raise the temperature to 400 degrees F and set for 5 more minutes.
8. Tear a piece of aluminum foil that will fit to wrap the rack. Take it out of the basket with tongs and put it in the middle of the foil. Carefully wrap and let sit about 10 minutes. Unwrap and serve.

Nutrition Calories 282 Fat 23 g Protein 26 g Fiber 23 g

525. Lamb Roast with Root Vegetables

Preparation Time: 35 Minutes
Cooking Time: 1 h 15 Minutes
Servings: 6

Ingredients
- 4cloves garlic, peeled and sliced thin, divided
- 2springs fresh rosemary, leaves pulled off, divided
- 4pounds leg of lamb
- salt and pepper to taste, divided
- medium-sized sweet potatoes, peeled and cut into wedges
- 1tablespoon oil, divided
- 1cups baby carrots
- 1 teaspoon butter
- large red potatoes, cubed

Directions
1. Slice the garlic and take the leaves of the rosemary.
2. Cut about 5 to 6 slits in the top of the lamb and insert slices of garlic and some rosemary in each. Salt and pepper the roast to your taste and set aside to cook after the vegetables are done.
3. Coat the sweet potatoes in 1 tablespoon of olive oil and season with salt and pepper.
4. Spray the basket of the air fryer with cooking spray and put it in the wedges. You may have to do two batches. Set for 400 degrees F and air fry 8 minutes, shake and cook another 8 minutes or so. Dump into a bowl and cover with foil.
5. Place the carrots in some foil to cover and put the butter on top of them. Enclose them in the foil and place them in the air fryer. Set for 400 degrees for 20 minutes. Remove from the air fryer.
6. Coat the basket with cooking spray. Mix the red potatoes with the other tablespoon of oil and salt and pepper to taste. Place in the air fryer oven and cook at 400 degrees F for 20 minutes, shaking after 10 minutes have elapsed.
7. Use a foil tray or baking dish that fits into the air fryer and coat with cooking spray. Place the leftover garlic and rosemary in the bottom and place the lamb on top.
8. Set for 380 degrees F and cook 1 hour, checking after 30 minutes and 45 minutes to make sure it isn't getting too done. Increase the air fryer oven heat to 400 degrees F and cook for 10 to 15 minutes.
9. Remove the roast from the air fryer and set on a platter. Cover with foil and rest 10 minutes while you dump all the vegetables back in the basket and cooking at 350 degrees F for 8 to 10 minutes or until heated through.
10. Serve all together.

Nutrition Calories 398 Fat 5 g Protein 18 g Fiber 30.3 g

526. Lemon and Cumin Coated Rack of Lamb

Preparation Time: 15 Minutes
Cooking Time: 200 Minutes
Servings: 4

Ingredients
- 1 ½ to 1 ¾ pound Frenched rack of lamb
- Salt and pepper to taste
- ½ cup breadcrumbs
- 1 teaspoon cumin seed
- 1 teaspoon ground cumin
- ½ teaspoon salt
- 1 teaspoon garlic, peeled and grated
- Lemon zest (1/4 of a lemon)
- 1 teaspoon vegetable or olive oil
- 1 egg
- beaten

Directions
1. Season the lamb rack with pepper and salt to taste and set it aside.
2. In a large bowl, combine the breadcrumbs, cumin seed, ground cumin, salt, garlic, lemon zest, and oil and set aside.
3. In another bowl, beat the egg.
4. Preheat to air fryer to 250 degrees F for 5 minutes
5. Dip the rack in the egg to coat and then into the breadcrumb mixture. Make sure it is well coated.
6. Spray the basket of the air fryer using cooking spray and put the rack in. You may have to bend it a little to get it to fit.
7. Set for 250 degrees and cook 25 minutes.
8. Increase temperature to 400 degrees F and cook another 5 minutes. Check internal temperature to make sure it is 145 degrees for medium-rare or more.
9. Remove rack when done and cover with foil for 10 minutes before separating ribs into individual servings.

Nutrition Calories 276 Fat 24 g Protein 33 g Fiber 12.3 g

527. Macadamia Rack of Lamb

Preparation Time: 20 Minutes
Cooking Time: 32 Minutes
Servings: 4

Ingredients
- 1 tablespoon olive oil
- 1 clove garlic, peeled and minced
- 1 ½ to 1 ¾ pound rack of lamb
- Salt and pepper to taste
- ¾ cup unsalted macadamia nuts
- 1 tablespoon fresh rosemary, chopped
- 1 tablespoon breadcrumbs
- 1 egg
- beaten

Directions
1. Mix together the olive oil and garlic and brush it all over the rack of lamb. Season with salt and pepper.
2. Preheat the air fryer 250 degrees F for 8 minutes.
3. Chop the macadamia nuts as fine as possible and put them in a bowl.
4. Mix in the rosemary and breadcrumbs and set it aside.
5. Beat the egg in another bowl.
6. Dip the rack in the egg mixture to coat completely.
7. Place the rack in the breadcrumb mixture and coat well.
8. Spray the basket of the air fryer using cooking spray and place the rack inside.
9. Cook at 250 degrees for 25 minutes and then increase to 400 and cook another 5 to 10 minutes or until done.
10. Cover with foil paper for 10 minutes, uncover and separate into chops and serve.

Nutrition Calories 321 Fat 9 g Protein 12 g Fiber 8.3 g

528. Perfect Lamb Burgers

Preparation Time: 10 Minutes
Cooking Time: 20 Minutes
Servings: 4

Ingredients
- For the Moroccan spice mix:
- 1 teaspoon ground ginger
- 1 teaspoon ground cumin
- 1 teaspoon sea salt
- ¾ teaspoon ground black pepper
- ½ teaspoon ground coriander
- ½ teaspoon ground allspice
- ½ teaspoon ground cloves
- ½ teaspoon ground cinnamon
- ½ teaspoon cayenne
- For burgers and dip:
- 1 ½ pound ground lamb
- 1 teaspoon Harissa paste
- 1tablespoons Moroccan spice mix, divided
- 1teaspoons garlic, peeled and minced
- ¼ teaspoon fresh chopped oregano
- 1tablespoons plain Greek yogurt
- 1 small lemon, juiced

Directions
6. Moroccan Spice Mix:
7. Whisk the ginger, cumin, salt, pepper, coriander, allspice, cloves, cinnamon, and cayenne in a small bowl and set aside.
8. Burgers and dip:
9. Place the lamb in a large bowl and add the Harissa sauce, 1 tablespoon of the homemade Moroccan spice mix, and the garlic. Mix in everything with the hands and form 4 patties.
10. Preheat the air fryer to 360 degrees for 5 minutes while making the patties.
11. Spray the basket of the air fryer using cooking spray and place two of the burgers in.
12. Cook a total of 12 minutes, flipping after 6 minutes.
13. Repeat with the other two burgers.
14. While burgers cook, make the dip by chopping the fresh oregano and placing it in a bowl with the yogurt, 1 teaspoon of the Moroccan spice mix, and the juice of the lemon. Whisk this with a fork and divide it into small containers to serve with the burgers when they are done.

Nutrition Calories 534 Fat 8 g Protein 21 g Fiber 8.7 g

529. Simple Yet Tasty Lamb Chops

Preparation Time: 15 Minutes
Cooking Time: 30 Minutes
Servings: 4

Ingredients
- 1 clove of garlic separated from the head of garlic (maybe 2)
- 1 ½ tablespoons olive oil
- 1lamb chops
- ½ tablespoon fresh oregano, chopped
- Salt and pepper to taste

Directions
1. Preheat the air fryer oven to 400 degrees F for 6 minutes.
2. Take a little of the olive oil and coat the garlic clove(s). Place in the basket of the air fryer and roast 12 minutes.
3. While the garlic is cooking
4. mix the oregano, salt, and pepper in a small bowl. Add all the remaining olive oil and mix well.
5. Spread a thin coating of the oregano mixture on both sides of the lamb chops and reserve the rest.
6. Remove the clove(s) of garlic from the basket of the air fryer with rubber-tipped tongs. Be careful because the cloves will be very soft and you don't want them to break open quite yet.
7. Spray the basket of the air fryer using cooking spray and place the lamb chops in, 2 at a time in 2 batches. Cook 5 minutes, turn and cook another 4 minutes.
8. When chops are done, squeeze the garlic out of the papery shell into the rest of the oregano mixture and mix it in. Serve this on the side like ketchup.

Nutrition Calories 542 Fat 4 g Protein 23 g Fiber 6 g

530. Tandoori Lamb

Preparation Time: 10 Minutes
Cooking Time: 20 Minutes
Servings: 4

Ingredients
- ½ onion, peeled and quartered
- 5cloves garlic, peeled
- 1slices fresh ginger, peeled
- 1 teaspoon ground fennel
- 1 teaspoon Garam Masala
- 1 teaspoon ground cinnamon
- ½ teaspoon ground cardamom
- ½ teaspoon cayenne
- 1 teaspoon salt
- 1 pound boneless lamb sirloin steaks

Directions

1. Place the onion, garlic, ginger, fennel, Garam Masala, cinnamon, cardamom, cayenne, and salt in a blender and pulse 4 to 6 times until ground.
2. Place the lamb steaks in a large bowl and slash the meat so the spices will permeate into it.
3. Pour the spice mix over top and rub it on both sides. Let sit room temperature 30 minutes or cover and refrigerate overnight.
4. Preheat the air fryer to 350 degrees F for 10 minutes.
5. Spray the basket using cooking spray and place lamb steaks in without letting them overlap much. You may have to do this in batches.
6. Cook 7 minutes, turn and cook another 8 minutes.
7. Test with the meat thermometer to make sure they are done. The medium-well will be 150 degrees F.

Nutrition Calories 232 Fat 20 g Protein 42 g Fiber 5 g

531. Barbecue Flavored Pork Ribs

Preparation Time: 5 Minutes
Cooking Time: 15 Minutes
Servings: 6

Ingredients

- ¼ cup honey, divided
- ¾ cup BBQ sauce
- 2 tablespoons tomato ketchup
- 1 tablespoon Worcestershire sauce
- 1 tablespoon soy sauce
- ½ teaspoon garlic powder
- Freshly ground white pepper, to taste
- 1¾ pound pork ribs

Directions

1. In a large bowl, mix together 3 tablespoons of honey and remaining ingredients except for the pork ribs.
2. Refrigerate to marinate for about 20 minutes.
3. Preheat the Air fryer oven to 355 degrees F.
4. Place the ribs in an Air fryer rack/basket.
5. Cook for about 13 minutes.
6. Remove the ribs from the Air fryer oven and coat with remaining honey.
7. Serve hot.

Nutrition Calories 376 Fat 20 g Protein 32 g Fiber 12 g

532. Rustic Pork Ribs

Preparation Time: 5 Minutes
Cooking Time: 15 Minutes
Servings: 4

Ingredients

- 1 rack of pork ribs
- 1 tablespoons dry red wine
- 1 tablespoon soy sauce
- 1/2 teaspoon dried thyme
- 1/2 teaspoon onion powder
- 1/2 teaspoon garlic powder
- 1/2 teaspoon ground black pepper
- 1 teaspoon smoked salt
- 1 tablespoon cornstarch
- 1/2 teaspoon olive oil

Directions

1. Begin by preheating your Air fryer oven to 390 degrees F. Place all ingredients in a mixing bowl and let them marinate at least 1 hour.
2. Air Frying:
3. Cook the marinated ribs approximately 25 minutes at 390 degrees F.
4. Serve hot.

Nutrition Calories 326 Fat 14 g Protein 23 g Fiber 13 g

533. Italian Parmesan Breaded Pork Chops

Preparation Time: 5 Minutes
Cooking Time: 25 Minutes
Servings: 5

Ingredients

- 5 (3½- to 5-ounce) pork chops (bone-in or boneless)
- 1 teaspoon Italian seasoning
- Seasoning salt
- Pepper
- ¼ cup all-purpose flour
- 1 tablespoons Italian bread crumbs
- 1 tablespoons finely grated Parmesan cheese
- Cooking oil

Directions

1. Season the pork chops with the Italian seasoning and seasoning salt and pepper to taste.
2. Sprinkle the flour on each side of the pork chops, then coat both sides with the bread crumbs and Parmesan cheese.
3. Place the pork chops in the air fryer oven. Stacking them is okay. Spray the pork chops with cooking oil. Set temperature to 360°F. Cook for 6 minutes.
4. Open the air fryer oven and flip the pork chops. Cook for an additional 6 minutes.
5. Cool before serving. Instead of seasoning salt, you can use either chicken or pork rub for additional flavor. You can find these rubs in the spice aisle of the grocery store.

Nutrition Calories 334 Fat 7 g Protein 34 g Fiber 0 g

534. Crispy Breaded Pork Chops

Preparation Time: 10 Minutes
Cooking Time: 15 Minutes
Servings: 8

Ingredients

- 1/8 tsp. pepper
- ¼ tsp. chili powder
- ½ tsp. onion powder
- ½ tsp. garlic powder
- 1 ¼ tsp. sweet paprika
- 1 tbsp. grated parmesan cheese
- 1/3 C. crushed cornflake crumbs
- ½ C. panko breadcrumbs
- 1 beaten egg
- center-cut boneless pork chops

Directions

1. Ensure that your air fryer is preheated to 400 degrees. Spray the basket with olive oil.
2. With ½ teaspoon salt and pepper, season both sides of pork chops.
3. Combine ¾ teaspoon salt with pepper, chili powder, onion powder, garlic powder, paprika, cornflake crumbs, panko breadcrumbs, and parmesan cheese.
4. Beat egg in another bowl.
5. Dip the pork chops into the egg and then crumb mixture.
6. Add pork chops to air fryer and spritz with olive oil.

7. Air Frying:
8. Set temperature to 400°F, and set time to 12 minutes. Cook 12 minutes, making sure to flip over halfway through the cooking process.
9. Only add 3 chops in at a time and repeat the process with remaining pork chops.

Nutrition Calories 378 Fat 13 g Protein 33 g Sugar 1 g

535. Caramelized Pork Shoulder

Preparation Time: 10 Minutes
Cooking Time: 20 Minutes
Servings: 8

Ingredients
- 1/3 cup soy sauce
- 1tablespoons sugar
- 1 tablespoon honey
- 2pounds pork shoulder, cut into 1½-inch thick slices

Directions
1. In a bowl, mix all the ingredients except pork.
2. Add pork and coat with marinade generously.
3. Cover and refrigerate o marinate for about 2-8 hours.
4. Preheat the Air fryer oven to 335 degrees F.
5. Place the pork in an Air fryer rack/basket.
6. Cook for about 10 minutes.
7. Now, set the Air fryer oven to 390 degrees F. Cook for about 10 minutes.

Nutrition Calories 268 Fat 10 g Protein 23 g Sugar 5 g

536. Roasted Pork Tenderloin

Preparation Time: 5 Minutes
Cooking Time: 1 h
Servings: 4

Ingredients
- 1 (3-pound) pork tenderloin
- 1tablespoons extra-virgin olive oil
- 2garlic cloves, minced
- 1 teaspoon dried basil
- 1 teaspoon dried oregano
- 1 teaspoon dried thyme
- Salt
- Pepper

Directions
1. Dip the pork fillet in olive oil.
2. Grate the garlic, basil, oregano, thyme, and salt and pepper to taste throughout the steak.
3. Place the steak in the oven of the deep fryer. Cook for 45 minutes.
4. Use a meat thermometer to check for politeness
5. Open the Air Fryer and flip the pork fillet. Cook for 15 more minutes.
6. Take the cooked pork out of the deep fryer and let it rest for 10 minutes before slicing it.

Nutrition Calories 283 Fat 10 g Protein 48 g

537. Bacon-Wrapped Pork Tenderloin

Preparation Time: 5 Minutes
Cooking Time: 15 Minutes
Servings: 4

Ingredients
- Pork:
- 1-2 tbsp. Dijon mustard
- 3-4 strips of bacon
- 1 pork tenderloin
- 1Apple Gravy:
- ½ - 1 tsp. Dijon mustard
- 1 tbsp. almond flour
- 1tbsp. ghee
- 1 chopped onion
- 2-3 Granny Smith apples
- 1 C. vegetable broth

Directions
1. Spread Dijon mustard all over the tenderloin and wrap the meat with strips of bacon.
2. Place into the Air fryer oven, set the temperature to 360°F, and set time to 15 minutes, and cook 10-15 minutes at 360 degrees.
3. To make sauce, heat ghee in a pan and add shallots. Cook 1-2 minutes.
4. Then add apples, cooking 3-5 minutes until softened.
5. Add flour and ghee to make a roux. Add broth and mustard, stirring well to combine.
6. When the sauce starts to bubble, add 1 cup of sautéed apples, cooking till sauce thickens.
7. Once the pork tenderloin is cooked, let it sit 5-10 minutes to rest before slicing.
8. Serve topped with apple gravy.

Nutrition Calories 552 Fat 25 g Protein 29 g Sugar 6 g

538. Dijon Garlic Pork Tenderloin

Preparation Time: 5 Minutes
Cooking Time: 10 Minutes
Servings: 6

Ingredients
- 1 C. breadcrumbs
- Pinch of cayenne pepper
- 1Crushed garlic cloves
- 2tbsp. ground ginger
- 2tbsp. Dijon mustard
- 2tbsp. raw honey
- 2tbsp. water
- 2tsp. salt
- 1 pound pork tenderloin, sliced into 1-inch rounds

Directions
1. With pepper and salt, season all sides of the tenderloin.
2. Combine cayenne pepper, garlic, ginger, mustard, honey, and water until smooth.
3. Dip pork rounds into the honey mixture and then into breadcrumbs, ensuring they all get coated well.
4. Place coated pork rounds into your Air fryer oven.
5. Set temperature to 400°F, and set time to 10 minutes. Cook 10 minutes at 400 degrees. Flip and then cook an additional 5 minutes until golden in color.

Nutrition Calories 423 Fat 18 g Protein 31 g Sugar 3 g

539. Pork Neck with Salad

Preparation Time: 10 Minutes
Cooking Time: 12 Minutes
Servings: 2

Ingredients
- For Pork:
- 1 tablespoon soy sauce
- 1 tablespoon fish sauce
- ½ tablespoon oyster sauce
- ½ pound pork neck
- For Salad:
- 1 ripe tomato, sliced tickly
- 8-10 Thai shallots, sliced
- 1 scallion, chopped
- 1 bunch fresh basil leaves
- 1 bunch fresh cilantro leaves
- For Dressing:
- 1 Tablespoons fish sauce
- tablespoons olive oil
- 1 teaspoon apple cider vinegar
- 1 tablespoon palm sugar
- 1 bird's eye chili
- 1 tablespoon garlic, minced

Directions
1. For the pork:
2. In a bowl, mix all the ingredients except the pork.
3. Add the pork neck and marinade layer evenly. Refrigerate for about 2-3 hours.
4. Preheat the deep fryer oven to 340 degrees F.
5. Air fry. Place the pork neck in a grill pan. Cook for about 12 minutes.
6. Meanwhile, in a large bowl, combine all of the salad ingredients.
7. In a bowl, add all the dressing ingredients and beat until well combined.
8. Remove the pork neck from the fryer and cut it into the desired slices.
9. Place the pork slices on top of the salad.

Nutrition Calories 296 Fat: 20 g Protein 24 g Sugar 8 g

540. Chinese Braised Pork Belly

Preparation Time: 5 Minutes
Cooking Time: 20 Minutes
Servings: 8

Ingredients
- 1 lb. pork belly, sliced
- 1 tbsp. oyster sauce
- 1 tbsp. sugar
- Red fermented bean curds
- 1 tbsp. red fermented bean curd paste
- 1 tbsp. cooking wine
- 1/2 tbsp. soy sauce
- 1 tsp sesame oil
- 1 cup all-purpose flour

Directions
1. Preheat the Air fryer oven to 390 degrees.
2. In a small bowl, mix up the ingredients together and rub the pork thoroughly with this mixture
3. Set aside to marinate for at least 30 minutes or preferably overnight for the flavors to permeate the meat
4. Coat each marinated pork belly slice in flour and place in the Air fryer oven tray
5. Cook for 20 minutes until crispy and tender.

Nutrition Calories 409 Fat 14 g Protein 19 g Sugar 9 g

541. Air Fryer Sweet and Sour Pork

Preparation Time: 10 Minutes
Cooking Time: 12 Minutes
Servings: 6

Ingredients
- Tbsp. olive oil
- 1/16 tsp. Chinese five-spice
- ¼ tsp. pepper
- ½ tsp. sea salt
- 1 tsp. pure sesame oil
- eggs
- 1 C. almond flour
- pounds pork, sliced into chunks
- Sweet and Sour sauce:
- ¼ tsp. sea salt
- ½ tsp. garlic powder
- 1 tbsp. low-sodium soy sauce
- ½ C. rice vinegar
- 1 tbsp. tomato paste
- 1/8 tsp. water
- ½ C. sweetener of choice

Directions
1. To make the dipping sauce, whisk all sauce ingredients together over medium heat, stirring 5 minutes. Simmer uncovered 5 minutes till thickened.
2. Meanwhile, combine almond flour, five-spice, pepper, and salt.
3. In another bowl, mix eggs with sesame oil.
4. Dredge pork in flour mixture and then in the egg mixture. Shake any excess off before adding to the air fryer rack/basket.
5. Set temperature to 340°F, and set time to 12 minutes.
6. Serve with sweet and sour dipping sauce!

Nutrition Calories 371 Fat 17 g Protein 27 g Sugar 1 g

542. Juicy Pork Ribs Ole

Preparation Time: 10 Minutes
Cooking Time: 25 Minutes
Servings: 4

Ingredients
- 1 rack of pork ribs
- 1/2 cup low-fat milk
- 1 tablespoon envelope taco seasoning mix
- 1 can tomato sauce
- 1/2 teaspoon ground black pepper
- 1 teaspoon seasoned salt
- 1 tablespoon cornstarch
- 1 teaspoon canola oil

Directions
1. Place all ingredients in a mixing dish; let them marinate for 1 hour.
2. Cook the marinated ribs approximately 25 minutes at 390 degrees F
3. Work with batches. Enjoy.

Nutrition Calories 218 Fat 8 g Protein 11 g Sugar 1 g

543. Teriyaki Pork Rolls

Preparation Time: 10 Minutes
Cooking Time: 8 Minutes
Servings: 6
Ingredients
- 1 tsp. almond flour
- 1 tbsp. low-sodium soy sauce
- 1 tbsp. mirin
- 1 tbsp. brown sugar
- Thumb-sized amount of ginger, chopped
- Pork belly slices
- Enoki mushrooms

Directions
1. Mix brown sugar, mirin, soy sauce, almond flour, and ginger until brown sugar dissolves.
2. Take pork belly slices and wrap around a bundle of mushrooms. Brush each roll with teriyaki sauce. Chill half an hour.
3. Preheat your Air fryer oven to 350 degrees and add marinated pork rolls.
4. Set temperature to 350°F, and set time to 8 minutes.

Nutrition Calories 412 Fat 9 g Protein 19 g Sugar 4 g

544. Glazed Pork Tenderloin

Preparation Time: 15 minutes
Cooking time: 20 minutes
Servings: 3
Ingredients:
- 1-pound pork tenderloin
- tablespoons Sriracha
- tablespoons honey
- Salt, as required

Directions
1. Insert the rotisserie rod through the pork tenderloin.
2. Insert the rotisserie forks, one on each side of the rod to secure the pork tenderloin.
3. In a small bowl, add the Sriracha, honey and salt and mix well.
4. Brush the pork tenderloin with honey mixture evenly.
5. Arrange the drip pan in the bottom of Air fryer oven cooking chamber.
6. Select "Air Fry" and then adjust the temperature to 350 F.
7. Set the timer for 20 minutes and press the "Start".
8. When the display shows "Add Food" press the red lever down and load the left side of the rod into the oven.
9. Now, slide the rod's left side into the groove along the metal bar so it doesn't move.
10. Then, close the door and touch "Rotate".
11. When cooking time is complete, press the red lever to release the rod.
12. Remove the pork from oven and place onto a platter for about 10 minutes before slicing.
13. With a sharp knife, cut the roast into desired sized slices and serve.

Nutrition: Calories 269 Fat 5.3g Saturated Fat 1.8g Cholesterol 110mg Sodium 207mg Total Carbs 13.5g Sugar 11.6g Protein 39.7g

545. Crusted Rack Of Lamb

Preparation Time: 15 minutes
Cooking time: 19 minutes
Servings: 4
Ingredients:
- 1 rack of lamb, trimmed all fat and frenched
- Salt and ground black pepper, as required
- 1/3 cup pistachios, chopped finely
- 2 tablespoons panko breadcrumbs
- teaspoons fresh thyme, chopped finely
- 1 teaspoon fresh rosemary, chopped finely
- 1 tablespoon butter, melted
- 1 tablespoon Dijon mustard

Directions
1. Insert the rotisserie rod through the rack on the meaty side of the ribs, right next to the bone.
2. Insert the rotisserie forks, one on each side of the rod to secure the rack.
3. Season the rack with salt and black pepper evenly.
4. Arrange the drip pan in the bottom of Air fryer oven cooking chamber.
5. Select "Air Fry" and then adjust the temperature to 380 F.
6. Set the timer for 12 minutes and press the "Start".
7. When the display shows "Add Food" press the red lever down and load the left side of the rod into the oven.
8. Now, slide the rod's left side into the groove along the metal bar so it doesn't move.
9. Then, close the door and touch "Rotate".
10. Meanwhile, in a small bowl, mix together the remaining ingredients except the mustard.
11. When cooking time is complete, press the red lever to release the rod.
12. Remove the rack from oven and brush the meaty side with the mustard.
13. Then, coat the pistachio mixture on all sides of the rack and press firmly.
14. Now, place the rack of lamb onto the cooking tray, meat side up.
15. Select "Air Fry" and adjust the temperature to 380 F.
16. Set the timer for 7 minutes and press the "Start".
17. When the display shows "Add Food" insert the cooking tray in the center position.
18. When the display shows "Turn Food" do nothing.
19. When cooking time is complete, remove the tray from oven and place the rack onto a cutting board for at least 10 minutes.
20. Cut the rack into individual chops and serve.

Nutrition: Calories 824 Fat 39.3g Saturated Fat 14.2g Cholesterol 233mg Sodium 373mg Carbs 10.3g Fiber 1.2g Sugar 0.2g Protein 72g

546. Greek Rotisserie Lamb Leg

Preparation Time: 25 minutes
Cooking time: 1 hour 30 minutes
Servings: 4 to 6
Ingredients:
- `3 pounds (1.4 kg) leg of lamb, boned in
- `For the Marinade:
- `1 tablespoon lemon zest (about 1 lemon)
- `3 tablespoons lemon juice (about 1½ lemons)
- `3 cloves garlic, minced
- `1 teaspoon onion powder
- `1 teaspoon fresh thyme
- `¼ cup fresh oregano

- `¼ cup olive oil
- `1 teaspoon ground black pepper
- `For the Herb Dressing:
- `1 tablespoon lemon juice (about ½ lemon)
- `¼ cup chopped fresh oregano
- `1 teaspoon fresh thyme
- `1 tablespoon olive oil
- `1 teaspoon sea salt
- `Ground black pepper, to taste

Directions
1. Place lamb leg into a large resealable plastic bag. Combine the ingredients for the marinade in a small bowl. Stir to mix well.
2. Pour the marinade over the lamb, making sure the meat is completely coated. Seal the bag and place in the refrigerator. Marinate for 4 to 6 hours before grilling.
3. Remove the lamb leg from the marinade. Using the rotisserie shaft, push through the lamb leg and attach the rotisserie forks.
4. If desired, place aluminum foil onto the drip pan. (It makes for easier clean-up!)
5. Set the oven to Roast, set temperature to 350 F (180 degrees Celsius), Rotate, and set time to 1 hour 30 minutes. Press Start to begin preheating.
6. Once preheated, place the prepared lamb leg with rotisserie shaft into the oven. Baste with marinade for every 30 minutes.
7. Meanwhile, combine the ingredients for the herb dressing in a bowl. Stir to mix well.
8. When cooking is complete, remove the lamb leg using the rotisserie handle and, using hot pads or gloves, carefully remove the lamb leg from the shaft.
9. Cover lightly with aluminum foil for 8 to 10 minutes.
10. Carve the leg and arrange on a platter,. Drizzle with herb dressing. Serve immediately.

Nutrition: Calories 824 Fat 39.3g Saturated Fat 14.2g Cholesterol 233mg Sodium 373mg Carbs 10.3g Fiber 1.2g Sugar 0.2g Protein 72g

547. Duo Crisp Ribs

Preparation Time: 10 minutes
Cooking Time: 50 minutes
Servings: 2
Ingredients:
- 1 rack of pork ribs
- Rub
- 1 1/2 cup broth
- 3 tablespoons Liquid Smoke
- 1 cup Barbecue Sauce

Directions:
1. Rub the rib rack with spice rub generously.
2. Pour the liquid into the Air fryer.
3. Set an Air Fryer Basket into the Pot and place the rib rack in the basket.
4. Put on the pressure-cooking lid and seal it.
5. Hit the "Pressure Button" and select 30 minutes of Cooking Time, then press "Start."
6. Once the Air fryer beeps, do a quick release and remove its lid.
7. Remove the ribs and rub them with barbecue sauce.
8. Empty the pot and place the Air Fryer Basket in it.
9. Set the ribs in the basket, and Air fry them for 20 minutes.
10. Serve.

Nutrition: Calories 306 Total Fat 6.4g Saturated Fat 2g Cholesterol 32mg Sodium 196mg Carbs 46g Fiber 0.8g Sugars 33.1g Protein 14.7g

WRAP AND SANDWICH

WRAP AND SANDWICH

548. Cheesy Chicken Wraps

Preparation Time: 30 minutes
Cooking Time: 5 minutes
Servings: 12

Ingredients:
- 2 large-sized chicken breasts, cooked and shredded
- 2 spring onions, chopped
- 10 ounces (284 g) Ricotta cheese
- 1 tablespoon rice vinegar
- 1 tablespoon molasses
- 1 teaspoon grated fresh ginger
- ¼ cup soy sauce
- 1/3 teaspoon sea salt
- ¼ teaspoon ground black pepper, or more to taste
- 48 wonton wrappers
- Cooking spray

Directions:
1. Spritz the air fry basket with cooking spray.
2. Combine all the ingredients, except for the wrappers in a large bowl. Toss to mix well.
3. Unfold the wrappers on a clean work surface, then divide and spoon the mixture in the middle of the wrappers.
4. Dab a little water on the edges of the wrappers, then fold the edge close to you over the filling. Tuck the edge under the filling and roll up to seal.
5. Arrange the wraps in the basket.
6. Place the basket on the air fry position.
7. Select Air Fry, set temperature to 375°F (190°C) and set time to 5 minutes. Flip the wraps halfway through the cooking time.
8. When cooking is complete, the wraps should be lightly browned.
9. Serve immediately.

Nutrition: Calories 246 Carbs 0.1g Fat 2.8g Protein 10.8g

549. Chicken-Lettuce Wraps

Preparation time: 15 minutes
Cooking time: 12 to 16 minutes
Servings: 2 to 4

Ingredients:
- 1 pound (454 g) boneless, skinless chicken thighs, trimmed
- 1 teaspoon vegetable oil
- tablespoons lime juice
- 1 shallot, minced
- 1 tablespoon fish sauce, plus extra for serving
- 1 teaspoons packed brown sugar
- 1 garlic clove, minced
- ⅛ teaspoon red pepper flakes
- 1 mango, peeled, pitted, and cut into ¼-inch pieces
- ⅓ cup chopped fresh mint
- ⅓ cup chopped fresh cilantro
- ⅓ cup chopped fresh Thai basil
- 1 head Bibb lettuce, leaves separated (8 ounces / 227 g)
- ¼ cup chopped dry-roasted peanuts
- Thai chiles, stemmed and sliced thin

Directions
1. Pat the chicken dry with paper towels and rub with oil. Place the chicken in air fryer basket. Select the Air Fry function and cook at 400 F (204 degrees Celsius) for 12 to 16 minutes, or until the chicken registers 175 F (79 degrees Celsius), flipping and rotating chicken halfway through cooking.
2. Meanwhile, whisk lime juice, shallot, fish sauce, sugar, garlic, and pepper flakes together in large bowl; set aside.
3. Transfer chicken to cutting board, let cool slightly, then shred into bite-size pieces using 2 forks. Add the shredded chicken, mango, mint, cilantro, and basil to bowl with dressing and toss to coat.
4. Serve the chicken in the lettuce leaves, passing peanuts, Thai chiles, and extra fish sauce separately.

Nutrition: Calories 311 Fat 11g Carbs 22g Protein 31g

550. Chicken Pita Sandwich

Preparation time: 10 minutes
Cooking time: 9 to 11 minutes
Servings: 4

Ingredients:
- 2 boneless, skinless chicken breasts, cut into 1-inch cubes
- 1 small red onion, sliced
- 1 red bell pepper, sliced
- ⅓ cup Italian salad dressing, divided
- ½ teaspoon dried thyme
- 4 pita pockets, split
- 2 cups torn butter lettuce
- 1 cup chopped cherry tomatoes

Directions
1. Select the Bake function and preheat Maxx to 380 F (193 degrees Celsius).
2. Place the chicken, onion, and bell pepper in the air fryer basket. Drizzle with 1 tablespoon of the Italian salad dressing, add the thyme, and toss.
3. Bake for 9 to 11 minutes, or until the chicken is 165 F (74 degrees Celsius) on a food thermometer, stirring once during cooking time.
4. Transfer the chicken and vegetables to a bowl and toss with the remaining salad dressing.
5. Assemble sandwiches with the pita pockets, butter lettuce, and cherry tomatoes. Serve immediately.

Nutrition: Calories 311 Fat 11g Carbs 22g Protein 31g

551. Veggie Salsa Wraps

Preparation time: 5 minutes
Cooking time: 7 minutes
Servings: 4

Ingredients:
- 1 cup red onion, sliced
- 1 zucchini, chopped
- 1 poblano pepper, deseeded and finely chopped
- 1 head lettuce
- ½ cup salsa
- 8 ounces (227 g) Mozzarella cheese

Directions
1. Place the red onion, zucchini, and poblano pepper in the air fryer basket. Select the Air Fry function and cook at 390 F (199 degrees Celsius) for 7 minutes, or until they are tender and fragrant.
2. Divide the veggie mixture among the lettuce leaves and spoon the salsa over the top. Finish off with Mozzarella cheese. Wrap the lettuce leaves around the filling.
3. Serve immediately.

Nutrition: Calories 140 Fat 4g Fiber 3g Carbs 5g Protein 7g

552. Cheesy Shrimp Sandwich

Preparation time: 10 minutes
Cooking time: 5 to 7 minutes
Servings: 4
Ingredients:
- 1¼ cups shredded Colby, Cheddar, or Havarti cheese
- 1 (6-ounce / 170-g) can tiny shrimp, drained
- 3 tablespoons mayonnaise
- 2 tablespoons minced green onion
- 4 slices whole grain or whole-wheat bread
- 2 tablespoons softened butter

Directions
1. In a medium bowl, combine the cheese, shrimp, mayonnaise, and green onion, and mix well.
2. Spread this mixture on two of the slices of bread. Top with the other slices of bread to make two sandwiches. Spread the sandwiches lightly with butter.
3. Select the Air Fry function and cook at 400 F (204 degrees Celsius) for 5 to 7 minutes, or until the bread is browned and crisp and the cheese is melted.
4. Cut in half and serve warm.

Nutrition: Calories 602 Fat 23.9g Carbs 46.5g Sugar 2.9g Protein 11.3g Sodium 886mg

553. Smoky Chicken Sandwich

Preparation time: 10 minutes
Cooking time: 11 minutes
Servings: 2
Ingredients:
- 2 boneless, skinless chicken breasts (8 ounces / 227 g each), sliced horizontally in half and separated into 4 thinner cutlets
- Kosher salt and freshly ground black pepper, to taste
- ½ cup all-purpose flour
- 3 large eggs, lightly beaten
- ½ cup dried bread crumbs
- 1 tablespoon smoked paprika
- Cooking spray
- ½ cup marinara sauce
- 6 ounces (170 g) smoked Mozzarella cheese, grated
- 2 store-bought soft, sesame-seed hamburger or Italian buns, split

Directions
1. Season the chicken cutlets all over with salt and pepper. Set up three shallow bowls: Place the flour in the first bowl, the eggs in the second, and stir together the bread crumbs and smoked paprika in the third. Coat the chicken pieces in the flour, then dip fully in the egg. Dredge in the paprika bread crumbs, then transfer to a wire rack set over a baking sheet and spray both sides liberally with cooking spray.
2. Transfer 2 of the chicken cutlets to the air fryer oven. Select the Air Fry function and cook at 350 F (177 degrees Celsius) for 6 minutes, or until beginning to brown. Spread each cutlet with 2 tablespoons of the marinara sauce and sprinkle with one-quarter of the smoked Mozzarella.
3. Increase the temperature to 400 F (204 degrees Celsius) and air fry for 5 minutes more, or until the chicken is cooked through and crisp and the cheese is melted and golden brown.
4. Transfer the cutlets to a plate, stack on top of each other, and place inside a bun. Repeat with the remaining chicken cutlets, marinara, smoked Mozzarella, and bun.
5. Serve the sandwiches warm.

Nutrition: Calories 311 Fat 11g Carbs 22g Protein 31g

554. Nugget and Veggie Taco Wraps

Preparation time: 5 minutes
Cooking time: 15 minutes
Servings: 4
Ingredients:
- 1 tablespoon water
- 4 pieces commercial vegan nuggets, chopped
- 1 small yellow onion, diced
- 1 small red bell pepper, chopped
- 2 cobs grilled corn kernels
- 4 large corn tortillas
- Mixed greens, for garnish

Directions
1. Over a medium heat, sauté the nuggets in the water with the onion, corn kernels and bell pepper in a skillet, then remove from the heat.
2. Fill the tortillas with the nuggets and vegetables and fold them up. Transfer to the air fryer basket. Select the Air Fry function and cook at 400 F (204 degrees Celsius) for 15 minutes.
3. Once crispy, serve immediately, garnished with the mixed greens.

Nutrition: Calories 140 Fat 4g Fiber 3g Carbs 5g Protein 7g

555. Cheesy Greens Sandwich

Preparation time: 15 minutes
Cooking time: 10 to 13 minutes
Servings: 4
Ingredients:
- 1½ cups chopped mixed greens
- 2 garlic cloves, thinly sliced
- 2 teaspoons olive oil
- 2 slices low-sodium low-fat Swiss cheese
- 4 slices low-sodium whole-wheat bread
- Cooking spray

Directions
1. Select the Bake function and preheat Maxx to 400 F (204 degrees Celsius).
2. In a baking pan, mix the greens, garlic, and olive oil. Bake for 4 to 5 minutes, stirring once, until the vegetables are tender. Drain, if necessary.
3. Make 2 sandwiches, dividing half of the greens and 1 slice of Swiss cheese between 2 slices of bread. Lightly spray the outsides of the sandwiches with cooking spray.
4. Bake the sandwiches in the air fryer oven for 6 to 8 minutes, turning with tongs halfway through, until the bread is toasted and the cheese melts.
5. Cut each sandwich in half and serve.

Nutrition: Calories 140 Fat 4g Fiber 3g Carbs 5g Protein 7g

556. Cheesy Chicken Sandwich

Preparation time: 10 minutes
Cooking time: 5 to 7 minutes
Servings: 1

Ingredients:
- ⅓ cup chicken, cooked and shredded
- 2 Mozzarella slices
- 1 hamburger bun
- ¼ cup shredded cabbage
- 1 teaspoon mayonnaise
- 2 teaspoons butter, melted
- 1 teaspoon olive oil
- ½ teaspoon balsamic vinegar
- ¼ teaspoon smoked paprika
- ¼ teaspoon black pepper
- ¼ teaspoon garlic powder
- Pinch of salt

Directions
1. Select the Bake function and preheat Maxx to 370 F (188 degrees Celsius).
2. Brush some butter onto the outside of the hamburger bun.
3. In a bowl, coat the chicken with the garlic powder, salt, pepper, and paprika.
4. In a separate bowl, stir together the mayonnaise, olive oil, cabbage, and balsamic vinegar to make coleslaw.
5. Slice the bun in two. Start building the sandwich, starting with the chicken, followed by the Mozzarella, the coleslaw, and finally the top bun.
6. Transfer the sandwich to the air fryer oven and bake for 5 to 7 minutes.
7. Serve immediately.

Nutrition: Calories 311 Fat 11g Carbs 22g Protein 31g

557. Thai Pork Burgers

Preparation Time: 10 minutes
Cooking Time: 14 minutes
Servings: 6

Ingredients:
- 1 pound (454 g) ground pork
- 1 tablespoon Thai curry paste
- 1 1/2 tablespoons fish sauce
- ¼ cup thinly sliced scallions, white and green parts
- 2 tablespoons minced peeled fresh ginger
- 1 tablespoon light brown sugar
- 1 teaspoon ground black pepper
- 6 slider buns, split open lengthwise, warmed
- Cooking spray

Directions:
1. Spritz the air fry basket with cooking spray.
2. Combine all the ingredients, except for the buns in a large bowl. Stir to mix well.
3. Divide and shape the mixture into six balls, then bash the balls into six 3-inch-diameter patties.
4. Arrange the patties in the basket and spritz with cooking spray.
5. Place the basket on the air fry position.
6. Select Air Fry, set temperature to 375°F (190°C) and set time to 14 minutes. Flip the patties halfway through the cooking time.
7. When cooked, the patties should be well browned.
8. Assemble the buns with patties to make the sliders and serve immediately.

Nutrition: Calories 226 Carbs 0.1g Fat 2.8g Protein 2.8g

558. Easy Homemade Hamburgers

Preparation time: 5 minutes
Cooking time: 15 minutes
Servings: 2

Ingredients:
- 3/4 pound lean ground chuck
- Kosher salt and ground black pepper, to taste
- 3 tablespoons onion, minced
- 1 teaspoon garlic, minced
- 1 teaspoon soy sauce
- 1/2 teaspoon smoked paprika
- 1/4 teaspoon ground cumin
- 1/2 teaspoon cayenne pepper
- 1/2 teaspoon mustard seeds
- 2 burger buns

Directions
1. Thoroughly combine the ground chuck, salt, black pepper, onion, garlic and soy sauce in a mixing dish.
2. Season with smoked paprika, ground cumin, cayenne pepper and mustard seeds. Mix to combine well.
3. Shape the mixture into 2 equal patties.
4. Spritz your patties with a nonstick cooking spray. Air fry your burgers at 380 degrees F for about 11 minutes or to your desired degree of doneness.
5. Place your burgers on burger buns and serve with favorite toppings. Devour!

Nutrition: Calories 433 Fat 17.4g Carbs 40g Protein 39.2g Sugars 6.4g

559. Easy Beef Burritos

Preparation time: 5 minutes
Cooking time: 25 minutes
Servings: 3

Ingredients:
- 1 pound rump steak
- Sea salt and crushed red pepper, to taste
- 1/2 teaspoon shallot powder
- 1/2 teaspoon porcini powder
- 1/2 teaspoon celery seeds
- 1/2 teaspoon dried Mexican oregano
- 1 teaspoon piri piri powder
- 1 teaspoon lard, melted
- 3 (approx 7-8" dia) whole-wheat tortillas

Directions
1. Toss the rump steak with the spices and melted lard.
2. Cook in your Air Fryer at 390 F for 20 minutes, turning it halfway through the cooking time. Place on a cutting board to cool slightly.
3. Slice against the grain into thin strips.
4. Spoon the beef strips onto wheat tortillas; top with your favorite fixings, roll them up and serve. Enjoy!

Nutrition: Calories 368 Fat 13g Carbs 20.2g Protein 35.1g Sugars 2.7g

560. Beef and Seeds Burgers

Preparation Time: 15 minutes
Cooking Time: 10 minutes
Servings: 4

Ingredients:
- 1 teaspoon cumin seeds
- 1 teaspoon mustard seeds
- 1 teaspoon coriander seeds
- 1 teaspoon dried minced garlic
- 1 teaspoon dried red pepper flakes
- 1 teaspoon kosher salt
- 2 teaspoons ground black pepper
- 1 pound (454 g) 85% lean ground beef
- 2 tablespoons Worcestershire sauce
- 4 hamburger buns
- Mayonnaise, for serving
- Cooking spray

Directions:
1. Spritz the air fry basket with cooking spray.
2. Put the garlic, seeds, salt, red pepper flakes, and ground black pepper in a food processor. Pulse to coarsely ground the mixture.
3. Put the ground beef in a large bowl. Pour in the seed mixture and drizzle with Worcestershire sauce. Stir to mix well.
4. Divide the mixture into four parts and shape each part into a ball, then bash each ball into a patty. Arrange the patties in the basket.
5. Place the basket on the air fry position.
6. Select Air Fry, set temperature to 350°F (180°C) and set time to 10 minutes. Flip the patties with tongs halfway through the cooking time.
7. When cooked, the patties will be well browned.
8. Assemble the buns with the patties, then drizzle the mayo over the patties to make the burgers. Serve immediately.

Nutrition: Calories 246 Carbs 0.1g Fat 2.8g Protein 10.8g

561. Chicago-Style Beef Sandwich

Preparation time: 5 minutes
Cooking time: 25 minutes
Servings: 2

Ingredients:
- 1/2 pound chuck, boneless
- 1 tablespoon olive oil
- 1 tablespoon soy sauce
- 1/4 teaspoon ground bay laurel
- 1/2 teaspoon shallot powder
- 1/4 teaspoon porcini powder
- 1/2 teaspoon garlic powder
- 1/2 teaspoon cayenne pepper
- Kosher salt and ground black pepper, to taste
- 1 cup pickled vegetables, chopped
- 2 ciabatta rolls, sliced in half

Preparation
1. Toss the chuck roast with olive oil, soy sauce and spices until well coated.
2. Cook in the preheated Air Fryer at 400 F for 20 minutes, turning over halfway through the cooking time.
3. Shred the meat with two forks and adjust seasonings.
4. Top the bottom halves of the ciabatta rolls with a generous portion of the meat and pickled vegetables. Place the tops of the ciabatta rolls on the sandwiches. Serve immediately and enjoy!

Nutrition: Calories 385 Fat 17.4g Carbs 28g Protein 29.8g Sugars 6.2g

562. Air Fryer Veggie Quesadillas

Preparation Time: 20 minutes
Cooking Time: 20 minutes
Servings: 4

Ingredients:
- 4 sprouted whole-grain flour tortillas (6-in.)
- 1 cup sliced red bell pepper
- 4 ounces reduced-fat Cheddar cheese, shredded
- 1 cup sliced zucchini
- 1 cup canned black beans, Dry out and rinsed (no salt)
- Cooking spray
- 2 ounces plain 2% reduced-fat Greek yogurt
- 1 teaspoon lime zest
- 1 Tbsp. fresh juice (from 1 lime)
- ¼ tsp. ground cumin
- 2 tablespoons chopped fresh cilantro
- 1/2 cup Dry out refrigerated pico de gallo

Directions:
1. Place tortillas on work surface, sprinkle 2 tablespoons shredded cheese over half of each tortilla and top with cheese on each tortilla with 1/4 cup each red pepper slices, zucchini slices, and black beans. Sprinkle evenly with remaining 1/2 cup cheese.
2. Fold tortillas over to form half-moon shaped quesadillas, lightly coat with cooking spray, and secure with toothpicks.
3. Lightly spray air fryer basket with cooking spray. Place 2 quesadillas in the basket, and cook at 400°F for 10 minutes until tortillas are golden brown and slightly crispy, cheese is melted, and vegetables are slightly softened. Turn quesadillas over halfway through cooking.
4. Repeat with remaining quesadillas. Meanwhile, stir yogurt, lime juice, lime zest and cumin in a small bowl. Cut each quesadilla into wedges and sprinkle with cilantro.
5. Serve with 1 tablespoon cumin cream and 2 tablespoons pico de gallo each.

Nutrition: Calories 291 Fat 8g Protein 17g Carbs 36g

563. Crispy Cheesy Vegan Quesarito

Preparation Time: 5 minutes
Cooking Time: 10 minutes
Servings: 4

Ingredients:
- 2 large gluten free tortillas
- 4 tablespoons Vegan Queso (divided)
- 2-3 tablespoons grated cheese
- 3 tablespoons Meaty Crumbles
- 3-4 tablespoons Simple Spanish rice
- 1-2 tablespoons Spicy Almond Sauce
- 1 tablespoon cashew cream or dairy free sour cream
- Added ingredients
- Fresh baby spinach, Fresh bell peppers
- Roasted red peppers

Directions:
1. Lay first tortilla flat on prep surface.
2. Cut about an inch from around the entire edge of the second tortilla using a knife, making one smaller tortilla and then set aside.
3. On the first tortilla, spread the vegan queso around the middle of the tortilla, in a circle the size of the smaller tortilla.

WRAP AND SANDWICH

4. Add 3 tablespoons grated cheese to the top of the queso, in an even layer across the small circle (1 tablespoon grated cheese)
5. Top the queso / cheese circle with the smaller second tortilla, and press down slightly.
6. Spoon a line of the meaty crumbles onto the middle of the second smaller tortilla, spoon the Spanish rice on top of the meaty crumbles, followed by the tangy cream sauce and cashew cream / sour cream.
7. Carefully fold and roll burrito tightly. Secure the edge with the reserved 1 tablespoon grated cheese. Place the burrito cheese sealed side down in air fryer basket.
8. Fry for 6-7 minutes at 370°F, or until lightly golden and crisp.

Nutrition: Calories 514 Fat 18g Carbs 13g Protein 22g

564. Mozzarella-Spinach Stuffed Burgers

Preparation Time: 5 minutes
Cooking Time: 20 minutes
Servings: 4

Ingredients:
- 1 ½ lbs. ground chuck
- 2 tbsp. parmesan, grated
- 2 cups fresh spinach
- ½ cup shredded mozzarella cheese
- Pepper and salt as desired

Directions:
1. In a standard mixing bowl, join ground chuck and season accordingly. Then scoop about 1/3 cup of meat mixture and shape into 8 patties about ½ inch thick. Set in refrigerator.
2. Cook spinach over medium heat for a couple minutes until the spinach wilts. Drain spinach and let it cool before squeezing out excess liquid.
3. Move spinach to cutting board and chop the spinach. Add spinach, mozzarella cheese, and parmesan to a separate mixing bowl. Stir all ingredients together.
4. Take beef patties out of the fridge and scoop about ¼ cup of stuffing and place in the center of 4 patties.
5. Cover with remaining beef patties and press edges together firmly to seal the stuffing inside the patties. Round out the edges of the patties to create a single thick patty.
6. Heat a pan or grill to medium-high and prepare stuffed burgers for 5 to 6 minutes on, grilling equally on each side.

Nutrition: Calories: 414 Protein: 36g Net Carbs: 1g Fat 29g

565. Crispy Baked Avocado Tacos

Preparation Time: 20 minutes
Cooking Time: 10 minutes
Servings: 4

Ingredients:
- Salsa:
- 1/2 jalapeno finely sliced
- 1 tomato finely chopped
- 1 clove garlic minced
- 1/2 red bell pepper finely chopped
- 1/2 of a medium red onion 1/2 cup, finely sliced
- 1 cup crushed pineapple
- Pinch each cumin and salt
- Avocado Tacos:
- 1 avocado
- 1/4 cup all-purpose flour
- Pinch each salt and pepper
- flour tortillas click for recipe
- 1/2 cup panko crumbs
- 1 large egg beaten
- Adobo Sauce:
- 1/4 tsp lemon juice
- 1 Tbsp adobo sauce from a jar of chipotle peppers
- 1/4 cup white yogurt
- 2 Tbsp mayonnaise

Directions:
1. Salsa: Combine all the salsa ingredients and put them in the fridge.
2. Prepare avocado: Halve the length of the avocado and remove the pit. Lay the avocado skin face down and cut each half into 4 equal pieces. Then gently peel off the skin.
3. Preparation station: Preheat the oven to 230 ° C or the air fryer to 190 ° C. Arrange your work area so that you have a bowl of flour, a bowl of whisk, a bowl of Panko with S&P, and a baking sheet lined with parchment at the end.
4. Coat: Dip each avocado slice first in the flour, then in the egg and then in the panko. Place on the prepared baking sheet and bake for 10 minutes or fry in the air. Lightly brown after half of the cooking process.
5. Sauce: While cooking avocados, combine all the sauce ingredients.
6. Servings: Put salsa on a tortilla, top with 2 pieces of avocado and drizzle with sauce. Serve immediately and enjoy!

Nutrition: Calories: 630 kcal Protein: 13.7 g Fat: 35 g Carbs: 69 g

566. Quick Sausage and Veggie Sandwiches

Preparation time: 5 minutes
Cooking time: 35 minutes
Servings: 4

Ingredients:
- 4 bell peppers
- 2 tablespoons canola oil
- 4 medium-sized tomatoes, halved
- 4 spring onions
- 4 beef sausages
- 4 hot dog buns
- 1 tablespoon mustard

Preparation
1. Start by preheating your Air Fryer to 400 F.
2. Add the bell peppers to the cooking basket. Drizzle 1 tablespoon of canola oil all over the bell peppers.
3. Cook for 5 minutes. Turn the temperature down to 350 F. Add the tomatoes and spring onions to the cooking basket and cook an additional 10 minutes.
4. Reserve your vegetables.
5. Then, add the sausages to the cooking basket. Drizzle with the remaining tablespoon of canola oil.
6. Cook in the preheated Air Fryer at 380 F for 15 minutes, flipping them halfway through the cooking time.
7. Add the sausage to a hot dog bun; top with the air-fried vegetables and mustard; serve.

Nutrition: Calories 627 Fat 42g Carbs 41.3g Protein 23.2g Sugars 9.3g

567. Cheesy Beef Burrito

Preparation time: 5 minutes
Cooking time: 20 minutes
Servings: 4
Ingredients:
- 1 pound rump steak
- 1 teaspoon garlic powder
- 1/2 teaspoon onion powder
- 1/2 teaspoon cayenne pepper
- 1 teaspoon piri piri powder
- 1 teaspoon Mexican oregano
- Salt and ground black pepper, to taste
- 1 cup Mexican cheese blend
- 4 large whole wheat tortillas
- 1 cup iceberg lettuce, shredded

Directions
1. Toss the rump steak with the garlic powder, onion powder, cayenne pepper, piri piri powder, Mexican oregano, salt, and black pepper.
2. Cook in the preheated Air Fryer at 390 F for 10 minutes. Slice against the grain into thin strips. Add the cheese blend and cook for 2 minutes more.
3. Spoon the beef mixture onto the wheat tortillas; top with lettuce; roll up burrito-style and serve.

Nutrition: Calories 468 Fat 23.5g Carbs 22g Protein 42.7g Sugars 2.3g

568. Cheeseburger Egg Rolls

Preparation Time: 10 minutes
Cooking Time: 7 minutes
Servings: 6
Ingredients:
- 6 egg roll wrappers
- 6 chopped dill pickle chips
- 1 tbsp. yellow mustard
- 3 tbsp. cream cheese
- 3 tbsp. shredded cheddar cheese
- ½ C. chopped onion
- ½ C. chopped bell pepper
- ¼ tsp. onion powder
- ¼ tsp. garlic powder
- 8 ounces of raw lean ground beef

Directions:
1. In a skillet, add seasonings, beef, onion, and bell pepper. Stir and crumble beef till fully cooked, and vegetables are soft.
2. Take skillet off the heat and add cream cheese, mustard, and cheddar cheese, stirring till melted.
3. Pour beef mixture into a bowl and fold in pickles.
4. Lay out egg wrappers and place 1/6th of beef mixture into each one. Moisten egg roll wrapper edges with water. Fold sides to the middle and seal with water.
5. Repeat with all other egg rolls.
6. Place rolls into air fryer, one batch at a time.
7. Pour into the Oven rack/basket. Place the Rack on the middle-shelf of the Air Fryer Oven. Set temperature to 392°F, and set time to 7 minutes

Nutrition: Calories 153 Cal Fat 4 g Carbs 0 g Protein 12 g

569. Juicy Cheeseburgers

Preparation Time: 5 minutes
Cooking Time: 15 minutes
Servings: 4
Ingredients:
- 1 pound 93% lean ground beef
- 1 teaspoon Worcestershire sauce
- 1 tablespoon burger seasoning
- Salt
- Pepper
- Cooking oil
- 4 slices cheese
- Buns

Directions:
1. In a large bowl, mix the ground beef, Worcestershire, burger seasoning, and salt and pepper to taste until well blended.
2. Spray the air fryer basket with cooking oil. You will need only a quick sprits. The burgers will produce oil as they cook. Shape the mixture into 4 patties. Place the burgers in the air fryer. The burgers should fit without the need to stack, but stacking is okay if necessary.
3. Pour into the Oven rack/basket. Place the Rack on the middle-shelf of the Air Fryer Oven. Set temperature to 375°F, and set time to 8 minutes
4. Cook for 8 minutes Open the air fryer and flip the burgers.
5. Cook for an additional 3 to 4 minutes Check the inside of the burgers to determine if they have finished cooking. You can stick a knife or fork in the center to examine the color.
6. Top each burger with a slice of cheese. Cook for an additional minute, or until the cheese has melted
7. Serve on buns with any additional toppings of your choice.

Nutrition: Calories 566 Cal Fat 39 g Carbs 0 g Protein 29 g

570. Crunchy Chicken Egg Rolls

Preparation Time: 10 minutes
Cooking Time: 24 minutes
Servings: 4
Ingredients:
- 1 pound (454 g) ground chicken
- 2 teaspoons olive oil
- 2 garlic cloves, minced
- 1 teaspoon grated fresh ginger
- 2 cups white cabbage, shredded
- 1 onion, chopped
- ¼ cup soy sauce
- 8 egg roll wrappers
- 1 egg, beaten
- Cooking spray

Directions:
1. Spritz the air fry basket with cooking spray.
2. Heat olive oil in a saucepan over medium heat. Sauté the garlic and ginger in the olive oil for 1 minute, or until fragrant. Add the ground chicken to the saucepan. Sauté for 5 minutes, or until the chicken is cooked through. Add the cabbage, onion and soy sauce and sauté for 5 to 6 minutes, or until the vegetables become soft. Remove the saucepan from the heat.
3. Unfold the egg roll wrappers on a clean work surface. Divide the chicken mixture among the wrappers and brush the edges of the wrappers with the beaten egg. Tightly roll up the egg rolls, enclosing the filling. Arrange the rolls in the basket.
4. Place the basket on the air fry position.

5. Select Air Fry, set temperature to 370°F (188°C) and set time to 12 minutes. Flip the rolls halfway through the cooking time.
6. When cooked, the rolls will be crispy and golden brown.
7. Transfer to a platter and let cool for 5 minutes before serving.

Nutrition: Calories 246 Carbs 0.1g Fat 2.8g Protein 8.8g

571. Panko-Crusted Avocado and Slaw Tacos

Preparation Time: 15 minutes
Cooking Time: 6 minutes
Servings: 4

Ingredients:
- ¼ cup all-purpose flour
- ¼ teaspoon salt, plus more as needed
- ¼ teaspoon ground black pepper
- 2 large egg whites
- 1¼ cups panko bread crumbs
- 2 tablespoons olive oil
- 2 avocados, peeled and halved, cut into 1/2-inch-thick slices
- 1/2 small red cabbage, thinly sliced
- 1 deseeded jalapeño, thinly sliced
- 2 green onions, thinly sliced
- 1/2 cup cilantro leaves
- ¼ cup mayonnaise
- Juice and zest of 1 lime
- 4 corn tortillas, warmed
- 1/2 cup sour cream
- Cooking spray

Directions:
1. Spritz the air fry basket with cooking spray.
2. Pour the flour in a large bowl and sprinkle with salt and black pepper, then stir to mix well.
3. Whisk the egg whites in a separate bowl. Combine the panko with olive oil on a shallow dish.
4. Dredge the avocado slices in the bowl of flour, then into the egg to coat. Shake the excess off, then roll the slices over the panko.
5. Arrange the avocado slices in a single layer in the basket and spritz the cooking spray.
6. Place the basket on the air fry position.
7. Select Air Fry, set temperature to 400°F (205°C) and set time to 6 minutes. Flip the slices halfway through with tongs.
8. When cooking is complete, the avocado slices should be tender and lightly browned.
9. Combine the cabbage, onions, jalapeño, cilantro leaves, lime juice, mayo, and zest, and a touch of salt in a separate large bowl. Toss to mix well.
10. Unfold the tortillas on a clean work surface, then spread with cabbage slaw and air fried avocados. Top with sour cream and serve.

Nutrition: Calories 278 Carbs 0.1g Fat 2.8g Protein 4.8g

572. Golden Cabbage and Mushroom Spring Rolls

Preparation Time: 20 minutes
Cooking Time: 14 minutes
Servings: 14

Ingredients:
- 2 tablespoons vegetable oil
- 4 cups sliced Napa cabbage
- 5 ounces (142 g) shiitake mushrooms, diced
- 3 carrots, cut into thin matchsticks
- 1 tablespoon minced fresh ginger
- 1 tablespoon minced garlic
- 1 bunch scallions, white and light green parts only, sliced
- 2 tablespoons soy sauce
- 1 (4-ounce / 113-g) package cellophane noodles
- ¼ teaspoon cornstarch
- 1 (12-ounce / 340-g) package frozen spring roll wrappers, thawed
- Cooking spray

Directions:
1. Heat the olive oil in a nonstick skillet over medium-high heat until shimmering.
2. Add the cabbage, carrots, and mushrooms and sauté for 3 minutes or until tender.
3. Add the garlic, scallions, and ginger and sauté for 1 minutes or until fragrant.
4. Mix in the soy sauce and turn off the heat. Discard any liquid remains in the skillet and allow to cool for a few minutes.
5. Bring a pot of water to a boil, then turn off the heat and pour in the noodles. Let sit for 10 minutes or until the noodles are al dente. Transfer 1 cup of the noodles in the skillet and toss with the cooked vegetables. Reserve the remaining noodles for other use.
6. Dissolve the cornstarch in a small dish of water, then place the wrappers on a clean work surface. Dab the edges of the wrappers with cornstarch.
7. Scoop up 3 tablespoons of filling in the center of each wrapper, then fold the corner in front of you over the filling. Tuck the wrapper under the filling, then fold the corners on both sides into the center. Keep rolling to seal the wrapper. Repeat with remaining wrappers.
8. Spritz the air fry basket with cooking spray. Arrange the wrappers in the basket and spritz with cooking spray.
9. Place the basket on the air fry position.
10. Select Air Fry, set temperature to 400°F (205°C) and set time to 10 minutes. Flip the wrappers halfway through the cooking time.
11. When cooking is complete, the wrappers will be golden brown.
12. Serve immediately.

Nutrition: Calories 246 Carbs 0.1g Fat 2.8g Protein 10.8g

573. Korean Beef and Onion Tacos

Preparation Time: 1 hour 15 minutes
Cooking Time: 12 minutes
Servings: 6
Ingredients:
- 2 tablespoons gochujang
- 1 tablespoon soy sauce
- 2 tablespoons sesame seeds
- 2 teaspoons minced fresh ginger
- 2 cloves garlic, minced
- 2 tablespoons toasted sesame oil
- 2 teaspoons sugar
- 1/2 teaspoon kosher salt
- 1 1/2 pounds (680 g) thinly sliced beef chuck
- 1 medium red onion, sliced
- 6 corn tortillas, warmed
- ¼ cup chopped fresh cilantro
- 1/2 cup kimchi
- 1/2 cup chopped green onions

Directions:
1. Combine the ginger, garlic, gochujang, sesame seeds, soy sauce, sesame oil, salt, and sugar in a large bowl. Stir to mix well.
2. Dunk the beef chunk in the large bowl. Press to submerge, then wrap the bowl in plastic and refrigerate to marinate for at least 1 hour.
3. Remove the beef chunk from the marinade and transfer to the air fry basket. Add the onion to the basket.
4. Place the basket on the air fry position.
5. Select Air Fry, set temperature to 400°F (205°C) and set time to 12 minutes. Stir the mixture halfway through the cooking time.
6. When cooked, the beef will be well browned.
7. Unfold the tortillas on a clean work surface, then divide the fried beef and onion on the tortillas. Spread the green onions, kimchi, and cilantro on top.
8. Serve immediately.

Nutrition: Calories 246 Carbs 0.1g Fat 2.8g Protein 10.8g

574. Cabbage and Prawn Wraps

Preparation time: 20 minutes
Cooking time: 18 minutes
Servings: 4
Ingredients:
- 2 tablespoons olive oil
- 1 carrot, cut into strips
- 1-inch piece fresh ginger, grated
- 1 tablespoon minced garlic
- 2 tablespoons soy sauce
- ¼ cup chicken broth
- 1 tablespoon sugar
- 1 cup shredded Napa cabbage
- 1 tablespoon sesame oil
- 8 cooked prawns, minced
- 8 egg roll wrappers
- 1 egg, beaten
- Cooking spray

Directions
1. Spritz the perforated pan with cooking spray. Set aside.
2. Heat the olive oil in a nonstick skillet over medium heat until shimmering.
3. Add the carrot, ginger, and garlic and sauté for 2 minutes or until fragrant.
4. Pour in the soy sauce, broth, and sugar. Bring to a boil. Keep stirring.
5. Add the cabbage and simmer for 4 minutes or until the cabbage is tender.
6. Turn off the heat and mix in the sesame oil. Let sit for 15 minutes.
7. Use a strainer to remove the vegetables from the liquid, then combine with the minced prawns.
8. Unfold the egg roll wrappers on a clean work surface, then divide the prawn mixture in the center of wrappers.
9. Dab the edges of a wrapper with the beaten egg, then fold a corner over the filling and tuck the corner under the filling. Fold the left and right corner into the center. Roll the wrapper up and press to seal. Repeat with remaining wrappers.
10. Arrange the wrappers in the pan and spritz with cooking spray.
11. Select Air Fry. Set temperature to 370 F (188 degrees Celsius) and set time to 12 minutes. Press Start to begin preheating.
12. Once the oven has preheated, place the pan into the oven. Flip the wrappers halfway through the cooking time.
13. When cooking is complete, the wrappers should be golden.
14. Serve immediately.

Nutrition: Calories 339 Fat 15.9g Total Carbs 27.5g Protein 24.2g

575. Ricotta Spinach and Basil Pockets

Preparation time: 20 minutes
Cooking time: 10 minutes
Servings: 8 pockets
Ingredients:
- 2 large eggs, divided
- 1 tablespoon water
- 1 cup baby spinach, roughly chopped
- ¼ cup sun-dried tomatoes, finely chopped
- 1 cup ricotta cheese
- 1 cup basil, chopped
- ¼ teaspoon red pepper flakes
- ¼ teaspoon kosher salt
- 2 refrigerated rolled pie crusts
- 2 tablespoons sesame seeds

Directions
1. Spritz the perforated pan with cooking spray.
2. Whisk an egg with water in a small bowl.
3. Combine the spinach, tomatoes, the other egg, ricotta cheese, basil, red pepper flakes, and salt in a large bowl. Whisk to mix well.
4. Unfold the pie crusts on a clean work surface and slice each crust into 4 wedges. Scoop up 3 tablespoons of the spinach mixture on each crust and leave ½ inch space from edges.
5. Fold the crust wedges in half to wrap the filling and press the edges with a fork to seal.
6. Arrange the wraps in the pan and spritz with cooking spray. Sprinkle with sesame seeds.
7. Select Air Fry. Set temperature to 380 F (193 degrees Celsius) and set time to 10 minutes. Press Start to begin preheating.
8. Once the oven has preheated, place the pan into the oven. Flip the wraps halfway through the cooking time.
9. When cooked, the wraps will be crispy and golden.
10. Serve immediately.

Nutrition: Calories 175 Fat 13.4g Total Carbs 2g Protein 11.9g

WRAP AND SANDWICH

576. Avocado and Tomato Wraps

Preparation time: 10 minutes
Cooking time: 5 minutes
Servings: 5

Ingredients:
- 10 egg roll wrappers
- 3 avocados, peeled and pitted
- 1 tomato, diced
- Salt and ground black pepper, to taste
- Cooking spray

Directions
1. Spritz the perforated pan with cooking spray.
2. Put the tomato and avocados in a food processor. Sprinkle with salt and ground black pepper. Pulse to mix and coarsely mash until smooth.
3. Unfold the wrappers on a clean work surface, then divide the mixture in the center of each wrapper. Roll the wrapper up and press to seal.
4. Transfer the rolls to the pan and spritz with cooking spray.
5. Select Air Fry. Set temperature to 350 F (180 degrees Celsius) and set time to 5 minutes. Press Start to begin preheating.
6. Once the oven has preheated, place the pan into the oven. Flip the rolls halfway through the cooking time.
7. When cooked, the rolls should be golden brown.
8. Serve immediately.

Nutrition: Calories 419 Fat 14g Total Carbs 39g Protein 33g

577. Hot Bacon Sandwiches

Preparation time: 10 minutes
Cooking time: 7 minutes
Servings: 4

Ingredients:
- 1/3 cup bbq sauce
- 8 bacon slices, cooked and cut into thirds
- 1 red bell pepper, sliced
- 2 tablespoon honey
- butter
- 1 and ¼ cup lettuce leaves, torn
- 3 pita pockets, halved
- 8 tomatoes, sliced
- 1 yellow bell pepper, sliced

Directions
1. Mix honey and bbq sauce in a bowl and whisk properly.
2. Brush bell peppers and bacon with some of this mixture
3. Set them in your air fryer, and cook for around 4 minutes at 350 F
4. Shaking the fryer and cook them for about 2 minutes extra.
5. Stuff pita pockets with bacon mix, and also stuff with lettuce and tomatoes.
6. Expand the bottom of the bbq sauce and serve them for lunch.

Nutrition: Calories 186 Fiber 9g Carbs 14g Fat 6g Protein 4g

578. Chicken Sandwiches

Preparation time: 10 minutes
Cooking time: 10 minutes
Servings: 4

Ingredients:
- 2 chicken breasts, skinless, boneless and cubed
- 1 red bell pepper, sliced
- 1 red onion, chopped
- ½ teaspoon thyme, dried
- ½ cup Italian seasoning
- 2 cups butter lettuce, torn
- 4 pita pockets
- 1 tablespoon olive oil
- 1 cup cherry tomatoes, halved

Directions
1. Mix chicken with bell pepper, onion, oil, and Italian seasoning in your air fryer, toss well, and cook for 10 minutes at 380 F.
2. Transfer the mixture to a bowl, add butter, lettuce, thyme, cherry, tomatoes, and toss well.
3. Stuff pita pockets with the mixture and then serve them for lunch.

Nutrition: Calories 126 Fiber 8g Carbs 14g Fat 4g Protein 4g

579. Easy Hot Dogs

Preparation time: 10 minutes
Cooking time: 7 minutes
Servings: 2

Ingredients:
- 2 hot dog buns
- Dijon mustard (1 tablespoon)
- 2 hot dogs
- cheddar cheese, grated (2 tablespoons)

Directions
1. Put hot dogs in the preheated air fryer and cook them for around 5 minutes at 390 F.
2. Arrange hot dogs into the hot dog buns, expand cheese, and mustard.
3. Return everything to the air fryer and cook at 390 F for 2 minutes extra.
4. Serve them for lunch.

Nutrition: Calories 211 Fiber 8g Carbs 12g Fat 3g Protein 4g

580. Turkey Burgers

Preparation time: 10 minutes
Cooking time: 8 minutes
Servings: 4

Ingredients:
- 1 shallot, minced
- 1 pound turkey meat, ground
- Zest from 1 lime, grated
- 1 small jalapeno pepper, minced
- 2 teaspoons lime juice
- A drizzle of olive oil
- black pepper and salt
- 1 teaspoon cumin, ground
- Guacamole for serving
- 1 teaspoon sweet paprika

Directions
1. Mix turkey meat with pepper, cumin, paprika, jalapeno, lime juice, shallot, and zest in a bowl, stir well, shape burgers from this mix, drizzle the oil over them, introduce in the preheated air fryer and cook them for around 8 minutes on all side at 370 F.
2. Distribute between plates and serve them with guacamole on top.

Nutrition: Calories 200 Fat 12g Protein 12g

581. Prosciutto Sandwich

Preparation time: 10 minutes
Cooking time: 5 minutes
Servings: 1
Ingredients:
- 2 mozzarella slices
- 1 teaspoon olive oil
- 2 bread slices
- 2 prosciutto slices
- 2 tomato slices
- 2 basil leaves
- A pinch of black pepper and salt

Directions
1. Arrange prosciutto and mozzarella on a bread piece.
2. Season with pepper and salt, put them in your air fryer, and cook for 5 minutes at 400 F.
3. Drizzle oil above prosciutto, add basil and tomato cover with the other bread piece, chopped sandwich in half and serve them.
4. Enjoy!

Nutrition: Calories 172 Fiber 7g Carbs 9g Fat 3g Protein 5g

582. Tasty Cheeseburgers

Preparation time: 10 minutes
Cooking time: 20 minutes
Servings: 2
Ingredients:
- teaspoons
- 4 cheddar cheese slices
- 2 teaspoons
- 12 ounces lean beef, ground
- 2 tablespoons yellow onion, chopped
- black pepper and salt
- 2 burger buns, halved

Directions
1. Mix beef with ketchup, salt mustard, onion, and pepper in a bowl; stir well and shape four patties out of the mixture.
2. Arrange cheese on two patties and the top with another two patties.
3. Put them in a preheated air fryer at 370 F and stir-fry them for around 20 minutes.
4. Place the cheeseburger on two bread bun halves, and the top with another two halves, and serve for lunch.

Nutrition: Calories 261 Fiber 10g Carbs 20g Fat 6g Protein 6g

583. Rolled Salmon Sandwich

Preparation Time: 5 minutes
Cooking time: 5 minutes
Servings: 1
Ingredients:
- 1 piece of flatbread
- 1 salmon filet
- Pinch of salt
- 1 tablespoon green onion, chopped
- 1/4 teaspoon dried sumac
- 1/2 teaspoon thyme
- 1/2 teaspoon sesame seeds
- 1/4 English cucumber
- 1 tablespoon yogurt

Directions
1. Start by peeling and chopping the cucumber. Cut the salmon at a 45-degree angle into 4 slices and lay them flat on the flatbread.
2. Sprinkle salmon with salt to taste. Sprinkle onions, thyme, sumac, and sesame seeds evenly over the salmon.
3. Broil the salmon for at least 3 minutes, but longer if you want a more well-done fish.
4. While you broil your salmon, mix the yogurt and cucumber. Remove your flatbread from the toaster oven, put it on a plate, and spoon the yogurt mix over the salmon.
5. Fold the flatbread sides in and roll it up for a gourmet lunch that you can take on the go.

Nutrition: Calories 347 Sodium 397mg Dietary Fiber 1.6g Fat 12.4g Total Carbs 20.6g Protein 38.9g

584. Chicken Capers Sandwich

Preparation Time: 3 minutes
Cooking time: 3 minutes
Servings: 2
Ingredients:
- 2 leftover chicken breasts or pre-cooked breaded chicken
- 1 large ripe tomato
- 2 ounces' mozzarella cheese slices
- 3 slices of whole-grain bread
- 1/4 cup olive oil
- 1/3 cup fresh basil leaves
- Salt and pepper to taste

Directions
1. Start by slicing tomatoes into thin slices.
2. Layer tomatoes, then cheese over two slices of bread and place on a greased baking sheet.
3. Grill for about 3 minutes
4. Heat chicken while the cheese melts.
5. Remove from oven, sprinkle with basil, and add chicken.
6. Sprinkle with oil and add salt and pepper.
7. Top with other slices of bread and serve.

Nutrition: Calories 808 Sodium 847mg Dietary Fiber 5.2g Fat 43.6g Total Carbs 30.7g Protein 78.4g

585. Easy Prosciutto Grilled Cheese

Preparation Time: 5 minutes
Cooking time: 5 minutes
Servings: 1
Ingredients:
- 2 slices muenster cheese
- 2 slices white bread
- 2 thinly-shaved pieces of prosciutto
- 1 tablespoon sweet and spicy pickles

Directions
1. Set air fryer oven to the Toast setting.
2. Put one slice of cheese on each piece of bread.
3. Put prosciutto on one slice and pickles on the other.
4. Take it to a baking sheet and toast for 4 minutes or until the cheese is melted.
5. Combine the sides, cut, and serve.

Nutrition: Calories 460 Sodium 2180mg Fat 25.2g Carbs 11.9g Protein 44.2g

586. Persimmon Toast with Sour Cream and Cinnamon

Preparation Time: 5 minutes
Cooking time: 5 minutes
Servings: 1

Ingredients:
- 1 slice of wheat bread
- 1/2 persimmon
- Sour cream to taste
- Sugar to taste
- Cinnamon to taste

Directions
1. Apply a thin layer of sour cream across the bread.
2. Slice the persimmon into 1/4 inch pieces and lay them across the bread.
3. Sprinkle cinnamon and sugar over persimmon.
4. Toast in the air fryer oven until bread and persimmon begin to brown.

Nutrition: Calories 89 Sodium 133mg Dietary Fiber 2.0g Fat 1.1g Total Carbs 16.5g Protein 3.8g

587. Roasted Grape and Goat Cheese Crostinis

Preparation Time: 30 minutes
Cooking time: 5 minutes
Servings: 10

Ingredients:
- 1 pound seedless red grapes
- 1 teaspoon chopped rosemary
- 2 tablespoons olive oil
- 1 rustic French baguette
- 1 cup sliced shallots
- 2 tablespoons unsalted butter
- 2 ounces' goat cheese
- 1 tablespoon honey

Directions
1. Start by preheating the air fryer oven to 400 F.
2. Toss grapes, rosemary, and 1 tablespoon of olive oil in a large bowl.
3. Take it to a roasting pan and roast for 20 minutes.
4. Remove the pan from the oven and set aside to cool.
5. Slice the baguette into 1/2-inch-thick pieces.
6. Rub each slice with olive oil and place on a baking sheet.
7. Cook for 8 minutes, then remove from oven and set aside.
8. In a medium skillet, add butter and one tablespoon of olive oil.
9. Add shallots and sauté for about 10 minutes.
10. Mix goat cheese and honey in a medium bowl, then add the shallot pan and mix thoroughly.
11. Spread shallot mixture onto a baguette, top with grapes, and serve.

Nutrition: Calories 238 Sodium 139mg Dietary Fiber 0.6g Fat 16.3g Total Carbs 16.4g Protein 8.4g

588. Veggies on Toast

Preparation Time: 12 minutes
Cooking time: 11 minutes
Servings: 4

Ingredients:
- 1 red bell pepper, cut into ½-inch strips
- 1 cup sliced button or cremini mushrooms
- 1 small yellow squash, sliced
- 2 green onions, cut into ½-inch cuts
- Extra light olive oil
- 3 to 6 pieces sliced French bread
- 2 tablespoons softened butter
- ½ cup soft goat cheese

Directions
1. Mix the red pepper, mushrooms, squash, and green onions in the air fryer and mist with oil.
2. Cook for 15 minutes until the vegetables are tender, shaking the basket once during cooking time.
3. Take out the vegetables from the basket and set aside.
4. Put the bread with butter and place in the air fryer.
5. Heat up for 2 to 4 minutes or until golden brown.
6. Put the goat cheese on the toasted bread and top with the vegetables; serve warm.

Nutrition: Calories 162 Sodium 160mg Fiber 2g Fat 11g Saturated Fat 7g Carbs 9g Protein 7g Cholesterol 30mg

589. Mushroom Pita Pizzas

Preparation Time: 10 minutes
Cooking time: 5 minutes
Servings: 4

Ingredients:
- 4 (3-inch) pitas
- 1 tablespoon olive oil
- ¾ cup pizza sauce
- 1 (4-ounce) jar sliced mushrooms, drained
- ½ teaspoon dried basil
- 2 green onions, minced
- 1 cup grated mozzarella or provolone cheese
- 1 cup sliced grape tomatoes

Directions
1. Put each piece of pita with oil and top with the pizza sauce.
2. Put the mushrooms and sprinkle with basil and green onions. Put with the grated cheese.
3. Bake for 5 to 10 minutes or until the cheese is melted and starts to brown. Put with the grape tomatoes.

Nutrition: Calories 231 Sodium 500mg Fiber 2g Fat 9g Saturated Fat 4g Carbs 25g Protein 13g Cholesterol 15mg

590. French Toast Sticks with Sugar and Berries

Preparation Time: 10 Minutes
Cooking time: 10 Minutes
Servings: 4
Ingredients:
- 4(2-inch thick) bread slices
- 2large eggs
- ¼ cup whole milk
- ¼ cup brown sugar
- 1 tbsp maple syrup
- 1 tsp cinnamon powder
- A pinch nutmeg powders
- pinches icing sugar for topping
- 2Fresh blueberries and raspberries for topping

Directions
1. Insert the drip pan at the bottom rack of the device and preheat the air fryer at Air Fryer mode at 350 F for 3 to 4 minutes.
2. Cut each bread slice into 4 long strips and set aside.
3. Open the eggs into a bowl then whisk in the milk, maple syrup, cinnamon powder, and nutmeg powder.
4. Place the cooking tray to your side. Working in batches, dip 7 to 8 bread strips into the egg mixture and arrange widthwise on the tray.
5. Open the oven and fit in the cooking tray on the middle rack. Set the timer for 10 minutes, then cook until the timer reads to the end.
6. Open the oven, remove the tray and check the toasts, which should not be wet but crispy and sweet.
7. Transfer to serving plates and make the remaining toasts.
8. To serve, sprinkle with the icing sugar and enjoy warm with the berries.

Nutrition: Calories 132 Fat 4g Total Carbs 17.12g Fiber 1.7g Protein 6.77g Sugar 3.82g Sodium 190mg

591. Coconut Sandwich with Tomato and Avocado

Preparation Time: 5 Minutes
Cooking time: 15 Minutes
Servings: 4
Ingredients:
- ½ cup almond flour
- ¼ teaspoon salt
- ¼ teaspoon baking soda
- 2eggs
- 2tablespoons coconut oil
- 2tablespoons coconut milk
- 1 ripe avocado
- 1 large red tomato

Directions
1. Combine the almond flour with salt and baking soda then mix well.
2. Make a hole in the center of the flour mixture then add eggs, coconut oil, and coconut milk to it. Stir until incorporated.
3. Line a baking pan that fits the Air fryer oven then grease it with cooking spray.
4. Transfer the batter to the prepared baking pan and spread it evenly.
5. Next, install the crisper plate into the basket of your Air fryer oven then preheat the for 3 minutes.
6. Select the "Bake" menu then set the temperature to 325 F and adjust the time to 10 minutes.
7. Insert the baking pan to the air fryer basket then press the "Start/Stop" button to begin. Bake the bread.
8. Once the Air Fryer beeps and the bread is done, remove it from the Air Fryer and take the bread out of the pan.
9. Cut the bread into thick slices then top each slice of bread with avocado and tomato slices.
10. Serve and enjoy.

Nutrition: 242 Calories, 22.6g Fats, 2.9g Net Carbs, 5g Protein

592. Avocado Taco Fry

Preparation Time: 5 Minutes
Cooking time: 20 Minutes
Servings: 12
Ingredients:
- 1 peeled avocado, sliced
- 1 beaten egg
- 1/2 cup panko bread crumbs
- Salt
- Tortillas and toppings

Directions
1. Using a bowl, add in the egg.
2. Using a separate bowl, set in the breadcrumbs.
3. Dip the avocado into the bowl with the beaten egg and coat with the breadcrumbs. Sprinkle the coated wedges with a bit of salt.
4. Arrange them in the cooking basket in a single layer.
5. Set the Air Fryer to 392 F and cook for 15 minutes. Shake the basket halfway through the cooking process.
6. Put them on tortillas with your preferred toppings.

Nutrition: Calories 140 Fat 8.8g Carbs 12g Protein 6g

593. Breakfast Cheese Bread Cups

Preparation Time: 6 Minutes
Cooking time: 15 Minutes
Servings: 2
Ingredients:
- 2eggs
- 2tbsps. grated cheddar cheese
- Salt and pepper
- 1 ham slice cut into two pieces
- 4bread slices flatted with a rolling pin

Directions
1. Spray both sides of the ramekins with cooking spray.
2. Place two slices of bread into each ramekin.
3. Add the ham slice pieces into each ramekin.
4. Crack an egg in each ramekin, then sprinkle with cheese.
5. Season with salt and pepper.
6. Place the ramekins into the air fryer at 300 F for 15 minutes.
7. Serve warm.

Nutrition: Calories 162 Fat 8g Carbs 10g Protein 11g

594. Cheese and Egg Breakfast Sandwich

Preparation Time: 3 Minutes
Cooking time: 6 Minutes
Servings: 1

Ingredients:
- 1 egg
- 2 slices of cheddar or Swiss cheese
- A bit of butter
- 1 roll either English muffin or Kaiser bun halved

Directions
1. Butter the sliced rolls on both sides.
2. Whisk the eggs in an oven-safe dish.
3. Place the cheese, egg dish, and rolls into the air fryer. Make sure the buttered sides of the roll are facing upwards.
4. Adjust the air fryer to 390 F. Cook for 6 minutes.
5. Place the egg and cheese between the pieces of roll. Serve warm.

Nutrition: Calories 212 Fat 11.2g Carbs 9.3g Protein 12.4g

595. Breakfast Muffins

Preparation Time: 3 Minutes
Cooking time: 6 Minutes
Servings: 2

Ingredients:
- 2 whole-wheat English muffins
- 4 slices of bacon
- Pepper
- 2 eggs

Directions
1. Crack an egg each into ramekins, then season with pepper.
2. Place the ramekins in your preheated air fryer at 390 F.
3. Allow cooking for 6-minutes with the bacon and muffins alongside.
4. Remove the muffins from the air fryer after a few minutes and split them.
5. When the bacon and eggs are done cooking, add two bacon pieces and one egg to each egg muffin. Serve when hot.

Nutrition: Calories 276 Fat 12g Carbs 10.2g Protein 17.3g

596. Tomato and Mozzarella Bruschetta

Preparation Time: 5 Minutes
Cooking time: 4 Minutes
Servings: 1

Ingredients:
- 6 small loaf slices
- ½ cup tomatoes, finely chopped
- 3 ounces (85 g) Mozzarella cheese, grated
- 1 tablespoon fresh basil, chopped
- 1 tablespoon olive oil

Directions
1. Press Start/Cancel. Preheat the air fryer oven to 350 F (177 degrees Celsius).
2. Put the loaf slices in the fry basket and insert the fry basket at mid position.
3. Select Air Fry, Convection, and set time to 3 minutes.
4. Add the tomato, Mozzarella, basil, and olive oil on top.
5. Air fry for an additional minute before serving.

Nutrition: Calories 166 Fat 12g Carbs 11g Protein 3g

597. All-in-One Toast

Preparation Time: 10 Minutes
Cooking time: 10 Minutes
Servings: 1

Ingredients:
- 1 strip bacon, diced
- 1 slice 1-inch thick bread
- 1 egg
- Salt and freshly ground black pepper, to taste
- ¼ cup grated Colby cheese

Directions
1. Press Start/Cancel. Preheat the air fryer oven to 400 F (204 degrees Celsius).
2. Place the bacon in the fry basket. Insert the fry basket at mid position.
3. Select Air Fry, Convection, and set time to 3 minutes, shaking the basket once or twice while it cooks. Remove the bacon to a paper towel-lined plate and set aside.
4. Use a sharp paring knife to score a large circle in the middle of the bread slice, cutting halfway through but not through to the cutting board. Press down on the circle in the center of the bread slice to create an indentation.
5. Transfer the slice of bread, hole side up, to the fry basket. Crack the egg into the center of the bread and season with salt and pepper.
6. Adjust the air fryer oven temperature to 380 F (193 degrees Celsius) and air fry for 5 minutes. Sprinkle the grated cheese around the bread's edges, leaving the yolk's center uncovered, and top with the cooked bacon. Press the cheese and bacon into the bread lightly to help anchor it to the bread and prevent it from blowing around in the air fryer oven.
7. Air fry for two more minutes, just to melt the cheese and finish cooking the egg. Serve immediately.

Nutrition: Calories 243 Fat 14.5g Carbs 15.4g Protein 12.6g

598. Jalapeño Tacos with Guacamole

Preparation Time: 10 Minutes
Cooking time: 30 Minutes
Servings: 3

Ingredients:
- 3 soft taco shells
- 1 cup kidney beans, drained
- 1 cup black beans, drained
- ½ cup tomato puree
- 1 fresh jalapeño pepper, chopped
- 1 cup fresh cilantro, chopped
- 1 cup corn kernels
- ½ tsp ground cumin
- ½ tsp cayenne pepper
- Salt and black pepper to taste
- 1 cup grated mozzarella cheese
- Guacamole to serve

Directions
1. In a bowl, add beans, beans, tomato puree, chili, cilantro, corn, cumin, cayenne, salt and pepper; stir well.
2. Spoon the mixture onto one half of the taco, sprinkle the cheese over the top and fold over.
3. Spray the frying basket, and lay the tacos inside.
4. Cook for 14 minutes at 360 F, until the cheese melts.
5. Serve hot with guacamole.

Nutrition: Calories 419 Fat 14g Total Carbs 39g Protein 33g

APPETIZER AND SNACK

APPETIZER AND SNACK

599. Air Fried Buffalo Chicken Strips

Preparation time: 5 minutes
Cooking time: 15 minutes
Servings: 4
Ingredients:
- 12 ounces chicken breast strips
- ¼ cup of flour
- 1 egg (or liquid egg whites)
- Buffalo Sauce - (We used about 1/2 cup)
- Garlic salt and pepper to taste

Directions:
1. In a separate bowl, place egg, and flour
2. Spray a little cooking spray on the bottom of your Air fryer. Dip chicken in the flour, and then the egg, until well coated.
3. Place the chicken in your Air fryer, spray the top of the chicken with a little more cooking spray.
4. Set the timer to fry at 375°F for about 10 minutes. After the 10 minutes, flip and cook for an additional 3 to 5 minutes.
5. When the time is up, remove chicken from your Air fryer. Place in a mixing bowl and toss in buffalo sauce until well coated.
6. Serve with celery, carrots and ranch.
7. Serve and enjoy!

Nutrition: Calories: 220 Carbs: 14 g Fat: 10 g Protein: 21 g

600. Allspice Chicken Wings

Preparation Time:
Cooking Time: 45 minutes
Servings: 8
Ingredients:
- ½ tsp celery salt
- ½ tsp bay leaf powder
- ½ tsp ground black pepper
- ½ tsp paprika
- ¼ tsp dry mustard
- ¼ tsp cayenne pepper
- ¼ tsp allspice
- 2 pounds chicken wings

Directions:
1. Grease the air fryer basket and preheat to 340 F. In a bowl, mix celery salt, bay leaf powder, black pepper, paprika, dry mustard, cayenne pepper, and allspice. Coat the wings thoroughly in this mixture.
2. Arrange the wings in an even layer in the basket of the air fryer. Cook the chicken until it's no longer pink around the bone, for 30 minutes then, increase the temperature to 380 F and cook for 6 minutes more, until crispy on the outside.

Nutrition: Calories 332 Fat 10.1 g Carbs 31.3 g Protein 12 g

601. Friday Night Pineapple Sticky Ribs

Preparation Time: 10 minutes
Cooking Time: 20 minutes
Servings: 4
Ingredients:
- 2 lb. cut spareribs
- 7 oz salad dressing
- 1 (5-oz) can pineapple juice
- 2 cups water
- Garlic salt to taste
- Salt and black pepper

Directions:
1. Sprinkle the ribs with salt and pepper, and place them in a saucepan. Pour water and cook the ribs for 12 minutes on high heat.
2. Dry out the ribs and arrange them in the fryer; sprinkle with garlic salt. Cook it for 15minutes at 390 F.
3. Prepare the sauce by combining the salad dressing and the pineapple juice. Serve the ribs drizzled with the sauce.

Nutrition: Calories 316 Fat 3.1 g Carbs 1.9 g Protein 5 g

602. Egg Roll Wrapped with Cabbage and Prawns

Preparation Time: 10 minutes
Cooking Time: 40 minutes
Servings: 4
Ingredients:
- 2 tbsp. vegetable oil
- 1-inch piece fresh ginger, grated
- 1 tbsp. minced garlic
- 1 carrot, cut into strips
- ¼ cup chicken broth
- 2 tbsp. reduced-sodium soy sauce
- 1 tbsp. sugar
- 1 cup shredded Napa cabbage
- 1 tbsp. sesame oil
- 8 cooked prawns, minced
- 1 egg
- 8 egg roll wrappers

Directions:
1. In a skillet over high heat, heat vegetable oil, and cook ginger and garlic for 40 seconds, until fragrant. Stir in carrot and cook for another 2 minutes Pour in chicken broth, soy sauce, and sugar and bring to a boil.
2. Add cabbage and let simmer until softened, for 4 minutes Remove skillet from the heat and stir in sesame oil. Let cool for 15 minutes Strain cabbage mixture, and fold in minced prawns. Whisk an egg in a small bowl. Fill each egg roll wrapper with prawn mixture, arranging the mixture just below the center of the wrapper.
3. Fold the bottom part over the filling and tuck under. Fold in both sides and tightly roll up. Use the whisked egg to seal the wrapper. Repeat until all egg rolls are ready. Place the rolls into a greased air fryer basket, spray them with oil and cook for 12 minutes at 370 F, turning once halfway through.

Nutrition: Calories 215 Fat 7.9 g Carbs 6.7 g Protein 8 g

603. Sesame Garlic Chicken Wings

Preparation Time: 10 minutes
Cooking Time: 40 minutes
Servings: 4
Ingredients:
- 1-pound chicken wings
- 1 cup soy sauce, divided
- ½ cup brown sugar
- ½ cup apple cider vinegar
- 2 tbsp. fresh ginger, minced
- 2 tbsp. fresh garlic, minced
- 1 tsp finely ground black pepper
- 2 tbsp. cornstarch
- 2 tbsp. cold water
- 1 tsp sesame seeds

Directions:
1. In a bowl, add chicken wings, and pour in half cup soy sauce. Refrigerate for 20 minutes; Dry out and pat dry. Arrange the wings in the air fryer and cook for 30 minutes at 380 F, turning once halfway through. Make sure you check them towards the end to avoid overcooking.
2. In a skillet and over medium heat, stir sugar, half cup soy sauce, vinegar, ginger, garlic, and black pepper. Cook until sauce has reduced slightly, about 4 to 6 minutes.
3. Dissolve 2 tbsp. of cornstarch in cold water, in a bowl, and stir in the slurry into the sauce, until it thickens, for 2 minutes Pour the sauce over wings and sprinkle with sesame seeds.

Nutrition: Calories 413 Fat 8.3 g Carbs 7 g Protein 8.3 g

604. Sausage and Onion Rolls

Preparation time: 15 minutes
Cooking time: 15 minutes
Servings: 12
Ingredients:
- 1-pound (454 g) bulk breakfast sausage
- ½ cup finely chopped onion
- ½ cup fresh bread crumbs
- ½ teaspoon dried mustard
- ½ teaspoon dried sage
- ¼ teaspoon cayenne pepper
- 1 large egg, beaten
- 1 garlic clove, minced
- 2 sheets frozen puff pastry, thawed
- All-purpose flour, for dusting

Directions
1. In a medium bowl, break up the sausage. Stir in the onion, bread crumbs, mustard, sage, cayenne pepper, egg, and garlic.
2. Divide the sausage mixture in half and tightly wrap each half in plastic wrap. Refrigerate for 5 to 10 minutes.
3. Lay the pastry sheets on a lightly floured work surface. Lightly roll out the pastry to smooth out the dough.
4. Take out one of the sausage packages and form the sausage into a long roll. Remove the plastic wrap and place the sausage on top of the puff pastry about 1 inch from one of the long edges.
5. Roll the pastry around the sausage and pinch the edges of the dough together to seal. Repeat with the other pastry sheet and sausage.
6. Slice the logs into lengths about 1½ inches long. Place the sausage rolls in the baking pan, cut-side down.
7. Choose 'Roast", temperature to 350 F (180 degrees Celsius), and set time to 15 minutes.
8. Let cool for 5 minutes before serving.

Nutrition: Calories 94 Carbs: 10g Fat 4g Protein 3g

605. Green Chilis Nachos

Preparation time: 15 minutes
Cooking time: 10 minutes
Servings: 6
Ingredients:
- 8oz (227g) tortilla chips
- 3 cups shredded Monterey Jack cheese, divided
- 2 (7oz/198g) cans chopped green chilies, drained
- 1 (8oz/227g) can tomato sauce
- ¼ teaspoon dried oregano
- ¼ teaspoon granulated garlic
- ¼ teaspoon freshly ground black pepper
- Pinch cinnamon
- Pinch cayenne pepper

Directions
1. Arrange the tortilla chips close together in a single layer in the baking pan. Sprinkle 1½ cups of the cheese over the chips.
2. Arrange the green chilies over the cheese as evenly as possible. Top with the remaining 1½ cups of the cheese.
3. Select "Roast," temperature to 375 F (190 degrees Celsius), and set time to 10 minutes.
4. Meanwhile, stir the remaining ingredients in a bowl for the sauce.
5. Remove from when done, then drizzle the sauce over the nachos and serve warm.

Nutrition: Calories 5 Carbs 1g

606. Dehydrated Candied Bacon

Preparation time: 3 hours
Cooking time: 4 hours and 10 minutes
Servings: 4
Ingredients:
- 6 slices bacon
- 3 tablespoons light brown sugar
- 2 tablespoons rice vinegar
- 2 tablespoons chili paste
- 1 tablespoon soy sauce

Directions:
1. Mix brown sugar, rice vinegar, chili paste, and soy sauce together in a bowl.
2. Add bacon slices and mix until all are evenly coated.
3. Set aside for up to 3 hours or up until ready to dehydrate.
4. Then put the bacon on the food tray.
5. Set bacon on the air fryer 's wire rack, then insert the rack at mid-position in the air fryer toaster oven.
6. Select the Dehydrate function on the Air Fryer, set time to 4 hours, then press Start.
7. Remove the tray once done baking and let the bacon cool for 5 minutes, then serve.

Nutrition: Calories 137 Total Fat 8.8g Total Carbs 6.9g Protein 7.6g

607. Cheesy Roasted Jalapeño Poppers

Preparation time: 15 minutes
Cooking time: 15 minutes
Servings: 8
Ingredients:
- 6oz (170g) cream cheese, at room temperature
- 4oz (113g) shredded Cheddar cheese
- 1 teaspoon chili powder
- 12 large jalapeño peppers, deseeded and sliced in half lengthwise
- 2 slices cooked bacon, chopped
- ¼ cup panko bread crumbs
- 1 tablespoon butter, melted

Directions
1. Mix the cream cheese, Cheddar cheese, and chili powder in a medium bowl. Spoon the cheese mixture into the jalapeño halves and arrange them in the baking pan.
2. In a small bowl, stir the bacon, bread crumbs, and butter. Sprinkle the mixture over the jalapeño halves.
3. Roast, then temperature to 375 F (190 degrees Celsius) and set time to 15 minutes.
4. Remove, then let the poppers cool for 5 minutes before serving.

Nutrition: Calories 280 Carbs 24g Fat 19g Protein 4g

608. Salty Baked Almonds

Preparation time: 5 minutes
Cooking time: 25 minutes
Servings: 4
Ingredients:
- 1 cup of raw almonds
- 1 egg white, beaten
- ½ teaspoon coarse sea salt

Directions
1. Spread the almonds in the baking pan in an even layer.
2. Choose the "Convection Bake" set temperature to 350 F (180 degrees Celsius) and set time to 20 minutes.
3. Remove, then coat the almonds with the egg white and sprinkle with the salt. Return the pan to the oven within 5 minutes.
4. Cool completely before serving.

Nutrition: Calories 180 Carbs 5g Fat 16g Protein: 6g

609. Dehydrated Spiced Orange Slices

Preparation time: 10 minutes
Cooking time: 6 hours
Servings: 3
Ingredients:
- 2 large oranges, cut into ⅛-inch-thick slices
- ½ teaspoon ground star anise
- ½ teaspoon ground cinnamon
- 1 tbsp. Choco-hazelnut spread

Directions:
1. Dash seasonings on the orange slices.
2. Place into the fry basket, then insert the basket at mid-position in the Air Fryer.
3. Select the Dehydrate function, fix the time to 6 hours and temperature to 140°F, then press Start.
4. Remove once done, and if desired serve with chocolate hazelnut spread.

Nutrition: Calories 99 Total Fat 2.2g Total Carbs 18.2g Protein 1.6g

610. Spicy and Sweet Roasted Nuts

Preparation time: 5 minutes
Cooking time: 15 minutes
Servings: 4
Ingredients:
- 1-pound (454g) walnut halves and pieces
- ½ cup granulated sugar
- 3 tablespoons vegetable oil
- 1 teaspoon cayenne pepper
- ½ teaspoon fine salt

Directions
1. Soak the walnuts in a large bowl with boiling water for a minute or two. Drain the walnuts.
2. Stir in the sugar, oil, and cayenne pepper to coat well. Spread the walnuts in a single layer in the baking pan.
3. Select "Roast" set temperature to 325 F (163 degrees Celsius) and set time to 15 minutes.
4. After 7 or 8 minutes, remove, and stir the nuts. Return, and check frequently.
5. When done, the walnuts should be dark golden brown. Sprinkle the nuts with the salt and let cool. Serve warm.

Nutrition: Calories 205 Carbs 5g Fat 20g Protein 4g

611. Steamed Pot Stickers

Preparation time: 20 minutes
Cooking time: 10 minutes
Servings: 30
Ingredients:
- ½ cup finely chopped cabbage
- 2 teaspoons low-sodium soy sauce
- 2 tablespoons cocktail sauce
- 30 wonton wrappers
- ¼ cup finely chopped red bell pepper
- 3 tablespoons water, and more for brushing the wrappers
- 2 green onions, finely chopped
- 1 egg, beaten

Directions
1. Combine the cabbage, bell pepper, chives, egg, cocktail sauce in a small bowl, and soy sauce and mix well.
2. Put exactly 1 teaspoon of the mixture in the middle of each wonton wrapper. Fold the wrap in half, covering the filling. wet the edges with water and seal. You can fold the edges of the wrapper with your fingers so they look like the stickers you get at restaurants. Brush them with water.
3. Put 3 tablespoons of water in the skillet under the fryer basket. Cook potstickers in 2 batches for 9 to 10 minutes or until potstickers are hot and the bottom is light.

Nutrition: Calories 291 Fat 2g Cholesterol 35mg Sodium 649mg Carbs 57g Fiber 3g Protein 10g

612. Beef and Mango Skewers

Preparation time: 10 minutes
Cooking time: 5 minutes
Servings: 4
Ingredients:
- 2 tablespoons balsamic vinegar
- 1 tablespoon olive oil
- 1 tablespoon honey
- ½ teaspoon dried marjoram
- A pinch of salt
- Freshly ground black pepper
- 1 mango
- ¾ pound beef sirloin (cut into 1-inch cubes)

Directions
1. Put the meat cubes in a medium bowl and add the balsamic vinegar, olive oil, honey, marjoram, salt, and pepper. Mix well and then massage the marinade into the meat with your hands. Set aside.
2. To prepare the mango, leave it last and cut the skin with a sharp blade.
3. Then gently cut around the oval pit to remove the pulp. Cut the mango into 1-inch cubes.
4. The metal wire skewers alternate with three cubes of meat and two cubes of mango.
5. Bake the skewers in the skillet for 4 to 7 minutes or until the meat is browned and at least 145 F.

Nutrition: Calories 242 Fat 9g Saturated Fat 3g Cholesterol 76mg Sodium 96mg Carbs 13g Fiber 1g Protein 26g

613. Curried Sweet Potato Fries

Preparation time: 5 minutes
Cooking time: 12 minutes
Servings: 4
Ingredients:
- ½ cup sour cream
- ½ cup mango chutney
- 3 teaspoons curry powder, divided
- 4 cups frozen sweet potato fries
- 1 tablespoon olive oil
- A pinch of salt
- Freshly ground black pepper

Directions
1. In a bowl, add together sour cream, chutney, and 1½ teaspoon curry powder. Mix well and let stand.
2. Place the sweet potatoes in a sizeable bowl. Pour over the olive oil and sprinkle with the remaining 1½ teaspoon curry powder, salt, and pepper.
3. Put the potatoes in the fryer basket. Cook 8 to 12 minutes or until crisp, hot and golden, shaking the basket once during cooking.
4. Place the potatoes in a basket and serve with the teaspoon.

Nutrition: Calories 323 Fat 10g Saturated Fat 4g Cholesterol 13mg Sodium 138mg Carbs 58g Fiber 7g Protein 3g

614. Spicy Kale Chips with Yogurt Sauce

Preparation time: 10 minutes
Cooking time: 5 minutes
Servings: 4
Ingredients:
- 1 cup Greek yogurt
- 3 tablespoons lemon juice
- 2 tablespoons honey mustard
- ½ teaspoon dried oregano
- 1 bunch curly kale
- 2 tablespoons olive oil
- ½ teaspoon salt
- ⅛ teaspoon pepper

Preparation
1. In a bowl, add together the yogurt, lemon juice, honey mustard, and oregano and set aside.
2. Remove the stems and ribs from the cabbage with a sharp knife. Cut the leaves into 2 to 3-inch pieces.
3. Toss the cabbage with olive oil, salt, and pepper. Massage the oil with your hands.
4. Fry the kale in batches until crisp, about 5 minutes, shaking the basket once during cooking. Serve with yogurt sauce.

Nutrition: Calories 154 Fat 8g Saturated Fat 2g Cholesterol 3mg Sodium 378mg Carbs 13g Fiber 1g Protein 8g

615. Phyllo Artichoke Triangles

Preparation time: 15 minutes
Cooking time: 9 minutes
Servings: 18
Ingredients:
- ¼ cup ricotta cheese
- 1 egg white
- ⅓ cup minced drained artichoke hearts
- 3 tablespoons grated mozzarella cheese
- ½ teaspoon dried thyme
- 6 sheets frozen phyllo dough, thawed
- 2 tablespoons melted butter

Directions
1. In a bowl, combine ricotta cheese, egg white, artichoke hearts, mozzarella cheese, and thyme and mix well.
2. Cover the dough with a damp kitchen towel while you work so it doesn't dry out. Using one sheet at a time, lay it out on your work surface and cut into thirds lengthwise.
3. Apply 1½ tsp of filling on each strip at the base. Fold the bottom-right edge of the sheet over the filling to meet the other side in a triangle, then continue folding into a triangle. Brush each angle with butter to seal the edges. Repeat with the remaining dough and filling.

Nutrition: Calories 271 Fat 17g Saturated Fat 7g Cholesterol 19mg Sodium 232mg Carbs 23g Fiber 5g Protein 9g

616. Arancini

Preparation time: 15 minutes
Cooking time: 22 minutes
Servings: 16
Ingredients:
- eggs, beaten
- 1½ cups panko bread crumbs, divided
- ½ cup grated Parmesan cheese
- 2 tablespoons minced fresh basil
- 2 cups cooked rice or leftover risotto
- 16 ¾-inch cubes mozzarella cheese
- 2 tablespoons olive oil

Preparation
1. In a medium bowl, add together the rice, eggs, a cup of breadcrumbs, Parmesan, and basil. Shape this mixture into 16 1-inch balls.
2. Create a hole in each of the balls with your finger and place a cube of mozzarella. Glue the rice mixture firmly around the cheese.
3. On a shallow plate, add together the remaining 1 cup of breadcrumbs with the olive oil and mix well. Wrap the rice balls in the breadcrumbs for color.
4. Cook the arancini in batches for 8 to 11 minutes or until golden brown.

Nutrition: Calories 378 Fat 11g Saturated Fat 4g Cholesterol 57mg Sodium 361mg Carbs 53g Fiber 2g Protein 16g

617. Pesto Bruschetta

Preparation time: 10 minutes
Cooking time: 8 minutes
Servings: 4
Ingredients:
- 8 slices French bread, ½ inch thick
- 2 tablespoons softened butter
- 1 cup shredded mozzarella cheese
- ½ cup basil pesto
- 1 cup chopped grape tomatoes
- 2 green onions, thinly sliced

Directions
1. Butter the bread and place the butter in the deep fryer basket. Bake 3 to 5 minutes or until bread is lightly golden.
2. Take the bread out of the basket and fill each piece with a little cheese. Return to the basket in batches and bake until cheese is melted, for about 1 to 3 minutes.

3. Meanwhile, combine pesto, tomatoes, and chives in a small bowl.
4. When the cheese is melted, remove the bread from the fryer and place it on a plate. Fill each slice with a little pesto mix and serve.

Nutrition: Calories 462 Fat 25g Saturated Fat 10g Cholesterol 38mg Sodium 822mg Carbs 41g Fiber 3g Protein 19g

618. Fried Tortellini with Spicy Dipping Sauce

Preparation time: 8 minutes
Cooking time: 20 minutes
Servings: 4
Ingredients:
- ¾ cup mayonnaise
- 2tablespoons mustard
- 1 egg
- ½ cup flour
- ½ teaspoon dried oregano
- 1½ cups bread crumbs
- 2tablespoons olive oil
- 2cups frozen cheese tortellini

Directions
1. In a small bowl, add together the mayonnaise and mustard and mix well. Set aside.
2. In a shallow bowl, beat the egg. In a separate bowl, combine the flour and oregano. In another bowl, combine the breadcrumbs and olive oil and mix well.
3. Add the tortellini, a few at a time, to the egg, then the flour, then the egg again, then the breadcrumbs to coat. Place in the fryer basket, cooking in batches.
4. Air fry for about 10 minutes, stirring halfway through cooking time, or until tortellini are crisp and golden on the outside. Serve with mayonnaise.

Nutrition: Calories 698 Fat 31g Saturated Fat 4g Cholesterol 66mg Sodium 832mg Carbs 88g Fiber 3g Protein 18g

619. Shrimp Toast

Preparation time: 15 minutes
Cooking time: 12 minutes
Servings: 12
Ingredients:
- 3slices firm white bread
- ⅔ cup finely chopped peeled and deveined raw shrimp
- 1 egg white
- 2cloves garlic, minced
- 2tablespoons cornstarch
- ¼ teaspoon ground ginger
- A pinch of salt
- Freshly ground black pepper
- 2tablespoons olive oil

Directions
1. Cut the crust from the bread with a sharp knife. crumble the crusts to make breadcrumbs. Set aside.
2. In a small bowl, add together the shrimp, egg white, garlic, cornstarch, ginger, salt, and pepper and mix well.
3. Spread the shrimp mixture evenly over the pan around the edges. With a sharp blade or knife, cut each slice into 4 strips.
4. Mix the breadcrumbs with the olive oil and beat with the shrimp mixture. Arrange the shrimp tostadas in the fryer basket in one layer. You may need to cook in batches.
5. Air fry for 3 to 6 minutes, until crisp and golden.

Nutrition: Calories 121 Fat 6g Saturated Fat 1g Cholesterol 72mg Sodium 158mg Carbs 7g Protein 9g

620. Bacon Tater Tots

Preparation time: 5 minutes
Cooking time: 17 minutes
Servings: 4
Ingredients:
- 24 frozen tater tots
- 6slices precooked bacon
- 2tablespoons maple syrup
- 1 cup shredded Cheddar cheese

Directions
1. Put the tattoos in the fryer basket. Fry for 10 minutes, shaking the fryer basket halfway through the cooking time.
2. Cut the bacon into 1-inch pieces and slice the cheese.
3. Remove the hook from the fryer basket and place it in a 6-by-6-by-2-inch pot. Fill the bacon with the maple syrup. Air fry 5 minutes or until spoons and bacon are crisp.
4. Fill with cheese and air fry for 2 minutes or until cheese is melted.

Nutrition: Calories 374 Fat 22g Saturated Fat 9g Cholesterol 40mg Sodium 857mg Carbs 34g Fiber 2g Protein 13g

621. Hash Brown Bruschetta

Preparation time: 7 minutes
Cooking time: 8 minutes
Servings: 4
Ingredients:
- 4frozen hash brown patties
- 1 tablespoon olive oil
- ⅓ cup chopped cherry tomatoes
- 3tablespoons diced fresh mozzarella
- 2tablespoons grated Parmesan cheese
- 1 tablespoon balsamic vinegar
- 1 tablespoon minced fresh basil

Preparation
1. Place the brown cake patties in the air fryer in a single layer. Air fry for 8 minutes or until the potatoes are crisp, hot, and golden.
2. Meanwhile, combine olive oil, tomatoes, mozzarella, Parmesan, vinegar, and basil in a small bowl.
3. When the potatoes are cooked, carefully remove them from the basket and place them on a plate. Fill with tomato mixture and serve.

Nutrition: Calories 123 Fat 6g Saturated Fat 2g Cholesterol 6mg Sodium 81mg Carbs 14g Fiber 2g Protein 5g

622. Mini Burgers

Preparation Time: 5 minutes
Cooking time: 25 minutes
Servings: 4

Ingredients:
- 500g Minced pork
- Salt
- Ground pepper
- Garlic Powder
- Fresh parsley
- Spices
- 1 egg
- 1 tbsp grated bread
- Mini Bread for Burgers

Direction:
1. Dress the meat of the hamburgers.
2. Add some salt to the ground beef, some ground pepper, garlic powder, a tablespoon of chopped fresh parsley, a teaspoon of spices.
3. Now, throw an egg and one or two teaspoons of breadcrumbs, so that the meat becomes more consistent. Stir all ingredients well until everything is integrated
4. Then, cover it with transparent and let it rest in the refrigerator for at least half an hour or more. It will be easier after handling the meat and giving it the shape of a hamburger.
5. Once the time has elapsed, take out the meat. Take it out of the paper that surrounds the container and begins to mold and make the mini burger.
6. To prepare them in the fryer:
7. First, heat the fryer. So, adjust the thermostat to 200 degrees Celsius and the timer for about 5 minutes. When it is hot, the pilot or the green light will go out.
8. When half the time has passed, turn around so that they are done well by both parties.

Nutrition: Calories 219 Fat 17g Protein 18g Cholesterol 70mg

623. Honey Roasted Carrots

Preparation time: 5 minutes
Cooking time: 20 minutes
Servings: 4

Ingredients:
- 1 Tablespoon Honey, Raw
- 3 Cups Baby Carrots
- 1 Tablespoon Olive Oil
- Sea Salt & Black Pepper to Taste

Directions:
1. Put all of the ingredients in a bowl, then heat your air fryer to 390.
2. Cook for twelve minutes and serve warm.

Nutrition: Calories: 82 Protein: 1g Fat: 3.2g Carbs: 2.1

624. Potato Balls Stuffed with Ham and Cheese from the Air Fryer

Preparation Time: 5 minutes
Cooking time: 25 minutes
Servings: 4

Ingredients:
- 4 potatoes
- 100g cooked ham
- 100g of grated or grated cheese
- Salt
- Ground pepper
- Flour
- Oil

Direction:
1. Peel the potatoes and cut into quarters.
2. Put in a pot with water and bring to the fire, let cook until tender.
3. Drain and squeeze with a fork until the potatoes are made dough and season.
4. Add the ham and cheese.
5. Let's link everything.
6. Make balls and pass through the flour.
7. Spray with oil and go to the basket of the air fryer.
8. Select 20 minutes, 200 degrees Celsius for each batch of balls you put. Do not pile up because they would break down. From time to time remove from the basket so that they are made on all sides, you have to shake the basket so that the balls roll a little and serve.

Nutrition: Calories 224 Fat 14g Carbs 19g Sugar 1g Protein 4g

625. Garlic Mozzarella Sticks

Preparation time: 1 hour and 5 minutes
Cooking time: 10 minutes
Servings: 4

Ingredients:
- 1 Tablespoon Italian Seasoning
- 1 Cup Parmesan Cheese
- 8 String Cheeses, Diced
- 2 Eggs, Beaten
- 1 Clove Garlic, Minced

Directions:
1. Start by combining your parmesan, garlic and Italian seasoning in a bowl. Dip your cheese into the egg, and mix well.
2. Roll it into your cheese crumbles, and then press the crumbs into the cheese.
3. Place them in the fridge for an hour, and then preheat your air fryer to 375.
4. Spray your air fryer down with oil, and then arrange the cheese strings into the basket. Cook for eight to nine minutes at 365.
5. Allow them to cool for at least five minutes before serving.

Nutrition: Calories: 80 Protein: 7g Fat: 6.2g Net Carbs: 3g

626. Sausages and Chorizos

Preparation Time: 10 minutes
Cooking time: 20 minutes
Servings: 2-4

Ingredients:
- 300g of sausage or frozen sausages
- One tablespoon olive oil

Direction:
1. Remove sausages directly from the freezer and place them in the fryer basket.
2. To defrost sausages and remove some of their fat, you must boil them for 5 to 10 minutes, and then prick food to remove all the remaining fat.
3. Then separate the sausages and chorizos on a tray or bowl.
4. Add a tablespoon of your favorite oil (preferably olive oil) in the bowl and mix the sausage well with the oil.
5. Then place the sausages and chorizos in the fryer basket.
6. Program your fryer at a temperature of 190 degrees Celsius and the timer in about 10 minutes.
7. Then turn the sausage as well as chorizos and perform the same process with the fryer.
8. And finally, after 10 minutes, serve and enjoy them.

Nutrition: Calories 356 Fat 29.3g Carbs 1.9g Protein 21.18g Cholesterol 1.9mg Cholesterol 72.60mg

627. Air Fried French Fries

Preparation Time: 10 minutes
Cooking time: 1 hour
Servings: 4

Ingredients:
- 2tbsps. olive oil
- 6peeled russet potatoes

Directions
1. Slice the peeled potatoes into strips.
2. Allow to soak in water for 30 minutes.
3. Drain and pat excess moisture with paper towels. Put them in a bowl and add oil. Toss until coated.
4. Put the potato slices in the cooking basket.
5. Cook for 30 minutes at 360 F. Shake twice during the cooking process.

Nutrition: Calories 497 Fat 7.19g Carbs 100g Protein 11.84g

628. Double-Baked Stuffed Potato

Preparation Time: 15 minutes
Cooking time: 75 minutes
Servings: 2

Ingredients:
- 2large russet potatoes
- 2tablespoons butter
- ½ cup heavy whipping cream
- ¼ teaspoon kosher salt
- ¼ cup sour cream
- ¼ cup shredded cheddar cheese
- 2slices cooked bacon, cut into bits
- 1 green onion, sliced

Directions
1. Select Bake, set time to 1 hour, and temperature to 350 F.
2. Put the potatoes on the wire rack and insert them at mid-position in the preheated air fryer oven.
3. Remove, then cool it for 5 minutes.
4. Scoop out the insides of the potatoes into a large bowl.
5. Put the butter, heavy whipping cream, and kosher salt to the bowl and mash it.
6. Put the mashed potatoes into the potato skins and put back in the air fryer toaster oven.
7. Bake again, set time to 15 minutes and temperature to 350 F, then press Start/Cancel twice to forgo preheating.
8. Remove potatoes and garnish with sour cream, cheddar cheese, bacon bits, and green onion.

Nutrition: Calories 694 Fat 41.7g Carbs 61.1g Protein 18.6g

629. Homemade Peanut Corn Nuts

Preparation time: 5 minutes
Cooking time: 20 minutes
Servings: 4

Ingredients:
- 6 oz dried hominy, soaked overnight
- 3 tbsp. peanut oil
- 2 tbsp. old bay seasoning
- Salt to taste

Directions
1. Preheat air fryer to 390 F.
2. Pat dry hominy and season with salt and old bay seasoning. Drizzle with oil and toss to coat. Spread in the air fryer basket and Air Fry for 10-12 minutes. Remove to shake up and return to cook for 10 more minutes until crispy. Transfer to a towel-lined plate to soak up the excess fat. Let cool and serve.

Nutrition: Calories: 100 Carbs: 3 g Fat: 3 g Protein: 5 g

630. Walnut & Cheese Filled Mushrooms

Preparation time: 5 minutes
Cooking time: 10 minutes
Servings: 4

Ingredients:
- 4 large portobello mushroom caps
- ⅓ cup walnuts, minced
- 1 tbsp. canola oil
- ½ cup mozzarella cheese, shredded
- 2 tbsp. fresh parsley, chopped

Directions
1. Preheat air fryer to 350 F. Grease the air fryer basket with cooking spray.
2. Rub the mushrooms with canola oil and fill them with mozzarella cheese. Top with minced walnuts and arrange on the bottom of the greased air fryer basket. Bake for 10 minutes or until golden on top. Remove, let cool for a few minutes and sprinkle with freshly chopped parsley to serve.

Nutrition: Calories: 110 Carbs: 6 g Fat: 5 g Protein: 8 g

631. Cauliflower and Broccoli Dish

Preparation Time: 15 minutes
Cooking time: 20 minutes
Servings: 4
Ingredients:
- 1 and ½ cups broccoli, cut into 1-inch pieces
- 1 and ½ cups cauliflower, cut into 1-inch pieces
- 1 tablespoon olive oil
- Salt as needed

Directions
1. Take a bowl and add vegetables, oil, and salt. Toss well and coat them well
2. Press "Power Button" on your Air Fryer and select "Air Fry" mode
3. Press the Time Button and set time to 20 minutes
4. Push Temp Button and set temp to 375 F.
5. Press the "Start/Pause" button and start the device
6. Arrange the vegetable mixture into your Air Fryer Basket and push it into the oven, let it cook until the timer runs out
7. Serve and enjoy!

Nutrition: Calories 60 Fat 4g Saturated Fat 0.5g Carbs 4g Fiber 2g Sodium 61mg Protein 2g

632. Hearty Lemon Green Beans

Preparation Time: 15 minutes
Cooking time: 12 minutes
Servings: 4
Ingredients:
- 1-pound green beans, trimmed
- 1 tablespoon butter, melted
- 1 tablespoon fresh lemon juice
- ¼ teaspoon garlic powder
- Salt and pepper to taste
- ½ teaspoon lemon zest, grated

Directions
1. Take a large-sized bowl and add all listed ingredients, except lemon zest
2. Toss and coat well
3. Press "Power Button" on your Air Fryer and select "Air Fry" mode
4. Press the Time Button and set time to 12 minutes
5. Push Temp Button and set temp to 400 F
6. Press the "Start/Pause" button and start the device
7. Arrange the green beans into Air Fryer basket and push into the oven, let it cook until the timer runs out
8. Serve warm with a garnish with lemon zest!

Nutrition: Calories 60 Fat 3g Saturated Fat 1.9g Carbs 8g Fiber 3g Sodium 67mg Protein 2g

633. Stuffing hushpuppies

Preparation Time: 10 minutes
Cooking Time: 12 minutes
Servings: 3
Ingredients:
- Cooking trays
- 3 cups of cold stuffing
- 1 large egg

Directions:
1. Place the egg in a large bowl and beat it. Add 3 cups of stuffing and stir until they are well combined.
2. Preheat your air fryer to 375 F and set it to 12 minutes
3. Remove the cooking tray and spray it with a cooking spray before adding the hushpuppies into the racks. Spray on top of the hushpuppies as well. Cook for 6 minutes before flipping.
4. Once you are halfway flip the hushpuppies to allow for the other side to cook well. Repeat this with the remaining hushpuppies.
5. Serve with a sauce of your choice.

Nutrition: Calories 237.4 Fat 16.6g Carbs 18.8g Proteins 3.2g

634. Quick Zucchini Cakes

Preparation Time: 10 minutes
Cooking time: 12 minutes
Servings: 12
Ingredients:
- ½ cup whole wheat flour
- 1 yellow onion; chopped
- Cooking spray
- ½ cup dill; chopped
- 1 egg
- 2 garlic cloves; minced
- 3 zucchinis; grated
- Salt and black pepper to the taste

Directions
1. In a bowl; mix zucchinis with garlic, onion, flour, salt, pepper, egg, and dill; stir well, shape small patties out of this mix, spray them with cooking spray; place them in your air fryer's basket and cook at 370 F, for 6 minutes on each side.
2. Serve them as a snack right away.

Nutrition: Calories 60 Protein 2g Fat 1g Carbs 6g

635. Apple Cider Donuts

Preparation Time: 25 minutes
Cooking Time: 45 minutes
Servings: 6
Ingredients:
- 3 cups all-purpose flour
- 2 cups apple cider
- ½ cup light brown sugar
- 2 tsp baking powder
- 1 tsp ground cinnamon
- 1 tsp ground ginger
- 8 tsp unsalted butter
- ½ tsp baking soda
- 1 tsp kosher salt
- For finishing:
- ¼ cup all-purpose flour
- 8 tsp unsalted butter
- 1 cup granulated sugar
- 1 tsp cinnamon

Directions:
1. Pour 2 cups of apple cider into a pan and bring it to boil transfer the reduced apple dicer once it is half the volume and allow it to cool completely.
2. Put 3 cups all-purpose flour, ½ cup brown sugar, 1 tsp ground cinnamon, 2 tsp baking soda, ½ tsp kosher salt and 1 tsp ground ginger in a bowl and whisk them properly.
3. Grate 8 pieces cold unsalted butter and add it to the mixture using your fingers and incorporate the butter into the dough well. Make it perfect at the center of the mixture and add 1 cup of reduce cider and ½ cup of cold milk as well and use a spatula to mix the dough together.

4. Sprinkle the dough on a surface and have a few table spoons of flour on the surface for shaping the dough. Pat the dough into an even layer about an inch thick and sprinkle more flour. Fold and repeat the procedure again until the dough is less springy. Pat the dough into a 9x13 inch rectangular about ½ inches thick.
5. Cut the donut out of the dough using a floured donut cutter.
6. Transfer your donuts into a baking sheet and gather the scraps before patting the dough again and repeat this process until you have 18 donuts.
7. Preheat your air fryer and put it at 375 F.
8. Melt the remaining butter in a medium pan and add granulated sugar and 1 tsp of ground cinnamon and whisk them together.
9. Depending on the size of the air fryer, you can bake a batch at a time until you have ready donuts. Serve the donuts warm once it is golden brown with warm cider for dipping.

Nutrition: Calories 322 Fat 12.4g Carbs 49.1g Proteins 3.5g

636. Berry Crumble

Preparation Time: 5 minutes
Cooking time: 30 minutes
Servings: 6
Ingredients:
- 12oz. fresh strawberries
- 7oz. fresh raspberries
- 5oz. fresh blueberries
- 5tablespoons cold butter
- T2ablespoons lemon juice
- 1 cup flour
- A ½ cup of sugar
- 1 tablespoon water
- A pinch of salt

Directions
1. Gently mass the berries, but make sure there are chunks left. Mix with the lemon juice and 2 tablespoons of the sugar.
2. Place the berry mixture at the bottom of a prepared round cake. Combine the flour with the salt and sugar, in a bowl.
3. Add the water and rub the butter with your fingers until the mixture becomes crumbled.
4. Arrange the crisp batter over the berries. Cook in the air fryer at 390 F for 20 minutes. Serve chilled.

Nutrition: Calories 261 Protein 2.6g Fat 9.6g Carbs 42.7g

637. Butternut Squash with Thyme

Preparation Time: 5 minutes
Cooking time: 20 minutes
Servings: 4
Ingredients:
- 2cups peeled, butternut squash, cubed
- 1 tbsp olive oil
- ¼ tsp salt
- ¼ tsp black pepper
- ¼ tsp dried thyme
- 1 tbsp finely chopped fresh parsley

Directions
1. In a bowl, add squash, oil, salt, pepper, and thyme, and toss until squash is well-coated.
2. Place squash in the air fryer and cook for 14 minutes at 360 F.
3. When ready, sprinkle with freshly chopped parsley and serve chilled.

Nutrition: Calories 219 Protein 7.8g Fat 4.3g Carbs 9.4g

638. Chicken Breasts in Golden Crumb

Preparation Time: 10 minutes
Cooking time: 25 minutes
Servings: 4
Ingredients:
- 1 ½ lb. chicken breasts, boneless, cut into strips
- 1 egg, lightly beaten
- 1 cup seasoned breadcrumbs
- Salt and black pepper to taste
- ½ tsp dried oregano

Directions
1. Preheat the air fryer to 390 F. Season the chicken with oregano, salt, and black pepper. In a small bowl, whisk in some salt and pepper to the beaten egg. In a separate bowl, add the crumbs. Dip chicken tenders in the egg wash, then in the crumbs.
2. Roll the strips in the breadcrumbs and press firmly, so the breadcrumbs stick well. Spray the chicken tenders with cooking spray and arrange them in the air fryer. Cook for 14 minutes, until no longer pink in the center, and nice and crispy on the outside.

Nutrition: Calories 223 Protein 5g Fat 3.2g Carbs 4.3g

639. Yogurt Chicken Tacos

Preparation Time: 5 minutes
Cooking time: 20 minutes
Servings: 4
Ingredients:
- 1 cup cooked chicken, shredded
- 1 cup shredded mozzarella cheese
- ¼ cup salsa
- ¼ cup Greek yogurt
- Salt and ground black pepper
- 8flour tortillas

Directions
1. In a bowl, mix chicken, cheese, salsa, and yogurt, and season with salt and pepper. Spray one side of the tortilla with cooking spray. Lay 2 tbsp of the chicken mixture at the center of the non-oiled side of each tortilla.
2. Roll tightly around the mixture. Arrange taquitos into your air fryer basket, without overcrowding. Cook in batches if needed. Place the seam side down, or it will unravel during cooking crisps.
3. Cook it for 12 to 14 minutes, or until crispy, at 380 F.

Nutrition: Calories 312 Protein 6.2g Fat 3g Carbs 6.5g

640. Flawless Kale Chips

Preparation Time: 5 minutes
Cooking time: 20 minutes
Servings: 4
Ingredients:
- 4cups chopped kale leaves; stems removed
- 2tbsp olive oil
- 1 tsp garlic powder
- ½ tsp salt
- ¼ tsp onion powder
- ¼ tsp black pepper

Directions
1. In a bowl, mix kale and oil together, until well-coated. Add in garlic, salt, onion, and pepper and toss until well-coated. Arrange half the kale leaves to air fryer, in a single layer.
2. Cook for 8 minutes at 350 F, shaking once halfway through. Remove chips to a sheet to cool; do not touch.

Nutrition: Calories 312 Protein 7g Fat 5.3g Carbs 5g

641. Cheese Fish Balls

Preparation Time: 5 minutes
Cooking time: 40 minutes
Servings: 6
Ingredients:
- 1 cup smoked fish, flaked
- 2 cups cooked rice
- 2 eggs, lightly beaten
- 1 cup grated Grana Padano cheese
- ¼ cup finely chopped thyme
- Salt and black pepper to taste
- 1 cup panko crumbs

Directions
1. In a bowl, add fish, rice, eggs, Parmesan cheese, thyme, salt and pepper into a bowl; stir to combine. Shape the mixture into 12 even-sized balls. Roll the balls in the crumbs then spray with oil.
2. Arrange the balls into the fryer and cook for 16 minutes at 400 F, until crispy.

Nutrition: Calories 234 Protein 6.2g Fat 5.2g Carbs 4.3g

642. Vermicelli Noodles and Vegetables Rolls

Preparation Time: 5 minutes
Cooking time: 25 minutes
Servings: 8
Ingredients:
- 8 spring roll wrappers
- 1 cup cooked and cooled vermicelli noodles
- garlic cloves, finely chopped
- 1 tbsp minced fresh ginger
- 2 tbsp soy sauce
- 1 tsp sesame oil
- 1 red bell pepper, seeds removed, chopped
- 1 cup finely chopped mushrooms
- 1 cup finely chopped carrot
- ½ cup finely chopped scallions

Directions
1. In a saucepan, add garlic, ginger, soy sauce, pepper, mushroom, carrot and scallions, and stir-fry over high heat for a few minutes, until soft. Add in vermicelli noodles; remove from the heat.
2. Place the spring roll wrappers onto a working board. Spoon the dollops of veggie and noodle mixture at the center of each spring roll wrapper. Roll the spring rolls and tuck the corners and edges in to create neat and secure rolls.
3. Spray with oil and transfer them to the air fryer. Cook for 12 minutes at 340 F, turning once halfway through. Cook until golden and crispy. Serve with soy or sweet chili sauce.

Nutrition: Calories 312 Protein 3g Fat 5g Carbs 5.4g

643. Dehydrated Spiced Cauliflower

Preparation Time: 10 minutes
Cooking Time: 1 hour
Servings: 3
Ingredients:
- ½ tsp nutmeg
- 2 lb. head of cauliflower
- 1 tsp olive oil
- 1 tsp smoked paprika
- 1 tsp hot sauce
- 1 tsp lime juice
- 1 tsp cumin

Directions:
1. Chop the cauliflower into tiny sizes that can fit on your thumb. In your large bowl combine cauliflower and the remaining ingredients and toss to coat them evenly.
2. Divide the cauliflower and make an even layer in a baking tray. Place a drip pan at the bottom of the cooking chamber and insert a tray at the top most position and another at the bottom.
3. Used the display panel and choose DEHYDRATE and adjust the temperature to 130 degrees and touch START. When the dehydration processes are over, Press START again and removes the popcorn and serve immediately.

Nutrition: Calories 30 Fat 2g Carbs 3g Proteins 0g

644. Roasted Pumpkin Seeds

Preparation Time: 10 minutes
Cooking time: 40 minutes
Servings: 4
Ingredients:
- 1 cup pumpkin seeds, pulp removed, rinsed
- 1 tbsp butter, melted
- 1 tbsp brown sugar
- 1 tsp orange zest
- ½ tsp cardamom
- ½ tsp salt

Directions
1. Cook the seeds for 4 minutes at 320 F, in your air fryer, to avoid moisture. In a bowl, whisk melted butter, sugar, zest, cardamom and salt.
2. Add the seeds to the bowl and toss to coat thoroughly.
3. Transfer the seeds to the air fryer and cook for 35 minutes at 300 F, shaking the basket every 10-12 minutes. Cook until lightly browned.

Nutrition: Calories 536 Fat 42.86g Calcium 71g Sodium 571mg

645. Buttery Parmesan Broccoli Florets

Preparation Time: 5 minutes
Cooking time: 20 minutes
Servings: 2
Ingredients:
- 2 tbsp butter, melted
- 1 egg white
- 1 garlic clove, grated
- ¼ tsp salt
- A pinch of black pepper
- ½ lb. broccoli florets
- ⅓ cup grated Parmesan cheese

Directions
1. In a bowl, whisk together the butter, egg, garlic, salt, and black pepper.
2. Toss in broccoli to coat well.
3. Top with Parmesan cheese and; toss to coat.
4. Arrange broccoli in a single layer in the air fryer, without overcrowding.
5. Cook it in batches for 10 minutes at 360 F.
6. Remove to a serving plate and sprinkle with Parmesan cheese.

Nutrition: Calories 350 Fat 27g Carbs 20g Protein 15g

646. Spicy Chickpeas

Preparation Time: 5 minutes
Cooking time: 10 minutes
Servings: 4
Ingredients:
- 1 (15-oz.) can chickpeas rinsed and Dry-out
- 1 tablespoon olive oil
- ½ teaspoon ground cumin
- ½ teaspoon cayenne pepper
- ½ teaspoon smoked paprika
- Salt, as required

Directions
1. In a bowl, add all the ingredients and toss to coat well.
2. Press "Power Button" of Air Fry Oven and turn the dial to select the "Air Fry" mode.
3. Press the Time button and again turn the dial to set the cooking time to 10 minutes
4. Now push the Temp button and rotate the dial to set the temperature at 390 F.
5. Press "Start/Pause" button to start.
6. When the unit beeps to show that it is preheated, open the lid.
7. Arrange the chickpeas in "Air Fry Basket" and insert in the oven.
8. Serve warm.

Nutrition: Calories 146 Fat 4.5g Carbs 18.8g Protein 6.3g

647. Roasted Peanuts

Preparation Time: 5 minutes
Cooking time: 14 minutes
Servings: 6
Ingredients:
- 1½ cups raw peanuts
- Nonstick cooking spray

Directions
1. Press "Power Button" of Air Fry Oven and turn the dial to select the "Air Fry" mode. Press the Time button and again turn the dial to set the cooking time to 14 minutes
2. Now push the Temp button and rotate the dial to set the temperature at 320 F. Press "Start/Pause" button to start.
3. When the unit beeps to show that it is preheated, open the lid.
4. Arrange the peanuts in "Air Fry Basket" and insert in the oven.
5. Toss the peanuts twice.
6. After 9 minutes of cooking, spray the peanuts with cooking spray.
7. Serve warm.

Nutrition: Calories 207 Fat 18g Carbs 5.9g Protein 9.4g

648. Roasted Cashews

Preparation Time: 5 minutes
Cooking time: 5 minutes
Servings: 6
Ingredients:
- 1½ cups raw cashew nuts
- 1 teaspoon butter, melted
- Salt and freshly ground black pepper, as needed

Directions
1. In a bowl, mix together all the ingredients.
2. Press "Power Button" of Air Fry Oven and turn the dial to select the "Air Fry" mode.
3. Press the Time button and again turn the dial to set the cooking time to 5 minutes
4. Now push the Temp button and rotate the dial to set the temperature at 355 F.
5. Press "Start/Pause" button to start.
6. When the unit beeps to show that it is preheated, open the lid.
7. Arrange the cashews in "Air Fry Basket" and insert in the oven.
8. Shake the cashews once halfway through.

Nutrition: Calories 202 Fat 16.5g Carbs 11.2g Protein 5.3g

649. French Fries

Preparation Time: 15 minutes
Cooking time: 30 minutes
Servings: 4
Ingredients:
- 1 lb. potatoes, peeled and cut into strips
- 3 tablespoons olive oil
- ½ teaspoon onion powder
- ½ teaspoon garlic powder
- 1 teaspoon paprika

Directions
1. In a large bowl of water, soak the potato strips for about 1 hour.
2. Dry out the potato strips well and pat them dry with the paper towels.
3. In a large bowl, add the potato strips and the remaining ingredients and toss to coat well.
4. Press "Power Button" of Air Fry Oven and turn the dial to select the "Air Fry" mode.
5. Press the Time button and again turn the dial to set the cooking time to 30 minutes
6. Now push the Temp button and rotate the dial to set the temperature at 375 F.
7. Press "Start/Pause" button to start.
8. When the unit beeps to show that it is preheated, open the lid.
9. Arrange the potato fries in "Air Fry Basket" and insert in the oven.
10. Serve warm.

Nutrition: Calories 172 Fat 10.7g Carbs 18.6g Protein 2.1g

650. Mini Popovers

Preparation Time: 10 minutes
Cooking Time: 15 minutes
Servings: 4
Ingredients:
- 1 tsp butter melted
- 2 eggs at room temperature
- 1 cup of milk at room temperature
- 1 cup all-purpose flour
- Salt and pepper to taste

Directions:
1. Generously coat a mini popover with nonstick spray.
2. Add all the ingredients to a blender and process it at medium speed.
3. Fill each mold with 2 tsp batter. Place a drip pan at the bottom of the cooking chamber.
4. Using the display panel selects AIRFRY and adjusts it to 400 F and a time of 20 minutes then touch START.
5. When the display panel indicates 'add food' place the egg bite mold on the lower side of the cooking tray. When the display indicates "TURNFOOD" do not touch anything. When the popovers are brown open the cooking chamber and pierce them to release steam and cook for a minute or so.
6. Serve immediately.

Nutrition: Calories 53 Fat 1g Carbs 9g Proteins 2g

651. Fried Up Avocados

Preparation Time: 10 Minutes
Cooking time: 20 Minutes
Servings: 6
Ingredients:
- ½ cup almond meal
- ½ teaspoon salt
- 1 Hass avocado, peeled, pitted, and sliced
- Aquafaba from one bean can (bean liquid)

Directions:
1. Take a shallow bowl and add almond meal, salt
2. Pour aquafaba in another bowl, dredge avocado slices in aquafaba and then into the crumbs to get a nice coating
3. Assemble them in a single layer in your Air Fryer cooking basket, don't overlap
4. Cook for 10 minutes at 390 F, give the basket a shake, and cook for 5 minutes more
5. Serve.

Nutrition: Calories 356 Fat 14g Carbs 8g Protein 23g

652. Hearty Green Beans

Preparation Time: 5 Minutes
Cooking time: 10 to 15 Minutes
Servings: 6
Ingredients:
- 1-pound green beans washed and de-stemmed
- 1 lemon
- Pinch of salt
- ¼ teaspoon oil

Directions:
1. Add beans to your Air Fryer cooking basket
2. Squeeze a few drops of lemon
3. Season with salt and pepper
4. Drizzle olive oil on top
5. Cook for 10-12 minutes at 400 F.
6. Once done, serve.

Nutrition: Calories 84 Fat 5g Carbs 7g Protein 2g

653. Parmesan Cabbage Wedges

Preparation Time: 5 Minutes
Cooking time: 20 Minutes
Servings: 4
Ingredients:
- ½ a head cabbage
- 2 cups parmesan
- Four tablespoons melted butter
- Salt and pepper to taste

Directions:
1. Preheat your Air Fryer to 380 F.
2. Take a container and add melted butter, and season with salt and pepper.
3. Cover cabbages with your melted butter.
4. Coat cabbages with parmesan.
5. Transfer the coated cabbages to your Air Fryer and bake for 20 minutes.
6. Serve with cheesy sauce.

Nutrition: Calories 108 Fat 7g Carbs 11g Protein 2g

654. Extreme Zucchini Fries

Preparation Time: 10 Minutes
Cooking time: 15 to 20 Minutes
Servings: 4
Ingredients:
- 3 medium zucchinis, sliced
- 2 egg whites
- ½ cup seasoned almond meal
- 2 tablespoons grated parmesan cheese
- ¼ teaspoon garlic powder

Directions:
1. Pre-heat your Fryer to 425 F.
2. Take the Air Fryer cooking basket and place a cooling rack.
3. Coat the rack with cooking spray.
4. Take a bowl, add egg whites, beat it well, and season with some pepper and salt.
5. Take another bowl and add garlic powder, cheese, and almond meal
6. Take the Zucchini sticks and dredge them in the egg and finally breadcrumbs.
7. Transfer the Zucchini to your cooking basket and spray a bit of oil.
8. Bake for 20 minutes and serve with Ranch sauce.

Nutrition: Calories 367 Fat 28g Carbs 5g Protein 4g

655. Easy Fried Tomatoes

Preparation Time: 5 Minutes
Cooking time: 10 Minutes
Servings: 3
Ingredients:
- 1 green tomato
- ¼ tablespoon Creole seasoning
- Salt and pepper to taste
- ¼ cup almond flour
- ½ cup buttermilk

Directions:
1. Add flour to your plate and take another plate and add buttermilk
2. Cut tomatoes and season with salt and pepper

3. Make a mix of creole seasoning and crumbs
4. Take tomato slice and cover with flour, place in buttermilk and then into crumbs
5. Repeat with all tomatoes
6. Preheat your fryer to 400 F
7. Cook the tomato slices for 5 minutes
8. Serve with basil.

Nutrition: Calories 166 Fat 12g Carbs 1g Protein 3g

656. Caprese Stuffed Garlic Butter Portobellos

Preparation Time: 5 minutes
Cooking Time: 10 minutes
Servings: 6
Ingredients:
- For Garlic butter
- 2 tsp of butter
- 2 cloves garlic 1 tsp parsley finely chopped
- For the mushrooms
- 6 large Portobello mushrooms, washed and dried well with paper towel
- 6 mozzarella cheese balls thinly sliced
- 1 cup grape tomatoes thinly sliced
- Fresh basil for garnishing
- For balsamic glaze
- 2 tsp brown sugar
- ¼ cup balsamic vinegar

Directions:
1. Preheat the oven to broil setting on high heat. Arrange the oven shelf and place it in the right direction. Combine the garlic butter ingredients in a small pan and melt until the garlic begins to be fragrant. Brush the bottoms of the mushroom and place them on the buttered part of the baking tray.
2. Flip and brush the remaining garlic over each cap. Fill each mushroom with tomatoes and mozzarella slices and grill until the cheese has melted. Drizzle with the balsamic glaze and sprinkle some salt to taste. If you are making the balsamic glaze from scratch, combine the sugar and vinegar in a small pan and reduce the heat to low. Allow it to simmer for 6 minutes or until the mixture has thickened well.

Nutrition: Calories 101 Fat 5g, Carbs 12g, Proteins 2g

657. Roasted Brussels and Pine Nuts

Preparation Time: 10 Minutes
Cooking time: 35 Minutes
Servings: 6
Ingredients:
- 15ounces Brussels sprouts
- 1 tablespoon olive oil
- 1 and ¾ ounces raisins, drained
- Juice of 1 orange
- 1 and ¾ ounces toasted pine nuts

Directions:
1. Take a pot of boiling water, then add sprouts and boil them for 4 minutes.
2. Transfer the sprouts to cold water and drain them well.
3. Place them in a freezer and cool them.
4. Take your raisins and soak them in orange juice for 20 minutes.
5. Warm your Air Fryer to a temperature of 392-degree Fahrenheit.
6. Take a pan and pour oil, and stir the sprouts.
7. Take the sprouts and transfer them to your Air Fryer.
8. Roast for 15 minutes.
9. Serve the sprouts with pine nuts, orange juice, and raisins!

Nutrition: Calories 260 Fat 20g Carbs 10g Protein 7g

658. Low-Calorie Beets Dish

Preparation Time: 10 Minutes
Cooking time: 10 Minutes
Servings: 2
Ingredients:
- 4whole beets
- 1 tablespoon balsamic vinegar
- 1 tablespoon olive oil
- Salt and pepper to taste
- 2springs rosemary

Directions:
1. Wash your beets and peel them
2. Cut beets into cubes
3. Take a bowl and mix in rosemary, pepper, salt, vinegar
4. Cover beets with the prepared sauce
5. Coat the beets with olive oil
6. Pre-heat your Fryer to 400 F
7. Transfer beets to Air Fryer cooking basket and cook for 10 minutes
8. Serve with your cheese sauce.

Nutrition: Calories 149 Fat 1g Carbs 5g Protein 30g

659. Grilled Avocado Caprese Crostini

Preparation Time: 10 minutes
Cooking Time: 20 minutes
Servings: 2
Ingredients:
- 1 avocado thinly sliced
- 9 ounces ripened cherry tomatoes
- Ounces fresh bocconcini in water
- 2 tsp balsamic glaze
- 8 pieces Italian baguette
- ½ cup basil leaves

Directions:
1. Preheat your oven to 375 F
2. Arrange your baking sheet properly before spraying them on top with olive oil.
3. Bake your item of choice until they are well done or golden brown. Rub your crostini with the cut side of garlic while they are still warm and you can season them with pepper and salt.
4. Divide the basil leaves on each side of bread and top up with tomato halves, avocado slices and bocconcini. Season it with pepper and salt.
5. Broil it for 4 minutes and when the cheese starts to melt through remove and Drizzle with balsamic glaze before serving.

Nutrition: Calories 278 Fat 10g Carbs 37g Proteins 10g

660. Bacon and Asparagus Spears

Preparation Time: 15 Minutes
Cooking time: 8 Minutes
Servings: 4
Ingredients:
- 20 spears asparagus
- 4 bacon slices
- 1 tablespoon olive oil
- 1 tablespoon sesame oil
- 1 garlic clove, crushed

Directions:
1. Warm your Air Fryer to 380 F.
2. Take a small bowl and add oil, crushed garlic, and mix
3. Separate asparagus into four bunches and wrap them in bacon
4. Brush wraps with oil and garlic mix, transfer to your Air Fryer basket
5. Cook for 8 minutes
6. Serve.

Nutrition: Calories 175 Fat 15g Carbs 6g Protein 5g

661. Healthy Low Carb Fish Nugget

Preparation Time: 5 Minutes
Cooking time: 10 Minutes
Servings: 4
Ingredients:
- 1-pound fresh cod
- 2 tablespoons olive oil
- ½ cup almond flour
- 2 larges finely beaten eggs
- 1-2 cups almond meal

Directions:
1. Preheat your Air Fryer to 388 F.
2. Take a food processor and add olive oil, almond meal, salt, and blend
3. Take three bowls and add almond flour, almond meal, beaten eggs individually
4. Take cods and cut them into slices of 1-inch thickness and 2-inch length
5. Dredge slices into flour, eggs, and crumbs
6. Transfer nuggets to Air Fryer cooking basket and cook for 10 minutes until golden
7. Serve.

Nutrition: Calories 196 Fat 14g Carbs 6g Protein 14g

662. Fried Up Pumpkin Seeds

Preparation Time: 10 Minutes
Cooking time: 60 Minutes
Servings: 2
Ingredients:
- 1 and ½ cups pumpkin seeds
- Olive oil as needed
- 1 and ½ teaspoons salt
- 1 teaspoon smoked paprika

Directions:
1. Cut pumpkin and scrape out seeds and flesh
2. Separate flesh from seeds and rinse the seeds under cold water
3. Bring two-quarter of salted water to boil and add seeds, boil for 10 minutes
4. Drain seeds and spread them on a kitchen towel
5. Dry for 20 minutes
6. Preheat your fryer to 350 F
7. Take a bowl and add seeds, smoked paprika, and olive oil
8. Season with salt and transfer to your Air Fryer cooking basket
9. Cook for 35 minutes, then serve.

Nutrition: Calories 237 Fat 21g Carbs 4g Protein 12g

663. Decisive Tiger Shrimp Platter

Preparation Time: 5 Minutes
Cooking time: 10 Minutes
Servings: 6
Ingredients:
- 1 ¼ pound tiger shrimp, or a count of about 16 to 20
- ¼ teaspoons cayenne pepper
- ½ teaspoons old bay seasoning
- ¼ teaspoons smoked paprika
- 1 tablespoon olive oil

Directions:
1. Pre-heat your Fryer to 390 F
2. Take a bowl and add the listed ingredients
3. Mix well
4. Transfer the shrimp to your fryer cooking basket and cook for 5 minutes
5. Remove and serve the shrimp over cauliflower rice if preferred

Nutrition: Calories 251 Fat 19g Carbs 3g Protein 17g

664. Jalapeno Poppers

Preparation Time: 5 Minutes
Cooking time: 10 Minutes
Servings: 4
Ingredients:
- jalapeno poppers halved and deseeded
- ounces cashew cream
- ¼ cup fresh parsley
- ¾ cup almond meal

Directions:
1. Take a bowl and mix ½ of almond meal and cashew cream
2. Add parsley and stuff the pepper with the mixture
3. Press the top gently with remaining crumbs and make an even topping
4. Transfer to Air Fryer cooking basket and cook for 8 minutes at 370 F.
5. Let it cool and serve.

Nutrition: Calories 456 Fat 60g Carbs 7g Protein 15g

665. Jicama Fries

Preparation Time: 5 Minutes
Cooking time: 30 Minutes
Servings: 4
Ingredients:
- 1 small jicama, peeled.
- ¼ tsp. onion powder.
- ¾ tsp. chili powder
- ¼ tsp. ground black pepper
- ¼ tsp. garlic powder.

Directions:
1. Cut jicama into matchstick-sized pieces.
2. Place pieces into a small bowl and sprinkle with remaining ingredients. Place the fries into the air fryer basket

APPETIZER AND SNACK

3. Adjust the temperature to 350 F and set the timer for 20 minutes. Toss the basket 2 or 3 times during cooking. Serve warm.

Nutrition: Calories 37 Fat 0.1g Carbs 8.7g Protein 0.8g Fiber 4.7g

666. Parmesan Potatoes

Preparation Time: 10 minutes
Cooking Time: 45 minutes
Servings: 2

Ingredients:
- 5 medium potatoes, peeled and cut into 1/2-inch pieces
- 3 tbsp olive oil
- 1 tsp garlic powder
- 1 tsp paprika
- 1/2 cup parmesan cheese, grated
- Salt

Directions:
1. Line cooking pan with parchment paper and set aside.
2. In a mixing bowl, add potatoes and remaining ingredients and toss to coat.
3. Arrange potatoes on a prepared cooking pan.
4. Select bake mode and set the omni to 450 F for 30 minutes once the oven beeps, place the cooking pan into the oven.
5. Turn potatoes and bake for 10-15 minutes more.
6. Serve and enjoy.

Nutrition: Calories 635 Fat 27 g Carbs 86.2 g Sugar 6.6 g Protein 17.4 g Cholesterol 18 mg

667. Tasty Zucchini Fritters

Preparation Time: 10 minutes
Cooking Time: 25 minutes
Servings: 4

Ingredients:
- 1 egg
- 1 tsp garlic powder
- 2 tbsp dill, chopped
- tbsp chives, chopped
- 1/4 cup parmesan cheese, grated
- 1/2 cup cheddar cheese, shredded
- 1 1/4 cups oat flour
- 2 medium zucchini, shredded and squeeze out all liquid
- 1 tsp kosher salt

Directions:
1. Line cooking pan with parchment paper and set aside.
2. Add all ingredients into the mixing bowl and mix until well combined.
3. Make small patties from mixture and place onto the prepared cooking pan.
4. Select bake mode and set the omni to 375 F for 25 minutes once the oven beeps, place the cooking pan into the oven.
5. Serve and enjoy.

Nutrition: Calories 228 Fat 9.3 g Carbs 24.9 g Sugar 2.1 g Protein 12.4 g Cholesterol 60 mg

668. Crispy Beef Cubes

Preparation Time: 10 minutes
Cooking Time: 20 minutes
Servings: 4

Ingredients:
- 1-pound sirloin tip, cut into 1-inch cubes
- 1 cup cheese pasta sauce (from a 16-ounce jar)
- 1½ cups soft bread crumbs
- 2 tablespoons olive oil
- ½ teaspoon dried marjoram

Directions:
1. In a medium bowl, toss the beef with the pasta sauce to coat.
2. In a shallow bowl, combine the bread crumbs, oil, and marjoram, and mix well. Drop the beef cubes, one at a time, into the bread crumb mixture to coat thoroughly.
3. Cook the beef in two batches for 6 to 8 minutes, shaking the basket once during cooking time, until the beef is at least 145°F and the outside is crisp and brown. Serve with toothpicks or little forks.

Nutrition: Calories 554 Fat 22g Carbs 43g Protein 44g

669. Healthy Carrot Fries

Preparation Time: 10 minutes
Cooking Time: 25 minutes
Servings: 4

Ingredients:
- 4 medium carrots, peeled and cut into fries shape
- 1 tsp cumin powder
- 1/2 tbsp paprika
- 1 1/2 tbsp olive oil
- 1/2 tsp salt

Directions:
1. Line cooking pan with parchment paper and set aside.
2. Add carrot fries and remaining ingredients into the mixing bowl and toss well.
3. Arrange carrot fries on the prepared cooking pan in a single layer.
4. Select bake mode and set the omni to 450 F for 10 minutes once the oven beeps, place the cooking pan into the oven.
5. Turn carrot fries and bake for 15 minutes more.
6. Serve and enjoy.

Nutrition: Calories 75 Fat 5.5 g Carbs 6.7 g Sugar 3.1 g Protein 0.7 g

670. Easy Baked Potato Wedges

Preparation Time: 10 minutes
Cooking Time: 30 minutes
Servings: 4

Ingredients:
- 2 large potatoes, cut into wedges
- 2 tbsp olive oil
- 1 tbsp ranch seasoning

Directions:
1. Line cooking pan with parchment paper and set aside.
2. Add potato wedges, oil, and ranch seasoning in mixing bowl and toss well.
3. Arrange potato wedges onto the prepared cooking pan.
4. Select bake mode and set the omni to 400 F for 15 minutes once the oven beeps, place the cooking pan into the oven.
5. Turn potato wedges and bake for 15 minutes more.
6. Serve and enjoy.

Nutrition: Calories 195 Fat 7.2 g Carbs 29 g Sugar 2.1 g Protein 3.1 g

671. Waffle Fry Poutine

Preparation Time: 10 minutes
Cooking Time: 20 minutes
Servings: 4
Ingredients:
- 2 cups frozen waffle cut fries
- 2 teaspoons olive oil
- 1 red bell pepper, chopped
- 2 green onions, sliced
- 1 cup shredded Swiss cheese
- ½ cup bottled chicken gravy

Directions:
1. Toss the waffle fries with olive oil and place in the air fryer basket. Air-fry for 10 to 12 minutes or until the fries are crisp and light golden brown, shaking the basket halfway through the cooking time.
2. Transfer the fries to a 6-by-6-by-2-inch pan and top with the pepper, green onions, and cheese. Air-fry for 3 minutes until the vegetables are crisp and tender.
3. Remove the pan from the air fryer and Drizzle with the gravy over the fries. Air-fry for 2 minutes or until the gravy is hot. Serve immediately.

Nutrition: Calories 347; Fat 19g Carbs 33g Protein 12g

672. Spicy Almonds

Preparation Time: 10 minutes
Cooking Time: 20 minutes
Servings: 6
Ingredients:
- 1 1/2 cups raw almonds
- 1/2 tsp cayenne
- 1/4 tsp onion powder
- 1/4 tsp dried basil
- 1/2 tsp garlic powder
- 1/2 tsp cumin
- 1 1/2 tsp chili powder
- 2tsp Worcestershire sauce
- 2tbsp butter, melted
- 1/2 tsp sea salt

Directions:
1. Line cooking pan with parchment paper and set aside.
2. In a mixing bowl, whisk together butter, Worcestershire sauce, chili powder, cumin, garlic powder, basil, onion powder, cayenne, and salt.
3. Add almonds and toss to coat.
4. Spread almonds onto the prepared cooking pan.
5. Select bake mode and set the omni to 350 F for 20 minutes once the oven beeps, place the cooking pan into the oven.
6. Serve and enjoy.

Nutrition: Calories 117 Fat 15.9 g Carbs 6.2 g Sugar 1.5 g Protein 5.2 g Cholesterol 10 mg

673. Onion Pakora

Preparation Time: 10 minutes
Cooking Time: 10 minutes
Servings: 4
Ingredients:
- 1 cupg Flour
- 1/4 cup almond flour
- 2 teaspoons olive oil
- 4 whole onions
- 2 green chili
- 1 tablespoon coriander
- 1/4 teaspoon carom
- 1/8 teaspoon chili powder
- Salt as needed

Directions:
1. Slice your onion into individual slices. Chop the green chilies
2. Cut up the coriander into equal-sized portions
3. Take a bowl and add carom, turmeric powder, salt, and chili powder
4. Add onion, chilies, and coriander; Mix well
5. Add water and keep mixing until you have a dough-like consistency
6. Mix the dough and form balls
7. Pre-heat your Fryer to 390 F in "AIR FRY" mode. Cook for 8 minutes
8. Make sure to keep checking after every 6 minutes to ensure that they are not burnt

Nutrition: Calories 280 Fat 20 g, Carbs 28g Protein 8g

674. Juicy Fish Nuggets

Preparation Time: 10 minutes
Cooking Time: 10 minutes
Servings: 4
Ingredients:
- 1-pound fresh cod
- 2 tablespoons olive oil
- 1/2 cup almond flour
- 2 large finely beaten eggs
- 1-2 cups almond meal
- Salt as needed

Directions:
1. Preheat your Air Fryer to 380 degrees F in "AIR FRY" mode.
2. Take a food processor and add olive oil, almond meal, salt and blend
3. Take three bowls and add almond flour, almond meal, beaten eggs individually
4. Take costs and cut them into slices of 1-inch thickness and 2-inch length
5. Dredge slices into flour, eggs and in crumbs
6. Transfer nuggets to Air Fryer cooking basket and cook for 10 minutes until golden
7. Serve and enjoy!

Nutrition: Calories 200 Fat 14 g, Carbs 6 g, Protein 14g

675. Cheese Stuffed Jalapenos

Preparation Time: 10 minutes
Cooking Time: 25 minutes
Servings: 4

Ingredients:
- 10 jalapeno peppers, halved, remove seeds & membranes
- 1 tsp onion powder
- 1 tsp garlic powder
- 1 oz cheddar cheese, shredded
- 6 oz cream cheese

Directions:
1. Spray cooking pan with cooking spray and set aside.
2. In a small bowl, mix together cream cheese, garlic powder, and onion powder.
3. Stuff cream cheese mixture into each jalapeno halves.
4. Place jalapeno halves onto the prepared cooking pan and top with shredded cheddar cheese.
5. Select bake mode and set the omni to 350 F for 25 minutes once the oven beeps, place the cooking pan into the oven.
6. Serve and enjoy.

Nutrition: Calories 196 Fat 17.7 g Carbs 4.8 g Sugar 1.7 g Protein 5.7 g Cholesterol 54 mg

676. Ranch Chickpeas

Preparation Time: 10 minutes
Cooking Time: 12 minutes
Servings: 12

Ingredients:
- 15 oz can chickpeas, rinsed, drained, and pat dry
- 2 tbsp ranch seasoning
- 1 tsp olive oil

Directions:
1. Line cooking pan with parchment paper and set aside.
2. In a mixing bowl, toss chickpeas with ranch seasoning and oil.
3. Spread chickpeas onto the prepared cooking pan.
4. Place cooking pan into the oven and select air fry mode set omni to the 380 F for 12 minutes. Stir chickpeas twice.
5. Serve and enjoy.

Nutrition: Calories 51 Fat 0.8 g Carbs 8 g Sugar 0 g Protein 1.8 g

677. Cauliflower Hummus

Preparation Time: 10 minutes
Cooking Time: 35 minutes
Servings: 8

Ingredients:
- 1 cauliflower head, cut into florets
- 3 tbsp olive oil
- 1/2 tsp ground cumin
- 1 tsp garlic, chopped
- tbsp fresh lemon juice
- 1/3 cup tahini
- Pepper
- Salt

Directions:
1. Spray cooking pan with cooking spray.
2. Spread cauliflower florets onto the prepared cooking pan.
3. Select bake mode and set the omni to 400 F for 35 minutes once the oven beeps, place the cooking pan into the oven. Turn cauliflower florets halfway through.
4. Transfer cauliflower florets into the food processor along with remaining ingredients and process until smooth.
5. Serve and enjoy.

Nutrition: Calories 115 Fat 10.7 g Carbs 4.2 g Sugar 1 g Protein 2.4 g

678. Tortilla Chips

Preparation Time: 10 minutes
Cooking Time: 3 minutes
Servings: 3

Ingredients:
- 4 corn tortillas cut into triangles
- 1 tablespoon olive oil
- Salt, to taste

Directions:
1. Coat the tortilla chips with oil and then, sprinkle each side of the tortillas with salt.
2. Press "Power Button" of Air Fry Oven and turn the dial to select the "Air Fry" mode.
3. Press the Time button and again turn the dial to set the cooking time to 3 minutes.
4. Now push the Temp button and rotate the dial to set the temperature at 390 degrees F.
5. Press "Start/Pause" button to start.
6. When the unit beeps to show that it is preheated, open the lid.
7. Arrange the tortilla chips in "Air Fry Basket" and insert in the oven.
8. Serve warm.

Nutrition: Calories 110 Fat 5.6 g Carbs 14.3 g Protein 1.8 g

679. Apple Chips

Preparation Time: 10 minutes
Cooking Time: 8 minutes
Servings: 2

Ingredients:
- 1 apple, peeled, cored and thinly sliced
- 1 tablespoon sugar
- ½ teaspoon ground cinnamon
- Pinch of ground cardamom
- Pinch of ground ginger
- Pinch of salt

Directions:
1. In a bowl, add all the ingredients and toss to coat well.
2. Press "Power Button" of Air Fry Oven and turn the dial to select the "Air Fry" mode.
3. Press the Time button and again turn the dial to set the cooking time to 8 minutes
4. Now push the Temp button and rotate the dial to set the temperature at 390 degrees F.
5. Press "Start/Pause" button to start.
6. When the unit beeps to show that it is preheated, open the lid.
7. Arrange the apple chips in "Air Fry Basket" and insert in the oven.

Nutrition: Calories 83 Fat 0.2 g Carbs 22 g Protein 0.3 g

680. Herb Mushrooms

Preparation Time: 10 minutes
Cooking Time: 14 minutes
Servings: 4
Ingredients:
- 1 lb mushrooms
- 1/2 tsp ground coriander
- 1 tsp rosemary, chopped
- 1 tbsp basil, minced
- 1 garlic clove, minced
- 1/2 tbsp vinegar
- Pepper
- Salt

Directions:
1. Add all ingredients into the large bowl and toss well.
2. Spread mushrooms onto the cooking pan.
3. Place cooking pan into the oven and select air fry mode set omni to the 350 F for 14 minutes. Stir halfway through.
4. Serve and enjoy.

Nutrition: Calories 27 Fat 0.4 g Carbs 4.2 g Sugar 2 g Protein 3.6 g

681. Cinnamon Sweet Potato Bites

Preparation Time: 10 minutes
Cooking Time: 15 minutes
Servings: 2
Ingredients:
- 2 sweet potato, diced into 1-inch cubes
- 1 1/2 tsp cinnamon
- 2 tbsp olive oil
- 2 tbsp honey
- 1 tsp red chili flakes
- 1/2 cup fresh parsley, chopped

Directions:
1. Add all ingredients into the bowl and toss well.
2. Spread sweet potato cubes onto the cooking pan.
3. Place cooking pan into the oven and select air fry mode set omni to the 350 F for 15 minutes. Stir halfway through.
4. Serve and enjoy.

Nutrition: Calories 297 Fat 14.3 g Carbs 43.2 g Sugar 24.8 g Protein 2.9 g Cholesterol 0 mg

682. Spicy Mix Nuts

Preparation Time: 10 minutes
Cooking Time: 4 minutes
Servings: 2
Ingredients:
- cup mixed nuts
- 1 tsp ground cumin
- 1 tbsp olive oil
- 1 tsp chili powder
- 1 tsp pepper
- 1 tsp salt

Directions:
1. Add nuts and remaining ingredients into the mixing bowl and toss well.
2. Spread nuts onto the cooking pan.
3. Place cooking pan into the oven and select air fry mode set omni to the 350 F for 4 minutes. Stir halfway through.
4. Serve and enjoy.

Nutrition: Calories 956 Fat 88g Carbs 34 g Sugar 8.8 g Protein 22.8 g

683. Easy Roasted Walnuts

Preparation Time: 10 minutes
Cooking Time: 5 minutes
Servings: 6
Ingredients:
- 2 cups walnuts
- 1/4 tsp chili powder
- 1/8 tsp paprika
- 1 tsp olive oil
- Pepper
- Salt

Directions:
1. Add walnuts, chili powder, paprika, oil, pepper, and salt into the bowl and toss well.
2. Spread walnuts onto the cooking pan.
3. Place cooking pan into the oven and select air fry mode set omni to the 320 F for 5 minutes.
4. Serve and enjoy.

Nutrition: Calories 265 Fat 25.4 g Carbs 4g Sugar 0.5 g Protein 10 g

684. Rosemary Cauliflower Bites

Preparation Time: 10 minutes
Cooking Time: 15 minutes
Servings: 4
Ingredients:
- 1 lb cauliflower florets
- 1 1/2 tsp garlic powder
- 1 tbsp olive oil
- 1 tsp sesame seeds
- 1 tsp ground coriander
- 1/2 tsp dried rosemary
- Pepper
- Salt

Directions:
1. Add cauliflower florets and remaining ingredients into the large bowl and toss well.
2. Spread cauliflower florets onto the cooking pan.
3. Select bake mode and set the omni to 400 F for 15 minutes once the oven beeps, place the cooking pan into the oven.
4. Serve and enjoy.

Nutrition: Calories 67 Fat 4 g Carbs 7.1 g Sugar 3 g Protein 2.6 g Cholesterol 0 mg

685. Sweet Potato Croquettes

Preparation Time: 10 minutes
Cooking Time: 60 minutes
Servings: 6
Ingredients:
- 2 cups cooked quinoa
- 2 tsp Italian seasoning
- 2 cups sweet potatoes, mashed
- 1/4 cup scallions, chopped
- 1/4 cup parsley, chopped
- 1/4 cup flour
- 1 garlic clove, minced
- 1/4 cup celery, diced
- Pepper
- Salt

Directions:
1. Spray cooking pan with cooking spray and set aside.

2. Add all ingredients into the large bowl and mix until well combined.
3. Make 1-inch round croquettes from mixture and place on a prepared cooking pan.
4. Select bake mode and set the omni to 375 F for 60 minutes once the oven beeps, place the cooking pan into the oven.
5. Serve and enjoy.

Nutrition: Calories 295 Fat 4.1 g Carbs 55.2 g Sugar 0.6 g Protein 9.5 g Cholesterol 1 mg

686. Sweet & Spicy Mixed Nuts

Preparation Time: 10 minutes
Cooking Time: 20 minutes
Servings: 16
Ingredients:
- 4cups mixed nuts
- 2tbsp butter
- 1 tbsp maple syrup
- 1 tsp chili powder
- 1 1/2 tsp salt

Directions:
1. In a mixing bowl, mix together melted butter, maple syrup, chili powder, and salt.
2. Add mixed nuts and toss to coat.
3. Spread nuts onto the parchment-lined cooking pan
4. Select bake mode and set the omni to 300 F for 20 minutes once the oven beeps, place the cooking pan into the oven.
5. Serve and enjoy.

Nutrition: Calories 238 Fat 21.7 g Carbs 9 g Sugar 2.3 g Protein 5.6 g Cholesterol 4 mg

687. Cheese Dip

Preparation Time: 10 minutes
Cooking Time: 10 minutes
Servings: 4
Ingredients:
- 10oz goat cheese
- 2tbsp olive oil
- 1/4 cup parmesan cheese
- 2garlic cloves, minced
- 1/4 tsp sage
- 1/4 tsp thyme
- Pepper
- Salt

Directions:
1. Spray a baking dish with cooking spray and set aside.
2. Add all ingredients into the food processor and process until just combined.
3. Pour mixture into the prepared baking dish and spread well.
4. Select bake mode and set the omni to 400 F for 10 minutes once the oven beeps, place the baking dish into the oven.
5. Serve and enjoy.

Nutrition: Calories 403 Fat 33.6 g Carbs 2.3 g Sugar 1.6 g Protein 23.8 g Cholesterol 79 mg

688. Creamy Zucchini Dip

Preparation Time: 10 minutes
Cooking Time: 15 minutes
Servings: 6
Ingredients:
- 1 lb zucchini, grated & squeeze out all liquid
- 1 tbsp lime juice
- 1 tbsp olive oil
- 1 cup heavy cream
- 1 tsp garlic, minced
- 1 tsp dill, chopped
- Pepper
- Salt

Directions:
1. Spray a baking dish with cooking spray and set aside.
2. Add all ingredients into the large bowl and mix until well combined.
3. Pour zucchini mixture into the prepared baking dish.
4. Place baking dish into the oven and select air fry mode set omni to the 375 F for 15 minutes.
5. Serve and enjoy.

Nutrition: Calories 104 Fat 9.9 g Carbs 4 g Sugar 1.5 g Protein 1.4 g Cholesterol 27 mg

DESSERT

DESSERT

689. Lemon Mousse

Preparation Time: 10 minutes
Cooking time: 12 minutes
Servings: 2
Ingredients:
- 4ounces cream cheese, softened
- ½ cup heavy cream
- 2tablespoons fresh lemon juice
- 2tablespoons honey
- Pinch of salt

Directions
1. In a bowl, add all the ingredients and mix until well combined.
2. Transfer the mixture into 2 ramekins.
3. Select "Bake" of Air fryer oven and then adjust the temperature to 350 F.
4. Set the timer for 12 minutes and press "Start/Stop" to begin cooking.
5. When the unit beeps to show that it is preheated, place the ramekins over the air rack and insert in the Air fryer oven.
6. When cooking time is complete, remove the ramekin from Air fryer oven and place onto a wire rack to cool completely.
7. Refrigerate the ramekins for at least 3 hours before serving.

Nutrition: Calories 369 Fat 31g Cholesterol 103mg Sodium 261mg Total Carbs 20g Fiber 0.1gSugar 17.7g Protein 5.1g

690. Glazed Banana

Preparation Time: 10 minutes
Cooking time: 10 minutes
Servings: 4
Ingredients:
- 2ripe bananas, peeled and sliced lengthwise
- 1 teaspoon fresh lime juice
- 4teaspoons maple syrup
- 1/8 teaspoon ground cinnamon

Directions
1. Coat each banana half with lime juice.
2. Arrange the banana halves onto the greased "baking pan" cut sides up.
3. Drizzle the banana halves with maple syrup and sprinkle with cinnamon.
4. Select "Air Fry" of Air fryer oven and then adjust the temperature to 350 F.
5. Set the timer for 10 minutes and press "Start/Stop" to begin cooking.
6. When the unit beeps to show that it is preheated, insert the baking pan in the Air fryer oven.
7. When cooking time is complete, remove the baking pan from Air fryer oven and serve immediately.

Nutrition: Calories 70 Fat 0.2g Saturated Fat 0.1g Sodium 1mg Carbs 18g Fiber 1.6g Sugar 11.2g Protein 0.6g

691. Raspberry Danish

Preparation Time: 20 minutes
Cooking time: 25 minutes
Servings: 6
Ingredients:
- 1 tube full-sheet crescent roll dough
- 4ounces cream cheese, softened
- ¼ cup raspberry jam
- ½ cup fresh raspberries, chopped
- 1 cup powdered sugar
- 2-3 tablespoons heavy whipping cream

Directions
1. Place the sheet of crescent roll dough onto a flat surface and unroll it.
2. In a microwave-safe bowl, add the cream cheese and microwave for about 20-30 seconds.
3. Remove from microwave and stir until creamy and smooth.
4. Spread the cream cheese over the dough sheet, followed by the strawberry jam.
5. Now, place the raspberry pieces evenly across the top.
6. From the short side, roll the dough and pinch the seam to seal.
7. Arrange a greased parchment paper onto the steak tray of oven.
8. Carefully, curve the rolled pastry into a horseshoe shape and arrange onto the prepared tray.
9. Select "Air Fry" of Air fryer oven and then adjust the temperature to 350 F.
10. Set the timer for 25 minutes and press "Start/Stop" to begin cooking.
11. When the unit beeps to show that it is preheated, insert the tray in the Air fryer oven.
12. When cooking time is complete, remove the tray from Air fryer oven and place onto a rack to cool.
13. Meanwhile, in a bowl, mix together the powdered sugar and cream.
14. Drizzle the cream mixture over cooled Danish and serve.

Nutrition: Calories 335 Fat 15.3g Saturated Fat 8g Cholesterol 28mg Sodium 342mg Carbs 45.3g Fiber 0.7g Sugar 30.1g Protein 4.4g

692. Blueberry Muffins

Preparation Time: 15 minutes
Cooking time: 15 minutes
Servings: 8
Ingredients:
- ¼ cup unsweetened coconut milk
- 2large eggs
- ½ teaspoon vanilla extract
- 1½ cups almond flour
- ¼ cup Swerve
- 1 teaspoon baking powder
- ¼ teaspoon ground cinnamon
- Pinch of ground cloves
- Pinch of ground nutmeg
- 1/8 teaspoon salt
- ½ cup fresh blueberries
- ¼ cup pecans, chopped

Directions
1. In a blender, add the almond milk, eggs and vanilla extract and pulse for about 20-30 seconds.
2. Add the almond flour, Swerve, baking powder, spices and salt and pulse for about 30-45 seconds until well blended.

3. Transfer the mixture into a bowl
4. Gently, fold in half of the blueberries and pecans.
5. Place the mixture into 8 silicone muffin cups and top each with remaining blueberries.
6. Select "Air Fry" of Air fryer oven and then adjust the temperature to 325 F.
7. Set the timer for 15 minutes and press "Start/Stop" to begin cooking.
8. When the unit beeps to show that it is preheated, place the cups over the air rack and insert in the Air fryer oven.
9. When cooking time is complete, remove the cups from Air fryer oven and place onto a wire rack to cool for about 10 minutes.
10. Carefully, invert the muffins onto the wire rack to completely cool before serving.

Nutrition: Calories 191 Fat 16.5g Cholesterol 47mg Sodium 54mg Total Carbs 14.8g Fiber 3.2g Sugar 9.7g Protein 6.8g

693. Cranberry Cupcakes

Preparation Time: 15 minutes
Cooking time: 15 minutes
Servings: 10
Ingredients:
- 4½ ounces self-rising flour
- ½ teaspoon baking powder
- Pinch of salt
- ½ ounce cream cheese, softened
- 4¾ ounces butter, softened
- 4¼ ounces caster sugar
- 2 eggs
- 2 teaspoons fresh lemon juice
- ½ cup fresh cranberries

Directions
1. In a bowl, mix together the flour, baking powder, and salt.
2. In another bowl, mix together the cream cheese, and butter.
3. Add the sugar and beat until fluffy and light.
4. Add the eggs, one at a time and whisk until just combined.
5. Add the flour mixture and stir until well combined.
6. Stir in the lemon juice.
7. Place the mixture into silicone cups and top each with cranberries evenly, pressing slightly.
8. Select "Air Fry" of Air fryer oven and then adjust the temperature to 365 F.
9. Set the timer for 15 minutes and press "Start/Stop" to begin cooking.
10. When the unit beeps to show that it is preheated, place the cups over the air rack and insert in the Air fryer oven.
11. When cooking time is complete, remove the cups from Air fryer oven and place onto a wire rack to cool for about 10 minutes.
12. Carefully, invert the cupcakes onto the wire rack to completely cool before serving.

Nutrition: Calories 209 Fat 12.4g Cholesterol 63mg Sodium 110mg Total Carbs 22.6g Fiber 0.6g Sugar 12.4g Protein 2.7g

694. Zucchini Mug Cake

Preparation Time: 10 minutes
Cooking time: 20 minutes
Servings: 1
Ingredients:
- ¼ cup whole-wheat pastry flour
- 1 tablespoon sugar
- ¼ teaspoon baking powder
- ¼ teaspoon ground cinnamon
- Pinch of salt
- 2 tablespoons plus 2 teaspoons milk
- 2 tablespoons zucchini, grated and squeezed
- 2 tablespoons almonds, chopped
- 1 tablespoon raisins
- 2 teaspoons maple syrup

Directions
1. In a bowl, mix together the flour, sugar, baking powder, cinnamon and salt.
2. Add the remaining ingredients and mix until well combined.
3. Place the mixture into a lightly greased ramekin.
4. Select "Bake" of Air fryer oven and then adjust the temperature to 350 F.
5. Set the timer for 20 minutes and press "Start/Stop" to begin cooking.
6. When the unit beeps to show that it is preheated, place the ramekin over the air rack and insert in the Air fryer oven.
7. When cooking time is complete, remove the ramekin from Air fryer oven and place onto a wire rack to cool slightly before serving.

Nutrition: Calories 310 Fat 7g Cholesterol 3mg Sodium 175mg Total Carbs 57.5g Fiber 3.2g Sugar 27.5g Protein 7.2g

695. Chocolate Brownies

Preparation Time: 15 minutes
Cooking time: 15 minutes
Servings: 4
Ingredients:
- ½ cup all-purpose flour
- ¾ cup sugar
- 6 tablespoons cacao powder
- ¼ teaspoon baking powder
- ¼ teaspoon salt
- ¼ cup butter, melted
- 2 large eggs
- 1 tablespoon olive oil
- ½ teaspoon pure vanilla extract

Directions
1. Grease a 7-inch baking dish generously. Set aside.
2. In a bowl, add all the ingredients and mix until well combined.
3. Place the mixture into the prepared baking dish and with the back of a spoon, smooth the top surface.
4. Arrange the baking pan of oven in the bottom of Air Fryer Oven.
5. Select "Air Fry" of Air fryer oven and then adjust the temperature to 320 F.
6. Set the timer for 30 minutes and press "Start/Stop" to begin cooking.
7. When the unit beeps to show that it is preheated, place the baking dish over the baking pan and insert in the Air fryer oven.
8. When cooking time is complete, remove the pan from Air fryer oven and place onto a wire rack to cool completely before cutting.
9. Cut the brownie into desired-sized squares and serve.

Nutrition: Calories 367 Fat 19.2g Cholesterol 124mg Sodium 265mg Total Carbs 53.6g Fiber 2.7g Sugar 37.8g Protein 6.4g

DESSERT

696. Apple Crisp

Preparation Time: 15 minutes
Cooking time: 40 minutes
Servings: 2

Ingredients:
- 1½ cups apple, peeled, cored and sliced
- ¼ cup sugar, divided
- 1½ teaspoons cornstarch
- 3 tablespoons all-purpose flour
- ¼ teaspoon ground cinnamon
- Pinch of salt
- 1½ tablespoons cold butter, chopped
- 3 tablespoons rolled oats

Directions
1. In a bowl, place apple slices, 1 teaspoon of sugar and cornstarch and toss to coat well.
2. Divide the plum mixture into lightly greased 2 (8-ounce) ramekins.
3. In a bowl, mix together the flour, remaining sugar, cinnamon and salt.
4. With 2 forks, blend in the butter until a crumbly mixture form.
5. Add the oats and gently, stir to combine.
6. Place the oat mixture over apple slices into each ramekin.
7. Select "Bake" of Air fryer oven and then adjust the temperature to 350 F.
8. Set the timer for 40 minutes and press "Start/Stop" to begin cooking.
9. When the unit beeps to show that it is preheated, place the ramekins over the air rack and insert in the Air fryer oven.
10. When cooking time is complete, remove the ramekins from Air fryer oven and place onto a wire rack to cool for about 10 minutes before serving.

Nutrition: Calories 337 Fat 9.6g Cholesterol 23mg Sodium 141mg Total Carbs 64.3g Fiber 5.3g Sugar 42.5g Protein 2.8g

697. Banana and Walnut Cake

Preparation time: 10 minutes
Cooking time: 25 minutes
Servings: 6

Ingredients:
- 1 pound (454g) bananas, mashed
- 8 ounces (227g) flour
- 6 ounces (170g) sugar
- 3.5 ounces (99g) walnuts, chopped
- 3.5 ounces (71g) butter, melted
- 2 eggs, lightly beaten
- ¼ teaspoon baking soda

Directions
1. Select the Bake function and preheat Maxx to 355 F (179 degrees Celsius).
2. In a bowl, combine the sugar, butter, egg, flour, and baking soda with a whisk. Stir in the bananas and walnuts.
3. Transfer the mixture to a greased baking dish. Put the dish in the air fryer oven and bake for 10 minutes.
4. Reduce the temperature to 330 F (166 degrees Celsius) and bake for another 15 minutes. Serve hot.

Nutrition: Calories 70 Fat 0.2g Saturated Fat 0.1g Sodium 1mg Total Carbs 18g Fiber 1.6g Sugar 11.2g Protein 0.6g

698. Perfect Cinnamon Toast

Preparation time: 10 minutes
Cooking time: 5 minutes
Servings: 6

Ingredients:
- 2 tsp. pepper
- 1 ½ tsp. vanilla extract
- 1 ½ tsp. cinnamon
- ½ C. sweetener of choice
- 1 C. coconut oil
- 12 slices whole wheat bread

Directions
1. Melt coconut oil and mix with sweetener until dissolved. Mix in remaining ingredients minus bread till incorporated.
2. Spread mixture onto bread, covering all area.
3. Pour the coated pieces of bread into the Oven rack/basket. Place the Rack on the middle-shelf of the Air fryer oven. Set temperature to 400 F, and set time to 5 minutes.
4. Remove and cut diagonally. Enjoy!

Nutrition: Calories 124 Fat 2g Sugar 4g

699. Easy Baked Chocolate Mug Cake

Preparation time: 5 minutes
Cooking time: 15 minutes
Servings: 3

Ingredients:
- ½ cup cocoa powder
- ½ cup stevia powder
- 1 cup coconut cream
- 1 package cream cheese, room temperature
- 1 tablespoon vanilla extract
- 1 tablespoons butter

Directions
1. Preheat the air fryer oven for 5 minutes.
2. In a mixing bowl, combine all ingredients.
3. Use a hand mixer to mix everything until fluffy.
4. Pour into greased mugs.
5. Place the mugs in the fryer basket.
6. Bake for 15 minutes at 350 F.
7. Place in the fridge to chill before serving.

Nutrition: Calories 744 Fat 69.7g Protein 13.9g Sugar 4g

700. Angel Food Cake

Preparation time: 5 minutes
Cooking time: 30 minutes
Servings: 12

Ingredients:
- ¼ cup butter, melted
- 1 cup powdered erythritol
- 1 teaspoon strawberry extract
- 12 egg whites
- 2 teaspoons cream of tartar
- A pinch of salt

Directions
1. Preheat the air fryer oven for 5 minutes.
2. Mix the egg whites and cream of tartar.
3. Use a hand mixer and whisk until white and fluffy.
4. Add the rest of the ingredients except for the butter and whisk for another minute.
5. Pour into a baking dish.

6. Place in the air fryer basket and cook for 30 minutes at 400 F or if a toothpick inserted in the middle comes out clean.
7. Drizzle with melted butter once cooled.

Nutrition: Calories 65 Fat 5g Protein 3.1g Fiber 1g

701. Sweet Pear Stew

Preparation Time: 10 minutes
Cooking Time: 15 minutes
Servings: 4

Ingredients:
- 4 pears, cored and cut into wedges
- 1 tsp vanilla
- 1/4 cup apple juice
- 2 cups grapes, halved

Directions:
1. Put all of the ingredients in the inner pot of air fryer and stir well.
2. Seal pot and cook on high for 15 minutes.
3. As soon as the cooking is done, let it release pressure naturally for 10 minutes then release remaining using quick release. Remove lid.
4. Stir and serve.

Nutrition: Calories – 162 Protein – 1.1 g. Fat – 0.5 g. Carbs – 41.6 g.

702. Apple Dumplings

Preparation time: 10 minutes
Cooking time: 25 minutes
Servings: 4

Ingredients:
- 2tbsp. melted coconut oil
- 2puff pastry sheets
- 1 tbsp. brown sugar
- 2tbsp. raisins
- 2small apples of choice

Directions
1. Ensure your air fryer oven is preheated to 356 F.
2. Core and peel apples and mix with raisins and sugar.
3. Place a bit of apple mixture into puff pastry sheets and brush sides with melted coconut oil.
4. Place into the air fryer. Cook 25 minutes, turning halfway through. Will be golden when done.

Nutrition: Calories 367 Fat 7g Protein 2g Sugar 5g

703. Apple Pie in Air Fryer

Preparation time: 5 minutes
Cooking time: 35 minutes
Servings: 4

Ingredients:
- ½ teaspoon vanilla extract
- 1 beaten egg
- 1 large apple, chopped
- 1 Pillsbury Refrigerator pie crust
- 1 tablespoon butter
- 1 tablespoon ground cinnamon
- 1 tablespoon raw sugar
- 2tablespoon sugar
- 2teaspoons lemon juice
- Baking spray

Directions
1. Lightly grease baking pan of air fryer oven with cooking spray. Spread pie crust on bottom of pan up to the sides.
2. In a bowl, mix vanilla, sugar, cinnamon, lemon juice, and apples. Pour on top of pie crust. Top apples with butter slices.
3. Cover apples with the other pie crust. Pierce with knife the tops of pie.
4. Spread beaten egg on top of crust and sprinkle sugar.
5. Cover with foil.
6. For 25 minutes, cook on 390 F.
7. Remove foil cook for 10 minutes at 330oF until tops are browned.
8. Serve and enjoy.

Nutrition: Calories 372 Fat 19g Protein 4.2g Sugar 5g

704. Air Fryer Chocolate Cake

Preparation time: 5 minutes
Cooking time: 35 minutes
Servings: 8-10

Ingredients:
- ½ cup hot water
- 1 tsp. vanilla
- ¼ cup olive oil
- ½ cup almond milk
- 1 egg
- ½ tsp. salt
- ¾ tsp. baking soda
- ¾ tsp. baking powder
- ½ cup unsweetened cocoa powder
- 2cup almond flour
- 1 cup brown sugar

Directions
1. Preheat your air fryer oven to 356 F.
2. Stir all dry ingredients together. Then stir in wet ingredients. Add hot water last.
3. The batter will be thin, no worries.
4. Pour cake batter into a pan that fits into the fryer. Cover with foil and poke holes into the foil.
5. Bake 35 minutes.
6. Discard foil and then bake another 10 minutes.

Nutrition: Calories 378 Fat 9g Protein 4g Sugar 5g

705. Banana-Choco Brownies

Preparation time: 5 minutes
Cooking time: 30 minutes
Servings: 12

Ingredients:
- 2cups almond flour
- 2teaspoons baking powder
- ½ teaspoon baking powder
- ½ teaspoon baking soda
- ½ teaspoon salt
- 1 over-ripe banana
- 3large eggs
- ½ teaspoon stevia powder
- ¼ cup coconut oil
- 1 tablespoon vinegar
- 1/3 cup almond flour
- 1/3 cup cocoa powder

Directions
1. Preheat the air fryer oven for 5 minutes.
2. Combine all ingredients in a food processor and pulse until well-combined.

3. Pour into a baking dish that will fit in the air fryer.
4. Place in the air fryer basket and cook for 30 minutes at 350 F or if a toothpick inserted in the middle comes out clean.

Nutrition: Calories 75 Fat 6.5g Protein 1.7g Sugar 2g

706. Chocolate Donuts

Preparation time: 5 minutes
Cooking time: 20 minutes
Servings: 8-10
Ingredients:
- 1 (8-ounce) can jumbo biscuits
- Cooking oil
- Chocolate sauce, such as Hershey's

Directions
1. Separate the biscuit dough into 8 biscuits and place them on a flat work surface. Use a small circle cookie cutter or a biscuit cutter to cut a hole in the center of each biscuit. You can also cut the holes using a knife.
2. Spray the air fryer basket with cooking oil.
3. Place 4 donuts in the air fryer oven. Do not stack. Spray with cooking oil. Cook for 4 minutes.
4. Open the air fryer and flip the donuts. Cook for an additional 4 minutes.
5. Remove the cooked donuts from the air fryer oven, then repeat for the remaining 4 donuts.
6. Drizzle chocolate sauce over the donuts and enjoy while warm.

Nutrition: Calories 181 Fat 98g Protein 3g Fiber 1g

707. Easy Air Fryer Donuts

Preparation time: 5 minutes
Cooking time: 5 minutes
Servings: 8
Ingredients:
- Pinch of allspice
- 4tbsp. dark brown sugar
- ½ - 1 tsp. cinnamon
- 1/3 cup granulated sweetener
- 3tbsp. melted coconut oil
- 1 can of biscuits

Directions
1. Mix allspice, sugar, sweetener, and cinnamon together.
2. Take out biscuits from can and with a circle cookie cutter, cut holes from centers and place into air fryer.
3. Cook 5 minutes at 350 F. As batches are cooked, use a brush to coat with melted coconut oil and dip each into sugar mixture.
4. Serve warm!

Nutrition: Calories 209 Fat 4g Sugar 3g

708. Chocolate Soufflé for Two

Preparation time: 5 minutes
Cooking time: 14 minutes
Servings: 2
Ingredients:
- 2tbsp. almond flour
- ½ tsp. vanilla
- 3tbsp. sweetener
- 2separated eggs
- ¼ cup melted coconut oil
- 3ounces of semi-sweet chocolate, chopped

Directions
1. Brush coconut oil and sweetener onto ramekins.
2. Melt coconut oil and chocolate together.
3. Beat egg yolks well, adding vanilla and sweetener. Stir in flour and ensure there are no lumps.
4. Preheat the air fryer oven to 330 F.
5. Whisk egg whites till they reach peak state and fold them into chocolate mixture.
6. Pour batter into ramekins and place into the air fryer oven.
7. Cook 14 minutes.
8. Serve with powdered sugar dusted on top.

Nutrition: Calories 238 Fat 6g Protein 1g Sugar 4g

709. Blueberry Lemon Muffins

Preparation time: 5 minutes
Cooking time: 10 minutes
Servings: 12
Ingredients:
- 1 tsp. vanilla
- Juice and zest of 1 lemon
- 2eggs
- 1 cup blueberries
- ½ cup cream
- ¼ cup avocado oil
- ½ cup monk fruit
- 2 ½ cup almond flour

Directions
1. Mix monk fruit and flour together.
2. In another bowl, mix vanilla, egg, lemon juice, and cream together. Add mixtures together and blend well.
3. Spoon batter into cupcake holders.
4. Place in air fryer oven. Bake 10 minutes at 320 F, checking at 6 minutes to ensure you don't overbake them.

Nutrition: Calories 317 Fat 11g Protein 3g Sugar 5g

710. Sweet Cream Cheese Wontons

Preparation time: 5 minutes
Cooking time: 5 minutes
Servings: 16
Ingredients:
- 1 egg mixed with a bit of water
- Wonton wrappers
- ½ cup powdered erythritol
- 8ounces softened cream cheese
- Olive oil

Directions
1. Mix sweetener and cream cheese together.
2. Lay out 4 wontons at a time and cover with a dish towel to prevent drying out.
3. Place ½ of a teaspoon of cream cheese mixture into each wrapper.
4. Dip finger into egg/water mixture and fold diagonally to form a triangle. Seal edges well.
5. Repeat with remaining ingredients.
6. Place filled wontons into the air fryer oven and cook 5 minutes at 400 F, shaking halfway through cooking.

Nutrition: Calories 303 Fat 3g Protein 0.5g Sugar 4g

711. Air Fryer Cinnamon Rolls

Preparation time: 15 minutes
Cooking time: 5 minutes
Servings: 8

Ingredients:
- 1 ½ tbsp. cinnamon
- ¾ cup brown sugar
- ¼ cup melted coconut oil
- 1 pound frozen bread dough, thawed
- Glaze:
- ½ tsp. vanilla
- 1 ¼ cup powdered erythritol
- 2 tbsp. softened ghee
- 2 ounces softened cream cheese

Directions
1. Lay out bread dough and roll out into a rectangle. Brush melted ghee over dough and leave a 1-inch border along edges.
2. Mix cinnamon and sweetener together and then sprinkle over dough.
3. Roll dough tightly and slice into 8 pieces. Let sit 1-2 hours to rise.
4. To make the glaze, simply mix ingredients together till smooth.
5. Once rolls rise, place into air fryer and cook 5 minutes at 350 F.
6. Serve rolls drizzled in cream cheese glaze. Enjoy!

Nutrition: Calories 390 Fat 8g Protein 1g Sugar 7g

712. Raspberry Cream Rol-Ups

Preparation time: 10 minutes
Cooking time: 25 minutes
Servings: 4

Ingredients:
- 1 cup of fresh raspberries rinsed and patted dry
- ½ cup of cream cheese softened to room temperature
- ¼ cup of brown sugar
- ¼ cup of sweetened condensed milk
- 1 egg
- 1 teaspoon of corn starch
- 6 spring roll wrappers (any brand will do, we like Blue Dragon or Tasty Joy, both available through Target or Walmart, or any large grocery chain)
- ¼ cup of water

Directions
1. Preparing the Ingredients. Cover the basket of the air fryer with a lining of tin foil, leaving the edges uncovered to allow air to circulate through the basket. Preheat the air fryer to 350 F.
2. In a mixing bowl, combine the cream cheese, brown sugar, condensed milk, cornstarch, and egg. Beat or whip thoroughly, until all ingredients are completely mixed and fluffy, thick and stiff.
3. Spoon even amounts of the creamy filling into each spring roll wrapper, then top each dollop of filling with several raspberries.
4. Roll up the wraps around the creamy raspberry filling, and seal the seams with a few dabs of water.
5. Place each roll on the foil-lined air fryer basket, seams facing down.
6. Air Frying. Set the air fryer timer to 10 minutes. During cooking, shake the handle of the fryer basket to ensure a nice even surface crisp.
7. After 10 minutes, when the air fryer shuts off, the spring rolls should be golden brown and perfect on the outside, while the raspberries and cream filling will have cooked together in a glorious fusion. Remove with tongs and serve hot or cold.

Nutrition: Calories 335 Fat 15.3g Cholesterol 28mg Sodium 342mg Total Carbs 45.3g Fiber 0.7g Sugar 30.1g Protein 4.4g

713. Apple Hand Pies

Preparation time: 5 minutes
Cooking time: 8 minutes
Servings: 6

Ingredients:
- 15-ounces no-sugar-added apple pie filling
- 1 store-bought crust

Directions
1. Preparing the Ingredients. Lay out pie crust and slice into equal-sized squares.
2. Place 2 tbsp. filling into each square and seal crust with a fork.
3. Air Frying. Place into the air fryer. Cook 8 minutes at 390 F until golden in color.

Nutrition: Calories 278 Fat 10g Sugar 4g Protein 5g

714. Chocolaty Banana Muffins

Preparation time: 5 minutes
Cooking time: 25 minutes
Servings: 12

Ingredients:
- ¾ cup whole wheat flour
- ¾ cup plain flour
- ¼ cup cocoa powder
- ¼ teaspoon baking powder
- 1 teaspoon baking soda
- ¼ teaspoon salt
- 2 large bananas, peeled and mashed
- 1 cup sugar
- 1/3 cup canola oil
- 1 egg
- ½ teaspoon vanilla essence
- 1 cup mini chocolate chips

Directions
1. Preparing the Ingredients. In a large bowl, mix together flour, cocoa powder, baking powder, baking soda, and salt.
2. In another bowl, add bananas, sugar, oil, egg and vanilla extract and beat till well combined.
3. Slowly, add flour mixture in egg mixture and mix till just combined.
4. Fold in chocolate chips.
5. Preheat the Air Fryer to 345 F. Grease 12 muffin molds.
6. Air Frying. Transfer the mixture into prepared muffin molds evenly and cook for about 20-25 minutes or till a toothpick inserted in the center comes out clean.
7. Remove the muffin molds from Air fryer and keep on wire rack to cool for about 10 minutes. Carefully turn on a wire rack to cool completely before serving.

Nutrition: Calories 75 Fat 6.5g Protein 1.7g Sugar 2g

DESSERT

715. Chocolate Rice

Preparation Time: 10 minutes
Cooking Time: 20 minutes
Servings: 4
Ingredients:
1. 1 cup of rice
2. 1 tbsp. cocoa powder
3. 2 tbsp. maple syrup
4. 2 cups almond milk

Directions:
- Put all of the ingredients in the inner pot of air fryer and stir well.
- Seal pot and cook on high for 20 minutes.
- As soon as the cooking is done, let it release pressure naturally for 10 minutes then release remaining using quick release. Remove lid.
- Stir and serve.

Nutrition: Calories – 474 Protein – 6.3 g. Fat – 29.1 g. Carbs – 51.1 g.

716. Cinnamon Fried Bananas

Preparation time: 5 minutes
Cooking time: 10 minutes
Servings: 2-3
Ingredients:
- 1 cup panko breadcrumbs
- 3 tbsp. cinnamon
- ½ cup almond flour
- 3 egg whites
- 8 ripe bananas
- 3 tbsp. vegan coconut oil

Directions
1. Preparing the Ingredients. Heat coconut oil and add breadcrumbs. Mix around 2-3 minutes until golden. Pour into bowl.
2. Peel and cut bananas in half. Roll each bananas half into flour, eggs, and crumb mixture.
3. Air Frying. Place into the air fryer. Cook 10 minutes at 280 F.
4. A great addition to a healthy banana split!

Nutrition: Calories 219 Fat 10g Protein 3g Sugar 5g

717. Awesome Chinese Doughnuts

Preparation time: 10 minutes
Cooking time: 8 minutes
Servings: 8
Ingredients:
- 1 tbsp. baking powder
- 1 tbsps. coconut oil
- ¾ cup of coconut milk
- 6 tsps. sugar
- 2 cup all-purpose flour
- ½ tsp. sea salt

Directions
1. Preheat the air fryer to 350 F.
2. Mix baking powder, flour, sugar, and salt in a bowl.
3. Add coconut oil and mix well. Add coconut milk and mix until well combined.
4. Knead dough for 3-4 minutes.
5. Roll dough half inch thick and using cookie cutter cut doughnuts.
6. Place doughnuts in cake pan and brush with oil. Place cake pan in air fryer basket and air fry doughnuts for 5 minutes. Turn doughnuts to other side and air fry for 3 minutes more.
7. Serve and enjoy.

Nutrition: Calories 259 Fat 15.9g Carbs 27g Protein 3.8g

718. Crispy Bananas

Preparation time: 10 minutes
Cooking time: 10 minutes
Servings: 4
Ingredients:
- 4 sliced ripe bananas
- 1 egg
- ½ cup breadcrumbs
- 1 ½ tbsps. cinnamon sugar
- 1 tbsp. almond meal
- 1 ½ tbsps. coconut oil
- 1 tbsp. crushed cashew
- ¼ cup corn flour

Directions
1. Set the pan on fire to heat the coconut oil over medium heat and add breadcrumbs in the pan and stir for 3-4 minutes.
2. Remove pan from heat and transfer breadcrumbs in a bowl.
3. Add almond meal and crush cashew in breadcrumbs and mix well.
4. Dip banana half in corn flour then in egg and finally coat with breadcrumbs.
5. Place coated banana in air fryer basket. Sprinkle with Cinnamon Sugar.
6. Air fry at 350 F/ 176 degrees Celsius for 10 minutes.
7. Serve and enjoy.

Nutrition: Calories 282 Fat 9g Carbs 46g Protein 5g

719. Air Fried Banana and Walnuts Muffins

Preparation time: 10 minutes
Cooking time: 10 minutes
Servings: 2
Ingredients:
- ¼ cup flour
- ½ tsp. baking powder
- ¼ cup mashed banana
- ¼ cup butter
- 1 tbsp. chopped walnuts
- ¼ cup oats

Directions
1. Spray four muffin molds with cooking spray and set aside.
2. In a bowl, mix together mashed bananas, walnuts, sugar, and butter.
3. In another bowl, mix oat flour, and baking powder.
4. Combine the flour mixture to the banana mixture.
5. Pour batter into prepared muffin mold.
6. Place in air fryer basket and cook at 320 F/ 160 degrees Celsius for 10 minutes.
7. Remove muffins from air fryer and allow to cool completely.
8. Serve and enjoy.

Nutrition: Calories 192 Fat 12.3g Carbs 19.4g Protein 1.9g

720. Nutty Mix

Preparation time: 5 minutes
Cooking time: 4 minutes
Servings: 6
Ingredients:
- 2cup mix nuts
- 1 tsp. ground cumin
- 1 tsp. chili powder
- 1 tbsp. melted butter
- 1 tsp. salt
- 1 tsp. pepper

Directions
1. Set all ingredients in a large bowl and toss until well coated.
2. Preheat the air fryer at 350 F for 5 minutes.
3. Add mix nuts in air fryer basket and air fry for 4 minutes. Shake basket halfway through.
4. Serve and enjoy.

Nutrition: Calories 316 Fat 29g Carbs 11.3g Protein 7.6g

721. Vanilla Spiced Soufflé

Preparation time: 20 minutes
Cooking time: 32 minutes
Servings: 6
Ingredients:
- ¼ cup all-purpose flour
- 1 cup whole milk
- 2tsps. vanilla extract
- 1 tsp. cream of tartar
- 1 vanilla bean
- 4egg yolks
- 1-oz. sugar
- ¼ cup softened butter
- ¼ cup sugar
- 5egg whites

Directions
1. Combine flour and butter in a bowl until the mixture becomes a smooth paste.
2. Set the pan over medium flame to heat the milk. Add sugar and stir until dissolved.
3. Mix in the vanilla bean and bring to a boil.
4. Beat the mixture using a wire whisk as you add the butter and flour mixture.
5. Lower the heat to simmer until thick. Discard the vanilla bean. Turn off the heat.
6. Place them on an ice bath and allow to cool for 10 minutes.
7. Grease 6 ramekins with butter. Sprinkle each with a bit of sugar.
8. Beat the egg yolks in a bowl. Add the vanilla extract and milk mixture. Mix until combined.
9. Whisk together the tartar cream, egg whites, and sugar until it forms medium stiff peaks.
10. Gradually fold egg whites into the soufflé base. Transfer the mixture to the ramekins.
11. Put 3 ramekins in the cooking basket at a time. Cook for 16 minutes at 330 F. Move to a wire rack for cooling and cook the rest.
12. Sprinkle powdered sugar on top and drizzle with chocolate sauce before serving.

Nutrition: Calories 215 Fat 12.2g Carbs 18.98g Protein 6.66g

722. Chocolate Cup Cakes

Preparation time: 5 minutes
Cooking time: 12 minutes
Servings: 6
Ingredients:
- 3eggs
- ¼ cup caster sugar
- ¼ cup cocoa powder
- 1 tsp. baking powder
- 1 cup milk
- ¼ tsp. vanilla essence
- 2cup all-purpose flour
- 4tbsps. butter

Directions
1. Preheat your Air Fryer to a temperature of 400 F (200 degrees Celsius).
2. Beat eggs with sugar in a bowl until creamy.
3. Add butter and beat again for 1-2 minutes.
4. Now add flour, cocoa powder, milk, baking powder, and vanilla essence, mix with a spatula.
5. Fill ¾ of muffin tins with the mixture and place them into Air Fryer basket.
6. Let cook for 12 minutes.
7. Serve!

Nutrition: Calories 289 Fat 11.5g Carbs 38.94g Protein 8.72g

723. Air Baked Cheesecake

Preparation time: 20 minutes
Cooking time: 20 minutes
Servings: 8-12
Ingredients:
Crust
- 1/2 cup dates, chopped, soaked in water for at least 15 min., soaking liquid reserved
- 1/2 cup walnuts
- 1 cup quick oats

Filling
- 1/2 cup vanilla almond milk
- 1/4 cup coconut palm sugar
- 1/2 cup coconut flour
- 1 cup cashews, soaked in water for at least 2 hours
- 1 tsp. vanilla extract
- 2tbsp. lemon juice
- 1 to 2 tsp. grated lemon zest
- 1/2 cup fresh berries or 6 figs, sliced
- 1 tbsp. arrowroot powder

Directions:
1. Make the crust: in a food processor, process together all the crust ingredients until smooth and press the mixture into the bottom of a spring form pan.
2. Make the filling: add cashews along with soaking liquid to a blender and process until very smooth; add milk, palm sugar, coconut flour, lemon juice, lemon zest, and vanilla and blend until well combined; add arrowroot and continue blending until mixed and pour into the crust. Smooth the top and cover the spring form pan with foil.
3. Place the pan in your air fry toaster oven and bake at 375 F for 20 minutes.
4. Carefully remove the pan from the fryer and remove the foil; let the cake cool completely and top with fruit to serve.

Nutrition: Calories 423 Fat 3.1g Carbs 33.5g Protein 1.2g

724. Air Roasted Nuts

Preparation time: 10 minutes
Cooking time: 20 minutes
Servings: 8

Ingredients:
- 1 cup raw peanuts
- 1/2 teaspoon cayenne pepper
- 3 teaspoons seafood seasoning
- 2 tablespoons olive oil
- salt

Directions:
1. Preheat your air fryer toast oven to 320 F.
2. In a bowl, whisk together cayenne pepper, olive oil, and seafood seasoning; stir in peanuts until well coated.
3. Transfer to the fryer basket and air roast for 10 minutes; toss well and then cook for another 10 minutes.
4. Transfer the peanuts to a dish and season with salt. Let cool before serving.

Nutrition: Calories 193 Fat 17.4g Carbs 4.9g Protein 7.4g

725. Air Fried White Corn

Preparation time: 10 minutes
Cooking time: 40 minutes
Servings: 8

Ingredients
- 2 cups giant white corn
- 3 tablespoons olive oil
- 1-1/2 teaspoons sea salt

Directions:
1. Soak the corn in a bowl of water for at least 8 hours or overnight; drain and spread in a single layer on a baking tray; pat dry with paper towels.
2. Preheat your air fryer toast oven to 400 F.
3. In a bowl, mix corn, olive oil and salt and toss to coat well.
4. Air fry corn in batches in the preheated air fryer toast oven for 20 minutes, shaking the basket halfway through cooking.
5. Let the corn cool for at least 20 minutes or until crisp.

Nutrition: Calories 225 Fat 7.4g Carbs 35.8g Protein 5.9g

726. Fruit Cake

Preparation time: 5 minutes
Cooking time: 45 minutes
Servings: 4-6

Ingredients:
Dry Ingredients
- 1/8 teaspoon sea salt
- 1/2 teaspoon baking powder
- 1/2 teaspoon baking soda
- 1/2 teaspoon ground cardamom
- 1-1/4 cup whole wheat flour

Wet Ingredients
- 2 tablespoons coconut oil
- 1/2 cup unsweetened nondairy milk
- 2 tablespoons ground flax seeds
- 1/4 cup agave
- 1-1/2 cups water

Mix-Ins
- 1/2 cup chopped cranberries
- 1 cup chopped pear

Directions
1. Grease a Bundt pan; set aside.
2. In a mixing, mix all dry ingredients together. In another bowl, combine together the wet ingredients; whisk the wet ingredients into the dry until smooth.
3. Fold in the add-ins and spread the mixture into the pan; cover with foil.
4. Place pan in your air fryer toast oven and add water in the bottom and bake at 370 F for 35 minutes.
5. When done, use a toothpick to check for doneness. Of it comes out clean, then the cake is ready, if not, bake for 5-10 more minutes, checking frequently to avoid burning.
6. Remove the cake and let stand for 10 minutes before transferring from the pan.
7. Enjoy!

Nutrition: Calories 309 Fat 27g Carbs 14.7g Protein 22.6g

727. Hydrated Apples

Preparation time: 5 minutes
Cooking time: 15 minutes
Servings: 6

Ingredients:
- apples, cored
- 1 teaspoon cinnamon powder
- 1/2 cup sugar
- 1 cup red wine
- 1/4 cup raisins

Directions
1. Add apples to your air fryer toast oven's pan and then add wine, cinnamon powder, sugar and raisins.
2. Hydrate for 20 minutes and remove from air fry toaster oven.
3. Serve the apples in small serving bowls drizzled with lots of cooking juices.
4. Enjoy!

Nutrition: Calories 229 Fat 0.4g Carbs 53.3g Protein 0.8g

728. Nutty Slice

Preparation time: 10 minutes
Cooking time: 30 minutes
Servings: 4

Ingredients:
- 4 cups fresh or frozen mixed berries
- 1 cup almond meal
- 1/2 cup almond butter
- 1 cup oven roasted walnuts, sunflower seeds, pistachios.
- 1/2 tsp. ground cinnamon

Directions:
1. Preheat air fryer toast oven to 375 F.
2. Crush the nuts using a mortar and pestle.
3. In a bowl, combine the nut mix, almond meal, cinnamon and ghee and combine well.
4. In a pie dish, spread half the nut mixture over the bottom of the dish, then top with the berries and finish with the rest of the nut mixture.
5. Bake for 30 minutes. Slice and serve warm with natural vanilla yogurt.
6. Yum!

Nutrition: Calories 278 Fat 15.7g Carbs 10.3g Protein 13.8g

729. Energy Brownies

Preparation time: 10 minutes
Cooking time: 35 minutes
Servings: 10
Ingredients:
- 1-1/2 cups unsweetened shredded coconut
- 1/2 cup dried cranberries
- 1/2 cup golden flax meal
- 1/2 cup coconut butter
- 1 cup hemp seeds
- A good pinch of sea salt

Directions
1. Combine the cranberries, flax, and hemp seeds in the bowl of your food processor and pulse until well-ground.
2. Add the shredded coconut, coconut butter, stevia, and salt and pulse until it forms thick dough.
3. Transfer the dough to a baking dish and bake for 10 minutes in your air fryer toast oven at 370 F, then remove from air fryer toast oven.
4. Let cool completely, then chill in the fridge to firm up. Slice it into bars and enjoy!

Nutrition: Calories 314 Fat 10.1g Carbs 19.8g Protein 7.8g

730. Air Fry Toaster Oven Bars

Preparation time: 5 minutes
Cooking time: 25 minutes
Servings: 4
Ingredients:
- 1 cup chopped chocolate
- 2 ripe avocados
- 1 tsp. raw honey
- 2 tsp. vanilla extract
- 4 eggs
- 1 cup ground almonds
- 1/2 cup cocoa powder
- 1/4 tsp. salt

Directions:
1. Prepare an 8-inch baking pan by lining it with foil and then coating with non-stick cooking spray.
2. Add chocolate to a bowl and place over a large saucepan of boiling water.
3. Stir until chocolate is melted. Remove from heat and let cool.
4. Meanwhile, prepare the batter: in a bowl, mash the avocados; add honey and stir to combine.
5. Whisk in vanilla extract and eggs until well blended. Gradually whisk in the chocolate until well incorporated.
6. Stir in ground almonds, cocoa powder, and salt until well blended.
7. Transfer the batter to the prepared baking pan and cover with a paper towel and then with aluminum foil.
8. Place the pan in your air fryer toast oven and bake at 375 F for 30 minutes or until done to desire.
9. Let cool completely before cutting into squares. These brownies are best served chilled.

Nutrition: Calories 512 Fat 12.3g Carbs 31.2g Protein 14.4g

731. Self-Saucing Banana Pudding

Preparation time: 5 minutes
Cooking time: 60 minutes
Servings: 6-8
Ingredients:
- 1 cup caster sugar
- 1 1/2 cups self-rising flour, sifted
- 1/3 cup butter, melted and cooled
- 1 tsp. vanilla extract
- 1/4 cup mashed banana
- 1 egg, lightly beaten
- 3/4 cups milk
- 1/2 cup packed brown sugar
- 1/8 tsp. nutmeg
- 1 tsp. cinnamon
- 1/2 cups boiling water
- ice cream, to serve

Directions
1. Preheat air fryer oven for 10 minutes.
2. Grease the air fryer oven pan with butter using wax paper.
3. Combine the first 7 ingredients above in a large mixing bowl; whisk until well-combined.
4. Fold into the air fryer oven pan. Sift sugar, nutmeg, and cinnamon over the pudding mix.
5. Spoon the boiling water gently and evenly over the mixture.
6. Lock lid in place and cook for 1 hour.
7. Serve hot with a scoop of ice cream on top!

Nutrition: Calories 307 Sodium 76mg Dietary Fiber 0.9g Fat 9g Carbs 54.3g Protein 4g

732. Chocolate Lava Cake

Preparation time: 5 minutes
Cooking time: 1 hour 10 minutes
Servings: 6-8
Ingredients:
- 1 box of Devil's Food Chocolate Cake mix, prepared according to box instructions
- 1 (15 oz.) can of milk chocolate frosting, divided
- Non-stick cooking spray

Directions
1. Spray the air fryer oven pan with cooking spray.
2. Add cake batter prepared as instructed on the box.
3. Spoon half of the chocolate frosting into the middle of the cake batter.
4. Cook for 1 hour.
5. Flip the air fryer oven pan upside down over a cake plate. Heat the remaining frosting in a microwave for 25 seconds, and pour over the warm cake, and serve.

Nutrition: Calories 172 Sodium 91mg Fat 7.6g Carbs 27g Protein 0.3g

733. Banana Bread

Preparation time: 5 minutes
Cooking time: 1 hour 10 minutes
Servings: 6-8
Ingredients:
- 1 1/2 cup unbleached flour
- 1/2 cup sugar or sugar substitute
- 2 tsp. baking powder
- 1/2 tsp. baking soda
- 1/2 tsp. vanilla extract

- 1/2 tsp. sea salt
- 1 cup ripe bananas, mashed
- 1/3 cup softened butter
- 1/4 cup milk
- 1 egg
- 1/4 cup walnuts chopped

Directions
1. Combine the flour, sugar, baking powder, baking soda and salt in a large mixing bowl; whisk until the ingredients are well mixed.
2. Fold in the bananas, butter, milk, egg and vanilla extract. Use an electric mixer to mix until the batter has a uniform thick consistency.
3. Fold in chopped walnuts.
4. Grease the bottom of the air fryer oven pan with non-stick cooking spray.
5. Pour batter into air fryer oven pan and cook for 1 hour. Transfer to plate and let cool for one hour before serving.

Nutrition: Calories 255 Sodium 211mg Dietary Fiber 1.4g Fat 11g Carbs 36.1g Protein 4.6g

734. Choco-Peanut Mug Cake

Preparation time: 5 minutes
Cooking time: 20 minutes
Servings: 1

Ingredients:
- 1 tsp Softened butter
- 1 Egg
- 1 tsp butter
- 1 tsp Vanilla extract
- 2 tbsps Erythritol
- 2 tbsps Unsweetened cocoa powder
- ¼ tsp Baking powder
- 1 tbsp Heavy cream

Directions
1. Preheat the air fryer for 5 minutes.
2. Combine all ingredients in a mixing bowl.
3. Pour into a greased mug.
4. Set in the air fryer basket and cook for 20 minutes at 400 F

Nutrition: Calories 293 Protein 12.4g Fat 23.3g Carbs 8.5g

735. Raspberry-Coco Desert

Preparation time: 5 minutes
Cooking time: 20 minutes
Servings: 12

Ingredients:
- 1 tsp Vanilla bean
- 1 cup Pulsed raspberries
- 1 cup Coconut milk
- 3 cups Desiccated coconut
- ¼ cup Coconut oil
- 1/3 cup Erythritol powder

Directions
1. Preheat the air fryer for 5 minutes.
2. Combine all ingredients in a mixing bowl.
3. Pour into a greased baking dish.
4. Bake in the air fryer for 20 minutes at 375 F.

Nutrition: Calories 132 Protein 1.5g Fat 9.7g Carbs 9.7g

736. Almond Cherry Bars

Preparation time: 5 minutes
Cooking time: 35 minutes
Servings: 12

Ingredients:
- 1 tbsp Xanthan gum
- 1 ½ cup Almond flour
- ½ tsp Salt
- 1 cup Pitted fresh cherries
- ½ cup Softened butter
- 2 Eggs
- ¼ cup Water
- ½ tsp Vanilla
- 1 cup Erythritol

Directions
1. Combine almond flour, softened butter, salt, vanilla, eggs, and erythritol in a large bowl until you form a dough.
2. Press the dough in a baking dish that will fit in the air fryer.
3. Set in the air fryer and bake for 10 minutes at 375 F.
4. Meanwhile, mix the cherries, water, and xanthan gum in a bowl.
5. Take the dough out and pour over the cherry mixture.
6. Cook again for 25 minutes more at 375 F in the air fryer.

Nutrition: Calories 99 Protein 1.8g Fat 9.3g Carbs 2.1g

737. Coffee Flavored Doughnuts

Preparation time: 5 minutes
Cooking time: 6 minutes
Servings: 6

Ingredients:
- 1 tsp Baking powder
- ½ tsp Salt
- 1 tbsp Sunflower oil
- ¼ cup Coffee
- ¼ cup Coconut sugar
- 1 cup White all-purpose flour
- 2 tbsps Aquafaba

Directions
1. Combine sugar, flour, baking powder, salt in a mixing bowl.
2. In another bowl, combine the aquafaba, sunflower oil, and coffee.
3. Mix to form a dough.
4. Let the dough rest inside the fridge.
5. Preheat the air fryer to 400 F.
6. Knead the dough and create doughnuts.
7. Arrange inside the air fryer in single layer and cook for 6 minutes.
8. Do not shake so that the donut maintains its shape.

Nutrition: Calories 113 Protein 21.6g Fat 2.54g Carbs 20.45g

738. Simple Strawberry Cobbler

Preparation time: 10 minutes
Cooking time: 25 minutes
Servings: 4

Ingredients:
- ¼ cup Heavy whipping cream
- 1 ½ tsps Cornstarch
- 1 ½ tsps White sugar
- ½ cup Water
- ¼ tsp Salt

- 2tsps Butter
- 1 ½ cup Hulled strawberries
- 1 ½ tsps White sugar
- 1 tbsp Diced butter
- 1 tbsp Butter
- ½ cup All-purpose flour
- ¾ tsp Baking powder

Directions
1. Lightly grease baking pan of air fryer with cooking spray. Add water, cornstarch, and sugar. Cook for 10 minutes 390 F or until hot and thick. Add strawberries and mix well. Dot tops with 1 tablespoon butter.
2. In a bowl, mix well salt, baking powder, sugar, and flour. Cut in 2 teaspoons butter. Mix in cream. Spoon on top of berries.
3. Cook for 15 minutes at 390 F, until tops are lightly browned.
4. Serve and enjoy.

Nutrition: Calories 255 Protein 2.4g Fat 13g Carbs 32g

739. Easy Pumpkin Pie

Preparation time: 5 minutes
Cooking time: 35 minutes
Servings: 8

Ingredients:
- 2 Egg yolks
- 1 Large egg
- ½ tsp. Ground ginger
- ½ tsp Fine salt
- 1/8 tsp Chinese 5-spice powder
- 1 9-inch Unbaked pie crust
- ¼ tsp Freshly grated nutmeg
- 14oz Sweetened condensed milk
- 15oz Pumpkin puree
- 1 tsp Ground cinnamon

Directions
1. Lightly grease baking pan of air fryer with cooking spray. Press pie crust on bottom of pan, stretching all the way up to the sides of the pan. Pierce all over with fork.
2. In blender, blend well egg, egg yolks, and pumpkin puree. Add Chinese 5-spice powder, nutmeg, salt, ginger, cinnamon, and condensed milk. Pour on top of pie crust.
3. Cover pan with foil.
4. For 15 minutes, cook on preheated 390 F air fryer.
5. Cook for 20 more minutes at 330 F without the foil until middle is set.
6. Allow to cool in air fryer completely.
7. Serve and enjoy.

Nutrition: Calories 326 Protein 7.6g Fat 14.2g Carbs 41.9g

740. Simple Cheesecake

Preparation time: 10 minutes
Cooking time: 19 minutes
Servings: 5

Ingredients:
- 1 cup Crumbled graham crackers
- ½ tsp. Vanilla extract
- 4tbsps. Sugar
- 2 tbsps. Butter
- 1 lb. Cream cheese
- 2 Eggs

Directions
1. Mix crackers with the butter in a bowl.
2. Press crackers mixture on the bottom of a lined cake pan.
3. Transfer to the air fryer to cook at 350 F for 4 minutes.
4. Meanwhile, in a bowl, mix eggs, cream cheese, sugar and vanilla, and whisk well.
5. Spread filling over crackers crust and cook in the air fryer at 310 F for 15 minutes.
6. Cool and keep in the refrigerator for 3 hours.
7. Slice and serve.

Nutrition: Calories 245 Protein 3g Fat 12g Carbs 20g

741. Strawberry Donuts

Preparation time: 10 minutes
Cooking time: 15 minutes
Servings: 4

Ingredients:
- 4oz Whole milk
- 1 Egg
- 1 tsp. Baking powder
- 1 tbsp. Brown sugar
- 1 tbsp. White sugar
- 8oz. Flour
- ½ tbsps. Butter
- For the strawberry icing:
- 1 tbsp Whipped cream
- ½ tsp Pink coloring
- 2tbsps Butter
- ¼ cup Chopped strawberries

Directions
1. In a bowl, mix flour, 1 tbsp. white sugar, 1 tbsp. brown sugar and butter, and stir.
2. Stir together the egg with milk, and 1 ½ tbsp. butter in another bowl.
3. Combine the 2 mixtures, stir, then shape donuts from this mix.
4. Cook the doughnuts in the air fryer at 3600 F for 15 minutes.
5. Mix strawberry puree, whipped cream, food coloring, icing sugar and 1 tbsp. butter, and whisk well.
6. Arrange donuts on a platter and serve with strawberry icing on top.

Nutrition: Calories 250 Protein 4g Fat 12g Carbs 32g

742. Apricot Blackberry Crumble

Preparation time: 10 minutes
Cooking time: 20 minutes
Servings: 8

Ingredients:
- 1 cup Flour
- 2tbsps Lemon juice
- 2oz Cubed and deseeded fresh apricots
- ½ cup Sugar
- 2tbsps. Cold butter
- 5.5 oz Fresh blackberries
- Salt.

Directions
1. Put the apricots and blackberries in a bowl. Add lemon juice and 2 tablespoons of sugar. Mix until combined. Transfer the mixture to a baking dish.
2. Mix flour, the rest of the sugar, and a pinch of salt in a bowl.
3. Add a tablespoon of cold butter. Combine the mixture until it becomes crumbly. Put this on top of the fruit mixture and press it down lightly.

4. Move the baking dish in the cooking basket. Cook for 20 minutes at 390 F.
5. Allow to cool before slicing and serving.

Nutrition: Calories 217 Protein 2.3g Fat 7.44g Carbs 36.2g

743. Ginger Cheesecake

Preparation time: 2 hours 10 minutes
Cooking time: 20 minutes
Servings: 6

Ingredients:
- ½ tsp. Ground nutmeg
- oz. Soft cream cheese
- 1 tsp. Rum
- ½ cup Crumbled ginger cookies
- ½ tsp. Vanilla extract
- tsps. Melted butter
- Eggs
- ½ cup Sugar

Directions
1. Grease a pan with butter and spread cookie crumbs on the bottom.
2. In a bowl, beat cream cheese, eggs, rum, vanilla and nutmeg. Whisk well and spread over the cookie crumbs.
3. Place in the air fryer and cook at 340 F for 20 minutes.
4. Cool and keep in the refrigerator.
5. Slice and serve.

Nutrition: Calories 412 Protein 6g Fat 12g Carbs 20g

744. Coconut Donuts

Preparation Time: 5 minutes
Cooking time: 15 minutes
Servings: 4

Ingredients:
- 8ounces coconut flour
- 1 egg, whisked
- 2and ½ tablespoons butter, melted
- 4ounces coconut milk
- 1 teaspoon baking powder

Directions
1. In a bowl, put all of the ingredients and mix well.
2. Shape donuts from this mix, place them in your air fryer's basket and cook at 370 F for 15 minutes.
3. Serve warm.

Nutrition: Calories 190 Protein 6g Fat 12g Carbs 4g

745. Blueberry Cream

Preparation Time: 4 minutes
Cooking time: 20 minutes
Servings: 6

Ingredients:
- 2cups blueberries
- Juice of ½ lemon
- 2tablespoons water
- 1 teaspoon vanilla extract
- 2tablespoons swerve

Directions
1. In a large bowl, put all ingredients and mix well.
2. Divide this into 6 ramekins, put them in the air fryer and cook at 340 F for 20 minutes
3. Cool down and serve.

Nutrition: Calories 123 Protein 3g Fat 2g Carbs 4g

746. Blackberry Chia Jam

Preparation Time: 10 minutes
Cooking time: 30 minutes
Servings: 12

Ingredients:
- 3cups blackberries
- ¼ cup swerve
- 4tablespoonslemon juice
- 4tablespoonschia seeds

Directions
1. In a pan that suits the air fryer, combine all the ingredients and toss.
2. Put the pan in the fryer and cook at 300 F for 30 minutes.
3. Divide into cups and serve cold.

Nutrition: Calories 100 Protein 1g Fat 2g Carbs 3g

747. Mixed Berries Cream

Preparation Time: 5 minutes
Cooking time: 30 minutes
Servings: 6

Ingredients:
- 12ounces blackberries
- 6ounces raspberries
- 12ounces blueberries
- ¾ cup swerve
- 2ounces coconut cream

Directions
1. In a bowl, put all the ingredients and mix well.
2. Divide this into 6 ramekins, put them in your air fryer and cook at 320 F for 30 minutes.
3. Cool down and serve it.

Nutrition: Calories 100 Protein 2g Fat 1g Carbs 2g

748. Cinnamon-Spiced Acorn Squash

Preparation Time: 5 minutes
Cooking time: 15 minutes
Servings: 2

Ingredients:
- 1 medium acorn squash, halved crosswise and deseeded
- 1 teaspoon coconut oil
- 1 teaspoon light brown sugar
- Few dashes of ground cinnamon
- Few dashes of ground nutmeg

Directions
1. On a clean work surface, rub the cut sides of the acorn squash with coconut oil. Scatter with the brown sugar, cinnamon, and nutmeg.
2. Put the squash halves in the air fryer basket, cut-side up.
3. Put in the air fryer basket and cook at 325 F for 15 minutes.
4. When cooking is complete, the squash halves should be just tender when pierced in the center with a paring knife. Remove from the oven. Rest for 5 to 10 minutes and serve warm.

Nutrition: Calories 172 Protein 3.9g Fat 9.8g Carbs 17.5g

749. Pear Sauce

Preparation Time: 10 minutes
Cooking time: 15 minutes
Servings: 6
Ingredients:
- 10 pears, sliced
- 1 cup apple juice
- 1 1/2 tsp cinnamon
- 1/4 tsp nutmeg

Directions:
1. Put all of the ingredients in the air fryer and stir well.
2. Seal pot and cook on high for 15 minutes.
3. Once done, allow to release pressure naturally for 10 minutes then release remaining using quick release. Remove lid.
4. Blend the pear mixture using an immersion blender until smooth.
5. Serve and enjoy.

Nutrition: Calories 222 Protein 1.3g Fat 0.6g Carbs 58.2g

750. Brownie Muffins

Preparation Time: 10 minutes
Cooking time: 10 minutes
Servings: 12
Ingredients:
- 1 package Betty Crocker fudge brownie mix
- ¼ cup walnuts, chopped
- 1 egg
- 1/3 cup vegetable oil
- 2 teaspoons water

Directions:
1. Grease 12 muffin molds. Set aside.
2. In a bowl, put all ingredients together.
3. Place the mixture into the prepared muffin molds.
4. Press "Power Button" of Air Fry Oven and turn the dial to select the "Air Fry" mode.
5. Press the Time button and again turn the dial to set the cooking time to 10 minutes.
6. Now push the Temp button and rotate the dial to set the temperature at 300 F.
7. Press the "Start/Pause" button to start.
8. When the unit beeps to show that it is preheated, open the lid.
9. Arrange the muffin molds in "Air Fry Basket" and insert them in the oven.
10. Place the muffin molds onto a wire rack to cool for about 10 minutes.
11. Carefully, invert the muffins onto the wire rack to completely cool before serving.

Nutrition: Calories 168 Protein 2g Fat 8.9g Carbs 20.8g

751. Chocolate Mug Cake

Preparation Time: 7 minutes
Cooking time: 13 minutes
Servings: 3
Ingredients:
- ½ cup of cocoa powder
- ½ cup stevia powder
- 1 cup coconut cream
- 1 package cream cheese, room temperature
- 1 tbsp. vanilla extract
- 1 tbsp. butter

Directions:
1. Preheat the Smart Air Fryer Oven for 5 minutes at 350 F.
2. In a mixing bowl, combine all the listed ingredients using a hand mixer until fluffy.
3. Pour into greased mugs.
4. Place the mugs in the fryer basket and bake for 13 minutes at 350 F.
5. Serve when cool.

Nutrition: Calories 100 Protein 3g Carbs 21g

752. Warm Peach Compote

Preparation Time: 10 minutes
Cooking Time: 1 minute
Servings: 4
Ingredients:
1. 4 peaches, peeled and chopped
2. 1 tbsp. water
3. 1/2 tbsp. cornstarch
4. 1 tsp vanilla

Directions:
- Add water, vanilla, and peaches into the air fryer basket.
- Seal pot and cook on high for 1 minute.
- Once done, allow to release pressure naturally. Remove lid.
- In a small bowl, whisk together 1 tablespoon of water and cornstarch and pour into the pot and stir well.
- Serve and enjoy.

Nutrition: Calories – 66 Protein – 1.4 g. Fat – 0.4 g. Carbs – 15 g.

753. Chocolate Cake

Preparation Time: 6 minutes
Cooking time: 35 minutes
Servings: 9
Ingredients:
- ½ cups hot water
- 1 tsp. vanilla
- ¼ cups olive oil
- ½ cups almond milk
- 1 egg
- ½ tsp. Salt
- ¾ tsp. Baking soda
- ¾ tsp. baking powder
- ½ cups unsweetened cocoa powder
- 2 cups almond flour
- 1 cup brown sugar

Directions:
1. Preheat your Smart Air Fryer Oven to 356 F.
2. Stir all dry ingredients together and then stir in wet ingredients.
3. Add hot water last.
4. The batter should be thin.
5. Pour cake batter into a pan that fits into the fryer.
6. Bake for 35 minutes.

Nutrition: Calories 378 Protein 4g Fat 9g Carbs 5g

DESSERT

754. Chocolate Chip Air Fryer Cookies

Preparation Time: 10 minutes
Cooking time: 16 minutes
Servings: 3
Ingredients
- 75g Self Raising Flour
- 100g Butter
- 75g Brown Sugar
- 75g Milk Chocolate
- 30 milliliters Honey
- 30 milliliters Whole Milk

Directions:
1. Beat the butter until smooth and fluffy. Add the butter to the sugar and beat together in a smooth mixture. Now add and mix in the milk, sugar, chocolate (broken into small chunks/chips), and flour. Preheat your air fryer to 360 F. Shape the mixture into cookie shapes and put them on a baking sheet that will sit 16 minutes or until cooked through in the air fryer Bake.

Nutrition: Calories 515 Protein 4g Fat 9g Carbs 5g

755. Doughnuts

Preparation Time: 35 minutes
Cooking time: 60 minutes
Servings: 8
Ingredients
- 1/4 cup warm water, warmed (100 F to 110 F)
- 1 tablespoon active yeast
- 1/4 cup, plus half tsp. Granulated Sugar, divided
- 2 cups (about 8 1/2 oz.) all-purpose flour
- 1/4 teaspoon kosher salt
- 1/4 cup whole milk, at room temperature
- 2 tablespoons unsalted butter, melted
- 1 large egg, beaten
- 1 cup (about 4 oz.) powdered sugar
- 4 teaspoons tap water

Directions:
1. Mix water, yeast, and 1/2 teaspoon of the granulated sugar in a small bowl; let stand until foamy, around five minutes. Combine flour, salt, and remaining 1/4 cup granulated sugar in a medium bowl. Add yeast mixture, milk, butter, and egg; stir it with a wooden spoon until a soft dough comes together. Turn dough out onto a lightly floured surface and knead until smooth, 1 to 2 minutes. Switch dough to a lightly greased tub. Cover and let rise in a warm place until doubled in volume, around 1 hour.
2. Turn dough out onto a lightly floured surface. Gently roll to 1/4-inch thickness. Cut out eight doughnuts using a 3-inch round cutter and a 1-inch round cutter to delete core: place doughnuts and doughnuts holes on a lightly floured surface. Cover loosely with plastic wrap and let stand for about 30 minutes, until doubled in volume.
3. Place two doughnuts and two doughnuts holes in a single layer in an air fryer pan, and cook at 350 F until golden brown, 4 to 5 minutes. Continue with doughnuts and holes remaining on.
4. Whisk powdered sugar together and tap water until smooth in a medium bowl. In a glaze, dip doughnuts and doughnut holes, place them on a wire rack set above a rimmed baking sheet to allow excess glaze to drip off. Let stand for about 10 minutes, until the glaze hardens.

Nutrition: Calories 378 Protein 4g Fat 9g Carbs 5g

756. Cherry-Choco Bars

Preparation Time: 7 minutes
Cooking time: 15 minutes
Servings: 8
Ingredients:
- ¼ tsp. salt
- ½ cup almonds, sliced
- ½ cup chia seeds
- ½ cup dark chocolate, chopped
- ½ cup dried cherries, chopped
- ½ cup prunes, pureed
- ½ cup quinoa, cooked
- ¾ cup almond butter
- 1/3 cup honey
- 2 cups oats
- 2 tbsp. coconut oil

Directions:
1. Preheat the Air Fryer Oven to 375 F.
2. In a bowl, combine the oats, quinoa, chia seeds, almond, cherries, and chocolate.
3. In a saucepan, heat the almond butter, honey, and coconut oil.
4. Pour the butter mixture over the dry mix, then add salt and prunes and mix until well combined.
5. Pour over a baking dish that can fit inside the air fryer.
6. Bake for 15 minutes.
7. Let it cool before slicing into bars.

Nutrition: Calories 378 Protein 4g Fat 9g Carbs 5g

757. Crusty Apple Hand Pies

Preparation Time: 7 minutes
Cooking time: 8 minutes
Servings: 6
Ingredients:
- 15-oz. no-sugar-added apple pie filling
- 1 store-bought crust

Directions:
1. Lay out pie crust and slice into equal-sized squares.
2. Place 2 tbsp. filling into each square and seal crust with a fork.
3. Pour into the Oven rack/basket.
4. Place the Rack on the middle-shelf of the Smart Air Fryer Oven.
5. Set temperature to 390 F and set time to 8 minutes until golden in color.

Nutrition: Calories 378 Protein 4g Fat 9g Carbs 5g

758. Pancakes Nutella-Stuffed

Preparation Time: 15 minutes
Cooking time: 20 minutes
Servings: 12
Ingredients
- 4 teaspoons of chocolate-hazelnut spread, such as Nutella ®, at room temperature
- 1/4 cup vegetable oil, plus
- 1/4 cup grid all-purpose flour
- 1 1/4 cup buttermilk
- 1/4 cup of granulated sugar
- 1 teaspoon baking soda
- 1 teaspoon baking soda
- 1 egg

- A pinch of salt
- Sugar for dusting
- Maple syrup for serving

Directions:
1. Line a parchment baking sheet and drop 12 different teaspoonful mounds of chocolate-hazelnut spread over it. Place the baking sheet on a counter to flatten the dollops and freeze for about 15 minutes until firm.
2. In the meantime, preheat a griddle over low heat and brush with oil lightly.
3. In a large bowl, whisk together the flour, buttermilk, oil, granulated sugar, baking powder, baking soda, egg, and a pinch of salt until smooth.
4. Pour batter pools on the hot griddle and cook until bubbles just start forming on the pancake's surface and the bottoms are golden, 1 to 2 minutes. Place a frozen chocolate-hazelnut dish spread on 4 of the pancakes and flip the remaining four pancakes on top of those, so the wet batter envelopes the disks. Put the rest of the discs back into the freezer. Continue cooking the pancakes for about 1 minute, flipping halfway, until the edges are set. Repeat with the remaining batters and disks, oiling the grid lightly in between lots.
5. Stub the pancakes with the sugar of the confectioners and serve warmly with syrup.

Nutrition: Calories 151 Protein 4g Fat 9g Carbs 5g

759. Spiced Pear Sauce

Preparation Time: 10 minutes
Cooking time: 6 hours
Servings: 12

Ingredients:
- `8 pears, cored and diced
- `1/2 tsp ground cinnamon
- `1/4 tsp ground nutmeg
- `1/4 tsp ground cardamom
- `1 cup of water

Directions:
1. Put all of the ingredients in the air fryer and stir well.
2. Seal the pot with a lid and select slow cook mode and cook on low for 6 hours.
3. Mash the sauce using a potato masher.
4. Pour into the container and store.

Nutrition: Calories 81 Protein 0.5g Fat 0.2g Carbs 21.4g

760. Saucy Fried Bananas

Preparation Time: 7 minutes
Cooking time: 10 minutes
Servings: 2

Ingredients:
- `1 large egg
- ¼ cup cornstarch
- ¼ cup plain breadcrumbs
- `2 bananas, halved crosswise
- `Cooking oil
- `Chocolate sauce

Directions:
1. Preheat your Air fryer oven to 350 F.
2. In a small bowl, beat the egg.
3. In another bowl, place the cornstarch.
4. Place the breadcrumbs in a different bowl.
5. Dip the bananas in the cornstarch, then the egg, and then the breadcrumbs.
6. Spray the basket with cooking oil. Place the bananas in the basket and spray them with cooking oil.
7. Cook for 5 minutes.
8. Open the air fryer and flip the bananas then cook for an additional 2 minutes.
9. Transfer the bananas to plates.
10. Drizzle the chocolate sauce over the bananas and serve.

Nutrition: Calories 378 Protein 4g Fat 9g Carbs 5g

761. Easy cheesecake

Preparation time: 10 minutes
cooking time: 19 minutes
servings: 15

Ingredients:
- `1 lb. Cream cheese
- `1/2 tsp. Vanilla extract
- `1 cup graham crackers, crumbled
- `2 tbsp. Butter
- `2 eggs
- `4 tbsp. Sugar

Directions:
1. In a bowl mix crackers with butter.
2. Press crackers mix on the bottom of a lined cake pan, introduce in your air fryer and cook at 350 °f, for 4 minutes
3. Meanwhile in a bowl, mix sugar with cream cheese, eggs and vanilla and whisk well.
4. Spread filling over crackers crust and cook your cheesecake in your air fryer at 310 °f for 15 minutes.
5. Leave cake in the fridge for 3 hours, slice and serve

Nutrition: Calories 245 fats: 12 g carbs 20 g proteins 3 g

762. Macaroons

Preparation time: 10 minutes
cooking time: 8 minutes
servings: 20

Ingredients:
- `2 tbsp. Sugar
- `2 cup coconut, shredded
- `4 egg whites
- `1 tsp. Vanilla extract

Directions:
1. In a bowl mix egg whites with stevia and beat using your mixer
2. Add coconut and vanilla extract, whisk again, shape small balls out of this mix, introduce them in your air fryer and cook at 340 °f for 8 minutes.
3. Serve macaroons cold

Nutrition: Calories 55 fats: 6 g carbs 2 g proteins 1 g

763. Orange cake

Preparation time: 10 minutes
cooking time: 16 minutes
servings: 12

Ingredients:
- `1 orange, peeled and cut into quarters
- `1 tsp. Vanilla extract
- `6 eggs
- `2 tbsp. Orange zest
- `4 oz. Cream cheese
- `1 tsp. Baking powder

- `9 oz. Flour
- `2 oz. Sugar+ 2 tbsp.
- `4 oz. Yogurt

Directions:
1. In your food processor, pulse orange very well
2. Add flour, 2 tbsp. Sugar, eggs, baking powder, vanilla extract and pulse well again.
3. Transfer this into 2 spring form pans, introduce each in your fryer and cook at 330 °f, for 16 minutes
4. Meanwhile in a bowl, mix cream cheese with orange zest, yogurt and the rest of the sugar and stir well.
5. Place one cake layer on a plate, add half of the cream cheese mix, add the other cake layer and top with the rest of the cream cheese mix.
6. Spread it well, slice and serve.

Nutrition: Calories 200 fats: 13 g carbs 9 g proteins 8 g

764. Bread dough and amaretto

Preparation time: 7 minutes
cooking time: 8 minutes
servings: 12

Ingredients:
- `1 lb. Bread dough
- `1 cup heavy cream
- `12 oz. Chocolate chips
- `1 cup sugar
- `1/2 cup butter, melted
- `2 tbsp. Amaretto liqueur

Directions:
1. Roll dough, cut into 20 slices and then cut each slice in halves.
2. Brush dough pieces with butter, sprinkle sugar, place them in your air fryer's basket after you've brushed it some butter, cook them at 350 °f for 5 minutes flip them, cook for 3 minutes more and transfer to a platter
3. Heat up a pan with the heavy cream over medium heat, add chocolate chips and stir until they melt. Add liqueur stir again.
4. Transfer to a bowl and serve bread dippers with this sauce

Nutrition: Calories 200 fats: 1 g carbs 6 g proteins 6 g

765. Carrot cake

Preparation time: 10 minutes
cooking time: 45 minutes
servings: 6

Ingredients:
- `5 oz. Flour
- `3/4 tsp. Baking powder
- `1/4 tsp. Nutmeg
- `ground
- `1/2 tsp. Baking soda
- `1/2 tsp. Cinnamon powder
- `1/2 cup sugar
- `1/3 cup carrots, grated
- `1/3 cup pecans, toasted and chopped.
- `1/4 cup pineapple juice
- `1/2 tsp. Allspice
- `1 egg
- `3 tbsp. Yogurt
- `4 tbsp. Sunflower oil
- `1/3 cup coconut flakes; shredded
- `Cooking spray

Directions:
1. In a bowl mix flour with baking soda and powder, salt, allspice, cinnamon and nutmeg and stir.
2. In another bowl, mix egg with yogurt, sugar, pineapple juice, oil, carrots, pecans and coconut flakes and stir well
3. Combine the two mixtures and stir well, pour this into a spring form pan that fits your air fryer which you've greased with some cooking spray, transfer to your air fryer and cook on 320 °f for 45 minutes.
4. Leave cake to cool down, then cut and serve it.

Nutrition: Calories 200 fats: 6 g carbs, 22 g proteins 4 g

766. Sweet Peach Jam

Preparation Time: 10 minutes
Cooking Time: 16 minutes
Servings: 20

Ingredients:
1. 1 1/2 lb fresh peaches, pitted and chopped
2. 1/2 tbsp. vanilla
3. 1/4 cup maple syrup

Directions:
- Put all of the ingredients in the air fryer and stir well.
- Seal pot and cook on high for 1 minute.
- Once done, allow to release pressure naturally. Remove lid.
- Set pot on sauté mode and cook for 15 minutes or until jam thickened.
- Pour into the container and store it in the fridge.

Nutrition: Calories – 16 Protein – 0.1 g. Fat – 0 g. Carbs – 3.7 g.

767. Easy granola

Preparation time: 20 minutes
cooking time: 25 minutes
servings: 4

Ingredients:
- `1 cup coconut, shredded
- `1/2 cup almonds
- `1/2 cup pecans, chopped.
- `2 tbsp. Sugar
- `1/2 cup pumpkin seeds
- `1/2 cup sunflower seeds
- `2 tbsp. Sunflower oil
- `1 tsp. Nutmeg
- `ground
- `1 tsp. Apple pie spice mix

Directions:
1. In a bowl mix almonds and pecans with pumpkin seeds, sunflower seeds, coconut, nutmeg and apple pie spice mix and stir well
2. Heat up a pan with the oil over medium heat, add sugar and stir well.
3. Pour this over nuts and coconut mix and stir well
4. Spread this on a lined baking sheet that fits your air fryer, introduce in your air fryer and cook at 300 °f and bake for 25 minutes.
5. Leave your granola to cool down, cut and serve.

Nutrition: Calories 322 fats: 7 g carbs 12 g proteins 7 g

768. Pears and espresso cream

Preparation time: 10 minutes
cooking time: 30 minutes
servings: 4

Ingredients:
- `4 pears, halved and cored
- `2 tbsp. Water
- `2 tbsp. Lemon juice
- `1 tbsp. Sugar
- `2 tbsp. Butter
- `For the cream:
- `1 cup whipping cream
- `2 tbsp. Espresso, cold
- `1 cup mascarpone
- `1/3 cup sugar

Directions:
1. In a bowl mix pears halves with lemon juice, 1 tbsp. Sugar, butter and water, toss well, transfer them to your air fryer and cook at 360 °f for 30 minutes
2. Meanwhile in a bowl, mix whipping cream with mascarpone, ⅓ cup sugar and espresso, whisk really well and keep in the fridge until pears are done.
3. Divide pears on plates, top with espresso cream and serve them

Nutrition: Calories 211 fats: 5 g carbs 8 g proteins 7 g

769. Vanilla Apple Compote

Preparation Time: 10 minutes
Cooking Time: 15 minutes
Servings: 6

Ingredients:
- 3 cups apples, cored and cubed
- 1 tsp vanilla
- 3/4 cup coconut sugar
- 1 cup of water
- 2 tbsp. fresh lime juice

Directions:
Put all of the ingredients in the inner pot of air fryer and stir well.
Seal pot and cook on high for 15 minutes.
As soon as the cooking is done, let it release pressure naturally for 10 minutes then release remaining using quick release. Remove lid.
Stir and serve.

Nutrition: Calories – 76 Protein – 0.5 g. Fat – 0.2 g. Carbs – 19.1 g

770. Raisins Cinnamon Peaches

Preparation Time: 10 minutes
Cooking Time: 15 minutes
Servings: 4

Ingredients:
- 4 peaches, cored and cut into chunks
- 1 tsp vanilla
- 1 tsp cinnamon
- 1/2 cup raisins
- 1 cup of water

Directions:
1. Put all of the ingredients in the inner pot of air fryer and stir well.
2. Seal pot and cook on high for 15 minutes.
3. As soon as the cooking is done, let it release pressure naturally for 10 minutes then release remaining using quick release. Remove lid.
4. Stir and serve.

Nutrition: Calories – 118 Protein – 2 g. Fat – 0.5 g. Carbs – 29 g.

771. Air Fried Butter Cake

Preparation Time: 10 minutes
Cooking Time: 15 minutes
Servings: 4

Ingredients:
- 7 Tablespoons of butter, at ambient temperature
- White sugar: ¼ cup plus 2 tablespoons
- All-purpose flour: 1 ⅔ cups
- Salt: 1 pinch or to taste
- Milk: 6 tablespoons

Directions:
1. Preheat an air fryer to 350 F (180 C). Spray the cooking spray on a tiny fluted tube pan.
2. Take a large bowl and add ¼ cup butter and 2 tablespoons of sugar in it.
3. Take an electric mixer to beat the sugar and butter until smooth and fluffy. Stir in salt and flour. Stir in the milk and thoroughly combine batter. Move batter to the prepared saucepan; use a spoon back to level the surface.
4. Place the pan inside the basket of the air fryer. Set the timer within 15 minutes. Bake the batter until a toothpick comes out clean when inserted into the cake.
5. Turn the cake out of the saucepan and allow it to cool for about five minutes.

Nutrition: Calories – 470 Protein – 7.9 g. Fat – 22.4 g. Carbs – 59.7 g.

772. Dried Raspberries

Preparation Time: 10 minutes
Cooking Time: 15 hours
Servings: 4

Ingredients:
- 4 cups raspberries, wash and dry
- 1/4 cup fresh lemon juice

Directions:
1. Add raspberries and lemon juice in a bowl and toss well.
2. Arrange raspberries on air fryer oven tray and dehydrate at 135 F for 12-15 hours.
3. Store in an air-tight container.

Nutrition: Calories – 68 Protein – 1.6 g. Fat – 0.9 g. Carbs – 15 g.

773. Fried peaches

Preparation time: 2 hours 10 minutes
cooking time: 15 minutes
Servings: 4

Ingredients
- `4 ripe peaches (1/2 a peach = 1 serving)
- `1 1/2 cups flour
- `Salt
- `2 egg yolks
- `3/4 cups cold water
- `1 1/2 tablespoons olive oil
- `2 tablespoons brandy
- `4 egg whites
- `Cinnamon/sugar mix

Directions:
1. Mix flour, egg yolks, and salt in a mixing bowl. Slowly mix in water, then add brandy. Set the mixture aside for 2 hours and go do something for 1 hour 45 minutes.
2. Boil a large pot of water and cut and x at the bottom of each peach. While the water boils fill another large bowl with water and ice. Boil each peach for about a minute, then plunge it in the ice bath. Now the peels should basically fall off the peach. Beat the egg whites and mix into the batter mix. Dip each peach in the mix to coat.
3. Pour the coated peach into the oven rack/basket. Place the rack on the middle-shelf of the air fryer oven. Set temperature to 360°f, and set time to 10 minutes.
4. Prepare a plate with cinnamon/sugar mix, roll peaches in mix and serve.

Nutrition: calories: 306 Fat:3g protein:10g fiber:2.7g

774. Air Fryer Oreo Cookies

Preparation Time: 5 minutes
Cooking Time: 5 minutes
Servings: 9

Ingredients:
- Pancake Mix: ½ cup
- Water: ½ cup
- Cooking spray
- Chocolate sandwich cookies: 9 (e.g. Oreo)
- Confectioners' sugar: 1 tablespoon, or to taste

Directions:
1. Blend the pancake mixture with the water until well mixed.
2. Line the parchment paper on the basket of an air fryer. Spray nonstick cooking spray on parchment paper. Dip each cookie into the mixture of the pancake and place it in the basket. Make sure they do not touch; if possible, cook in batches.
3. The air fryer is preheated to 400 degrees F (200 degrees C). Add basket and cook for 4 to 5 minutes; flip until golden brown, 2 to 3 more minutes. Sprinkle the sugar over the cookies and serve.

Nutrition: Calories – 77 Protein – 1.2 g. Fat – 2.1 g. Carbs – 13.7 g.

775. Peanut Butter Cookies

Preparation Time: 2 minutes
Cooking Time: 5 minutes
Servings: 10

Ingredients:
- Peanut Butter: 1 cup
- Sugar: 1 cup
- 1 Egg

Directions:
1. Blend all of the ingredients with a hand mixer.
2. Spray trays of air fryer with canola oil. (Alternatively, parchment paper can also be used, but it will take longer to cook your cookies)
3. Set the air fryer temperature to 350 degrees and preheat it.
4. Place rounded dough balls onto air fryer trays. Press down softly with the back of a fork.
5. Place air fryer tray in your air fryer in the middle place. Cook for five minutes.
6. Use milk to serve with cookies.

Nutrition: Calories – 236 Protein – 6 g. Fat – 13 g. Carbs – 26 g.

776. Grilled Peaches

Preparation Time: 10 minutes
Cooking Time: 10 minutes
Servings: 2

Ingredients:
- 2 peaches, cut into wedges and remove pits
- ¼ cup butter, diced into pieces
- ¼ cup brown sugar
- ¼ cup graham cracker crumbs

Directions:
1. Arrange peach wedges on air fryer oven rack and air fry at 350 F for 5 minutes.
2. In a bowl, put the butter, graham cracker crumbs, and brown sugar together.
3. Turn peaches skin side down.
4. Spoon butter mixture over top of peaches and air fry for 5 minutes more.
5. Top with whipped cream and serve.

Nutrition: Calories – 378 Protein – 2.3 g. Fat – 24.4 g. Carbs – 40.5 g.

777. Honey Fruit Compote

Preparation Time: 10 minutes
Cooking Time: 3 minutes
Servings: 4

Ingredients:
1. 1/3 cup honey
2. 1 1/2 cups blueberries
3. 1 1/2 cups raspberries

Directions:
- Put all of the ingredients in the air fryer basket and stir well.
- Seal pot with lid and cook on high for 3 minutes.
- Once done, allow to release pressure naturally. Remove lid.
- Serve and enjoy.

Nutrition: Calories – 141 Protein – 1 g. Fat – 0.5 g. Carbs – 36.7 g.

778. Lemon Pear Compote

Preparation Time: 10 minutes
Cooking Time: 15 minutes
Servings: 6

Ingredients:
1. 3 cups pears, cored and cut into chunks
2. 1 tsp vanilla
3. 1 tsp liquid stevia
4. 1 tbsp. lemon zest, grated
5. 2 tbsp. lemon juice

Directions:
- Put all of the ingredients in the inner pot of air fryer and stir well.
- Seal pot and cook on high for 15 minutes.
- As soon as the cooking is done, let it release pressure naturally for 10 minutes then release remaining using quick release. Remove lid.
- Stir and serve.

Nutrition: Calories – 50 Protein – 0.4 g. Fat – 0.2 g. Carbs – 12.7 g.

779. Simple & Delicious Spiced Apples

Preparation Time: 10 minutes
Cooking Time: 10 minutes
Servings: 4
Ingredients:
- 4 apples, sliced
- 1 tsp apple pie spice
- 2 tbsp. sugar
- 2 tbsp. ghee, melted

Directions:
1. Add apple slices into the mixing bowl.
2. Add remaining ingredients on top of apple slices and toss until well coated.
3. Transfer apple slices on air fryer oven pan and air fry at 350 F for 10 minutes.
4. Top with ice cream and serve.

Nutrition: Calories – 196 Protein – 0.6 g. Fat – 6.8 g. Carbs – 37.1

780. Cinnamon Pear Jam

Preparation Time: 10 minutes
Cooking Time: 4 minutes
Servings: 12
Ingredients:
1. 8 pears, cored and cut into quarters
2. 1 tsp cinnamon
3. 1/4 cup apple juice
4. 2 apples, peeled, cored and diced

Directions:
- Put all of the ingredients in the inner pot of air fryer and stir well.
- Seal pot and cook on high for 4 minutes.
- As soon as the cooking is done, let it release pressure naturally. Remove lid.
- Blend pear apple mixture using an immersion blender until smooth.
- Serve and enjoy.

Nutrition: Calories – 103 Protein – 0.6 g. Fat – 0.3 g. Carbs – 27.1 g.

781. Fried bananas with chocolate sauce

Preparation time: 10 minutes
cooking time: 10 minutes
Servings: 2
Ingredients
- `1 large egg
- `¼ cup cornstarch
- `¼ cup plain bread crumbs
- `3 bananas, halved crosswise
- `Cooking oil
- `Chocolate sauce (see ingredient tip)

Directions:
1. In a small bowl, beat the egg. In another bowl, place the cornstarch. Place the bread crumbs in a third bowl. Dip the bananas in the cornstarch, then the egg
2. and then the bread crumbs.
3. Spray the air fryer basket with cooking oil. Place the bananas in the basket and spray them with cooking oil.
4. Set temperature to 360°f and cook for 5 minutes. Open the air fryer and flip the bananas. Cook for an additional 2 minutes. Transfer the bananas to plates.
5. Drizzle the chocolate sauce over the bananas, and serve.
6. You can make your own chocolate sauce using 2 tablespoons milk and ¼ cup chocolate chips. Heat a saucepan over medium-high heat. Add the milk and stir for 1 to 2 minutes. Add the chocolate chips. Stir for 2 minutes, or until the chocolate has melted.

Nutrition: calories: 203 Fat:6g protein:3g fiber:3g

782. Air Fryer S'mores

Preparation Time: 5 minutes
Cooking Time: 3 minutes
Servings: 4
Ingredients:
- Four graham crackers (each half split to make 2 squares, for a total of 8 squares)
- 8 Squares of Hershey's chocolate bar, broken into squares
- 4 Marshmallows

Directions:
1. Take deliberate steps. Air-fryers use hot air for cooking food. Marshmallows are light and fluffy, and this should keep the marshmallows from flying around the basket if you follow these steps.
2. Put 4 squares of graham crackers on a basket of the air fryer.
3. Place 2 squares of chocolate bars on each cracker.
4. Place back the basket in the air fryer and fry on air at 390 °F for 1 minute. It is barely long enough for the chocolate to melt. Remove basket from air fryer.
5. Top with a marshmallow over each cracker. Throw the marshmallow down a little bit into the melted chocolate. This will help to make the marshmallow stay over the chocolate.
6. Put back the basket in the air fryer and fry at 390 °F for 2 minutes. (The marshmallows should be puffed up and browned at the tops.)
7. Using tongs to carefully remove each cracker from the basket of the air fryer and place it on a platter. Top each marshmallow with another square of graham crackers.
8. Enjoy it right away!

Nutrition: Calories – 200 Protein – 2.6 g. Fat – 3.1 g. Carbs – 15.7 g.

783. Walnut Apple Pear Mix

Preparation Time: 10 minutes
Cooking Time: 10 minutes
Servings: 4
Ingredients:
1. 2 apples, cored and cut into wedges
2. 1/2 tsp vanilla
3. 1 cup apple juice
4. 2 tbsp. walnuts, chopped
5. 2 apples, cored and cut into wedges

Directions:
- Put all of the ingredients in the inner pot of air fryer and stir well.
- Seal pot and cook on high for 10 minutes.
- As soon as the cooking is done, let it release pressure naturally for 10 minutes then release remaining using quick release. Remove lid.
- Serve and enjoy.

Nutrition: Calories – 132 Protein – 1.3 g. Fat – 2.6 g. Carbs – 28.3 g.

784. Apple Dates Mix

Preparation Time: 10 minutes
Cooking Time: 15 minutes
Servings: 4
Ingredients:
1. 4 apples, cored and cut into chunks
2. 1 tsp vanilla
3. 1 tsp cinnamon
4. 1/2 cup dates, pitted
5. 1 1/2 cups apple juice

Directions:
- Put all of the ingredients in the inner pot of air fryer and stir well.
- Seal and cook on high for 15 minutes.
- As soon as the cooking is done, let it release pressure naturally for 10 minutes then release remaining using quick release. Remove lid.
- Stir and serve.

Nutrition: Calories – 226 Protein – 1.3 g. Fat – 0.6 g. Carbs – 58.6 g.

785. Tangy Mango Slices

Preparation Time: 10 minutes
Cooking Time: 12 hours
Servings: 6
Ingredients:
- 4 mangoes, peel and cut into ¼-inch slices
- 1/4 cup fresh lemon juice
- 1 tbsp. honey

Directions:
1. In a big bowl, combine together honey and lemon juice and set aside.
2. Add mango slices in lemon-honey mixture and coat well.
3. Arrange mango slices on air fryer rack and dehydrate at 135 F for 12 hours.

Nutrition: Calories – 147 Protein – 1.9 g. Fat – 0.9 g. Carbs – 36.7 g.

786. Bread pudding with cranberry

Preparation time: 5 minutes
cooking time: 45 minutes
Servings: 4
Ingredients
- `1-1/2 cups milk
- `2-1/2 eggs
- `1/2 cup cranberries1 teaspoon butter
- `1/4 cup and 2 tablespoons white sugar
- `1/4 cup golden raisins
- `1/8 teaspoon ground cinnamon
- `3/4 cup heavy whipping cream
- `3/4 teaspoon lemon zest
- `3/4 teaspoon kosher salt
- `3/4 french baguettes, cut into 2-inch slices
- `3/8 vanilla bean, split and seeds scraped away

Directions:
1. Lightly grease baking pan of air fryer with cooking spray. Spread baguette slices, cranberries, and raisins.
2. In blender, blend well vanilla bean, cinnamon, salt, lemon zest, eggs, sugar, and cream. Pour over baguette slices. Let it soak for an hour.
3. Cover pan with foil.
4. For 35 minutes, cook on 330°f.
5. Let it rest for 10 minutes.
6. Serve and enjoy.

Nutrition: calories: 581 Fat:23.8g protein:15.8g sugar:7g

787. Black and white brownies

Preparation time: 10 minutes
cooking time: 20 minutes
Servings: 8
Ingredients
- `1 egg
- ¼ cup brown sugar
- `2 tablespoons white sugar
- `2 tablespoons safflower oil
- `1 teaspoon vanilla
- ¼ cup cocoa powder
- `⅓ cup all-purpose flour
- ¼ cup white chocolate chips
- Nonstick baking spray with flour

Directions:
1. In a medium bowl, beat the egg with the brown sugar and white sugar. Beat in the oil and vanilla.
2. Add the cocoa powder and flour, and stir just until combined. Fold in the white chocolate chips.
3. Spray a 6-by-6-by-2-inch baking pan with nonstick spray. Spoon the brownie batter into the pan.
4. Pour the pan into the oven rack/basket. Place the rack on the middle-shelf of the air fryer oven. Set temperature to 390°f, and set time to 20 minutes. Bake for 20 minutes or until the brownies are set when lightly touched with a finger. Let cool for 30 minutes before slicing to serve.

Nutrition: calories: 81 Fat:4g protein:1g fiber:1g

788. French toast bites

Preparation time: 5 minutes
cooking time: 15 minutes
Servings: 8
Ingredients
- `Almond milk
- `Cinnamon
- `Sweetener
- `3 eggs
- `4 pieces wheat bread

Directions:
1. Preheat the air fryer oven to 360 degrees.
2. Whisk eggs and thin out with almond milk.
3. Mix 1/3 cup of sweetener with lots of cinnamon.
4. Tear bread in half, ball up pieces and press together to form a ball.
5. Soak bread balls in egg and then roll into cinnamon sugar, making sure to thoroughly coat.
6. Place coated bread balls into the air fryer oven and bake 15 minutes.

Nutrition: calories: 289 Fat:11g protein:0g sugar:4g

789. Baked apple

Preparation time: 5 minutes
cooking time: 20 minutes
Servings: 4

Ingredients
- ¼ c. Water
- ¼ tsp. Nutmeg
- ¼ tsp. Cinnamon
- 1 ½ tsp. Melted ghee
- 2 tbsp. Raisins
- 2 tbsp. Chopped walnuts
- 1 medium apple

Directions:
1. Preheat your air fryer to 350 degrees.
2. Slice apple in half and discard some of the flesh from the center.
3. Place into frying pan.
4. Mix remaining ingredients together except water. Spoon mixture to the middle of apple halves.
5. Pour water over filled apples.
6. Place pan with apple halves into the air fryer oven, bake 20 minutes.

Nutrition: calories: 199 Fat:9g protein:1g sugar:3g

790. Coffee and blueberry cake

Preparation time: 5 minutes
cooking time: 35 minutes
Servings: 6

Ingredients
- 1 cup white sugar
- 1 egg
- 1/2 cup butter, softened
- 1/2 cup fresh or frozen blueberries
- 1/2 cup sour cream
- 1/2 teaspoon baking powder
- 1/2 teaspoon ground cinnamon
- 1/2 teaspoon vanilla extract
- 1/4 cup brown sugar
- 1/4 cup chopped pecans
- 1/8 teaspoon salt
- 1-1/2 teaspoons confectioners' sugar for dusting
- 3/4 cup and 1 tablespoon all-purpose flour

Directions:
1. In a small bowl, whisk well pecans, cinnamon, and brown sugar.
2. In a blender, blend well all wet ingredients. Add dry ingredients except for confectioner's sugar and blueberries. Blend well until smooth and creamy.
3. Lightly grease baking pan of air fryer with cooking spray.
4. Pour half of batter in pan. Sprinkle half of pecan mixture on top. Pour the remaining batter. And then topped with remaining pecan mixture.
5. Cover pan with foil.
6. For 35 minutes, cook on 330°f.
7. Serve and enjoy with a dusting of confectioner's sugar.

Nutrition: calories: 471 Fat:24g protein:4.1g sugar:6g

791. Cinnamon sugar roasted chickpeas

Preparation time: 5 minutes
cooking time: 10 minutes
Servings: 2

Ingredients
- 1 tbsp. Sweetener
- 1 tbsp. Cinnamon
- 1 c. Chickpeas

Directions:
1. Preheat air fryer oven to 390 degrees.
2. Rinse and drain chickpeas.
3. Mix all ingredients together and add to air fryer.
4. Pour into the oven rack/basket. Place the rack on the middle-shelf of the air fryer oven. Set temperature to 390°f, and set time to 10 minutes.

Nutrition: calories: 111 Fat:19g protein:16g sugar:5g

792. Strawberry Stew

Preparation Time: 10 minutes
Cooking Time: 15 minutes
Servings: 4

Ingredients:
1. 12 oz fresh strawberries, sliced
2. 1 tsp vanilla
3. 1 1/2 cups water
4. 1 tsp liquid stevia
5. 2 tbsp. lime juice

Directions:
- Put all of the ingredients in the inner pot of air fryer and stir well.
- Seal pot and cook on high for 15 minutes.
- As soon as the cooking is done, let it release pressure naturally for 10 minutes then release remaining using quick release. Remove lid.
- Stir and serve.

Nutrition: Calories – 36 Protein – 0.7 g. Fat – 0.3 g. Carbs – 8.5 g.

793. Sweet Peach Wedges

Preparation Time: 10 minutes
Cooking Time: 8 hours
Servings: 4

Ingredients:
- 3 peaches, cut and remove pits and sliced
- 1/2 cup fresh lemon juice

Directions:
1. Add lemon juice and peach slices into the bowl and toss well.
2. Arrange peach slices on air fryer oven rack and dehydrate at 135 F for 6-8 hours.
3. Serve and enjoy.

Nutrition: Calories – 52 Protein – 1.3 g. Fat – 0.5 g. Carbs – 11.1 g.

794. Coconutty lemon bars

Preparation time: 5 minutes
cooking time: 25 minutes
Servings: 12

Ingredients
- ¼ cup cashew
- ¼ cup fresh lemon juice, freshly squeezed
- ¾ cup coconut milk
- ¾ cup erythritol
- 1 cup desiccated coconut

- `1 teaspoon baking powder
- `2 eggs, beaten
- `2 tablespoons coconut oil
- ` air fryer of salt

Directions:
1. Preheat the air fryer oven for 5 minutes. In a mixing bowl, combine all ingredients. Use a hand mixer to mix everything. Pour into a baking dish that will fit in the air fryer.
2. Bake for 25 minutes at 350°f or until a toothpick inserted in the middle comes out clean.

Nutrition: calories: 118 Fat:10g protein:2.6g sugar:5g

795. Simple Coffee Cake

Preparation Time: 10 minutes
Cooking time: 20 minutes
Servings: 2

Ingredients:
- ¼ cup butter
- ½ teaspoon instant coffee
- 1 tablespoon black coffee, brewed
- 1 egg
- A ¼ cup of sugar
- ¼ cup flour
- 1 teaspoon of cocoa powder
- A pinch of salt
- Powdered sugar, for icing

Directions
1. 1.Preheat the air fryer to 330 F and grease a small ring cake pan.
2. 2.Beat the sugar and egg along in a very bowl. Beat in cocoa, instant and black coffee; stir in salt and flour.
3. 3.Transfer the batter to the prepared pan. Cook for 15 minutes.

Nutrition: Calories 418 Protein 5.1g Fat 25.5g Carbs 44.8g

796. Lime Cheesecake

Preparation Time: 5 minutes
Cooking time: 4 hours 14 minutes
Servings: 10

Ingredients:
- 2tablespoons butter, melted
- 2teaspoons sugar
- 4ounces flour
- ¼ cup coconut, shredded
- For the filling:
- 1 pound cream cheese
- Zest from 1 lime, grated
- Juice from 1 lime
- 2cups hot water
- 2sachets lime jelly

Directions
1. In a bowl, mix coconut with flour, butter, and sugar, stir well and press this on the bottom of a pan that fits your air fryer.
2. Meanwhile, put the hot water in a bowl, add jelly sachets and until it dissolves.
3. Put cream cheese in a bowl, add jelly, lime juice, and zest and whisk really well.
4. Add this over the crust, spread, introduce in the air fryer and cook at 300 F. for 4 minutes.
5. Keep in the fridge for 4 hours before serving.
6. Enjoy!

Nutrition: Calories 260 Protein 7g Fat 23g Carbs 5g

797. Marvelous Lemon Biscuits

Preparation Time: 5 minutes
Cooking time: 10 minutes
Servings: 4

Ingredients:
- ½ cup softened unsalted butter
- 5cups of coconut flour
- 1 lemon juice and zest
- 2cups of coconut milk
- 2teaspoons of yeast
- A ¼ cup of granulated sugar
- 1 teaspoon of salt
- 1 teaspoon of baking soda
- 1 teaspoon of baking powder

Directions
1. Preheat your air fryer to 360 F.
2. Using a bowl, add and stir the coconut flour, yeast, baking soda, baking powder, salt, and granulated sugar.
3. Add and stir in the coconut milk, lemon juice, lemon zest, unsalted butter and mix it properly until it has soft dough's texture.
4. Roll out the pastry and cut it into biscuits.
5. Place the biscuits on a baking sheet and cook it for 5 minutes at a 360 F.
6. Remove and allow it to cool off until it is cool enough to eat.
7. Sprinkle it with icing sugar.
8. Serve and enjoy!

Nutrition: Calories 170 Protein 2g Fat 7g Carbs 26g

798. Banana Fritters

Preparation Time: 5 minutes
Cooking time: 15 minutes
Servings: 8

Ingredients:
- 8bananas
- 3tablespoons vegetable oil
- 3tablespoons corn flour
- 1 egg white
- ¾ cup breadcrumbs

Directions
1. Preheat the air fryer to 350 F and combine the oil and breadcrumbs, in a small bowl. Coat the bananas with the corn flour first, brush them with egg white, and dip them in the breadcrumb mixture.
2. Arrange on a lined baking sheet and cook for 8 minutes.

Nutrition: Calories 203 Protein 3.4g Fat 6.3g Carbs 36.05g

799. Tasty Banana Snack

Preparation Time: 5 minutes
Cooking time: 15 minutes
Servings: 8

Ingredients:
- 16baking cups crust
- 1 banana; peeled and sliced into 16 pieces
- ¼ cup peanut butter
- A ¾ cup of chocolate chips
- 1 tablespoon vegetable oil

Directions
1. Put chocolate chips in a small pot, heat up over low heat; stir until it melts and takes off heat.
2. In a bowl; mix peanut butter with coconut oil and whisk well.
3. Spoon 1 teaspoon chocolates mix in a cup, add 1 banana slice and top with 1 teaspoon butter mix.
4. Repeat with rest of the cups, place them all into a dish that fits your air fryer, cook at 320 F for 5 minutes; transfer to a freezer and keep there until you serve them as a snack.

Nutrition: Calories 70 Protein 1g Fat 4g Carbs 10g

800. Strawberry Cobbler

Preparation Time: 5 minutes
Cooking time: 35 minutes
Servings: 6
Ingredients:
- A ¾ cup of sugar
- 6cups strawberries, halved
- 1/8 teaspoon baking powder
- 1 tablespoon lemon juice
- ½ cup flour
- A pinch of baking soda
- A ½ cup of water
- 3and ½ tablespoon olive oil
- Cooking spray

Directions
1. In a bowl, mix strawberries with half of the sugar, sprinkle some flour, add lemon juice, whisk and pour into the baking dish that fits your air fryer and greased with cooking spray.
2. In another bowl, mix flour with the rest of the sugar, baking powder and soda and stir well.
3. Add the olive oil and mix until the whole thing with your hands.
4. Add ½ cup water and spread over strawberries.
5. Introduce in the fryer at 355 F and bake for 25 minutes.
6. Leave cobbler aside to cool down, slice and serve.
7. Enjoy!

Nutrition: Calories 221 Protein 9g Fat 3g Carbs 6g

801. Super Yummy Brownies

Preparation Time: 5 minutes
Cooking time: 25 minutes
Servings: 4
Ingredients:
- 4-ounces of softened unsalted butter
- 8-ounces of bittersweet chocolate chips
- 3eggs
- 1 cup of granulated sugar
- ½ teaspoon of salt
- 1 cup of all-purpose flour

Directions
1. Preheat your air fryer to 350 F.
2. Grease a heat-safe dish that is convenient with your air fryer.
3. Using a saucepan, soften the butter and chocolate.
4. Then using a large bowl, add and mix all the ingredients properly.
5. Add the brownie batter to the greased heat-safe dish and smoothen the surface.
6. Place it in your air fryer and cook it for 25 minutes or until a toothpick comes out clean in the center.
7. Remove the brownies and allow it to chill it is cool enough to eat, thereafter cut it into squares.
8. Serve and enjoy!

Nutrition: Calories 130 Protein 2g Fat 5g Carbs 21g

802. Air Fryer Churros with Chocolate Sauce

Preparation Time: 5 minutes
Cooking Time: 10 minutes
Servings: 4
Ingredients:
- 1/2 cup water 1/4 teaspoon kosher salt
- Unsalted butter, split half cup
- 2 tbsp. All-purpose flour
- 2 large eggs
- 1/3 cup granulated sugar cinnamon

Directions:
1. Bring 1/4 cup of water, salt, and butter to a boil in a small saucepan over medium-high. Reduce heat from medium to low; Add the flour, and stir vigorously with a wooden spoon until the dough is smooth about 30 seconds.
2. Continue cooking, stirring continuously, until the dough starts to move away from the sides of the pan and leave a movie variety on the back of the pan for 2 to 3 minutes.
3. Transfer the dough to a medium bowl. Stir continuously for about 1 minute, until slightly cooled. Add eggs, 1 at a time, stirring continuously until completely smooth after each addition. Transfer the mixture to a piping bag equipped with a medium celebrity tip. Chill 30 minutes.
4. Pipe 6 (3 inches long) pieces into one layer in an air fryer basket. Cook at 380 ° F, about 10 minutes, until golden. Repeat with the last flour.
5. In a medium bowl, collectively stir the sugar and cinnamon. Brush the cooked churros with the remaining 2 tablespoons of melted butter, and roll in a sugar mixture.
6. Serve churros with chocolate sauce.

Nutrition: Calories: 108 Fat:6 Carbs: 12 Protein:1

CASSEROLE, FRITTATA AND QUICHE

803. Cheesy Chicken Divan

Preparation Time: 5 minutes
Cooking Time: 2 minutes
Servings: 4

Ingredients:
- 4 chicken breasts
- Salt and ground black pepper, to taste
- 1 head broccoli, cut into florets
- 1/2 cup cream of mushroom soup
- 1 cup shredded Cheddar cheese
- 1/2 cup croutons
- Cooking spray

Directions:
1. Spritz the air fry basket with cooking spray.
2. Put the chicken breasts in the air fry basket and sprinkle with salt and ground black pepper.
3. Place the basket on the air fry position.
4. Select Air Fry. Set temperature to 390°F (199°C) and set time to 14 minutes. Flip the breasts halfway through the cooking time.
5. When cooking is complete, the breasts should be well browned and tender.
6. Remove the breasts from the air fryer grill and allow to cool for a few minutes on a plate, then cut the breasts into bite-size pieces.
7. Combine the chicken, broccoli, mushroom soup, and Cheddar cheese in a large bowl. Stir to mix well.
8. Spritz a baking pan with cooking spray. Pour the chicken mixture into the pan. Spread the croutons over the mixture.
9. Place the pan on the bake position.
10. Select Bake. Set time to 10 minutes.
11. When cooking is complete, the croutons should be lightly browned and the mixture should be set.
12. Remove the baking pan from the air fryer grill and serve immediately.

Nutrition: Calories 246 Carbs 0.1g Fat 2.8g Protein 10.8g

804. Cheesy-Creamy Broccoli Casserole

Preparation Time: 5 minutes
Cooking Time: 30 minutes
Servings: 4

Ingredients:
- 4 cups broccoli florets
- ¼ cup heavy whipping cream
- 1/2 cup sharp Cheddar cheese, shredded
- ¼ cup ranch dressing
- Kosher salt and ground black pepper, to taste

Directions:
1. Combine all the ingredients in a large bowl. Toss to coat well broccoli well.
2. Pour the mixture into a baking pan.
3. Place the pan on the bake position.
2. Select Bake, set temperature to 375°F (190°C) and set time to 30 minutes.
3. When cooking is complete, the broccoli should be tender.
4. Remove the baking pan from the air fryer grill and serve immediately.

Nutrition: Calories 246 Carbs 2.1g Fat 7.8g Protein 10.8g

805. Cheesy Chorizo, Corn, and Potato Frittata

Preparation Time: 8 minutes
Cooking Time: 12 minutes
Servings: 4

Ingredients:
- 2 tablespoons olive oil
- 1 chorizo, sliced
- 4 eggs
- 1/2 cup corn
- 1 large potato, boiled and cubed
- 1 tablespoon chopped parsley
- 1/2 cup feta cheese, crumbled
- Salt and ground black pepper, to taste

Directions:
1. Heat the olive oil in a nonstick skillet over medium heat until shimmering.
2. Add the chorizo and cook for 4 minutes or until golden brown.
3. Whisk the eggs in a bowl, then sprinkle with salt and ground black pepper.
4. Mix the remaining ingredients in the egg mixture, then pour the chorizo and its fat into a baking pan. Pour in the egg mixture.
5. Place the pan on the bake position.
6. Select Bake, set temperature to 330°F (166°C) and set time to 8 minutes. Stir the mixture halfway through.
5. When cooking is complete, the eggs should be set.
6. Serve immediately.

Nutrition: Calories 246 Carbs 0.1g Fat 2.8g Protein 10.8g

806. Taco Beef and Green Chile Casserole

Preparation Time: 10 minutes
Cooking Time: 15 minutes
Servings: 4

Ingredients:
- 1 pound (454 g) 85% lean ground beef
- 1 tablespoon taco seasoning
- 1 (7-ounce / 198-g) can diced mild green chiles
- 1/2 cup milk
- 2 large eggs
- 1 cup shredded Mexican cheese blend
- 2 tablespoons all-purpose flour
- 1/2 teaspoon kosher salt
- Cooking spray

Directions:
1. Spritz a baking pan with cooking spray.
2. Toss the ground beef with taco seasoning in a large bowl to mix well. Pour the seasoned ground beef in the prepared baking pan.
3. Combing the remaining ingredients in a medium bowl. Whisk to mix well, then pour the mixture over the ground beef.
4. Place the pan on the bake position.
5. Select Bake, set temperature to 350°F (180°C) and set time to 15 minutes.
6. When cooking is complete, a toothpick inserted in the center should come out clean.
7. Remove the casserole from the air fryer grill and allow to cool for 5 minutes, then slice to serve.

Nutrition: Calories 266 Carbs 3.1g Fat 2.8g Protein 10.8g

807. Golden Asparagus Frittata

Preparation Time: 5 minutes
Cooking Time: 25 minutes
Servings: 4

Ingredients:
- 1 cup asparagus spears, cut into 1-inch pieces
- 1 teaspoon vegetable oil
- 1 tablespoon milk
- 6 eggs, beaten
- 2 ounces (57 g) goat cheese, crumbled
- 1 tablespoon minced chives, optional
- Kosher salt and pepper, to taste

Directions:
2. Add the asparagus spears to a small bowl and drizzle with the vegetable oil. Toss until well coated and transfer to the air fry basket.
3. Place the basket on the air fry position.
4. Select Air Fry. Set temperature to 400°F (205°C) and set time to 5 minutes. Flip the asparagus halfway through.
5. When cooking is complete, the asparagus should be tender and slightly wilted.
6. Remove the asparagus from the air fryer grill to a baking pan.
7. Stir together the milk and eggs in a medium bowl. Pour the mixture over the asparagus in the pan. Sprinkle with the goat cheese and the chives (if using) over the eggs. Season with salt and pepper.
8. Place the pan on the bake position.
9. Select Bake, set temperature to 320°F (160°C) and set time to 20 minutes.
10. When cooking is complete, the top should be golden and the eggs should be set.
11. Transfer to a serving dish. Slice and serve.

Nutrition: Calories 286 Carbs 0.1g Fat 2.8g Protein 10.8g

808. Corn and Bell Pepper Casserole

Preparation Time: 10 minutes
Cooking Time: 20 minutes
Servings: 4

Ingredients:
- 1 cup corn kernels
- ¼ cup bell pepper, finely chopped
- 1/2 cup low-fat milk
- 1 large egg, beaten
- 1/2 cup yellow cornmeal
- 1/2 cup all-purpose flour
- 1/2 teaspoon baking powder
- 2 tablespoons melted unsalted butter
- 1 tablespoon granulated sugar
- Pinch of cayenne pepper
- ¼ teaspoon kosher salt
- Cooking spray

Directions:
1. Spritz a baking pan with cooking spray.
2. Combine all the ingredients in a large bowl. Stir to mix well. Pour the mixture into the baking pan.
3. Place the pan on the bake position.
4. Select Bake, set temperature to 330°F (166°C) and set time to 20 minutes.
5. When cooking is complete, the casserole should be lightly browned and set.
6. Remove the baking pan from the air fryer grill and serve immediately.

Nutrition: Calories 279 Carbs 2.1g Fat 2.8g Protein 10.8g

809. Creamy-Mustard Pork Gratin

Preparation Time: 15 minutes
Cooking Time: 21 minutes
Servings: 4

Ingredients:
- 2 tablespoons olive oil
- 2 pounds (907 g) pork tenderloin, cut into serving-size pieces
- 1 teaspoon dried marjoram
- ¼ teaspoon chili powder
- 1 teaspoon coarse sea salt
- 1/2 teaspoon freshly ground black pepper
- 1 cup Ricotta cheese
- 11/2 cups chicken broth
- 1 tablespoon mustard
- Cooking spray

Directions:
1. Spritz a baking pan with cooking spray.
2. Heat the olive oil in a nonstick skillet over medium-high heat until shimmering.
3. Add the pork and sauté for 6 minutes or until lightly browned.
4. Transfer the pork to the prepared baking pan and sprinkle with marjoram, salt, chili powder, and ground black pepper.
5. Combine the remaining ingredients in a large bowl. Stir to mix well. Pour the mixture over the pork in the pan.
6. Place the pan on the bake position.
7. Select Bake, set temperature to 350°F (180°C) and set time to 15 minutes. Stir the mixture halfway through.
8. When cooking is complete, the mixture should be frothy and the cheese should be melted.
9. Serve immediately.

Nutrition: Calories 246 Carbs 0.1g Fat 2.8g Protein 10.8g

810. Broccoli, Carrot, and Tomato Quiche

Preparation Time: 6 minutes
Cooking Time: 14 minutes
Servings: 4

Ingredients:
- 4 eggs
- 1 teaspoon dried thyme
- 1 cup whole milk
- 1 steamed carrots, diced
- 2 cups steamed broccoli florets
- 2 medium tomatoes, diced
- ¼ cup crumbled feta cheese
- 1 cup grated Cheddar cheese
- 1 teaspoon chopped parsley
- Salt and ground black pepper, to taste
- Cooking spray

Directions:
1. Spritz a baking pan with cooking spray.
2. Whisk together the eggs, salt, thyme, and ground black pepper in a bowl and fold in the milk while mixing.
3. Put the broccoli, carrots, and tomatoes in the prepared baking pan, then spread with 1/2 cup Cheddar cheese and feta cheese. Pour the egg mixture over, then scatter with remaining Cheddar on top.

4. Place the pan on the bake position.
5. Select Bake, set temperature to 350°F (180°C) and set time to 14 minutes.
6. When cooking is complete, the egg should be set and the quiche should be puffed.
7. Remove the quiche from the air fryer grill and top with chopped parsley, then slice to serve.

Nutrition: Calories 216 Carbs 0.1g Fat 2.8g Protein 6.8g

811. Herbed Cheddar Cheese Frittata

Preparation Time: 10 minutes
Cooking Time: 20 minutes
Servings: 4
Ingredients:
- 1/2 cup shredded Cheddar cheese
- 1/2 cup half-and-half
- 4 large eggs
- 2 tablespoons chopped scallion greens
- 2 tablespoons chopped fresh parsley
- 1/2 teaspoon kosher salt
- 1/2 teaspoon ground black pepper
- Cooking spray

Directions:
1. Spritz a baking pan with cooking spray.
2. Whisk together all the ingredients in a large bowl, then pour the mixture into the prepared baking pan.
3. Place the pan on the bake position.
4. Select Bake, set temperature to 300°F (150°C) and set time to 20 minutes. Stir the mixture halfway through.
5. When cooking is complete, the eggs should be set.
6. Serve immediately.

Nutrition: Calories 246 Carbs 0.1g Fat 2.8g Protein 3.8g

812. Cauliflower, Okra, and Pepper Casserole

Preparation Time: 8 minutes
Cooking Time: 12 minutes
Servings: 4
Ingredients:
- 1 head cauliflower, cut into florets
- 1 cup okra, chopped
- 1 yellow bell pepper, chopped
- 2 eggs, beaten
- 1/2 cup chopped onion
- 1 tablespoon soy sauce
- 2 tablespoons olive oil
- Salt and ground black pepper, to taste

Directions:
1. Spritz a baking pan with cooking spray.
2. Put the cauliflower in a food processor and pulse to rice the cauliflower.
3. Pour the cauliflower rice in the baking pan and add the remaining ingredients. Stir to mix well.
4. Place the pan on the bake position.
5. Select Bake, set temperature to 380°F (193°C) and set time to 12 minutes.
6. When cooking is complete, the eggs should be set.
7. Remove the baking pan from the air fryer grill and serve immediately.

Nutrition: Calories 246 Carbs 0.1g Fat 2.8g Protein 10.8g

813. Sumptuous Chicken and Vegetable Casserole

Preparation Time: 15 minutes
Cooking Time: 15 minutes
Servings: 4
Ingredients:
- 4 boneless and skinless chicken breasts, cut into cubes
- 2 carrots, sliced
- 1 yellow bell pepper, cut into strips
- 1 red bell pepper, cut into strips
- 15 ounces (425 g) broccoli florets
- 1 cup snow peas
- 1 scallion, sliced
- Cooking spray
- Sauce:
- 1 teaspoon Sriracha
- 3 tablespoons soy sauce
- 2 tablespoons oyster sauce
- 1 tablespoon rice wine vinegar
- 1 teaspoon cornstarch
- 1 tablespoon grated ginger
- 2 garlic cloves, minced
- 1 teaspoon sesame oil
- 1 tablespoon brown sugar

Directions:
1. Spritz a baking pan with cooking spray.
2. Combine the chicken, bell peppers, and carrot in a large bowl. Stir to mix well.
3. Combine the ingredients for the sauce in a separate bowl. Stir to mix well.
4. Pour the chicken mixture into the baking pan, then pour the sauce over. Stir to coat well.
5. Place the pan on the bake position.
6. Select Bake, set temperature to 370°F (188°C) and set time to 13 minutes. Add the broccoli and snow peas to the pan halfway through.
7. When cooking is complete, the vegetables should be tender.
8. Remove the pan from the air fryer grill and sprinkle with sliced scallion before serving.

Nutrition: Calories 206 Carbs 0.1g Fat 2.8g Protein 5.8g

CASSEROLE, FRITTATA AND QUICHE

814. Easy Chickpea and Spinach Casserole

Preparation Time: 10 minutes
Cooking Time: 22 minutes
Servings: 4
Ingredients:
- 2 tablespoons olive oil
- 2 garlic cloves, minced
- 1 tablespoon ginger, minced
- 1 onion, chopped
- 1 chili pepper, minced
- Salt and ground black pepper, to taste
- 1 pound (454 g) spinach
- 1 can coconut milk
- 1/2 cup dried tomatoes, chopped
- 1 (14-ounce / 397-g) can chickpeas, drained

Directions:
1. Heat the olive oil in a saucepan over medium heat. Sauté the ginger and garlic in the olive oil for 1 minute, or until fragrant.
2. Add the chili pepper, onion, salt and pepper to the saucepan. Sauté for 3 minutes.
3. Mix in the spinach and sauté for 3 to 4 minutes or until the vegetables become soft. Remove from heat.
4. Pour the vegetable mixture into a baking pan. Stir in chickpeas, dried tomatoes and coconut milk until well blended.
5. Place the pan on the bake position.
6. Select Bake, set temperature to 370°F (188°C) and set time to 15 minutes.
7. When cooking is complete, transfer the casserole to a serving dish. Let cool for 5 minutes before serving.

Nutrition: Calories 246 Carbs 1.1g Fat 2.8g Protein 2.8g

815. Classic Mediterranean Quiche

Preparation Time: 10 minutes
Cooking Time: 30 minutes
Servings: 4
Ingredients:
- 4 eggs
- ¼ cup chopped Kalamata olives
- 1/2 cup chopped tomatoes
- ¼ cup chopped onion
- 1/2 cup milk
- 1 cup crumbled feta cheese
- 1/2 tablespoon chopped oregano
- 1/2 tablespoon chopped basil
- Salt and ground black pepper, to taste
- Cooking spray

Directions:
1. Spritz a baking pan with cooking spray.
2. Whisk the eggs with remaining ingredients in a large bowl. Stir to mix well.
3. Pour the mixture into the prepared baking pan.
4. Place the pan on the bake position.
5. Select Bake, set temperature to 340°F (171°C) and set time to 30 minutes.
6. When cooking is complete, the eggs should be set and a toothpick inserted in the center should come out clean.
7. Serve immediately.

Nutrition: Calories 246 Carbs 0.1g Fat 2.8g Protein 10.8g

816. Cheesy Mushrooms and Spinach Frittata

Preparation Time: 7 minutes
Cooking Time: 8 minutes
Servings: 2
Ingredients:
- 1 cup chopped mushrooms
- 2 cups spinach, chopped
- 4 eggs, lightly beaten
- 3 ounces (85 g) feta cheese, crumbled
- 2 tablespoons heavy cream
- A handful of fresh parsley, chopped
- Salt and ground black pepper, to taste
- Cooking spray

Directions:
1. Spritz a baking pan with cooking spray.
2. Whisk together all the ingredients in a large bowl. Stir to mix well.
3. Pour the mixture in the prepared baking pan.
4. Place the pan on the bake position.
5. Select Bake, set temperature to 350°F (180°C) and set time to 8 minutes. Stir the mixture halfway through.
6. When cooking is complete, the eggs should be set.
7. Serve immediately.

Nutrition: Calories 243 Carbs 0.1g Fat 2.8g Protein 10.8g

817. Broccoli-Rice 'n Cheese Casserole

Preparation Time: 5 minutes
Cooking Time: 30 minutes
Servings: 4
Ingredients:
- 1 (10 ounce) can chunk chicken, Dry out
- 1 cup uncooked instant rice
- 1 cup water
- 1/2 (10.75 ounce) can condensed cream of chicken soup
- 1/2 (10.75 ounce) can condensed cream of mushroom soup
- 1/2 cup milk
- 1/2 small white onion, chopped
- 1/2-pound processed cheese food
- 2 tablespoons butter
- 8-ounce frozen chopped broccoli

Directions:
1. Lightly grease baking pan of air fryer with cooking spray. Add water and bring to a boil at 390oF. Stir in rice and cook for 3 minutes.
2. Stir in processed cheese, onion, broccoli, milk, butter, chicken soup, mushroom soup, and chicken. Mix well. Cook for 15 minutes at 390oF, fluff mixture and continue cooking for another 10 minutes until tops are browned. Serve and enjoy.

Nutrition: Calories 752 Carbs 82.7g Protein 36.0g Fat 30.8g

818. Beefy 'n Cheesy Spanish Rice Casserole

Preparation Time: 10 minutes
Cooking Time: 50 minutes
Servings: 3
Ingredients:
- 2 tablespoons chopped green bell pepper
- 1 tablespoon chopped fresh cilantro
- 1/2-pound lean ground beef
- 1/2 cup water
- 1/2 teaspoon salt
- 1/2 teaspoon brown sugar
- 1/2 pinch ground black pepper
- 1/3 cup uncooked long grain rice
- 1/4 cup finely chopped onion
- 1/4 cup chili sauce
- 1/4 teaspoon ground cumin
- 1/4 teaspoon Worcestershire sauce
- 1/4 cup shredded Cheddar cheese
- 1/2 (14.5 ounce) can canned tomatoes

Directions:
1. Lightly grease baking pan of air fryer with cooking spray. Add ground beef.
2. For 10 minutes, cook on 360°F Halfway through cooking time, stir and crumble beef. Discard excess fat,
3. Stir in pepper, Worcestershire sauce, cumin, brown sugar, salt, chili sauce, rice, water, tomatoes, green bell pepper, and onion. Mix well. Cover pan with foil and cook for 25 minutes. Stirring occasionally
4. Give it one last good stir, press down firmly and sprinkle cheese on top.
5. Cook uncovered for 15 minutes at 390°F until tops are lightly browned.
6. Serve and enjoy with chopped cilantro.

Nutrition: Calories 346 Cal Fat 19.1 g Carbs 0 g Protein 18.5 g

819. Air Fryer Beef Casserole

Preparation Time: 5 minutes
Cooking Time: 30 minutes
Servings: 4
Ingredients:
- 1 green bell pepper, seeded and chopped
- 1 onion, chopped
- 1-pound ground beef
- 3 cloves of garlic, minced
- 3 tablespoons olive oil
- 6 cups eggs, beaten
- Salt and pepper to taste

Directions:
1. Preheat the Air Fryer Oven for 5 minutes
2. In a baking dish that will fit in the air fryer, mix the ground beef, onion, garlic, olive oil, and bell pepper. Season it with salt and pepper to taste.
3. Pour in the beaten eggs and give a good stir.
4. Place the dish with the beef and egg mixture in the air fryer.
5. Pour into the Oven rack/basket. Place the Rack on the middle-shelf of the Air Fryer Oven. Set temperature to 325°F, and set time to 30 minutes. Bake it for 30 minutes

Nutrition: Calories 1520 Cal Fat 125.11 g Carbs 0 g Protein 87.9 g

820. Broccoli Creamy Casserole

Preparation Time: 5 minutes
Cooking Time: 30 minutes
Servings: 4
Ingredients:
- 1 cup diced ham
- 1 (14-ounce) bags frozen broccoli
- 4 ounces' cream cheese, softened
- ½ cup plain full-fat greek yogurt
- ¼ cup mayonnaise
- ½ teaspoon garlic salt
- ½ teaspoon onion powder
- ½ teaspoon dried basil
- ½ teaspoon smoked paprika
- ¼ teaspoon rosemary
- ¼ teaspoon thyme
- ½ cup shredded cheese
- ½ cup crushed pork rinds

Directions:
1. Preheat air fryer to 350-degrees F. Spray a 6-inch soufflé dish with non-stick cooking spray; set aside.
2. Mix the ham, broccoli, cream cheese, yoghurt, mayonnaise, garlic salt, onion powder, basil, smoked paprika, rosemary and thyme in a large bowl.
3. Pour the batter into a oiled pan and cover the pan with grated cheese and shredded rinds. Bake it for 25 minutes or until the pan is golden and bubbly.

Nutrition: Calories 273 Fat 17.4g Carbs 9.7g Protein 17.4g

821. Chicken, Feta, and Olive Casserole

Preparation Time: 5 minutes
Cooking Time: 30 minutes
Servings: 4
Ingredients:
- Chicken Casserole
- 1½ pounds boneless chicken thighs
- Salt and pepper, to taste
- 2 tablespoons butter
- 3 ounces pesto
- 1¼ cups coconut cream
- 3 ounces' green olives
- 5 ounces diced feta cheese
- 1 clove garlic, finely chopped

For Servings:
- 5 ounces leafy greens
- 4 tablespoons coconut oil
- Salt and pepper, to taste

Directions:
1. Preheat air fryer to 350-degrees F. Spray a 6-inch soufflé dish with non-stick cooking spray; set aside.
2. Put the butter in a large saucepan. Heat the pan until the butter is melt, then sauté the chicken pieces until golden.
3. Combine pesto and cream in a container to make the sauce. Put the chicken, olives, feta, and garlic and pesto sauce in a saucepan.
4. Mix well and Bake it for 30 minutes in air fryer or until the edges are hot and brown

Nutrition: Calories 643 Fat 56.7g Carbs: 5.7g Protein 28.5g

822. Turkey Taco Casserole

Preparation Time: 5 minutes
Cooking Time: 40 minutes
Servings: 6
Ingredients:
- 8 oz. shredded cheese
- 1 ½ - 2 lbs. ground turkey
- 1 cup salsa
- 2 tbsp. taco seasoning
- 16 oz. cottage cheese

Directions:
1. Switch on the oven to 400 degrees.
2. In a sizeable casserole dish, put in the ground meat and mix in the taco seasoning—Bake for 20 minutes.
3. While ground turkey is baking, mix 1 cup of shredded cheese, cottage cheese, and salsa.
4. Take the casserole from the oven and strain out any leftover juices from the ground meat.
5. Pound and crush the meat into smaller pieces and then layer the cottage cheese and salsa combo over the meat. Sprinkle remaining cheese on top of the ground meat.
6. Put the casserole back into the oven and bake for 15-20 minutes until the meat cooks all the way through. And the cheese is melted and bubbling.

Nutrition: Calories: 367 Protein: 45g Net Carbs: 6g Fat 18g

823. Italian Chicken Casserole

Preparation Time: 10 minutes
Cooking Time: 25 minutes
Servings: 6
Ingredients:
- ¾ lbs. chicken breasts
- 2 tablespoons pesto sauce
- ½ (14 oz) can tomatoes, diced
- 1 cup Mozzarella cheese, shredded
- 2 tablespoon fresh basil, chopped

Directions:
- Place the flattened chicken breasts in the Air fryer and top them with pesto. Add tomatoes, cheese, and basil on top of each chicken piece.
- Put on the Air Fryer and cook on Bake mode for 25 minutes at 355 degrees F. Once done, remove the lid and serve warm.

Nutrition: Calories: 537 Protein: 37.8g Carbs: 25.1g Fat: 19.8g

SAUCE, DIP AND DRESSING

SAUCE, DIP AND DRESSING

824. Spicy Buffalo Chicken Dip

Preparation time: 10 minutes
Cooking time: 10 minutes
Servings: 4
Ingredients:
- 1 cup cooked, diced chicken breast
- 2 ounces full-fat cream cheese, softened
- ½ cup buffalo sauce
- ⅓ cup full-fat ranch dressing
- ⅓ cup chopped pickled jalapeños
- 1½ cups shredded medium Cheddar cheese, divided
- scallions, sliced on the bias

Directions
1. Place chicken into a large bowl. Add cream cheese, buffalo sauce, and ranch dressing. Stir until the sauces are well mixed and mostly smooth. Fold in jalapeños and 1 cup Cheddar.
2. Pour the mixture into a 4-cup round baking dish and place remaining Cheddar on top. Place dish into the air fryer basket.
3. Adjust the temperature to 350 F and set the timer for 10 minutes.
4. When done, the top will be brown and the dip bubbling. Top with sliced scallions. Serve warm.

Nutrition: Calories 472 Protein 25.6g Fiber 0.6g Net Carbs 8.5mg Fat 32.0g Sodium 1532mg Carbs 9.1g Sugar 7.4g

825. Bacon Cheeseburger Dip

Preparation time: 20 minutes
Cooking time: 10 minutes
Servings: 6
Ingredients:
- 8 ounces full-fat cream cheese
- ¼ cup full-fat mayonnaise
- ¼ cup full-fat sour cream
- ¼ cup chopped onion
- 1 teaspoon garlic powder
- 1 tablespoon Worcestershire sauce
- 1¼ cups shredded medium Cheddar cheese, divided
- ½ pound cooked 80/20 ground beef
- 6 slices sugar-free bacon, cooked and crumbled
- 2 large pickle spears, chopped

Directions
1. Place cream cheese in a large microwave-safe bowl and microwave for 45 seconds. Stir in mayonnaise, sour cream, onion, garlic powder, Worcestershire sauce, and 1 cup Cheddar. Add cooked ground beef and bacon. Sprinkle remaining Cheddar on top.
2. Place in 6" bowl and put into the air fryer basket.
3. Adjust the temperature to 400 F and set the timer for 10 minutes.
4. Dip is done when top is golden and bubbling. Sprinkle pickles over dish. Serve warm.

Nutrition: Calories 457 Protein 21.6g Fiber 0.2g Net Carbs 3.6mg Fat 35.0g Sodium 589mg Carbs 3.8g Sugar 2.2g

826. Spicy Spinach Artichoke Dip

Preparation time: 10 minutes
Cooking time: 10 minutes
Servings: 6
Ingredients:
- 10 ounces frozen spinach, drained and thawed
- 1 (14-ounce) can artichoke hearts, drained and chopped
- ¼ cup chopped pickled jalapeños
- 8 ounces full-fat cream cheese, softened
- ¼ cup full-fat mayonnaise
- ¼ cup full-fat sour cream
- ½ teaspoon garlic powder
- ¼ cup grated Parmesan cheese
- 1 cup shredded pepper jack cheese

Directions
1. Mix all ingredients in a 4-cup baking bowl. Place into the air fryer basket.
2. Adjust the temperature to 320 F and set the timer for 10 minutes.
3. Remove when brown and bubbling. Serve warm.

Nutrition: Calories 226 Protein 10.0g Fiber 3.7g Net Carbs 6.5g Fat 15.9g Sodium 776mg Carbs 10.2g Sugar 3.4g

827. Peppers and Cheese Dip

Preparation Time: 5 Minutes
Cooking time: 25 Minutes
Servings: 6
Ingredients:
- Two bacon slices, cooked and crumbled
- 4oz. parmesan; grated
- 4oz. mozzarella; grated
- 8oz. cream cheese, soft
- Two roasted red peppers; chopped.
- A pinch of salt and black pepper

Directions
1. Mix all the ingredients, and whisk well.
2. Introduce the pan to the fryer and cook at 400 F for 20 minutes. Divide into bowls and serve cold.

Nutrition: Calories 173 Fat 8g Fiber 2g Carbs 4g Protein 11g

828. Fennel Spread

Preparation Time: 5 Minutes
Cooking time: 25 Minutes
Servings: 8
Ingredients:
- Three fennel bulbs; trimmed and cut into wedges
- Four garlic cloves; minced
- ¼ cup parmesan; grated
- 3 tbsp. olive oil
- A pinch of salt and black pepper

Directions
1. Put the fennel in the air fryer's basket and bake at 380 F for 20 minutes.
2. In a blender, combine the roasted fennel with the rest of the ingredients and pulse well
3. Put the spread in a ramekin, introduce it in the fryer and cook at 380 F for 5 minutes more
4. Divide into bowls and serve as a dip.

Nutrition: Calories 240 Fat 11g Fiber 3g Carbs 4g Protein 12g

829. Spinach Dip

Preparation Time: 10 Minutes
Cooking time: 25 Minutes
Servings: 8
Ingredients:
- 8ounces softened cream cheese
- 1 cup of sour cream
- 10ounces fresh spinach leaves
- 1 tsp minced garlic
- 1/2 tsp salt
- 1/4 tsp pepper
- 1/2 cup of grated parmesan cheese
- Shredded mozzarella cheese, (1 1/2 cup)
- 1 tbsp chopped parsley
- bread, crackers and vegetables for serving
- cooking spray

Directions
1. Steam the spinach or saute it until wilted. Let it cool off then wring all the excess water out. Chop the spinach coarsely.
2. To 375 F. Preheat the oven. Using cooking spray to grease a shallow baking dish or skillet.
3. In a mug, add the cream cheese, sour cream, cooked spinach, garlic, salt, pepper, parmesan cheese, and 3/4 cup mozzarella cheese. Stir once mixed properly.
4. In the prepared dish, scatter the spinach mixture. Place the leftover mozzarella cheese on top.
5. Bake until the dip is bubbly and the cheese is melting, or for 20 minutes. Turn the oven to broil and cook for another 2-3 minutes or until the cheese is browning.
6. Sprinkle with minced parsley and serve with pizza, vegetables and crackers.

Nutrition: Calories 226 Protein 10.0g Fiber 3.7g Net Carbs 6.5g Fat 15.9g Sodium 776mg Carbs 10.2g Sugar 3.4g

830. Spicy Sweet Potato Dip

Preparation Time: 15 Minutes
Cooking time: 30 Minutes
Servings: 6
Ingredients:
- 1 large sweet potato (1.5lbs)
- 1-2 tsp healthy oil
- salt and pepper, as need
- 3tbsp tahini paste
- 2cloves garlic
- 1/2-1 tsp salt (season)
- 1/2 tsp cayenne pepper
- 1/4 tsp smoked paprika
- 1/4 tsp cumin
- 1/2 lime

Directions
1. Pre-heat the oven to 375 F. With parchment paper, cover a baking/roasting plate.
2. Peel and carve the sweet potato into one-inch cubes. Smash/flatten the cloves of garlic with a knife.
3. Spread the garlic and sweet potato on a baking/roasting tray lined with parchment, and drizzle with oil. Sprinkle with salt and pepper and roast with a fork for 30 minutes or until soft and easy to mash.
4. Enable to cool slowly, then add and puree until smooth in a blender or food processor.
5. Combine the tahini, cinnamon, cayenne pepper, smoked paprika, cumin and 1/2 of the lime juice. Blend thoroughly.

Add a little water (1 tbsp at a time) for a thinner consistency and begin blending until smooth and creamy. I like an extra dense one of mine!
6. Pour the contents into a small serving bowl and surround the soft flatbread, pita chips, and carrot sticks with your pick. Using the dip as a tasty basis for your favorite protein and vegetables for a side-dish vibe. Enjoy!

Nutrition: Calories 240 Fat 11g Fiber 3g Carbs 4g Protein 12g

831. Smoked Salmon Dip

Preparation Time: 5 Minutes
Cooking time: 10 Minutes
Servings: 2 cups
Ingredients:
- 1 cup (8 ounces) of cream cheese
- 1/4 cup of sour cream
- 1/4 cup of mayonnaise
- 1 tbsp fresh lemon juice
- tbsp drained capers
- 1/4 tsp Tasbasco
- 4ounces smoked salmon, roughly chopped
- 2tbsps fresh chopped dill
- 2tbsps fresh chopped chives
- Salt, to taste

Directions
1. In a food processor equipped with a metal blade, mix the cream cheese, sour cream, mayonnaise, lemon juice, capers and Tabasco; pulse until combined. Add the salmon, dill and chives and pulse until the salmon is finely sliced, scraping the sides of the bowl as desired. If appropriate, taste and add salt (I normally add around 1/4 tsp, but it depends on the smoked salmon's saltiness). Serve with crackers or bagel chips as a sauce, or with bagels as a spread.
2. Make it ahead: You should make this dip a couple days ahead of time. It gets very firm in the fridge, however, so let it sit out before serving at room temperature, otherwise it would be difficult to scoop.

Nutrition: Calories 472 Protein 25.6g Fiber 0.6g Net Carbs 8.5mg Fat 32.0g Sodium 1532mg Carbs 9.1g Sugar 7.4g

832. Blue Cheese Dressing

Preparation Time: 10 Minutes
Cooking time: 0 Minutes
Servings: 2 ¼ cups
Ingredients:
- 1 cup of mayonnaise
- 1/2 cup of crumbled Maytag or other blue cheese (3 ounces), divided
- 1/2 cup of half and half
- 2tbsps sour cream
- 1 tbsp od freshly squeezed lemon juice
- Worcestershire sauce (1/4 tsp)
- kosher salt (1/2 tsp)
- Freshly ground black pepper

Preparation
1. Mix the mayonnaise, 1/4 cup of blue cheese, half and half, sour cream, lemon juice, Worcestershire, and salt together in a medium bowl, until smooth. Stir the remaining 1/4 of a cup of blue cheese gently and season with pepper to taste. Using it now or store it in the fridge for up to 3 days.

Nutrition: Calories 457 Protein 21.6g Fiber 0.2g Net Carbs 3.6mg Fat 35.0g Sodium 589mg Carbs 3.8g Sugar 2.2g

SAUCE, DIP AND DRESSING

833. Broccoli Dip

Preparation Time: 5 minutes
Cooking time: 20 minutes
Servings: 4
Ingredients:
- 1 ½ cups veggie stock
- 1/3 cup coconut milk
- 3 cups broccoli florets
- 2 garlic cloves; minced
- 1 tbsp. olive oil
- 1 tbsp. balsamic vinegar
- Salt and black pepper to taste.

Directions
1. In a pan that fits your air fryer, mix all the ingredients, toss.
2. Introduce in the fryer and cook at 390 F for 15 minutes. Divide into bowls and serve

Nutrition: Calories 163 Fat 4g Fiber 2g Carbs 4g Protein 5g

834. Crab and Artichoke Dip

Preparation Time: 5 minutes
Cooking time: 20 minutes
Servings: 4
Ingredients:
- 8oz. cream cheese, soft
- 12oz. jumbo crab meat
- 1 bunch green onions; minced
- 14oz. canned artichoke hearts, drained and chopped.
- 1 cup coconut cream
- 1 ½ cups mozzarella; shredded
- 1 tbsp. lemon juice
- 1 tbsp. lemon juice
- A pinch of salt and black pepper

Directions
1. In a bowl, combine all the ingredients except half of the cheese and whisk them really well.
2. Transfer this to a pan that fits your air fryer, introduce in the machine and cook at 400 F for 15 minutes
3. Sprinkle the rest of the mozzarella on top and cook for 5 minutes more. Divide the mix into bowls and serve as a party dip

Nutrition: Calories 240 Fat 8g Fiber 2g Carbs 4g Protein 14g

835. Feta Cheese Dip

Preparation Time: 5 minutes
Cooking time: 5 minutes
Servings: 6
Ingredients:
- 2 avocados, peeled, pitted and mashed
- ¼ cup spring onion; chopped.
- 1 garlic clove; minced
- ¼ cup parsley; chopped.
- ½ cup feta cheese, crumbled
- 1 tbsp. jalapeno; minced
- Juice of 1 lime

Directions
1. In a ramekin, mix all the ingredients and whisk them well.
2. Introduce in the fryer and cook at 380 F for 5 minutes. Serve as a party dip right away

Nutrition: Calories 200 Fat 12g Fiber 2g Carbs 4g Protein 9g

836. Eggplant Dip

Preparation Time: 5 minutes
Cooking time: 15 minutes
Servings: 4
Ingredients:
- 1 eggplant, peeled
- 1 garlic clove, peeled
- 1 tablespoon sesame oil
- ¼ teaspoon ginger, grated
- 1 chili pepper, minced
- ½ tablespoon spring onions, chopped
- ½ teaspoon chili powder
- ¼ teaspoon ground coriander
- ¼ teaspoon turmeric
- ½ teaspoon fresh cilantro, chopped

Directions
1. Chop the eggplant into the cubes and put it in the air fryer. Add garlic and cook the vegetables at 400 F for 15 minutes. Shake the vegetables every 5 minutes. After this, transfer the soft eggplants and garlic in the bowl and mash them with the help of the fork. Add sesame oil, ginger, minced chili pepper, onion, chili powder, ground coriander, and turmeric. Stir the mixture until homogenous and top with cilantro.

Nutrition: Calories 226 Protein 10.0g Fiber 3.7g Net Carbs 6.5g Fat 15.9g Sodium 776mg Carbs 10.2g Sugar 3.4g

837. Naan Bread Dippers

Preparation Time: 10 minutes
Cooking time: 40 minutes
Servings: 10
Ingredients:
- `4 naan bread, cut into 2-inch strips
- `3 tbsp. butter, melted
- `12 oz. light cream cheese, softened
- `1 cup plain yogurt
- `2 tsp. curry powder
- `2 cups cooked chicken, shredded
- `4 scallions, minced
- `⅓ cup golden raisins
- `6 oz. Monterey Jack cheese, grated [about 2 cups]
- `¼ cup fresh cilantro, chopped
- `Salt and freshly ground black pepper
- `½ cup slices
- `½ cup Major Grey's Chutney

Directions
1. Pre-heat Air Fryer to 400 F.
2. Slice up the naan in thirds lengthwise before cutting crosswise into 2-inch strips. In a bowl, toss the strips with the melted butter.
3. Move the naan strips to Air Fryer basket. Toast for 5 minutes, shaking the basket halfway through. You will have to do this in two batches.
4. Mix together the softened cream cheese and yogurt with a hand mixer or in a food processor. Add in the curry powder and combine evenly.
5. Fold in the shredded chicken, scallions, golden raisins, Monterey Jack cheese and chopped cilantro.
6. Sprinkle with salt and freshly ground black pepper as desired.
7. Pour the mixture into a 1-quart baking dish and spread out evenly. Arrange the slices on top. Air-fry at 300 F for 25 minutes.

8. Put a dollop of Major Grey's chutney in the center of the dip and scatter the scallions on top.
9. Serve the naan dippers with the hot dip.

Nutrition: Calories 472 Protein 25.6g Fiber 0.6g Net Carbs 8.5mg Fat 32.0g Sodium 1532mg Carbs 9.1g Sugar 7.4g

838. Cheese Artichoke Arugula Dip

Preparation Time: 5 minutes
Cooking time: 17 minutes
Servings: 10
Ingredients:
- `1/2 cup mozzarella cheese, shredded
- `3 cups arugula leaves, chopped
- `1/2 cup mayonnaise
- `7 oz brie cheese
- `1/3 tsp dried basil
- `2 garlic cloves, minced
- `1/3 cup sour cream
- `1/3 can artichoke hearts, drained and chopped
- `1/3 tsp pepper
- `1 tsp sea salt

Directions
1. Add all ingredients except mozzarella cheese into the air fryer baking dish and mix until well combined.
2. Spread mozzarella cheese on top and place dish in the air fryer.
3. Cook at 325 F for 17 minutes.
4. Serve and enjoy.

Nutrition: Calories 226 Protein 10.0g Fiber 3.7g Net Carbs 6.5g Fat 15.9g Sodium 776mg Carbs 10.2g Sugar 3.4g

839. Mozzarella, Brie and Artichoke Dip

Preparation Time: 5 minutes
Cooking time: 20 minutes
Servings: 10
Ingredients:
- cups arugula leaves, torn into pieces
- 1/3 can artichoke hearts, drained and chopped
- 1/2 cup Mozzarella cheese, shredded
- 1/3 cup sour cream
- cloves garlic, minced
- 1/3 teaspoon dried basil
- 1 teaspoon sea salt
- ounces Brie cheese
- 1/2 cup mayonnaise
- 1/3 teaspoon ground black pepper, or more to taste
- A pinch of ground allspice

Directions
1. Combine together the Brie cheese, mayonnaise, sour cream, garlic, basil, salt, ground black pepper, and the allspice.
2. Throw in the artichoke hearts and arugula; gently stir to combine. Transfer the prepared mixture to a baking dish. Now, scatter the Mozzarella cheese evenly over the top.
3. Bake in your Air Fryer at 325 F for 17 minutes. Serve with keto veggie sticks. Bon appétit!

Nutrition: Calories 240 Fat 8g Fiber 2g Carbs 4g Protein 14g

840. Garlic Cheese Dip

Preparation Time: 10 minutes
Cooking time: 15 minutes
Servings: 10
Ingredients:
- 1 lb. mozzarella; shredded
- garlic cloves; minced
- tbsp. olive oil
- 1 tbsp. thyme; chopped.
- 1 tsp. rosemary; chopped.
- A pinch of salt and black pepper

Directions
1. In a pan that fits your air fryer, mix all the ingredients, whisk really well, introduce in the air fryer and cook at 370 F for 10 minutes. Divide into bowls and serve right away.

Nutrition: Calories 184 Fat 11g Carbs 5g Protein 7g

841. Cheesy Beef Dip

Preparation Time: 10 minutes
Cooking time: 25 minutes
Servings: 12
Ingredients:
- 1 lb corned beef, diced
- ¾ cup mayonnaise
- oz can sauerkraut, drained
- oz Swiss cheese, shredded
- Pepper
- Salt

Directions
1. Fit the Air fryer oven with the rack in position, add all ingredients into the bowl and mix well and pour into the greased baking dish. Set to bake at 400 F for 30 minutes. After 5 minutes place the baking dish in the preheated oven. Serve and enjoy.

Nutrition: Calories 283 Fat 25g Carbs 3g Protein 12g

842. Cheesy Spinach Dip

Preparation Time: 8 minutes
Cooking time: 20 minutes
Servings: 12
Ingredients:
- oz frozen spinach, defrosted and chopped
- 1 cup sour cream
- 1 tsp garlic salt
- cups cheddar cheese, shredded
- oz cream cheese

Directions
1. Fit the Air fryer oven with the rack in position, add all ingredients into the mixing bowl and mix well. Transfer mixture into the baking dish. Set to bake at 350 F for 25 minutes. After 5 minutes place the baking dish in the preheated oven. Serve and enjoy.

Nutrition: Calories 185 Fat 16.9g Carbs 2g Protein 7g

843. Tomatoes Dip

Preparation Time: 5 minutes
Cooking time: 15 minutes
Servings: 6
Ingredients:
- 12 oz. cream cheese, soft
- oz. mozzarella cheese; grated ¼ cup basil; chopped.
- ¼ cup parmesan; grated
- garlic cloves; minced
- 1 pint grape tomatoes; halved
- tbsp. thyme; chopped.
- ½ tbsp. oregano; chopped.
- 1 tsp. olive oil
- A pinch of salt and black pepper

Directions
1. Put the tomatoes in your air fryer's basket and cook them at 400 F for 15 minutes, in a blender, combine the fried tomatoes with the rest of the ingredients and pulse well. Transfer this to a ramekin, place it in the air fryer and cook at 400 F for 5 - 6 minutes more. Serve as a snack.

Nutrition: Calories 184 Fat 8gCarbs 4g Protein 8g

844. Easy Buffalo Chicken Dip

Preparation Time: 10 minutes
Cooking time: 25 minutes
Servings: 8
Ingredients:
- chicken breasts, skinless, boneless, cooked and shredded
- 1 cup Monterey jack cheese, shredded
- 1 cup cheddar cheese, shredded
- 1/4 cup blue cheese, crumbled
- 1/2 cup ranch dressing
- 1/2 cup buffalo wing sauce
- oz cream cheese, softened

Directions
1. Spray a 1.5-quart casserole dish with cooking spray and set aside.
2. Insert wire rack in rack position 4. Select bake, set temperature 350 F, timer for 25 minutes. Press start to preheat the oven.
3. Add cream cheese into the casserole dish and top with shredded chicken, ranch dressing, and buffalo sauce.
4. Sprinkle cheddar cheese, Monterey jack cheese and blue cheese on top of chicken mixture.
5. Bake for 25 minutes.
6. Serve and enjoy.

Nutrition: Calories 298 Fat 22.8g Carbs 2g Sugar 0.6g Protein 20.8g Cholesterol 94mg

845. Perfect Goat Cheese Dip

Preparation Time: 10 minutes
Cooking time: 20 minutes
Servings: 8
Ingredients:
- 12 oz goat cheese
- tsp rosemary, chopped
- 1 tsp red pepper flakes
- garlic cloves, minced
- tbsp olive oil
- 1/2 cup parmesan cheese, shredded
- oz cream cheese
- 1/2 tsp salt

Directions
1. Spray a baking dish with cooking spray and set aside.
2. Insert wire rack in rack position 4. Select bake, set temperature 390 F, timer for 20 minutes. Press start to preheat the oven.
3. Add all ingredients into the mixing bowl and mix until well combined. Pour mixture into the baking dish and bake for 20 minutes.
4. Serve and enjoy.

Nutrition: Calories 294 Fat 24.9g Carbs 2.3g Sugar 1g Protein 16g Cholesterol 64mg

846. Easy Taco Dip

Preparation Time: 10 minutes
Cooking time: 25 minutes
Servings: 2
Ingredients:
- 1/4 cup salsa
- tbsp red pepper, chopped
- tbsp onion, chopped
- 1 cup cheddar cheese, shredded
- 1/2 cup sour cream
- 1/2 cup miracle whip
- 1 oz taco seasoning

Directions
1. Spray a baking dish with cooking spray and set aside.
2. Insert wire rack in rack position 4. Select bake, set temperature 350 F, timer for 25 minutes. Press start to preheat the oven.
3. In a bowl, mix together all ingredients and pour into the baking dish and bake for 25 minutes.
4. Serve and enjoy.

Nutrition: Calories 661 Fat 52.5g Carbs 31.4g Sugar 11.6g Protein 19.9g Cholesterol 105mg

847. Spicy Mexican Cheese Dip

Preparation Time: 10 minutes
Cooking time: 30 minutes
Servings: 10
Ingredients:
- oz cream cheese, softened
- 1/2 cup hot salsa
- cups cheddar cheese, shredded
- 1 cup sour cream

Directions
1. Spray an 8*8-inch baking dish with cooking spray and set aside.
2. Insert wire rack in rack position 4. Select bake, set temperature 350 F, timer for 25 minutes. Press start to preheat the oven.
3. In a mixing bowl, mix together all ingredients until well combined and pour into the baking dish and bake for 30 minutes.
4. Serve and enjoy.

Nutrition: Calories 348 Fat 31.9g Carbs 3.4g Sugar 0.7g Protein 12.8g Cholesterol 96mg

848. Cheesy Crab Dip

Preparation Time: 10 minutes
Cooking time: 15 minutes
Servings: 4
Ingredients:
- oz crab meat
- 1/4 tsp paprika
- 1/2 tsp garlic powder
- 1/4 cup onion, chopped
- 1 1/2 tsp garlic, minced
- 1 cup cheddar cheese, shredded
- 1/2 cup sour cream
- 1/4 cup mayonnaise
- oz cream cheese, softened
- Pepper
- Salt

Directions
1. Spray a baking dish with cooking spray and set aside.
2. Insert wire rack in rack position 4. Select bake, set temperature 390 F, timer for 15 minutes. Press start to preheat the oven.
3. Add all ingredients into the bowl and mix until well combined. Pour mixture into the baking dish and bake for 15 minutes.
4. Serve and enjoy.

Nutrition: Calories 487 Fat 41.1g Carbs 9g Sugar 1.7g Protein 19.7g Cholesterol 139mg

849. Perfect Crab Dip

Preparation Time: 5 minutes
Cooking time: 7 minutes
Servings: 4
Ingredients:
- 1 cup crabmeat
- tbsp parsley, chopped
- tbsp fresh lemon juice
- tbsp hot sauce
- 1/2 cup green onion, sliced
- cups cheese, grated
- 1/4 cup mayonnaise
- 1/4 tsp pepper
- 1/2 tsp salt

Directions
1. In a 6-inch dish, mix together crabmeat, hot sauce, cheese, mayo, pepper, and salt.
2. Place dish in air fryer basket and cook dip at 400 F for 7 minutes.
3. Remove dish from air fryer.
4. Drizzle dip with lemon juice and garnish with parsley.
5. Serve and enjoy.

Nutrition: Calories 313 Fat 23.9g Carbs 8.8g Sugar 3.1g Protein 16.2g Cholesterol 67mg

850. Yummy Chicken Dip

Preparation Time: 10 minutes
Cooking time: 20 minutes
Servings: 6
Ingredients:
- cups chicken, cooked and shredded
- 3/4 cup sour cream
- 1/4 tsp onion powder
- oz cream cheese, softened
- tbsp hot sauce
- 1/4 tsp garlic powder

Directions
1. Preheat the air fryer to 325 F.
2. Add all ingredients in a large bowl and mix until well combined.
3. Transfer mixture in air fryer baking dish and place in the air fryer.
4. Cook chicken dip for 20 minutes.
5. Serve and enjoy.

Nutrition: Calories 245 Fat 17g Carbs 1.5g Sugar 0.2g Protein 16g Cholesterol 85mg

851. Creamy Mushroom Dip

Preparation time: 10 minutes
Cooking time: 10 minutes
Servings: 10
Ingredients:
- oz. Cremona mushrooms; chopped.
  - oz. Portobello mushrooms; chopped.
- 1 cup chicken stock
- 1/4 cup coconut cream
- 1 oz. Parmesan cheese; grated.
- 1/4 cup olive oil
- garlic cloves; minced.
- 1 yellow onion; chopped.
- 1 tbsp. Thyme; chopped.
- 1 tbsp. Cilantro; chopped.
- Salt and black pepper to the taste

Directions
1. Set the Air Fryer Oven on Sauté mode, add the oil, heat it up, add the onion and the garlic, stir and cook for 5 minutes.
2. Place the pressure lid on and cook on High for 20 minutes. Release the pressure naturally for 10 minutes, divide into bowls and serve as party dip

Nutrition: Calories 329 Fat 30g Carbs 6g Protein 310g Sodium 813g | Fiber 2g Saturated Fat 8g

852. Different Hummus

Preparation time: 10 minutes
Cooking time: 8 minutes
Servings: 2
Ingredients:
- garlic cloves; minced.
- 1/2 cup veggie stock
- 1/4 cup lemon juice
- cups carrots; chopped.
- 1/4 cup olive oil
- 1 cup canned chickpeas; drained.
- A pinch of salt and black pepper
- 1 tsp. sweet paprika

SAUCE, DIP AND DRESSING

Directions
1. In the bowl, mix the carrots with the oil, salt, and pepper, toss and leave aside for 10 minutes.
2. Put the carrots in the Air Fryer oven basket and put the basket inside.
3. Set the machine on Baking mode and cook at 400 F for 20 minutes. In the blender, mix roasted carrots with all the other ingredients, pulse well, divide into bowls and serve as snack

Nutrition: Calories 171 Fat 15.7g Carbs 3.7g Protein 4.9g Fiber 1.3g Sugar 1.2g Saturated Fat 9.7g

853. Hot Spread

Preparation Time: 5 minutes
Cooking time: 10 minutes
Servings: 4

Ingredients:
- red chilies, dried, seedless and chopped
- 1/4 cup veggie stock
- garlic cloves; minced.
- tbsp. apple cider vinegar
- 1 tsp. sugar
- 1/2 tsp. Oregano; chopped.
- Salt and black pepper to the taste

Directions
1. In your Air Fryer Oven, combine all the ingredients, toss, put the pressure lid on and cook on High for 10 minutes. Release the pressure naturally for 10 minutes, blend everything using an immersion blender, divide into bowls and serve

Nutrition: Calories 171 Fat 15.7g Carbs 3.7g Protein 4.9g Fiber 1.3g Sugar 1.2g Saturated Fat 9.7g

854. Basil Cream Cheese Dip

Preparation Time: 5 minutes
Cooking time: 10 minutes
Servings: 4

Ingredients:
- 10 calamite olives, pitted and minced
- oz. bacon, cooked and crumbled
- oz. cream cheese
- 1 tbsp. Basil; chopped.
- tbsp. basil pesto
- Salt and black pepper to the taste

Directions
1. In your Air Fryer Oven's baking pan, combine all the ingredients, and stir well. Put the reversible rack in the Air Fryer Oven, put the pan in the machine, set it on Baking mode, and cook at 360 F for 8 minutes. Divide the dip into bowls and serve

Nutrition: Calories 171 Fat 15.7g Carbs 3.7g Protein 4.9g Fiber 1.3g Sugar 1.2g Saturated Fat 9.7g

855. Honey Tomato Dip

Preparation time: 15 minutes
Cooking time: 9 minutes
Servings: 4

Ingredients:
- 1 yellow onion; chopped.
- garlic cloves; minced.
- 1 cup tomato puree
- 1 tbsp. olive oil
- tbsp. white vinegar
- tbsp. honey
- 1 tsp. Tabasco sauce
- Salt and black pepper to the taste

Directions
1. In your Air Fryer Oven machine, combine all the ingredients, toss, put the pressure lid on, set on high, and cook for 12 minutes. Release the pressure naturally for 10 minutes, stir the mix again, divide into bowls and serve

Nutrition: Calories 301 Fat 12g Carbs 1.5g Protein 28g

856. Tofu Dip

Preparation time: 15 minutes
Cooking time: 10 minutes
Servings: 20

Ingredients:
- oz. cream cheese, soft
- 1 yellow onion; chopped.
- 1 tbsp. olive oil
- tbsp. white vinegar
- 1/3 cup sour cream
- 1/2 cup firm tofu
- A pinch of salt and black pepper

Directions
1. In your Air Fryer oven, combine all the ingredients, put the pressure lid on, set the machine on High, and cook for 10 minutes. Release the pressure naturally for 10 minutes, blend everything with an immersion blender, divide into bowls and serve

Nutrition: Calories 164 Fat 3g Total Carbs 28g Protein 6g Sugar 2g

857. Mango and Chili Spread

Preparation time: 15 minutes
Cooking time: 25 minutes
Servings: 4

Ingredients:
- spring onions; chopped.
- 1 1/4 cup sugar
- 1 1/4 apple cider vinegar
- mangos, peeled chopped
- red hot chilies; chopped.
- 1 tbsp. olive oil
- tbsp. Ginger; minced.
- 1/2 tsp. cinnamon powder

Directions
1. Set the Air Fryer oven on Sauté mode, add the oil, heat it up, add the onions, stir and cook for 2 minutes. Add the other ingredients, put the pressure lid, on and cook on High for 12 minutes
2. Release the pressure naturally for 10 minutes, blend everything using an immersion blender, divide into bowls, and serve.

Nutrition: Calories 171 Fat 3.6g Total Carbs 26.8g Protein 7.3g Cholesterol 18mg Sodium 324mg

858. Smoked Dip

Preparation time: 15 minutes
Cooking time: 20 minutes
Servings: 6
Ingredients:
- o oz. Red peppers; chopped.
- 1 1/4 cups apple cider vinegar
- 1 tbsp. smoked paprika
- 1 tsp. liquid smoke
- Salt and black pepper to the taste

Directions
1. In your Air Fryer oven, combine all the ingredients, put the pressure lid on, and cook on High for 8 minutes. Release the pressure naturally for 10 minutes, blend using an immersion blender, divide into bowls, and serve.

Nutrition: Calories 166 Fat 4g Carbs 26g Protein 6g Sodium 209mg

859. Meat Sauce

Preparation time: 3 minutes
Cooking time: 10 minutes
Servings: 3
Ingredients:
- 1/2 large, chopped purple onion
- 1-1.5 pounds of ground beef
- 1 teaspoon of minced garlic
- cans of 15 ounces of tomato sauce
- ½ tablespoon of dried oregano
- ½ tablespoon of dried basil
- 1 teaspoon of crushed red pepper flakes
- ½ teaspoon of garlic powder
- ½ teaspoon of sea salt
- 1-2 cups of freshly chopped basil

Directions:
1. Preheat your air fryer oven by pressing the setting function sauté on the display panel
2. Add in the diced purple onion and sauté this chopped purple onion
3. Add in the minced garlic and combine with the sautéed purple onion
4. Add in the ground beef and the onion mixture to your air fryer oven pan.
5. Crumble the ground beef and sauté it it until it becomes brown
6. Excess any grease from the air fryer oven pan.
7. Add in the tomato sauce, the oregano, the dried basil, the crushed red pepper flakes, the garlic powder, and the sea salt to the mixture of the beef and let simmer for about 10 minutes
8. Press the button Cancel/Keep Warm and let the meat keep warm for about 10 minutes
9. Scoop the sauce and Sprinkle with fresh basil
10. Serve the sauce over Zucchini noodles and enjoy your dish!

Nutrition: Calories 263 Fat 18.6g Carbs 10.6g Fiber 3g Protein 11.8g

860. Mushroom Broth

Preparation time: 5 minutes
Cooking time: 13 minutes
Servings: 5-6
Ingredients:
- cups of water
- ½ Cup of dried porcini mushrooms
- Medium peeled and smashed garlic cloves of garlic
- 1 Teaspoon of scant
- 1 teaspoon of fine grain sea salt
- ½ teaspoon of freshly ground pepper
- 1 or 2 sprigs of fresh thyme

Directions:
1. Combine the dried mushrooms with the water and the garlic in your air fryer oven pan
2. Pressure cook on high for about 10 minutes.
3. Carefully quick release; then gently shake or tap.
4. Season with the pepper and the salt as well as the thyme; then wait for 1 to 2 minutes and stir
5. Adjust the taste of salt to your liking
6. Store the broth in the refrigerator for days!

Nutrition: Calories 5 Carbs 1g

861. Red Lentil Mushroom Ragu

Preparation time: 5 minutes
Cooking time: 13 minutes
Servings: 6
Ingredients:
- cups (950 ml) vegetable broth
- 1 large yellow onion, diced
- stalks celery, diced
- medium carrots, diced
- 12 ounces (340g) Cremini mushrooms, quartered
- cloves garlic, diced
- 1½ cups (300g) red lentils, rinsed
- 1½ teaspoons (7.5 ml) sea salt
- teaspoons (10 ml) thyme
- teaspoons (10 ml) oregano
- 1 teaspoon (5 ml) basil
- ¼ teaspoon (1.25 ml) red pepper flakes
- 28 ounces (795g) crushed tomatoes, canned
- 28 ounces (795g) diced tomatoes, canned
- tablespoons (45 ml) tomato paste

Directions:
1. Prepare all the ingredients per the list of ingredients.
2. Add all the ingredients, in the order given, to the inner liner of your air fryer oven pan.
3. Do not stir and make sure the broth is on the bottom.
4. Close and lock the lid ensuring the Pressure Valve is in the Sealing Position.
5. Select the Pressure Cook/Manual button and set the cooking time for 2 minutes.
6. Once the cooking time is complete, allow a 5-minute Natural Pressure Release, then carefully turn the Pressure Valve from Sealing to Venting to release any remaining pressure.
7. Once all the pressure has been released and the Float Valve has dropped, carefully remove the lid.
8. Then, carefully remove the inner pot to a heatproof surface.
9. Stir well and serve immediately or refrigerate or freeze for later use.

SAUCE, DIP AND DRESSING

Nutrition: Calories 311 Calories from Fat 10 Total Carbs 62.96g Fat 1.12g Protein 18.87g Sodium 3040mg Potassium 1645mg

862. Fresh Tomato Marinara Sauce

Preparation time: 5 minutes
Cooking time: 13 minutes
Servings: 20 (½ cup servings)
Ingredients:
- 4½ pounds (2 kg) Roma (plum) tomatoes, diced
- 1 medium yellow onion, chopped
- cloves garlic, minced
- 1 bay leaf
- 1 cup (240 ml) red wine
- tablespoons (25g) sugar, can substitute honey if you wish but it won't be vegan
- tablespoons (30 ml) dried basil
- 1 tablespoon (15 ml) dried oregano
- 1 tablespoon (15 ml) dried thyme
- 1 tablespoon (15 ml) sea salt
- 1 teaspoon (5 ml) black pepper, freshly ground
- tablespoons (30 ml) balsamic vinegar

Directions:
1. Combine all of the ingredients, with the exception of the balsamic vinegar, in the inner pot of your air fryer oven and stir well.
2. Close and lock the lid ensuring the Pressure Valve is in the Sealing position.
3. Select Pressure Cook/Manual mode and set the cooking time for 5minutes.
4. When cooking time is complete do a 10-minute Natural Pressure Release followed by a Quick Release by carefully turning the Pressure Valve from Sealing to Venting.
5. Once all the pressure has been released and the Float Valve has dropped, carefully remove the lid.
6. Add the vinegar and stir well.
7. Carefully remove the inner pot to a heatproof surface and blend with an immersion blender until smooth. If you don't have an immersion blender, you can use a regular blender and blend the sauce in batches until smooth.
8. Transfer the sauce to sterilized canning jars and allow to cool.
9. Refrigerate or freeze for later use.

Nutrition: Calories 106 Calories from Fat 5 Total Carbs 21.41g Fat 0.65g Protein 4.4g Sodium 373mg Potassium 1149mg

863. Fresh Tomato Basil Sauce

Preparation time: 5 minutes
Cooking time: 13 minutes
Servings: 20 (½ cup servings)
Ingredients:
- 4½ pounds (2 kg) Roma (plum) tomatoes, diced
- 1 medium yellow onion, diced
- cloves garlic, minced
- 1 tablespoon (15 ml) sea salt
- ½ teaspoon (2.5 ml) black pepper, freshly ground 1½ teaspoons (7.5 ml) marjoram, dried
- 1½ teaspoons (7.5 ml) oregano, dried
- ¼ teaspoon (1.25 ml) crushed red pepper
- 1 medium bay leaf
- ¼ cup (6g) fresh basil, chopped
- ¼ cup (15g) fresh parsley, chopped

Directions:
1. Combine all of the ingredients in the inner pot of your air fryer oven pan and stir well.
2. Close and lock the lid ensuring the Pressure Valve is in the Sealing position.
3. Select Pressure Cook/Manual mode and set the cooking time for 8 minutes.
4. When cooking time is complete do a Quick Release by carefully turning the Pressure Valve from Sealing to Venting.
5. Once all the pressure has been released and the Float Valve has dropped, carefully remove the lid.
6. Stir well.
7. Carefully remove the inner pot to a heatproof surface and blend with an immersion blender until smooth. If you don't have an immersion blender, you can use a regular blender and blend the sauce in batches until smooth.
8. Transfer the sauce to sterilized canning jars and allow to cool.
9. Refrigerate or freeze for later use.

Nutrition: Calories 35 Calories from Fat 2 Total Carbs 8.07g Fat 0.23g Protein 1.49g Sodium 1483mg Potassium 319mg

864. Red Onion Marmalade

Preparation Time: 10 Minutes
Cooking time: 30 Minutes
Servings: 8
Ingredients:
- 1 tablespoon of butter
- ¼ cup of white sugar
- ¼ cup of balsamic vinegar
- tablespoons of olive oil
- large red onions, should be thinly sliced
- 1 cup of dry red wine
- 1 pinch of salt to taste

Direction:
1. Heat butter together with olive oil in a large skillet and place on medium heat. Cook and stir sugar and onions in hot oil until the onions start to caramelize in about 15 minutes. Then stir balsamic vinegar and red wine into the onion mixture and let it boil. Reduce the heat to medium-low and simmer until all the liquid is evaporated in about 15-20 minutes—finally, season with salt.

Nutrition: Calories 111.5 Carbs 11.7g Protein 0.5g Fat 4.9g Cholesterol 3.8mg Sodium 14.9mg

865. Louisiana Crab Dip

Preparation Time: 15 Minutes
Cooking time: 50 Minutes
Servings: 8
Ingredients:
- tablespoons unsalted butter
- garlic cloves, minced
- ½ cup mayonnaise
- 1 pound (16 ounces) whipped or room temperature cream cheese
- teaspoons Worcestershire sauce
- teaspoons hot sauce
- teaspoons freshly squeezed lemon juice
- teaspoons Creole seasoning
- ¾ cup Parmesan cheese
- 1-pound lump crab meat

Directions:
1. Let preheat for 3 minutes.
2. Add the butter and garlic and sauté for 2 minutes.
3. Add the mayonnaise, cream cheese, Worcestershire sauce, hot sauce, lemon juice, Creole seasoning, and Parmesan cheese. Stir well.
4. Add the crab meat and lightly fold to incorporate. Close air fryer oven lid.
5. Set the temperature to 350 F, and set the time to 40 minutes. Select Start/Stop to begin
6. When cooking is complete, open the lid. Let cool for 10 minutes before serving.

Nutrition: Calories 391 Fat 39g Saturated Fat 18g Cholesterol 114mg Sodium 976mg Carbs 4g Protein 16g

866. Three-Layer Taco Dip

Preparation Time: 10 Minutes
Cooking time: 15 Minutes
Servings: 6

Ingredients:
- (15.5-ounce) cans pinto beans, rinsed and drained
- 1 white onion, chopped
- garlic cloves, chopped
- 1 (14.5-ounce) can diced tomatoes
- 1 serrano chile, seeded and chopped
- 1 teaspoon kosher salt
- teaspoons ground cumin
- teaspoons chili powder
- cups shredded Mexican blend cheese
- 1 cup shredded iceberg lettuce

Directions:
1. Place the beans, onions, garlic, tomatoes, chile, salt, cumin, and chili powder in the pot. Assemble the pressure lid, making sure the pressure release valve is in the SEAL position.
2. Set the temperature to 375 F and set time to 5 minutes. Select Start/Stop to begin.
3. Using a silicone spatula, stir the mixture in the pot. Sprinkle shredded cheese across the top of the bean mixture. Close crisping lid.
4. Set the time to 10 minutes. Select Start/Stop to begin.
5. When cooking is complete, open the lid. Let cool for 5 minutes, then add the shredded lettuce. Serve immediately.

Nutrition: Calories 327 Fat 14g Saturated Fat 9g Cholesterol 46mg Sodium 612mg Carbs 33g Fiber 10g Protein 19g

867. Mexican Street Corn Queso Dip

Preparation Time: 10 Minutes
Cooking time: 20 Minutes
Servings: 8

Ingredients:
- 1 (8-ounce) package cream cheese, quartered
- ounces cotija cheese, crumbled, 2 ounces reserved for topping
- 1 (10-ounce) can fire-roasted tomatoes with chiles
- ½ cup mayonnaise
- Zest of 2 limes
- Juice of 2 limes
- (8-ounce) packages shredded Mexican cheese blend, divided
- 1 garlic clove, grated
- 1 (14.75-ounce) can cream corn
- 1 cup of frozen corn
- Kosher salt
- Freshly ground black pepper

Directions:
1. Pour the cream cheese, 4 ounces of cotija cheese, tomatoes with chiles, mayonnaise, lime zest, and juice, one 8-ounce package Mexican cheese blend, garlic, cream corn, and frozen corn in the pot. Season with salt and pepper and stir. Close crisping lid.
2. Set the temperature to 375 F, and set the time to 20 minutes. Select Start/Stop to begin.
3. After 10 minutes, open the lid and sprinkle the dip with the remaining 2 ounces of cotija cheese and remaining 8-ounce package of Mexican blend cheese. Close the crisping lid and continue cooking.
4. When cooking is complete, the cheese will be melted and the dip hot and bubbling at the edges. Open the lid and let the dip cool for 5 to 10 minutes before serving. Serve topped with chopped cilantro, hot sauce, and chili powder, if desired.

Nutrition: Calories 538 Fat 45g Saturated Fat 22g Cholesterol 109mg Sodium 807mg Carbs 18g Fiber 2g Protein 20g

868. Cheesy Bacon Dipping Sauce

Preparation Time: 10 Minutes
Cooking time: 20 Minutes
Servings: 8

Ingredients:
- cloves Garlic, minced
- ounces Cream cheese, softened
- ½ cup Sour cream
- 1 cup Shredded mozzarella cheese
- 1 cup Shredded cheddar
- ounces Bacon, cooked and crumbled
- oz. Diced tomatoes

Directions:
1. Add tomatoes, cream cheese, and sour cream and allow to warm.
2. Add the onion and mix.
3. Cook on low for 2 hours.
4. Add bacon pieces and mix. Cook for 1 hour more.
5. Sprinkle with cheddar and serve with veggies.

Nutrition: Calories 200 Fat 17.7g Carbs 3.9g Protein 7.1g

869. Caramel Sauce

Preparation Time: 10 Minutes
Cooking time: 10 Minutes
Servings: 4

Ingredients:
- tbsp. Butter
- tbsp. Heavy cream
- 1 tsp. Confectioners swerve
- 1 tbsp. Stevia caramel flavor
- Salt to taste

Directions:
1. In a pan, sauté butter until golden brown.
2. Add the swerve and salt, and mix.
3. Add cream and mix well.
4. Remove from the heat and add the extract.
5. Cool and serve.

Nutrition: Calories 154 Fat 17.1g Carbs 1.7g Protein 0.4g

870. Alfredo Sauce

Cook time: 10 minutes
Servings: 4
Ingredients
- Butter – 2 tbsp.
- Minced garlic – 4 cloves
- Heavy cream – 1 cup
- Grated Parmesan cheese – 7 tbsp.
- Freshly ground nutmeg – ½ tsp.
- Salt and pepper to taste

Directions:
1. Add butter in a hot skillet and sauté with garlic for 1 minute.
2. Add the heavy cream and mix.
3. Add the Parmesan, 1 tbsp. at a time and mix after each edition. Add nutmeg and mix. Stir continuously for 5 to 10 minutes, being careful not to boil the sauce.
4. Season with salt and pepper, cool and serve.

Nutrition: Calories: 131 Fat: 13.1g Carbs: 1.4g Protein: 2.9g

871. Beef Spaghetti Sauce

Cook time: 8 hours
Servings: 4
Ingredients
- Ground beef – 1 lb.
- Onion – 1, sliced
- Diced tomatoes – 1 (16 oz.) can
- Oregano, salt, pepper, and Italian seasoning to taste

Directions:
1. Brown the ground beef.
2. Add the beef to the Crock-Pot.
3. Add diced tomatoes to the pot.
4. Caramelize the onions and add to the Crock-Pot.
5. Add spices to the taste.
6. Mix and cook on low for 8 hours.
7. Serve.

Nutrition: Calories: 248 Fat: 7.7g Carbs: 7g Protein: 35.8g

872. Spaghetti Sauce

Cook time: 8 hours
Servings: 10
Ingredients
- Olive oil – ¼ cup
- Salt pork – 2 ounces, sliced
- Onion – 3 tbsp., minced
- Garlic – 2 cloves, minced
- Crushed tomatoes – 2 (28 oz.) cans
- Fresh basil leaves – 6
- Dried oregano – ½ tsp.
- Salt and pepper to taste

Directions:
1. Heat the oil in a pan.
2. Add the salted pork and cook until the fat is rendered.
3. Remove the pork from the pan and add garlic and onion to the pan.
4. Sauté until the onion is translucent. Add the onion mixture and crushed tomatoes to the Crock-Pot.
5. Cook the pork in the same pan until cooked through. Add the meat to the pot.
6. Cover and cook on low for 8 hours.
7. Garnish with basil, oregano, and season to taste and serve.

Nutrition: Calories: 113 Fat: 9.2g Carbs: 7.4g Protein: 2.1g

EMILY ROMERO

BREAD, BAGEL AND PIZZA

873. Bread Roll

Preparation time: 11 minutes
Cooking time: 16 minutes
Servings: 4
Ingredients:
- 1/2 tsp. of turmeric powder
- chopped green chilies
- slices of bread
- Black pepper and salt
- boiled and mashed potatoes
- curry leaves
- chopped yellow onions
- 1/2 tsp. of mustard seeds
- 1 chopped coriander brunch
- tbsp. of olive oil

Directions
1. Put mustard seeds, 1 tsp. of oil, and turmeric in a pan and heat over medium heat
2. Add onion, pepper, curry leaves, mashed potatoes, chilies, and salt. Stir, remove from heat, and allow cooling
3. Sprinkle water on the slices of bread.
4. Put one piece on a flat surface, put a little potato mix in it. Wrap the bread round the mix
5. Do the same for the remaining potato mix
6. Place the bread roll in the Air fryer oven
7. Set the air fryer to air fry mode at bake preset.
8. Cook for 12 minutes at 400 F
9. Serve immediately as breakfast

Nutrition: Calories 131 Carbs 27g Proteins 5g

874. Ham Rolls

Preparation time: 11 minutes
Cooking time: 11 minutes
Servings: 4
Ingredients:
- tsp. of mustard
- 1 sheet puff pastry
- slices of chopped ham
- handful of grated gruyere cheese

Directions
1. Spread the puff pastry sheet on a working surface
2. Put ham, mustard, and cheese on it
3. Roll the pastry tight and cut to your desired medium
4. Put the rolls in the Air fryer oven
5. Set to air fry mode at pastry preset
6. Cook at 375 F for 10 minutes
7. Serve immediately.

Nutrition: Calories 211 Fat 5g Carbs 31g Proteins 13g

875. Raspberry Roll

Preparation time: 30 minutes
Cooking time: 22 minutes
Servings: 6
Ingredients:
- 1 egg
- 1 lemon zest
- tbsp. of butter
- 1 tsp. of vanilla extract
- 12 ounces of raspberries
- tbsp. of sugar
- tsp. of yeast
- 1 tbsp. of cornstarch
- 1/4 cup of sugar
- ounces of cream cheese
- 3-1/4 cups of flour
- 1 cup of milk

Directions
1. Mix sugar, yeast, and flour in a bowl.
2. Add egg and milk, mix until it forms a dough
3. Place the dough on a flat surface
4. Mix vanilla, cream cheese, lemon zest, and sugar in another bowl.
5. Mix corn starch and raspberries in a third bowl, pour it on the cream cheese mixture
6. Pour the mix on the dough
7. Roll the dough and cut to your desired medium. Spray with cooking oil
8. Place the dough in the Air fryer oven
9. Set the air fryer to air fry mode at bake preset
10. Cook for 30 minutes at 400 F

Nutrition: Calories 211 Fat 5g Carbs 42g Proteins 5g

876. Egg Rolls

Preparation time: 11 minutes
Cooking time: 16 minutes
Servings: 4
Ingredients:
- 1 egg
- 1/2 cup of mushroom
- chopped green onion
- 1 tbsp. of cornstarch
- 1/2 cup of carrots
- tbsp. of soy sauce
- 1/2 cup of grated zucchini
- wrappers of egg roll

Directions
1. Mix zucchini, carrots, soy sauce, mushroom, and green onion in a bowl.
2. Place the egg roll wrappers on a flat surface
3. Put the veggie mixture on the egg roll
4. Mix egg and corn starch in another bowl
5. Rub the egg mix over the egg rolls
6. Transfer the egg rolls to the Air fryer oven
7. Set to air fry mode at toast preset
8. Cook for 15 minutes at 400 F
9. Serve immediately

Nutrition: Calories 198 Fat 5g Carbs 30g Proteins 11g

877. Garlic with Bacon Pizza

Preparation time: 11 minutes
Cooking time: 11 minutes
Servings: 4
Ingredients:
- 1/2 tsp. of garlic powder
- Cooking spray
- dinner rolls
- slices of bacon
- cloves of garlic
- 1 cup of tomato sauce
- 1-1/4 cup of cheddar cheese
- 1/2 tsp. of dried oregano

Directions
1. Put the dinner rolls on a flat surface. Press it well.
2. Drizzle with cooking spray
3. Place it in the Air fryer oven.
4. Set the air fryer to air fry mode at bake preset.
5. Cook for 2 minutes at 375 F
6. Put bacon, garlic, tomato sauce, cheese, and tomato sauce on the dinner roll
7. Put it back in the air fryer and bake for another 8 minutes at 3750F
8. Serve immediately

Nutrition: Calories 411 Fat 23g Carbs 41g Proteins 16g

878. Spring Roll

Preparation time: 11 minutes
Cooking time: 26 minutes
Servings: 7
Ingredients:
- 1 grated carrot
- Black pepper and salt
- tbsp. of water
- cups of green cabbage
- sheets of spring roll
- 1 tbsp. of grated ginger
- chopped yellow onions
- tbsp. of olive oil
- 1 tsp. of soy sauce
- 1/2 chili pepper
- tbsp. of cornflour
- 1 tsp. of sugar
- cloves of garlic

Directions
1. Put the oil in the pan and heat over medium heat.
2. Add soy sauce, ginger, onion, sugar, cabbage, salt, chili pepper, pepper, and carrots.
3. Cook for about 3 minutes
4. Place the spring roll sheet on a flat surface.
5. Put the cabbage mix on the roll sheet, and seal well
6. Place the roll in the air fryer
7. Set the Air fryer oven to air fry mode at bake preset.
8. Cook for 10 minutes at 375 F
9. Serve immediately

Nutrition: Calories 155 Fat 9g Carbs 5g Proteins 17g

879. Chicken Roll

Preparation time: 11 minutes
Cooking time: 23 minutes
Servings: 4
Ingredients:
- 1 cup of sun-dried tomatoes
- cups of baby spinach
- Olive oil, a drizzle
- 1-1/2 tbsp. of Italian seasoning
- chicken breasts
- slices of mozzarella
- Black pepper and salt

Directions
1. Use a meat tenderizer to flatten the chicken breast.
2. Put spinach, tomato, and mozzarella on it, add Italian seasoning, pepper, and salt, then roll and seal
3. Put the rolls in the Air fryer oven
4. Set the air fryer to rotisserie mode and press rotate for the rolls to cook evenly
5. Cook for 20 minutes at 435 F.
6. Serve immediately

Nutrition: Calories 130 Fat 5g Carbs 4g Proteins 128g

880. Barbeque Bacon With Chicken Pizza

Preparation time: 10 minutes
Cooking time: 10 minutes
Servings: 2
Ingredients:
- 1/4 cup of barbeque sauce
- 1/2 cup of cooked bacon, chopped
- pizza crust
- 10 ounces of roasted chicken
- 1/4 cup of chopped green onion
- 3/4 cup of mozzarella cheese
- 1/4 cup of bell pepper and tomato

Directions
1. Place the pizza crust on a working surface
2. Spread barbecue sauce on it, add tomato, chicken breast, cheese, pepper, onion, and bacon
3. Place it in the Air fryer oven
4. Set the air fryer to air fry mode at pizza preset.
5. Bake at 450 F for 10 minutes

Nutrition: Calories 278 Fat 15g Carbs 17g Proteins 20g

881. Turkey and Artichoke Pizza

Preparation time: 10 minutes
Cooking time: 10 minutes
Servings: 1
Ingredients:
- 1 cup of cooked turkey, chopped
- 1 baked pizza crust
- 1/2 cup of shredded parmesan cheese
- 1-1/2 cup of mozzarella cheese
- 1 can of artichoke heart
- 1 can of diced tomatoes
- 1 tsp. of garlic, basil, and oregano
- 1 can of black olives

Directions
1. Put the pizza crust on a working surface
2. Put mozzarella cheese on it, add olives, tomatoes, artichokes, basil, oregano, turkey, parmesan cheese, and garlic.
3. Place the pizza crust in the Air fryer oven
4. Set to air fry mode at pizza preset
5. Bake for 10 minutes at 450 F

Nutrition: Calories 176 Fat 9g Carbs 14g Proteins 12g

882. Beef Stuffed Pizza

Preparation time: 10 minutes
Cooking time: 18 minutes
Servings: 1
Ingredients:
- 1 cup of torn romaine lettuce
- 1/3 cup of mayonnaise
- 1/2 cup of mozzarella cheese
- big sliced tomatoes
- 1 bread shell
- slices of cooked beef

Directions
1. Put beef, mayonnaise, cheese, and tomatoes on the bread shell
2. Place it in the Air fryer oven
3. Set to bake mode at pizza preset.
4. Bake for 18 minutes at 450 F
5. Serve immediately

Nutrition: Calories 365 Fat 16g Carbs 39g Proteins 18g

883. Vanilla and Mango Bread with Cinnamon

Preparation time: 10 minutes
Cooking time: 30 minutes
Servings: 6
Ingredients:
- ½ cup butter, melted
- 1 egg, lightly beaten
- ½ cup brown sugar
- 1 tsp vanilla extract
- ripe mango, mashed
- 1 ½ cups plain flour
- 1 tsp baking powder
- ½ tsp grated nutmeg
- ½ tsp ground cinnamon

Directions
1. Line a baking pan with parchment paper. In a bowl, whisk butter, egg, sugar, vanilla, and mango. Sift in flour, baking powder, nutmeg, and cinnamon and stir without overmixing.
2. Pour the batter into the pan and place it in the oven. Press Start and cook for 25 minutes at 350 F on Bake function. Let cool before slicing.

Nutrition: Calories 365 Fat 16g Carbs 39g Proteins 18g

884. Cinnamon and Vanilla Toast

Preparation time: 5 minutes
Cooking time: 10 minutes
Servings: 6
Ingredients:
- 12 bread slices
- ½ cup sugar
- 1 ½ tsp cinnamon
- 1 stick of butter, softened
- 1 tsp vanilla extract

Preparation
1. Preheat on Toast function to 300 F. Combine all ingredients, except the bread, in a bowl. Spread the buttery cinnamon mixture onto the bread slices. Place the bread slices in the oven and press Start. Cook for 8 minutes. Serve.

Nutrition: Calories 176 Fat 9g Carbs 14g Proteins 12g

885. Basil Parmesan Bagel

Preparation time: 5 minutes
Cooking time: 10 minutes
Servings: 1
Ingredients:
- 2 tbsp butter, softened
- ¼ tsp dried basil
- 1 tsp garlic powder
- 1 tbsp Parmesan cheese, grated
- Salt and black pepper to taste
- 1 bagel

Directions
1. Preheat on Bake function to 370 degrees Fahrenheit. Cut the bagel in half. Combine the butter, Parmesan cheese, garlic, and basil in a small bowl. Season with salt and pepper. Spread the mixture onto the halved bagel. Place the bagel in the basket and press Start. Cook for 5-6 minutes.

Nutrition: Calories 131 Carbs 27g Proteins 5g

886. Buttery Orange Toasts

Preparation time: 5 minutes
Cooking time: 10 minutes
Servings: 6
Ingredients:
- 12 bread slices
- ½ cup sugar
- 1 stick butter
- 1 ½ tbsp vanilla extract
- 1 ½ tbsp cinnamon
- 2 oranges, zested

Directions
1. Mix butter, sugar, and vanilla extract and microwave the mixture for 30 seconds until it melts. Add in orange zest. Spread the mixture onto bread slices. Lay the bread slices on the cooking basket and cook in the oven for 5 minutes at 400 F on Toast function. Serve warm.

Nutrition: Calories 131 Carbs 27g Proteins 5g

887. Basil Prosciutto Crostini with Mozzarella

Preparation time: 5 minutes
Cooking time: 10 minutes
Servings: 1
Ingredients:
- ½ cup tomatoes, chopped
- 3 oz mozzarella cheese, chopped
- 3 prosciutto slices, chopped
- 1 tbsp olive oil
- 1 tsp dried basil
- 6 small slices of French bread

Preparation
1. Preheat on Toast function to 350 degrees F. Place in the bread slices and toast them for 5 minutes. Top the bread with tomatoes, prosciutto, and mozzarella. Sprinkle with basil. Drizzle with olive oil. Return to oven and cook for 1 more minute, enough to become melty and warm.

Nutrition: Calories 411 Fat 23g Carbs 41g Proteins 16g

888. Soda Brad

Preparation Time: 15 minutes
Cooking time: 30 minutes
Servings: 10
Ingredients:
- 3 cups whole-wheat flour
- 1 tablespoon sugar
- 2 teaspoon caraway seeds
- 1 teaspoon baking soda
- 1 teaspoon sea salt
- ¼ cup chilled butter, cubed into small pieces
- 1 large egg, beaten
- 1½ cups buttermilk

Directions
1. In a large bowl, mix together the flour, sugar, caraway seeds, baking soda and salt and mix well.
2. With a pastry cutter, cut in the butter flour until coarse crumbs like mixture is formed.
3. Make a well in the center of flour mixture.
4. In the well, add the egg, followed by the buttermilk and with a spatula, mix until well combined.
5. With floured hand, shape the dough into a ball.
6. Place the dough onto a floured surface and lightly knead it.
7. Shape the dough into a 6-inch ball.
8. With a serrated knife, score an X on the top of the dough.
9. Press "Power Button" of Air Fry Oven and turn the dial to select the "Air Crisp" mode.
10. Press the Time button and again turn the dial to set the cooking time to 30 minutes.
11. Now push the Temp button and rotate the dial to set the temperature at 350 F.
12. Press "Start/Pause" button to start.
13. When the unit beeps to show that it is preheated, open the lid.
14. Arrange the dough in lightly greased "Air Fry Basket" and insert in the oven.
15. Place the pan onto a wire rack to cool for about 10 minutes.
16. Carefully, invert the bread onto wire rack to cool completely before slicing.
17. Cut the bread into desired-sized slices and serve.

Nutrition: Calories 205 Fat 5.9g Saturated Fat 3.3g Cholesterol 32mg Sodium 392mg Total Carbs 31.8g Fiber 1.2g Sugar 3.1g Protein 5.9g

889. Baguette Bread

Preparation Time: 15 minutes
Cooking time: 20 minutes
Servings: 8
Ingredients:
- ¾ cup warm water
- ¾ teaspoon quick yeast
- ½ teaspoon demerara sugar
- 1 cup bread flour
- ½ cup whole-wheat flour
- ½ cup oat flour
- 1¼ teaspoons salt

Directions
1. In a large bowl, place the water and sprinkle with yeast and sugar.
2. Set aside for 5 minutes or until foamy.
3. Add the bread flour and salt mix until a stiff dough forms.
4. Put the dough onto a floured surface and with your hands, knead until smooth and elastic.
5. Now, shape the dough into a ball.
6. Place the dough into a slightly oiled bowl and turn to coat well.
7. With a plastic wrap, cover the bowl and place in a warm place for about 1 hour or until doubled in size.
8. With your hands, punch down the dough and form into a long slender loaf.
9. Place the loaf onto a lightly greased baking sheet and set aside in warm place, uncovered, for about 30 minutes.
10. Press "Power Button" of Air Fry Oven and turn the dial to select the "Air Bake" mode.
11. Press the Time button and again turn the dial to set the cooking time to 20 minutes.
12. Now push the Temp button and rotate the dial to set the temperature at 450 F.
13. Press "Start/Pause" button to start.
14. When the unit beeps to show that it is preheated, open the lid.
15. Carefully, arrange the dough onto the "Wire Rack" and insert in the oven.
16. Carefully, invert the bread onto wire rack to cool completely before slicing.
17. Cut the bread into desired-sized slices and serve.

Nutrition: Calories 114 Fat 0.8g Saturated Fat 0.1g Sodium 366mg Total Carbs 22.8g Fiber 2.1g Sugar 0.3g Protein 3.8g

890. Yogurt Bread

Preparation Time: 20 minutes
Cooking time: 40 minutes
Servings: 10
Ingredients:
- 1½ cups warm water, divided
- 1½ teaspoons active dry yeast
- 1 teaspoon sugar
- 3 cups all-purpose flour
- 1 cup plain Greek yogurt
- 2 teaspoons kosher salt

Directions
1. Add ½ cup of the warm water, yeast and sugar in the bowl of a stand mixer, fitted with the dough hook attachment and mix well.
2. Set aside for about 5 minutes.
3. Add the flour, yogurt, and salt and mix on medium-low speed until the dough comes together.
4. Then, mix on medium speed for 5 minutes.
5. Place the dough into a bowl.
6. With a plastic wrap, cover the bowl and place in a warm place for about 2-3 hours or until doubled in size.
7. Transfer the dough onto a lightly floured surface and shape into a smooth ball.
8. Place the dough onto a greased parchment paper-lined rack.
9. With a kitchen towel, cover the dough and let rest for 15 minutes.
10. With a very sharp knife, cut a 4x½-inch deep cut down the center of the dough.
11. Press "Power Button" of Air Fry Oven and turn the dial to select the "Air Roast" mode.
12. Press the Time button and again turn the dial to set the cooking time to 40 minutes.
13. Now push the Temp button and rotate the dial to set the temperature at 325 F.
14. Press "Start/Pause" button to start.
15. When the unit beeps to show that it is preheated, open the lid.
16. Carefully, arrange the dough onto the "Wire Rack" and insert in the oven.

17. Carefully, invert the bread onto wire rack to cool completely before slicing.
18. Cut the bread into desired-sized slices and serve.

Nutrition: Calories 157 Fat 0.7g Saturated Fat 0.3g Cholesterol 1mg Sodium 484mg Total Carbs 31g Fiber 1.1g Sugar 2.2g Protein 5.5g

891. Sunflower Seed Bread

Preparation Time: 15 minutes
Cooking time: 18 minutes
Servings: 6

Ingredients:
- 2/3 cup whole-wheat flour
- 2/3 cup plain flour
- 1/3 cup sunflower seeds
- ½ sachet instant yeast
- 1 teaspoon salt
- 2/3-1 cup lukewarm water

Directions
1. In a bowl, mix together the flours, sunflower seeds, yeast, and salt.
2. Slowly, add in the water, stirring continuously until a soft dough ball forms.
3. Now, move the dough onto a lightly floured surface and knead for about 5 minutes using your hands.
4. Make a ball from the dough and place into a bowl.
5. With a plastic wrap, cover the bowl and place at a warm place for about 30 minutes.
6. Grease a cake pan.
7. Coat the top of dough with water and place into the prepared cake pan.
8. Press "Power Button" of Air Fry Oven and turn the dial to select the "Air Crisp" mode.
9. Press the Time button and again turn the dial to set the cooking time to 18 minutes.
10. Now push the Temp button and rotate the dial to set the temperature at 390 degrees F.
11. Press "Start/Pause" button to start.
12. When the unit beeps to show that it is preheated, open the lid.
13. Arrange the pan in "Air Fry Basket" and insert in the oven.
14. Place the pan onto a wire rack to cool for about 10 minutes.
15. Carefully, invert the bread onto wire rack to cool completely before slicing.
16. Cut the bread into desired-sized slices and serve.

Nutrition: Calories 132 Fat 1.7g Saturated Fat 0.1g Sodium 390mg Total Carbs 24.4g Fiber 1.6g Sugar 0.1g Protein 4.9g

892. Date Bread

Preparation Time: 15 minutes
Cooking time: 22 minutes
Servings: 10

Ingredients:
- 2½ cup dates, pitted and chopped
- ¼ cup butter
- 1 cup hot water
- 1½ cups flour
- ½ cup brown sugar
- 1 teaspoon baking powder
- 1 teaspoon baking soda
- ½ teaspoon salt
- 1 egg

Directions
1. In a large bowl, add the dates, butter and top with the hot water.
2. Set aside for about 5 minutes.
3. In another bowl, mix together the flour, brown sugar, baking powder, baking soda, and salt.
4. In the same bowl of dates, mix well the flour mixture, and egg.
5. Grease a baking pan.
6. Place the mixture into the prepared pan.
7. Press "Power Button" of Air Fry Oven and turn the dial to select the "Air Crisp" mode.
8. Press the Time button and again turn the dial to set the cooking time to 22 minutes.
9. Now push the Temp button and rotate the dial to set the temperature at 340 F.
10. Press "Start/Pause" button to start.
11. When the unit beeps to show that it is preheated, open the lid.
12. Arrange the pan in "Air Fry Basket" and insert in the oven.
13. Place the pan onto a wire rack to cool for about 10 minutes.
14. Carefully, invert the bread onto wire rack to cool completely before slicing.
15. Cut the bread into desired-sized slices and serve.

Nutrition: Calories 269 Fat 5.4g Saturated Fat 3.1g Cholesterol 29mg Sodium 285mg Total Carbs 55.1g Fiber 4.1g Sugar 35.3g Protein 3.6g

893. Date and Walnut Bread

Preparation Time: 15 minutes
Cooking time: 35 minutes
Servings: 5

Ingredients:
- 1 cup dates, pitted and sliced
- ¾ cup walnuts, chopped
- 1 tablespoon instant coffee powder
- 1 tablespoon hot water
- 1¼ cups plain flour
- ¼ teaspoon salt
- ½ teaspoon baking powder
- ½ teaspoon baking soda
- ½ cup condensed milk
- ½ cup butter, softened
- ½ teaspoon vanilla essence

Directions
1. In a large bowl, add the dates, butter and top with the hot water.
2. Set aside for about 30 minutes.
3. Drain well and set aside.
4. In a small bowl, add the coffee powder and hot water and mix well.
5. In a large bowl, mix together the flour, baking powder, baking soda and salt.
6. In another large bowl, add the condensed milk and butter and beat until smooth.
7. Add the flour mixture, coffee mixture and vanilla essence and mix until well combined.
8. Fold in dates and ½ cup of walnut.
9. Line a baking pan with a lightly greased parchment paper.
10. Place the mixture into the prepared pan and sprinkle with the remainng walnuts.
11. Press "Power Button" of Air Fry Oven and turn the dial to select the "Air Crisp" mode.
12. Press the Time button and again turn the dial to set the cooking time to 35 minutes.

13. Now push the Temp button and rotate the dial to set the temperature at 320 F.
14. Press "Start/Pause" button to start.
15. When the unit beeps to show that it is preheated, open the lid.
16. Arrange the pan in "Air Fry Basket" and insert in the oven.
17. Place the pan onto a wire rack to cool for about 10 minutes.
18. Carefully, invert the bread onto wire rack to cool completely before slicing.
19. Cut the bread into desired-sized slices and serve.

Nutrition: Calories 593 Fat 32.6g Saturated Fat 14g Cholesterol 59mg Sodium 414mg Total Carbs 69.4g Fiber 5g Sugar 39.6g Protein 11.2g

894. Pizza Toast

Preparation Time: 10 minutes
Cooking time: 10 minutes
Servings: 4
Ingredients:
- 4 Slices of Bread
- 1/3 cup of Pizza Sauce
- 1 cup of Grated Mozzarella
- 1 thinly sliced Tomato
- 1 tsp Dried Oregano

Directions
1. Heat the grill oven.
2. Toast your bread lightly.
3. Place the toast in a baking and spread the pizza sauce on each slice.
4. Top the mozzarella cheese on each slice, then the tomato slices, and then a pinch of dried oregano per piece.
5. Put it under the grill for about 5 minutes or until the cheese is melted, blast and start turning golden.

Nutrition: Calcium 176mg Fat 7g Saturated Fat 3g Protein 10g Cholesterol 21mg Sugar 3g Sodium 384mg Fiber 2g Carbs 14g

895. Blueberry Overload French Toast

Preparation Time: 5 minutes
Cooking time: 40 minutes
Servings: 5
Ingredients:
- 1 (8 ounce) package cream cheese, cut into 1-inch cubes
- 1 cup fresh blueberries, divided
- 1 cup milk
- 1 tablespoon cornstarch
- 1/2 cup water
- 1/2 cup white sugar
- 1/2 teaspoon vanilla extract
- 1-1/2 teaspoons butter
- 2 tablespoons and 2 teaspoons maple syrup
- 6 eggs, beaten
- 6 slices day-old bread, cut into 1-inch cubes

Directions
1. Lightly grease baking pan of air fryer with cooking spray.
2. Evenly spread half of the bread on bottom of pan. Sprinkle evenly the cream cheese and ½ cup blueberries. Add remaining bread on top.
3. In a large bowl, whisk well eggs, milk, syrup, and vanilla extract. Pour over bread mixture.
4. Cover air fryer baking pan with foil and refrigerate overnight.
5. Preheat air fryer to 330 F.
6. Cook for 25 minutes covered in foil, remove foil and cook for another 20 minutes or until middle is set.
7. Meanwhile, make the sauce by mixing cornstarch, water, and sugar in a saucepan and bring to a boil. Stir in remaining blueberries and simmer until thickened and blueberries have burst.
8. Serve and enjoy with blueberry syrup.

Nutrition: Calories 492 Carbs 51.9g Protein 15.1g Fat 24.8g

896. Meat Lovers' Pizza

Preparation Time: 10 minutes
Cooking time: 12 minutes
Servings: 2
Ingredients:
- 1 pre-prepared 7-inch pizza pie crust, defrosted if necessary
- 1/3 cup of marinara sauce
- ounces of grilled steak, sliced into bite-sized pieces
- ounces of salami, sliced fine
- ounces of pepperoni, sliced fine
- ¼ cup of American cheese
- ¼ cup of shredded mozzarella cheese

Directions
1. Preheat the Air Fryer Oven to 350 F. Lay the pizza dough flat on a sheet of parchment paper or tin foil, cut large enough to hold the entire pie crust, but small enough that it will leave the edges of the air frying basket uncovered to allow for air circulation. Using a fork, stab the pizza dough several times across the surface – piercing the pie crust will allow air to circulate throughout the crust and ensure even cooking. With a deep soup spoon, ladle the marinara sauce onto the pizza dough, and spread evenly in expanding circles over the surface of the pie-crust. Be sure to leave at least ½ inch of bare dough around the edges, to ensure that extra-crispy crunchy first bite of the crust! Distribute the pieces of steak and the slices of salami and pepperoni evenly over the sauce-covered dough, then sprinkle the cheese in an even layer on top.
2. Set the air fryer timer to 12 minutes, and place the pizza with foil or paper on the fryer's basket surface. Again, be sure to leave the edges of the basket uncovered to allow for proper air circulation, and don't let your bare fingers touch the hot surface. After 12 minutes, when the Air Fryer Oven shuts off, the cheese should be perfectly melted and lightly crisped, and the pie crust should be golden brown. Using a spatula – or two, if necessary, remove the pizza from the air fryer basket and set on a serving plate. Wait a few minutes until the pie is cool enough to handle, then cut into slices and serve.

Nutrition: Calories 390 Carbs 34g Calories from Fat 21g Fiber 3g

897. Easy Peasy Pizza

Preparation Time: 5 minutes
Cooking time: 10 minutes
Servings: 4
Ingredients:
- Cooking oil spray (coconut, sunflower, or safflower)
- 1 flour tortilla, preferably sprouted or whole grain
- ¼ cup vegan pizza or marinara sauce
- ⅓ cup grated vegan mozzarella cheese or Cheesy Sauce
- Toppings of your choice

Directions
1. Spray the air fryer basket with oil. Place the tortilla in the air fryer basket. If the tortilla is a little bigger than the base, no

problem! Simply fold the edges up a bit to form a semblance of a "crust."
2. Pour the sauce in the center, and evenly distribute it around the tortilla "crust" (I like to use the back of a spoon for this purpose).
3. Sprinkle evenly with vegan cheese, and add your toppings. Bake it for 9 minutes, or until nicely browned. Remove carefully, cut into four pieces, and enjoy.

Nutrition: Calories 210 Carbs 33g Fat 6g Protein 5g

898. Mexican Pizza

Preparation Time: 10 minutes
Cooking time: 7 to 9 minutes
Servings: 4
Ingredients:
- ¾ cup refried beans (from a 16-ounce can)
- ½ cup salsa
- 10 frozen precooked beef meatballs, thawed and sliced
- 1 jalapeño pepper, sliced
- 4 whole-wheat pita breads
- 1 cup shredded pepper Jack cheese
- ½ cup shredded Colby cheese
- ⅓ cup sour cream

Directions
1. In a medium bowl, combine the refried beans, salsa, meatballs, and jalapeño pepper.
2. Preheat the air fryer 370 F for 3 to 4 minutes or until hot.
3. Top the pitas with the refried bean mixture and sprinkle with the cheeses.
4. Bake for 7 to 9 minutes or until the pizza is crisp and the cheese is melted and starts to brown.
5. Top each pizza with a dollop of sour cream and serve warm.

Nutrition: Calories 510 Fat 24g Saturated Fat 12g Cholesterol 64mg Sodium 1196mg Carbs 50g Fiber 9g Protein 31g

899. Bacon Garlic Pizza

Preparation Time: 10 minutes
Cooking time: 20 minutes
Servings: 4
Ingredients:
- Flour, for dusting
- Nonstick baking spray with flour
- 4 frozen large whole-wheat dinner rolls, thawed
- 5 cloves garlic, minced
- ¾ cup pizza sauce
- ½ teaspoon dried oregano
- ½ teaspoon garlic salt
- 8 slices precooked bacon, cut into 1-inch pieces
- 1¼ cups shredded Cheddar cheese

Directions
1. On a lightly floured surface, press out each dinner roll to a 5-by-3-inch oval.
2. Spray four 6-by-4-inch pieces of heavy duty foil with nonstick spray and place one crust on each piece.
3. Bake at 370 F, two at a time, for 2 minutes or until the crusts are set, but not browned.
4. Meanwhile, in a small bowl, combine the garlic, pizza sauce, oregano, and garlic salt. When the pizza crusts are set, spread each with some of the sauce. Top with the bacon pieces and Cheddar cheese.
5. Bake, two at a time, for another 8 minutes or until the crust is browned and the cheese is melted and starting to brown.

Nutrition: Calories 739 Fat 42g Saturated Fat 19g Cholesterol 102mg Sodium 1685mg Carbs 53g Fiber 3g Protein 37g

900. Tomato and Cheese Pizza

Preparation Time: 10 minutes
Cooking time: 12 minutes
Servings: 2
Ingredients:
- 12 inches pizza dough
- 1 teaspoon olive oil
- 1 tablespoon tomato sauce
- Buffalo mozzarella

Preparation
1. Roll out the dough to the size of two personal pan pizzas.
2. Lightly brush the dough with olive oil.
3. Spread a layer of tomato sauce.
4. Top with chunks of buffalo mozzarella.
5. Place the dough on a greased baking pan.
6. Select the bake function on your air fryer oven.
7. Bake at 375 F for 7 minutes.

Nutrition: Calories 411 Fat 23g Carbs 41g Proteins 16g

901. Low-Calorie Calzones

Preparation Time: 10 minutes
Cooking time: 27 minutes
Servings: 2
Ingredients:
- 2 oz. rotisserie chicken breast, shredded
- 1/3 cup low-sodium marinara sauce
- 1/4 cup red onion, finely chopped
- 1 teaspoon olive oil
- 3 oz. baby spinach leaves
- 6 oz. whole wheat pizza dough
- 1-1/2 oz. mozzarella cheese, shredded
- Cooking spray

Directions
1. Heat the olive oil in a non-stick skillet over medium to high setting.
2. Sauté the onion and spinach for 2 minutes.
3. Stir evenly with the chicken and marinara sauce.
4. Fill four 6-inch dough circles with the mix and cheese.
5. Evenly coat the calzones with cooking spray.
6. Select the bake function on your air fryer oven.
7. Bake at 325 F for 12 minutes.

Nutrition: Fat 7g Protein 10g Cholesterol 21mg Sugar 3g Fiber 2g Carbs 14g

902. Baked Turnovers with Pear

Preparation Time: 10 minutes
Cooking time: 30 minutes
Servings: 4
Ingredients:
- 1 medium pear, thinly sliced
- 1/4 lb. black forest deli ham, thinly sliced
- 1/4 cup toasted walnuts, chopped
- 2 tablespoons crumbled blue cheese
- 13.8 oz. refrigerated pizza crust, cut into 3x3-inch squares

Preparation
1. Layer all the ingredients on the pizza crust squares.
2. Fold into triangles, and seal with a fork.

3. Arrange in a single layer on a greased baking sheet.
4. Cook using the bake function at 400 F for 4 to 6 minutes on each side.

Nutrition: Calories 593 Fat 32.6g Cholesterol 59mg Carbs 69.4g Fiber 5g Sugar 39.6g Protein 11.2g

903. Creamy Beef Pockets

Preparation Time: 10 minutes
Cooking time: 30 minutes
Servings: 4
Ingredients:
- 1 large egg, beaten
- 2 tablespoons water
- 1 lb. ground beef, cooked
- 1-1/2 cups mushrooms, sliced and cooked
- 1/2 cup onion, chopped and cooked
- 1-1/2 teaspoons garlic, minced
- 4 teaspoons Worcestershire sauce
- 3/4 teaspoon dried rosemary, crushed
- 3/4 teaspoon paprika
- 1 sheet frozen puff pastry, thawed
- 1 cup Swiss cheese, shredded
- Salt and pepper to taste

Preparation
1. Beat egg and water, and then set aside.
2. Place all ingredients in a skillet, except for the egg mix and the puff pastry, and cook for 1 minute.
3. Stuff 4 puff pastry rectangles with the cooked filling and pinch the seams to seal.
4. Brush over with the egg mix, and place on a baking sheet.
5. Cook on bake mode at 375 F for 10 to 12 minutes, or until golden brown.

Nutrition: Calories 593 Fat 32.6g Cholesterol 59mg Carbs 69.4g Fiber 5g Sugar 39.6g Protein 11.2g

904. Mini Pizza

Preparation Time: 5 minutes
Cooking time: 20 minutes
Servings: 4
Ingredients:
- 1 tsp of Italian herb seasoning
- 1/4 cup of minced onion
- 6 toasted and split muffins
- 3 tbsp of steak sauce
- 2 cups of mozzarella cheese
- 1/4 cup of sliced green onion
- 1 can of tomato paste
- 3/4 pound of ground beef
- 2 cups of parmesan cheese

Directions
1. Crumble meat in a bowl, add onion, tomato paste, Italian herb, and steak sauce.
2. Stir well.
3. Spread the mixture on muffins and transfer to the Air fryer oven pan.
4. Set the Air fryer oven to pizza function.
5. Cook for about 20 minutes on both sides at 350 F.
6. Serve immediately with green onions and cheese.

Nutrition: Calories 273 Fat 27g Carbs 23g Proteins 21g

905. Artichoke with Red Pepper Pizza

Preparation Time: 5 minutes
Cooking time: 20 minutes
Servings: 1
Ingredients:
- 1 tsp of dried basil
- 1 can of artichoke hearts
- 1-1/2 cup of mozzarella cheese
- 1 cup of red bell pepper
- 5 cloves of garlic
- cracked pepper
- 1 tbsp of olive oil
- 1 pizza shell
- 1 tsp of oregano
- 1 jar of sliced mushroom

Directions
1. Mix artichoke hearts, basil, bell pepper, garlic, and cracked pepper in a bowl.
2. Add oregano, mushroom, and olive oil.
3. Place the mixture on the pizza shell
4. Transfer the pizza shell to Air fryer oven pan.
5. Set the Air fryer oven to pizza function.
6. Cook for about 20 minutes at 350 F.
7. Serve immediately

Nutrition: Calories 359 Fat 18g Carbs 43g Proteins 12g

906. Artichoke Turkey Pizza

Preparation Time: 5 minutes
Cooking time: 20 minutes
Servings: 2
Ingredients:
- 2 cups of chopped cooked turkey
- 1-1/2 cup of mozzarella cheese
- 2 baked pizza crust
- 1 can of black olives
- 1 can of diced tomatoes with garlic, oregano, and basil
- 1/2 cup of shredded parmesan cheese
- can of artichoke hearts

Directions
1. Place the pizza crusts on a working surface.
2. Place turkey, olive, tomatoes mix, parmesan cheese, olives, and artichokes on them.
3. Transfer the pizza crusts to the Air fryer oven pan.
4. Set the Air fryer oven to pizza function.
5. Cook for 10 minutes at 450 F
6. Serve immediately.

Nutrition: Calories 196 Fat 7g Carbs 28g Proteins 8g

907. Bacon Cheeseburger Pizza

Preparation Time: 5 minutes
Cooking time: 20 minutes
Servings: 2
Ingredients:
- 6 bacon strips
- 1/2 pound of ground beef
- 1 tsp of pizza seasoning
- 2 cups of mozzarella cheese
- 2 baked-bread crush
- 20 slices of dill pickles
- 1 chopped small onion

- 2 cups of shredded cheddar cheese
- 8 ounces of pizza sauce

Directions
1. Cook onion and beef over medium heat for about 5 minutes.
2. Drain the meat.
3. Add bacon, seasonings, sauce, cheeses, and pickles.
4. Place the bread crusts on a working surface.
5. Place the ingredients on them.
6. Transfer it to the Air fryer oven pan
7. Set the Air fryer oven to pizza function.
8. Cook for 10 minutes at 450 F

Nutrition: Calories 322 Fat 12g Carbs 42g Proteins 17g

908. Bacon Lettuce Tomato Pizza

Preparation Time: 5 minutes
Cooking time: 10 minutes
Servings: 2

Ingredients:
- 6 slices of plum tomatoes
- 1 cup of torn romaine lettuce
- 1/3 cup of mayonnaise
- 8 sliced of bacon
- 2 bread shell
- 1 cup of mozzarella cheese

Directions
1. Spread the bread shell on a working surface.
2. Put mayonnaise, cheese, bacon, and tomatoes on the bread shells.
3. Transfer to the Air fryer oven pan.
4. Set the Air fryer oven to pizza function.
5. Cook for 17 minutes at 450 F.
6. Serve immediately

Nutrition: Calories 132 Fat 8g Carbs 9g Proteins 8g

909. Bread Pudding

Preparation Time: 5 minutes
Cooking time: 1 hour 10 minutes
Servings: 8

Ingredients:
- 3 eggs
- 2 tbsp of vanilla
- 3 cups of whole milk
- 3 egg yolks
- 2 tsp of cinnamon
- 8 tbsp of butter
- 1 cups of cubed French bread
- 2 cups of granulated sugar
- 1/4 pyrex bowl

Directions
1. Mix milk and butter in a bowl and heat in the microwave.
2. Break the egg in another bowl and whisk.
3. Add cinnamon, sugar, eggs, and vanilla.
4. Add the milk mix.
5. Add dried bread, mix until the bread is soaked.
6. Put the mixture in a pyrex bowl
7. Place the pyrex bowl on the Air fryer oven pan.
8. Set the Air fryer oven to bagel/toast.
9. Cook 60 minutes at 270 F.
10. Allow cooling before serving

Nutrition: Calories 379 Fat 8g Carbs 70g Proteins 9g

910. Cheesy Bread

Preparation Time: 5 minutes
Cooking time: 20 minutes
Servings: 4

Ingredients:
- 4 cloves of garlic
- 1 cup of mozzarella cheese
- 8 slices of bread
- 6 tsp of sun-dried tomatoes
- 5 tbsp of melted butter

Directions
1. Place the bread slices on a flat surface.
2. Put butter on it, garlic, and tomato paste.
3. Add cheese
4. Place the bread on the Air fryer oven pan.
5. Set the Air fryer oven to toast/bagel function.
6. Cook for 8 minutes a 350 F.

Nutrition: Calories 226 Fat 8g Carbs 32g Proteins 8g

911. Peach Pie Mix

Preparation Time: 5 minutes
Cooking time: 50 minutes
Servings: 5

Ingredients:
- 1 tbsp of dark rum
- pie dough
- 2 tbsp of cornstarch
- Ground nutmeg
- 2 tbsp of butter
- 2 tbsp of flour
- 2-1/4 pound of peaches
- 1 tbsp of lemon juice
- 1/2 cup of sugar

Directions
1. Press the dough on the Air fryer oven pan
2. Mix sugar, nutmeg, lemon juice, cornstarch, and butter in a bowl.
3. Add peaches, rum, and flour.
4. Mix well
5. Pour the mixture into the dough.
6. Set the Air fryer oven to toast/bagel function.
7. Cook for 35 minutes at 350 F.
8. Serve immediately or allow cooling before serving

Nutrition: Calories 261 Fat 12g Carbs 39g Proteins 3g

912. Breakfast Pizza

Preparation Time: 10 minutes
Cooking time: 15 minutes
Servings: 5

Ingredients:
- 1 pound of bacon
- 8 ounces of crescent dinner rolls
- 1 cup of cheddar cheese
- 6 eggs

Directions
1. Place the rolls on the pizza pan.
2. Mix cheese, eggs, and bacon in a bowl.
3. Pour the mixture over the crust.
4. Place the pan in the Air fryer oven.
5. Set the Air fryer oven to pizza function.

6. Cook for 15 minutes at 370 F.
7. Serve immediately

Nutrition: Calories 311 Fat 11g Carbs 43g Proteins 15g

913. French Bread Pizza

Preparation Time: 10 minutes
Cooking time: 25 minutes
Servings: 4
Ingredients:
- 1 tsp of dried oregano
- 1/2 cup of fresh mushrooms
- 1 loaf of French bread
- 1/4 cup of parmesan cheese
- 1 cup of mozzarella cheese
- 1/2 green pepper
- 3/4 cup of spaghetti sauce

Directions
1. Put the spaghetti sauce on the French bread.
2. Add green pepper, cheeses, mushroom, and oregano.
3. Place it on the Air Fryer pan.
4. Set the Air Fryer to pizza function.
5. Cook for 15 minutes at 370 F.

Nutrition: Calories 303 Fat 7g Carbs 51g Proteins 13g

914. Quick Cheese Sticks

Preparation Time: 5 minutes
Cooking time: 10 minutes
Servings: 4
Ingredients:
- `6 oz bread cheese
- `2 tbsp butter
- `2 cups panko crumbs

Directions
1. Place the butter in a dish and melt it in the microwave, for 2 minutes; set aside. With a knife, cut the cheese into equal sized sticks.
2. Brush each stick with butter and dip into panko crumbs. Arrange the cheese sticks in a single layer on the fryer basket.
3. Cook at 390 F for 10 minutes. Flip them halfway through, to brown evenly; serve warm.

Nutrition: Calories 256 Fat 21g Carbs 8g Proteins 16g

915. Herbed Croutons with Brie Cheese

Preparation Time: 10 minutes
Cooking time: 10 minutes
Servings: 4
Ingredients:
- 2tbsp olive oil
- 1 tbsp french herbs
- 4oz brie cheese, chopped
- 1slices bread, halved

Directions:
1. Warm up your Air Fryer to 340 F. Using a bowl, mix oil with herbs. Dip the bread slices in the oil mixture to coat.
2. Place the coated slices on a flat surface. Lay the brie cheese on the slices.
3. Place the slices into your air fryer's basket and cook for 7 minutes.
4. Once the bread is ready, cut into cubes.

Nutrition: Calories 20 Fat 1.3g Carbs 1.5g Proteins 0.5g

916. Monkey Bread

Preparation Time: 20 minutes
Cooking time: 40 minutes
Servings: 8
Ingredients:
- `3 cans buttermilk biscuits
- `1 cup of sugar
- `2 tsp. (to 3 tsp) cinnamon
- `2 sticks butter
- `½ cup of brown sugar

Directions
1. Heat the oven to 350 F.
2. Open up all three cans of biscuits and cut into quarters of each biscuit.
3. Next, mix 2-3 tsp of cinnamon with the white sugar. Pour these into a 1 gallon zip bag and shake to combine evenly.
4. Through the cinnamon-sugar blend, drop all of the biscuit quarters. When it is in the bag, seal all the biscuit quarters and give it a vigorous shake. In the bundt pan, spread these nuggets out uniformly.
5. At this point, in a saucepan over medium-high heat, you'll want to melt the two sticks of butter together with 1/2 cup of brown sugar. It may be light sugar or dark brown sugar. Cook the butter/sugar mixture until the two become one, stirring for a couple of minutes. You can spill it over the biscuits until the brown sugar butter has become one color.
6. Bake until the crust is a rich dark brown on top, about 30-40 minutes. Remove it from the oven when it's finished cooking. If you have the willpower, allow it to cool before turning it on a plate for around 15-30 minutes.

Nutrition: Calories 379 Fat 8g Carbs 70g Proteins 9g

917. Southern Pimento Grilled Cheese

Preparation Time: 5 minutes
Cooking time: 35 minutes
Servings: 8
Ingredients:
- `3 oz. Cheese Cream
- `2 oz. Red Peppers Roasted
- `3 oz. Kale Kale
- `1 Tomato Roma
- `1 Red Onion
- `1/2 fl. Uh, oz. Vinegar with Seasoned Rice
- `1 Tsp. Oregano dried
- `3 oz. Cheddar-Cheese Jack, Shredded
- `1/4 oz. Dijon Mustard
- `4 Sourdough Slices for Bread

Directions
1. Cut into 1/4" dice. Stem kale and coarsely chop. Core Roma tomato and cut into ¾" cubes. Peel the onion and cut into 1/4" rounds.
2. In a large mixing bowl, whisk together seasoned rice vinegar, oregano, and 2 Tbsp. olive oil. Add kale, , Roma tomato and red onion. Toss with salt and pepper to combine and season to taste. Kale is a hearty green that benefits from soaking when cooking in vinaigrette.
3. Combine in a mixing bowl, cream cheese, shredded cheddar-jack, roasted red peppers, Dijon, and a pinch of salt and pepper. Mix until well mixed. Works better with a wooden spoon.
4. Heat 2 tsp. olive oil over medium heat in a large oven-safe non-stick pan. Spread two slices of sourdough bread with the cheese and top with the remaining slices. Place sandwiches

BREAD, BAGEL AND PIZZA

in a pan and cook for 3 minutes or until golden brown. Flip and transfer the pan to the oven carefully. Bake 5-6 minutes or until golden brown on the second side. Remove from the pan carefully and let stand 5 minutes before slicing.

Nutrition: Calories 226 Fat 8g Carbs 32g Proteins 8g

918. Fluffy Peanut Butter Marshmallow Turnovers

Preparation Time: 10 minutes
Cooking time: 10 minutes
Servings: 4

Ingredients:
- `4 Pastry Filo, defrosted sheets
- `4 tbsp. Peanut Butter Chunky
- `2 oz. Butter Melted
- `4 tsp Fluff of marshmallows
- `1 pinch Sea salt

Directions
1. Set the Air Fryer to a temperature of 360 F.
2. Brush 1 layer of the filo using the melted butter. Place the second sheet on top and then brush it with butter as well. When you have completed all 4 sheets, continue the operation.
3. Break the layers into 4 strips: 12-inch x 3-inch.
4. On the underside, put one teaspoon of the marshmallow fluff and one tablespoon of the peanut butter.
5. Fold the tip to form a triangle over the filo strip, ensuring that the filling is fully wrapped.
6. Using a small amount of butter to seal the ends. Place the completed turnovers for 3 to 5 minutes in the Air Fryer.
7. They'll be soft and golden brown when done.
8. For a sweet/salty combo, add a drop of sea salt. Just serve.

Nutrition: Calories 261 Fat 12g Carbs 39g Proteins 3g

919. Fast and Simple Doughnuts

Preparation Time: 10 minutes
Cooking time: 15 minutes
Servings: 8

Ingredients:
- `1 can Flaky jumbo refrigerated biscuits with dough
- `1 1/2 tsp. Cinnamon, ground
- `½ cup Granulated white sugar
- `Ghee or Coconut Oil (as needed)

Directions
1. Set the Air Fryer at 350 F.
2. On a cutting board, arrange the biscuits. To delete the cores, use a one-inch biscuit cutter. Grease the basket with ghee/oil.
3. Whisk in the cinnamon and sugar.
4. For 5 to 6 minutes, air-fry the doughnuts. For 3 to 4 minutes, fry the holes.
5. Using the butter to move to a dish and sweep, garnishing using a sprinkle of the cinnamon/sugar mixture.

Nutrition: Calories 379 Fat 8g Carbs 70g Proteins 9g

920. Raisin and Apple Dumplings

Preparation Time: 10 minutes
Cooking time: 30 minutes
Servings: 2

Ingredients:
- `2 tbsp. Raisins
- `2 Apples, small
- `1 tbsp Brown Sugar
- `2 sheets Puff Pastry
- `2 tbsp Butter Melted

Directions
1. To achieve 356 F, warm the Air Fryer.
2. Peel the apples and core them. Combine the sugar and the raisins. Place on the pastry sheets with the apples and fill with the raisin mixture.
3. To cover the fixings, fold the pastry over. Place them ontop a piece of foil to keep them from falling through the fryer. Brush them with butter that's melted.
4. Air-fry until it's golden brown (25 minutes).
5. Note: It is best to use tiny apples to cook them.

Nutrition: Calories 261 Fat 12g Carbs 39g Proteins 3g

921. Homemade Donuts

Preparation Time: 10 minutes
Cooking time: 59 minutes
Servings: 12

Ingredients:
- `1 cup milk, lukewarm (approximately 100 F)
- `2 1/2 tsp active dry yeast, or instant yeast, roughly
- `1/4 cup of granulated sugar, plus 1 teaspoon of sugar
- `1/2 TSP of salt
- `1 egg
- `1/4 cup unsalted, melted butter
- `All-purpose flour for 3 cups
- `Oil Mist, coconut oil functions best
- `About 6 Tbsp unsalted butter
- `Powdered sugar, 2 cups
- `2 tsp vanilla extract
- `4 Tbsp of hot water, or as needed,

Directions
1. Gently whisk together lukewarm milk, 1 tsp of sugar and yeast in the bowl of a stand mixer fitted with a dough handle. Let it sit for a period of 10 minutes till it becomes foamy.
2. To the milk mixture, add the sugar, salt, egg, melted butter and 2 cups of flour. Mix until mixed at low level, then add the remaining cup of flour slowly with the mixer going, until the dough no longer sticks to the bowl. Increase the pace to medium-low and knead until the dough is elastic and smooth for 5 minutes.
3. Place the dough inside a greased bowl and then cover it with plastic wrap. In a warm spot, let it rise until it doubles. If you create a dent with your finger and the indention remains, the dough is ready.
4. Turn the dough on a floured surface, punch it down and roll it out gently to a thickness of about 1/2 inch. To remove the middle, cut out 10-12 donuts using a 3-inch round cutter and a 1-inch round cutter.
5. Move to lightly floured parchment paper donuts and donut holes and cover loosely with greased plastic wrap. Allow the donuts rise for about 30 minutes, until the volume has doubled. Preheat the 350 F Air Fryer.

6. Spray the Air Fryer basket using oil spray and carefully move the donuts in a single layer to the Air Fryer basket. Use oil spray to spray donuts and cook at 350 F until golden brown, around 4 minutes. Repeat with donuts and holes left.
7. Melt the butter inside a small saucepan over medium heat while the donuts are in the Air Fryer. Stir in the powder with the sugar and vanilla extract until smooth. Remove from the heat and stir one tablespoon at a time in hot water until the icing is thin, but not watery. Merely set aside.
8. Dip hot donuts and donut holes into the glaze using forks to submerge them. Place it ontop a wire rack set over a rimmed baking sheet to allow the excess glaze to drip off. Let it sit till the glaze hardens for about 10 minutes.

Nutrition: Calories 379 Fat 8g Carbs 70g Proteins 9g

922. Mozzarella, Bacon and Turkey Calzone

Preparation Time: 10 minutes
Cooking time: 20 minutes
Servings: 4
Ingredients:
- `Pizza dough
- `4 oz cheddar cheese, grated
- `1 oz mozzarella cheese
- `1 oz bacon, diced
- `2 cups cooked and shredded turkey
- `1 egg, beaten
- `1 tsp thyme
- `4 tbsp tomato paste
- `1 tsp basil
- `1 tsp oregano
- `Salt and black pepper to taste

Directions
1. Preheat the Air fryer oven to 350 F.
2. Divide the pizza dough into 4 equal pieces so you have the dough for 4 small pizza crusts. Combine the tomato paste, basil, oregano, and thyme, in a small bowl.
3. Brush the mixture onto the crusts just make sure not to go all the way and avoid brushing near the edges on one half of each crust, place ½ turkey, and season the meat with some salt and pepper.
4. Top the meat with some bacon. Combine the cheddar and mozzarella and divide it between the pizzas, making sure that you layer only one half of the dough.
5. Brush the edges of the crust with the beaten egg. Fold the crust and seal with a fork. Cook for 10 minutes.

Nutrition: Calories 303 Fat 7g Carbs 51g Proteins 13g

923. Nutty Bread Pudding with Honey and Raisins

Preparation Time: 10 minutes
Cooking time: 45 minutes
Servings: 3
Ingredients:
- `8 slices of bread
- `½ cup buttermilk
- `¼ cup honey
- `1 cup milk
- `2 eggs
- `½ tsp vanilla extract
- `2 tbsp butter, softened
- `¼ cup sugar
- `4 tbsp raisins
- `2 tbsp chopped hazelnuts
- `Cinnamon for garnish

Directions
1. Preheat the Air fryer oven to 310 F. Beat the eggs along with the buttermilk, honey, milk, vanilla, sugar and butter. Stir in raisins and hazelnuts.
2. Cut the bread into cubes and place them in a bowl. Pour the milk mixture over the bread. Let soak for 10 minutes.
3. Cook the pudding for 30 minutes and garnish with cinnamon.

Nutrition: Calories 379 Fat 8g Carbs 70g Proteins 9g

924. Cheesy Berry-Flavored French Toast

Preparation Time: 10 minutes
Cooking time: 15 minutes
Servings: 4
Ingredients:
- `2 eggs, beaten
- `4 slices bread
- `3 tbsp sugar
- `1 ½ cups corn flakes
- `⅓ cup milk
- `¼ tsp nutmeg
- `4 tbsp berry-flavored cheese
- `¼ tsp salt

Directions
1. Preheat your Air Fryer oven to 400 F. In a bowl, mix sugar, eggs, nutmeg, salt and milk. In a separate bowl, mix blueberries and cheese. Take 2 bread slices and pour the blueberry mixture over the slices.
2. Top with the milk mixture. Cover with the remaining two slices to make sandwiches. Dredge the sandwiches over cornflakes to coat well.
3. Lay the sandwiches in the frying basket and cook for 8 minutes. Serve with berries and syrup.

Nutrition: Calories 492 Carbs 51.9g Protein 15.1g Fat 24.8g

925. Pita and Pepperoni Pizza

Preparation Time: 10 minutes
Cooking time: 6 minutes
Servings: 1
Ingredients:
- `1 teaspoon olive oil
- `1 tablespoon pizza sauce
- `1 pita bread
- `6 pepperoni slices
- `¼ cup grated Mozzarella cheese
- `¼ teaspoon garlic powder
- `¼ teaspoon dried oregano

Directions
1. Preheat the air fryer oven to 350 F (177 degrees Celsius). Grease the air fryer basket with olive oil.
2. Spread the pizza sauce on top of the pita bread. Put the pepperoni slices over the sauce, followed by the Mozzarella cheese.
3. Season with garlic powder and oregano, then transfer to the air fryer basket.

4. Place the air fryer basket onto the baking pan and slide into Rack Position 2, select Air Fry and set time to 6 minutes.
 5. Serve warm.

Nutrition: Calories 311 Fat 11g Carbs 43g Proteins 15g

926. Simple Cinnamon Toasts

Preparation Time: 5 minutes
Cooking time: 4 minutes
Servings: 4

Ingredients:
- `1 tablespoon salted butter
- `2 teaspoons ground cinnamon
- `4 tablespoons sugar
- `½ teaspoon vanilla extract
- `10 bread slices

Directions
 1. Preheat the air fryer oven to 380 F (193 degrees Celsius).
 2. In a bowl, combine the butter, cinnamon, sugar, and vanilla extract. Spread onto the slices of bread.
 3. Put the bread in a baking pan. Slide the baking pan into Rack Position 1, select Convection Bake and set time to 4 minutes, or until golden brown.
 4. Serve warm.

Nutrition: Calories 492 Carbs 51.9g Protein 15.1g Fat 24.8g

927. Sourdough Croutons

Preparation Time: 5 minutes
Cooking time: 6 minutes
Servings: 4 cups

Ingredients:
- `4 cups cubed sourdough bread, 1-inch cubes
- `1 tablespoon olive oil
- `1 teaspoon fresh thyme leaves
- `¼ teaspoon salt
- `Freshly ground black pepper, to taste

Directions
 1. Preheat the air fryer oven to 400 F (204 degrees Celsius).
 2. Combine all ingredients in a bowl. Put the bread cubes in the air fryer basket.
 3. Place the air fryer basket onto the baking pan and slide into Rack Position 2, select Air Fry and set time to 6 minutes, shaking the basket once or twice while they cook.
 4. Serve warm.

Nutrition: Calories 379 Fat 8g Carbs 70g Proteins 9g

928. American-Style BBQ Chicken Pizza

Preparation Time: 5 minutes
Cooking time: 15 minutes
Servings: 1

Ingredients:
- `¼ cup shredded Monterrey Jack cheese
- `1 piece naan bread
- `¼ cup barbeque sauce
- `¼ cup shredded mozzarella cheese
- `2 tbsp red onion, thinly sliced
- `½ chicken herby sausage
- `Chopped cilantro for garnish

Directions
 1. Preheat the Air fryer oven to 400 F on Bake function.
 2. Spray naan's bread bottom with cooking spray and arrange it on the oven/pizza rack.
 3. Brush well with barbeque sauce, sprinkle mozzarella cheese, Monterrey Jack cheese, and red onion on top.
 4. Top with the sausage over and spray the crust with cooking spray.
 5. Cook for 8 minutes.
 6. Serve and enjoy!

Nutrition: Calories 278 Fat 15g Carbs 17g Proteins 20g

929. Pizzas in Fryer Without Oil

Preparation Time: 5 minutes
Cooking time: 10 minutes
Servings: 1 pizza

Ingredients:
- `250g flour
- `6g salt
- `1 pinch sugar
- `1/2 over Instant Yeast
- `150ml warm water
- `1 dash of olive oil
- `sauce
- `1/2 onion
- `Ketchup
- `Ham
- `Mozzarella

Direction:
 1. Put the flour in a bowl with the salt a drizzle of olive oil, add the warm water and knead.
 2. Leave in the bowl in a warm place to double
 3. Then divide the dough into 4 and knead on discs that enter the air fryer pan without oil. Cut shortening paper on discs
 4. Place the dough on the paper and add the ham and cheese sauce. Put in a pan in a pan for about 7 minutes and soon.

Nutrition: Calories 311 Fat 11g Carbs 43g Proteins 15g

930. Avocado on Toast with Poached Egg

Preparation Time: 5 minutes
Cooking time: 10 minutes
Servings: 4

Ingredients:
- `1.2 country bread
- `6 pieces of eggs
- `100g spinach
- `3 mature avocado
- `100g butter
- `1-2 tbsp.vinegar
- `Salt pepper

Directions:
 1. Slice the country bread into slightly thicker slices. Cut the avocado in half, hollow it out with a spoon, slice it into thin slices, and even season with a little salt and pepper to marinate a bit.
 2. Now heat 1 liter of water, and 1-2 tablespoons of vinegar in the Air fryer baking pan at 392 F. Beat the eggs in a cup and set aside. Roast the slices of bread with butter in the pan, and then add leaf spinach.

3. When the water is hot, you can put the eggs into the water one at a time with a ladle and cook at 392 F for 3 minutes.
4. Now you can serve, first the spinach on the bread, then the avocado and finally on the top of two poached eggs. A little watercress for the spiciness, if necessary, a little salt and pepper for seasoning.

Nutrition: Calories 345 Fat 10g Carbs 35g Proteins 22g

931. Bread Roll and an Egg

Preparation Time: 5 minutes
Cooking time: 15 minutes
Servings: 4
Ingredients:
- `4 whole-grain bread rolls
- `4 eggs
- `40g spring onions
- `8 slicesbacon
- `50g butter
- `80g cheese
- `Salt pepper

Directions:
1. Cut in the rolls above and hollow out with the help of a spoon. Chop the spring onions, mix with the cheese and season a bit.
2. Spread buns with butter and cover with bacon, separate eggs. Add the egg whites to the spring onion and cheese and fill them with a spoon in the bread to fill. Put the egg yolk on top.
3. Bake the rolls at 320 F for 10-12 minutes in the baking tray of the Airfryer.

Nutrition: Calories 131 Carbs 27g Proteins 5g

932. Cheese Ham Pluck Bread

Preparation Time: 5 minutes
Cooking time: 1 hour 15 minutes
Servings: 4
Ingredients:
- `For the Dough
- `250ml milk
- `40g yeast
- `500g Flour
- `1 egg
- `70g butter
- `pinch of salt
- `20g sugar
- `Covering
- `150g cheese
- `180g cooked ham
- `For painting
- `100g butter
- `1 clove of garlic

Directions:
1. Heat the milk in a saucepan and dissolve the yeast in it. Add the flour and other ingredients and mix everything into a homogenous dough. Leave in a warm place for 30 - 60 minutes.
2. Cut the cheese and ham into strips about 3cm wide. Heat the butter and mix with minced garlic, set aside.
3. Now knead the dough vigorously and roll it out. Cut into 10 equal strips, brush with garlic butter, top with cheese and ham, and roll-up. Put the finished rolls into the back kit of the Air Fryer Oven and bake for 10 minutes at 320 F. Brush again with garlic butter and bake for another 5 minutes.

Nutrition: Calories 345 Fat 14g Carbs 25g Proteins 25g

933. Green Focaccia

Preparation Time: 5 minutes
Cooking time: 1 hour
Servings: 1 loaf
Ingredients:
- `225g wheat flour
- `40g yeast
- `4 tbsp.olive oil
- `2 bunch parsley
- `200ml water
- `30g Sun-dried tomatoes
- `40g green olives
- `40g black olives
- `2 sprigs of rosemary
- `Pinch of salt and sugar

Directions:
1. Preparation: Wash the parsley, finely chop and mix with the water. Sift flour and place in a bowl, chop rosemary, olives, and dried tomatoes.
2. Now press the soaked parsley through a sieve and knead with the flour, tomatoes, and olives to a homogeneous dough. Let it go for 30 minutes.
3. Knead the dough again after the rest period and distribute it in the baking tin of the Air Fryer Oven. Let it rest for another 10 minutes and then bake at 320 F for 18 minutes.

Nutrition: Calories 345 Fat 10g Carbs 35g Proteins 22g

934. Pizza Flammkuchen Style

Preparation Time: 5 minutes
Cooking time: 1 hour 15 minutes
Servings: 1 pizza
Ingredients:
- `For The Yeast Dough
- `300g Flour
- `pinch of sugar
- `pinch of salt
- `3 tbsp. oil
- `150ml water
- `1 Pack. Dry yeast
- `Alsatian dough
- `220g Flour
- `3 tbsp.olive oil
- `1 egg yolk
- `1/2 tsp salt
- `100ml Water, warm
- `For Covering
- `2 small onions, red
- `125g bacon
- `Handful of chives
- `2 Garlic cloves
- `1 cup of sour cream
- `1 Mug creme fraiche
- `Salt pepper
- `1 spring onion

Directions:

BREAD, BAGEL AND PIZZA

1. For the dough, dissolve the yeast in 50ml of water and add a pinch of sugar. In a bowl, mix the flour, pinch of salt, oil and the yeast water into a smooth dough. Let it go for 30 minutes. Mix flour, 2 tablespoons of olive oil, egg yolk, salt, and water to form a smooth dough. Spread dough ball with remaining oil and let it rest in foil for 30 minutes at room temperature.
2. Now the dough can be rolled out. For the pizza kit, he should have 26cm diameter.
3. Crème Fraiche, sour cream, garlic (pressed), and stir the chives. Season with salt and pepper and distribute about 3 tablespoons on a rolled out flatbread. Cover with bacon cubes and the onion. Bake at 392 degrees Celsius for 10 minutes.

Nutrition: Calories 345 Fat 14g Carbs 25g Proteins 25g

935. Beef and Onion BBQ Pizza

Preparation Time: 5 minutes
Cooking time: 1 hour 15 minutes
Servings: 1 pizza
Ingredients:
- `Pizza dough
- `60g minced meat
- `3 tbsp. sieved tomatoes
- `1 clove of garlic
- `1 tbsp. BBQ sauce
- `1 small red onion
- `Jalapeños, at will
- `1 teaspoon chili flakes
- `1.2 Mozzarella
- `Cheddar, at will
- `Parmesan, at will

Direction:
1. Roll out the dough thinly and place it on the pizza kit.
2. For the tomato sauce, pass tomatoes, BBQ sauce, crushed garlic, and chili flakes. Spread on the dough and top with the other ingredients.
3. Bake at 392 F for 6 minutes. If you like it darker 7 - 8 minutes.

Nutrition: Calories 345 Fat 10g Carbs 35g Proteins 22g

936. Cheese Sticks

Preparation Time: 5 minutes
Cooking time: 15 minutes
Servings: 3-4
Ingredients:
- `1 pack puff pastry
- `2 tbsp. tomato paste
- `100g Gouda, grated
- `50g Parmesan, grated
- `1 egg
- `1 Shot of milk
- `sesame to the sprinkling

Directions:
1. Roll out the puff pastry and spread with the tomato paste. Next, spread the Parmesan on the dough and then the Gouda. Press lightly so that not so much cheese is "lost" when turning.
2. Now cut the dough with a knife into 1 cm thick strips. Pick up both ends and twist like a cord (both ends in the opposite direction). To fit in the air fryer, divide the dough strands in the middle.
3. Whisk the egg and the milk and brush the sticks with it. Therefore, they get a nice appetizing color while baking, and the sesame seeds are much better! Sprinkle with sesame seeds and bake at 356 F for 8 minutes in the air fryer.

Nutrition: Calories 492 Carbs 51.9g Protein 15.1g Fat 24.8g

937. Baltic Garlic Bread Sticks with Yogurt Dip

Preparation Time: 5 minutes
Cooking time: 20 minutes
Servings: 3-4
Ingredients:
- `1 Loaf of bread, preferably black
- `6 tbsp.olive oil
- `2-3 Garlic cloves, pressed
- `1 tbsp. garlic powder
- `For The Dip
- `250g Yogurt / cottage cheese
- `1 Handful of parsley
- `1 Shot of olive oil
- `Salt pepper
- `Lemon, optional

Directions:
1. Cut the bread into finger-sized fries. Optionally, you can roast the bread at 356 F for about 8 minutes before.
2. In the meantime, the garlic can be squeezed into the olive oil, and the garlic powder added. Mix well and add a little salt.
3. Now to the dip. To do this, mix the yogurt / quark with the parsley, a dash of olive oil and salt and pepper.
4. Spread the crispy bread chips generously with the garlic oil and pour it into the air fryer for 10 minutes at 356 F.

Nutrition: Calories 525 Carbs 45g Protein 25g Fat 25g

938. Perfect Donuts

Preparation Time: 5 minutes
Cooking time: 1 hour 40 minutes
Servings: 3-4
Ingredients:
- `260ml warm milk
- `55g sugar
- `yeast
- `2 eggs
- `140g butter
- `440g Flour
- `1/2 tsp salt
- `melted butter to coat
- `For the glaze
- `200g chocolate jam
- `50g walnuts
- `30g coconut chips
- `200g powdered sugar
- `warm water

Directions:
1. For the dough, dissolve yeast, sugar, and salt in lukewarm milk and let rest for 10 minutes.
2. Melt butter and add to the milk with the eggs. Add the flour and let it rest for 1 hour.
3. Sprinkle the tray with flour and roll out the dough (but not too thin). Form the donuts (for example, with a glass) and let rest covered 20 minutes.
4. Put the donut blanks in the air fryer and brush with some melted butter. Bake at 320 F for 6-8 minutes.

5. For the chocolate icing, melt the chocolate jam. Mix the icing sugar with water and stir to get a creamy consistency. Now simply dip the finished donuts into the respective jam and sprinkle with coconut chips or walnuts – ready!

Nutrition: Calories 345 Carbs 25g Protein 25g Fat 14g

939. Three-grain Bread with the Airfryer Baking Pan

Preparation Time: 5 minutes
Cooking time: 1 hour 40 minutes
Servings: 2 loaves

Ingredients:
- `1kg Wheat flour (type 550)
- `250g spelled flour
- `750ml lukewarm water
- `1/2 cube
- `3.5 tbsp. fresh yeast
- `salt
- `1 teaspoon sugar
- `200g Sunflower seeds
- `200g linseed
- `100g sesame
- `some flour for kneading

Directions:
1. In a large bowl, dissolve the yeast cube in lukewarm water and stir with a whisk. Add salt and sugar and stir.
2. First, add the wheat flour and fold in. Once the flour has combined with the water, add the spelled flour and knead into a smooth dough. Finally, knead the linseeds, sunflower seeds, and sesame seeds. Cover the dough with a kitchen towel and leave for about an hour in a warm place until the greetings have doubled.
3. Cut the dough in half, shape it into two loaves with a little flour, cut into it and let it cover for another 20 minutes. Then coat with water, sprinkle with seeds and seeds and bake at 392 degrees Celsius for 35-40 minutes in the baking mold of the Airfryer.

Nutrition: Calories 345 Carbs 35g Protein 22g

940. Corn Bread

Preparation Time: 5 minutes
Cooking time: 30 minutes
Servings: 4

Ingredients:
- ½ cup whole milk
- ½ cup all-purpose flour
- ½ teaspoon kosher salt
- A ¼ cup of vegetable oil
- ½ cup corn kernels (fresh or frozen)
- ½ cup yellow cornmeal
- 2 tablespoons sugar
- 2 eggs
- 1 ½ teaspoon baking powder

Directions
1. Combine all the dry ingredients during a bowl and whisk.
2. In another bowl, put all the wet ingredients. Gently mix until combined. Gradually add the dry mixture into the bowl. Mix until smooth. Add the corn and mix until combined.
3. Transfer the mixture into a greased baking dish. Put it in the cooking basket. Cook for 25 minutes at 350 F.
4. Allow to cool transferring to a plated slice and serve.

Nutrition: Calories 372 Protein 8.8g Fat 20.16g Carbs 39.04g

SOUP AND STEW

941. Tortilla and White Beans Soup

Preparation Time: 10 minutes
Cooking Time: 27 minutes
Servings: 4
Ingredients:
- 1 cup white beans
- 4 tablespoons butter
- ¼ teaspoon white pepper
- 1 onion, roughly sliced
- 1 tablespoon sun dried tomatoes
- ¼ cup fresh cream
- 4 cups water
- 2 teaspoons salt
- 1 carrot, roughly chopped
- 4 garlic cloves, minced
- 4 tablespoons tomato paste
- Crunchy tortilla chips, for garnish

Directions:
1. Put the butter, garlic, carrots, onions and white pepper in the Air fryer and select "Sauté".
2. Sauté for 5 minutes and add white beans, potatoes, sun dried tomatoes, tomato paste, salt and water.
3. Set the Air fryer to "Soup" and cook for 12 minutes at high pressure.
4. Release the pressure naturally and add sour cream.
5. Blend the contents of the Air fryer to a smooth consistency and top with crunchy tortilla chips.

Nutrition: Calories: 353 Fat: 14.7g Carbs: 44.2g Sugars: 5.3g Protein: 14g

942. Mexican Beef Soup

Preparation Time: 30 minutes
Cooking time: 25 minutes
Servings: 4
Ingredients:
- 1-pound beef stew meat
- 3/4-pound potatoes cut into 3/4-inch cubes
- cups frozen corn, thawed
- medium carrots, cut into 1/2-inch slices
- 1 medium onion, chopped
- garlic cloves, minced
- 1-1/2 tsp. dried oregano
- 1 tsp. ground cumin
- 1/2 tsp. salt
- 1/4 tsp. crushed red pepper flakes
- cups beef stock
- 1 can diced tomatoes and green chilies

Directions
1. In a baking dish that fits your air fryer oven, mix the turkey with the rest of the ingredients except the parsley, toss, introduce the dish in the fryer, bake at 380 F for 25 minutes
2. Divide into bowls, sprinkle the parsley on top and serve.

Nutrition: Calories 250 Fat 11g Fiber 2g Carbs 6g Protein 12g

943. Zucchini and Cauliflower Stew

Preparation Time: 25 minutes
Cooking time: 20 minutes
Servings: 4
Ingredients:
- 1 cauliflower head, florets separated
- 1 ½ cups zucchinis; sliced
- 1 handful parsley leaves; chopped.
- ½ cup tomato puree
- green onions; chopped.
- 1 tbsp. balsamic vinegar
- 1 tbsp. olive oil
- Salt and black pepper to taste.

Directions
1. In a pan that fits your air fryer oven, mix the zucchinis with the rest of the ingredients except the parsley, toss, introduce the pan in the air fryer oven and cook at 380 F for 20 minutes
2. Divide into bowls and serve for lunch with parsley sprinkled on top.

Nutrition: Calories 193 Fat 5g Fiber 2g Carbs 4g Protein 7g

944. Butternut Squash and Apple Soup

Preparation Time: 35 minutes
Cooking time: 30 minutes
Servings: 6
Ingredients:
- 2tbsp. olive oil
- 1 onion, chopped
- 1 tsp. dried sage
- 1/3 cup Cashew Milk
- ¼ tsp. salt
- ¼ tsp. pepper
- cloves garlic, minced
- 1 (2 pounds) butternut squash, seeded, and cut into 1-inch cubes
- 2apples, cored and diced into 1-inch chunks
- 1cups vegetable stock

Directions
1. Grease a baking dish that fits your air fryer oven with the butter, add all the ingredients in the pan and toss them.
2. Introduce the dish in the fryer, cook at 360 F for 30 minutes, divide into bowls and serve

Nutrition: Calories 246 Fat 12g Fiber 2g Carbs 6g Protein 12g

945. Carrot Soup with Fowl

Preparation Time: 8 minutes
Cooking Time: 20 minutes
Servings: 4
Ingredients:
- ½ fowl or chicken
- 2 quarts of chicken broth
- ¼ Cup of coarsely chopped onion
- ½ Cup of coarsely chopped carrots
- ½ Cup of coarsely chopped celery
- 1 Teaspoon of saffron threads
- ¾ Cup of corn kernels
- ½ Cup of finely chopped celery
- 1 tablespoon of fresh chopped parsley
- 1 Cup of cooked egg noodles

Directions:
1. Start by combining all together the stewing chicken or fowl with the chicken broth in your Air fryer
2. Press sauté and add the onions, the carrots, the celery and the saffron
3. Now, close the lid and set at high pressure for around 20 minutes
4. Once the timer beeps, remove the chicken and shred it from the bone and cut it into small pieces
5. Strain your saffron broth with a fine sieve and then add the celery, the corn, the parsley, and the cooked noodles to your broth.
6. Return your soup to simmer for a few minutes
7. Serve and enjoy a delicious and nutritious soup

Nutrition: Calories: 154.4 Protein: 10.9 g. Fat: 0.8 g. Carbs: 27.2 g.

946. Lobster Bisque Soup

Preparation Time: 5 minutes
Cooking Time: 15 minutes
Servings: 4
Ingredients:
- 1 cups frozen or fresh lobster meat
- 1/2 cup homemade low-sodium vegetable or fish broth
- 1/4 cups unsweetened coconut cream
- 1 Tablespoons organic ghee (clarified butter)
- 1 medium yellow or red onion, finely chopped
- 2 garlic cloves, minced
- 1/2 cup dry white wine
- 1/2 cup carrots, finely chopped
- 1/2 cup celery, finely chopped
- 1/2 Tablespoon Worcestershire sauce
- 1/2 teaspoon smoked paprika or regular paprika
- 1/2 Tablespoon fresh parsley, chopped
- 1/2 teaspoon dried thyme
- Pinch of salt, pepper

Directions
1. Choose "Sauté" function on Air fryer. Add the ghee.
2. Once melted, add onion, celery, carrots, garlic. Cook 5 minutes.
3. Deglaze Air fryer with the wine. Simmer until reduced by half.
4. Stir in lobster meat, and broth.
5. Close, seal the lid. Press "Steam" function. Cook on HIGH 5 minutes.
6. When done, naturally release pressure. Remove the lid.
7. Stir in coconut cream, Worcestershire sauce, paprika, parsley, thyme, salt, and black pepper. Use an immersion blender to puree soup until smooth.
8. Ladle soup in bowls. Garnish with parsley, fresh ground black pepper. Serve.

Nutrition: Calories: 394 Fat: 29.3g Carbs: 5.3g Protein: 24.4g

947. Air fryer Angel Hair Soup

Preparation Time: 10 minutes
Cooking Time: 15 minutes
Servings: 4
Ingredients:
- 4 Cups of low sodium chicken broth
- 3 Tbsp of tomato sauce
- ½ lb of angel hair pasta
- 7 leaves of fresh basil
- 2 tbsp. of olive oil
- ¼ Cup of parmesan cheese to serve
- 2 Peeled and diced carrots
- 1 Peeled and cubed potato
- ¼ Cup of chickpeas

Directions:
1. Pour the oil, and add the broth, the chickpeas, the carrots, the tomato sauce and the basil in your Air fryer
2. Press sauté and let the ingredients simmer for around 5 minutes.
3. Add 1 and ½ cup of chicken broth or and close the lid of the Air fryer.
4. Set at high pressure for around 10 minutes.
5. Once the timer beeps, quick release the pressure and stir in the angel's hair pasta.
6. Boil the ingredients for 5 minutes
7. Add the basil and let cook for another minute.
8. Serve in bowl with a sprinkle of Parmesan cheese and tortilla strips.
9. Serve and enjoy!

Nutrition: Calories 216 Protein – 12.4 g. Fat – 3.8 g. Carbs – 35.1 g.

948. Vegetable Wild Rice Soup

Preparation Time: 10 minutes
Cooking time: 15 minutes
Servings: 4
Ingredients:
- `6 cups reduced-sodium vegetable broth
- `2 cans (14-1/2 ounces each) fire-roasted diced tomatoes, undrained
- `2 celery ribs, sliced
- `2 medium carrots, chopped
- `1-3/4 cups baby Portobello mushrooms, sliced
- `1 onion, chopped
- `1 parsnip, peeled and chopped
- `1 sweet potato, peeled and cubed
- `1 green pepper, chopped
- `1 cup uncooked wild rice
- `2 garlic cloves, minced
- `3/4 tsp. salt
- `1/4 tsp. pepper
- `2 bay leaves
- `2 fresh thyme sprigs

Directions
1. Set the Air fryer oven to 375 F for 5 minutes.
2. Put all ingredients in the cooking tray.
3. Insert the cooking tray in the oven.
4. Remove from the oven when Cooking Time is complete. Put the butter in a wok and add the garlic mixture, white beans, tomato paste, water, salt and white pepper.
5. Sauté for about 3 minutes and stir in the fresh cream. Secure the lid of the wok and cook for about 12 minutes on medium heat.

Nutrition: Calories 353 Fat 14.1g Carbs 44.7g Protein 14g

949. English Pub Split Pea Soup

Preparation Time: 5 minutes
Cooking time: 7 minutes
Servings: 4

Ingredients:
- `4 cups water
- `1 meaty ham bone
- `12-ounce light beer
- `1/4 tsp. pepper
- `1/2 tsp. salt
- `1/4 tsp. ground nutmeg
- `2 celery ribs, chopped
- `1 and a 1/3 cups dried green split peas
- `1 carrot, chopped
- `1 tbsp. English mustard
- `1 sweet onion, chopped
- `1/4 cup minced parsley
- `1/2 cup 2% milk

Directions
1. Set the Air fryer oven on Roast to 365 F for 7 minutes.
2. Put water, ham bone, beer, celery, peas, carrot, mustard and onion in the cooking tray.
3. Insert the cooking tray in the oven.
4. Remove from the oven when Cooking time is complete.
5. Serve warm.

Nutrition: Calories 174 Fat 10.4g Carbs 17.1g Protein 8.5g

950. Salmon Tortellini Soup

Preparation Time: 10 minutes
Cooking time: 20 minutes
Servings: 3

Ingredients:
- `2/3 cup diced onion
- `2 cloves garlic, minced
- `1–2 strips bacon, diced
- `12–16 ounces frozen boneless salmon
- `1 (10 oz.) package frozen mixed vegetables
- `10 ounces frozen tortellini
- `1-quart vegetable broth
- `1 tsp. paprika
- `1 tsp. Old Bay seasoning

Directions
1. Set the Air fryer oven to 375 F for 5 minutes.
2. Put the leeks, cob, garlic, and chives in the cooking tray.
3. Insert the cooking tray in the oven.
4. Remove from the Oven when Cooking Time is complete.
5. Sauté bacon, onions, and garlic for 3 minutes.
6. Add frozen salmon, frozen vegetables, frozen tortellini, broth, and seasonings to oven.
7. Set timer for 6 minutes.
8. Flake salmon into chunks.
9. Heat for about 3 minutes and ladle out in a bowl to serve hot.

Nutrition: Calories 323 Fat 11.5g Carbs 55.8g Protein 8.3g

951. Lentil Soup

Preparation Time: 10 minutes
Cooking time: 25 minutes
Servings: 4

Ingredients:
- `1/4 cup olive oil
- `1 1/2 cups lentils
- `28 ounce diced fire-roasted tomatoes
- `1-quart vegetable broth
- `1 cup water
- `1 onion
- `1 fennel bulb
- `2 large carrots
- `1 tsp. kosher salt
- `1 tbsp. paprika
- `1 tbsp. dried oregano
- `3 cups baby spinach
- `1 clove garlic, grated

Directions
1. Set the Air fryer oven to 375 F for 7 minutes.
2. Dice onions, fennel, and carrots.
3. Sauté onion and fennel for 7 minutes.
4. Add remaining ingredients except the last two.
5. Add spinach and garlic.
6. Insert the cooking tray in the oven.
7. Remove from the oven when Cooking Time is complete.
8. Puree the contents of the soup into the blender until smooth and serve warm.

Nutrition: Calories 435 Fat 25.4g Carbs 37.7g Protein 16.7g

952. Potato Soup

Preparation Time: 10 minutes
Cooking time: 23 minutes
Servings: 8

Ingredients:
- `4 slices bacon, diced
- `1 onion, chopped
- `1/2 cup shredded cheddar cheese
- `2 green onions, sliced
- `2 cloves garlic, minced
- `2 lbs. russet potatoes, cut into 1/2-inch pieces
- `4 cups chicken broth
- `1/4 cup sour cream

Directions
1. Set the Air fryer oven to 375 F for 7 minutes.
2. Sauté bacon in a pot until crisp. Remove.
3. Sauté yellow onion for 2 minutes.
4. Sauté garlic for 30 seconds.
5. Add the potatoes and broth.
6. Add sour cream.
7. Puree the soup.
8. Serve topped with the cheese, salt, pepper, bacon, and green onion
9. Remove from the oven when Cooking Time is complete.
10. Serve garnished with onion greens.

Nutrition: Calories 145 Fat 4.7g Carbs 22.6g Protein 4g

SOUP AND STEW

953. Noodle Soup with Tofu

Preparation Time: 10 minutes
Cooking time: 20 minutes
Servings: 5
Ingredients:
- `2 tsp. sesame oil
- `1 clove garlic, minced
- `1/2 tsp. Chinese five-spice
- `1/4 cup scallions, chopped
- `1 cup hot water
- `1/2 tsp. chicken base
- `1 1/2 oz. instant rice noodles
- `1 cup sugar snap peas
- `1 cup bean sprouts
- `1/2 cup tofu cubes

Directions
1. Set the Air fryer oven to 375 F for 5 minutes.
2. Sauté garlic and Chinese five-spice in oil for 1 minute.
3. Add water and chicken base at "Broil" and "More."
4. Add the rice noodles with pot off.
5. Add last 3 ingredients to a bowl.
6. Pour the broth over. Insert the cooking tray in the oven.
7. Remove from the Oven when Cooking Time is complete.
8. Put the olive oil in a wok and add the garlic, ginger, and onions. Sauté for about 3 minutes and add carrot mixture, vegetable stock, and Worcestershire sauce.
9. Serve with scallions and Sriracha sauce.

Nutrition: Calories 148 Fat 24.6g Carbs 4g Protein 4.6g

954. Tomato Soup

Preparation Time: 10 minutes
Cooking time: 7 minutes
Servings: 4
Ingredients:
- `2 tablespoons of homemade tomato sauce
- `2 teaspoons of dried basil, crushed
- `4 cups of low-sodium vegetable broth
- `1 tablespoon of balsamic vinegar
- `3 pounds of fresh tomatoes, chopped
- `1 tablespoon of olive oil
- `2 teaspoons of dried parsley, crushed
- `2 tablespoons of sugar
- `1 medium onion, chopped
- `Freshly ground black pepper, to taste
- `¼ cup of fresh basil, chopped
- `1 garlic clove, minced

Directions
1. Set the Air Fryer Oven on Air fryer to 365 F for 5 minutes. Put the tomatoes, garlic, onion, and fresh basil in the cooking tray. Insert the cooking tray in the Air Fryer Oven when it displays "Add Food".
2. Remove from the Air Fryer Oven when cooking time is complete. Put the olive oil in a wok and add the tomatoes mixture, tomato sauce, dried herbs, broth, and black pepper.
3. Secure the lid of the wok and cook for about 12 minutes on medium heat. Fold in the sugar and vinegar.
4. Pour into the immersion blender and puree the soup to serve hot.

Nutrition: Calories 146 Fat 4.5g Carbs 23.5g Protein 5.4g

955. Stewed Celery Stalk

Preparation Time: 10 minutes
Cooking time: 8 minutes
Servings: 6
Ingredients:
- `1-pound celery stalk
- `1 tablespoon butter
- `3 oz chive stems, diced
- `1 cup chicken stock
- `2 tablespoons heavy cream
- `1 teaspoon salt
- `1 tablespoon paprika

Directions
1. Chop the celery stalk roughly.
2. Pour the chicken stock into the air fryer basket tray and add the diced chives.
3. Preheat the air fryer to 400 F.
4. Cook the chives for 4 minutes.
5. After this, reduce the heat to 365 F.
6. Add the chopped celery stalk, butter, salt, paprika, and heavy cream.
7. Mix the vegetable mixture.
8. Cook the celery for 8 minutes more.
9. When the time is over – the celery stalk should be very soft.
10. Chill the side dish to the room temperature.
11. Serve it and enjoy!

Nutrition: Calories 59 Fat 13g Carbs 1.5g Protein 9.5g

956. Bacon and Cauliflower Soup

Preparation Time: 10 minutes
Cooking time: 20 minutes
Servings: 4
Ingredients:
- `2 tablespoons of butter
- `4 cups of chicken stock
- `1 large onion, chopped
- `4 potatoes, chopped
- `3 cups of cauliflower florets
- `½ cup of heavy cream
- `1 tablespoon of salt
- `1 tablespoon of black pepper
- `12 slices of bacon, crisp fried

Directions
1. Set the Air fryer oven on Air fryer to 375 F for 5 minutes Put the bacon, potatoes, and cauliflower in the cooking tray. Insert the cooking tray in the Air Fryer Oven when it displays "Add Food". Remove from the Air Fryer Oven when cooking time is complete. Put the butter in a wok and add the onions.
2. Sauté it for about 3 minutes and then stirs in the bacon mixture and the chicken stock. Secure the lid of the wok and cook for about 10 minutes on medium heat. Pour this mixture into an immersion blender and puree it. Ladle out in a bowl to serve.

Nutrition: Calories 344 Fat 16.7g Carbs 44.1g Protein 8.3g

957. Pork Stew

Preparation Time: 6 minutes
Cooking time: 12 minutes
Servings: 4
Ingredients:
- `2 lb. pork stew meat; cubed
- `1 eggplant; cubed
- `½ cup beef stock
- `2 zucchinis; cubed
- `½ tsp. smoked paprika
- `Salt and black pepper to taste.
- `A handful cilantro; chopped.

Directions
1. Preheat the air fryer to 370 F.
2. Mix all the ingredients in the air fryer pan. Toss and cook it in the air fryer and cook at 370 F for 30 minutes
3. Divide into bowls and serve right away.

Nutrition: Calories 245 Fat 12g Carbs 5g Protein 14g

958. Pumpkin Tomato Soup

Preparation Time: 10 minutes
Cooking time: 20 minutes
Servings: 4
Ingredients:
- `4 tablespoons of pumpkin puree
- `1 cup of tomatoes, chopped
- `4 cups of water
- `1 onion, roughly sliced
- `3 tablespoons of tomato paste
- `1 teaspoon of pumpkin spice powder
- `4 tablespoons of butter
- `1 carrot, roughly chopped
- `1 potato, roughly diced
- `3 tablespoons of sun-dried tomatoes
- `2 pinches of black pepper
- `2 teaspoons of salt

Directions
1. Set the Air fryer oven on Air fryer to 375 F for 5 minutes Put the tomatoes, carrots, potato, and sun-dried tomatoes in the cooking tray.
2. Insert the cooking tray in the Air Fryer Oven when it displays "Add Food". Remove from the Air Fryer Oven when cooking time is complete.
3. Put the butter in a wok and add the onions. Sauté for about 3 minutes and then stir in the tomato's mixture along with the remaining ingredients. Secure the lid of the wok and cook for about 12 minutes on medium heat.
4. Pour this mixture into an immersion blender and puree it. Ladle out in a bowl to serve.

Nutrition: Calories 190 Fat 12.7g Carbs 18.5g Protein 2.8g

959. Eggplant Stew

Preparation Time: 10 minutes
Cooking time: 13 minutes
Servings: 9
Ingredients:
- `1 eggplant
- `1 zucchini
- `4 oz chive stems
- `1 green pepper
- `2 garlic cloves, peeled
- `1 teaspoon turmeric
- `1 teaspoon paprika
- `1 teaspoon dried dill
- `1 teaspoon dried parsley
- `1 cup chicken stock
- `½ cup heavy cream
- `1 teaspoon kosher salt

Directions
1. Cut the zucchini and eggplant into the cubes.
2. Then sprinkle the vegetables with the dried parsley, dried dill, paprika, and turmeric.
3. Chop the garlic cloves.
4. Then chop the chives and green pepper.
5. Preheat the air fryer to 390 F.
6. Pour the chicken stock into the air fryer and add the eggplants.
7. Cook the eggplants for 2 minutes.
8. After this, add the chopped chives and green pepper.
9. Then add the chopped garlic cloves and heavy cream.
10. Cook the stew for 11 minutes more at the same temperature.
11. After this, transfer the cooked side dish in the serving plates.
12. Serve the meal hot.

Nutrition: Calories 49 Fat 13g Carbs 1.5g Protein 1g

960. Coconut Lime Soup

Preparation Time: 6 minutes
Cooking Time: 10 minutes
Servings: 3-4
Ingredients:
- ½ Tbsp of coconut Oil
- 1 Finely chopped onion
- 1 Teaspoon of ground coriander powder
- 1 Medium sized Cauliflower that are broken into large floret
- 3 Cups of Vegetable Broth
- ½ Cup of Coconut Milk
- 2-3 Tbsp of Lime Juice
- 1 Pinch of Salt to taste

Directions:
1. Start by heating the Air fryer and set the Manual button to sauté mode and sauté the onion for 6 minutes.
2. Add the coriander and keep stirring for a couple of minutes.
3. Add the rest of the ingredients; from the cauliflower, the vegetable broth and the coconut milk; then stir the ingredients to combine them.
4. Lock the lid and set the timer to 10 minutes.
5. Once the timer sets off; press the button keep warm and release the pressure
6. Blend the ingredients with a blender until it becomes soft
7. Add the lime juice and adjust the salt to taste
8. Serve and enjoy your soup!

Nutrition: Calories 262.8 Protein – 22 g. Fat – 12.7 g. Carbs – 16 g.

961. Garlic Soup with Almonds

Preparation Time: 5 minutes
Cooking Time: 15 minutes
Servings: 3
Ingredients:
- 3 and ¼ cups of freezing water
- 2 and ¼ cups of blanched almonds
- 5 Peeled and minced cloves of garlic
- 1 Baguette (remove the crusts removed and cut it into pieces)
- ½ Cup of coconuts oil
- 2 And ½ tbsp. of sherry vinegar
- 2 Drops of almond extract
- 1 Pinch of Kosher salt

Directions:
1. Start by combining the 2 cups of water in the Instant Processor with the almonds, the garlic, and the bread in the food processor.
2. Set the manual to the button Sauté; sauté the ingredients soften for around 5 minutes.
3. Add the remaining quantity of water, the coconut oil, the vinegar, the extract, and the salt.
4. Cancel the setting of the Sauté feature and set the timer to 10 minutes
5. Once the timer is off, release the pressure and blend the ingredients with the a food processor or blender
6. Garnish your soup with the halves of almonds.
7. Serve and enjoy your soup!

Nutrition: Calories 120 Protein – 7.1 g. Fat – 13.4 g. Carbs – 37.1 g.

962. Turkey And Broccoli Stew

Preparation Time: 5 minutes
Cooking time: 12 minutes
Servings: 4
Ingredients:
- `1 broccoli head, florets separated
- `1 turkey breast, skinless; boneless and cubed
- `1 cup tomato sauce
- `1 tbsp. parsley; chopped.
- `1 tbsp. olive oil
- `Salt and black pepper to taste.

Directions
1. Preheat the air fryer to 380 F.
2. In a baking dish that fits your air fryer, mix the turkey with the rest of the ingredients except the parsley, toss, introduce the dish in the fryer, bake at 380 F for 25 minutes
3. Divide into bowls, sprinkle the parsley on top and serve.

Nutrition: Calories 250 Fat 11g Carbs 6g Protein 12g

963. Leftover Stew

Preparation Time: 5 minutes
Cooking time: 20 minutes
Servings: 4
Ingredients:
- `1 tablespoon (15 mL) olive oil
- `1 large onion coarsely chopped
- `4 medium carrots cut in half lengthwise then in 2 inch (5 cm) pieces
- `2 stalks celery cut into 1 inch (2.5 cm) chunks
- `2 potatoes chopped in 1/2 inch (1.25 cm) pieces
- `3-4 cups (700-950 mL) broth (vegetable, beef or turkey) to cover, approximately
- `2 tablespoons (30 mL) bouillon (vegetable, beef or poultry)
- `2 cups (300g) leftover cooked meat of your choice, cut into bite-size pieces, approximately
- `Salt and pepper to taste

Directions
1. Select Sauté mode and allow the inner liner of your Air Fryer Oven to heat up.
2. Add the olive oil and allow it to heat up.
3. Add the onions and sauté for 2-3 minutes.
4. Press Cancel to turn off Sauté mode.
5. Add the rest of the ingredients, with the exception of the cooked meat.
6. Close and lock the lid ensuring the Pressure Valve is in the Sealing position.
7. Select Manual/Pressure Cook mode and set the cooking time for 4 minutes.
8. When the cooking time is complete, allow about a 5 minute Natural Pressure Release (just so you don't get broth spewing out of the valve) and then release the rest of the pressure by carefully turning the Pressure Valve from Sealing to Venting.
9. Once all of the pressure has been released and the Float Valve has dropped, carefully remove the lid.
10. Select Sauté mode and bring the liquid to a low simmer.
11. Add salt and pepper to taste.
12. If you find that the stew needs thickening, mixed together about a tablespoon (15 mL) of cornstarch with just enough water to make a pourable paste.
13. Slowly drizzle the cornstarch into the simmering liquid, stirring constantly until the desired consistency is reached.
14. If you plan to add dumplings now would be the time.
15. Press Cancel to turn off Sauté mode.
16. Add the leftover meat and allow it to heat through - about 5 minutes. Serve immediately, or cool and refrigerate to allow the flavors to blend, then reheat before serving.

Nutrition: Calories 245 Fat 12g Carbs 5g Protein 14g

964. Onion Soup

Preparation Time: 15 minutes
Cooking time: 5 hours 10 minutes
Servings: 6
Ingredients:
- `2 tablespoons olive oil
- `2 medium sweet onions, sliced
- `2 garlic cloves, minced
- `¼ cup low-sodium soy sauce
- `1 teaspoon unsweetened applesauce
- `1 teaspoon dried oregano, crushed
- `1 teaspoon dried basil, crushed
- `Ground black pepper, as required
- `5 cups vegetable broth
- `¼ cup Parmesan cheese, grated

Directions
1. In an oven-safe pan that will fit in the Air fryer oven, heat the oil over medium heat and cook the onion for about 8-9 minutes.
2. Add the garlic and cook for about 1 minute.
3. Remove from the heat and stir in the remaining ingredients except for cheese.
4. Cover the pan with a lid.
5. Arrange the pan over the wire rack.
6. Select "Slow Cooker" of Air fryer oven and set on "Low".
7. Set the timer for 5 hours and press "Start/Stop" to begin cooking.

8. When the cooking time is complete, remove the pan from the oven.
9. Remove the lid and stir in the cheese until melted completely.
10. Serve hot.

Nutrition: Calories 148 Fat 24.6g Carbs 4g Protein 4.6g

965. Mixed Veggies Soup

Preparation Time: 15 minutes
Cooking time: 8 hours 5 minutes
Servings: 6
Ingredients:
- `1 tablespoon olive oil
- `1 yellow onion, chopped
- `1 celery stalk, chopped
- `1 large carrot, peeled and chopped
- `2 garlic cloves, minced
- `1 teaspoon dried oregano, crushed
- `1 large zucchini, chopped
- `2 tomatoes, chopped
- `1 cup fresh spinach, chopped
- `4 cups homemade vegetable broth
- `Salt and ground black pepper, as required

Directions
1. In an oven-safe pan that will fit in the Air fryer oven, heat the oil over medium heat and sauté the onion, celery and carrot for about 3-4 minutes.
2. Add the garlic and thyme and sauté for about 1 minute.
3. Remove from the heat and stir in the remaining ingredients.
4. Cover the pan with a lid.
5. Arrange the pan over the wire rack.
6. Select "Slow Cooker" of Air fryer oven and set on "Low".
7. Set the timer for 8 hours and press "Start/Stop" to begin cooking.
8. When the cooking time is complete, remove the pan from the oven.
9. Remove the lid and stir the mixture well.
10. Serve hot.

Nutrition: Calories 193 Fat 5g Fiber 2g Carbs 4g Protein 7g

966. Lamb Stew

Preparation Time: 10 minutes
Cooking Time: 35 minutes
Servings: 5-6
Ingredients:
- 2 lbs of diced lamb stew meat
- 1 Large acorn squash
- 4 Medium carrots
- 2 Small yellow onions
- 2 Rosemary Sprigs.
- 1 bay leaf
- 6 sliced or minced cloves of garlic
- 3 Tbsp of broth or water
- ¼ Tbsp of sp salt (Adjust it to taste)

Directions:
1. Start by peeling and seeding, then cubing your acorn squash. You can use a nice trick which is to microwave the squash for 2 minutes.
2. Slice the carrots into quite thick circles.
3. Peel your onions and cut it into halves; then slice it into the shape of half-moons.
4. Now, place all of your ingredients in the Air fryer and set the feature Soup/ Stew button.

5. Lock the lid and set the timer to 35 minutes.
6. When the timer goes off; release the steam and pressure before opening the lid.
7. Serve and enjoy your stew.

Nutrition: Calories 332.7 Protein 28.9 g. Fat – 6.9 g. Carbs – 38.9 g.

967. Creamy Squash Soup

Preparation Time: 5 minutes
Cooking Time: 15 minutes
Servings: 4
Ingredients:
- 4 lbs. butternut squash, peeled, seeded, and cubed
- 4 cups beef stock
- ½ tsp. sage
- 1 tsp. thyme
- 2 garlic cloves, minced
- 1 onion, chopped
- 2 tbsp. olive oil
- Pepper
- Salt

Directions:
1. Add oil into air fryer and set on Sauté mode.
2. Add garlic and onion to the pot. Sauté for 5 minutes.
3. Add sage, thyme, pepper and salt. Stir for a minute.
4. Add squash and stock. Stir well.
5. Secure pot with lid and cook on manual high pressure for 10 minutes.
6. Quick release pressure then open the lid.
7. Puree the soup using an immersion blender until smooth and creamy. Serve and enjoy.

Nutrition: Calories 295 Protein – 7.7 g. Fat – 8.1 g. Carbs – 56.4 g.

968. Light Taco Soup

Preparation time: 24 minutes
Cooking time: 7 hours
Servings: 5
Ingredients:
- `7 oz. ground chicken
- `½ teaspoon sesame oil
- `3 cup vegetable stock
- `3 oz. yellow onion
- `1 cup tomato, canned
- `3 tomatoes
- `5 oz. corn kernels
- `1 jalapeno pepper, sliced
- `½ cup white beans, drained
- `3 tablespoon taco seasoning
- `¼ teaspoon salt
- `3 oz. black olives, sliced
- `5 corn tortillas, for serving

Directions
1. Peel the onion and dice it. Chop the fresh and canned tomatoes.
2. Place the ground chicken, sesame oil, vegetable stock, diced onion, chopped tomatoes, sliced black olives, sliced jalapeno pepper, and corn in an oven-safe pan that will fit in the Air fryer oven.
3. Add the white beans, taco seasoning, and salt.
4. Stir the soup mixture gently and close the lid.
5. Cook the soup for 7 hours on LOW. Meanwhile, cut the corn tortillas into the strips and bake them in the preheated to 365 F oven for 10 minutes.

6. When the soup is cooked, ladle it into the serving bowls and sprinkle with the baked corn tortilla strips. Enjoy!

Nutrition: Calories 328 Fat 9.6g Fiber 10g Carbs 45.19g Protein 18g

969. Spicy Mushroom Soup

Preparation Time: 5 minutes
Cooking Time: 11 minutes
Servings: 2

Ingredients:
- 1 cup mushrooms, chopped
- ½ tsp. chili powder
- 2 tsp. garam masala
- 3 tbsp. olive oil
- 1 tsp. fresh lemon juice
- 5 cups chicken stock
- ¼ cup fresh celery, chopped
- 2 garlic cloves, crushed
- 1 onion, chopped
- ½ tsp. black pepper
- 1 tsp. sea salt

Directions:
1. Add oil into air fryer and set on Sauté mode.
2. Add garlic and onion to the pot. Sauté for 5 minutes.
3. Add chili powder and garam masala. Cook for a minute.
4. Add remaining ingredients and stir well.
5. Secure pot with lid and cook on manual high pressure for 5 minutes.
6. Quick release pressure then open the lid.
7. Puree the soup using a blender and serve.

Nutrition: Calories 244 Protein – 3.9 g. Fat – 22.8 g. Carbs – 10.2 g.

970. Carrot Soup with Cardamom

Preparation time: 18 minutes
Cooking time: 12 hours
Servings: 9

Ingredients:
- `1-pound carrot
- `1 teaspoon ground cardamom
- `¼ teaspoon nutmeg
- `1 teaspoon salt
- `3 tablespoons fresh parsley
- `1 teaspoon honey
- `1 teaspoon marjoram
- `5 cups chicken stock
- `½ cup yellow onion, chopped
- `1 teaspoon butter

Directions
1. Toss the butter in a pan and add chopped onion.
2. Chop the carrot and add it to the pan too.
3. Roast the vegetables for 5 minutes on the low heat. After this, place the roasted vegetables in an oven-safe pan that will fit in the Air fryer oven. Add ground cardamom, nutmeg, salt, marjoram, and chicken stock.
4. Close the lid and cook the soup for 12 hours on LOW.
5. Chop the fresh parsley.
6. When the time is over, blend the soup with a hand blender until you get a smooth texture. Then ladle the soup into the serving bowls.
7. Sprinkle the prepared soup with the chopped fresh parsley and honey. Enjoy the soup immediately!

Nutrition: Calories 80 Fat 2.7g Fiber 2g Carbs 10.19g Protein 4g

971. Beef Noodle Soup

Preparation Time: 8 minutes
Cooking Time: 35 minutes
Servings: 4

Ingredients:
- ½ lb of beef shoulder
- 1 Tbsp of kosher salt
- ¼ Cup of fresh ground black pepper
- ½ Teaspoon of all spice
- ¼ Teaspoon of ground ginger
- 1 Tbsp of coconut oil
- 1 Piece of 1 inch of fresh ginger
- 4 Cups of chicken broth
- ¼ Cups of fish sauce
- 1 Medium head of bok choy
- 1 Head of cabbage
- 1 or 2 packages of Shriataki noodles
- 2 scallions
- ¼ Cup of cilantro
- 1 Cup of bean sprouts

Directions:
1. Cut the beef into one and small cubes of 1 inch each.
2. Blend all together the salt, the pepper, the all spice powder and the ginger.
3. Spice the quantity of beef cubes into the mixture of the spices.
4. Put the air fryer to the feature sauté, and once it becomes hot; then stir in the beef and sauté it until it becomes brown.
5. Add the broth of chicken
6. Add the fish sauce and the ginger
7. Now, lock the lid over the Air fryer and Put the air fryer to the Beef. Feature Stew and cook it for around 30 minutes. Meanwhile; cut the bok choy, the Napa cabbage and the scallions
8. When the cooking process is complete and the timer of the Air fryer gets off, vent your steam and remove its lid. Then set the feature of the Air fryer to the mode sauté
9. Add the Napa cabbage, the bok choy and the scallion; then simmer for around 5 minutes
10. Drain your noodles and rinse it; then add it to your air fryer. Let the ingredients simmer for around 2 minutes
11. Serve and enjoy your soup with cilantro for garnish and sprouts

Nutrition: Calories 204.4 Protein – 11.7 g. Fat – 7.5 g. Carbs – 27.8 g.

972. Asian Pork Soup

Preparation Time: 10 minutes
Cooking Time: 30 minutes
Servings: 5

Ingredients:
- 1 lb. ground pork
- 1 tsp. ground ginger
- ¼ cup soy sauce
- 4 cups beef broth
- ½ cabbage head, chopped
- 2 carrots, peeled and shredded
- 1 onion, chopped
- 1 tbsp. olive oil
- Pepper
- Salt

Directions:
1. Add oil into air fryer and set on Sauté mode.

2. Add meat to the pot and sauté for 5 minutes.
3. Add remaining ingredients and stir well.
4. Secure pot with lid and cook on manual high pressure for 25 minutes.
5. Quick release pressure then open the lid.
6. Stir well and serve hot.

Nutrition: Calories – 229 Protein – 29.8 g. Fat – 7.2 g. Carbs – 10.6 g.

973. Handmade Sausage Stew

Preparation time: 25 minutes
Cooking time: 3 hours
Servings: 3

Ingredients:
- `7 oz. ground pork
- `1 egg yolk
- `½ teaspoon salt
- `½ teaspoon ground black pepper
- `7 oz. broccoli, chopped
- `½ cup water
- `1 tomato, chopped
- `1 teaspoon butter

Directions
1. Mix the ground pork and yolk. Add salt and ground black pepper.
2. Stir the mixture and form small sausages with your hands.
3. Place the sausages in an oven-safe pan that will fit in the Air fryer oven.
4. Add the chopped broccoli and water.
5. Add chopped tomato and butter.
6. Close the lid and cook the stew for 3 hours on High.
7. Place the cooked stew in bowls and enjoy!

Nutrition: Calories 268 Fat 3g Fiber 4g Carbs 53.34g Protein 7g

974. Carrot Peanut Butter Soup

Preparation Time: 5 minutes
Cooking Time: 15 minutes
Servings: 4

Ingredients:
- 8 carrots, peeled and chopped
- 1 onion, chopped
- 3 garlic cloves, peeled
- 14 oz. coconut milk
- 1 ½ cup chicken stock
- ¼ cup peanut butter
- 1 tbsp. curry paste
- Pepper
- Salt

Directions:
1. Add all ingredients except salt and pepper into air fryer and stir well.
2. Secure pot with lid and cook on manual high pressure for 15 minutes.
3. Quick release pressure then open the lid.
4. Puree the soup using an immersion blender until smooth.
5. Season soup with pepper and salt.
6. Serve and enjoy.

Nutrition: Calories 416 Protein – 8.2 g. Fat – 34.2 g. Carbs – 25.3 g.

975. Taco Soup

Preparation time: 5 minutes
Cooking time: 1 hour
Servings: 6

Ingredients:
- `1 lb. chicken breast or tenders, diced
- `1 (15 oz) can hominy
- `1/2 medium onion, diced
- `1 clove garlic, minced
- `2 tsp. olive oil
- `5 cups chicken broth, low-sodium
- `1 (15 oz.) can diced tomatoes
- `1/2 cup brown rice
- `1/2 cup black beans, canned
- `Tortilla chips, for serving
- `Shredded cheese, for serving

Directions:
1. Add olive oil to inner pan and heat for 2 minutes; add onion and garlic and saute for 2 minutes.
2. Add diced chicken and brown for about 5 to 10 minutes.
3. Add remaining ingredients to the inner pan and cook for 45 minutes to 1 hour and serve topped with tortilla chips and shredded cheese.

Nutrition: Calories 321 Sodium 947mg Dietary Fiber 6.1g Fat 12.4g Carbs 38.8g Protein 31.5g

976. Kale Beef Soup

Preparation Time: 15 minutes
Cooking Time: 43 minutes
Servings: 4

Ingredients:
- 1 lb. beef stew meat
- 1 tsp. cayenne pepper
- 3 garlic cloves, crushed
- 4 cups chicken broth
- 2 tbsp. olive oil
- 1 cup kale, chopped
- 1 onion, sliced
- ¼ tsp. black pepper
- ½ tsp. salt

Directions:
1. Add oil into air fryer and set on Sauté mode.
2. Add garlic and onion. Sauté for 3 minutes.
3. Add meat and sauté for 5 minutes.
4. Add broth and season with cayenne pepper, pepper and salt. Stir well.
5. Secure pot with lid and cook on manual high pressure for 25 minutes.
6. Quick release pressure then open the lid.
7. Add kale and stir well. Sit for 10 minutes.
8. Stir well and serve.

Nutrition: Calories 333 Protein – 40.3 g. Fat – 15.6 g. Carbs – 6.3 g.

977. Chicken Daikon Soup

Preparation time: 5 minutes
Cooking time: 3 hours
Servings: 2-3
Ingredients:
- `1 lb. boneless, skinless chicken thighs
- `1 tsp. ginger, freshly sliced
- `1 daikon, peeled and cut into large chunks
- `1 small carrot, peeled and shredded
- `8 shiitake mushrooms, sliced and stems removed
- `1 tbsp. goji berries
- `3 conpoy or dried scallops
- `1/8 tsp. sea salt

Directions:
1. Add 4 cups of water to the inner pan and cook for 10 minutes; discard liquid and set aside blanched chicken pieces.
2. Add another 4 cups of water to the air fryer pan. Add chicken and remaining ingredients.
3. Lock the lid in place and cook for 45 minutes; allow to simmer for 1 hour.
4. Enjoy hot!

Nutrition: Calories 448 Sodium 783mg Dietary Fiber 5.4g Fat 12.2g Carbs 33.9g Protein 52.5g

978. Hearty Red Wine Stew

Preparation time: 5 minutes
Cooking time: 2 hours
Servings: 6-8
Ingredients:
- `2 pounds beef chuck, cut into 1 1/2 inch cubes
- `2 tbsp. all-purpose flour
- `1 tsp. garlic powder
- `1 tsp. sea salt
- `1 tsp. black pepper
- `1 tbsp. olive oil
- `3 shallots, peeled and quartered
- `1lb. small red potatoes halved
- `3 medium carrots, sliced large
- `3 sprigs fresh thyme
- `2 sprigs fresh rosemary
- `1 (15 oz.) can petite diced tomatoes
- `1 tbsp. balsamic vinegar
- `1 cup red wine
- `2 cups low-sodium beef broth

Directions:
1. Toss the beef cubes with the flour, garlic powder, salt and pepper to coat.
2. Add all the ingredients and toss well to combine.
3. Cook for 2 hours.
4. Ladle the stew into bowls and serve with your favorite, fresh bread.

Nutrition: Calories 296 Sodium 443mg Dietary Fiber 1.8g Fat 9g Carbs 11.1g Protein 36.6g

979. Butternut Cauliflower Soup

Preparation time: 5 minutes
Cooking time: 40 minutes
Servings: 6
Ingredients:
- `1 onion, diced
- `1 tsp. olive oil
- `3 garlic cloves, minced
- `1 lb. cauliflower, chopped
- `1 lb. butternut squash, cubed
- `2 cups chicken or vegetable broth
- `1/4 tsp. nutmeg
- `1/2 tsp. dried thyme
- `1/2 tsp. red pepper flakes
- `1/4 tsp. sea salt
- `1/2 cup half and half
- `1/2 cup sour cream
- `shredded cheddar cheese, for serving
- `crumbled bacon, for serving
- `sour cream, for serving

Directions:
1. Add olive oil and onion to the air fryer oven pan; cook 5 minutes. Add garlic and cook 2 minutes.
2. Fold in cauliflower, butternut squash, broth, and spices.
3. Cook for 25 minutes.
4. Add half and half and sour cream to inner pan. Use an immersion blender to cream the soup or allow soup to cool and blend in batches in a food processor or blender until smooth.
5. Top with cheese, bacon, and additional sour cream and serve.

Nutrition: Calories 301 Sodium 343mg Dietary Fiber 3.9g Fat 16.3g Carbs 17.2g Protein 23.2g

980. Pho

Preparation time: 5 minutes
Cooking time: 1 hour 10 minutes
Servings: 2-4
Ingredients:
- `4 lb. of beef bones
- `2 medium onions, sliced in half
- `2 cloves garlic, peeled and halved
- `2 medium carrots, sliced in half
- `1/2 cup fresh ginger
- `1 tbsp. apple cider vinegar
- `1 tsp. ground cinnamon
- `1 tsp. ground coriander
- `1 tsp. whole black peppercorns
- `2 tsp. sea salt
- `4 whole star anise
- `6 cups of water
- `Add-ins:
- `1 cup bean sprouts
- `1/2 lb. sirloin steak, sliced very thinly
- `1 lime, cut into wedges
- `2 scallions, sliced thinly
- `1 package of rice noodles
- `1 tbsp. fresh cilantro or mint
- `Fresh Hot Red Pepper, sliced

Directions:
1. Bring water to a boil in the air fryer oven pan. Add the bones and cook for 5 minutes.
2. Place onion, garlic, carrot, and ginger on a greased sheet-tray. Broil in the oven for 10 minutes, or until charred.
3. Add charred veggies, apple cider vinegar, spices, and more water, if needed, to cover the bones in the inner pan.
4. Lock lid in place and cook for 45 minutes. After cycle ends leave to rest, covered, for 15 minutes.
5. Cook the rice noodles by package instructions and set aside until ready to eat.
6. Strain the broth through a mesh strainer until it runs clear; about 3 times. Discard bones and veggies.
7. Return broth to inner pan and cook for 5 minutes.
8. Distribute bone broth, evenly into bowls, add in desired toppings, and enjoy!

Nutrition: Calories 325 Sodium 939mg Dietary Fiber 15.9g Fat 3.1g Carbs 70.2g Protein 9.3g

981. Beef and Guinness Stew

Preparation time: 5 minutes
Cooking time: 2 hours
Servings: 8
Ingredients:
- `1 lbs. stew beef, 1-inch pieces
- `salt and pepper to season
- `2 tsp. olive oil
- `1 small sweet onion, chopped
- `1 tsp. garlic powder
- `2 large carrots, peeled and chopped into thick slices
- `4 red potatoes, quartered
- `2 celery stalks, chopped into thick pieces
- `1/4 cup plain flour
- `2 cups stout beer, like Guinness
- `3 tbsp. tomato paste
- `2 cups beef broth
- `1 tsp. dried thyme

Directions:
1. Season beef generously with salt and pepper.
2. Heat olive oil in the inner pan and add beef; cook until browned. Transfer to a plate.
3. Add onion and sauté 5 minutes. Add the carrots, celery, and potatoes, and cook for an additional 5 minutes. Stir the flour into the vegetables in the inner pan and coat them evenly. Cook, stirring occasionally, for an additional 3 minutes.
4. Gently fold the Guinness into the stew; mix well to dissolve flour, then add the tomato paste, broth and thyme, scraping off any browned bits on the bottom of the inner pan with a wooden spoon or spatula.
5. Cook for 5 minutes. Fold the beef back into the pot cover and cook 1 hour.

Nutrition: Calories 235 Sodium 297mg Dietary Fiber 3g Fat 5.2g Carbs 26.4g Protein 17g

982. Mediterranean Bamyeh Okra Tomato Stew

Preparation Time: 5 minutes
Cooking Time: 7 minutes
Servings: 4
Ingredients:
- ¼ cup of water
- 2 tablespoons apple cider vinegar
- 1 cup onions, chopped
- 1 tablespoon minced garlic
- ounce canned tomatoes
- 1 tablespoon vegetable broth
- 1 teaspoon smoked paprika
- ½ teaspoon ground allspice
- 1 teaspoon salt
- 1 1/2 pounds fresh okra

Directions:
1. Place all ingredients except for the lemon juice and tomato paste into air fryer. Put in okra last.
2. Cook on high pressure for 2 minutes, let it rest for 5 minutes.
3. Quick release the pressure.
4. Open the lid carefully and add tomato paste in water and then the lemon juice. Stir gently and serve.

Nutrition: Calories – 85 Protein – 4 g. Fat – 5 g. Carbs – 19 g.

983. Beef Barley Soup

Preparation time: 5 minutes
Cooking time: 1 hour 30 minutes
Servings: 6-8
Ingredients:
- `1 lb. stew meat
- `Sea salt and pepper, to season stew meat
- `1 tsp. olive oil
- `10 key mushrooms, quartered
- `1/2 cup onion, chopped
- `1/2 cup celery, chopped
- `1/2 cup carrots, chopped
- `6 garlic cloves, minced
- `6 cups beef or vegetable broth
- `1 cup water
- `2 bay leaves
- `1/2 teaspoon dried thyme
- `2/3 cups pearl barley, rinsed

Directions:
1. Season the stew meat with sea salt and pepper. Heat olive oil in the inner pan. Add the stew meat and brown on all sides for about 3-5 minutes.
2. Add remaining ingredients and lock lid into place.
3. Cook for 20 minutes, serve and enjoy!

Nutrition: Calories 222 Sodium 188mg Dietary Fiber 3.4g Fat 7.7g Carbs 17.4g Protein 20.3g

984. Potato Leek Soup

Preparation time: 5 minutes
Cooking time: 30 minutes
Servings: 6-8
Ingredients:
- `1 leek, white and light green parts only, rinsed and diced
- `2 tbsp. olive oil
- `2 cloves garlic, minced
- `1/2 tsp. sea salt
- `1/2 tsp. black pepper
- `1/4 teaspoon thyme
- `Pinch of nutmeg
- `3 small baking potatoes, peeled and diced
- `3 cups chicken or vegetable broth
- `1/4 cup half and half
- `1/4 cup sour cream

Directions:
1. Add the leek, olive oil, garlic, salt, pepper, thyme, nutmeg, broth, and potatoes to the inner pan and cook for 30 minutes.
2. Add half and half and sour cream. Blend with an immersion blender until smooth, and garnish with additional black pepper.

Nutrition: Calories 191 Sodium 166mg Dietary Fiber 1.2g Fat 7.6g Carbs 14g Protein 17.2g

985. Chicken Soup

Preparation time: 5 minutes
Cooking time: 1 hour 16 minutes
Servings: 4
Ingredients:
- `4 chicken breasts, skinned and deboned
- `1 onion, sliced into rounds
- `2 tbsps. of extra virgin olive oil
- `16 ounces of chunky salsa
- `3 garlic cloves, grated
- `2 medium carrot, chopped
- `29 ounces of chicken stock
- `32 ounces of drained peas
- `29 ounces of canned diced tomatoes
- `1 Tbsp. of onion powder
- `Fresh parsley for garnish
- `1 Tbsp. of chili powder
- `1 tsp. garlic powder
- `15 ounces of frozen corn
- `Salt and black pepper, as desired

Directions:
1. Set the Air fryer oven to Air Fryer mode and set the time to 6 minutes.
2. Heat the oil, then add the sliced onions, stir and cook for 5 minutes. Stir in the garlic and cook for 1 minute.
3. Add the chicken breast, canned tomatoes, salsa, chicken broth, salt, parsley, black pepper, chili powder, onion powder, and garlic. Stir.
4. Close the cooker with the Pressure Lid. The short cooking program will have the chicken soup ready in 10 minutes.
5. Uncover the Air fryer oven and transfer the chicken to a chopping board. Shred and set it aside.
6. Add the frozen corn and pea to the Air fryer oven and cook for 2-3 minutes.
7. Combine the chicken soup and the beans mixture.
8. Divide into bowls, garnish with parsley, and serve.

Nutrition: Calories 110 Fat 4.4g Carbs 8g Protein 6g

986. Corn Soup

Preparation time: 5 minutes
Cooking time: 1 hour 15 minutes
Servings: 4
Ingredients:
- `2 Tbsps. of butter
- `Extra virgin olive oil
- `2 leeks, chopped
- `1 Tbsp. of fresh chives, chopped
- `2 garlic cloves, grated
- `1-quart of chicken stock
- `6 ears of corn, kernels removed and cobs reserved
- `4 tarragon sprigs, chopped
- `2 bay leaves
- `Boiled corn, for garnish
- `Salt and black pepper, as desired

Directions:
1. Set the Air fryer oven to Air Fryer mode and set the time to 6 minutes.
2. Melt the butter, then add garlic and chopped leeks, stir and cook for 4 minutes.
3. Add the corn, tarragon, bay leaves, 1/2 of the chicken broth. Cover with the Pressure Lid and cook for 3 minutes.
4. Uncover the Air fryer oven, then throw away the bay leaves and corn on the cob.
5. Transfer the other contents of the cooker to a food processor. Pulse to obtain a smooth soup, add the remaining stock, and stir again.
6. Season with the salt and black pepper and stir.
7. Divide the soup into equal portions and top with chives, boiled corn, and olive oil.
8. Serve.

Nutrition: Calories 300 Fat 8.3g Carbs 50g Protein 13g

987. Golden Lentil and Spinach Soup

Preparation Time: 10 minutes
Cooking Time: 25 minutes
Servings: 4
Ingredients:
- 2 teaspoons of olive oil
- ½ yellow onion, diced
- 2 carrots, peeled and diced
- 1 celery stock, diced
- 4 garlic cloves, minced
- 2 teaspoons ground cumin
- 1 teaspoon ground turmeric
- 1 teaspoon dried thyme
- 1 teaspoon kosher salt
- ¼ teaspoon freshly ground black pepper
- 1 cup dry brown lentils, rinsed well
- 4 cups low-sodium vegetable broth
- 8 ounces baby spinach

Directions:
1. Choose saute function of the air fryer and add oil. When hot, add onions, carrots, and celery. Saute, occasionally stirring, until tender, about 5 minutes.
2. Add garlic, cumin, turmeric, thyme, salt, and pepper. Cook and stir for one minute.
3. Stir in lentil and broth.

4. Place lid on air fryer and put the valve to "sealing." Press manual high pressure and set a timer for 12 minutes.
5. After 12 minutes, quick release pressure and then carefully remove the lid when done. Stir in the spinach, and add salt and pepper to taste.

Nutrition: Calories – 134 Protein – 9 g. Fat – 3 g. Carbs – 17 g.

988. Split Pea Soup

Preparation time: 5 minutes
Cooking time: 1 hour 30 minutes
Servings: 6
Ingredients:
- `1 pound of ground chicken sausage
- `2 Tbsps. of butter
- `1/2 cup carrots, chopped
- `1 yellow onion, sliced into rounds
- `1/2 cup of chopped celery
- `Salt and black pepper, as desired
- `2 garlic cloves, grated
- `29 ounces of chicken stock
- `16 ounces of split peas, rinsed
- `2 cups of water
- `1/4 tsp. red pepper flakes
- `1/2 cup half and half

Directions:
1. Set the Air fryer oven to Air Fryer mode. Add the sausage, brown on all sides and transfer to a plate.
2. Add the butter to the Air Fryer Oven and melt.
3. Add the celery and yellow onion, mix and cook for 4 minutes. Add the garlic, and cook for 1 minute. Add water, broth, a half and half, peas, and pepper flakes, cover with Glass Lid and cook for 20 minutes.
4. Transfer the mixture to a food processor and blend.
5. Divide the soup into equal portions, stir in the sausage and carrot
6. Serve.

Nutrition: Calories 60 Fat 1g Carbs 4g Protein 2g

989. Kale Cottage Cheese Soup

Preparation Time: 5 minutes
Cooking Time: 5 minutes
Servings: 4
Ingredients:
- 5 cups fresh kale, chopped
- 1 tbsp. olive oil
- 1 cup cottage cheese, cut into small chunks
- 3 cups chicken broth
- ½ tsp. black pepper
- ½ tsp. sea salt

Directions:
1. Add all ingredients except cottage cheese into air fryer and stir well.
2. Secure pot with lid and cook on manual high pressure for 5 minutes.
3. Quick release pressure then open the lid.
4. Add cottage cheese and stir well.
5. Serve hot and enjoy.

Nutrition: Calories 152 Protein – 13.9 g. Fat – 5.6 g. Carbs – 11.7 g.

990. Chicken and Wild Rice Soup

Preparation time: 5 minutes
Cooking time: 50 minutes
Servings: 6
Ingredients:
- `1 cup of chopped celery
- `1 cup of half and half
- `1 cup of grated carrots
- `1 Tbsp. of dried parsley
- `1 cup of sliced yellow onion
- `1 cup of milk
- `2 Tbsps. of butter
- `2 chicken breasts, shredded
- `6 ounces of wild rice
- `28 ounces of chicken stock
- `2 Tbsps. of cornstarch
- `Red pepper flakes
- `2 Tbsps. of water
- `Salt and black pepper, as desired

Directions:
1. Set the Air fryer oven to Air Fryer mode.
2. Melt the butter and add the carrot, onion, and celery. Cook for 5 minutes.
3. Add the rice, chicken, broth, parsley, salt, and pepper, cover with Glass Lid and cook for 10 minutes.
4. Uncover, add the cornstarch mixed with water, cheese, milk, and a half and a half. Keep cooking until the timer automatic timer runs out.
5. Transfer to bowls and serve.

Nutrition: Calories 200 Fat 7g Carbs 19g Protein 5g

991. Awesome Sea Bass Stew

Preparation time: 10 minutes
Cooking time: 20 minutes
Servings: 4
Ingredients:
- `10 ounces white rice
- `4 ounces peas
- `2 red bell pepper, chopped
- `28 ounces white wine
- ` 6 ounces of water
- `3 pounds sea bass fillets, skinless, boneless, and cubed
- `8 shrimp
- `Salt and black pepper to taste
- `2 tablespoon olive oil

Directions:
1. In your air fryer oven's pan, mix all ingredients and toss.
2. Set the temperature to 400 F, set the timer to 20 minutes, and set the mode to Air Fryer.
3. Place the pans in your air fryer baskets and cook at 400 F for 20 minutes, stirring halfway.
4. Divide into bowls, serve, and enjoy.

Nutrition: Calories 280 Fat 12g Carbs 16g Protein 11g

SOUP AND STEW

992. Hearty Orange Stew

Preparation time: 10 minutes
Cooking time: 20 minutes
Servings: 4
Ingredients:
- `4 oranges, peeled and cut into segments
- `2-1/4 cups white sugar
- `2 cups orange juice

Directions:
1. In a pan that fits your air fryer oven, mix the oranges with the sugar and orange juice; toss.
2. Set temperature to 320 F. Set the timer to 20 minutes
3. Place the pan in the air fryer oven and cook at 320 F for 20 minutes.
4. Divide the orange stew into cups, refrigerate, and serve cold.

Nutrition: Calories 171 Fat 1g Carbs 8g Protein 2g

993. Greek Vegetable Soup

Preparation Time: 15 minutes
Cooking Time: 40 minutes
Servings: 4
Ingredients:
- 3 tablespoons of olive oil
- 1 onion, chopped
- 1 clove garlic, minced
- 3 cups of cabbage, shredded
- 2 medium carrots, chopped
- 2 celery stocks, chopped
- 2 cups of cooked chickpeas
- 4 cups of vegetable broth
- 15-ounce fire-roasted tomatoes, diced
- salt and pepper to taste

Directions:
1. Put the olive oil in the air fryer and set to medium heat saute.
2. Add the onions and cook until soft. Add garlic and cabbage and cook for another 5 minutes. When the cabbage softens, add the carrots, celery, and chickpeas. Stir everything to combine and cook for 5 minutes longer
3. Add the broth and canned tomatoes, then season with salt and pepper.
4. Press cancel to end saute mode and cover the pot with the lid set to sealing mode.
5. Set to soup mode and adjust the time to 10 minutes.
6. After completion, release the pressure manually and serve immediately.
7. You may garnish the soup with parsley, feta, or anything you like on soup

Nutrition: Calories 412.9 Protein – 6.3 g. Fat – 26.1 g. Carbs – 43.2 g.

994. Autumn Stew

Preparation time: 10 minutes
Cooking time: 10-14 minutes
Servings: 6
Ingredients:
- `6 tablespoon avocado oil
- `2 white onion, chopped
- `12 white mushrooms, quartered
- `1 tablespoon oregano
- `6 cups Sebi friendly vegetable stock
- `Pinch of salt
- `4 zucchinis, chopped
- `2 tablespoon spelt flour

Directions:
1. Set the temperature to 300 F and set the timer to 10 minutes
2. Add oil to your cooking basket
3. Add onion, zucchini, mushrooms, oregano and cook for 3 minutes
4. Add spelt flour and stir well until thick
5. Add stock, salt divide the mixture between the baskets
6. Cook for 10 minutes more
7. Once done, serve and enjoy

Nutrition: Calories 117 Fat 6g Carbs 17g Protein 3g

995. Awesome Rosemary Stew

Preparation time: 10 minutes
Cooking time: 15 minutes
Servings: 4
Ingredients:
- `2 pounds beef roast
- `1 tablespoon olive oil
- `1 medium onion
- `1 teaspoon salt
- `2 teaspoons rosemary and thyme

Directions:
1. Place beef roast in Air Fryer cooking basket, rub it well with olive oil, rosemary, thyme, and onion
2. Set your temperature to 390 F with the timer set to 15 minutes
3. Transfer the meat to Air Fryer cooking baskets
4. Let them cook until the timer runs out
5. Serve and enjoy!

Nutrition: Calories 290 Fat 14g Carbs 8g Protein 32g

996. Turkey and Mushroom Stew

Preparation time: 30 minutes
Cooking time: 15 minutes
Servings: 4
Ingredients:
- `½ lb. Brown mushrooms, sliced
- `Salt
- `1 turkey breast, boneless and browned
- `black pepper
- `1 tbsp. Parsley, minced
- `tomato sauce

Directions:
1. Add mushrooms, pepper, turkey, tomato sauce and salt to your air fryer pan, mix well.
2. Arrange the pan in your air fryer.
3. Cook for around 15 minutes at 370 F.
4. Distribute among plates.
5. Sprinkle the parsley on the top, serve.

Nutrition: Calories 220 Fiber 2g Fat 12g Carbs 5g Protein 12g

997. Okra and Green Beans Stew

Preparation time: 20 minutes
Cooking time: 12 minutes
Servings: 4
Ingredients:
- `1 lb. Green beans, halved
- `Salt
- `4 garlic cloves; minced
- `Black pepper
- `1 tbsp. Thyme, chopped
- `tomato sauce
- `1 cup okra

Directions:
1. Add all the components in your pan, toss well.
2. Place the pan in your air fryer.
3. Cook for around 15 minutes at 370 F.
4. Distribute the stew within bowls, serve.

Nutrition: Calories 183 Fiber 2g Fat 5g Carbs 4g Protein 8g

998. Zucchini Stew

Preparation time: 17 minutes
Cooking time: 12 minutes
Servings: 4
Ingredients:
- `8 zucchinis, cubed
- `black pepper
- `olive oil
- `½ tsp Basil, chopped
- `Salt
- `¼ tsp. Rosemary, dried
- `tomato sauce

Directions:
1. Grease your air fryer pan with the oil. Add all the components, toss well. Place the pan in your fryer.
2. Cook for around 12 minutes at 350 F.
3. Distribute within bowls, serve.

Nutrition: Calories 200 Fiber 2g Fat 6g Carbs 4g Protein 6g

999. Asparagus Garlic Ham Soup

Preparation Time: 15 minutes
Cooking Time: 50 minutes
Servings: 4
Ingredients:
- 1 ½ lbs. asparagus, chopped
- 4 cups chicken stock
- 2 tsp. garlic, minced
- 3 tbsp. olive oil
- 1 onion, diced
- ¾ cup ham, diced
- ½ tsp. thyme

Directions:
1. Add oil into air fryer and set on Sauté mode.
2. Add onion and sauté for 4 minutes.
3. Add garlic and ham and cook for a minute.
4. Add stock and thyme. Stir well.
5. Seal pot with lid and cook on Soup mode for 45 minutes.
6. Quick release pressure then open the lid,
7. Stir well and serve.

Nutrition: Calories – 188 Protein – 9 g. Fat – 13.5 g. Carbs – 11.4 g

1000. Cabbage Soup

Preparation Time: 10 minutes
Cooking Time: 35 minutes
Servings: 6
Ingredients:
- 1 Onion, Chopped
- 1 Tablespoon Avocado Oil
- 1 lb. Ground Beef
- ½ Teaspoon Garlic Powder
- 1 Can Tomatoes, diced
- Sea Salt & Black Pepper to Taste
- 6 Cups Bone Broth
- 1 lb. Cabbage, Shredded
- 2 Bay Leaves

Directions:
1. Choose sauté, and then add in your oil. Once it heats up, sauté your beef and onions. Flavor with garlic, salt and pepper. Cook for 2 minutes, and then add in your bone broth, , cabbage, bay leaves and iced tomatoes.
2. Cook on high pressure for thirty minutes.
3. Use a quick release, and serve warm.

Nutrition: Calories 428 Protein 26.3 g. Fat 24.8 g. Carbs 9.2 g.

1001. Zoodle Soup

Preparation Time: 5 minutes
Cooking Time: 25 minutes
Servings: 6
Ingredients:
- 1 Tablespoon Olive oil
- 1 Onion, Diced
- 1 lb. Chicken Breasts, Boneless, Skinless & Sliced
- 2 Cloves Garlic, Minced
- 3 Carrots, Sliced
- 1 Bay leaf
- 6 Cups Chicken Broth
- 3 Stalks Celery, Sliced
- 1 Jalapeno Pepper, Diced
- 2 Tablespoons Apple Cider Vinegar
- 4 Zucchinis, Spiralized
- Sea Salt & Black Pepper to Taste

Directions:
1. Choose sauté, and then add in your garlic and onion. Cook until you can smell the aroma, and then add in your celery, carrots, jalapeno and chicken breasts. Stir for a minute before seasoning with salt and pepper.
2. Mix in your bay leaf, chicken broth, and apple cider vinegar. Close the lid, and cook on high pressure for 20 minutes before using a quick release.
3. Choose sauté again, and then add in your zucchini, cooking for another three minutes. Serve warm.

Nutrition: Calories 164 Protein 19 g. Fat 5 g. Carbs 10 g.

CONCLUSION

Most people who have tried using this air fryer are happy with everything about this cooking appliance. You will find that the food prepared with this air fryer is tasty and perfect for your daily diet.

This means that this product has everything covered so that you can make great dishes for your family or friends without having any problems at all. If you want to have a good time cooking, then you need to get this awesome air fryer.

The producers did their best so that their customers will be satisfied with what they have created, and I can tell already they have done a great job with designing and manufacturing this product.

The design of this product is simple and beautiful at the same time, but yet I am sure that it will make your cooking much more efficient.

The adventure of this company began by launching the Instant Pot multifunction electric pressure cooker.

After a series of improvements and evolutions based on the feedback received from their customers, they managed to turn it into the most desired and best-valued kitchen utensil.

A multifunction gadget capable of replacing many of the kitchen utensils present in any home kitchen.

If you are looking for an air fryer and are willing to experiment to learn how to use it, you may be satisfied. Just don't depend on the manual for much help. You may also like the rotisserie feature if you have the patience to figure out how to use it. However, there are already consumers complaining that the grill stopped working gives us a bit of concern about its durability.

And it also has an affordable price!

Remember that investing in products that involve cooking healthily is investing in health, don't think twice, healthy food and quality results!

CONVERSION CHART

Liquid Measure

8 ounces = 1 cup
2 cups = 1 pint
16 ounces = 1 pint
4 cups = 1 quart
1 gill = 1/2 cup or 1/4 pint
2 pints = 1 quart
4 quarts = 1 gallon
31.5 gal. = 1 barrel

3 tsp = 1 tbsp
2 tbsp = 1/8 cup or 1 fluid ounce
4 tbsp = 1/4 cup
8 tbsp = 1/2 cup
1 pinch = 1/8 tsp or less
1 tsp = 60 drops

Conversion of US Liquid Measure to Metric System

1 fluid oz. = 29.573 milliliters
1 cup = 230 milliliters
1 quart = .94635 liters
1 gallon = 3.7854 liters
.033814 fluid ounce = 1 milliliter
3.3814 fluid ounces = 1 deciliter
33.814 fluid oz. or 1.0567 qt. = 1 liter

Dry Measure

2 pints = 1 quart
4 quarts = 1 gallon
8 quarts = 2 gallons or 1 peck
4 pecks = 8 gallons or 1 bushel
16 ounces = 1 pound
2000 lbs. = 1 ton

Conversion of US Weight and Mass Measure to Metric System

.0353 ounces = 1 gram
1/4 ounce = 7 grams
1 ounce = 28.35 grams
4 ounces = 113.4 grams
8 ounces = 226.8 grams
1 pound = 454 grams
2.2046 pounds = 1 kilogram
.98421 long ton or 1.1023 short tons = 1 metric ton

Linear Measure

12 inches = 1 foot
3 feet = 1 yard
5.5 yards = 1 rod
40 rods = 1 furlong
8 furlongs (5280 feet) = 1 mile
6080 feet = 1 nautical mile

Conversion of US Linear Measure to Metric System

1 inch = 2.54 centimeters
1 foot = .3048 meters
1 yard = .9144 meters
1 mile = 1609.3 meters or 1.6093 kilometers
.03937 in. = 1 millimeter
.3937 in.= 1 centimeter
3.937 in.= 1 decimeter
39.37 in.= 1 meter
3280.8 ft. or .62137 miles = 1 kilometer

To convert a Fahrenheit temperature to Centigrade, do the following:
a. Subtract 32 b. Multiply by 5 c. Divide by 9

To convert Centigrade to Fahrenheit, do the following:
a. Multiply by 9 b. Divide by 5 c. Add 32

AIR FRYER COOKING TIMES

	Temperature (°F)	Time (min)		Temperature (°F)	Time (min)
Vegetables					
Asparagus (sliced 1-inch)	400°F	5	Onions (pearl)	400°F	10
Beets (whole)	400°F	40	Parsnips (½-inch chunks)	380°F	15
Broccoli (florets)	400°F	6	Peppers (1-inch chunks)	400°F	15
Brussels Sprouts (halved)	380°F	15	Potatoes (small baby, 1.5 lbs)	400°F	15
Carrots (sliced ½-inch)	380°F	15	Potatoes (1-inch chunks)	400°F	12
Cauliflower (florets)	400°F	12	Potatoes (baked whole)	400°F	40
Corn on the cob	390°F	6	Squash (½-inch chunks)	400°F	12
Eggplant (1½-inch cubes)	400°F	15	Sweet Potato (baked)	380°F	30 to 35
Fennel (quartered)	370°F	15	Tomatoes (cherry)	400°F	4
Green Beans	400°F	5	Tomatoes (halves)	350°F	10
Kale leaves	250°F	12	Zucchini (½-inch sticks)	400°F	12
Mushrooms (sliced ¼-inch)	400°F	5			
Chicken					
Breasts, bone in (1.25 lbs.)	370°F	25	Legs, bone in (1.75 lbs.)	380°F	30
Breasts, boneless (4 oz.)	380°F	12	Wings (2 lbs.)	400°F	12
Drumsticks (2.5 lbs.)	370°F	20	Game Hen (halved - 2 lbs.)	390°F	20
Thighs, bone in (2 lbs.)	380°F	22	Whole Chicken (6.5 lbs.)	360°F	75
Thighs, boneless (1.5 lbs.)	380°F	18 to 20	Tenders	360°F	8 to 10
Beef					
Burger (4 oz.)	370°F	16 to 20	Meatballs (3-inch)	380°F	10
Filet Mignon (8 oz.)	400°F	18	Ribeye, bone in (1-inch, 8 oz.)	400°F	10 to 15
Flank Steak (1.5 lbs.)	400°F	12	Sirloin steaks (1-inch, 12 oz.)	400°F	9 to 14
London Broil (2 lbs.)	400°F	20 to 28	Beef Eye Round Roast (4 lbs.)	390°F	45 to 55
Meatballs (1-inch)	380°F	7			
Pork and Lamb					
Loin (2 lbs.)	360°F	55	Bacon (thick cut)	400°F	6 to 10
Pork Chops, bone in (1-inch, 6.5 oz.)	400°F	12	Sausages	380°F	15
Tenderloin (1 lb.)	370°F	15	Lamb Loin Chops (1-inch thick)	400°F	8 to 12
Bacon (regular)	400°F	5 to 7	Rack of lamb (1.5 - 2 lbs.)	380°F	22
Fish and Seafood					
Calamari (8 oz.)	400°F	4	Tuna steak	400°F	7 to 10
Fish Fillet (1-inch, 8 oz.)	400°F	10	Scallops	400°F	5 to 7
Salmon, fillet (6 oz.)	380°F	12	Shrimp	400°F	5
Swordfish steak	400°F	10			

INDEX

A

Air Baked Cheesecake; 192
Air Fried Banana and Walnuts Muffins; 191
Air Fried Beef Tenderloin; 132
Air Fried Buffalo Chicken Strips; 165
Air Fried Butter Cake; 202
Air Fried Dragon Shrimp; 107
Air Fried French Fries; 171
Air Fried French Toast; 28
Air Fried Ground Beef; 133
Air Fried Kale Chips; 62
Air Fried Leeks; 40
Air Fried Spring Rolls; 29
Air Fried Strip Steak with Red Wine Sauce; 131
Air Fried Turkey Breast; 84
Air Fried White Corn; 193
Air Fry Toaster Oven Bars; 194
Air fryer Angel Hair Soup; 247
Air Fryer Asparagus; 44
Air Fryer Baby Back Ribs; 123
Air Fryer Baked Potato; 40
Air Fryer Beef Casserole; 214
Air Fryer Chicken and Waffles; 30
Air Fryer Chocolate Cake; 188
Air Fryer Churros with Chocolate Sauce; 208
Air Fryer Cinnamon Rolls; 190
Air Fryer Cornish Hen; 73
Air Fryer Crunchy Cauliflower; 44
Air Fryer Falafel Balls; 46
Air Fryer Fish Tacos; 115
Air fryer Golden Lentil and Spinach Soup; 257
Air Fryer Grilled Chicken Breasts; 72
Air Fryer Oreo Cookies; 203
Air Fryer Roast Beef; 128
Air Fryer Salmon; 97
Air Fryer Sausage Wraps; 29
Air Fryer S'mores; 204
Air Fryer Southern Fried Chicken; 72
Air Fryer Spicy Shrimp; 101
Air Fryer Sweet and Sour Pork; 147
Air Fryer Veg Buffalo Cauliflower; 44
Air Fryer Vegetables; 51
Air Fryer Veggie Quesadillas; 154
Air Roasted Nuts; 193
Air-Fried English Breakfast; 33
Air-Fried Lemon Olive Chicken; 85
Air-Fried Philly Cheesesteak; 141
Alfredo Sauce; 227
All-in-One Toast; 163
Allspice Chicken Wings; 165
Almond Cherry Bars; 195
Almond Flour Battered and Crisped Onion Rings; 44
Almond Flour Coco-Milk Battered Chicken; 80
American-Style BBQ Chicken Pizza; 241
Angel Food Cake; 187
Apple Chips; 181
Apple Cider Donuts; 172
Apple Crisp; 187
Apple Dates Mix; 205
Apple Dumplings; 188
Apple Hand Pies; 190
Apple Pie in Air Fryer; 188
Apricot Blackberry Crumble; 196
Arancini; 168
Argentinian Style Skirt Steak; 130
Artichoke Omelet; 36
Artichoke Turkey Pizza; 236
Artichoke with Red Pepper Pizza; 236
Asian Pork Soup; 253
Asian Swordfish; 105
Asparagus Garlic Ham Soup; 260
Autumn Stew; 259
Avocado and Spinach with Poached Eggs; 27
Avocado and Tomato Wraps; 159
Avocado on Toast with Poached Egg; 241
Avocado Shrimp; 102
Avocado Taco Fry; 162
Awesome Chinese Doughnuts; 191
Awesome Rosemary Stew; 259
Awesome Sea Bass Stew; 258

B

Bacon and Asparagus Spears; 178
Bacon and Cauliflower Soup; 249
Bacon Cheeseburger Dip; 217
Bacon Cheeseburger Pizza; 236
Bacon Garlic Pizza; 235
Bacon Lettuce Tomato Pizza; 237
Bacon Tater Tots; 169
Bacon Wrapped Filet Mignon; 135
Bacon Wrapped Scallops; 115
Bacon Wrapped Shrimp; 113
Bacon-Wrapped Pork Tenderloin; 146
Baguette Bread; 232
Baked apple; 206
Baked Butter Crayfish; 95
Baked Cheesy Eggplant with Marinara; 60
Baked Tilapia; 100
Baked Turnovers with Pear; 235
Balsamic-Glazed Chicken Breasts; 90
Baltic Garlic Bread Sticks with Yogurt Dip; 243
Banana and Walnut Cake; 187
Banana Bread; 194
Banana Fritters; 207
Banana-Choco Brownies; 188
Bang Bang Panko Breaded Fried Shrimp; 98
Barbecue Flavored Pork Ribs; 145
Barbecue with Chorizo and Chicken; 74
Barbeque Bacon With Chicken Pizza; 230
Basil Cream Cheese Dip; 223
Basil Parmesan Bagel; 231
Basil Prosciutto Crostini with Mozzarella; 231
Basil-Garlic Breaded Chicken Bake; 73
Bass Filet In Coconut Sauce; 108
BBQ Chicken Wings; 78
Beef & Lemon Schnitzel for One; 138
Beef and Guinness Stew; 256
Beef and Mango Skewers; 167
Beef and Onion BBQ Pizza; 243
Beef and Seeds Burgers; 154
Beef Barley Soup; 256
Beef Brisket Recipe from Texas; 136
Beef Burgers; 134
Beef Empanadas; 141
Beef Korma; 138
Beef Noodle Soup; 253
Beef Pot Pie; 141
Beef Ribeye Steak; 138
Beef Spaghetti Sauce; 227
Beef Steaks with Beans; 130
Beef Stroganoff; 137
Beef Stuffed Pizza; 231
Beef With Beans; 139
Beefy 'n Cheesy Spanish Rice Casserole; 214
Beefy Steak Topped with Chimichurri Sauce; 137

Beer Battered Cod Filet; 108
Beer Can Chicken; 89
Beer Potato Fish; 97
Bell PepperCorn Wrapped in Tortilla; 60
Berry Crumble; 173
Best Ever Jalapeño Poppers; 59
Black and white brownies; 205
Black Bean and Tomato Chili; 48
Blackberry Chia Jam; 197
Blackened Mahi Mahi; 102
Blue Cheese Dressing; 218
Blue Cheese Stuffed Burgers; 131
Blueberry Cream; 197
Blueberry Lemon Muffins; 189
Blueberry Muffins; 185
Blueberry Overload French Toast; 234
Bolognaise Sauce; 142
Braised Pork; 135
Bread dough and amaretto; 201
Bread Pudding; 237
Bread pudding with cranberry; 205
Bread Roll; 229
Bread Roll and an Egg; 242
Breaded Cheesy Broccoli Gratin; 52
Breaded Cod Sticks; 93
Breaded Flounder; 96
Breakfast Cheese Bread Cups; 162
Breakfast Muffins; 163
Breakfast Pizza; 237
Broccoli Bacon Ranch Chicken; 77
Broccoli Creamy Casserole; 214
Broccoli Dip; 219
Broccoli Salad Recipe; 47
Broccoli Stuffed Peppers; 32
Broccoli with Cauliflower; 53
Broccoli With Olives; 41
Broccoli, Carrot, and Tomato Quiche; 211
Broccoli-Rice 'n Cheese Casserole; 213
Broiled lobster tails; 118
Broiled Tilapia; 111
Brown Rice And Beef-Stuffed Bell Peppers; 126
Brown Rice, Spinach and Tofu Frittata; 61
Brownie Muffins; 198
Buckwheat with Pork Chunks; 125
Buffalo cauliflower; 56
Buffalo Chicken Tenders; 79
Butter Squash Fritters; 64
Butter Up Salmon; 106
Buttered Broccoli; 62
Buttered carrot-zucchini with mayo; 54
Butterflied Prawns with Garlic-Sriracha; 109
Buttermilk Chicken; 81
Buttermilk Fried Mushrooms; 59
Butternut Cauliflower Soup; 255
Butternut Squash and Apple Soup; 246
Butternut Squash with Thyme; 173

Buttery Chocolate Toast; 26
Buttery Orange Toasts; 231
Buttery Parmesan Broccoli Florets; 174
Buttery scallops; 118

C

Cabbage and Prawn Wraps; 158
Cabbage Soup; 260
Cajun Bacon Pork Loin Fillet; 128
Cajun Olives and Peppers; 47
Cajun Pork Steaks; 128
Cajun Rubbed Ribeye Steaks; 122
Cajun Shrimp; 107
Caprese Stuffed Garlic Butter Portobellos; 177
Caramel Sauce; 226
Caramelized Baby Carrots; 53
Caramelized Pork Shoulder; 146
Caramelized Salmon Fillet; 94
Carrot cake; 201
Carrot Fries; 47
Carrot Oatmeal; 36
Carrot Peanut Butter Soup; 254
Carrot Soup with Cardamom; 253
Carrot Soup with Fowl; 246
Carrots and Cauliflower Mix; 37
Carrots, Yellow Squash & Zucchini; 62
Cauliflower and Broccoli Dish; 172
Cauliflower Cakes Ole; 65
Cauliflower Faux Rice; 48
Cauliflower Fried Rice; 50
Cauliflower Hummus; 181
Cauliflower Pizza Crust; 42
Cauliflower Steak; 43
Cauliflower, Okra, and Pepper Casserole; 212
Celery and Carrot Croquettes; 66
Charred Onions And Steak Cube BBQ; 137
Cheddar, squash and zucchini casserole; 55
Cheese and Bacon Breakfast Bombs; 33
Cheese and Egg Breakfast Sandwich; 163
Cheese and Garlic Stuffed Chicken Breasts; 73
Cheese Artichoke Arugula Dip; 220
Cheese Broccoli Bake; 23
Cheese Dip; 183
Cheese Fish Balls; 174
Cheese Ham Omelette; 23
Cheese Ham Pluck Bread; 242
Cheese Soufflés; 31
Cheese Sticks; 243
Cheese Stuffed Jalapenos; 181
Cheese Toast; 37
Cheeseburger Egg Rolls; 156
Cheesy Bacon Dipping Sauce; 226

Cheesy Baked-Egg Toast; 26
Cheesy Beef Burrito; 156
Cheesy Beef Dip; 220
Cheesy Berry-Flavored French Toast; 240
Cheesy Bread; 237
Cheesy Broccoli Croquettes; 65
Cheesy cauliflower fritters; 53
Cheesy Chicken Divan; 210
Cheesy Chicken in Leek-Tomato Sauce; 89
Cheesy Chicken Sandwich; 153
Cheesy Chicken Wraps; 151
Cheesy Chorizo, Corn, and Potato Frittata; 210
Cheesy Crab Dip; 222
Cheesy Endives; 43
Cheesy Fish Gratin; 114
Cheesy Greens Sandwich; 152
Cheesy Ground Beef And Mac Taco Casserole; 137
Cheesy Mushrooms and Spinach Frittata; 213
Cheesy Roasted Jalapeño Poppers; 166
Cheesy Shrimp Sandwich; 152
Cheesy Spinach; 58
Cheesy Spinach Dip; 220
Cheesy Tater Tot Breakfast Bake; 35
Cheesy-Creamy Broccoli Casserole; 210
Cherry-Choco Bars; 199
Chicago-Style Beef Sandwich; 154
Chicken and Rice Casserole; 69
Chicken and Wild Rice Soup; 258
Chicken Breasts in Golden Crumb; 173
Chicken Breasts With Chimichurri; 70
Chicken Burrito; 36
Chicken Capers Sandwich; 160
Chicken Curry; 83
Chicken Daikon Soup; 255
Chicken Fajitas; 81
Chicken Fillets, Brie and Ham; 81
Chicken In Bacon Wrap; 85
Chicken in Beer; 75
Chicken Legs With Dilled Brussels Sprouts; 70
Chicken Parm; 79
Chicken Pie; 84
Chicken Pita Sandwich; 151
Chicken Roll; 230
Chicken Sandwiches; 159
Chicken Soup; 257
Chicken Wings With Prawn Paste; 71
Chicken with Avocado Mix; 82
Chicken with Coconut and Turmeric; 82
Chicken with Oregano-Orange Chimichurri & Arugula Salad; 87
Chicken, Feta, and Olive Casserole; 214
Chicken, Mushroom, And Pepper Kabobs; 86

Chicken, Potatoes & Cabbage; 86
Chicken-Lettuce Wraps; 151
Chili Cream Soufflé; 32
Chimichurri Skirt Steak; 136
Chinese Braised Pork Belly; 147
Chinese Salt and Pepper Pork Chop Stir-fry; 127
Chinese-Style Sticky Turkey Thighs; 79
Chocolate Brownies; 186
Chocolate Cake; 198
Chocolate Chip Air Fryer Cookies; 199
Chocolate Cup Cakes; 192
Chocolate Donuts; 189
Chocolate Filled Donut Holes; 30
Chocolate Lava Cake; 194
Chocolate Mug Cake; 198
Chocolate Rice; 191
Chocolate Soufflé for Two; 189
Chocolaty Banana Muffins; 190
Choco-Peanut Mug Cake; 195
Cilantro-Mint Pork BBQ Thai Style; 125
Cinnamon and Cheese Pancake; 22
Cinnamon and Honey Pancakes; 29
Cinnamon and Vanilla Toast; 231
Cinnamon butternut squash fries; 58
Cinnamon Fried Bananas; 191
Cinnamon Pancake; 22
Cinnamon Pear Jam; 204
Cinnamon sugar roasted chickpeas; 206
Cinnamon Sweet Potato Bites; 182
Cinnamon-Spiced Acorn Squash; 197
Classic Air Fried Drumstick; 88
Classic Beef Jerky; 133
Classic Corned Beef Hash and Eggs; 25
Classic Greek Chicken; 76
Classic Mediterranean Quiche; 213
Coconut Donuts; 197
Coconut Lime Soup; 250
Coconut Oil Artichokes; 45
Coconut Sandwich with Tomato and Avocado; 162
Coconutty lemon bars; 206
Cod and Endives; 112
Cod and Tomatoes; 112
Cod Fish Nuggets; 102
Coffee and blueberry cake; 206
Coffee Flavored Doughnuts; 195
Corn and Bell Pepper Casserole; 211
Corn Bread; 244
Corn Soup; 257
Cornish Hen with Montreal Chicken Seasoning; 91
Country Fried Steak; 128
Country Style Pork Tenderloin; 135
Crab and Artichoke Dip; 219
Crab Dip; 110
Crab Legs; 98
Cranberry Cupcakes; 186

Creamy and cheese broccoli bake; 56
Creamy Beef Pockets; 236
Creamy Burger & Potato Bake; 136
Creamy Cabbage; 42
Creamy Coconut Chicken; 69
Creamy Mushroom Dip; 222
Creamy Potatoes; 63
Creamy Spinach Quiche; 61
Creamy Squash Soup; 252
Creamy Zucchini Dip; 183
Creamy-Mustard Pork Gratin; 211
Cremini Mushrooms in Zesty Tahini Sauce; 65
Crime Chicken; 69
Crisp Chicken w/ Mustard Vinaigrette; 86
Crisped baked cheese stuffed chile pepper; 56
Crispy Air Fried Sushi Roll; 115
Crispy Air Fryer Butter Chicken; 71
Crispy and healthy avocado fingers; 57
Crispy Baked Avocado Tacos; 155
Crispy Bananas; 191
Crispy Beef Cubes; 179
Crispy Beef Schnitzel; 138
Crispy Breaded Pork Chops; 145
Crispy Brussels Sprouts; 44
Crispy Cheesy Asparagus; 50
Crispy Cheesy Vegan Quesarito; 154
Crispy Chicken Thighs; 76
Crispy Coated Scallops; 113
Crispy Dumplings; 130
Crispy Fried Pickle Spears; 64
Crispy Fried Pork Chops the Southern Way; 124
Crispy Ham Egg Cups; 28
Crispy jalapeno coins; 56
Crispy Mongolian Beef; 129
Crispy Mustard Pork Tenderloin; 121
Crispy Paprika Fish Fillets; 107
Crispy Roast Garlic-Salt Pork; 126
Crispy Salt and Pepper Tofu; 61
Crumbled Fish; 117
Crunchy Chicken Egg Rolls; 156
Crunchy Curry Chicken Strips; 82
Crunchy Golden Nuggets; 84
Crunchy Munchy Chicken Tenders With Peanuts; 78
Crusted Hake Fillets; 94
Crusted Rack Of Lamb; 148
Crusted scallops; 118
Crusty Apple Hand Pies; 199
Crusty Pesto Salmon; 99
Cumin-Paprika Rubbed Beef Brisket; 138
Curried Sweet Potato Fries; 168
Curry Pork Roast in Coconut Sauce; 125

D

Date and Walnut Bread; 233
Date Bread; 233
Decisive Tiger Shrimp Platter; 178
Deep Fried Prawns; 94
Dehydrated Candied Bacon; 166
Dehydrated Spiced Cauliflower; 174
Dehydrated Spiced Orange Slices; 167
Delicious Breakfast Soufflé; 33
Different Hummus; 222
Dijon Garlic Pork Tenderloin; 146
Double-Baked Stuffed Potato; 171
Doughnuts; 199
Dried Raspberries; 202
Dry Rub Baby Back Ribs; 125
Duck and Cherries; 89
Duck and Tea Sauce; 88
Duck Breast with Fig Sauce; 87
Duck Breasts and Raspberry Sauce; 88
Duck Breasts with Red Wine and Orange Sauce; 87
Duo Crisp Ribs; 149

E

Easy Air Fryer Donuts; 189
Easy Baked Chocolate Mug Cake; 187
Easy Baked Potato Wedges; 179
Easy Beef Burritos; 153
Easy Buffalo Chicken Dip; 221
Easy cheesecake; 200
Easy Chickpea and Spinach Casserole; 213
Easy Cinnamon Squash; 49
Easy Fish Sticks with Chili Ketchup Sauce; 110
Easy Fried Tomatoes; 176
Easy Frizzled Leeks; 65
Easy granola; 201
Easy Homemade Hamburgers; 153
Easy Hot Dogs; 159
Easy Lemon Chicken Thighs; 72
Easy Marinated Steak; 131
Easy Paprika Chicken; 84
Easy Peasy Pizza; 234
Easy Prosciutto Grilled Cheese; 160
Easy Pumpkin Pie; 196
Easy Ritzy Chicken Nuggets; 82
Easy Roasted Walnuts; 182
Easy Taco Dip; 221
Easy Turkey Breasts With Basil; 69
Egg Roll Wrapped with Cabbage and Prawns; 165
Egg Rolls; 229
Eggplant Dip; 219
Eggplant Parmesan; 51
Eggplant Stew; 250

Eggs Florentine; 24
Energy Brownies; 194
English Pub Split Pea Soup; 248
Extreme Zucchini Fries; 176

F

Faire-Worthy Turkey Legs; 77
Fast and Simple Doughnuts; 239
Fennel Spread; 217
Feta Cheese Dip; 219
Fish and Vegetable Tacos; 104
Fish in Parchment Paper; 117
Fish Tacos; 108
Fish Tacos Breakfast; 37
Flatbread; 42
Flavorful Chicken Drumsticks; 74
Flavors Balsamic Chicken; 78
Flawless Kale Chips; 173
Fluffy Peanut Butter Marshmallow Turnovers; 239
Flying Fish; 103
Foil Packet Lobster Tail; 101
Foil Packet Salmon; 100
French Bread Pizza; 238
French Fries; 175
French toast bites; 205
French Toast Sticks; 30
French Toast Sticks with Sugar and Berries; 162
Fresh Tomato Basil Sauce; 225
Fresh Tomato Marinara Sauce; 225
Friday Night Pineapple Sticky Ribs; 165
Fried bananas with chocolate sauce; 204
Fried Calamari; 104
Fried Chicken and Waffles; 35
Fried Egg; 22
Fried French Mussels; 111
Fried peaches; 202
Fried Pork Scotch Egg; 134
Fried Pork with Sweet and Sour Glaze; 127
Fried Scallops with Saffron Cream Sauce; 108
Fried Spicy Tofu; 41
Fried Tortellini with Spicy Dipping Sauce; 169
Fried Up Avocados; 176
Fried Up Pumpkin Seeds; 178
Friedamari; 116
Fruit Cake; 193

G

Garlic and Rosemary Lamb Cutlets; 142
Garlic Cheese Bread; 32
Garlic Cheese Dip; 220
Garlic Mozzarella Sticks; 170
Garlic Putter Pork Chops; 127
Garlic Sauced Lamb Chops; 142
Garlic Soup with Almonds; 251
Garlic Tilapia; 111
Garlic with Bacon Pizza; 229
Garlic-Roasted Red Potatoes; 50
Garlic-Rosemary Brussels Sprouts; 47
German Sausages with Peppers and Onions; 129
Ginger Cheesecake; 197
Glazed Banana; 185
Glazed Pork Tenderloin; 148
Gluten-Free Air Fried Chicken; 74
Golden Asparagus Frittata; 211
Golden Cabbage and Mushroom Spring Rolls; 157
Golden Garlicky Potatoes; 49
Golden Squash Croquettes; 51
Greek Rotisserie Lamb Leg; 148
Greek Style Lamb Chops; 130
Greek Vegetable Soup; 259
Green Beans and Cherry Tomatoes; 42
Green Beans and Shallots; 63
Green Beans with Sesame Seeds; 48
Green Chilis Nachos; 166
Green Focaccia; 242
Grilled Avocado Caprese Crostini; 177
Grilled Cheese; 26
Grilled Fish with Light Mayo Sauce; 96
Grilled Garlic Chicken; 86
Grilled Ham and Cheese; 31
Grilled Peaches; 203
Grilled Sardines; 93
Grilled Soy Salmon Fillets; 103

H

Ham and Cheese Bagel Sandwiches; 26
Ham and Cheese Patties; 36
Ham and Egg Toast Cups; 28
Ham Egg Brunch Bake; 23
Ham Rolls; 229
Handmade Sausage Stew; 254
Hanger Steak with Red wine sauce; 132
Harissa Chicken with Yogurt Sauce; 90
Harissa-Rubbed Cornish Game Hens; 71
Hash Brown Bruschetta; 169
Hashbrown Casserole; 24
Healthy Carrot Fries; 179
Healthy Chicken Popcorn; 75
Healthy Fish and Chips; 117
Healthy Low Carb Fish Nugget; 178
Hearty Green Beans; 176
Hearty Lemon Green Beans; 172
Hearty Orange Stew; 259
Hearty Red Wine Stew; 255
Hearty Spiced Salmon; 107
Herb Butter Rib-eye Steak; 133
Herb Crusted Lamb Chops; 122
Herb Encrusted Lamb Chops; 142
Herb Mushrooms; 182
Herbed Bell Peppers; 53
Herbed Cheddar Cheese Frittata; 212
Herbed Croutons with Brie Cheese; 238
Herbed Omelet; 37
Herbed Rack of Lamb; 143
Herbed Roast Beef; 141
Herbed Roasted Potatoes; 64
Herbed Tomatoes; 40
Herbed Turkey Breast; 75
Herby Chicken with Lime; 75
Home-Fried Potatoes; 34
Homemade Breaded Nugget In Doritos; 74
Homemade Cherry Breakfast Tarts; 34
Homemade Donuts; 239
Homemade Peanut Corn Nuts; 171
Honey and Wine Chicken Breasts; 81
Honey Duck Breasts; 69
Honey Fruit Compote; 203
Honey Glazed Salmon; 115
Honey Roasted Carrots; 170
Honey Tomato Dip; 223
Hot Bacon Sandwiches; 159
Hot Smoked Trout Frittata; 95
Hot Spread; 223
Hydrated Apples; 193

I

Indian Cauliflower Curry; 46
Indian Fish Fingers; 102
Indian-Style Garnet Sweet Potatoes; 64
-Ingredient Air Fryer Catfish; 117
Italian Beef Rolls; 122
Italian Chicken Casserole; 215
Italian Mushroom Mix; 64
Italian Parmesan Breaded Pork Chops; 145
Italian Ratatouille; 56
Italian Sausages with Peppers and Onions; 124

J

Jalapeno Breakfast Muffins; 22
Jalapeño cheese balls; 55
Jalapeno Poppers; 178
Jalapeño Tacos with Guacamole; 163
Jerk Chicken Legs; 77
Jicama fries; 57
Jicama Fries; 178
Juicy Cheeseburgers; 156
Juicy Fish Nuggets; 180
Juicy Pork Ribs Ole; 147

K

Kale Beef Soup; 254
Kale Cottage Cheese Soup; 258
Keto Parmesan Crusted Pork Chops; 124
Kimchi Stuffed Squid; 95
Korean Barbeque Beef; 134
Korean Beef and Onion Tacos; 158
Korean Beef Wraps; 132
Korean Chicken Wings; 71
Korean Style Meat Skewers; 131

L

Lamb Meatballs; 136
Lamb Roast with Root Vegetables; 143
Lamb Stew; 252
Lean Beef with Green Onions; 135
Leftover Stew; 251
Lemon and Cumin Coated Rack of Lamb; 143
Lemon and Honey Glazed Game Hen; 85
Lemon Asparagus; 42
Lemon Garlic Lamb Chops; 133
Lemon Garlic Rosemary Chicken; 83
Lemon Mousse; 185
Lemon Pear Compote; 203
Lemon-garlic Butter Lobster; 99
Lemon-Pepper Chicken Wings; 88
Lemony Tuna; 103
Lentil Soup; 248
Light Herbed Meatballs; 126
Light Taco Soup; 252
Lighter Fish and Chips; 104
Lime Cheesecake; 207
Lobster Bisque Soup; 247
Lobster tails with lemon butter; 119
Lobster tails with white wine sauce; 118
Louisiana Crab Dip; 225
Louisiana Shrimp Po Boy; 116
Low-Calorie Beets Dish; 177
Low-Calorie Calzones; 235

M

Macadamia Rack of Lamb; 144
Macaroons; 200
Mahi Mahi with Herby Buttery Drizzle; 108
Manchego and Potato Patties; 66
Mango and Chili Spread; 223
Marinara Sauce Cheese Chicken; 75
Marvelous Lemon Biscuits; 207
Maryland Crab Cakes; 113
Mashed Yams; 46
Mayo Brussels Sprouts; 63
Meat Lovers' Pizza; 234
Meat Sauce; 224

Mediterranean Air Fried Veggies; 49
Mediterranean Bamyeh Okra Tomato Stew; 256
Mediterranean Sole; 113
Mexican Beef Soup; 246
Mexican Pizza; 235
Mexican Street Corn Queso Dip; 226
Mini Burgers; 170
Mini Cinnamon Sticky Rolls; 25
Mini Pizza; 236
Mini Popovers; 176
Mint-Butter Stuffed Mushrooms; 66
Miso White Fish Fillets; 101
Mixed Berries Cream; 197
Mixed Veggies Soup; 252
Monkey Bread; 238
Monkfish with Olives and Capers; 95
Morning Mini Cheeseburger Sliders; 26
Morning Sandwich Cheesy Stuffed; 31
Mozzarella -Spinach Stuffed Burgers; 155
Mozzarella, Bacon and Turkey Calzone; 240
Mozzarella, Brie and Artichoke Dip; 220
Mushroom Broth; 224
Mushroom Pita Pizzas; 161
Mushroom with Peas; 58
Mushroom, Onion and Feta Frittata; 57
Mustard-Crusted Fish Fillets; 104

N

Naan Bread Dippers; 219
Noodle Soup with Tofu; 249
Nugget and Veggie Taco Wraps; 152
Nutty Bread Pudding with Honey and Raisins; 240
Nutty Mix; 192
Nutty Slice; 193

O

Okra and Green Beans Stew; 260
Old Bay Crab Cakes; 99
Olives and Artichokes; 42
Omelette Frittata; 31
Onion Pakora; 180
Onion rings; 57
Onion Soup; 251
Orange cake; 200
Orange Chicken Stir Fry; 82
Oregano-Paprika on Breaded Pork; 127
Oven-Fried Chicken Wings; 89

P

Packet Lobster Tail; 110
Pancakes Nutella-Stuffed; 199
Pandan Chicken; 83

Panko-Crusted Avocado and Slaw Tacos; 157
Panko-Crusted Tilapia; 116
Paprika Chicken Legs With Brussels Sprouts; 83
Paprika lobster tail; 119
Paprika Rotisserie-Style Chicken; 90
Parmesan Asparagus; 54
Parmesan Breaded Zucchini Chips; 60
Parmesan Cabbage Wedges; 176
Parmesan Chicken Meatballs; 70
Parmesan Cod; 112
Parmesan Potatoes; 179
Parmesan Shrimp; 99; 115
Peach Pie Mix; 237
Peanut Butter & Banana Sandwich; 25
Peanut Butter and Jelly Banana Boats; 27
Peanut Butter Cookies; 203
Pear Sauce; 198
Pears and espresso cream; 202
Pecan Brownies; 43
Pecan-crusted Catfish Fillets; 101
Pepper Jack Cauliflower Bites; 65
Peppers and Cheese Dip; 217
Peppers and Lettuce Salad; 36
Perfect Baked Chicken Breasts; 78
Perfect Brunch Baked Eggs; 24
Perfect Cinnamon Toast; 187
Perfect Crab Dip; 222
Perfect Donuts; 243
Perfect Goat Cheese Dip; 221
Perfect Juicy Chicken Breast; 76
Perfect Lamb Burgers; 144
Persimmon Toast with Sour Cream and Cinnamon; 161
Pesto Bruschetta; 168
Pho; 255
Phyllo Artichoke Triangles; 168
Pita and Pepperoni Pizza; 240
Pizza Flammkuchen Style; 242
Pizza Toast; 234
Pizzas in Fryer Without Oil; 241
Polish Sausage with Sauerkraut; 128
Porchetta-Style Pork Chops; 129
Pork And Fruit Kebabs; 123
Pork And Mixed Greens Salad; 121
Pork Burgers With Red Cabbage Salad; 121
Pork Cutlet Rolls; 133
Pork Milanese; 124
Pork Neck with Salad; 147
Pork Satay; 121
Pork Stew; 250
Pork Taquitos; 123
Potato Balls Stuffed with Ham and Cheese from the Air Fryer; 170
Potato Frittata; 37
Potato Leek Soup; 257

Potato Soup; 248
Potatoes with Zucchinis; 48
Prosciutto Sandwich; 160
Protein Packed Baked Chicken Breasts; 77
Pub Style Corned Beef Egg Rolls; 140
Pulled Pork; 126
Pumpkin and Pork Escallops; 123
Pumpkin Tomato Soup; 250

Q

Quick Cheese Sticks; 238
Quick Paella; 97
Quick Sausage and Veggie Sandwiches; 155
Quick Zucchini Cakes; 172
Quinoa Burgers; 51

R

Radish Hash Browns; 36
Raisin and Apple Dumplings; 239
Raisins Cinnamon Peaches; 202
Ranch Chickpeas; 181
Ranch Flavored Tilapia; 106
Raspberry Cream Rol-Ups; 190
Raspberry Danish; 185
Raspberry Roll; 229
Raspberry Smoked Pork Chops; 139
Raspberry-Coco Desert; 195
Red Lentil Mushroom Ragu; 224
Red Onion Marmalade; 225
Reuben Egg Rolls; 140
Rib Eye Steak; 132
Rice and Meatball Stuffed Bell Peppers; 140
Ricotta Spinach and Basil Pockets; 158
Roasted Brussels and Pine Nuts; 177
Roasted Butternut Squash With Brussels Sprouts and Sweet Potato Noodles; 41
Roasted Cashews; 175
Roasted Cauliflower with Nuts & Raisins; 55
Roasted Grape and Goat Cheese Crostinis; 161
Roasted Peanuts; 175
Roasted Pork Tenderloin; 146
Roasted Pumpkin Seeds; 174
Roasted vegetables salad; 54
Rolled All Beef Hot Dogs; 130
Rolled Salmon Sandwich; 160
Rosemary Air Fried Potatoes; 46
Rosemary Cauliflower Bites; 182
Rustic Pork Ribs; 145

S

Sage 'n Thyme Rubbed Porterhouse; 122
Salmon and Cauliflower Rice; 110
Salmon and Coconut Sauce; 111
Salmon and Sauce; 112
Salmon Burgers; 112
Salmon Cakes; 95
Salmon Croquettes; 116
Salmon Noodles; 103
Salmon on Bed of Fennel and Carrot; 106
Salmon Steak Grilled with Cilantro Garlic Sauce; 94
Salmon Tortellini Soup; 248
Salmon With Crisped Topped Crumbs; 93
Salmon with Pistachio Bark; 95
Salty Baked Almonds; 167
Salty Lemon Artichokes; 43
Saucy Fried Bananas; 200
Sausage and Cream Cheese Biscuits; 34
Sausage and Egg Breakfast Burrito; 33
Sausage and Onion Rolls; 166
Sausage Balls; 31
Sausages and Chorizos; 171
Sautéed Trout with Almonds; 96
Savory Cheese and Bacon Muffins; 35
Savory Cod Fish in Soy Sauce; 100
Scallion Sandwich; 22
Scallops and Spring Veggies; 99
Scallops with Green Vegetables; 106
Seasoned Carrots with Green Beans; 63
Seasoned Potatoes; 35
Seasoned Veggies; 63
Self-Saucing Banana Pudding; 194
Sesame Garlic Chicken Wings; 165
Sesame Seeds Coated Tuna; 98
Sesame Shrimp; 110
Sheet pan seafood bake; 119
Shrimp and Green Beans; 110
Shrimp Casserole Louisiana Style; 93
Shrimp Toast; 169
Simple & Delicious Spiced Apples; 204
Simple and Delicious Chicken Thighs; 78
Simple Balsamic-Glazed Carrots; 51
Simple Basil Potatoes; 47
Simple Cheesecake; 196
Simple Cinnamon Toasts; 241
Simple Coffee Cake; 207
Simple Egg Soufflé; 32
Simple Lemon Salmon; 101
Simple Strawberry Cobbler; 195
Simple Yet Tasty Lamb Chops; 144
Smoked Dip; 224
Smoked Salmon Dip; 218
Smoked Veggie Omelet; 66
Smoky Chicken Sandwich; 152
Snapper with Fruit; 105
Snow Peas With Ginger Salmon Steaks; 94
Soda Brad; 232
Sourdough Croutons; 241
Southern Pimento Grilled Cheese; 238
Southern Style Catfish with Green Beans; 97
Spaghetti Sauce; 227
Spaghetti squash tots; 57
Spiced Apple Turnovers; 25
Spiced Pear Sauce; 200
Spicy Almonds; 180
Spicy and Sweet Roasted Nuts; 167
Spicy Buffalo Chicken Dip; 217
Spicy Chicken Strips with Aioli Sauce; 76
Spicy Chickpeas; 175
Spicy Duck Legs; 87
Spicy Grilled Halibut; 114
Spicy Halibut; 100
Spicy Kale Chips with Yogurt Sauce; 168
Spicy Mackerel; 103
Spicy Mexican Cheese Dip; 221
Spicy Mix Nuts; 182
Spicy Mushroom Soup; 253
Spicy Roasted Chicken; 91
Spicy Rotisserie Chicken; 91
Spicy Spinach Artichoke Dip; 217
Spicy Sweet Potato Dip; 218
Spicy Sweet Potato Fries; 61
Spicy Winter Squash Bites; 64
Spinach Dip; 218
Split Pea Soup; 258
Spring Roll; 230
Squash Oat Muffins; 24
Steak and Asparagus Bundles; 139
Steak And Vegetable Kebabs; 123
Steak Bites and Mushrooms; 132
Steamed Pot Stickers; 167
Steamed Salmon and Sauce; 102
Stewed Celery Stalk; 249
Stir-Fried Chicken with Water Chestnuts; 87
Stir-Fried Steak and Cabbage; 140
Strawberry Cobbler; 208
Strawberry Donuts; 196
Strawberry Stew; 206
Stuffed Bell Peppers; 58
Stuffed Mushrooms; 47
Stuffed Okra; 40
Stuffing hushpuppies; 172
Sumptuous Chicken and Vegetable Casserole; 212
Sunflower Seed Bread; 233
Super Yummy Brownies; 208
Swedish Meatballs; 139
Sweet & Spicy Mixed Nuts; 183
Sweet and Sour Chicken; 80
Sweet and Spicy Parsnips; 52

Sweet Asian Style Salmon; 109
Sweet Cream Cheese Wontons; 189
Sweet Peach Jam; 201
Sweet Peach Wedges; 206
Sweet Pear Stew; 188
Sweet Potato and Carrot Croquettes; 66
Sweet Potato Croquettes; 182
Sweet Potato Frittata; 23
Sweet Potato Side Salad; 63

T

Taco Beef and Green Chile Casserole; 210
Taco Soup; 254
Tandoori Lamb; 144
Tangy Mango Slices; 205
Tarragon Yellow Squash; 41
Tasty Banana Snack; 207
Tasty Cheeseburgers; 160
Tasty Grilled Red Mullet; 106
Tasty Raspberry Scones; 29
Tasty Scramble Casserole; 30
Tasty Tuna Loaf; 113
Tasty Zucchini Fritters; 179
Tempura Shrimp; 109
Teriyaki Duck Legs; 80
Teriyaki Glazed Halibut Steak; 96
Teriyaki Pork Rolls; 148
Teriyaki Wings; 71
Texas Thighs; 84
Thai Green Curry Noodles; 67
Thai Pork Burgers; 153
Thai Red Duck with Candy Onion; 81
Three-grain Bread with the Airfryer Baking Pa; 244
Three-Layer Taco Dip; 226
Thyme Scallops; 105
Tilapia & Chives Sauce; 105
Tilapia Meunière With Vegetables; 100
Toasted Cinnamon Bananas; 27
Tofu and Bell Peppers; 38
Tofu Dip; 223
Tofu with Broccoli; 52
Tomato and Cheese Pizza; 235
Tomato and Mozzarella Bruschetta; 163
Tomato Basil Scallops; 114
Tomato Soup; 249
Tomatoes Dip; 221
Tomatta Spinacha Frittata; 27
Tortilla and White Beans Soup; 246
Tortilla Chips; 181
Tropical Shrimp Skewers; 114
Trout and Mint; 111
Tuna and Fruit Kebabs; 105
Tuna Patties; 111
Tuna Pie; 116
Tuna Sandwiches; 38
Tuna Veggie Stir-Fry; 98
Turkey And Almonds; 70
Turkey and Artichoke Pizza; 230
Turkey And Broccoli Stew; 251
Turkey and Mushroom Stew; 259
Turkey And Pepper Sandwich; 85
Turkey Burgers; 159
Turkey Taco Casserole; 215
Turkey Turnovers; 79
Turkey Wontons with Garlic-parmesan Sauce; 73
Twice-Baked Potatoes; 49

U

Ultimate Breakfast Burrito; 27
Ultimate Breakfast Sandwich; 28

V

Vanilla and Mango Bread with Cinnamon; 231
Vanilla Apple Compote; 202
Vanilla Oatmeal; 37
Vanilla Spiced Soufflé; 192
Vegetable Egg Soufflé; 32
Vegetable Medley; 50
Vegetable Sausage Egg Bake; 22
Vegetable Wild Rice Soup; 247
Veggie Salsa Wraps; 151
Veggie Stuffed Bell Peppers; 40
Veggies on Toast; 161
Veggies Rice; 59
Vermicelli Noodles and Vegetables Rolls; 174
Vinegar Green Beans; 53

W

Waffle Fry Poutine; 180
Walnut Apple Pear Mix; 204
Warm Peach Compote; 198
Warming Winter Beef with Celery; 137
Western Chicken Wings; 77
Wheat and Seed Bread; 28
Wine Glazed Mushrooms; 40
Winter Vegetarian Frittata; 62
Wonton Meatballs; 129
Wrapped Asparagus; 45

Y

Yogurt Bread; 232
Yogurt Chicken Tacos; 173
Yummy Breakfast Italian Frittata; 33
Yummy Chicken Dip; 222

Z

Zesty Ranch Fish Fillets; 109
Zingy and Nutty Chicken Wings; 80
Zoodle Soup; 260
Zucchini and Cauliflower Stew; 246
Zucchini Mug Cake; 186
Zucchini parmesan chips; 55
Zucchini Stew; 260
Zucchini with Tuna; 93

www.ingramcontent.com/pod-product-compliance
Lightning Source LLC
Chambersburg PA
CBHW081407080526
44589CB00016B/2491